24

Numbers in India's Periphery

Over the past two centuries, the deep and multifaceted relation between statistics and statecraft has emerged as a defining feature of modern states across the world. Governments increasingly depend upon statistics for planning and evaluation of interventions as well as self-representation. *Numbers in India's Periphery* examines systematic and deliberate errors in government statistics. Using field interviews, archival sources and secondary data, the book explores the shifting relations between various kinds of government statistics and charts their political career in Nagaland, a state located in India's landlocked ethno-geographic periphery stretching from Mizoram to Jammu and Kashmir.

This book examines the area (1951–2018), population (1951–2011) and National Sample Survey statistics (1973–2014) of Nagaland, treating them as part of a larger family of mutually constitutive statistics embedded in a shared context. It shows that Nagaland's government statistics suffer from sustained and large errors and examines the impact of inadequacies in the data generating processes on statistics of interest to policymakers. It argues that statistics are shaped by a combination of factors, including discontent with colonial borders, competition over resource-rich territories, political unrest, competition for government spending and contests over the delimitation of administrative units and electoral constituencies in the context of weak institutions and dominance of the state in the economy. It also engages with the shared experience of other states of India, including Assam, Jammu and Kashmir and Manipur, and other countries in Africa and Asia and non-governmental statistics such as church membership data.

Numbers in India's Periphery uncovers a mutually constitutive relationship between data, development and democracy deficits and offers an exciting account of how statistics are social artefacts dynamically shaped over their life cycle by political and economic factors. It contributes to the under-researched field of the political economy of statistics in developing countries.

Ankush Agrawal is Assistant Professor of Economics at the Indian Institute of Technology Delhi.

Vikas Kumar is Assistant Professor of Economics at Azim Premji University, Bengaluru.

Numbers in India's Periphery
The Political Economy of Government Statistics

Ankush Agrawal

Vikas Kumar

CAMBRIDGE
UNIVERSITY PRESS

CAMBRIDGE
UNIVERSITY PRESS

University Printing House, Cambridge CB2 8BS, United Kingdom

One Liberty Plaza, 20th Floor, New York, NY 10006, USA

477 Williamstown Road, Port Melbourne, VIC 3207, Australia

314–321, 3rd Floor, Plot 3, Splendor Forum, Jasola District Centre, New Delhi–110025, India

79 Anson Road, #06–04/06, Singapore 079906

Cambridge University Press is part of the University of Cambridge.

It furthers the University's mission by disseminating knowledge in the pursuit of education, learning and research at the highest international levels of excellence.

www.cambridge.org
Information on this title: www.cambridge.org/9781108486729

© Ankush Agrawal and Vikas Kumar 2020

First published 2020

Printed in India by Nutech Print Services, New Delhi 110020

A catalogue record for this publication is available from the British Library

Library of Congress Cataloging-in-Publication Data
Names: Agrawal, Ankush, author. | Kumar, Vikas, author.
Title: Numbers in India's periphery : the political economy of government statistics / Ankush Agrawal, Vikas Kumar.
Description: Cambridge, United Kingdom ; New York, NY : Cambridge University Press, 2020. | Includes bibliographical references and index.
Identifiers: LCCN 2020009125 (print) | LCCN 2020009126 (ebook) | ISBN 9781108486729 (hardback) | ISBN 9781108762229 (ebook)
Subjects: LCSH: India--Politics and government--Statistics--History--20th century. | India--Politics and government--Statistics--History--21st century. | India--Population--History--20th century. | India--Population--History--21st century. | Nāgāland (India)--Politics and government--Statistics--History--20th century. | Nāgāland (India)--Politics and government--Statistics--History--21st century. | Nāgāland (India)--Population--History--20th century. | Nāgāland (India)--Population--History--21st century.
Classification: LCC HA4585 .A37 2020 (print) | LCC HA4585 (ebook) | DDC 315.4--dc23
LC record available at https://lccn.loc.gov/2020009125
LC ebook record available at https://lccn.loc.gov/2020009126

ISBN 978-1-108-48672-9 Hardback

Contents

PART I   Introduction

PART II   Key Statistics

PART III   Policy Implications

Figures

Timelines

Maps

Tables

Abbreviations

AFSPA	Armed Forces (Special Powers) Act, 1958
ASA	Assam State Archives
CAGR	compound annual growth rate
CBR	crude birth rate
CDR	crude death rate
CPO	Chakhesang Public Organization
DCHB	*District Census Handbook*
DCI	Delimitation Commission of India
DCO	director of census operations
ECI	Election Commission of India
ENPO	Eastern Nagaland Peoples' Organisation
FFC	Fourteenth Finance Commission
FSU	First Stage Units
GHC	Gauhati High Court
GoI	Government of India
GoN	Government of Nagaland
GPT	*General Population Tables*
GSE	gross school enrolment
IAS	Indian Administrative Service
ILP	Inner Line Permit
IPS	Indian Police Service
ME	*Morung Express*
MGNREGS	Mahatma Gandhi National Rural Employment Guarantee Scheme
MOSPI	Ministry of Statistics and Programme Implementation
MPCE	monthly per capita consumer expenditure
NBCC	Nagaland Baptist Church Council
NEFA	North Eastern Frontier Agency
NFHS	National Family Health Survey

NGISRSC	Nagaland GIS & Remote Sensing Centre, Department of Planning & Coordination, Government of Nagaland
NGR	natural growth rate
NHBCC	Naga Hills Baptist Church Council
NHTA	Naga Hills-Tuensang Area
NNC	Naga National Council
NSA	Nagaland State Archives
NSCN-IM	National Socialist Council of Nagaland (Isak Muivah)
NSCN-K	National Socialist Council of Nagaland (Khaplang)
NSS	National Sample Survey
NSSO	National Sample Survey Office (formerly National Sample Survey Organisation)
NTC	Nagaland Tribes Council
ORGI	Office of the Registrar General of India
ORGI&CC	Office of the Registrar General of India & Census Commissioner
PCA	Primary Census Abstract
PCI	per capita income
PES	Post-Enumeration Survey (formerly Post-Enumeration Check)
PPF	Pochury Public Forum
PPT	*Provisional Population Totals*
RGCCI	Registrar General and Census Commissioner, India
RGI&CC	Registrar General of India & Census Commissioner
RGI	Registrar General of India
RSZ	Rengma Selo Zi
SATP	South Asia Terrorism Portal
SCO	superintendent of census operations
SC	Scheduled Caste
SCS	Special Category States
SCI	Supreme Court of India
SoI	Survey of India
SRS	Sample Registration System
ST	Scheduled Tribe
TFR	total fertility rate
UFS	Urban Frame Survey
UoI	Union of India
UT	union territories
VDB	Village Development Board

Preface

The long, sporadic prehistory of this book began when Vikas read former Chief Minister of Manipur Radhabinod Koijam's op-ed on the Naga peace process in the *Hindu* after finishing his undergraduate studies. Writing a few months after the 2001 Census, Koijam drew attention towards, among other things, the discrepancies between different estimates of Nagaland's area and population. An interview of Nagaland's Chief Minister Neiphiu Rio by Sanjoy Hazarika published in the *Statesman* in December 2005, when Vikas was back in the academe, briefly revived the interest in Nagaland's statistics. In the interview, Rio admitted that his state's headcount was flawed. This study though had to wait until 2011, when Ankush came across a news report on the 'contraction' of Nagaland's population between 2001 and 2011.

Our preliminary analysis of the census data suggested that conventional factors could not explain Nagaland's abnormal demographic trajectory. While it became clear that non-demographic factors were key to understanding changes in Nagaland's population and that fieldwork and archival research were indispensable, the scope of the study remained ill-defined until after we visited the state to obtain a first-hand idea of the scale and nature of the statistical 'mess'. Our conversations through the second half of 2011 coalesced into short-term project proposals at our respective institutions, Institute of Economic Growth and Azim Premji University. Little did we know then that Nagaland's statistics would engage us for the better part of the following decade and take us through the length and breadth of the state.

Studying maps was not part of our original plan. During our visits to Nagaland, we found a great diversity of maps on the walls of government offices and private establishments. Discussions with government officials and civil society leaders complicated the picture further. Finally, after a senior bureaucrat effectively told us that the estimate of the state's area was a state secret, we decided to examine maps and area statistics and realised that they were essential for conducting population censuses and sample surveys.

While examining our preliminary findings, we needed information on socio-economic and developmental indicators. We found that the incidence of poverty in

Nagaland was the lowest in the whole of the country in several years, which did not agree with our field observations. We then turned to the National Sample Surveys (NSSs), the source of data for government-appointed expert groups on the estimation of poverty.

So, two years into the project on Nagaland's demographic puzzle, we found ourselves working on three different types of statistics – area (and maps), census population and survey statistics. It took a while for us to realise that the seemingly parallel streams of work would converge. As our fieldwork unfolded, the significance of political and economic contexts as well as the interconnectedness of different statistics slowly became clearer. The logical sequence in which the material is presented in the book emerged midway when we began to put together the pieces of the puzzle to figure out the big picture. In other words, we have presented the chapters in the sequence we ought to have thought through the problem rather than the sequence that was actually followed.

We were still not sure whether the three strands should be presented together, let alone in the form of a book. Several factors pushed us in that direction, including acontextual debates on statistical reforms amidst the steady decline in India's statistical system and the growing clamour for evidence-based public policy. Also, while teaching courses at the interface of politics, statistics and policymaking, we found a dearth of material on the quality of data in India and, particularly, on the life cycle of data, interconnectedness of different types of data and context-dependence of data. Furthermore, we felt that government statistics, a key ingredient of public policy, do not receive sufficient attention in textbooks.

In the existing literature, most contributions deal with a particular type of statistics for a limited period, which impedes the emergence of a comprehensive understanding of the quality of data. Econometrics textbooks take students directly to techniques without introducing them to how the context shapes and is shaped by statistics or, at least, alerting them to the relevant literature in the social sciences. The discussion on the impact of data quality on econometric analyses is often limited to ex post robustness checks. The context of data is discussed in other social sciences, but those discussions are mostly theoretical and often happen in isolation from real data and, hence, do not directly challenge the complacence within economics. Unsurprisingly, most economists continue to work with the 'available' data without examining their quality. We believe that analyses of various statistics for the same territory over a long period informed by perspectives from different disciplines are needed to improve our understanding of the context-dependence of data.

This book begins with a brief survey of the problem of data deficit across countries and then takes readers to the context within which numbers are produced and consumed in Nagaland before introducing them to area, population and survey statistics, in that order. Each chapter emphasises the need to understand the context of data by supplementing statistical analyses with field interviews and, wherever possible, archival research. The concluding chapter explores the larger context of data deficit and extends the discussion on Nagaland to other states. While this book is focused on India, it might help illuminate the predicament facing other developing countries and trigger further research on the quality of data that is often circumscribed by a mutually constitutive relation among data, development and democracy deficits.

Acknowledgements

We have incurred many debts during our work on the book. If this book contributes to the understanding of the broader context within which statistics are produced and consumed in developing countries, we would have succeeded in repaying part of those debts.

As students of economics at Indira Gandhi Institute of Development Research, Mumbai (IGIDR), we were fortunate to sit through M. H. Suryanarayana's lectures on introductory econometrics that sowed seeds of doubt about the infallibility of statistics and P. G. Babu's lectures on advanced microeconomics that emphasised the embeddedness of phenomena.

Nearly a decade ago when we began exploring the census, Nagaland was just a name and a bunch of inconsistent statistics for us. The fieldwork for this project could not have been conceived without the support of C. M. Chang, R. N. Chhipa and Sanjoy Hazarika. They put us in touch with Charles Chasie, Visakono Sakhrie, Theja Therieh, Toshi Wungtung, V. Hekali Zhimomi and Lungsang Zeliang, who in turn introduced us to Nagaland. And, then we snowballed our way through the hills and plains of the state. Sanjoy Hazarika and K. Sreedhar Rao played a similar role in Assam. Rajesh Thapa and, for shorter periods, Akong, Ajay Lama, Chandra Limbo and Robin Swargiary provided invaluable travel support.

Village elders and leaders of youth/student organisations, civil society organisations and political parties across Nagaland, Manipur and Sarupathar circle of Golaghat district in Assam were generous with their time in sharing insights. Several current and former government officials in Nagaland, Manipur, Assam, Bengaluru and New Delhi offered valuable insights and helped with logistics whenever we found ourselves stranded.

Discussions with Metongmeren Ao, Charles Chasie, Fakharuddin, Kunal Ghosh, Hiren Gohain, Chandan Gowda, Nazrul Haque, late Lhusi Haralu, Sanjoy Hazarika, S. C. Jamir, R. Khing, S. K. Khemprai, L. L. Kuki, late Rajkumar Paira, L. Phom, Neiphiu Rio, Thaban Rongmei, Biswajit Sarmah, Khekiye Sema, Shürhozelie Liezietsu, late Devendra Swaroop, K. Therie, Theja Therieh, P. Tikhir, late B. G.

Verghese, N. N. Walling, Jelle J. P. Wouters, Toshi Wungtung, Hokiye Yepthomi and V. Hekali Zhimomi, among many others, enriched our understanding.

K. Achungla Chang, Rev. Anjo Keikung, Rev. Keviyiekielie Linyü and Rev. Father Dr Sojan Xavier helped us access church statistics. Alok Kanungo, Rev. V. K. Nuh and Peter van Ham allowed us access to valuable archival material in their possession. S. K. Khemprai, L. L. Kuki, Pius Lotha, H. Pushing, Thaban Rongmei, Theja Therieh, P. Tikhir, Toshi Wungtung and Hokiye Yepthomi shared with us unpublished documents.

The Office of the Commissioner Nagaland (Kohima) shared data on Inner Line Permits (ILPs). The ASA, Guwahati; Nagaland State Archives, Kohima (NSA); Naga Archives and Research Centre, Dimapur; Nagaland GIS and Remote Sensing Centre, Kohima; and Society for the Preservation and Promotion of Naga Heritage, Frankfurt provided access to maps and historical documents. Libraries at Azim Premji University, Bengaluru (APU); Department of Information and Public Relations, Kohima; Directorate of Census Operations, Kohima; Office of the Registrar General of India, New Delhi (ORGI); Institute of Economic Growth, Delhi (IEG); Indian Institute of Technology Delhi (IIT Delhi); Indian Statistical Institute, Delhi (ISI); National Council of Applied Economic Research, Delhi (NCAER); International Institute of Population Sciences, Mumbai (IIPS); IGIDR; Centre for Development Studies, Trivandrum (CDS); and Delhi School of Economics (DSE) provided access to various government publications. The staff of APU library, Lucy Tep (Directorate of Census Operations, Kohima) and Trilok Joshi (IEG) deserve special mention.

The audiences at the Adam Smith Seminar at the University of Munich; the First Annual Conference in Economics at IIT Delhi; the Annual Meeting of the European Public Choice Society (Freiburg, 2016) and seminars at APU; Erasmus University Rotterdam; IEG Delhi; South Asian University, New Delhi; IIT Gandhinagar and other places heard us out and offered valuable feedback. So did students of Political Economy of Government Statistics and Reading Nagaland at APU and Advanced Econometrics at IIT Delhi.

B. S. Arun (*Deccan Herald*), East Asia Forum, Sevanti Ninan (The Hoot) and Philip Steinberg (*Political Geography*) made room for Nagaland in their publications and helped us step outside our narrow disciplinary confines.

Soon after we finished the preliminary analysis of census data, Vikram Dayal motivated us to develop the research into a book. P. G. Babu, Chandan Gowda, Manfred Holler, Poonam Singh and M. H. Suryanarayana commented on early drafts of different parts of the book and, more importantly, were always available for discussions.

Two years ago, Anwesha Rana at Cambridge University Press helped us step out of the mountains of primary material we had collected and nudged us to put together a book. We would not have managed to complete the book without her encouragement and constant support. Tapajyoti Chaudhuri at Cambridge University Press carefully edited the manuscript and allowed us to make several rounds of changes. Without his support we would not have been able to incorporate the insights based on the data that were released after the completion of copy-editing.

APU, IEG and IIT Delhi offered much needed financial and institutional support. The Diocese of Kohima, Eastern Nagaland Peoples' Organization (ENPO), East Naga Students' Federation, Khiamniungan Tribal Council, Nagaland Baptist Church Council (NBCC), Rengma Hoho, Rengma Selo Zi (RSZ), Rotterdam Institute of Law and Economics, Western Sumi Hoho and Yimchunger Tribal Council extended valuable support at different stages.

We have been able to mention only a few of our Naga, Kachari, Kuki, Meitei, Assamese and other hosts and interlocutors based in the North-East, other states of India and Europe. Many more have been omitted for want of space and, in several cases, because of the need to maintain anonymity. We will remain indebted to all of them for their goodwill, warmth and candid exchanges.

To all of the above we offer the following line from *Aabhaar*, a poem by Shivmangal Singh 'Suman'.

जिस-जिस से पथ पर स्नेह मिला, उस-उस राही को धन्यवाद।

Part I
Introduction

1

State and Statistics

[In Nigeria,] the census figures became strong political weapons rather than statistical data to be used for planning for socio-economic development.

—Adepoju (1981: 35)

In a severely divided society ... an election can become an ethnic head count ... a census needs to be 'won'. So the election is a census, and the census is an election.

—Horowitz (2000: 196)

Introduction

Over the past two centuries, the deep and multifaceted relation between statistics and statecraft has emerged as one of the defining features of states across the world. Modern states depend on statistics for the planning and evaluation of interventions. The growing size and complexity of operations undertaken by states have deepened their dependence upon statistics.[1] Bureaucratisation[2] and technocratisation[3] of policymaking as well as the growing capacity of non-state actors to challenge government policies[4] have also pushed states towards statistics.

The relationship between state and statistics is not merely instrumental though. Given their intimate relation with the origin and evolution of modern states, statistics are integral to the self-imagination of states and, also, to how they are imagined by people.[5] In its earlier eighteenth-century sense, statistics was 'a set of administrative routines needed to describe a state and its population' (Desrosières 1998: 16), a description of the state by and for itself (ibid.: 147).[6] By the early nineteenth century, almost all Western countries had established statistical offices (Tooze 2003: 2; Urla 1993: 821) as 'national statistics' had come to be seen 'as one of the vital attributes of the nation-states then under construction or seeking to assert themselves' (Desrosières 2013: 10).[7] The quality of statistics produced by a country began to be seen as an attribute of its socio-economic and political development, with advanced economies and liberal democracies being associated with better statistical systems (Porter 1995: 80; see also Urla 1993: 821). Around the same time, statistics also began to be seen as enablers of public interest.[8] And the census 'became less concerned with what the people could be obliged to do for the state and more concerned with what the state could do for them' (Coleman 2012: 335) amidst an emerging 'shift towards willing participation [in state-sponsored data collection efforts] on the part of the respondents' (Bookman 2013: 51; see also Starr 1987: 12; Prewitt 2010: 239).

Democracy was another site for the intertwining of state and statistics. The origins and spread of modern democracy and state-sponsored human population censuses are closely related. The United States of America (USA), where decennial delimitation intertwined democracy and census in the late eighteenth century, was an early exemplar of this relationship. By the early twentieth century, conflicts over the delimitation of administrative units and electoral constituencies and, by implication, population censuses had almost become 'rites of passage in the lives of modern states outside the West' (Kumar 2019: 1).[9]

The long-standing and multifaceted relationship between state and statistics notwithstanding, government statistics of most (developing) countries are often not free of errors.[10] Errors result from definitional and measurement problems,[11] as well as from capacity constraints,[12] corruption[13] and unrealistic targets[14] (Figure 1.1). Non-governmental actors in most developing countries have limited expertise to question government data, let alone build alternative databases. Restrictions

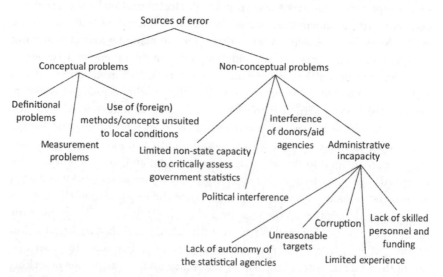

Figure 1.1   Sources of error in statistics of developing countries
Source: Authors.

on freedom of expression and media, weak judiciaries and lower rates of literacy further impede the scrutiny of government statistics in these countries. Developed countries face fewer problems because of a longer history of engagement with modern statistics, greater availability of skilled personnel and resources to build reliable databases, better quality of the general administration and greater non-governmental capacity to critically assess government statistics and build alternative databases.

Statistics are also susceptible to errors because of interference and contestation by interest groups competing for resources and power within and across countries. Countries manipulate economic statistics to attract international finance and secure preferential access to development funding. In the late 1990s, the World Bank 'lowered' the per capita income of China 'in line with the Chinese request' to allow it to access 'very cheap, long-term loans [offered by the International Development Association, the soft-loan arm of the World Bank] available to countries whose average income is below a certain level' (Wade 2012: 17). A decade later, the Chinese leader Le Keqiang noted that his country's national accounts were unreliable (Ninan 2018).[15] In 1987, Myanmarese leader Ne Win complained that 'political manipulation' and 'intentional falsification' had rendered economic statistics useless (Steinberg 2015: 10). In Pakistan, the 'basis for undermining the integrity of official statistics was laid in the 1990s when the Ministry of Finance engaged in systematic manipulation and misreporting of the public finances data … to "cheat" the IMF' (Sherani 2016). Michalski and Stoltz (2013: 591), who examine strategic falsification of economic statistics in a cross section of countries, point out that

> Argentina by misstating inflation figures avoided paying out higher interest on government bonds indexed to inflation … and raising the wages in the public sector. Greece enjoyed lower borrowing rates (close to Germany's) on its government debt … because investors did not know the entire extent of Greek budget troubles. (see also Coyle 2014: 3–4).

There is also a non-instrumental reason why developing countries manipulate data. These countries compete in both the real and symbolic realms. They are obsessed with global rankings as markers of status and, consequently, need to measure their progress relative to other countries, especially in the West.[16] Statistics allow easy, even if context-independent and, therefore, less meaningful, comparisons. 'India and China are', for instance, 'among the 60-plus countries that have government units dedicated to moving upwards [on the World Bank's ease of doing business ranking], almost as if it were an end in itself' (*Economist* 2018). Myanmar's military regime manipulated economic statistics 'to prove that their country was every bit as tigerish as its Asian rivals' (Cockett 2015: 158).

The Developing World's Experience

Most liberal democracies in the West have not seen deeply divisive ethnopolitical contests over census after the Second World War.[17] However, census has proven to be an arena of conflict across Asia and Africa as communities/regions indulge in competitive manipulation of statistics to secure favourable delimitation of administrative units and electoral constituencies and, by implication, a larger share of the public pie. The political history of independent Nigeria aptly illustrates the experience of developing countries. Adepoju (1981: 29, 35) points out that

> population issues play dominant roles and are largely responsible for major landmarks in the contemporary Nigerian political scene: it precipitated the constitutional crisis in the country in 1962; it played a major role in the crisis in the old Western Nigeria in 1965; was largely responsible for the military take-over in 1966; contributed greatly to the fall of Gowon's regime in 1975 and still looms large in the minds of Nigerians with the recent demand for the creation of even more states in the country; and revenue allocation among existing states soon after the return to civilian rule ... [ultimately,] the census figures became strong political weapons rather than statistical data to be used for planning for socio-economic development. (For a related discussion on Ethiopia, see *Economist* 2019)

In several countries, governments collect limited or no information on ethnicity, religion and language to avoid conflict (Horowitz 2000; Kertzer and Arel 2002b; Bookman 2013).[18] In others, governments delay the release of results.[19] In still other cases, data collection exercises are either indefinitely suspended to eliminate a source of conflict or cannot be conducted because rival groups resist the authority of the government to conduct surveys in their strongholds. Lebanon presents an extreme example in this regard. It did not conduct a census after 1932 as it feared that 'taking one would reveal such changes in the religious composition of the population as to make the marvelously intricate political arrangements designed to balance sectarian interests unviable' (Geertz 1973: 275; see also Horowitz 2000: 195).

Most countries in India's neighbourhood have not been able to conduct national censuses regularly.[20] The decennial cycle of census was disrupted in Pakistan when it postponed the 1971 Census. Pakistan has not been able conduct censuses regularly since then. It postponed the census five times between 1991 and 1998 fearing conflict in case the demographic balance among ethnolinguistic groups was altered and ultimately managed to produce figures that affirmed the status quo (Weiss 1999: 687, 691; see also Khan 1998: 481). In 2012, Sri Lanka conducted its first countrywide census in three decades (Government of Sri Lanka 2012). Myanmar conducted a census in 2014 after a gap of 31 years, but once again, it did not adequately cover the minorities (TNI-BCN 2014; Aung 2018). Afghanistan could not complete the 1979 Census due to political turmoil and has not been able to conduct a national census since then (Tolo News 2018). China did not conduct a census between 1964 and 1982 (*Global Times* 2011).

Africa abounds in examples of abandoned and delayed censuses (Lalasz 2006).[21] Even major African countries such as Nigeria have not been able to conduct regular and reliable censuses (Okolo 1999). Nigeria's 1962 Census had to be repeated in 1963 due to concerns about the quality of data. The next census was conducted in 1973, but it too proved to be controversial and the results were not published. Nigeria delayed censuses for a long time, fearing unrest and eventually conducted censuses that almost reproduced earlier federal population shares (Fawehinmi 2018).

In a survey of ethnic conflicts across the developing world, Horowitz highlights the mutually constitutive relation among ethnic conflict, elections and competitive manipulation of census:

> As an entitlement issue, the census is a splendid example of the blending of group anxiety with political domination.... Disputes over census results in ethnically divided societies are common.... In a severely divided society ... an election can become an ethnic head count. Now it is clear that a census needs to be 'won.' So the election is a census, and the census is an election. (Horowitz 2000: 194–6)[22]

Political considerations also affect sample surveys. In late colonial Ghana, the choice of the geographic scope of household budget surveys 'closely mirrored the political interests of those in power' (Serra 2014: 10).[23] Deaton and Kozel (2005: 190, 196) hint at the politically contested nature of India's National Sample Surveys (NSSs):

> The history of poverty lines in India is a case study in the interaction of science and politics, with political decisions often claiming a scientific basis.... There is no suggestion here that the statistical failures in India in the 1990s were the result of undue interference by politicians or policymakers in data collection or publication. Yet politics in the broad sense played a role. In evaluating the reforms, the political right had an interest in showing low poverty, and the political left in showing high poverty, and this undoubtedly intensified the debate on survey design and led to the unfortunate compromise design that temporarily undermined the poverty monitoring system.[24]

The contestations of the 1990s played out again towards the end of the following decade. The 66th round of the NSS (2009–10) proved to be controversial because it showed that employment generation fell significantly short of the target of the Eleventh Five Year Plan. This contradicted the presumptions of '[s]ome highly placed officials,' who instead of 'questioning their own priors ... decided that the data must be wrong, and castigated the NSSO for its faulty investigative methods' (Chandrasekhar and Ghosh 2011; see also *EPW* 2011). The then deputy chairman of the Planning Commission repeatedly argued that the results of the latest sample survey 'were not the best judge of the extent of impact government policies have had on the poor because it was a drought year' (*Economic Times* 2012; 2013a).[25] The 66th round was followed by another quinquennial survey in 2011–12. Chandrasekhar and Ghosh (2013) argue that

> for the UPA [United Progressive Alliance government], the 2009–10 figures must have been particularly disappointing.... It is possibly for this reason, and the fact that waning growth required finding other indicators to place before the electorate in 2014,[26] that the NSSO was encouraged to break from tradition and generate one more, large sample survey of employment relating to 2011–12.[27]

We have so far discussed select instances of politicisation of statistics from across the world. Different local factors explain the intertwining of politics and statistics in different countries. However, common to all of them 'is a constitutive interrelationship between quantification and democratic government' because numbers are 'intrinsic to the forms of justification that give legitimacy to political power in democracies' and 'integral to the technologies that seek to give effect to democracy as a particular set of mechanisms of rule' (Rose 1991: 675). In such settings, political and numerical controversies become inseparably intertwined and political disputes are often waged in the language of numbers (ibid.: 685). For instance, 'Arguments about numerical quotas, availability pools and demographic imbalance become a substitute for democratic discussion of the principles of equity and justice' (Kenneth Prewitt quoted in ibid.: 680). Since the process of creating equal opportunity conditions for minority/underprivileged groups is slow and uncertain, 'statistical proportionality' becomes 'a favored legal and administrative tool' (Prewitt 2003: 16). While our focus is on democratic states, the discussion can be extended to other kinds of states too.[28]

The conceptual vocabulary, categories and methods of measurement and modes of dissemination of data represent the government's political priorities and the balance of power in the society (notes 18 and 23 of this chapter). The legal–institutional architecture of government statistical infrastructure is negotiated 'between stakeholders from ... politics, the economy and law' (Heine and Oltmanns 2016: 205). Political elites are, however, not necessarily committed to the total welfare of the society and

> are likely to perceive four specific roles and objectives for official statistics: 1) a policymaking tool; 2) a signal to supporters and detractors; 3) a means for enhancing control over rents and revenues; and 4) a source of pressure and

competition to their position.... In addition, two factors influence elite decision-making on official statistics: their access to sources of financing and their political ideology. (Krätke and Byiers 2014: 26; see also Heine and Oltmanns 2016: 203, 207; Taylor 2016: 12–13).[29]

In short, statistics are sites of political contestation insofar as *what to count, how to count* and *how to use statistics* are inherently political choices. Or, as Bookman (2013: 71) puts it, 'who counts depends on who counts'. While it is true that statistics often serve elite interests, '[i]n the hands of the socially or politically disenfranchised, numbers may also be a language of social contestation, a way that ethnic groups, women, and minorities can make themselves visible, articulate their "differences" from the dominant society, and make claims upon the state and its services' (Urla 1993: 818; see also Goderle 2016: 87; Taylor 2016: 13). '[A]t stake in minority concerns with statistics are not only competing claims to resources but also competing claims to truth' because '[a]s part of a modern regime of truth that equates knowledge with measurement, statistics occupy a place of authority in contemporary modes of social description; they are technologies of truth production' (Urla 1993: 819).

Scope and Framework

Statistics of interest to social sciences are inherently prone to errors because of the difficulty in conducting designed experiments and the intrinsic randomness of human behaviour. We will, however, focus on erroneous statistics that are a product of deliberate human choices. We will examine errors engendered by deliberate intervention in the generative processes of government statistics and not merely their misuse or misinterpretation, which happens *after* statistics have already been collected. We will, however, not deal with conflicts over the choice of modes of statistical reasoning that can affect inferences derived from data (Schweber 2001) or with politically motivated changes in government policies that can alter the data generation process (Gregg 1994). Furthermore, our discussion is restricted not only to intra-national statistics but also to statistics produced and published domestically.[30] Even within the latter we do not deal with administrative statistics, that is, statistics generated by government departments as by-products of their routine operations or through statutory administrative returns (GoI n.d.16: para 14.3.1).[31] Chapter 4, though, discusses the quality of select administrative data that are compared with census data.

We will examine systematic and deliberate errors in key government statistics such as area, population and monthly per capita consumer expenditure (MPCE).[32] Area statistics and maps are essential for conducting population censuses.[33] 'The territory covered, along with any changes in its area in successive censuses, should be clearly and explicitly stated' because 'population figures have no meaning unless they refer to a well defined territory' (GoI 2009b: 5). The first few questions/entries in any census schedule help to uniquely and geographically locate the respondent. In fact, the primary, even if inadequately acknowledged, role of Houselisting and Housing Census – the first round of Indian censuses – is to help partition and map the territory into enumeration blocks consisting of numbered buildings.[34] Once data are collected, maps (and area statistics) are needed again to delimit and display them.

Maps and population are in turn essential for collecting most other statistics. Area and population are needed to calculate per unit estimates. Furthermore, population census provides information for planning sample surveys, identifying the sampling frame and estimating sample statistics (Kish and Verma 1986) and also provides 'benchmark data for evaluating the reasonableness of the over-all survey results' (GoI 2009b: 12). Maps are needed to locate sub-samples on the ground.

Most discussions on data quality examine statistics in isolation, overlooking the interrelationships between different kinds of statistics as well as the larger context of data deficit. The context can be understood if we locate *data* deficit, which includes both the unavailability and poor quality of data, in relation to *democracy* and *development* deficits. Figure 1.2 identifies some of the key interlinkages among the three.

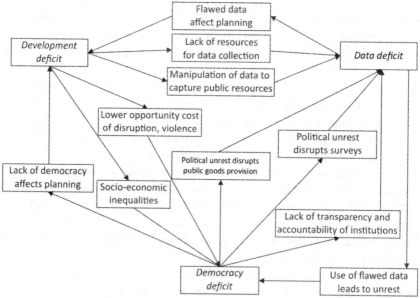

Figure 1.2   A triple deficit

Source: Authors.

It is well known that political unrest/instability is both a cause and consequence of underdevelopment (Alesina et al. 1996; Gyimah-Brempong and Traynor 1999), that is, *democracy*[35] and *development* deficits are interrelated. Furthermore, the availability and quality of data are affected by and affect democratic processes. The absence or weakness of democracy is associated with less transparent and less accountable institutions. Political conflict engendered by the breakdown of democratic institutions that can credibly guarantee equitable power-sharing and fair play is associated with poor public goods provision. It is, therefore, also associated with inadequate supply and poor quality of government statistics insofar as the latter are public goods.[36] The disruption of democratic processes can also affect the availability and quality of government data by restricting data collection. Surveyors might be unable to access sites due to disturbed conditions.[37] While the weakening of democracy affects statistics, democratic processes can themselves be affected by the quality of statistics. The use of flawed data in policymaking affects the relationship between the government and the beneficiaries of the flawed data, on the one hand, and aggrieved communities, on the other. Conflicts over redistribution on the basis of census are cases in point. In Nagaland, a state in north-eastern India, which will be explored in greater detail in the following chapters, flawed headcounts affected the sharing of public resources and divided the population into warring camps.[38] So, *democracy* and *data* deficits are also interrelated.

Data deficit is also related to development deficit. Underdevelopment limits resources available for non-essential activities such as data collection.[39] There is another more overt channel through which underdevelopment affects data quality. In societies with stagnant economies, where government spending apportioned among communities/regions according to reported population share and measured socio-economic disadvantage of groups plays an important role in everyday lives, statistics are manipulated to secure better representation in elected bodies and a larger share in public spending and employment. In India, the economies of insurgency-prone states such as Nagaland, located in the ethno-geographic periphery, are kept afloat by preferential federal transfers that account for more than half of the state budgets. In some of these states, communities resort to competitive manipulation of statistics. The resultant data deficit feeds back into development planning.[40] Thus, there is a bidirectional relationship between *data* and *development* deficits.

To sum up, *development, democracy* and *data* deficits are interrelated and as a result the quality of data is both affected by and affects political and economic processes. Statistics impact politics and policymaking, even as the latter intervene at various stages of production, dissemination and consumption of statistics. In other words, statistics are 'an integral part of the economic and social world, which they seek to describe', and, consequently, descriptions of statistics 'should be integrated within the wider history of the society that produces them' (Tooze 2003: 3; see also Diaz-Bone and Didier 2016: 9; Alonso and Starr 1987). However, the quality of data, let alone the mutually constitutive relationship among statistics, politics and economy, has not received sufficient scholarly attention. Demographers Guilmoto and Irudaya Rajan (2013: 69) note, 'In case of discrepancies, it is often found easier to dismiss statistical data than engage them, leading researchers to either credulously accept statistics or indiscriminately ignore them.' Likewise, in political science, researchers 'make heavy use of census statistics but have given scant attention to the politics behind the production of those statistics ...' (Prewitt 2010: 237). Given the interconnectedness of statistics and a variety of social phenomena, 'the relative paucity of studies of how statistics became what they are today is somewhat surprising' for historian Woolf (1989: 588). Others note the neglect of government statistics in academic research and university curriculum (Gal and Ograjenšek 2017: 80).

Economist Wade (2012: 17) points out that '[t]he sub-field of the political economy of statistics is notable for its absence', which is odd given that 'National and international statistical offices always operate in the tension between professional standards of objectivity and political insistence on certain results' (ibid.: 18). Srinivasan (1994: 4) observes that

> it would appear that researchers either are not aware of or, worse still, have chosen to ignore the fact that the published data, national and international, suffer from serious conceptual problems, measurement biases and errors, and lack of comparability over time within countries and across countries at a point in time. Of course this fact is neither new nor of recent origin. After all, three decades ago Morgenstern (1963) published his classic on the accuracy of economic and social data.

Commenting on the paucity of 'studies focusing on data adequacy and quality in India', Shetty (2012: 41, 43) suggests that 'collection of accurate statistics has a low priority in policymaking today and the intellectual community which studies India's economic problems also shows no concern for the deteriorating quality of the Indian database, which they otherwise studiously use for economic analysis or for various econometric exercises'.[41] Jerven (2013: xiv) too notes the 'surprising gap between knowing innately that these numbers cannot be good and an unwillingness [in economics] to study how bad they are' and adds that '[t]he scholars who are best equipped to analyze the validity and reliability of economic statistics are often data users themselves and are thus reluctant to undermine the datasets that are the bread and butter of scholarly work' (ibid.: 8). Philipsen (2015) highlights moral hazard on part of economists who avoid questioning the validity and usefulness of inherently problematic measures such as GDP. He adds that the lack of interest in the origin and evolution of economic measures is evident from the fact that 'files essential to the history of national accounts in the United States had not been checked out of the Library of Congress and the National Archives since the early 1970s' (ibid.: 320).

Numbers in India's Periphery tries to fill this gap in the literature by examining the political economy of government statistics. It views statistics as 'artefacts' produced by 'social actors in an effort to make sense of [and to manage] the complex and unmanageable reality that surrounds them' (Tooze 2003: 3; see also Urla 1993: 820, 837) and suggests that the processes that govern the generation of data need to be explicitly studied (Bowden 1989: x). The approach suggested here is necessitated by both the interdependence between different socio-economic processes, types of statistics and stages of data collection as well as the desirability of conceptual integrity, that is, we can be interested in the larger social context and body of statistics even if explicit causal relationships between them are not evident.[42]

This book tries to build a better understanding of the generative contexts of data and their use as follows.[43] First, it examines statistics across their life cycles rather than just at the stage of collection or publication (Figure 1.3).[44] Among other things, it pays attention to lay users, whose 'insurgent informational practices' (Wyly 2004: 7) are increasingly contesting their representation in government maps and data and, by implication, challenging the monopoly of the government over the collection, interpretation and dissemination of statistical facts. It also explores the afterlives of statistics that have been discarded or superseded. Second,

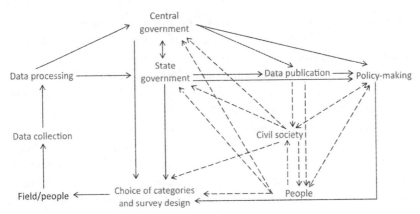

Figure 1.3   Life cycle of statistics

Source: Authors.

Note: Continuous (dashed) lines connect stakeholders through formal (informal) channels of communication.

it examines the quality of different types of statistics for a specific territory over a long period and as part of a larger family of interconnected statistics. Third, it not only situates map-making, censuses and sample surveys in a larger context but also tries to quantify the impact of political and economic factors on the statistics of interest to policymakers. Fourth, it discusses the relatively understudied problems of over-enumeration, non-sampling errors and the context dependence of data.

In other words, the book views statistics as embedded in specific contexts and combines political and economic perspectives to understand their quality across life cycle and over long periods; it also quantifies the impact of different factors on population and survey statistics. This book, which is based on, among other things, interviews conducted over several years and archival research, also contributes to the fledgling discipline of 'field economics'.[45]

Nagaland and, to a lesser extent, other states in India's ethno-geographic periphery are used to illustrate a way to read statistics in their proper context. Most academic studies on India that rely on statistics limit themselves to 'major' states for want of data and exclude the north-eastern region. We try to address this gap in research in the case of Nagaland. We also try to add a new dimension to the debate on India's north-eastern region that has for long been seen exclusively through the lenses of development and democracy deficits. We bring a new lens – data – to the debate and put together a fresh perspective by triangulating among data, development and democracy.

Why Nagaland?

A general explanation – numbers matter for political and economic outcomes in modern states – can explain the manipulation of government statistics. However, an intimate knowledge of the local context is needed to know why the general explanation works only in select localities and what accounts for the differences between localities otherwise governed by the same general explanation. In the absence of detailed local studies, it will be difficult to understand the specific mechanism(s) governing the manipulation of statistics and we will end up with global context-free measures to improve data quality that are unlikely to work on the ground. In this book, we focus on Nagaland to build a better understanding of the generative contexts of statistics and the mutually constitutive relationship between different types of statistics, as well as between them and their political and economic/developmental contexts.

Nagaland is located in the North-East of India, bound by the states of Assam, Arunachal Pradesh and Manipur on the west, north and south, respectively, and Myanmar on the east (Map 1.1). Its terrain is mostly rocky (about 95 per cent) (GSI

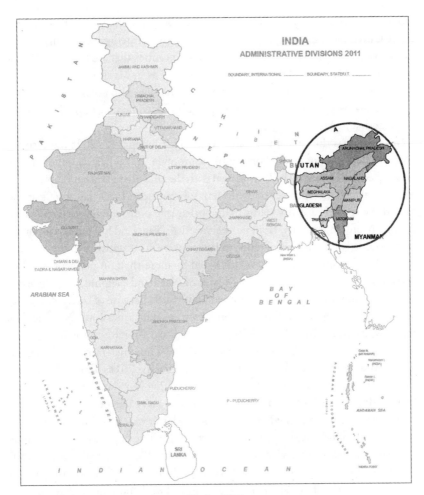

Map 1.1   States and union territories of India, 2011

Source: http://censusindia.gov.in/2011census/maps/administrative_maps/admmaps2011.html, accessed on 6 January 2020.

Notes: (i) Telangana is included within Andhra Pradesh as it was not a separate state during the 2011 Census. Similarly, Ladakh is included within Jammu and Kashmir as it was not a separate union territory in 2011. (ii) The circle shown in the map encompasses the states of the North-East.

Map not to scale and may not represent authentic international borders.

2011: 2) and forested (77.62 per cent) (FSI 2017: 255).[46] This small (16,579 square kilometres) and sparsely populated state is home to 14 Naga and four non-Naga indigenous tribes recognised by the state government and several other indigenous and non-indigenous tribal as well as non-tribal communities. The indigenous tribes accounted for about 86 per cent of Nagaland's population in 2011. The tribes are mostly Christian and speak more than 20 mutually unintelligible languages. It is also noteworthy that Nagaland is home to communities that are found across the border in neighbouring states within India as well as in Myanmar and has long-standing border disputes with its neighbours. The state also attracts immigrants from the plains of Assam and alleged illegal/undocumented immigrants from Bangladesh and Myanmar.

Nagaland was the first small state formed after independence. It was also the first state that was not created on linguistic grounds. It was carved out of Assam and granted full statehood in 1963 to deal with the first phase of what is now one of the oldest armed insurgencies of the Indian subcontinent. In the late 1960s, it was granted the special category status that entitled it to preferential access to federal funding. More importantly, from our perspective, Nagaland has perhaps seen the most sustained and substantial errors in basic government statistics in the country.

Nagaland's population was over-reported by more than 36 per cent in 2001. A few years later, the then Chief Minister of Nagaland Neiphiu Rio suggested that any attempt to conduct a recount would be futile because of intercommunity competition over the delimitation of constituencies (Hazarika 2005; Neiphiu Rio, interview, 27 May 2015, New Delhi). Eventually, delimitation was indefinitely postponed due to the threat of ethnic conflict. The chief minister, however, supported an initiative to conduct a clean census in 2011. The exercise was partially successful, and the 2011 Census reported that Nagaland's population had contracted between 2001 and 2011, even though a sizeable proportion of ghost entries seem to have remained undetected in the latter year too. Nagaland became the first state in independent India to register a negative population growth rate.

During an exploratory visit to the state to study the abnormalities in census data, we were struck by the multiplicity of mutually inconsistent maps displayed in government offices. The area *under* Nagaland's administration is underestimated by at least 3 per cent. Incorrect area and population estimates resulted in the overestimation of population density by as much as 40 per cent in 2001. We also noticed that Nagaland reported the lowest poverty rate among states during 2004–5, even though its poverty line was the highest in the country.

The presence of systematic, growing and interrelated errors in key government statistics and maps of Nagaland despite improvements in survey methods and data processing and map-making technologies challenges the technological determinism of some of the recent proposals for improving the statistical system and suggests that data deficit/quality cannot be understood in isolation from the larger context in which statistics are produced and consumed. This prompted us to explore the social and political-economic contexts of Nagaland's government statistics.

We have so far argued that Nagaland offers an opportunity to examine the context-dependence as well as interdependence of key government statistics. The choice of Nagaland for the study of India's government statistics offers other advantages too. In a country of the size of India, the choice of the unit of analysis is important. Decisions regarding key statistics are taken at the federal level in New Delhi and in state capitals, with different states operating independently of each other. The district administration simply supplies raw data. Therefore, states are more appropriate units of analysis than districts.

The choice of a specific state has to contend with the fact that some states are too large. The population of Uttar Pradesh is more than that of Brazil, the fifth most populous country in the world. Most other Indian states are comparable to large European countries in terms of population. The choice of a small state was necessary in the interest of tractability of fieldwork. Despite being remote and widely seen as a 'disturbed state', Nagaland helped us keep the logistics of field research manageable, while protecting the integrity of the data generation mechanism.

Choosing Nagaland over other small states afforded us several advantages. It was India's first small state formed in the early 1960s. This allows long-term comparisons (six censuses between 1961 and 2011) while keeping the borders fixed. Moreover, unlike smaller states in the north-west, Nagaland is highly diverse. About one-sixth of all the languages, with more than 10,000 speakers, reported in the 2011 Census of India were indigenous to Nagaland that accounts for less than 0.2 per cent of the country's population. Furthermore, the districts of Nagaland differ in terms of their colonial histories and there are also considerable geographical and climatic differences between different parts of the state. These differences have contributed to persistent socio-economic disparities within the state.

So, while Nagaland may not be representative of India in a strictly statistical sense, it shares several features associated with the country's population and its distribution, particularly, in its ethno-geographic periphery.[47] More importantly, the Nagaland government acknowledged the problems in the state's census and tried to make a new beginning by engaging different stakeholders ahead of the 2011 Census. States such as Jammu and Kashmir and Manipur that are facing similar problems have not yet had an inclusive public dialogue regarding the errors in their government statistics. So, the magnitude of errors in government statistics and the acknowledgement of the same from the government differentiate Nagaland from other states that also satisfy some of the conditions outlined above.

If Nagaland is not representative of India in any usual statistical sense, to what extent can it tell us something about India's government statistics as a whole? First, it will at least add to our understanding of statistics in insurgency-affected states in

India's ethno-geographic periphery (Maps 1.2 and 7.3) that suffer from a sustained data deficit (Map 7.1). Most national-level surveys either do not cover peripheral states or cover them irregularly. Even the surveys that cover them regularly do not have sufficiently representative samples to generate reliable estimates. An examination of Nagaland's experience will also add to our understanding of government statistics in the erstwhile special category states (Himachal Pradesh, Jammu and Kashmir, Sikkim, Uttarakhand and seven north-eastern states) (Map 7.4), states that enjoy special constitutional protections within the union (erstwhile Jammu and Kashmir and north-eastern states) and states where the last round of delimitation of constituencies had to be postponed until after the first census conducted after 2026 (Arunachal Pradesh, Assam, Jharkhand, Jammu and Kashmir, Manipur and Nagaland) or had to be conducted under constraints (Chhattisgarh, Meghalaya and Uttarakhand) (Map 7.2).

Second, as per the constitution, 'census' is a union subject (Art. 246, List 1, Item No. 69). Implementation happens in states under the direct supervision of the Ministry of Home Affairs (Census Act, 1948, Sections 3–4, 17A, 18). Union public servants posted in states are made answerable to the Office of the Registrar General & Census Commissioner, India, that designs and publishes the census schedules, processes the raw data and publishes reports without the interference of state governments. Likewise, the NSSs and cartographic surveys are directly conducted by central organisations.[48] In other words, authoritative population and area estimates of administrative units are published by central organisations. So, if there are serious and sustained errors in a state's maps, census and sample surveys, we have good reasons to suspect that similar problems could have affected government statistics in the rest of the country.[49]

Our discussion has wider relevance for developing countries.[50] As per the World Bank's Statistical Capacity Indicator, a composite score assessing the capacity of a country's statistical system, India scored 91.1 (out of 100) in 2017 compared to the average score of 75 for 140 developing countries (World Bank n.d.1).[51] Developing countries with weaker statistical systems are more likely to be susceptible to the problems that plague India's government statistics. In fact, it can be argued that the problems identified in Nagaland and other states of India might be unavoidable whenever and wherever the political status of a territory is contested and/or communities are locked into ethnopolitical competition over public resources under weak institutions.

Outline of the Book

We examine Nagaland's maps and area statistics (1951–2018), population census data (1951–2011) and MPCE estimates from the NSSs (1973–2014), treating each of them as part of a larger family of interrelated statistics, whose generative processes are embedded in shared socio-economic and political contexts. We also examine maps and area statistics published by insurgents, membership data published by churches and administrative data on electorate, school enrolment and inner line permits (ILPs).[52] In addition, we briefly discuss the experience of other states, including Assam, Jammu and Kashmir, Maharashtra, Manipur and Tripura.

The first part of the book introduces readers to larger debates at the interface of state and statistics (in this chapter) and statistical representations of Nagaland and the use of statistics in the state (Chapter 2, 'Nagaland and Numbers'). The latter chapter explores the use of statistics by politicians, bureaucrats, government statisticians and academicians. Four chapters in the second part analyse maps, population and National Sample Survey Office (NSSO) survey statistics (Chapters 3–6). Maps and population are the bedrock of government statistics, whereas NSSO data are the most widely used household-level socio-economic statistics in India. The chapters on maps and population are based on government as well as non-governmental publications collected from Nagaland and adjoining states and interviews/discussions conducted in these states as well as elsewhere in India and Europe between 2012 and 2019. The chapter on sample surveys is largely based on publicly available government statistics. The third part concludes with a reflection on the implications of the relationship among data, development and democracy deficits along India's ethno-geographic periphery (Chapter 7, 'Data, Development and Democracy'). Chapter 7 extends the discussion to other states of India and also emphasises the need to make data more transparent by making available adequate metadata, understand data deficit from the perspective of the life cycle and interconnectedness of data and not allow technological determinism to drive statistical reforms. The major insights of the key chapters in the second part are summarised here.

'Cartographic "Mess"', Chapter 3, examines the multiplicity of mutually inconsistent area statistics and maps of Nagaland published between 1951 and 2018. Both the number of 'incorrect' maps in circulation and the degree of 'inaccuracy' in maps have grown over time despite advances in map-making.[53] This chapter situates flaws in maps in the larger context that affects area as well as other statistics. It argues that the 'errors' can be attributed to a combination of political-geographic (popular demands to redraw 'artificial' colonial borders that divide Naga tribes between Myanmar and India and across states within India) and political-economic (the demand in the largely hilly Nagaland for fertile and resource-rich plains territory along the Assam–Nagaland border) factors. Naga resistance to colonial-era borders has spawned both vertical (involving union and state governments as well as non- and anti-state actors) and horizontal (involving neighbouring states) conflicts that affect both internal and external borders of the state.

The Nagaland government finds itself sandwiched between an irredentist insurgency on the one hand and status quoist neighbouring states and the union government on the other. The state government's balancing act is reflected in, among other things, competitive developmentalism along disputed borders and the diversity of conflicting maps published by different tiers and wings of the government. The state government, effectively, acts as a counter-mapper vis-à-vis colonial-origin borders and complements the civil society that relies upon counter-mapping and scale jumping to build a counter-narrative to cartographic/territorial/political status quo.

Nagaland's cartographic predicament is rooted in the as yet inconclusive search for a stable basis for Naga identity and the ongoing dispute over its place within the Union of India. Its disputed borders are, in fact, sites of a meta-conflict insofar as they are the loci of intersection of different conceptions of nationhood (Indian and Naga) and understandings of constitutional federalism. As a result, the 'errors' in Nagaland's maps are not amenable to resolution through the introduction of better survey methods.

The twin chapters (Chapters 4 and 5) on population, 'Demographic Somersault' and 'Winning Censuses', examine the plausibility of Nagaland's census population estimates. We assess the internal consistency of census data and also compare them with other government and non-governmental sources of information including data on electorate and school enrolment, data from the Sample Registration System (SRS), the National Family Health Survey (NFHS) and church membership records. We disaggregate data across administrative units, electoral constituencies and socio-demographic categories such as religion, tribe, sex and place of residence (rural/urban). We show that demographic and political-geographic factors, political transitions, insurgency and changes in the area covered by the Census cannot explain the dramatic changes in Nagaland's population (or any of its subgroups) between 1981 and 2011.

We argue that a conjunction of political-economic factors, ethnic conflicts and weak state institutions explain Nagaland's *demographic somersault* – decades of unusually high population growth followed by a sudden 'contraction' of population. The headcount was inflated due to competitive manipulation by Naga tribes demanding new administrative units and fighting for a larger share of legislative assembly seats.

The literature on census is largely focused on content errors (errors in the sub-classification of headcount) from the perspective of the ability of dominant groups to shape the choice of categories and influence the process of counting and processing of data. Chapters 4 and 5, however, examine the historical and political-economic context of coverage errors (errors in the overall headcount) as well as content errors and also try to quantify these errors.[54] The chapter 'Winning

Censuses' also explores the relationship between meta-electoral competition over delimitation and statistics, and in doing so contributes to the small but growing literature on (electoral) politics in Nagaland.

Chapter 6, 'Flawed Surveys', explores factors other than small sample size that affect the quality of survey statistics. It highlights the problem of frame and sample non-coverage in the context of household surveys in India, which has received scant attention in the literature, and identifies gaps in NSS reports with regard to information necesssary for understanding the sampling frame and assessing the nature and extent of non-coverage. This chapter examines the quality of NSSO data for Nagaland (and Jammu and Kashmir, Manipur and Tripura) over a long period and shows that during 1973–2014 the NSSs lacked representativeness and inter-temporal comparability for Nagaland due to faulty sampling frames, frame non-coverage and biased samples. Since census is used as the sampling frame in household surveys, errors in Nagaland's headcount affected survey statistics. Frame non-coverage due to the arbitrary restriction of sample to accessible areas of Nagaland too affected the estimates of survey statistics. Moreover, the systematic differences between the areas covered in surveys and those left out biased the NSSO samples. The chapter quantifies the impact of non-coverage on survey statistics (such as MPCE) that in turn affect statistics of interest to policymakers (such as poverty rate). The degree of non-coverage and bias were so high that in most years between 1993 and 2012 Nagaland's poverty headcount ratio was the lowest in the country despite the possible overestimation of its poverty line. Further, the decline in Nagaland's average MPCE relative to the rest of the country over the years is partly an artefact of the changing sampling frame.

Taken together, the poor quality of a whole range of statistics for Nagaland and other states in India's ethno-geographic periphery over the past several decades highlights a serious problem. Some of the states that suffer from sustained development and democracy deficits and need greater attention from the government, academia and media are also the ones that suffer from a sustained data deficit. We argue that the problem can be understood and appropriate corrective policy measures can be identified only if we pay attention to the generative contexts of statistics, namely, the mutually constitutive relationship between democracy/politics, development/economy and data/information. Attempts to mechanically fix the problem by introducing better data collection and data processing tools will not be effective, as data deficit is often enmeshed with other deficits.

A Note on Terminology and Spellings

A few words on some of the terms used in this book are in order to clarify the context of their use. We will begin with the phrase 'government statistics' that is used here for what is generally referred to as 'official statistics'[55] in, for example, *Guide to Official Statistics* published by India's Central Statistics Organisation (later renamed Central Statistics Office), the UN Economic and Social Council's *Fundamental Principles of National Official Statistics, International Association for Official Statistics* and *Journal of Official Statistics*. Our preference for *government statistics* is dictated by the fact that governments no longer enjoy a monopoly over statistics. Non-state actors increasingly command sufficient resources to publish their own 'official' databases (note 4 of this chapter).

We use 'census' to refer to the mundane process of enumeration, whereas 'Census' refers to the state machinery and constitutionally mandated practices that outlive any particular round of enumeration of population. Furthermore, '1991 Census' refers to the census conducted in 1991 in its entirety, including pre- and post-census operations.

The phrase 'ethno-geographic periphery' refers to landlocked states that share a land border with another country (Map 1.2A) and where a majority speaks non-scheduled languages (Map 1.2B), belongs to Scheduled Tribes (STs) (Map 1.2C) and/or follows non-Hindu religions (Map 1.2D). Lakshadweep, a marine union territory, also satisfies some of these conditions and so do some of the districts in the landlocked tribal areas in the 'mainland'.

'North-East' refers to the states of Arunachal Pradesh, Assam, Manipur, Meghalaya, Mizoram, Nagaland and Tripura and does not include Sikkim (except in Table 6.1) and Darjeeling and the adjoining areas in West Bengal. Government ministries and agencies such as the Ministry of Development of North Eastern Region and the North Eastern Council include Sikkim in the North-East though. While the category 'North East India' is contentious (Baruah 2005: 4–5, 40–1; Misra 2012: 1–10; Haokip 2012; Wouters 2018: xv–xvi), it has found growing acceptance within and outside the region (Baruah 2005: 4; Borgohain and Borgohain 2011: 58, 190–1; McDuie-Ra 2012; Ngaihte 2013; Hazarika 2018). Political platforms launched in the past few years such as North-East Regional Political Front and the North-East Democratic Alliance are cases in point. We use the category for want of a better substitute. Insurgent organisations have crafted new labels such as 'Western South East Asia' to refer to the North-East (*Hindustan Times* 2013b). Also, note that we refer to India's South East Asian neighbour by its new name Myanmar rather than Burma. See Cockett (2015: xv–xvi) and Steinberg (2015: 3) for discussions in this regard. Furthermore, we treat Jammu and Kashmir as a state and Telangana as part of the state of Andhra Pradesh in accordance with the constitutional status of the respective territories at the time of the 2011 Census.

Following Jones (2009a: 180), we use 'border' for lines on maps as well as the corresponding infrastructure on the ground that divides jurisdictions and

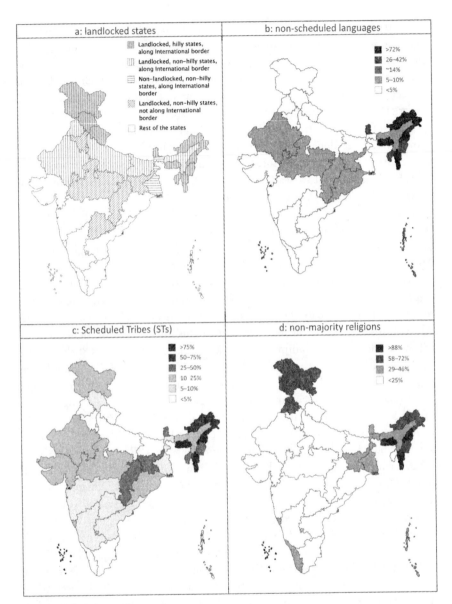

Map 1.2   India's periphery

Source: Prepared by authors. These maps have been generated using a template available at https://mapchart.net/india.html and the 2011 Census data on language, tribe and religion. They are used solely for depicting select geographic and demographic characteristics.

Note: The census data have *not* been adjusted for content and coverage errors identified in the book.

Maps not to scale and may not represent authentic international borders.

'boundary' for the larger set of tangible and intangible delineating practices. Nagaland is divided into 12 districts that are further divided into administrative units called 'circles.' We will have to work with 11 districts that existed at the time of the 2011 Census as the borders of Noklak district, which was formed in December 2017, have not yet been demarcated and it does not yet figure as a district in some of the government records (GoN 2019a). 'Sub-division' refers to a unit of administration between district and circle. There are four kinds of administrative headquarters in districts: the district headquarter that is the seat of the deputy commissioner and sub-district administrative headquarters including circle headquarters that are seats of additional deputy commissioners, subdivisional officers and extra-assistant commissioners.

The communities that lived in the hills of Nagaland before the advent of colonialism are referred to as 'tribe'. The word has no parallel in Naga languages or the languages of the non-tribal communities in their immediate neighbourhood. More than a century after it was first introduced, the term 'tribe' remains controversial even though its use continues to grow.[56] Unless otherwise stated 'tribe' refers to the STs, a constitutional-administrative category that includes tribes recognised by the state for the purpose of affirmative action, among other things. All recognised tribes of Nagaland are indigenous inhabitants. Recognised Naga tribes include Angami (Kohima), Ao (Mokokchung), Chakhesang (Phek), Chang (Tuensang), Khiamniungan* (Noklak), Konyak* (Mon), Lotha (Wokha), Phom (Longleng), Pochury (Phek), Rengma (Kohima), Sangtam (Kiphire and Tuensang), Sumi (Zunheboto), Yimchunger* (Kiphire and Tuensang) and Zeliang (Peren) (Table 5.1). The native district of each tribe is mentioned within parentheses, while asterisks identify tribes distributed between India and Myanmar. Zeliangs are distributed across Assam, Manipur and Nagaland. Recognised non-Naga tribes include Garo, Kachari, Kuki and Mikir (Karbi). Kukis are distributed across Assam, Manipur and Nagaland, while the rest inhabit Dimapur and the neighbouring states of Assam and/or Meghalaya. The Census also provides information on categories of Nagas who do not belong to any recognised indigenous Naga tribe. They are variously referred to as 'Naga' (including Naga not classified) (1991); 'Naga,' that is 'Those who wrote their tribe name "Naga"' (1981, 2001, 2011); and 'Unclassified Nagas' (2001, 2011) in census reports. We refer to these different categories as 'Other Nagas'. In addition, there are non-indigenous tribal immigrants from neighbouring states and even Myanmar as well as non-tribal indigenous inhabitants in the state. Legally, indigenous inhabitants are persons (or their descendants) whose names were recorded in the first electoral roll of the state (5.12.1963) and/or who had been paying house tax or had acquired property before the formation of the state (1.12.1963) (GoN 2010: 143).

Phrases such as 'backward tribe/district/area/region' are used in some places for want of better alternatives, but wherever possible we use *educationally and economically weaker/disadvantaged* or other suitable phrases instead of *backward*. Government (GoN 2010), non-governmental organisations (ENPO 2010), media and people routinely use the word 'backward' in discussions on socio-economic development in Nagaland.[57] Depending on the context, backward community/district could refer to one or more of the following in Nagaland: low per capita income, *kuchcha* (thatched roof) houses, low literacy rate, poor public infrastructure, poor representation in salaried jobs and even alleged underrepresentation in the legislature. The belated end of headhunting and continued use of opium are sometimes added to this list.

Nagas are prone to refer to their languages as dialects, while admitting that most of these 'dialects' are mutually unintelligible.[58] Outsiders often accept this and refer to Nagas as a whole as *a* tribe (Raza and Ahmad 1990: Plate 17) and their languages as dialects (Gundevia 1975: 4; Nibedon 1978: 8; SoI 2010).[59] We will use 'dialect' only when we deal with a dialect per se.

Most Naga languages adopted orthographic conventions in the recent past that have not yet been fully internalised.[60] For the names of tribes, languages and places, we follow the spellings used in the most recent census reports and state government's publication *Basic Facts*. In particular, we use the latest spellings for the names of the Khiamniungan and Yimchunger tribes that continue to be misspelled in union government (GoI 2018c) and, even, state government (*ME* 2018ai) publications. In one case, however, we deviate from the census. The Sema tribe changed the spelling of its name to Sumi. *Basic Facts* switched to 'Sumi' in 1995, but 'Sema' continues to be used in census reports and other government publications. Also, note that 'Sumi' is spelled in two ways. We prefer 'Sumi' to 'Sümi' as the former is more widely used.

We use an awkward expression *illegal/undocumented* to qualify alleged immigrants from neighbouring countries, who are not recorded as international immigrants in the Census. In popular parlance they are referred to as *mian* or *miya*, which is a derogatory term in the North-East (Hazarika 2018: 184, 205, 395). While the popular estimates of international immigrants in Nagaland range between 50,000 and 500,000, as per the 2001 (2011) Census 7,984 (7,108) persons born outside India were enumerated in Nagaland, which includes foreign immigrants irrespective of country of origin and their duration of stay in Nagaland (GoI n.d.2, 2019: D1-Appendix). From the perspective of the state government, migrants are non-indigenous residents of Nagaland. Depending on the context, 'illegal' migrants can include Indian nationals who enter the hills without the ILP or stay beyond the permitted period and foreign nationals who enter India illegally or overstay their visa/permit. These legal–administrative distinctions are immaterial from the perspective of the extended de facto (synchronous) method of enumeration under which the people are simultaneously counted (where they are actually found during the enumeration period) across the country over an extended period (of three weeks). All that matters is the place of last residence within the stipulated period. Those who incorrectly report their migrant status in the census can be referred to as undocumented immigrants and they contribute to content errors in the headcount. However, in Nagaland, as in the rest of the North-East, politicians (Rio 2006: 200; Rio 2010b: 12; Neiphu Rio, interview, 27 May 2015, New Delhi), bureaucrats (*Nagaland Post* 2013), non-governmental organisations (CPO et al. 2003: 2; *ME* 2012), media (see sources referred to in Kumar 2015c) and academics (Amarjeet Singh 2009: 17) routinely use the word 'illegal' in this context. This label serves the immediate goal of regulating the sociopolitical and, by implication, economic status of immigrants, for example, Malays living in Southern Thailand for generations are still referred to as 'khaek' that means *visitor* (Horowitz 2000: 33). Our expression, *illegal/undocumented*, captures both the demographic and legal-administrative as well as popular and political perspectives.

Insurgency has been an integral part of the lives of the people of Nagaland.[61] We engage with insurgency insofar as it impinges on government statistics and offers alternatives to the state's hegemony over cartographical and statistical representations of the land and its people. We distinguish between insurgents/ national workers/the underground (or UG as they are popularly known), partisans of independence and partisans of integration of Naga-inhabited areas within India. The first two differ insofar as the former are armed, even during ceasefire.

Notes

1. In developed countries the length of census schedules grew with the share of government spending in national income (Coleman 2012: 335). The Indian census schedule had 29 questions in 2011, compared to 14 in 1951 (GoI n.d.7). The number of tables generated by the Census of India also increased from 123 in 1961 to 257 in 1991 (Maheshwari 1996: 180). Likewise, the number of questions in India's National Sample Surveys (NSSs) (reports of various rounds) and National Family Health Surveys (NFHSs) (Irudaya Rajan and James 2008: 34) has grown over the years.

2. Porter (1995: 8) argues that 'The appeal of numbers is especially compelling to bureaucratic officials who lack the mandate of a popular election, or divine right. Arbitrariness and bias are the most usual grounds upon which such officials are criticized. A decision made by the numbers (or by explicit rules of some other sort) has at least the appearance of being fair and impersonal.'

3. Pioneers of modern statistics such as Karl Pearson believed that statistics 'provided the proper discipline to reasoning in ... government and administration, which for too long had been in the hands of scientifically illiterate gentlemen and

aristocrats' (Porter 1995: 20). In nineteenth-century Austria, statisticians presented themselves as 'men who served their respective states less by following political guidelines than by employing science and its universal validity in the state's interest' (Göderle 2016: 69). In early-twentieth century United States of America (USA), Wesley Mitchell suggested that 'the use of facts for the guidance of policy' sets the modern civilisation apart from the 'savage past' (Philipsen 2015: 61) and that 'social sciences' and 'quantitative analysis' 'promised a better way forward' than 'Reform by agitiation or class struggle' (ibid.: 62). His contemporary in England, John Maynard Keynes equated the lack of data on economic variables with the state of 'barbaric darkness' (Keynes 1927: 565). More recently, Michael Boskin claimed that without national accounts 'we would be in the economic dark age' (Philipsen 2015: 149). The use of words such as 'dark', 'barbaric' and 'savage' in the context of data deficit is noteworthy.

4. The extensive use of maps and statistics by Basque nationalists in Spain (Urla 1993) is an example of the growing non-governmental capacity to challenge the representation of people and territory by the state. The same holds true of the partisans of independence or greater provincial autonomy in the state of Nagaland in India, whose use of maps and numbers is discussed at length in this book. A third example relates to linguistic surveys in India. The government-sponsored Linguistic Survey of India (LSI) that was launched in the early 1980s has so far managed to publish only a few volumes. On the other hand, the Peoples' Linguistic Survey of India (PLSI), 'a right based movement for carrying out a nation-wide survey of Indian languages' that was launched in 2010, has already published more than 40 volumes covering most of the country; see http://peopleslinguisticsurvey. org/aboutus.aspx?page=PLSI. The quality of PLSI publications requires a separate discussion, but see notes 22 of Chapter 2, 91 of Chapter 4 and 30 of Chapter 7 for preliminary observations.

5. The nascent relationship between statistics and statecraft in nineteenth-century Europe was part of a larger web of relationships generated by co-evolving processes including the emergence of global scientific discourses and engineering practices, standardisation of measurement, industrialisation of economy, emergence of nation states, unification of national economies and currencies and globalisation of capital and trade (Porter 1995; Diaz-Bone and Didier 2016). However, as Woolf (1989) points out, statistics and other fields that appear naturally intertwined today got entangled through non-linear and often unconnected historical processes contingent on conditions that varied across countries and fields of knowledge.

6. 'The term statistics has its roots in the Latin word *status* which means the state, and it was coined ... about the middle of eighteenth century to mean collection, processing and use of data by the state' (C. R. Rao 1999: 45; see also Lepenies 2016: 20). The discipline of statistics was initially known as *political arithmetic* and its purpose was to make 'discoveries which are useful to the art of governing peoples' (Diderot [1751] 2008) and serve as 'the eyes and ears of the government' (C. R. Rao 1999: 46) and a 'compass' or 'lighthouse' to statesmen (Woolf 1989: 602). By the early twentieth century it became necessary for states to be able to

describe themselves in numerically precise ways. Article 1 (and also Articles 2 and 9) of the *Montevideo Convention on Rights and Duties of States 1933*, for instance, suggests that a state is an entity with, among other things, 'a permanent population and a defined territory' (League of Nations 1936: 25).

7. In late eighteenth-century France, 'The Bureau de Statistique ... hoped that by gathering up and disseminating great masses of information about all the regions ... they could promote national unity and an informed citizenry' (Porter 1995: 35; see also Woolf 1989). Mid nineteenth-century Italy (Woolf 1989: 602) and Austria (Göderle 2016: 64) too hoped that census would help consolidate the state. The Indian census continues to be eulogised as a 'nation-building process' with participation in it being 'a true reflection of the national spirit of unity in diversity' (GoI n.d.8).

8. As a French champion of 'progress through public information' announced, 'wherever the struggle resurfaces between the champions of the general interest and that of private interest, you will find us [statisticians] at our post, armed and ready to march' (Porter 1995: 80; see also Holt 2008: 324–6).

9. India's last colonial census conducted in 1941 (GoI 1953a: 9) and Nigeria's first postcolonial census conducted in 1962 (Government of Nigeria n.d.; Jerven 2013: 57) were marred by competitive manipulation. Likewise, the journey of South Sudan, the latest member of the United Nations, towards independence was also marked by controversies over census and delimitation (Santschi 2008). More recently, soon after its formation, India's newest state 'Telangana' launched a controversial Intensive Household Survey (*Times of India* 2014). It is also noteworthy that laws governing census have been among the earliest legislative interventions in several newly independent countries (Kumar 2019). India's Census Act, 1948, for instance, predates the adoption of its constitution.

10. Accuracy, precision, credibility, comparability, usability/interpretability, relevance, accessibility, timeliness and completeness are among the key dimensions of data quality (Biemer 2010: 819). Most discussions on the quality of data in India focus on accuracy and comparability. Other dimensions such as timelines and accessibility (Agrawal and Kumar 2019a) have not received much attention. Note that 'data quality' is different from 'information quality' (Kenett and Shmueli 2014).

11. The mismatch between India's national income estimates from the National Accounts and National Sample Survey Office (NSSO) surveys (Suryanarayana and Iyengar 1986; Deaton and Kozel 2005) and between estimates of unemployment rate from the Census and NSSO surveys (Kasturi 2015) have been attributed to definitional differences. Omkarnath (2012: 236) suggests that India's employment data are of little help to those interested in the informal and rural economy because its employment accounting 'uncritically imitates, albeit with some modifications, accounting appropriate for industrially advanced countries'. More generally, the national income of developing countries is underestimated due to the difficulty of measuring the informal economy (Jerven 2013). Furthermore, income inequality is likely to be underestimated if the distribution of consumption expenditure is used in

lieu of income due to the unavailability of data on income. For a group of countries where comparable data on consumption and income are available, Deininger and Squire (1996: 581) found that the use of consumption-based measures resulted in the underestimation of income inequality and the average difference between the two Gini coefficients was 6.6 points.

12. See S. Bhalla (2014), Shetty (2012) and Chandrasekhar and Ghosh (2011) for manpower constraints faced by India's NSSO, GoI (1991:4) for computing capacity constraints faced by the Census of India and Devarajan (2013) and Jerven (2013) for capacity constraints in Africa.

13. Headcount-linked schemes offer incentives for manipulation, especially when the government lacks the ability to independently verify claims due to either corruption or capacity constraints. The Karnataka government identified about 1.8 million illegal cooking gas connections, that is, more than a fifth of all domestic connections in the state (*Hindu* 2012). In neighbouring Andhra Pradesh, the government identified several hundred thousand duplicate ration cards (*Indian Express* 2012). Wade (1985: 72) highlights the connivance of government officials in such situations in his discussion on the falsification of information about sowing of water-intensive crops in southern India. Similar problems have been reported in other countries. Housing rationing in erstwhile Yugoslavia seems to have provided incentives to inflate headcount in the 1953 Census (Zarkovich 1989), whereas sugar rationing allegedly played a similar role in parts of Sudan in 1993 (A. H. Ahmed n.d.). International donors and aid agencies routinely struggle with manipulation of data in developing countries. Sandefur and Glassman (2015: 129) discuss the manipulation of vaccination and school enrolment statistics in Africa due to 'perverse incentives created by connecting data to financial incentives without checks and balances'. Morgenstern (1973: 20–1) draws attention to manipulation of data by the beneficiaries of the Marshall Plan in Europe.

14. Measures linked to government intervention are susceptible to misreporting by bureaucracy under pressure to achieve targets. Rwanda, India, Nigeria and Malawi seem to have manipulated data on agricultural reforms (Jerven 2013: 63, 75–9; Desiere, Staelens and D'Haese 2016). The Indian government also seems to have overestimated the number of births averted through family planning policies (Dandekar 2004: 44–8) and the impact of structural reforms on economic growth (Jerven 2013: 53) and poverty reduction (Deaton and Kozel 2005: 196).

15. More recently, He (2014) argued that China disputed the World Bank's estimates that suggested that it was close to becoming the largest economy in purchasing power parity (PPP) terms, possibly because it was not prepared to shoulder the international responsibilities entailed by the number-one status. Moreover, it feared that embracing that status could fuel nationalism, which would constrain its foreign policy.

16. Even in the West, the origin and spread of statistics were closely associated with international economic comparisons (Diderot [1751] 2008; Woolf 1989; Coyle 2014; Philipsen 2015; Lepenies 2016).

17. Steve Wilkinson (cited in Alesina and La Ferrara 2005: 790) notes an abrupt change in the composition of a Bohemian town, 'where about a third of the respondents who had declared to be "Germans" in the 1910 Census switched to "Czech" in 1921'. Comparisons of censuses in Europe before and after the world wars and transition to and from communism reveal several examples of abrupt change in the ethnolinguistic composition of the population (Kertzer and Arel 2002a). One of the last major census controversies in Western Europe relates to the use of statistics by the Nazi regime (Aly and Roth 2004; Tooze 2001: 36–9, 285–7) that left a lasting impact, which is reflected in, among other things, census boycott movements in West Germany during the 1980s (Hannah 2009: 71). For a survey of demographic engineering in post-1945 Europe, see Bookman (2013). There is a massive literature on the USA, where minorities have long complained of under-enumeration in the census and under-representation in the legislature (McWorter and Alkalimat 1980; Choldin 1986; Lujan 1990; Anderson and Fienberg 2000; Behrens, Uggen and Manza 2003) and the correction/adjustment of population estimates used for electoral delimitation and federal redistribution has been a subject of litigation (Bradshaw 1996; Goldin 2000). Prewitt (2010: 244–5) discusses the politicisation and 'racialization' of census and how 'sampling became political ideology' in the USA.

18. 'In the United States, the prohibition of religious classification extends to the national census. On one occasion when the Bureau of the Census asked a question about religion, it was prevented from publishing any data on the grounds that even a statistical inquiry into religious practices overstepped the state's authority' (Starr 1992: 290). Britain asked a question on religion in 1851 (Jones 1981: 76–7) and then in 2001 (Kumar 2019), but it was not mandatory to answer it on either occasion. India's founding fathers curtailed census data on caste (Chandrasekhar 1972: 31; GoI 1975c: Note; Maheshwari 1996: 142, 179; GoI 2009b: 28; Roy Burman 1998) and religion (Wilkinson 2004: 40; GoI 2004b: v, xv; Khalidi 2006), while the leadership later restricted the release of data on language to mother tongues spoken by more than 10,000 speakers (GoI 1976c: i; Saxena 1997: 269; *Hindu* 2013). As Mohanty (1996: 165) puts it, in postcolonial India 'the census organization has shown completely stoic indifference to the key cultural and ethnic variables.... Perhaps, the fears were that such tabulation might lead to social unrest' (see also Maheshwari 1996: 179).

19. The Indian government has also been guilty of motivated delays. Data on religion from the 2001 (Engineer 2004) and 2011 (Kumar 2015a) censuses were published after long delays. For examples of delays in various countries and a detailed analysis of delays in the release of India's census data (1951–2011), see Agrawal and Kumar (2019a).

20. On a few occasions census could not be conducted in two states of India, Assam (1981) and Jammu and Kashmir (1951, 1991), which account for about 3.5 per cent of both India's population and area. Other surveys such as geological surveys, cartographic surveys, NSSO surveys, Rural Economic and Demographic Surveys

and District Level Household and Facility Surveys too do not adequately and/or regularly cover smaller/peripheral states.

21. In Africa 'only 32 countries representing 65 percent of the total population have had a census during the last 10 years' (Devarajan 2013: S11; see also Chamie 1994: 140 for a longer-term global assessment of gaps in demographic data). Survey-based statistics such as poverty rate are similarly patchy: 'During the ten year period between 2002 and 2011, among the 155 countries for which the World Bank monitors poverty data using the WDI database, 29 countries do not have any poverty data point and 28 countries have only one poverty data point' (Serajuddin et al. 2015: 3; see also Devarajan 2013: S12 for Africa). Also, twenty-four of the forty-five sub-Saharan countries covered by the Penn World Tables (version 6.1) 'did not have any benchmark study of prices' (Young 2012: 696).

22. Others have equated census in such settings with 'plebiscite' and 'political campaign' (Kertzer and Arel 2002b: 28), 'opinion polls' (Abramson 2002: 178), 'show of strength' (Hekali Zhimomi, DCO, Nagaland, interview, 25 June 2013, Kohima), 'weapon' (Karmakar 2010), 'negotiation' (Government of Nigeria n.d.; Okolo 1999: 323; Aung 2018), 'political weapons' (Adepoju 1981: 35; Fawehinmi 2018; see also Siddiqui and McCarthy 2019 for a similar usage in the USA), 'political document' (Brass 1974: 75, 77) and 'war' (Khan Bahadur Sheikh Fazl-i-Ilahi, SCO, Delhi quoted in I. Ahmed 1999: 124). Commenting on the politicisation of economic statistics in Greece, the head of the Hellenic Statistical Authority pointed out that statistics was 'a combat sport' in his country (Coyle 2014: 1). On the other hand, Russell Weigley quipped that the Second World War was a 'gross national product war' (quoted in Lepenies 2016: 123).

23. Surveys in the cocoa-producing areas of Ghana incorporated different cognitive tools compared to other areas to 'provide a more rigorous assessment of farmers' income' (Serra 2014: 18). Jerven (2013) discusses the colonial state's statistical priorities in Africa where the government collected data mostly on the export-oriented sectors, ignoring the inland trade. The absence of statistics on unemployment in the early-twentieth century USA likewise reflected the lack of political interest in the problem (Philipsen 2015: 71, 76–7). As discussed in Chapter 7, such 'uneven statistical topography' (Serra 2014) reflects the balance of power in the underlying political economy.

24. In this case, interference, if any, was limited to the choice of measures and does not amount to politically-motivated manipulation of the data generation process or data.

25. Around this time, the government was questioning a variety of inconvenient statistics including estimates of poverty rate, unemployment rate and inflation indices (*EPW* 2011). When the NFHS-IV was allegedly 'called off,' the government was accused of cancelling data collection to 'suppress ... unflattering findings', with regard to health and nutrition (*Times of India* 2012a; *Mint* 2012). The next round of NFHS was conducted in 2015–16.

26. For delays in the release of data ahead of elections, see Devarajan (2013: S14), Taylor (2016: 13) and Agrawal and Kumar (2019a). Most recently, members of India's National Statistical Commission resigned protesting against delays in the release of the Periodic Labour Force Survey data (*Business Standard* 2019). The government seemed to be uncomfortable with releasing dismal employment data ahead of parliamentary elections. This, however, is not the first instance of its kind. In the 1970s, B. S. Minhas resigned from the Planning Commission due to differences over the use of 'distorted or juggled' data for economic planning (Weinraub 1973). Likewise, B. K. Roy Burman (1992: viii) dissociated himself from the Second Backward Classes Commission.

27. Pronab Sen and TCA Anant, who succeeded Sen as chief statistician, argued that a fresh quinquennial survey became necessary as gross domestic product (GDP) could not have been rebased using NSSO data from an 'abnormal year' (*Forbes India* 2013). The 2009–10 round of NSSO was marred by recession and drought and rebasing could not have been postponed until the 2014–15 quinquennial survey. Anant added that the preparatory work for a fresh survey was completed before the 2009–10 survey results were released. The repeated attacks on the NSSO by the Planning Commission deputy chairman, however, gave the impression that politics played a role as well. This, though, was not the first time that a quinquennial round was repeated. 'To meet some ad hoc requirement, a Consumer Expenditure survey [conducted in the 27th round, 1972–73] was also conducted in 1973–74 (NSS 28th round)' (GoI 1986b: S-3). For further discussion, see note 30 of Chapter 6. Most recently, the government decided against releasing 'the Consumer Expenditure Survey results of 2017–2018 [75th round of NSS]' because, among other things, it 'is not an appropriate year to be used as the new base year [for rebasing the national accounts]' (GoI 2019b).

28. Democracy is a not a necessary condition for the intertwining of politics and statistics. By the early nineteenth century, Indians had started using statistics to communicate with the colonial government and contest and influence its policies (Kumar 2015b). A century later, Indians began communicating with each other using statistics and even manipulating statistics to promote community interests within the narrow confines of the colonial polity (Maheshwari 1996: 116–36; see also I. Ahmed 1999: 124; Dhulipala 2015: 142, 273–8; Kumar 2015b). More recent evidence comes from a variety of non-democratic countries. The under-enumeration of Blacks in apartheid-era South Africa (Lipton 1972), Tutsis in Rwanda (Uvin 2002), Tajiks in Uzbekistan (Abramson 2002) and Russians in Turkmenistan (Goble 2015) are cases in point. Saudi Arabia did not publish census results for a long time fearing that 'publishing an exact count (showing their own population to be smaller than many supposed) might encourage enemies to invade the country or promote subversion [in the Shia-dominated oil-rich Eastern province]' (Alonso and Starr 1985: 96). Incidentally, even the nascent USA was 'worried that a small population would tempt ... enemies to military action' (Prewitt 2003: 6). Similar considerations seem to have affected headcounts in Bhutan (Chandrasekharan 2013) and Turkmenistan (Goble 2015).

29. Taylor (2016: 13–14) discusses competing incentives facing politicians vis-à-vis the design of a national statistical system, namely, short-term losses because of greater public oversight and long-term gains in monitoring and constraining sucessors.

30. Data published by international agencies such as the World Bank and the International Monetary Fund are the preferred sources of cross-country data (Jerven 2013: 34). These data are susceptible to additional errors insofar as communication between international agencies and national authorities is less than perfect and 'the compulsion to publish numbers that purport to be actual observations for a given year and country ... appears to have won over a sober assessment of the quality [and often even the availability] of the underlying data' (Srinivasan 1994: 17, see also Srinivasan 2003: 304; Mishra 1999; Wade 2012; Jerven 2013). Poor quality notwithstanding, international datasets are uncritically used as hardly anyone has 'the expertise or the time' to question them and, as a result, 'only a few statisticians and economists [working on international comparisons] concern themselves with the matters of detail' (Coyle 2014: 48, 55, 80).

31. Administrative statistics are as important as census and survey statistics examined here. The decline in the quality of administrative statistics is, in fact, one of the biggest challenges facing India's statistical system (Vidwans 2002a).

32. The quality of a variety of other government statistics is questionable as well. National income (Nagaraj 2015), agricultural (Jerven 2013: 77), service (Nagaraj 2009) and industrial (Subbarao 2011) sector outputs, unemployment and wages (GoI 2017; Subbarao 2011), livestock (Mishra 1999), morbidity and mortality (Subramanian et al. 2009) and child immunisation (Irudaya Rajan and James 2008) are cases in point.

33. Woolf (1989) and Göderle (2016) discuss how (mapped) territory is integral to the conceptualisation of modern statistics. Göderle (2016: 87) argues, 'All of the practices that rendered the modern census possible involved techniques to make space controllable.... A territorial conception of the modern state is a precondition of the census procedure.' He further points out that nineteenth-century Austrian censuses were 'In the first place ... not at all concerned with citizens, but rather with space' (Göderle 2016: 71). Pre-war censuses in Czech regions and Belgium conflated headcounts and ethnic borders (Arel 2002: 102, 106). We can, therefore, 'think of the census as a map – a map of the society rather than of the territory' (Prewitt 2003: 1).

34. The conferences of the directors of census operations held before Indian censuses devote substantial time to the geography of census operations. Also, the first few circulars issued before censuses freeze jurisdictional borders as per the Census Rules, 1990 (Art. 8(iv)) (Circular No. 1, dated 22.12.17 for the 2021 Census) and issue directives for the compilation of jurisdictional changes (Circular No. 1) and changes in the status of village and urban areas (Circular No. 2, dated 4.9.18 and Circular No. 3, dated 12.11.18) in the preceding intercensal period.

35. We refer to democracy deficit in our discussion because India is a democratic country, and political unrest is, therefore, associated with the weakening or

breakdown of democratic structures/processes. A more general nomenclature is needed to cover non-democratic states.

36. Heine and Oltmanns (2016: 207) argue that 'data from the statistical infrastructure can be ascribed the characteristics of public goods, because statistical data can be consumed on a non-competing basis.... The marginal costs of production are zero and therefore the price-mechanism does not work. On the other hand the exclusion principle can be applied; in principle it is possible to limit the access of users to data. As a result, data are a good to which a property right can be assigned (exclusion), but market pricing does not work properly (non-rivalry in consumption).' Note that the marginal cost of expanding the coverage of surveys or the dissemination of results is very small; also that the exclusion principle is inapplicable to government statistics in democracies with an independent judiciary and a free media. Moreover, in India, the Right to Information Act, 2005 allows access to most of the information collected by the state.

37. Chapter 6 discusses an example of restrictions on surveys due to political disturbance. Under such circumstances, even journalists and researchers are unable to collect information either due to the difficulty in physically accessing sites amidst unrest or because the government and/or non-governmental groups restrict the freedom of expression and movement. Researchers working on India's North-East have complained that both the state (Wouters 2018: xiv, xviii–xix, 22–3, 27; Prabhakara 2012: 226) and its competitors (Amarjeet Singh 2009: 18–19; Prabhakara 2012: 223–7) impede field work.

38. Dissatisfaction with census-based redistribution of resources and electoral seats has been reported in countries as diverse as Pakistan (Kiani 2019; Khan 1998: 481; Weiss 1999: 683, 688), Nigeria (Okolo 1999: 322; Jerven 2013: 57) and the USA (Goldin 2000; Prewitt 2003).

39. Initiatives to improve the statistical capacity of developing countries are often driven by donors and aid agencies that need to identify requirements and opportunities and later measure the impact of their intervention. International development loans often 'include investments in statistical systems' to address the incapacity of recipients (World Bank n.d.2, see also Shetty 2012: 44; Krätke and Byiers 2014: Table 1; OECD 2017; PARIS21 2017). India's Thirteenth Finance Commission offered grants to states to improve their statistical capacities at the district level (GoI 2009a: 37, 224). More recently, the Indian government has extended support to states under the Support for Statistical Strengthening scheme (*ME* 2018g).

40. A high-level UN Panel on the Post-2015 Development Agenda noted that 'too often, development efforts are hampered by a lack of the most basic data about the social and economic circumstances in which people live' (Krätke and Byiers 2014: 6).

41. Srinivasan (2003: 306) suggests that 'the [macroeconomic] data situation continues to be alarming' in India because of the rudimentary state of macroeconomic analysis in the country. In other words, there is a lack of demand for better data.

42. This two-layered justification is inspired by a comprehensive approach to study law and development suggested by Sen (2006).

43. There are contributions on survey data quality (Bertrand and Mullainathan 2001; Biemer et al. 2004; Meyer, Mok and Sullivan 2015), the evolution of measures of economic activity (Jerven 2013; Coyle 2014; Philipsen 2015; Lepenies 2016), the quality of census data (Bose, Gupta and Raychaudhuri 1977; Barrier 1981; Preston, Heuveline and Guillot 2001), the politics of numbers (Alonso and Starr 1987; Horowitz 2000; Kertzer and Arel 2002a; Bookman 2013; Morland 2018) and the politics of mapping (Winichakul 1994; Wood 2010). There are monographs examining a variety of statistics for Western countries, for example, Maier and Imazeki (2013) for the USA and Crook and O'Hara (2005) and Levitas and Guy (1996) for Great Britain. Similar contributions on India include the multivolume *Database of Indian Economy* (Dandekar and Venkataramaiah 1975) published in the 1970s and the report of the National Statistical Commission. Others such as Saluja (2017) merely compile sources of government statistics without examining data quality. There are also journal issues devoted to data quality (for example, *Canadian Journal of Development Studies* 35:1; *Journal of Development Economics* 44:1, 98:1; *Journal of Development Studies* 51:2). Most collections that deal with multiple statistics or locations examine different statistics for different periods and places, do not engage with the politics of numbers and do not correlate the findings for different kinds of statistics.

44. Diaz-Bone and Didier (2016: 9) identify four stages in the lives of data: identification of categories, conversion of knowledge into numbers, communication of numbers and the subsequent use of numbers.

45. The phrase 'field economics' is borrowed from Frederick Cooper and Randall Packard quoted in Jerven (2013: 89).

46. Estimates of Nagaland's forest cover vary considerably (Rio 2006: 251–3; 2007: 111, 258), possibly due to differences in definitions.

47. The partisans of independence in Nagaland stress the uniqueness of Nagas and their culture and history vis-à-vis the rest of the country (note 49 of Chapter 3). We have highlighted only a few broad structural similarities between the composition of the population of Nagaland and the country as a whole.

48. The Directorates of Economics and Statistics (DES)/State Statistical Bureaus (SSB) 'participate in NSS by following the same sample design and canvassing the same enquiry schedules through their personnel. The sample First Stage Units (FSUs) for DES/SSB of all the States/UTs are selected by NSSO and supplied to them' (GoI 2011a: 14–15). The central and state samples are not pooled, though, and the NSSO's official results are based exclusively on the central sample. The NSSO takes the help of the DES/SSB for conducting field surveys in a few states such as Arunachal Pradesh, Manipur, Mizoram and Tripura (GoI 2011a: 2). In a few rounds, it has also taken the help of its state counterpart to survey inaccessible parts of Jammu and Kashmir, such as Ladakh (Agrawal and Kumar 2017b).

49. The problems identified in this book are not limited to Nagaland. Errors in data on tribes (Sharad Kulkarni 1991; Verma 2013), caste (Maheshwari 1996; Verma 2013), religion (Gill 2007) and languages (Brass 1974; Gill 2007) of various states and overestimates of the overall headcount of Kashmir Valley (Guilmoto and Irudaya Rajan 2013) and the northern districts of Manipur (Chapter 7) are cases in point.

50. For insightful discussions of government statistics in the Indian subcontinent, see Kansakar (1977), Begum and Miranda (1979) and Mishra (1999).

51. India is perhaps unique in the developing world insofar as it can boast of a long-time series for a wide range of statistics. Moreover, India has been known for advances in the fields of census and sample surveys and has contributed to the development of the relevant international statistical standards (C. R. Rao 1973; Maheshwari 1996; T. J. Rao 2010). However, as Shetty (2012: 41) puts it, 'India's pride in being a nation with a strong base in statistics is getting increasingly punctured' as its 'official statistical collection machinery has been in decline for more than two decades' (see also Mishra 1999; Vidwans 2002a–b; Srinivasan 2003).

52. Except for 'census' data for 22 villages in Phek (Office of the Razou Peyu Phek Sub-region Chakhesang 1992), we could not access data generated by Nagaland's insurgent organisations that purportedly 'conduct population count in villages' across 'their regions and "union territories"' in India and Myanmar, carry out 'delimitation exercise of constituencies' (*Telegraph* 2011a) and collect 'taxes'. While much of this could be rejected as play-acting, as discussed later, people are sensitive to a specific aspect of these exercises. Further, it bears noting that in 2010, that is, more than a decade after the signing of the ceasefire, the largest Naga insurgent organisation admitted that 'a complete official census has not been possible yet due to the compelling political situation' (GPRN 2010 [2007]: 2). It is highly unlikely that insurgents could collect statistics amidst active conflict before the signing of ceasefire, but reports (*Nagaland Post* 2011) suggest that they interfere with government censuses in favour of communities aligned with them. In neighbouring Manipur, several government officials confirmed that insurgents interfere with data collection (interviews, 7 October 2019, Chandel; 8 October 2019, Senapati). Also note that we do not have access to cartographic (note 3 of Chapter 3) and demographic (note 34 of Chapter 4) information purportedly collected by the armed forces.

53. Incorrect is placed within scare quotes as we are not sure if correct maps exist or can be prepared before the Naga political problem is addressed.

54. Historically, people tried to avoid census, fearing it to be a prelude to higher taxes, conscription or more intrusive presence of the state. Religious beliefs and customs also interfered with census. These factors combined with the general difficulty in tracking everyone, inaccessibility of remote areas, the moral hazard of enumerators and the limited reach of the government in rebellious areas and slums often caused undercounting of population. Commenting on the results of the 1991 Census, the doyen of demographic research in India, Ashish Bose (1991: 31) wrote, 'I do not rule out the possibility of a large undercount in disturbed districts of Punjab,

Jammu & Kashmir and Assam. In my view, the extent of undercount may be even 20 per cent in the big cities.' Likewise, Srivastava (1972: 139) suggests that over-enumeration seems 'to be less frequent than under-enumeration'. The literature on coverage errors has, therefore, mostly focused on undercount. We, however, focus on the possibility of overcount in a postcolonial setting.

55. India's draft 'National Policy on Official Statistics' defines official statistics as 'statistics derived by the Government agencies from statistical surveys, administrative and registration records and other forms and papers, the statistical analyses of which are published regularly, or planned to be published regularly, or could reasonably be published regularly' (GoI 2018b: 3). Following Pronab Sen, the first chief statistician of India, we can add that official statistics also include statistics collected by non-governmental organisations, but endorsed by the government (interview, 11 December 2018, New Delhi).

56. For the debate on the colonial genealogy of the category of tribe and its postcolonial acceptance in India, see Beteille (1960), Desai (1960), Sharad Kulkarni (1991), Skaria (1997, 1998), Xaxa (2003), Roy Burman (2009), Nongkynrih (2010), *ME* (2016) and Wouters (2018). See also Chapter 7.

57. For a discussion of the colonial origins of the widespread use of the twin words *backward* and *advanced* in developing countries, see Horowitz (2000: 147–9). Even within nineteenth-century Europe, certain countries, regions within countries and sectors of the economy were seen as backward (Woolf 1989: 601, 603). In India, the British referred to tribal areas excluded from the usual administration as 'Backward tracts' in 1919 that were later renamed 'Excluded areas' and 'Partially excluded areas' in 1935 (note 38 of Chapter 3). For the colonial-missionary origins of the characterisation of the pre-Christian Naga society as backward and the acceptance of this among Nagas, see Thomas (2016). Wouters (2018: 220–1) points out that now the backwardness is self-perceived and people are infatuated 'with the discourse of backwardness'. See, for instance, *CPO & Anr. vs. SoN & Ors.* 2010.

58. Vizol (n.d.: 57), Sema (1984: 94, 244), Horam (1988: 29, 198), S. C. Jamir (2003: 182), Rio (2011: 16; 2014: 7), *ME* (2013d) and GoN (2014: 18, 72, 128). Others use 'language' and 'dialect' interchangeably (Alemchiba 1970: 3, 24–5; Gundevia 1975: 4, 91; Boruah 2014: xxix).

59. The historical–political origins of this conflation of 'language' and 'tribe' requires a separate discussion.

60. See Sachdeva (2001) and the relevant publications of the Central Institute of Indian Languages, Mysore. The degree of orthographic fluidity should be evident from the fact that Naga language newspapers can spell their own names in three different ways in the same issue (Kumar 2015i).

61. There is a large literature on insurgency (and related issues) in Nagaland: Alemchiba (1970), Yonuo (1974), Gundevia (1975), Nibedon (1978), Horam (1988), Hazarika (1995, 2018), Chasie (2000), Iralu (2009), Borgohain and Borgohain (2011), Lintner (2012), Misra (2012), Thomas (2016) and Wouters (2018).

2

Nagaland and Numbers

Introduction

Until the late nineteenth century, when the British established control over parts of the Naga Hills[1] and Ao Nagas were exposed to Christianity, the Naga society was non-literate. Unlike other parts of the Indian subcontinent that had prior exposure to collection of information by premodern states and could influence early colonial statistical categories and practices to some extent (Peabody 2001; Guha 2003), Nagas were first exposed to statistics only in the late nineteenth century beginning with the record-keeping of the Baptist Church and colonial administration.[2] Yet within a generation, numbers and written documents became key ingredients of political debates in the Naga Hills and began to play an important role in the Naga nationalist discourse.[3]

The Memorandum on the Naga Hills to the Simon Commission (1929), the foundational document of the Naga political history (Timeline 2.1), contains arguments based on government statistics and statistical comparisons. The memorandum notes,

> [O]ur population numbering 1,02,000 is very small in comparison with the population of the plains districts in the Province [Assam], and any representation that may be allotted to us in the Council will be negligible and will carry no weight whatsoever ... if we are forced to enter the Council of the majority all these rights [private rights recognised by the British Government] may be extinguished by an unsympathetic Council, the majority of whose number is sure to belong to the Plain District ... we should not be thrust to the mercy of the people who could never subjugate us, but leave us alone to determine ourselves as in ancient times.[4] (Chasie 2000: Appendix A.I)

The adjusted 1921 population of the Naga Hills district was 158,801 after accounting for the transfer of the Diger Mauza from Kohima subdivision to North Cachar subdivision in 1923 (NSA, 2:587). Furthermore, according to the 1921 Census, the population of the Naga tribes of Assam, including Nagas outside the Naga Hills district, was 220,619 (Marten 1923: 160). The members of the Naga Club who submitted the memorandum belonged to Angami (including Eastern Angami, that is, Chakhesang), Kacha Naga, Kuki, Sumi, Lotha and Rengma tribes. The population of the speakers of the corresponding 'vernaculars' was 121,759 (ibid.: 98). The figure quoted in the memorandum is, however, close to 102,402, the 1901 Census population estimate (Allen 1902: 32; McSwiney 1912: Table II).

About two decades later, a memorandum submitted by the Naga National Council (NNC) to the government (on 19 February 1947) argued that a million Nagas 'will be wiped out of existence' amidst 'forty crores [400 million] of Indians' (Iralu 2009: 391). 'Forty crores' is close to 389 million, the population of undivided India according to the 1941 Census, but the corresponding population of the Naga Hills was only 189,641 (GoI 1946: 57, 126).

The fear of demographic invasion also figures in the plebiscite speech (16 May 1951) delivered by A. Z. Phizo, the father of Naga nationalism: 'being surrounded by world's biggest nations around us (in matters of human population).... Being a small nation (almost a 1000th part of India), we can easily be submerged and get lost ...' (NNC 1951: 8, 10; Zinyü 2014: 288–313).[5] In that plebiscite, 99.99 per cent of Nagas are reported to have supported independence (Nuh 2002: 111, 131). This number quickly emerged as a politically salient and iconic figure and remains so until this day, but has not yet received a critical scrutiny.

In 1980, the National Socialist Council of Nagaland (NSCN), a splinter of the NNC, too highlighted the demographic threat in its manifesto:

> The involuntary influx of Indian nationals from overpopulated India into our country has set all Nagaland under constant threat of eventual submersion ... before the year 1947, there was not a single Indian in Nagaland. It has now more than two hundred thousand Indians. If, with a greater ratio of influx, another twenty years would go let alone a generation, what would be the state of affairs.... (NSCN 1993: 15).

Contrary to the NSCN's claim, Nagaland's non-tribal population was about 120,000 in 1981. Also, it is not true that there were no non-Nagas/Indians in the Naga Hills/Nagaland before 1947. There were four indigenous non-Naga tribes in Nagaland and Nagaland's commercial capital Dimapur, which was the capital of the indigenous medieval Kachari tribal kingdom, was resettled in the colonial period by non-tribal entrepreneurs from across the Indian subcontinent.

To sum up, since the late 1920s, Nagas have used comparative demographic statistics to argue that they were small in numbers as well as culturally and ethnolinguistically distinct from their neighbours within India and, therefore,

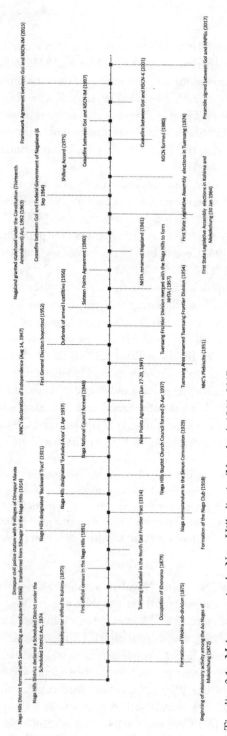

Timeline 2.1   Major events in the Naga Hills district/Nagaland, 1866–2017

Source: Authors' compilation, using various sources (see note 61 of Chapter 1).

deserved political autonomy/independence. On the other hand, independence and even statehood for the Naga Hills were opposed on grounds of its small size equated with unviability (Palat 2015: 176).[6] So, 'smallness' was central to both the self-perception of Nagas and the outside world's perception of the Naga Hills (Horam 1988: 224; Borgohain and Borgohain 2011: 147). Nagas responded to the perceived 'smallness' by taking inspiration from small countries such as Singapore (Ramunny 1988: 215) and by resorting to scale jumping, investing in the idea of integration of Naga areas and insisting on their unique political history and culture and independence since time immemorial (Chapter 3).

Insurgency was another site for the politicisation of numbers. Right from the beginning, the insurgency was fought both on the physical terrain as well as in the realm of information. The two sides routinely published conflicting information on their area of influence, number of casualties and relative numerical strength of the armed forces and insurgents. An interesting early example of the information war is found in the pages of the *Statesman* (ASA, TAD/CON-78/54). The *Statesman* (10 October 1954) referred to a Press Trust of India (PTI) report that suggested that the partisans of independence had established a republican government covering 5,000 square miles and 700,000 people in the unadministered part of the Naga Hills, that is, the Tuensang Frontier Division of the North Eastern Frontier Agency (NEFA). A day later it published another story covering the refutation by the NEFA authorities who pointed out that the Tuensang was spread over 2,000 square miles and had a population of about 100,000. Neither side had any reliable estimate of the population, though, as only a small portion of Tuensang was enumerated in 1951.[7]

Once numbers were accorded primacy in debates with 'outsiders', it was only a matter of time before they began to shape internal debates on creation of new states out of Nagaland (ZPC 1983; ENPO 2010), formation of new districts within Nagaland (KTC 2008; Rengma Hoho 2016), delimitation of assembly constituencies (Chapter 5), recognition of indigenous tribes (NTC 2013), affirmative action in government jobs (*CPO & Anr. vs. SoN & Ors.* 2010) and immigration (Rio 2010b: 12).

Small circles demanding district status stress their political uniqueness and ethnic particularity and argue that (small) numbers have to be read in their historical and political contexts.[8] Khiamniungans demanded district status on grounds of remoteness, underdevelopment, their role in giving refuge to Nagas escaping religious persecution in Myanmar and their contribution to the Naga national movement (KTC 2008: 3–4). In a memorandum demanding district status for Tseminyu and Tsogin circles of Kohima district, the Rengma Hoho (2016: 5–6) first catalogued the Rengma tribe's contributions to the Naga nationalist movement. It then appreciated the creation of a sub-district administrative unit for the lone village of Khezhakeno in Phek district 'based on its historical importance in the history of Nagas' and called for the creation of a district for Rengmas 'in the same manner ... on ground of unique historical importance ... and ... distinct background of Rengma tribe'. Leaders of the Rengma Hoho and the Rengma Selo Zi (Rengma Youth Organisation) (interview, 13 December 2018, Tseminyu) argue that they have been discriminated against and denied a fair share in legislative assembly, development funds and government jobs within Nagaland because India's democracy favours the majority over justice to the minorities. Elsewhere in Nagaland, the Eastern Nagaland Peoples' Organization (ENPO 2010: 5–6; Kumar 2015d) demands the separation of five districts to form 'Frontier Nagaland' state in response to the decades long political, economic and social neglect within Nagaland. The ENPO propaganda relies on an array of cartographic and demographic data interpreted in light of historical facts and the geopolitical importance of the Eastern Naga people and their territory. The arguments of the KTC, Rengma Hoho and ENPO are reminiscent of the Naga nationalist discourse that stresses historical uniqueness and laments that the Indian democracy invariably sidelines minorities.[9] Communities do not take chances though and, as shown in later chapters, try to bolster their numbers even as they celeberate their (smallness and) uniqueness.

A *Nagaland Post* (2009) editorial noted that manipulation of headcount was 'hinged on (a) politics, where more people means more votes, and (b) [development] funds, where the size of population means more money'. Such explanations of abnormal population figures were endorsed by the *Provisional Population Totals* (*PPT*) of the 2011 Census (GoI 2011c: viii). The Naga Hoho, which was the most influential tribal organisation in Nagaland at the time of the 2011 Census, lamented that 'the Census has been a much misunderstood exercise in Nagaland with the people equating it with the electoral roll listing or a data that is solely used by the Government of India' and appealed against viewing census through the lens of 'political or tribal interest' (*Eastern Panorama* 2011; *Meghalaya Times* 2010).

Given the long-standing use of demographic arguments and facts in Naga politics, one expects a careful use of numbers. However, as discussed below, uncritical reliance on statistics and their selective use seem to be the norm in the government as well as academia.[10]

Do Chief Ministers Know Their State's Population?

Political leaders can perhaps not be expected to consistently quote correct statistics in their public speeches. Nevertheless, their speeches merit attention in light of the multiplicity of conflicting government statistics in circulation in Nagaland and the fact that some of the chief ministers had themselves expressed concern at the quality of government statistics (Vamuzo n.d.: 37; 1991: 11–12; Hazarika 2005). Table 2.1 compiles population figures mentioned in speeches of political leaders between 1969 and 2016.[11] In most cases the stated figures were were less than the corresponding census estimates.[12] This systematic divergence needs to be read in light of the fact that the Census had overestimated Nagaland's population, at least, until 2001. If headcounts used in public discourse can diverge so much from the Census, one can only imagine how well other more complex statistics are understood.[13]

Politicians not only refer to 'incorrect' numbers, but they also interpret data conveniently. After the 2001 Census reported abnormal population growth, Nagaland's Chief Minister Neiphiu Rio adopted different stands on the issue of high population growth rates. On the occasion of inauguration of new districts, which had seen massive over-reporting of headcount in the 2001 Census, he (Rio 2004: 14, 30) noted that the decision fulfilled the aspirations of 'a population of approximately over four lakh [400,000] people'. The population of these three districts, which were among the epicentres of the manipulation of census data, was 318,942 in 2001 and contracted to 219,580 in 2011. The chief minister overlooked his government's doubts regarding the veracity of headcount (GoN 2003a) and even his own concerns about the poor quality of government records in the state (Rio 2004: 32; 2010b: 107–8). In 2005, Rio admitted that the population had been inflated possibly by more than half a million in 2001 by tribes competing for favourable delimitation of constituencies (Hazarika 2005).[14] Years after blaming inter-tribal competition for high population growth rate, Rio (2010b: 12) drew attention to the growth of mosques and religious seminaries [15] to argue that 'the increase in the influx of illegal Bangladeshi immigrants' explains the 'abnormal' population growth.[16] Also note that in 2003, he had drawn attention towards the possibility of 'illegal immigration' from Bangladesh as well as Myanmar (Rio 2003: 117), whereas in 2010 he highlighted only the former (Rio 2010a).[17]

Policymaking

Unlike political leaders, official publications of the government are expected to use statistics carefully. However, the bureaucracy too uses erroneous statistics uncritically. Long after the state government rejected the 2001 Census (GoN 2003a), its statistical bureaucracy continued to produce and use projections based on that census (GoN 2004b). The flawed headcount affected the whole range of secondary statistics calculated using population, for example, population density and per capita income, and resulted in abnormal swings in socio-economic indicators that vitiated intertemporal and interstate comparisons.[18]

Table 2.1 Nagaland's population in speeches/writings/interviews of political leaders, 1970–2016

Year[‡]	Date of speech/ publication	Chief minister/ leader	Population (in statement)	Census figure[†]	Difference (in %)[††]	Source
1963	30 Nov. 1970	Hokishe Sema	From 0.3 to 0.4 million	394,834	From –24.02 to 1.31	H. Sema (1984: 216)
1970	15 Aug. 1970		About 0.4 million	499,403	–19.9	H. Sema (1984: 7)
1970	26 Nov. 1970		Over 0.4 million	499,403	—	H. Sema (1984: 105)
1976	23–4 Sept. 1978	Vizol	A little less than 0.7 million	632,623	10.65	Vizol (n.d.: 15) as per a state government survey
1979	10 Jun. 1979		Not more than 650,000	714,522	–9.03	Vizol (n.d.: 74)
1994	26 Oct. 1994	S. C. Jamir	A little more than 1.2 million	1,404,410	–14.55	S. C. Jamir (1996: 10)
1997	15 Jan. 1997		Around one-and-a-half-million population	1,551,464	–3.32	S. C. Jamir (1998: 11)
1998	15 Aug. 1998/2 Sept. 1998		A million and a half	1,713,915	–12.48	S. C. Jamir (1999: 49, 66, 68, 70)
1999	12 Nov. 1999		1.4 million	1,801,413	–22.28	S. C. Jamir (n.d.3: 133)
2000	19 Oct. 1985		More than 1 million	1,893,377	—	S. C. Jamir (n.d.1: 48)
2000	26 Oct. 1994		From 1.8 to 2 million	1,893,377	From –4.93 to 5.63	S. C. Jamir (1996: 10)
2000	18 Sept. 2000		Estimated at about 1.7 million	1,893,377	–10.21	S. C. Jamir (n.d.4: 109)
2000	21 Jan. 2001		About 1.8 million	1,893,377	–4.93	S. C. Jamir (n.d.5: 26)
2001	13 Jul. 2001	R. Koijam*	1.6 million	1,990,036	–19.6	Koijam (2001)
2001	24 Dec. 2005	N. Rio	1.4 million	1,990,036	–29.65	Hazarika (2005)
2011	17 Jun. 2012	K. Therie*	1.4 million	1,978,502	–29.24	Times of India (2012b)
2016	1 Apr. 2016	S. C. Jamir*	2.275 million	n/a	—	S. C. Jamir (2016)

Source: Compiled by authors using collections of speeches and other sources.

Notes: [‡] 'Year' is the period to which the 'Population (in statement)' corresponds. The use of population projections (Table 4.1) instead of census figures will not affect our inferences. [†] Interpolated figures have been reported for intercensal periods. [††] Indicates the difference between the stated and census populations divided by the latter; a positive (negative) difference indicates that the census population is smaller (larger) than the stated population, for example, the non-census source over- (under-) estimates the population vis-à-vis the census. 'n/a' indicates that we have not extrapolated the population. * Except for these, the rest are based on statements of the respective chief ministers of Nagaland. S. C. Jamir was not in office in 2016.

Government reports drew erroneous inferences from published statistics. The *Nagaland State Human Development Report* (GoN 2004a: 15), for instance, argued that '[t]his unprecedented growth rate of population is a cause of serious concern to the demographers and policy planners in the State' and called 'for policy intervention to tackle this spiralling population growth, which can seriously hamper the planning process and development aspirations'. Similar sentiments are echoed in Nagaland's *Economic Survey 2002–2003* that used the 2001 population data to argue that the state's rapid population growth posed an 'enormous problem' because it aggravates unemployment (GoN 2005a: 1). Both these were published after the census population estimate was challenged by the state government itself. More recently, a senior government official misunderstood the census data and blamed 'migration ... beyond expectation' for the contraction of rural population during 2001–11 (*ME* 2019b).

At the national level, most academic analyses of development challenges are restricted to 'major' states, invariably leaving out the ethno-geographic periphery. However, policymakers and government-appointed committees often end up using flawed data as they cannot avoid smaller states.

The Committee on Optimum Sample Sizes for North Eastern States (GoI 2011a) used incorrect population estimates for Nagaland. The Committee for Evolving a Composite Development Index of States (GoI 2013e: 26–7) was expected to suggest, among other things, an index that could be used for deciding the devolution of funds from the centre to states. The committee used population and household amenities data from the Census and consumption and educational data from the NSSO for ranking states on the basis of backwardness. (To the best of our knowledge the proposed index was not put to its intended use.) Later chapters show these sources to be flawed in case of Nagaland.

The *Report of the High Level Committee on Socio-economic, Health and Educational Status of Tribal Communities*[19] compared the heavily inflated 2001 headcount with the 2011 Census figures and expressed concern at the contraction of the population long after the former figures were rejected.

> Health of the ten crores [100 million] vulnerable people should become an important national concern. At the same time negative Scheduled Tribe population growth in Nagaland and in the Great Andamanese tribe in Andaman & Nicobar is a concern. (GoI 2014c: 240, see also 40–1, 192)

This is an alarmist reading. The drop in Nagaland's population was a result of better vigilance that checked ghost enumeration.[20] Also, Nagaland that is dominated by Naga tribes is different from Andaman and Nicobar where tribes constitute a small and isolated minority.

Under the Fourteenth Finance Commission (FFC), Nagaland's inter se share of taxes increased to 0.498 (GoI 2015a: 95) from 0.314, the share recommended by the previous commission (GoI 2009a: 122). This spike can be explained by the use of population projections for the period from 2010–11 to 2012–13 that were based on the flawed 2001 headcount and the 2011 population estimate that is not entirely free of errors either (Chapter 7). Furthermore, the indicator used by the commission for measuring fiscal capacity distance/income distance makes use of per capita figures that are also distorted by errors in the headcount.

While it can be argued that the committees referred to above were end users and had to use *published* government data, the same cannot be said for the expert groups on population projections. Successive expert groups used flawed headcounts as baselines and arrived at highly inaccurate projections of Nagaland's population. The magnitude of projection errors grew over the years and, most recently, the direction/sign of projection error reversed (Figure 2.1).

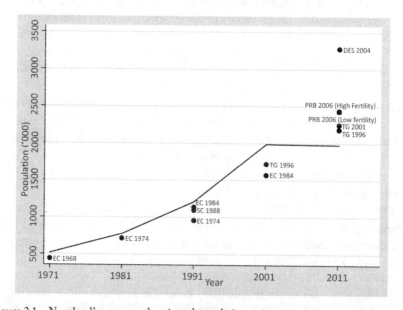

Figure 2.1   Nagaland's census and projected population estimates

Source: Prepared by authors using EC 1968: GoI (2011b: 169), EC 1974: GoI (1979a: 48–9), EC 1984: GoI (1988b: 28), SC 1988: Nath (1991), TG 1996: GoI (1996b: 64), TG 2001: GoI (2006a: 36), DES (2004): GoN (2004b: 28) and PFI-PRB (2007): PFI-PRB (2007: 6, 11).

Notes: (i) EC, SC and TG stand for Expert Committee, Standing Committee and Technical Group, respectively. (ii) The continuous line indicates the census population estimates, while dots indicate projected population estimates. A dot below (above) the line indicates under-(over-) projection. (iii) See also Notes to Table 4.1.

Sample Surveys

Several national-level surveys do not cover the smaller states of the North-East such as Nagaland. Most states in the North-East were not covered in the Rural Economic and Demographic Surveys and the surveys conducted by the National Nutrition Monitoring Bureau. Furthermore, not all national surveys regularly cover these states. The District Level Household and Facility Survey did not cover Nagaland in 2007–8. Even the surveys conducted by the NSSO that regularly cover the North-East did not fully survey Nagaland until recently.

Errors in headcount bias survey estimates because sample surveys use census as the sampling frame.[21] However, census data are poorly understood. The 1991 and 2001 Censuses overestimated Nagaland's population and the NSSO used the inflated headcounts for its projections, even after the state government had rejected the flawed census data. The overcount was corrected to an extent in the 2011 Census, when the government tried to curtail ghost enumeration. The growth rate turned negative because the 2011 population was less than the manipulated headcount of 2001. The NSSO interpreted the correction as a contraction and used a negative growth rate to project Nagaland's rural population (NSS Report No. 564: Appendix C). This highlights a lack of attention to even essential statistics that influence sampling design. It is also noteworthy that the share of tribal households in NSSO samples has increased substantially over the years, even though the composition of Nagaland's population has been largely stable (Chapter 6).

Academic Research

The uncritical use of flawed statistics on Nagaland is quite widespread among researchers. We will discuss a few examples related to fertility, migration and language and show how inferences are drawn without without paying due attention to the quality of data.

Guilmoto and Irudaya Rajan estimate fertility for districts for different censuses. They used the 2001 Census data without noting that the abnormally high growth rate of Nagaland was not in agreement with other sources of demographic information. Guilmoto and Irudaya Rajan (2001: 723) noted, 'By the late 1980s, fertility in Manipur and Nagaland was as low as in south Indian states [that is, among the lowest in India].' However, a year later Guilmoto and Irudaya Rajan (2002: 667) arrived at much higher estimates of Nagaland's fertility: 'the recently released National Population Policy document says that the total fertility rate (TFR) in Nagaland and Delhi are 1.5 and 1.6 whereas the NFHS estimates [3.77 for Nagaland] and ours [3.16] are much higher.' After the 2011 Census, Guilmoto and Irudaya Rajan (2013: 59) telegraphically note the 'apparent stagnation' in

Nagaland's population without asking how the population can stagnate when their own estimates of the TFR were much higher than the replacement rate in both 2001 (3.16) and 2011 (2.82), and the rate of out-migration has not been high either. They do not reflect on Nagaland's case even though they discuss at some length how politically-motivated manipulation seems to have vitiated Jammu and Kashmir's headcount in 2011.

Others accept population growth statistics and explain glaring discrepancies by invoking assumed trends of migration. Several studies attribute the high population growth rates of Nagaland to immigration: 'The high tribal growth rate ... is *largely* due to the immigration of tribal groups from the adjoining foreign territories' (Sharma and Kar 1997: 87), 'The influx of migrants and immigrants ... has been the cause [of high growth rate]' (Shimray 2007: 8),[22] '*Evidently*, the silent and unchecked influx of illegal immigrants in the state has played a crucial role' (Amarjeet Singh 2009: 17), 'We will have to highlight ... another factor of population growth, viz., the migration ... *particularly* from Bangladesh' (Gogoi at al 2009: 298), '*obviously* because of immigration, not natural growth' (Shimray and Devi 2009: 13) and 'The impact of Bangladeshi migrants is also *visible* in the *unstable demographic profile* of the state' (Nag 2014: 41) (emphases added). Interestingly, others arrive at an opposite conclusion using the same data. Misra (2012: 203) suggests that 'the indigenous population of these [northeastern] states [such as Nagaland] is not being threatened by the influx of outsiders' as 'the scheduled tribes population registered a marked rise'. Misra overlooks the fact that Nagaland's population was overestimated in successive censuses with indigenous tribes accounting for most of the overcount. When the growth rate fell precipitously, Chaurasia (2011: 15) attributed the decrease in population during 2001–11 to out-migration: 'there are indications of a very heavy out migration'. Kundu and Kundu (2011) attributed the decrease to a drop in in-migration: 'the tendency of the people in the so-called heartland to go to these states to grab employment and business opportunities seems to have weakened'. (The 2011 Census data on migration were released much later.) To these we can add a much longer list of statements of political and civil society leaders, who assume that Nagaland's population changes can be explained by illegal/undocumented immigrants allegedly of Bangladeshi origin (S. C. Jamir n.d.4: 12–13; Rio 2010a).

We will examine the contribution of migration to Nagaland's population in Chapter 4, but a few observations about the migration-based explanations are in order. First, researchers drew conclusions about migration from population growth rates, rather than the data on migration. The 2001 Census suggests that there was net out-migration from Nagaland between 1991 and 2001 (GoI n.d.23). Second, researchers did not question the quality of data. Third, flawed/misinterpreted statistics have been used to whip up sentiments against alleged illegal/undocumented (Bangladeshi Muslim) immigrants in Nagaland.

Researchers misinterpret census data on identity too. According to the Census, the most widely spoken languages of Nagaland are tribal languages. However, Nagamese, which is not reported in the Census, is the most widely spoken (second) language in the state and is the only indigenous inter-tribal language (Kumar 2014b). Scholars ignore Nagamese as it is occluded by key sources of information such as the Census (excursus of Chapter 4).

Varshney (2013) discusses, among other things, the implications of the distribution of linguistic and religious groups across the states of India. Using census data, Varshney (2013: 57–8) suggests that 'in Northeastern India, some states, especially Nagaland and Mizoram, are not only tribe-based, but those tribes are linguistically as well as religiously distinct from the rest of Indians. Their respective vernaculars are the first languages of Nagaland and Mizoram, not Hindi and both are Christian-majority states (ibid.: Table 6). It is in these states that the attempts at secession have been made'. Varshney overlooks subsidiary languages and Nagamese, the lingua franca of the state. Stepan, Linz and Yadav (2011: 107) too ignore Nagamese and claim that Ao was 'the most common language in the state'.

A few observations on the treatment of language data in Stepan, Linz and Yadav and Varshney are in order. First, both use the 2001 Census statistics, which were rejected many years ago, without any caveat. In fact, Varshney (2013: Tables 5–6) used the 1991 Census data even though he refers to the 2001 Census as the source. In Nagaland, the ranking of languages by census population shares changed between 1991 and 2001. Second, Stepan, Linz and Yadav's claim is barely true insofar as Ao was the largest mother tongue community as per the 2001 Census. Otherwise, Ao language is not common in any sense. It is spoken only by the Ao tribe in Mokokchung district and by out-migrants from there. It is not understood by other tribes except for some in the eastern districts along Myanmar border, where people were exposed to it because of the evangelical and educational initiatives of Aos, the location of pioneering religious and educational institutions in Mokokchung and intermarriage between upwardly mobile eastern Naga men and Ao women. These factors have weakened in the recent decades because of the emergence of indigenous cadres of missionaries and teachers, opening of new colleges in the eastern districts and migration to the 'mainland' for higher education. In fact, Ao may not even be the most widely spoken mother tongue of the state after content and coverage errors are accounted for. Third, we wonder if Varshney would have emphasised the linguistic chasm between the 'mainland' and Nagaland and Stepan, Linz and Yadav would have emphasised the fragmentation of the Naga society as much if the Census also reported the number of those who spoke Nagamese as the second or third language, and placed tables on link languages before the tables on mother tongues in its publications. Nagamese is the most widely spoken second language of Nagaland that is used in all the districts.

It is used in the state legislative assembly as well as in insurgent camps, on the one hand, and bazaars, classrooms, political rallies and multi-community churches, on the other. Nagamese and Assamese are to a large extent mutually intelligible. Under favourable conditions, Nagamese might have mitigated the 'fragmentation' of the Naga society and, perhaps, also the disconnect between Nagaland and, say, Assam. We are not suggesting that the widespread prevalence of Nagamese negates the conventional understanding that there has been an emotional and cultural disconnect between states such as Nagaland and the 'mainland', which has compounded the constitutional-political conflict. However, explanations of the origins and persistence of insurgency have to go beyond statistical catalogues of differences. More nuanced explanations of the relationship between identity (and its official accounting) and conflict are needed in complex settings such as Nagaland because people do not enter conflicts with preformed, statistically assessable identities.

Academics are not alone in misinterpreting language data from the Census. The report of the National Commission for Religious and Linguistic Minorities too identifies Ao language as 'Main language' and 'Major' language and the rest, including Angami, Kuki, Lotha, Sema, Chokri, Konyak, as 'Minority Language' (GoI 2007b: Table 4.2) and 'Minor' languages (GoI 2007b: Table 4.4). Nothing could be farther from truth though. There is no hierarchy among Naga languages. The speakers of Angami, the only Naga language taught at the Nagaland University, would bristle at such a classification.

Fourth, it seems that 'quantification processes *in and of themselves* [have begun to] constitute our most basic understandings' of the world around us (Urla 1993: 820, emphasis in original). The widespread neglect of Nagamese, which is not enumerated, is a good example of the stranglehold of (government) statistics on scholarly and public imagination. By the same token, enumeration is often treated as an evidence of timeless existence. Tikhirs treat their community's enumeration in successive censuses as evidence of their long-standing separation from the neighbouring Yimchungers (TSU 2006: 21). The latter, however, claim that Tikhirs are their sub-tribe because, among other things, Tikhir is a dialect of Yimchunger as per the Census (various interviews; Shahoto 2001: 180; Yimchungrü 2002; PLSI 2016: 258[23]).

The composition of the tribal population of Nagaland is also often misunderstood. In *An Atlas of Tribal India*, using the 1961 Census data, Raza and Ahmad (1990: 60) classify Nagaland as 'mono-tribal'. This erroneous classification is explained by the ad hoc practice of the Census to report aggregate statistics for a number of tribes collectively known as Naga (GoI 1966: 66). However, the category 'Naga' includes 14 recognised indigenous tribes and a few unrecognised indigenous tribes, which speak mutually unintelligible languages. The Census also publishes statistics for each of these tribes.

An example regarding the use of sample survey data is also in order. An interstate study on human development ranked Nagaland as the second best in India (Suryanarayana and Agrawal 2013). The authors relied upon NSSO surveys to calculate income and education sub-indices. Nagaland outperformed all states along both these dimensions, but these findings are likely to be driven by the inadequacies of the NSSO samples for Nagaland (Chapter 6).

Concluding Remarks

We have seen how the Naga political discourse has been intertwined with statistics since the colonial period. The extensive use of numbers in and numbers about Nagaland has, however, not meant a careful scrutiny of their quality. We eclectically highlighted assorted instances of the misuse and misinterpretation of data in politics, policymaking, sample surveys and academic research. Government bodies (and often even researchers) can only use the published estimates of population as the Census Act, 1948, does not provide for the revision of published figures (Kumar 2019). However, the Census should at least alert users to the errors. In most cases discussed in this chapter, bureaucratic and academic users did not even note the faulty nature of statistics, let alone examine the implications of using the flawed data or the generative contexts of data. Context refers to both the immediate setting in which data were collected (such as the politicisation of the headcount in 2001 and the absence of any provision in the Census Act, 1948, for the correction of faulty statistics) and the broader setting in and for which data are collected (such as the close relationship between a tribe, its language and its territory in Nagaland). The following chapters suggest ways of reading statistics by locating them in a proper context and contribute to the understudied field of the political economy of statistics in developing countries.

Notes

1. The Naga Hills district of Assam and the Tuensang Frontier Division (erstwhile Naga Tribal Areas) of the North Eastern Frontier Agency (NEFA) were merged in 1957 to create the Naga Hills–Tuensang Area (NHTA), which was later renamed as Nagaland (Timeline 2.1, Maps 3.10A–E). Unlike the Naga Tribal Areas, the Naga Hills district was an administered territory during the colonial period.
2. Thomas (2016: 26) points out that Rev. William Pettigrew served as the 'superintendent of the first census of the hill tribes [of Manipur] (1910–11)' as the colonial presence in the hills was limited and 'only the missionary had a working knowledge of the language and customs'. This was one of the many ways in which the missionary enterprise was intertwined with the colonial state and later its

postcolonial avatar in Naga areas (Thomas 2016). Missionaries seem to have been generally supportive of census in the colonial era (Maheshwari 1996: 29–30).

3. Longkumer (2018) discusses how the use of English language and Roman script shaped the Naga nationalist discourse and helped the otherwise isolated and divided people to come together and transcend their traditional divisions. Nagas were exposed to maps in the late nineteenth century, but soon enough maps too became an integral part of the Naga nationalist propaganda (Chapter 3). It can be argued that statistics and maps played an equally important and complementary role in the making of the community.

4. Nisier, a signatory to the Simon Commission memorandum, also pushed for making the church 'autonomous of the plains' (Thomas 2016: 131–2). The separation of the Baptist Churches of Assam and the Naga Hills took place in the 1930s, whereas the political separation had to wait until the late 1950s.

5. Phizo's plebiscite speech abounds in demographic arguments and 'facts' and is the most extensive statement of the demographic concerns, among others, that motivate the Naga insurgency/nationalist movement.

6. *Bedrock of Naga Society*, the most detailed critique of Naga nationalist movement from within Nagaland, highlighted the smallness of territory and population, among other things, to argue against independence (NPCC 2000: 17).

7. Stracey (1968: 82) draws attention to the departmental politics within the government that influenced statistical assessments of the strength of the insurgents.

8. Wouters (2018: 258–60) suggests that the village he studied enjoyed hegemonic status in the precolonial period. This village 'thought it not just justifiable but *historically* inevitable that they would dominate numerically on the constituency's electoral list' (emphasis added). So, the electoral roll is viewed as an arena for status contests, with the vote share of a village in its constituency's electorate being a reflection of relative substantive power, rather than a mere list of adult population.

9. Pleas for contextual reading of numbers are not unique to the Naga Hills. The Sikhs unsuccessfully demanded 33 per cent seats in the legislature of Punjab on the basis of their contribution to the economy and the colonial army (Singh 1999: 220–3). Even Muslims used similar numbers *plus* arguments ('political importance and value of the contribution ... to the defence of the Empire') to bolster their claims (Jones 1981: 89; see also Guha 2003: 160). After independence, the Constituent Assembly of India provided for disproportionate representation to the Anglo-Indian community taking into consideration historical factors and their contribution to certain important fields (Ashraf 2013). The community accounted for a large part of the country's human capital in certain sectors of the formal economy.

10. The following discussion omits the media, where there are fewer resources and lesser expertise compared to the bureaucracy and academia to critically examine data. A senior journalist, who extensively covered the politicisation of census in Assam, used Nagaland's flawed headcount without any reservation even as it was being questioned within the state (see Prabhakara 2012: 238). More recently, a

news report published in a leading, local daily informed readers that 'the urban population in the state has been increasing over the years – from 19% in 2001 to 28% in 2011' (*ME* 2018h) without alerting them that the correction of the rural population explains a large part of this jump in the rate of urbanisation. In fact, even the current chief minister, whose government facilitated the correction of the inflated headcount of 2001, too noted that Nagaland 'recorded highest urbanization rate in the nation during the last two consecutive census[es] 2001 and 2011' (*ME* 2019k).

11. Area statistics are not referred to in speeches as frequently as headcounts, but as discussed at length in Chapter 3, government as well as non-governmental sources report a variety of mutually inconsistent figures. For instance, state and central government sources provide widely differing estimates of the area of the newly formed district of Longleng. On the occasion of the inauguration of the district the chief minister stated that the area of the district was 885 square kilometres (Rio 2004: 31; see also https://longleng.nic.in/), but the area is only 562 square kilometres as per census (GoI n.d.5; 2018a: Table A-1) and other government (FSI 2017: 258) publications.

12. We also compiled references to headcount and the number of households for villages and districts in chief ministers' speeches and found that most statements were inconsistent with census estimates.

13. For a brief but insightful observation about the larger problem of data disuse in India, see Srinivasan (2003: 306).

14. We have not been able to locate the collection of Rio's speeches delivered in 2005, which could have helped us to understand what made the chief minister change his opinion between early 2004 and late 2005.

15. It is even claimed that 'there are already a considerable number of militant [Islamic] fundamentalist groups operating in the bordering areas of Nagaland with a design to overrun our land and resources' (*Times of India* 2012c) and that Dimapur has become a 'Jihadi hub' (*ME* 2012). It is commonplace in Nagaland to refer to 'a sea of skull caps' or 'shuttered shops' in Dimapur during Muslim festivals as evidence of massive illegal immigration (Naga IAS officer, interview, 22 November 2012, Kohima; retired Naga IAS officer, interview, 16 November 2013, Dimapur; Amarjeet Singh 2009: 23–4).

16. In 2000, Rio's predecessor S. C. Jamir (n.d.4: 12–13) highlighted 'demographic invasion' involving illegal immigrants from Bangladesh that threatened 'to swamp the local population completely'. In fact, Rio (2003: 117) too referred to illegal Bangladeshi immigration in 2003, but he did not link it to high population growth (see also *Telegraph* 2003a).

17. When we discussed the issue of alleged Bangladeshi immigrants after the 2011 Census with Neiphu Rio, he suggested that the foothills, especially Dimapur, Tuli and Baghty were more vulnerable to illegal immigration and that there must be about 200,000 'floating' illegal immigrants in Dimapur. He added that the state government had directed the officials to not count them (interview, 27 May 2015, New Delhi).

18. The trend of the ratio of Nagaland's gross school enrolment to its 0–14 year population (Figure 4.5) and its electorate to population (Figure 4.6) behave abnormally vis-à-vis the rest of the country.

19. This report was not officially released by the government (*Indian Express* 2014). Copies are, however, available on the Internet. We retrieved one from http://www. indiaenvironmentportal.org.in/files/file/Tribal%20Committee%20Report,%20 May-June%202014.pdf on 8 July 2019.

20. Recently, the *Down to Earth* (2019) magazine carried a report, which concluded that the Sema/Sumi language now had 'few takers' as the Census reported a 90 per cent decline in the number of speakers of the language. In reality, the Sema/ Sumi language is one of the most vibrant tribal languages of Nagaland and the decline in the strength of its speakers is an artefact of content errors (see excursus of Chapter 4).

21. Surveys also compare the actual sample drawn with the Census to check the ex post representativeness of their sample (for example, Lokniti 2008: 3–4). Such comparisons or benchmarkings are vitiated by errors in census data.

22. Shimray (2007) trusted the Census insofar as it supported his claim that Nagas faced a serious demographic threat from 'outsiders' (ibid.: 8, 34–5), but blamed the under-enumeration of Naga women due to 'enumerators' negligence' and ignorance about census among people for the decrease in sex ratio in 1991 (ibid.: 31, 34).

23. Elsewhere, PLSI (2016: 4) suggests that Tikhir belongs to Khiamniungan language rather than Yimchunger.

Part II
Key Statistics

3

Cartographic 'Mess'[*]

Introduction

In the run-up to the February 2018 Assembly Elections, the website of Nagaland's chief electoral officer hosted two different types of constituency maps. One was legally correct with regard to the external borders (Maps 3.1 and 3.3[b]), and the other was factually correct with regard to constituency borders and the location of polling booths in the disputed territory between Assam and Nagaland (Maps 3.2 and 3.3[a]). This is not the first time though that the Nagaland government has published mutually inconsistent maps of constituencies (Agrawal and Kumar 2017a: Map 5).[1] Moreover, election maps are not the only conflicting maps released by the state government. Maps published by the Census (Maps 3.8 and 3.10E) and the Nagaland GIS and Remote Sensing Centre (NGISRSC) (Maps 3.5–3.7) also differ with respect to the external borders. In some cases, even maps published on the same sheet are mutually inconsistent (Map 3.4).[2] The diversity of government maps is supplemented by a wide variety of maps published by civil society organisations, non-governmental organisations, insurgent groups and partisans of independence, which are often displayed in government offices as well.[3]

When we first visited Nagaland about eight years ago, we were struck by this multiplicity of inconsistent maps and estimates of area of the state. Unable to find any authoritative estimate of area, one of us interviewed a senior official in-charge of border affairs in Kohima (25 June 2013). Initially, the official denied the cartographic diversity, but later argued that maps released by different departments varied with their footprints. So, the education department's map of schools differs from the health department's map of dispensaries. This can at best explain the differences within the borders of the state but not the differences between maps in terms of the external borders. The official finally admitted that there might be discrepancies due to border disputes but expressed an inability to share the estimate of Nagaland's area as the matter was sub judice (*SoA vs. UoI & Ors.* 1988)

[*]This chapter is a substantially expanded and updated version of a paper published in *Political Geography* (Agrawal and Kumar 2017a).

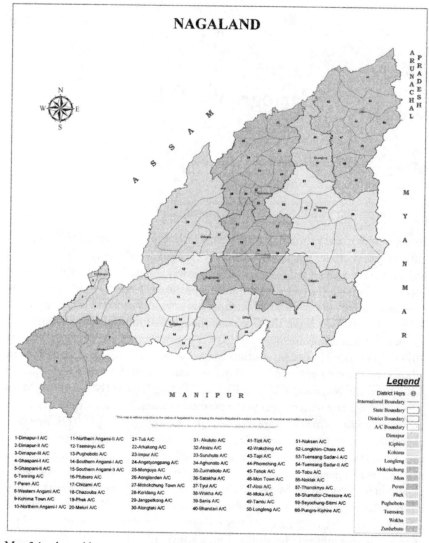

Map 3.1   Assembly constituencies, 2018

Source: Adapted from CEO Nagaland, http://www.ceonagaland.nic.in/ac-map.

Note: Map not to scale and may not represent authentic international borders.

and referred the interviewer to existing government publications.[4] Another official argued that geographic information system (GIS) maps were not entirely accurate for forested, hilly terrain (interview, 19 September 2012, Kohima). However, the maps of Nagaland are more erroneous around the Assam–Nagaland border that runs through plains and foothills, where the vegetation is not dense.

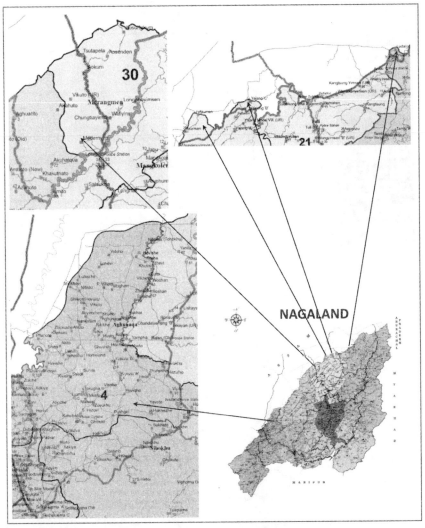

Map 3.2   Political Map, 2018

Source: Adapted from CEO Nagaland, http://www.ceonagaland.nic.in/maps/Atlas%20Maps/img/Nagaland%20Political%20Map.jpg.

Note: The disputed territory included in the inset map (of Nagaland) is expanded in the adjoining fragments.

Map not to scale and may not represent authentic international borders.

We will argue that the persistent and growing 'errors' in Nagaland's maps suggest that we are not faced with an instance of, what Monmonier (1991: 43) would call, 'cartographic carelessness'. Map-making in Nagaland faces inherent

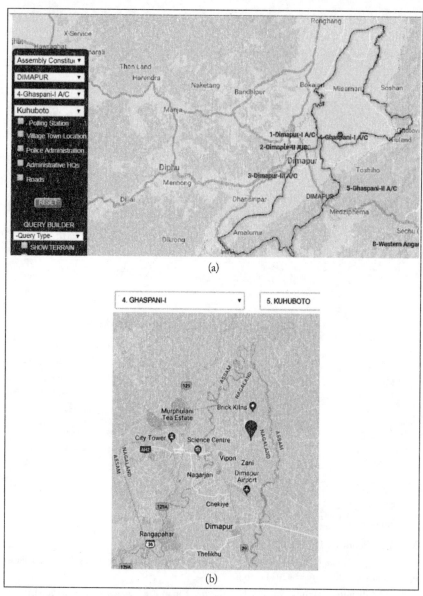

(a)

(b)

Map 3.3   Constituencies (a) and polling stations (b) maps, 2018

Sources: Adapted from CEO Nagaland, http://117.242.184.23/maps/NagalandMaps.php and http://ceonagaland.nic.in/locate-polling-station.

Note: The polling stations map shows an incorrect location for Kuhoboto polling station of Ghaspani I constituency in Dimapur. Several other polling stations of constituencies along the Assam–Nagaland border are incorrectly marked on these maps.

Maps not to scale and may not represent authentic borders.

indeterminacies that result from multidimensional cartographic/territorial conflicts. Three prominent interfaces – centre–state, interstate and government–civil society – are sites of cartographic mismatches and conflicts. The Nagaland government is sandwiched between an irredentist insurgency and partisans of independence/integration of Naga areas within India in the civil society, on the one hand, and status quoist neighbouring states and the union government, on the other. This chapter examines the cartographic, statistical and administrative implications of the state government's balancing act. More generally, it explores postcolonial responses to colonial-era borders and the resultant horizontal

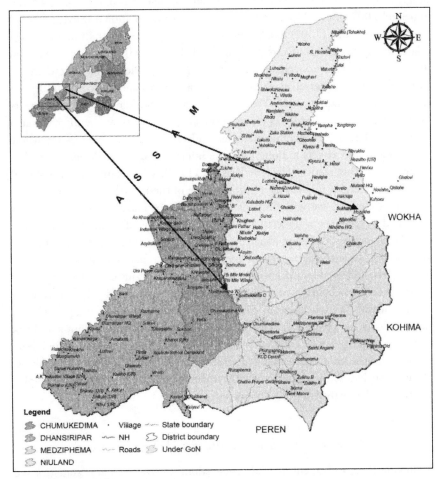

Map 3.4   Administrative blocks, Dimapur

Source: Adapted from http://nagalandgis.in/document_files/DIMAPUR%20ADM%20BLOCK.pdf, accessed on 20 December 2019.

Note: Map not to scale and may not represent authentic borders.

(interstate, inter-district) and vertical (centre–state, state–district, state–civil society) conflicts over territory as well as its representations.

Studies in the Indian context have examined map-making as a scientific enterprise in the construction and legitimisation of the British Empire as a unified entity (Edney 1997; Barrow 2003), the impact of colonial map-making on the self-image of the British people (Barrow 2003), the scalar structure of colonial India (Legg 2009; 2016), the demarcation of borders between British India and nominally independent states (Cederlöf 2014), boundary-making in colonial frontiers (Phanjoubam 2016), late colonial boundary commissions (Talbot and Singh 1999; Chester 2008) and postcolonial international (Chatterji 1999, van Schendel 2002; Jones 2009b; Shewly 2013) and intra-national (Suykens 2013) borders. Corbridge (2002) touches upon the idea of 'Greater Jharkhand', which relates to our discussion of 'Greater Nagaland'. Urla (1993) and Crampton (1996) discuss similar cases from Spain and Bosnia. The extension of Naga settlements in the disputed border areas shares similarities with Israel's growing footprint in Palestine (Weizman 2007; Wood 2010). Unlike Suykens (2013), who treats Nagaland's disputed border as an exceptional space, we treat the disputed area as part of a larger cartographic-statistical indeterminacy that engulfs the whole of Nagaland and affects it along both the internal and external margins.[5] This chapter is in this respect close to Krishna (1994), who examines postcolonial India's cartographic anxiety using the example of the Indo-Bangladesh border.[6]

In this chapter, we will first discuss changes in Nagaland's area statistics unrelated to changes in its territory, the long afterlives of earlier estimates, the mutual inconsistency of maps issued by different tiers and wings of the government and the impact of the cartographic 'mess' on other statistics such as population. This will be followed by a discussion of the colonial origins of conflicting maps, Naga irredentism, conflicts over the units of measurement and political economy of irredentism. We will then discuss how the state government and partisans of independence or greater autonomy have used competitive developmentalism, counter-mapping, scalar competition and scale jumping to contest colonial-era borders and the union government's constitutional monopoly over map-making. We will conclude with a discussion on the implications of this complex cartographic politics for the quality of government statistics.

Disconnect between Territory and Area Statistics

Following the government official's suggestion, we compiled area statistics and maps from census reports. Estimates of the state's area changed over the years without changes in its external borders. Census publications of the 1950s and 1960s provide three estimates of the 1951 area: 16,397.21, 16,451.60 and 16,487.90 square

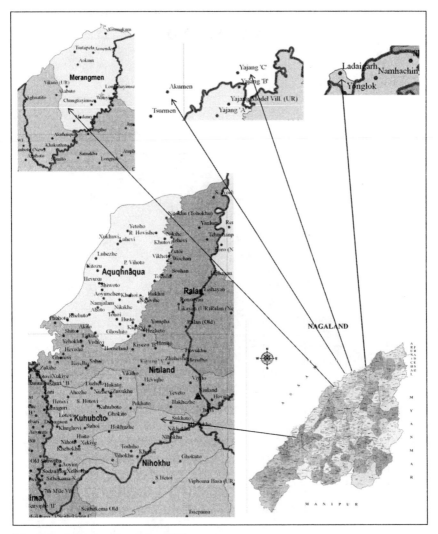

Map 3.5   Administrative circles, 2013

Source: Adapted from Nagaland GIS & Remote Sensing Centre (NGISRSC) (2013).

Note: The disputed territory included in the inset map (of Nagaland) is expanded in the adjoining fragments.

Map not to scale and may not represent authentic international borders.

kilometres (Table 3.1).[7] The 1961 estimate of area, 16,487.9 square kilometres, agrees with one of the 1951 estimates. The estimate was revised to 16,527 square kilometres in 1971, with the intercensal increase being attributed to changes in 'computational techniques' (GoI 1973a: 23, 40). As per the 1981 Census,

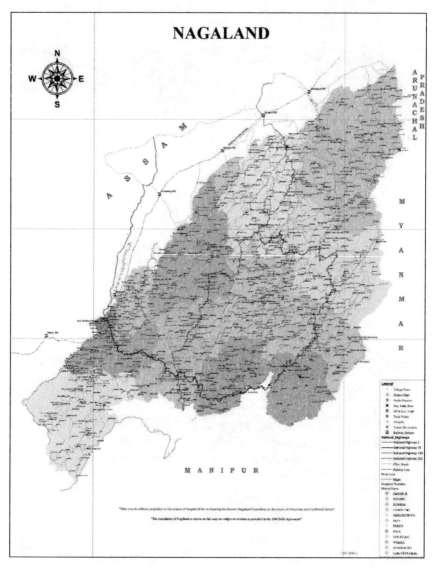

Map 3.6   *Index Map*, 2013

Source: Adapted from NGISRSC (2013).

Notes: The areas that lie in the disputed territory are referred to in the legends as territories 'Under GON [Government of Nagaland] Admin'.

Map not to scale and may not represent authentic international borders.

Map 3.7   Circle map, 2013

Source: Adapted from NGISRSC (2013).

Note: The disputed areas, partly or wholly under Nagaland's administration, lie outside the state's border marked by a thick line.

Map not to scale and may not represent authentic international borders.

Table 3.1 Area (in sq km) of Nagaland's districts, 1951–2011

District	Year									
	1951	1961	1971	1981	1991	2001	2011†	2011††	2011	2011
Source(s)	GoI (1956: 3, 55) [GoI (1966: 42)] (GoI (1966: 50)) {GoI (1956: 3, 55)}	GoI (1966: 37)	GoI (1973a: 26, 40)	GoI (1984b: 26–38)	GoI (1998: 46)	GoI (2005a: 59)	GoI (2012a)	GoI (2011c: xiv, 59)	GoI (n.d.5)	GoA (n.d.1)
Kohima (1971)	6,171.94 (6,148.7)	6,148.7	7,209	6,067	6,067	6,067	6,065	5,937	6,067	6,067 + 354.55*
Kohima			7,209	4,041	4,041	3,114	1,472	1,268	1,463	
Dimapur						927	746	926	927	
Peren							1,833	1,726	1,651	
Phek				2,026	2,026	2,026	2,014	2,016	2,026	
Mokokchung (1971)	4,957.24 (4,983.1)	4,983.1	3,852	4,498	4,498	4,498	4,508	4,499	4,498	4,498 + 239.86*
Mokokchung			3,852	1,615	1,615	1,615	1,629	1,610	1,615	
Wokha				1,628	1,628	1,628	1,608	1,630	1,628	
Zunheboto				1,255	1,255	1,255	1,272	1,259	1,255	
Tuensang (1971)	5,322.43 (5,356.1)	5,356.1	5,466	6,014	6,014	6,014	6,004	5,667	6,014	6,014 + 0.00*
Tuensang			5,466	4,228	4,228	4,228	2,132	2,187	2,536	
Kiphire							1,130	1,122	1,130	
Longleng							562	568	562	
Mon				1,786	1,786	1,786	2,180	1,791	1,786	
Total area	16,451.60 [16,451.7] (16,487.9) [16,397.21]	16,487.9	16,527	16,579	16,579	16,579	16,576.8†	16,103 (16,644‡)	16,579	16,579 + 594.41 (= 17,173.41)

Source: Authors.

Notes: (i) The census reported area statistics in sq miles in 1951, both in sq miles and sq km in 1961 and in sq km later. (ii) †The sum of the areas of the districts is 16,576.8 sq km, but the area was 16,579 sq km as per GoI (2012a: 1). (iii) ††Calculated using data on population density and population (GoI 2011c). The area of the state calculated by adding up the area of districts is 16,103 sq km, which is 3 per cent less than the 2001 area possibly due to inaccurate distribution of area between Kohima and Tuensang and their successor districts. (iv) ‡Area calculated using the overall population and population density is 0.4 per cent more than the 2001 area. The difference could possibly be attributed to rounding-off errors. (v) *Correction in the 2011 area using the Assam government's estimate of the territory under Nagaland's administration (GoA n.d.1). (vi) Contrary to all census reports, GoN (1981: 35) suggests that Tuensang's area was 5,466 sq km in 1961, of which only 5,356 sq km was enumerated.

Nagaland's area was 16,579 square kilometres and the intercensal difference was attributed 'to adoption of different technique' (GoI 1984b: 13).[8] Subsequent censuses use this figure. The Census reports for 1961 and 1971 are silent about crucial cartographic moments, namely, the 1967 Boundary Agreement between India and Myanmar, which might have affected Nagaland's overall area,[9] and the formation of Nagaland's precursor the Naga Hills-Tuensang Area (NHTA) in 1957 through the merger of the Naga Hills district of Assam and the Tuensang Frontier Division (erstwhile Naga Tribal Areas) of the North Eastern Frontier Agency (NEFA), which affected the borders of districts.[10]

Each of the pre-1981 estimates of area has enjoyed a long afterlife. The state government continued to use the 1961 figure as late as 1979. State government publications such as *1979 Nagaland Basic Facts* (GoN 1979: 1, 7) reported the 1961 estimate of area, whereas *Nagaland 1980 Basic Facts* (GoN 1980: 1, 12) reported estimates (16,572 and 16,572.9 square kilometres) closer to the figure published in the 1981 Census (16,579 square kilometres). The biennial *State of Forest Report* used the figure 16,530 square kilometres until 1989 (FSI 1989: 19), which is close to the 1971 estimate. The *1991 State of Forest Report* switched to the 1981 estimate, with the increase being attributed to the 'correction in the geographical area' (FSI 1991: 15, 24). Likewise, until recently, the Geological Survey of India (GSI) used the 1971 estimate of Nagaland's area (GSI 2011: 2). Surprisingly, even a recent Survey of India map mentions the 1971 area (SoI 2010). Since multiple figures including those superseded are in circulation, researchers and even government agencies end up using outdated estimates.[11]

Nagaland's territorial dispute with Assam, which predates its formation, adds another dimension to the problem. Decades of occupation and counter-occupation in pursuit of a favourable alignment of the resource-rich Assam–Nagaland border have denuded Assam's reserved forests and transformed them into a patchwork of Assamese and Naga villages that cannot be separated into mutually exclusive zones. So, while these villages are administered by the respective state governments, it is difficult to neatly divide the disputed territory between the two states. The Nagaland government's maps show a large part of the disputed territory – including Assamese villages administered by Assam – to be under its administration, even though its census did not enumerate the Assamese villages in the disputed territory. Unlike the maps published by the Nagaland government (Maps 3.5–3.7), census maps of Nagaland do not include any part of the disputed territory (Maps 3.8 and 3.10E).

Nagaland and Assam are not the only states locked into a territorial dispute, but the union government does not follow uniform norms for reporting such disputes. Four different cases can be identified with regard to intra-national border disputes.[12] In some, the Census explicitly identifies disputes.[13] In others, disputes are noted without identifying the size of the disputed territory.[14] The third category of territorial disputes such as between Maharashtra and Karnataka and Odisha and its neighbours are not noted in government maps. Some of the earlier publications for Odisha, though, noted the disputed character of its border with Andhra Pradesh (GoI 1997e: 18). Nagaland's case is different. A vague and, mostly, evasive approach is followed in case of the Assam–Nagaland border dispute. While Assam has disputes with all its successor states, government maps note the disputed nature of borders in case of Arunachal Pradesh and Meghalaya and do not carry any comparable note for Nagaland (GoI 2011f: ii; GoI n.d.4). In fact, even a SoI (2010) map of Nagaland is silent about the Assam–Nagaland border dispute, while it notes the tentative nature of the other borders of Assam.

The cartographic confusion along Nagaland's external margins is matched by confusion along the internal margins. Changes in area estimates and borders of sub-state units have often not matched changes on the ground. Without the addition of any new territory, Tuensang's area reported in the Census changed from 5,356.1 square kilometres in 1961 to 5,466 square kilometres in 1971 and 6,014 square kilometres in 1981 (Table 3.1).[15] During the same period, the area of Kohima decreased and that of Mokokchung increased marginally. The next census adjusted the population, but not the area, of the six districts affected by territorial changes in the 1980s (Figure 3.1; GoI 1998: 76). Three villages were transferred from Mokokchung to Wokha in 1987. The entire Tobu subdivision comprising of Monyakshu, Mopong and Tobu circles was transferred from Tuensang to Mon in 1986. Pughoboto and Ghathashi circles were transferred from Kohima to Zunheboto in 1986. In fact, even after the creation of new districts in 2004 and 2017, the state's area has not yet been properly apportioned among districts (note 11 of Chapter 2).

The problem is not restricted to the apportionment of the state's area between districts. In several cases, borders of circles have changed contrary to exchange of territory.[16] Peren's border shifted northward into Dimapur between 1981 and 1991 despite the net transfer of territory to the latter (Agrawal and Kumar 2017a: Map 8; GoI 1988a: Map 16; GoN n.d.5; SoI 2010). One village each from Pedi (Moava) and Jalukie (Kiyevi A) circles of Peren were transferred to Medziphema and Dhansiripar circles of Dimapur, respectively (GoI 1998). Likewise, maps of electoral constituencies such as Ghaspani I, Ghaspani II and Tseminyu vary across election cycles and even within the same electoral cycle without the redistribution of the electorate. Stray maps in other government reports show further variations in the state's internal borders (see, for instance, GoI 2013c: 6).[17]

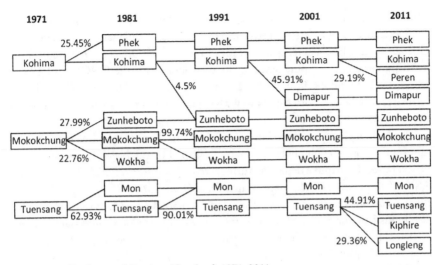

Figure 3.1 Evolution of districts, Nagaland, 1971–2011

Sources: Prepared using information from Kumar and Somanathan (2009) for 1971–2001 and GoI (2011c) for 2001–11.

Notes: Numbers adjacent to arrows denote the share of the population (in the preceding census) of the parent district that was transferred to a new/existing district before the next census. A new district Noklak was created in 2017, but its borders have not yet been demarcated.

Many Maps

Nagaland exercised administrative control over at least 594.4 square kilometres of Assam's territory as of 2013. This territory is mostly in Golaghat district adjoining Nagaland's commercial capital Dimapur and to a lesser extent in Karbi Anglong, Jorhat and Sivasagar districts of Assam (Table 3.1).[18] The Census does not include the area of this territory in Nagaland's area, even though the corresponding population is added to the state's population as settlers in villages administered by Nagaland refuse to cooperate with enumerators from Assam. Census reports for Assam have consistently maintained that Golaghat's area is 3,502 square kilometres (GoI 1996a: 22; GoI 2008a: 22; GoI 2018a: Table A-1), even though the state government's own estimates indicate the loss of at least 362.94 square kilometres territory of this district to Nagaland (GoA n.d.1). The census reports for Assam add that Nagaland claims territory in Golaghat 'to be under their jurisdiction and administrative control', but 'as per the Survey of India maps these 62 villages are located' in Assam (GoI 1996a: 22; GoI 2008a: 22). The Assam government has not reduced the area in its records because that might weaken its case in the Supreme Court and also trigger protests within the state. It indirectly admits the absence of administrative presence in these villages, where it could not conduct census due to 'strong resistance by the [Naga] villagers' (GoI 1996a: 22; GoI 2008: 22). Elsewhere, both Andhra Pradesh and Odisha conducted census in 'disputed area … in pursuance of the instructions of' the ORGI (GoI 1997e: 18–21; GoI 2005a: 24; GoI 2008c: 18–20) and Odisha tabulated the population estimates supplied by both the states with explanations of the differences between the two sets of figures.

The lack of clarity over the borders of circles in the disputed area is the source of several inconsistencies between maps published by the Nagaland government. For instance, Dimapur's depiction varies across *Administrative Atlas of India* (Map 3.8), *Administrative Circles* map (Map 3.5), *Administrative Blocks* map (Map 3.4), *District Census Handbook, Index Map* (Map 3.6) and *Political Map* (Map 3.2). This also holds true for circles of some of the other districts along the Assam border.

Nagaland has established and expanded its administration in the disputed area and altered the status quo even as the border dispute is sub judice. It ostensibly maintains status quo by publishing a set of maps that do not show any administrative presence in the disputed area. In these maps, four circles – Niuland, Nihoku, Kuhoboto and Aquqhnaqua – are arbitrarily squeezed into the north-eastern part of Dimapur, even though perhaps only the first two lie partly within the state's officially recognised border. Some government sources indirectly hint at this anomaly by noting that the borders of 'newly created' circles in the disputed area – Aquqhnaqua (Dimapur) and Merangmen (Mokokchung) – 'could not be drawn due to technical difficulty' (GoI 2011f: 39; 2012). Some election maps too arbitrarily fit polling stations of the disputed area into the official borders of the state (Map 3.1; see also 2013 Nagaland Assembly Constituencies map [1.25 inches = 5 miles], mentioned in note 1 of this chapter).

Cartographic manoeuvring along the Assam border has had a domino effect on other circles including Rengma-dominated Tseminyu (Agrawal and Kumar 2017a: 133). In earlier maps (1971–81 Censuses), Tseminyu (subsequently bifurcated into Tseminyu and Tsogin circles) shared a border with Assam, whereas in later maps (1991–2011 Censuses) Dimapur's new circles separate it from Assam (Map 3.10E; GoN n.d.5: 10). This change took place between 1985 and 1988 (cf. GoI 1985a; 1990a) without the transfer of any territory from Tseminyu to Dimapur.[19] Surprisingly, Tseminyu still shares a border with Assam in the 2010 SoI map of Nagaland (SoI 2010), India Administrative Divisions map of 2011 (Agrawal and Kumar 2017a: Map 1), administrative circles map of 2013 (Map 3.5), assembly constituencies map of 2013 (Agrawal and Kumar 2017a: Map 5), assembly constituencies map of 2018 (Map 3.1) and political map of 2018 (Map 3.2). On the Assam side of the border, the demarcation of reserved forests does not agree with the ground reality. Large parts of the reserved forests of Golaghat marked on maps do not exist on the ground (Map 3.9).[20] De-reservation of forest land,

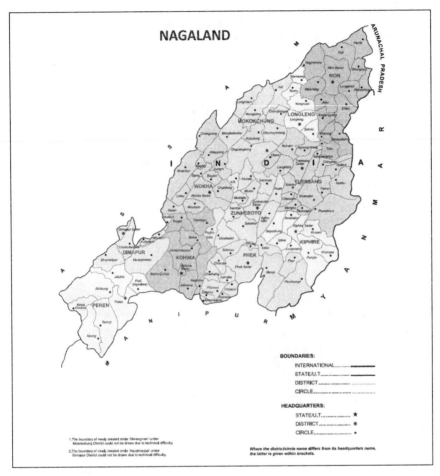

Map 3.8   Administrative divisions map, 2011

Source: Adapted from GoI (2011f).

Note: Map not to scale and may not represent authentic international borders.

which is a complicated process even under normal circumstances, is particularly difficult in this case as the Supreme Court and Nagaland demand status quo.

Counting amidst Cartographic Fluidity

Both Assam and Nagaland try to mould the fluid situation in the disputed area in their favour. This has tempted them to conduct census in villages not under their administration. In the 2011 Census, for instance, enumerators from Nagaland

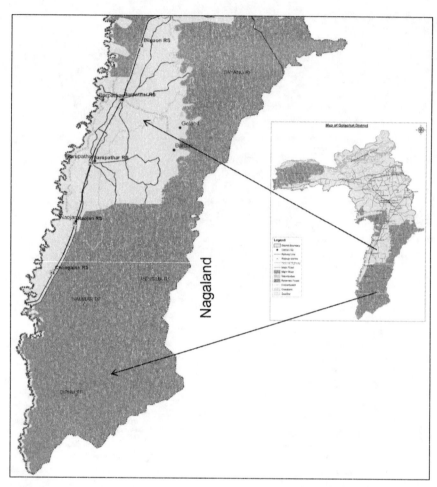

Map 3.9 Reserved forests, Golaghat district, Assam

Source: Adapted from http://online.assam.gov.in/assammaps, accessed on 23 August 2011.

Note: The areas highlighted with dark grey, including the one bordering Nagaland, indicate reserved forests.

Map not to scale and may not represent authentic borders.

tried to cover seven non-Naga villages in Uriamghat area/Sector C of the disputed territory, where Nagaland has a thin presence.[21] Nagaland has conducted at least four censuses in parts of the disputed territory – in 1981 (GoI 1984a),[22] 1991 (GoI 1996a: 22–4), 2001 (GoI 2005a: 24) and 2011 (GoI 2018a; Assam government official, interview, 5 June 2013, Sarupathar, Assam; Naga IAS officer, interview, 25 June 2013, Kohima).[23] The growing reach of Nagaland's census in the disputed area suggests that the area *under* Nagaland's administration has grown over the years. However, the state's declared area has not changed since 1981. While census maps and reports for Nagaland do not say anything about the disputed territory, census reports for Assam (GoI 1996a: 22; 2008a: 22) and India (GoI 2005a: 24) note that there are 62 Naga villages in the disputed territory. The actual number of villages is twice as much.[24]

It seems conducting census in the disputed area is not as difficult as including its headcount in the state's overall population. Both state governments continue to struggle to contain dynamic populations within frozen cartographic frames. This is reflected in several anomalies discussed as follows.

First, in 2001, the reported population densities of sparsely populated, entirely rural administrative circles located in the disputed territory was about six times the density of Nagaland and one and a half times that of Dimapur, the state's commercial capital (Table 3.2). The disputed area is located close to Nagaland's commercial hub and Assam's rail and road networks and consists of fertile plains where wet cultivation is practiced. This area should be able to support more population than economically isolated hills, where shifting cultivation is practised. Yet, the average number of persons and households in the villages located in the disputed area is much lower than that in the rest of the state (Figure 3.2). So, the disputed area villages are smaller in terms of population than the villages in the hills, but their population density is far greater than the latter and, even, the highly urbanised district of Dimapur. The density of these circles has, in fact, been overestimated as they have been arbitrarily fitted into Nagaland by extracting some area from the nearest circle inside the recognised border. In other words, the inclusion of the disputed territory's population in Nagaland, but not the respective area, inflates the population density.

Table 3.2   Area, population and population density of select circles of Dimapur

Circle/district/state	Area (in sq km) (2011)*	Population		Population density (persons per sq km)	
		2001	2011	2001	2011
Niuland & Aquqhnaqua[†]	30.57	31,479	21,069	1,029.63	689.13
Nihoku	70.00	12,155	8,699	173.65	124.28
Kuhoboto	23.84	12,699	12,519	532.63	525.08
Dimapur	927	309,224	378,811	333.57	408.64
Nagaland	16,579	1,990,036	1,978,502	120.03	119.34

Sources: Prepared by authors using 'Table A-1: Number of Villages, Towns, Households, Population and Area', http://www.censusindia.gov.in/2011census/A-1_NO_OF_VILLAGES_TOWNS_HOUSEHOLDS_POPULATION_AND_AREA.xlsx; GoI (2014b).

Notes: *We could not retrieve the circle-wise area estimates for 2001. [†]Separate estimates of the area of Niuland and Aquqhnaqua circles are not available.

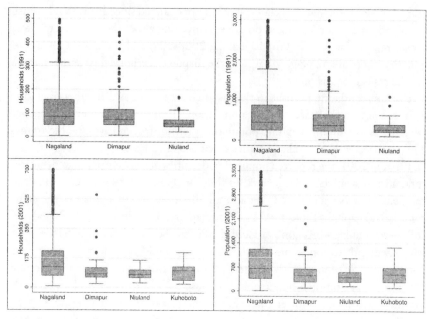

Figure 3.2   Distribution of households and population of villages in the disputed area and Nagaland

Sources: Preapred by authors using data from GoI (n.d.1; n.d.2).

Notes: The box plots show the distribution of households and population of villages in Nagaland, Dimapur district and Dimapur's circles lying in the disputed territory. In 1991 – when Dimapur was a part of Kohima district – Dhansiripar, Chumukedima, Medziphema, Niuland and Nihokhu circles are treated as a part of Dimapur for the sake of comparison across years. We have excluded the villages having two or less households. There were 11 (3) such villages in 1991 (2001). Further, the box plots for households exclude villages with more than 500 (700) households in 1991 (2001). In Nagaland (Dimapur district), there were 46 (none) such villages in 1991 and 52 (none) in 2001. The truncation points for box plots for population are 3,000 and 3,500 in 1991 and 2001, respectively, resulting in the exclusion of 56 (none) and 102 (none) villages in case of Nagaland (Dimapur district). The aforesaid truncation does not affect the distribution for Dimapur or any of its circles. Nihokhu circle that has very few villages is not shown separately in this figure.

We can correct the densities by either excluding the population or including the area of the disputed territory. We choose the latter as information on the location of the villages vis-à-vis the recognised border is not available. Dimapur's population density drops by 27.66 per cent from 409 (reported in the 2011 Census) to 296 persons per square kilometre if the disputed territory under Nagaland's administration is accounted for. Similarly, Nagaland's population density drops by 3.46 per cent, from 119 to 115 persons per square kilometre.

Second, the territory of Assam under Nagaland's administration is shown in maps of both the states. Yet, their estimates of the disputed area's population do not agree.[25] Nagaland does not identify non-Naga villages that are, in fact, more numerous. The maps of Nagaland simply erase 'others' living in the midst of Nagas and show the entire territory under Nagaland, even though the Assamese villages do not maintain any contact with Nagaland's administration and access public services provided by the Assam government. The Government of Assam, on the other hand, classifies villages as Naga and non-Naga and reports statistics for both. However, Assam's statistics for Naga villages in the disputed territory suffer from both coverage and content errors. In 1991, according to Assam, the population of 62 disputed villages (referred to as the Naojan forest areas of Golaghat district) under Nagaland's administration was 23,063. The population of these villages (referred to as Sarupathar Revenue Circle of Golaghat district) dropped to 10,931 in 2001 (GoI 1996a: 22–4; 2008a: 23), which is not in agreement with the very high growth rates reported across Nagaland in the corresponding census decade.

The figures cited above cover only Sectors A through C of the disputed territory.[26] Our compilation based on Nagaland's census of Naga villages located in these sectors indicates that the population of Nagas in the disputed territory was 37,785, 56,372 and 43,488, respectively, in 1991, 2001 and 2011 (GoI n.d.1; n.d.2; n.d.9), which are much higher than the estimates provided by the census reports of Assam but compare favourably with the estimates reported by other departments of the Assam government (GoA n.d.3). These figures imply a 49.19 per cent growth in 2001 (compared to Nagaland's overall population growth rate of 64.53 per cent) and 22.85 per cent decline in 2011 (compared to 5.26 per cent decline in Nagaland's rural population after adjusting for the notification of 11 new towns).

Third, Assam's census also suffers from content errors. In 1991 (2001), of the 14,034 (10,645) Sumi speakers enumerated outside Nagaland, 13,836 (10,346) were enumerated in Assam; almost all of them were based in Sarupathar circle of Golaghat district, that is, the site of the largest Naga settlement in the disputed territory in the vicinity of Dimapur. Given the general pattern of over-reporting of headcount in Nagaland in 2001 and migration of Sumis to the disputed territory, the population should have increased. Either the Census of Assam overestimated the Naga population of the disputed territory in 1991,[27] or it undercounted Nagas in 2001. In Golaghat (Assam), the population of Sumis further dropped to 26 (1,945) in 2011. The drop cannot be explained by conventional demographic factors and seems to be an artefact of content errors discussed in Chapter 4 (excursus) and a sudden drop in the number of Naga villages covered by Assam's census (note 24 of this chapter).

Assam's census data on Yimchunger Nagas of the disputed territory, who are a much smaller community, are even more misleading. In Golaghat, the number of Yimchunger-speakers, historically inhabitants of the hills adjoining Myanmar, dropped from 1,347 in 1991 to 26 in 2001. Interestingly, as per the 2001 Census, all Yimchunger-speakers belonged to the Tikhir community (GoI n.d.1; n.d.2), but Tikhirs of Dimapur Town are not aware of their kith and kin living in the disputed territory (Tikhir leaders, interview, 10 April 2013, Dimapur). At the same time, the Yimchungers who have a long-standing presence in that area were not reported in Assam's census. In 2011, the Census reported 450 Yimchunger speakers in Assam including 374 Chirr, 70 Yimchunger and 6 Tikhir speakers, but none of them were in Golaghat. According to the census data from Nagaland, in 2001 and 2011, respectively, there were 2,408 and 1,934 Yimchunger speakers in the disputed area of Golaghat under Nagaland's administration (GoI n.d.2; n.d.9).

Fourth, the anomalous accounting of population of the disputed territory has an impact, howsoever small, on the national level statistics, as both Assam and Nagaland provide separate estimates for this territory. The census mechanically aggregates the populations of states and union territories (UTs) to arrive at the all-India population estimates. As a result, the disputed area's population is added twice as part of the population of Assam as well as Nagaland. This anomaly also affects national level sample surveys, including NSSO surveys that use the census as the sampling frame.

A Border among Ethno-ecological Boundaries

The Ahom dynasty ruled over large parts of Assam's Brahmaputra Valley between the thirteenth and nineteenth centuries. The hills and the plains/valley were separated by porous ethno-ecological boundaries that allowed sociocultural exchange, marital relations, trade and migration. The boundary was sensitive, among other things, to the changing balance of power between the hills and the plains and the degree of forest cover along the foothills.[28] More importantly, neither side claimed absolute/exclusive ownership over the grey area along the boundary, while both enjoyed customary use rights over certain resources on the other side.[29] A crucial difference between the precolonial and colonial borders/boundaries is the discontinuity of the former. The precolonial boundaries were often a collection of separate points on the terrain. The Ahom–Naga boundary was marked by *duars* through which different tribes approached the plains. The British inherited this arrangement from the Ahoms, but regulated exchange between people to discourage traditional hills–plains synergies (see, for instance, ASA, Government of Bengal Papers, 24–28/1873).

The contemporary cartographic confusion and conflicts along Nagaland's borders can be traced back to colonial attempts to impose a rigid modern border over ethno-ecological boundaries.[30] The intensely territorial headhunting Naga tribes were mapped by colonial administration without their knowledge, let alone consent,[31] which reminds of Bernard Nietschmann's quip, 'More indigenous territory has been claimed by maps than by guns' (Wood 2010: 135).[32] The British secured about half of the territory directly and the rest was cartographically claimed on the basis of stray punitive and exploratory expeditions and often under the legal fiction that the British succeeded the Ahom and Burmese kingdoms in these areas.[33] This was part of a larger pattern of nominal engagement with the periphery. Just like maps were prepared without proper surveys, the population was reported without actual enumeration. However, once published, maps and headcounts created an illusion of knowledge and control.[34] While the tribes were initially not aware of the significance of map-making and census, they were nevertheless opposed to these activities as they intuitively understood them to be disruptive of their ways of life.[35]

The colonial borders separating the hills and plains were governed by the Bengal Eastern Frontier Regulations, 1873, popularly known as the Inner Line Regulations (ILR). These regulations are among the most enduring colonial initiatives in the hills adjoining Assam and Bengal. They allowed the exclusion of certain territories from the legal and administrative framework applicable to the plains and effectively limited the size of government in the revenue-deficit hills. Furthermore, the ILR restricted the mobility of labour and capital. Travel across inner lines was regulated to avoid conflict between 'simple' hill tribes and 'cunning' outsiders/plainsmen,[36] which in turn regulated hills–plains trade and circumscribed the ability of outsiders to acquire land in the hills.[37]

While the inner lines placed the revenue-deficit hill/tribal areas beyond direct administration, they nevertheless served the purpose of containing non-state spaces that fell within British India. Territories beyond the inner lines were first categorised as 'backward tracts' under the Government of India Act, 1919, and then as 'excluded areas' under the Government of India Act, 1935.[38] These borders can be viewed as instantiations of colonial biopolitics that regulated the flow of populations believed to be incapable of self-discipline (Legg 2005) and colonial scalar politics that placed territories allegedly 'unsuited to modern democracy and governmentality' under a lighter administration (Legg 2016: 62). Commenting on the logic that underwrote such colonial restrictions and their long-term implications, Horowitz (2000: 158–9, 147–9, 243–59) noted

Internal migration was sometimes regulated as well, typically as part of a policy of 'protecting' the inhabitants of one region from incursions by migrants from another.... The protected groups were felt to be at a competitive disadvantage [vis-à-vis traders and agriculturalists from other parts of the colony or other colonies], and it was also believed that special protection would be repaid by loyalty to the colonial power. This expectation generally proved correct. Protected peoples tended to stay aloof from anti-colonial movements.... After independence, several such groups became strongly separatist. Protection implies separate development, and it was accompanied by separate administration and specialized administrators who developed distinctive biases.... Protection emphasized and accentuated the backwardness of backward groups.

This 'protection' was overlaid by an enhanced reliance on 'outsiders' for administration (ibid.: 159–60). The biopolitics and scalar politics that isolated the hills from the plains was also replicated within the hills. The Naga Hills were divided into the (minimally) administered areas adjoining Assam and the (completely) unadministered areas adjoining Myanmar. As in other colonial frontiers, the administered areas grew at the expense of the unadministered areas.

International factors too contributed to the making of the borders of the Naga Hills as the north-eastern region was close to China and French colonies in South East Asia. The protection of productive colonies from competing powers and securing existing and potential trade routes were among the priorities of the colonial administration. Colonies were notionally divided into concentric circles consisting of the core surrounded by a ring of protectorates in the buffer/frontier zone that were in turn surrounded by spheres of influence and spheres of interest (Curzon 1908: 42). Administrative presence and the accuracy of borders decreased as one moved away from the core. The border between Assam, in the core, and the Naga Hills, in the frontier, was marked by clearer inner lines than the border between the Naga Hills and Myanmar. However, neither of these borders were identified as clearly as the borders of the provinces within the core of the colony. Interestingly, the border between the Naga Hills and Myanmar was marked on maps without field surveys and despite the fact that the territory on the other side was part of a British colony. This betrays a 'cartographic anxiety', that is, the fear of unbounded/unconquered territory that had to be rendered legible and controllable through mapping (Painter 2008; Krishna 1994).[39]

While larger international considerations governed the nature, purpose and location of borders, their precise shape depended upon the competing political-economic interests of the revenue/civil and defence wings of the colonial government and the imperial bureaucracy as well as the personal interests of the officials responsible for the actual survey of the territory and enforcement of borders (Cederlöf 2014; Phanjoubam 2016). The administration had to protect the interests of the cash crop and natural resource businesses expanding from the plains towards the foothills, while defending the revenue-surplus plains from tribal raiders based in the hills. There was hardly any room for the legitimate interests of the people in the colonial calculus though. And, in any case, colonial borders were not meant to resolve postcolonial ethno-territorial conflicts. A few key features of colonial borders bear emphasising in this regard.

First, colonial borders primarily served administrative expediency and the defence of expanding frontiers and economic interests and were responsive to the changing priorities of these interests. The administered part of the Naga Hills expanded through the colonial period. Initially, the small administered territory of the Naga Hills was attached to a larger plains territory to make a viable district, whose capital was located in the plains/foothills. Over the years with the expansion of the administered territory in the Naga Hills, the district and its headquarter shifted eastwards into the hills culminating in an administrative unit beyond the present Assam–Nagaland border that was entirely in the hills except the plains territory around Dimapur (Maps 3.10A–E, GoI 1973a: 4). The area of the district was 4,900 square miles in 1872, 5,300 square miles in 1876 and 6,400 square miles in 1881 but dropped to 3,070 square miles in 1911 before increasing to 4,293 square miles in 1931. The area dropped marginally to 4,289 square miles in 1941 before rebounding to 4,297 square miles in 1951 (Timeline 3.1).[40] During this period Dimapur was first assigned to the Naga Hills and then to Sibsagar before returning to the former (ASA, General XVI 64/20; see also Maps 3.10A–D). Dimapur, which was traditionally inhabited by a non-Naga tribe, was included on grounds of administrative convenience and also because its economy was entirely dependent upon being an entrepôt to the Naga Hills (ibid.). Dimapur Town was not covered by the ILR, though. The shifting frontiers left behind several maps (Maps 3.10A–E and Timeline 3.1), allowing each side to cherry-pick a convenient colonial border and bestow it with 'historical' sanctity. This partly explains the divergence between the positions of Assam and Nagaland and is a major obstacle to the resolution of the border dispute.

Second, the quest for 'strategic defensible borders' resulted in the alignment of border with topographical features 'without too much regard for populations' (Crampton 2010a: 72).[41] This was particularly problematic as most Naga tribes settle on ridges. The Indo-Myanmar border cuts through the territories of Konyak, Khiamniungan and Yimchunger Nagas. Longwa village, which straddles the Indo-Myanmar border, has emerged as a major tourist attraction as the border seems to cut across the chieftain's house, dividing his living room between the two countries. While governments fear open, uncontrolled borders that facilitate illicit trade, arms and drug trafficking and easy movement of insurgents (Rio 2006: 162, 279; 2007: 16, 37, 51, 115, 261; 2008: 32; 2010: 13–14), the border cannot

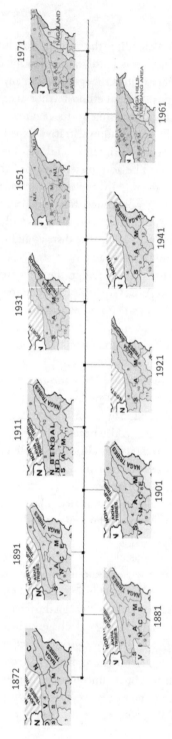

Timeline 3.1 Evolution of the Naga Hills district/Nagaland, 1872–1971

Source: Prepared by authors using maps from GoI (2011f).

Notes: (i) The Naga Hills district is identified in the maps by the following numbers/letters: 7 (1872), 8 (1881, 1891, 1901), 11 (1911), 9 (1921), 12 (1931, 1941) and NT (1951). (ii) The internal borders of the Naga Hills and Tuensang Area shown in the 1951 map are not correct. More generally, these low resolution maps are not entirely accurate in the vicinity of Dimapur and the western part of the present Peren district.

Maps not to scale and may not represent authentic borders.

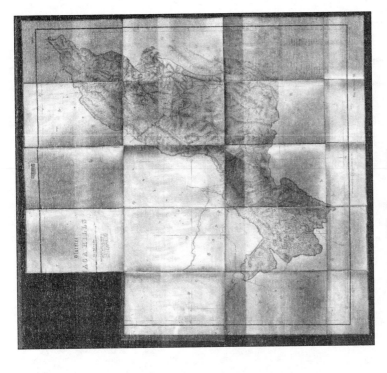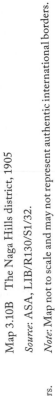

Map 3.10B   The Naga Hills district, 1905

Source: ASA, LIB/R130/S1/32.

Note: Map not to scale and may not represent authentic international borders.

Map 3.10A   The Naga Hills district, 1893

Source: ASA, LIB/R138/S3/17.

Note: Map not to scale and may not represent authentic international borders.

Map 3.10D   The Naga Hills district, 1931

Source: GoI (1932: 4).

Note: Map not to scale and may not represent authentic international borders.

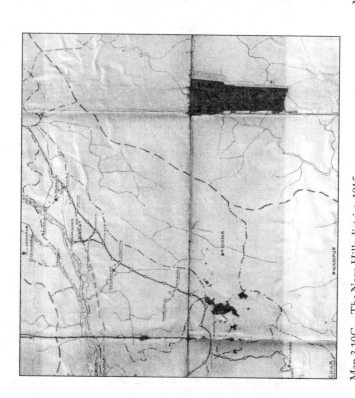

Map 3.10C   The Naga Hills district, 1915

Source: ASA, LIB/R136/S1/11.

Note: Inter-district (– · –) and inter-provincial (– – –) borders are marked by dashed lines.

Map not to scale and may not represent authentic international borders.

1951

1961

NAGALAND

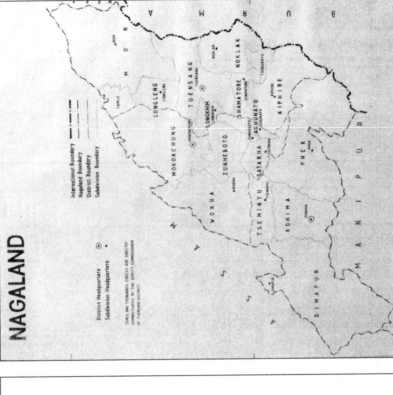

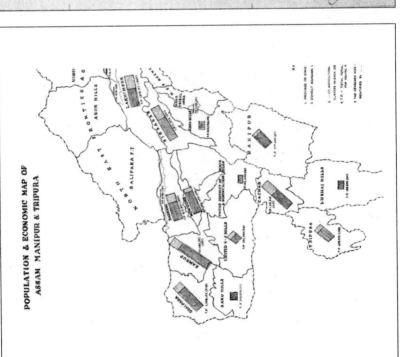

POPULATION & ECONOMIC MAP OF
ASSAM MANIPUR & TRIPURA

Map 3.10E contd

Map 3.10E contd

NAGALAND
1971

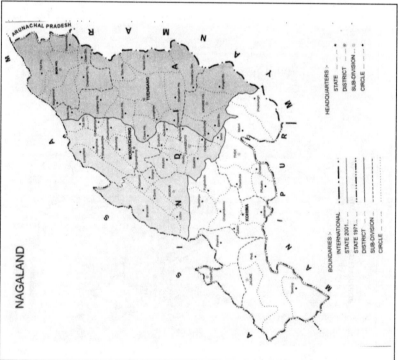

NAGALAND
1981

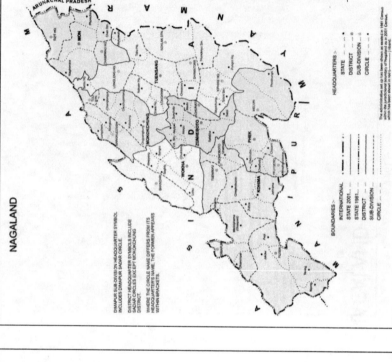

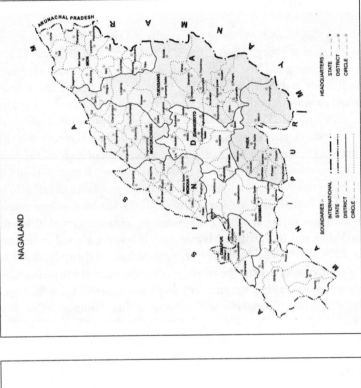

Map 3.10E   Administrative divisions maps, 1951–2001

Sources: Adapted from GoI (1954b; 1966) for 1951 and 1961 (first two maps) and the respective administrative atlases for the rest.

Note: Maps not to scale and may not represent authentic international borders.

be closed due to the difficult nature of the terrain and strong local opposition to the division of tribal territory.[42]

A source of amusement and fear for outsiders, the Indo-Myanmar border disrupts livelihoods and lives by separating villages from their fields, pastures and forests and grooms from the villages where they could find brides. Partisans of independence argue that 'some Indian and Burmese [Myanmarese] politicians may be thinking that some Nagas have their houses in Indian Territory and their fields in Burmese territory. But Nagas don't give a damn about such an imaginary Indian or Burmese boundary line' (Iralu 2018) that were drawn 'without the knowledge and consent of the indigenous Naga tribal people' (*ME* 2018ah; see also GPRN [2007] 2010: 3). This attitude towards the border has demographic consequences. Myanmarese and Bangladeshi immigrants are viewed differently (cf. Rio 2003: 117 and Rio 2010a). Myanmarese Nagas are viewed as 'Eastern' Nagas (Rio 2008: 47–8), with Myanmar being incidental to their identity. They need to be supported and, in extreme cases, even accommodated within Nagaland because they are persecuted in Myanmar for being Christians (KTC 2008: 3).[43] On the other hand, an alleged Bangladeshi Muslim is an 'illegal immigrant' or 'mian' (everyday usage), 'disease' (Borgohain and Borgohain 2011: 190), 'menace' (ibid.: 186, see also Shimray 2007: 35), 'demographic invasion' that 'threatens to swamp the local population completely' (S. C. Jamir n.d.4: 12–13, see also Borgohain and Borgohain 2011: 189), 'leech' (retired Naga IAS officer, interview, 9 April 2013, Kohima), 'hydra-headed monster' (*Nagaland Post* 2014a), 'like Niggers' (retired Naga IAS officer, interview, 16 November 2013, Dimapur), 'human time bomb' (*ME* 2018r; 2018x) and a 'real and frightening' problem (*ME* 2018r).[44]

Third, razor-sharp borders and the regulation of cross-border exchange divided both land and people. The British placed binaries across the border, with settled, arable, civilised and law-abiding territory/society on the one side and unproductive, uncivilised, violent and lawless territory/society on the other. This froze the ethnic identities of the people on the two sides for the purpose of governance. The borders disrupted traditional political and economic exchanges as well as the older pattern of sociocultural ties between the hills and plains along the margins. Henceforth, the Naga and the Assamese people who migrated to the other side of the border retained their 'original' identity forever, irrespective of the duration of their stay. And Nagas who came down to settle in the plain territory adjoining foothills transformed into 'outsiders', encroaching upon Assamese land (Kumar 2016b).[45] In a different era they would have been assimilated into the Assamese society, but now they are caught in the crossfire between the two states. The same is true of Assamese who would like to work in the relatively scarcely populated foothills. Ironically, the British inserted themselves between the 'headhunting' hills and 'cunning' plains, and both sides began to see them as the protector vis-à-vis the 'other' across the border.

The colonial administration not only cordoned off the Naga Hills from Assam using hard borders but it also reworked the internal boundaries of the Naga society to make it more 'governable'. A perceptive Naga newspaper editor pointed out, 'The colonial forces, through an interplay of indirect rule, and divide and conquer, fragmented the Naga people by categorizing and organizing the independent Naga village-states into a monolithic structure of a Tribe. In so doing the villages lost their autonomy and dynamism to externally imposed Tribe-centric identities and organizations that emerged therein' (*ME* 2016).[46] While this is true, Naga nationalism (and subsequent tribal factionalism in the insurgency) could not have been conceived without this (forced)[47] transition from a village/clan-centric society to tribe-centric society.

Overcoming 'Suffocation' and 'Dismemberment'

The demand for the reintegration of 'all Naga' areas divided by colonial borders has been a fixed point of Naga political discourse that emphasises the 'democratic desire of the Naga people to live together under one administrative umbrella' (*ME* 2018e) and 'natural right of the Nagas to unify their homeland into one Naga National Political entity called, Nagalim' (GPRN [2007] 2010: 6). Nagas argue that the colonial state encroached upon their territory along the foothills for timber, tea, minerals and building railways and also divided their 'traditional or 'historical' territory between India and Myanmar and further divided them across different administrative units within each country.[48] As a result, Nagas have not only been denied the right to live together with their kindred communities, but they have also been forced to live as minorities among non-Naga majorities that control the legislatures. Thus, Nagas simultaneously suffer, what Clifford Geertz (quoted in Englebert, Tarango and Carter 2002: 1094) calls, 'suffocation' (living with others including indigenous non-Naga tribal minorities) and 'dismemberment' (division of the community between India and Myanmar and across administrative units in each country) because of 'artificial borders'.[49] Moreover, they resent multiple layers and instances of their enclosure in (a) the Indian Union after 1947, (b) barricaded and grouped villages at the height of insurgency in the late 1950s and for a shorter period in the mid 1960s and (c) the state of Nagaland after 1963.[50]

These claims have been periodically reiterated over the past nine decades through memoranda, resolutions and agreements beginning with the Naga Club's memorandum to the Simon Commission (1929) that was the first statement of the Naga position legible in modern terms. It noted, 'Our country within the administered area consists of more than eight regions quite different from one another … and there are more regions outside the administered area which are not known at present' (Chasie 2000: 171).[51] The memorandum was followed by a series of expanding, open-ended descriptions of Naga territory that left the identification of 'Nagas' unspecified. Article 1 of the Yehzabo (Constitution) of the Naga National Council (NNC), the first pan-Naga organisation, described 'Nagaland' as 'all the territories inhabited by the indigenous Naga Tribes and such other territories as Tatar Hoho may by law admit ...' (FGN 1994).[52] The National Socialist Council of Nagaland (NSCN), a splinter of the NNC, claimed sovereignty 'over every inch of Nagaland whatever it may be and admit of no other existence whatever' (Hazarika 1995: 370). In the late 1980s, the NSCN (Isak-Muivah faction/NSCN-IM) called for the integration of the Naga-inhabited areas of India and Myanmar under a 'Greater Nagaland' (Hazarika 1995: 243).[53]

The above unilateral declarations and assertions have been buttressed by agreements between partisans of independence/integration of Naga territory within India and the government, such as the 1947 Nine Point Agreement (sixth point) (NSA, 5:21), 1960 Sixteen Point Agreement (twelfth and thirteenth points) (NSA, 5:22) and 1975 Shillong Accord (Chasie 2000: 185–7) and also six (1964, 1970, 1994, 2003, 2015 and 2018) Nagaland State Legislative Assembly resolutions (Chasie 2000: 50; Rio 2012: 91; *Nagaland Page* 2018a).

The rise of the Nagas of Manipur and Myanmar within the Naga insurgency bolstered irredentism, while the insurgency's fragmentation led to an escalation of claims. Broadly speaking, presently 'Greater Nagaland' includes the whole of Nagaland, several districts of Manipur (Chandel, Senapati, Tamenglong and Ukhrul), parts or whole of several districts of Assam (Dibrugarh, Golaghat, Jorhat, Karbi Anglong, North Cachar Hills/Dima Hasao, Sivasagar and Tinsukia) as well as Arunachal Pradesh (Changlang, Dibang Valley, Lohit, Longding and Tirap) and territory on both sides of the Chindwin River in Myanmar (Maps 3.11 and 4.1).[54]

Given the ambiguity surrounding the identification of 'Naga Lands,' 'all Naga areas,' 'Greater Nagaland' and Nagalim, it is difficult to accurately estimate the area claimed by Naga nationalists/irredentists. The estimates of the area of 'Greater Nagaland' have an elastic character: 20,000 square miles (51,800 square kilometres) (Yonuo 1974: 1–2; see also Horam 1988: 11), '30,000 sq miles [77,700 sq km] ... if not more' (Chasie 2000: 21, 166) and 47,000 square miles (121,729 square kilometres) (Nuh 2006: 24; see also Rio 2007: 240). The first two are about half of 120,000 square kilometres, the current claim of the GPRN ([2007] 2010: 2).[55] Among many others, Radhabinod Koijam (2001), a former chief minister of Manipur, noted the great disproportion between 'Greater Nagaland' that includes '120,000 sq km ... with a population of 35 lakhs [3.5 million]' and 'Nagaland [that] has an area of only 16,579 sq. km with a population of about 16 lakhs [1.6 million]'.

The remarkable documentary consistency across many decades, the expanding claims under the banner of 'Greater Nagaland' and the growing subscription

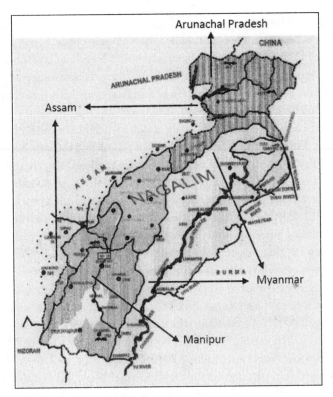

Map 3.11   A map of 'Greater Nagaland'

Source: NSCN-IM ([2007] 2010: 6).

Note: We have added arrows to identify the overlap between 'Greater Nagaland' and Assam, Manipur and Myanmar.

Map not to scale and may not represent authentic international borders.

of 'Greater Nagaland' among smaller tribal neighbours of Nagas[56] obscure the deeper contradictions of the irredentist project that serves as a pressure valve to avoid implosion within the Naga society-in-making that is bitterly divided over *who is a Naga* and *what are his (Naga women do not enjoy property rights) territorial entitlements.*[57]

The expansion of territorial claims and the simultaneous expansion of the definition of who is a Naga in the 1990s generated enormous stress within the Naga society that were initially managed by the newly formed pan-Naga civil society organisations such as the now dysfunctional Naga Hoho. The ostensible success of 'Greater Nagaland' project was read as the imminent dominance of the Tangkhul tribe of Manipur, which is over-represented in the NSCN-IM. This triggered a backlash in Nagaland, and one after another group of Naga tribes of

Nagaland beginning with the Eastern Nagas deserted pan-Naga organisations, and the NSCN-IM itself suffered splits. The Eastern Nagas are demanding a separate state called 'Frontier Nagaland' to be carved out of Nagaland (and possibly a few districts of Arunachal Pradesh) (ENPO 2010). There is also a long-standing, even if intermittent, demand for the creation of a Zeliangrong state, including parts of Assam, Manipur and Nagaland (ZPC 1983; *ME* 2018k).[58]

The irredentists have also burnt bridges with all neighbours, including Meiteis of Manipur, Assamese, Karbis and Dimasas of Assam and the non-Naga tribes of Arunachal Pradesh. Nagaland's neighbours have hardened their stand reducing the room for negotiation. Manipur maintains that 'as things stand today, integrity is no longer just territorial integrity but administrative integrity too' (*Sangai Express* 2018). Putting all Naga territories under one administration even for, say, sociocultural purposes without changing borders is not acceptable to other states as they feel that this concession will be projected as an admission of a lack of genuineness of their territorial claim. Neighbours are not only refusing to part with their territory but are also claiming parts of Nagaland. Dimasa Kacharis of Assam have intermittently campaigned for a Dimaraji state that would include parts of Nagaland around Dimapur, the site of their medieval kingdom (Sandeep Banerjee 2011, *ME* 2018j). The Kuki homeland includes parts of Manipur as well as Assam and Nagaland (Sinlung 2012; Haokip 2008: 1–2, 6–9, 386, maps). These proposed states overlap not only with 'Greater Nagaland' but also Nagaland (Kumar 2015d; 2015g). While Karbis are not demanding Nagaland's territory, they have repeatedly fought with their Rengma Naga neighbours within Assam due to the threat posed by 'Greater Nagaland'.

The most significant development, though, is the widespread support over the past few years for a new generation of sons-of-soil organisations in Nagaland and the opposition to the Tangkhul Naga-dominated NSCN-IM. This has, among other things, forced the state government to deny affirmative action benefits to Naga settlers of Manipuri origin (who are indigenous inhabitants for administrative purposes by virtue of having settled in the state before its formation),[59] shrunk the support base of the NSCN-IM-dominated pan-Naga organisations in Nagaland and facilitated the formation of a Working Group of insurgent groups that are headed by Nagas of Nagaland. The working group has attacked the 'theatrical politics' of the NSCN-IM 'in their nonexistent land called Nagalim ["Greater Nagaland"]' (*ME* 2017a). Likewise, the Naga Hoho that is perceived to be close to the NSCN-IM has been criticised as 'entirely lopsided and helplessly drifting southward [toward Manipur] with imaginative domain which is null and void' (*Nagaland Page* 2018c).

Maps as Contested Units of Measurement

The 'Greater Nagaland' controversy does not merely contribute to the context within which the politics of maps and statistics unfolds in Nagaland. Rather 'Greater Nagaland' is itself an object of spatial–statistical dispute as it represents a (spatial) unit of measurement different from that adopted by the state. At a deeper level, the cartographic conflict in Nagaland is, therefore, also a conflict over the units of measurement. The government and the partisans of independence/integration of Naga areas within India differ over whether to measure and report statistics exclusively for the existing Nagaland state or include statistics for the adjoining areas claimed by it or, at least, areas under its administration. Urla (1993: 826–7) highlights a similar tension in Spain, where the partisans of Basqueland resist the naturalisation of the Basque Autonomous Community created by the government. She observes,

> The Basque government, armed at last with its own statistical data bank, has chosen to use this new administrative unit, the Basque Autonomous Community, rather than Euskalherria [Basqueland], as the unit of analysis in all of its maps and statistical charts ... [but] the 'units of measurement' are never innocent or without consequence. What concerns them [the radical Basque nationalists], very simply, is that with political recognition may come a gradual acceptance of the Autonomous Community as the 'natural' context for the discussion of Basque cultural issues.[60]

The controversy over the name of a territory can be as divisive as that over its delimitation. In the Basque case, 'There is no agreement even on the terminology with which to refer to the Basque Country or to the whole Basque area ... a full understanding of the different meanings of the concept "Basque Country" depends on both the interlocutor and the context' (Vieytez and Kallonen 2004: 253). The choice of terminology indeed shapes its geographical and cartographic correlates.

Charles Chasie points out that 'in Naga parlance, particularly in "Naga Nationalist" terminology, it was always Naga Lands or Naga Land which included all Naga areas. Nagaland came into being only in 1963 with the inauguration of statehood within Indian Union' (email communication, 26 November 2014; see also Chasie 2000: 174–5). Two imaginations clash at Nagaland's borders: 'The rest of the Indians think that it does not sound "Indian". On the other hand, to the Nagas living outside Nagaland the same is a "misnomer" because there is a sizeable Naga population living outside this present Nagaland proper' (Horam 1988: 10). So, Nagaland can be interpreted as 'the land where the Nagas are between the Chindwin and the Brahmaputra' or 'legally constituted Nagaland by the Government of India' (Yonuo 1974: 7). For Naga nationalists, the state of Nagaland is the biblical 'Golden Calf' (Elwin 1961: 63, 67), not to be confused with 'Naga-Land' (M. S. Jamir 2019).[61]

Some organisations use 'Nagaland' in their names even though they pursue pan-Naga goals, for example, the NSCN or the Council of Nagaland Churches. Other organisations use 'Nagalim' in their names to signal that they work across Naga areas, including those outside the state of Nagaland. In 1999, NSCN-IM replaced the word 'Nagaland' in 'National Socialist Council of Nagaland (IM)' with 'Nagalim' (Nag 2002: 308), but Nagalim is occasionally used along with Nagaland within parentheses – Nagalim (Nagaland) (see, for instance, GPRN [2007] 2010: 44, back cover).[62] Others simply use 'Naga' to signal their pan-Naga character, for example, the Naga Students' Federation and Naga People's Front. A striking example of the nominal realignments is offered by the church. After the formation of Nagaland, the Naga Hills Baptist Church Council (NHBCC) was renamed the Nagaland Baptist Church Council (NBCC), 'acknowledging and recognising the administrative and political unit put in place by the Indian state' (Thomas 2016: 139).[63] In contrast, an organisation formed with the aim of 'uniting all Naga tribes under one banner' was named the Council for Naga Baptist Churches and its battle cry is 'Nagas for Christ' rather than 'Nagaland for Christ' (ibid.: 197).

Every ceasefire between the government and insurgents since the 1960s has been rocked by differing interpretations of the cartographic correlate of 'Nagaland'. Nagaland's neighbouring states insist that the ceasefire has to be limited to Nagaland. However, insurgents claim immunity from arrest across Nagaland that signifies all Naga areas for them, including in neighbouring states, and use the geographical scope of ceasefires as endorsements of their territorial claims.[64] This matter is routinely contested across the length and breadth of Naga areas as the two sides test each other's resolve to defend claims (see *ME* 2018a for a recent instance). To sum up, we can argue that Nagaland's cartographic woes are manifestations of the larger dispute over the imagination and visualisation of the Naga nation.

The Political Economy of Irredentism

States and communities at the receiving end of Naga irredentism allege that encroachments, especially, along the Assam–Nagaland border are tolerated, if not encouraged, by the Nagaland government that allegedly coordinates with insurgents to reclaim the 'traditional' or 'historical' Naga territory. Gohain (2007: 3280, 3282) notes,

The modus operandi is sudden, unsuspected and unprovoked attack by armed gangs, reportedly including rebel Naga elements, who force people to flee abandoning their homesteads and farms, and then consolidate the possession by planting signboards of the Nagaland government overnight. Soon after government offices, schools and police stations are built ... [followed by the formation of] new administrative subdivisions on disputed territory.[65]

The Nagaland government's involvement in irredentism is not restricted to maps and the formation of administrative units in the disputed territory.[66] The state government has also not cooperated with the Survey of India for the authentication of the interstate border on the ground (*Telegraph* 2014), rejected the recommendations of several federal commissions that tried to settle the dispute (B. Bhattacharyya 1994; Gohain 2007), tried to extend the reach of the Nagaland Board of Secondary Education to Naga-inhabited areas outside Nagaland (Rio 2006: 213), conducted censuses and held elections in the disputed areas in Assam (Maps 3.1–3.3; B. Bhattacharyya 1994; Misra 1987: 2194; *Times of India* 2013) and published maps showing the territory of other states as part of Nagaland (see maps in this chapter; see also Agrawal and Kumar 2017a: Map 11).[67]

The Nagaland government was not always openly irredentist though. Initially, it used to omit maps from its publications to avoid endorsing the existing border, for example, the Kohima district gazetteer carried the following note: 'No map has been included in the publication as the Boundaries of Nagaland are subject to revision as provided for in the 1960 Delhi Agreement' (GoN 1970: xvi). Later publications included maps conforming to the border recognised by the union government (GoN 1979; 1981).

At present, the Nagaland government and Naga civil society claim that as much as 12,882 square kilometres of their 'ancestral' territory is under the 'illegal occupation' of Assam (*ME* 2018b; Talukdar 2014; Yeputhomi n.d.: 12–13; Assam government official, interview, 5 June 2013, Sarupathar, Assam). Nagaland's claim encompasses substantial territory far from the foothills, including areas where Nagas constitute a minuscule minority.[68] The Myanmar–Nagaland and Manipur–Nagaland borders are also contested. In fact, it seems that some of the earlier government maps of Nagaland, which we have not been able to access, 'did not demarcate the state's eastern and southern boundaries [with Myanmar and Manipur, respectively]' (Prabhakara 2012: 174; see also note 2 of Chapter 3). The location of border pillars and its implications for access to fields, pastures and forests, is the subject of daily contestation along the entire India–Myanmar border (*ME* 2018d). A recent controversy over the ownership of Dzükou Valley highlighted the territorial divide between Maos of Manipur and Southern Angamis of Nagaland. Other disputes along the Manipur–Nagaland border are centred around Jessami and Khezhakeno (*Nagaland Post* 2017a). However, neither Myanmar nor Manipur border has witnessed sustained irredentist activity, which is most intense along the Assam border.[69] Nagas inhabit both sides of Nagaland's borders with Arunachal Pradesh, Manipur and Myanmar, whereas 'others' are 'occupying' traditional Naga territory in Assam. However, there is more to this than meets the eye.[70] The Assam border abounds in a variety of natural resources including oil and coal in addition to timber and fertile agricultural land (Kikon 2019). Some of the earliest instances of 'encroachment' along Assam border seem to have been driven by economic considerations. Alleged encroachments in the vicinity of Diphu and Geleki Reserve Forests were linked to Nagaland Sugar Mills, Dimapur and Nagaland Pulp & Paper Co Ltd, Mokokchung (B. Bhattacharyya 1994: 18, 27, 36; ASA, Home Confidential PLB 70/1971; Sema 1984: 56–7), which required agricultural and forest products as inputs.

After these early corporate encroachments, later expansion of Naga settlements in the disputed area happened at the levels of individuals, clans and villages. Ecological stress, demographic pressure and lack of economic development have affected the living conditions in the hills. Aware of these problems, Naga leaders have been exhorting people to settle in the plains. A Naga politician 'highlighted the advantages of having settlements in plain areas and foothills, which are more easily accessible with more facilities especially water compared to the hilly areas, and encouraged the people to consider the suggestion' (*ME* 2017b). People also recognise that settlement in plains allows access to land for wet cultivation and markets (Kikon 2019: 30, 34, 66). However, Dimapur that accounts for most of the small plains territory of Nagaland is already overpopulated. The territory of Arunachal Pradesh, Manipur and Myanmar adjoining Nagaland is equally, if not more, inhospitable than the hills of Nagaland. So, Assam is the only outlet for Nagaland's growing population. Indeed, historically, the plains and valleys of Assam have been natural destinations for the excess population in the adjoining hills, but, as discussed above, the settlers began to be seen as outsiders and encroachers after the advent of rigid modern borders.

Presently, Naga settlers control a larger but sparsely populated part of the disputed area. They are not familiar with settled cultivation though and have to depend on Assamese settlers and alleged Bangladeshi immigrants, who are familiar with wet cultivation and can provide cheap, skilled and disciplined agricultural labour but do not have sufficient land. Such interdependence due to asymmetric distribution of land, capital and labour resources is commonplace in agrarian societies. Furthermore, Assam's towns bordering Nagaland serve as wholesale markets for the adjoining districts of Nagaland, the bulk of Nagaland's intra-state transport has to pass through the plains of Assam[71] and Nagaland is dependent upon supplies of agricultural and other commodities from Assam (and other states).

While the governments view shared spaces as a source of vulnerability and have securitised the border, cross-boundary relations cannot be eliminated because of the hard constraints imposed by geography and ecology on land-surplus settlers from the hills and land-scarce plainsmen. So, while 'others' are in occupation of ancestral Naga territory, a modus vivendi is arrived at as their agricultural skills and labour are indispensable to the sustenance of the Naga agrarian economy in the disputed territory. Similar transborder synergies that do not conform to the standard narrative of interstate conflict emerge in other fields such as coal-mining (Kikon 2019: 20, 47–8, 92, 126). Given the shared interest in maintenance of peace and livelihoods, Border Peace Coordination Committees have sprung up across the Assam–Nagaland border that are recognised by the local administration on both sides. These committees meet through the year (*ME* 2019e) and also respond to sudden developments that threaten peace (*Times of India* 2018). The regular meetings involve cultural events and even raffle draws.

The union government has shown remarkable indifference in the face of Nagaland's cartographic irredentism and 'encroachment' of the territory of other states. It has restricted itself to appointing commissions, whose recommendations are non-binding. It seems to believe that the border dispute has no solution at the national level due to constitutional and political constraints.

Nagaland elects one member of parliament (MP) each to the upper and lower houses compared to its neighbours – Arunachal Pradesh, Assam and Manipur – that elect 9 and 18 members, respectively. Of these, Assam alone accounts for 7 and 14 members in the upper and lower houses, respectively. Moreover, the ruling party in New Delhi has not been in power in Nagaland since 1995, while one or the other national party has been in power in all of Nagaland's neighbours during this period.[72] Thus, the national parties do not have any political incentive to move a constitutional amendment to redraw borders. Interstate territorial disputes are not amenable to legalistic solutions either. Not surprisingly, the union government is reluctant to get involved in Nagaland's territorial disputes involving several states.[73] It tolerates Nagaland's parchment transgressions and occasional physical 'encroachments' while leaving room for a local resolution of the problem.[74]

In fact, the union government has been cautious in this regard right since the inception of Nagaland, when it clarified that it 'could not make any commitment about the transfer of an area that forms part of another state' (NSA, 5:22).[75] And, that it could 'utmost' refer Nagaland's case to Assam, though it seemed to prefer 'direct' negotiations between Nagaland and Assam (ibid.). At the same time, the Assam government also rejected requests to leave behind parts of the erstwhile Naga Hills district in Assam (ASA, TAD/GA-112/57).

Similar considerations operate within Assam. The disputed areas along the Nagaland border can at best affect election outcomes in two constituencies in Assam. Moreover, Assamese villages in the disputed area are populated by communities that are not influential in the state politics. As a result, the resolution of the border dispute is not a priority for the Assam government. Add to this, the fact that the status quo supports Assam's most preferred border alignment. In contrast, Nagaland treats a favourable resolution of border dispute as essential for its survival. Its long-pending foothills road project aimed at reducing dependence upon Assam for road transport is presented as 'Survival Road Project' (*Nagaland Page* 2018b) and 'life line' (*ME* 2019g). Access to the fertile plains in the disputed area is also viewed as essential for the food security of the hilly state. A Naga civil society leader (interview, 22 June 2013, Dimapur) who was later elected to the state assembly told us that the disputed area 'cannot be given up by the Nagas. Too many things are at stake. It is our rice bowl. Dimapur being industrial cannot support agriculture. We have a few plains areas and we cannot give this up. This area also has pocket deposits of hydrocarbons' (see also Stracey 1968: 52–3 for an earlier account of similar sentiments in Nagaland). Add to this, the fact that almost 10 per cent of Nagaland's villages lie in the disputed area that accounts for more than half of the plains under Nagaland's administration. Last but not the least, the disputed area is inhabited by one of the most influential communities of the state. So, Nagaland, unlike Assam, is understandably impatient for an early and favourable resolution of the border dispute.

Faced with an aloof union government and status quoist neighbours, Nagaland relies on competitive developmentalism, scalar competition, scale jumping and counter-mapping to contest colonial era borders. The remainder of this chapter explores these strategies and their impact on maps and statistics.

'Development' as a Weapon

Despite the loss of hundreds of lives in border clashes and the inherent economic and ecological interdependence of the states that is unlikely to disappear anytime soon, the two governments are unwilling to cooperate. Instead of developing the border region as a belt of shared prosperity, the governments adopt different (spellings for the) names of villages in the disputed territory, condone exclusivist ethnic rhetoric and indulge in competitive developmentalism along the border to cultivate loyal villages. In some parts of the disputed area under Nagaland, roads are better than those in the state's political (Kohima) and commercial (Dimapur) capitals, while in others schools have been sanctioned for very small populations.[76] Electricity is supplied to neighbouring villages through parallel lines separately maintained by the two states (interviews with village elders and government officials in Dhupguri, Navapur and Sarupathar on 5–6 June 2013 and Husto, Tohoi and Niuland on 24 June 2015). Both governments issue documents to loyalists, including alleged illegal/undocumented Bangladeshi immigrants, to build documentary evidence in support of their claims. This is reminiscent of the growth of settlements along the Israel–Palestine border, where immigrants from Asia and Africa, some of questionable Jewish origins, are settled on the violent Israel–Palestinian frontier. Nagas allege that illegal/undocumented (Bangladeshi) immigrants have benefitted from the competition between the two states[77] and try to find common ground with the Assamese who are also bitterly opposed to Bangladeshi immigrants. However, absentee Naga landlords, including politicians, businessmen, insurgents and bureaucrats, are completely dependent upon the labour of alleged illegal/undocumented Bangladeshi immigrants and immigrants from other states of India.

Compared to Assam, Nagaland has been more active in the disputed area. Nagaland has encouraged the formation of new villages and created administrative circles for them. Between 1971 and 2011, the number of villages in Dimapur district (including the disputed area adjoining Dimapur) grew by 101 per cent, which accounts for a fourth of all the new villages formed in the state (Table 3.3).

Table 3.3   Number of inhabited villages and circles

Administrative unit	Villages			Circles	Villages per circle
	1971	2011	Growth[†]	2011	2011
Nagaland	960	1,400	46	114	12
Kohima (1971)	346	543	57	37	15
Dimapur	109*	219	101	8	27
Dimapur (circles in disputed area)	—	104	—	4	26
Mokokchung (1971)	326	449	38	34	13
Wokha	95	151	59	12	13
Tuensang (1971)	288	408	42	43	9
Nagaland (excl. Dimapur)	851	1,181	39	106	11
Nagaland (excl. Dimapur and Wokha)	756	1,030	36	94	11
Assam	21,995	25,372	15	184	138
Golaghat	664	1,032	55	6	172
Manipur	1,949	2,515	29	38	66
India	575,936	597,608	4	5,924	101

Sources: Prepared by authors using GoI (1973a; 1975a; 1996a; 2011f), 'Table A-1: Number of Villages, Towns, Households, Population and Area', http://www.censusindia.gov.in/2011census/A-1_NO_OF_VILLAGES_TOWNS_HOUSEHOLDS_POPULATION_AND_AREA.xlsx.

Notes: (i) Kohima (1971), etc. correspond to districts during the 1971 Census (Figure 3.1). (ii) [†]In per cent, calculated for the period 1971–2011. (iii) * Includes Dimapur and Pherima subdivisions. (iv) We have included the villages transferred during 1981–91 to Dimapur (one each from Pedi and Jalukie) and Wokha (three from Mangkolemba) in the respective 1971 village counts to ensure comparability across censuses. (v) Niuland, Nihoku, Kuhoboto and Aquqhnaqua circles are located in the disputed area.

Wokha, the other district adjoining the disputed area in the vicinity of Dimapur, also reported a large increase in the number of villages during this period (59 per cent). The corresponding figures for Nagaland as a whole and Assam were 46 per cent and 15 per cent, respectively. The figure for Nagaland excluding Dimapur is 39 per cent and drops to 36 per cent if we exclude Wokha as well. Wokha and Dimapur together account for 43 out of 120 unrecognised, that is, new villages in the state (*ME* 2018l).[78] It is also noteworthy that the Naga villages in the fertile disputed area, where wet cultivation is practised, are smaller than the villages in the hills, where shifting cultivation is practised. So, Nagaland is not only forming more villages in the disputed area, but these villages are also smaller in terms of population than their counterparts in Nagaland and Assam (Figure 3.2). This is true for the border circles of both Dimapur as well as Wokha.[79]

Assam has also tried to expand its footprint in the disputed territory and match Nagaland's fiscally ruinous administrative activism along the border. Golaghat district, which is the site of the most extensive 'encroachment' by Naga settlers, reported a 55 per cent growth in the number of villages, which is nearly four times the rate of growth of villages in Assam as a whole.[80] However, unlike Nagaland that anyway has small circles across its territory, densely populated Assam cannot afford to form too small circles in a district as that would trigger similar demands elsewhere in the state (senior official incharge of border affairs, interview, 3 June 2013, Guwahati).[81] So, even though the territory under Assam's control is more densely populated and poorly provisioned, it cannot afford to create smaller sub-district units to take public services closer to its loyalists. In 2011, Assam had a revenue circle for every 138 villages and Manipur had 1 subdivision for every 66 villages compared to Nagaland, where there was a circle for every 12 villages. This disproportion exists even if we restrict the comparison to the border districts. Along the Assam border, Nihokhu circle of Dimapur has just 10 villages, while Tamlu in Longleng has only 5 villages. Likewise, for the disputed Khezhakeno area on the Manipur border, Nagaland has created a circle for just two villages, including the circle headquarter.

There seem to be limits to Nagaland's competitive developmentalism too, though, both internal and external. On the one hand, Nagas themselves note the oddity of circles such as Khezhakeno. Tseminyu and Tsogin circles that are together demanding district status use, among other things, the example of Khezhakeno to justify their demand (Rengma Hoho 2016). On the other hand, courts demand status quo and have restrained the governments from putting in place a full-fledged administration in the disputed area. This has forced Nagaland to publish conflicting maps and gradually expand its visible administrative footprint to be able to argue that its hand has been guided by humanitarian considerations. The evolution of Aquqhnaqua as an administrative unit illustrates the gradualist approach. The villages of Aquqhnaqua were recognised before 2001. Aquqhnaqua circle was formed after 2001, and the Extra Additional Commissioner (EAC) office was sanctioned in 2009 (GoN 2009b), but offices were built a decade later in 2018 (*ME* 2018aa).

Settlers cope with the resultant uncertainty on the ground by publishing souvenir magazines and building village gates, celebrating centenaries of relatively recent settlements and preserving every shred of paper that somehow proves their *long-standing* presence in the area (interviews with village elders and government officials in Dhupguri, Navapur and Sarupathar on 5–6 June 2013 and Husto, Tohoi and Niuland on 24 June 2015; Kikon 2019: 30, 35, 127 for villages in Lotha and Konyak areas). People strategically invoke the state to improve their bargaining power vis-à-vis economic partners/competitors from across the border. They try to organise events such as health camps to draw in their government, boast about stray visits of government officials and try to goad their government by comparing it with the government on the other side of the border (Kikon 2019: 35, 64). At the same time when self-interest demands, they readily join with people from the other side to bypass their respective governments. Assamese traders help 'Naga villages ensure that lands marked for coal mines would come under the jurisdiction of Nagaland' where people own land and natural resources, that is, the government cannot demand royalties (ibid.: 47–8). The everyday struggles of people amidst legal–administrative uncertainties can be seen as a contribution to contesting 'state-making' projects because 'by choosing whom to bribe [officials of Assam or Nagaland], people living under the exception are not only trying to secure private benefits, but they are also … providing legitimacy to Assam or Nagaland' (Suykens 2013: 180). On the other hand, the state too selectively and strategically co-opts private infrastructure in the disputed area to claim sovereignty, thereby blurring the boundary between public and private goods (ibid.: 178). When the state fails the people, they turn to Naga insurgents who in turn exploit the opportunity to burnish their credentials as an alternative to the Indian state (ibid.: 180–1). As a result, the people in the border districts of Assam view Naga insurgent groups as 'an integral organ of the state in Nagaland' (Kikon 2019: 64, 109; see also Stracey 1968: 51; Gohain 2007: 3280).

Interstate competition, even within the bounds imposed by courts, has overshadowed the need to cooperate in face of shared challenges along the troubled border. Growing population and ecological crises (flooding, soil erosion and shrinking cycles of shifting cultivation) are pushing people from *both* the hills of Nagaland and the plains as well as tea gardens of Assam towards the fertile and relatively sparsely populated interstate border. Nagas occupy part of the disputed plains and most of the foothills and upstream area. Given rapid deforestation and erratic rainfall, the urgent task of forest and water management requires cooperation between the two states and their respective local stakeholders as watersheds cut across borders.[82] Not coincidentally, Nagaland's micro-watershed maps deviate the most from the existing border and include larger parts of Assam (Agrawal and Kumar 2017a: Map 11).[83] The two states also need to cooperate to address the ecological impact of logging, coal mining and petroleum extraction, sand mining and stone quarrying along the shared border. In absence of cooperation, non-state actors fill in the vacuum, often leading to 'inter-state' violence (*Sentinel* 2012). Usual quarrels between economic partners are allowed to escalate into interstate battles, disrupting local cross-border synergies (Assamese IAS officer 1, interview, 3 June 2013, Guwahati; *Nagaland Post* 2014c; Kikon 2019: 20, 92).

The irredentist rhetoric of the fragmented Naga insurgency, maximalist bargaining positions of the respective governments and opportunistic electoral politics have meant that there is not much room for cooperative solutions for shared problems.[84] As in Bosnia, non-ethnic alternative territorial divisions 'such as a (water) resource-based division, or even one based on journey to work, are hardly ever discussed' (Crampton 1996: 353, 358–9). However, identity-based partition does not lead to stability because, as Chatterji (1999: 241) demonstrates in case of the Indo-Pakistan border in Bengal, communal solidarity quickly falls apart 'along lines of territory, party, faction and personal ambition when it' runs 'into the reality of partition'.

Counter-Mapping

Other states of India have also witnessed irredentist demands after independence, but in most cases the demands lost support with the passage of time. Maharashtra remains locked in a territorial dispute with Karnataka over Marathi-speaking districts of the latter, but this is no longer a politically salient issue. Initially, there was a demand for a 'Greater Mizoram' (NSA, 2: 475), but over the years the debate has shifted in favour of cultural and linguistic unity of kindred tribes split across interstate and international borders (*ME* 2018s). The demand for 'Greater Jharkhand' (Corbridge 2002) and 'Greater Goa' (*Times of India* 2010) too lost vitality over the years. Odisha has territorial disputes with all its neighbours, involving 'Over 28,000 acre of land of 95 villages in 10 districts' (*Pioneer* 2016), but in recent times it seems to be focussed more on claiming exclusive ownership of cultural icons and desserts that predate modern interstate borders (*Hindustan Times* 2017). Elsewhere, communities such as Bhils occasionally demand states cutting across several existing states (*NDTV* 2018).

Nagaland's case is radically different. Its irredentist demands have persisted over a very long period during which the claims have grown. It is demanding a substantial portion of the territories of *all* its neighbours, for example, more than half of Manipur. The state government has been actively involved in territorial transgressions on the ground as well as counter-mapping. More importantly, Nagaland's territorial conflicts with neighbours have claimed *hundreds* of lives.

Given the limits to 'encroachment' across the border in neighbouring states, Naga irredentism has found its fullest expression in counter-mapping. Nagaland's counter-mapping broadly follows the general trajectory exemplified by, say, early Jewish settlers in Israel: map a territory, iconise it and then erase the inconvenient parts of the history (Wood 2010: 240; Jones 2010: 265). In the Naga Hills, colonial censuses categorised tribes which spoke mutually unintelligible languages and had limited contact with each other, as a population, that is, 'a bounded and quantifiable entity capable of, and indeed demanding, measurement ... with particular characteristics, rates of growth or attrition, and patterns of behaviour' (Urla 1993: 820, 834; see also Göderle 2016: 68).[85] The population later coalesced into a Naga 'majority' within colonial-era borders that were originally drawn to defend the revenue-surplus plains from tribal raiders, contain non-state spaces within the colonial state, introduce collective action problems between hills and plains and implement scalar differentiation to reduce administrative presence in revenue-deficit areas. The colonial demarcation of borders and the enumeration of the people enclosed by those borders under a common label brought together hitherto isolated tribes.

Naga counter-mappers used convenient colonial maps, census reports and ethnographic accounts to draw a compact but expanding 'Greater Nagaland' (Map 3.11).[86] The counter-mappers rhetorically traced back the map to a remote past and sacralised the enclosed territory simultaneously as the traditional/ancestral (that is, pre-Christian) land of Nagas as well as the citadel of Christianity (that is, *Nagaland for Christ*) in 'Hindu' India.[87] Two key features of Naga counter-mapping – nominal activism and the state government as a counter-mapper – are discussed as follows.

Renaming territories and places is an integral part of Naga counter-mapping as the nationalists view physical and nominal realms as mutually constitutive. Neighbouring territories which are populated or claimed by Nagas are nominally claimed as extensions of Nagaland.[88] Manipur's Naga areas are referred to as 'Southern Nagaland',[89] while the Naga areas of Myanmar are referred to as 'Eastern Nagaland' or 'Eastern Naga Areas'. The latter is a source of immense confusion as Nagaland's eastern districts, that is, Tuensang and its successor districts, are also referred to as 'Eastern Nagaland'. Earlier 'eastern' referred to Myamarese Naga areas, for example, the Eastern Naga National Council. However, this has changed after the rise of the Eastern Nagaland People's Organization (ENPO) that represents the eastern districts of Nagaland. In the Eastern Naga Students' Federation (ENSF), 'east' refers to Tuensang and its successor districts, whereas in Eastern Naga Students' Association (ENSA), it refers to Myanmar. Occasionally,

ENSA is referred to as Eastern (Myanmar) Naga Students' Association to avoid confusion (see, for instance, 'Order of Programme of a Lead-In General Public Meeting to the Centenary of the Naga Club' on p. 3 of *ME*, 29 October 2018). Likewise, Myanmar is appended to Eastern Konyak Union (*ME* 2019f) to clarify that it is not an affiliate of Nagaland's Konyak Union. Some observers in Nagaland are, however, sceptical of the nominal activism as they feel that 'simple phrases like East Nagas, West Nagas ... are now intentionally misrepresented by the adversaries to sow seeds of hatred and division' (*ME* 2018af) and reflect the internalisation of boundaries imposed by outsiders (Wouters 2018: 39).

The nominal activism is not limited to the external margins. Samaguting is now known as Chumukedima and there are demands to enforce the spelling Chümoukedima (*ME* 2017f). Likewise, Ghaspani is now Medziphema, even though the related constituencies continue to be known by the old name. Colonial era ethnonyms are also being replaced. Sema is now Sumi/*Sümi*, and Lhota is Lotha. Angamis have tried to promote their language by renaming it as Tenyidie to make it more acceptable to neighbouring tribes, loosely grouped as Tenyimia community. In most cases, colonial origin ethnonyms have persisted, though. Lothas have not been able to replace the exonym with 'Kyong', their endonym (Murry 2014). In fact, the experience of Khiamniungans suggests that even minor changes in the spelling can prove to be divisive (KSU 2013: 10). The usage of the colonial era label 'Naga' for the hill tribes of Nagaland (that is, excluding Dimapur) and the adjoining hill districts has grown steadily over the years.[90]

People are sensitive to the 'demarcation' and names of the regions (*ME* 2011, *Telegraph* 2011a) and tribes (*ME* 2018k; TSU 2006: 13–14, 21) recognised by the state, political parties, churches and even the self-styled governments of insurgent organisations. Rengmas (interview, 13 December 2018, Tseminyu), struggling for district status, point out that political parties treat their area as a separate district. Likewise, Tikhirs (various interviews, *details omitted*), who have not been recognised by the state government as a tribe, point to their recognition by insurgent factions, while their detractors point to their absence from the NBCC and so forth (various interviews, *details omitted*). A village in Phek protested against its exclusion from a map issued by a non-governmental body (*ME* 2019a), while the Rengma Selo Zi (RSZ) complained to the state government's GIS Cell (18 September 2018) against the exclusion of a Rengma village from the *Index Map*.

As the nominal controversies hint, the counter-mappers have to contend with subversive sub-Naga dreams that restrict the alignment of physical and nominal realms.[91] Dimapur continues to known by its Kachari name in absence of agreement among Nagas over an alternative.[92] It is believed that whoever – particularly, Angamis and Sumis – controls the nominal space in Dimapur will claim original landowner's rights over the only, truly multi-ethnic settlement in Nagaland. The original name serves everyone as it recognises the settlement as Kachari, but the respective community is numerically and politically marginal. Most of the district except for the old town has already been given Naga names by Naga settlers.

Further, Nagaland's case is particularly interesting as one of the tiers of the government complements the non-state counter-mappers.[93] The state government uses counter-mapping as a means of balancing contradictory pressures from status quoist union government and neighbouring states, on the one hand, and the irredentist insurgency, on the other. It publishes a variety of mutually inconsistent maps.[94]

The multiplicity of maps serves several purposes. First, it helps to superficially maintain status quo. A set of constituency maps that adhere to the status quo is published to satisfy courts[95] and another set that includes the disputed area along Assam border is meant for actual use by election officers. Second, it helps to gradually formalise claim over the 'encroached' area without direct confrontation with Assam and New Delhi. If Assam pushes back, 'incorrect' maps can be conveniently withdrawn. Otherwise, the circulation of an 'existing' map without any objection can be treated as an acknowledgement of Nagaland's 'historical' claim. Third, it helps the state government to satisfy civil society and voters. Civil society and government both cooperate as well as compete with each other qua counter-mappers. When the state government publishes a map claiming the territory of other states, it validates the claims of civil society and insurgent counter-mappers and bestows respectability to the irredentist cause, but, at the same time, it gets an opportunity to represent itself as a voice of people. Non-governmental counter-mappers, on the other hand, exploit the differences between the union and state governments to make the official map appear as ephemeral and promote the irredentist project.[96] This success notwithstanding, as in Crampton's (1996) Bosnia, Winichakul's (1994) Thailand and Wood's (2010) Israel, irredenstist maps of Nagaland are representations of an aspiration, that is, the creation of a singular 'social reality and identity for people in a given space' (Krishna 1994: 508), rather than reality. In other words, the counter-maps anticipate rather than reflect spatial reality. The aspirational nature of Nagaland's maps and the fragile nature of the underlying 'Greater Nagaland' project, engender a postcolonial cartographic anxiety. Under weak public institutions this anxiety triggers recurring outbursts against the 'other' (indigenous non-Naga tribes and non-indigenous/non-tribal communities) and the securitisation of boundaries.[97]

The aspiration of a Naga-dominated state that includes all Nagas is shaped by an early twentieth-century obsession with aligning states and nations to create stable non-irredentist states at peace with themselves (Crampton 1996). The feasibility of this rested upon the belief that populations could be exhaustively and exclusively classified into distinct, scientifically identifiable and immutable ethnic/racial categories (ibid.: 359). However, boundaries, identity and conflicts are mutually constitutive, that is, people do not enter conflicts with platonic ethnic identities (Baron and Hannan 1994: 1137; Abbott 1995; Jones 2009a). Not surprisingly, the road from colonial-era idealisations to the later emergence of a legible community has been long and tortuous everywhere and the completion of the journey is not guaranteed. Indeed, as pointed out above, 'Greater Nagaland' has begun to implode even before it could materialise.

Scalar Competition

After independence, the constituent assembly retained the colonial administrative arrangement because of its instrumentality in helping the tribes preserve their culture and way of life by protecting them from demographic pressure from the plains (Lok Sabha 1999: Vol. VII, 101–207). More importantly, it was hoped that administrative–political status quo would assuage the tribes that equated democracy with majoritarianism. The colonial scalar differentiation of territory into backward tracts/excluded areas and the rest has persisted as a result.[98] Naga nationalism/irredentism operates within the larger context of the scalar politics within the union.[99]

The cartographic divergence between the state and union governments can be viewed as a constitutional conflict over the distribution of powers. The union government is the sole constitutionally-empowered authority to alter international borders (Art. 2) and form new states or alter the areas, borders, or names of existing states (Art. 3). So, the Nagaland government's cartographic irredentism is repugnant to the constitution. Naga nationalists resent this distribution of cartographic powers within the union as it erases the 'unique' history of Nagaland's incorporation within the union (Yeputhomi 2018a).

Another dimension of scalar competition relates to safeguarding constitutional–legal provisions that protect customary institutions and practices and limit the mobility of national (and international) labour and capital across Nagaland's borders.[100] Some of these provisions are part of the constitution's 'Temporary, Transitional and Special Provisions', which engenders uncertainty about the permanence of the arrangement. In fact, these provisions were earlier known merely as 'Temporary and Transitional Provisions' and 'Special' was introduced through the Constitution (Thirteenth Amendment) Act enacted to grant statehood to Nagaland and add special provisions to protect its customary institutions (Art. 371A). Ever since Nagas have remained alert to potential erosion of the constitutional safeguards. Government's efforts to conserve forests have met with stiff opposition from villages (Stracey 1968: 133–5), which claim absolute ownership of their forests and control as much as 90 per cent of the state's forest area (GoN 2017: 56).[101] Petroleum exploration has been stalled for similar reasons. While it is true that oil royalties attract many claimants, including the 'traditional' apex tribal bodies formed in mid-twentieth century and the cash-strapped state government, the substance of constitutional federalism and democracy, and not just distribution of oil wealth, is also at stake. The state government argues that Nagaland's rights over its land and its resources under Art. 371A override the union government's monopoly over mineral resources. However, even exploration under a state law has been challenged as individual landowners and their respective (village and/or tribal) communities too claim priority under Art. 371A.[102]

Nagaland is also challenging the commensurability of provincial scales. In 2017, the civil society stalled the implementation of a federally mandated 33 per cent reservation of seats for women in urban local bodies as it purportedly violates constitutionally-guaranteed customary laws (Lohe 2017) and is even otherwise needed only in the plains and not in the purportedly traditionally egalitarian societies of the hills (Kumar 2017a). Opposition to urban local bodies is rooted in the fear that their power to impose taxes will dilute the absolute control of the people over land.[103] More than a decade ago, Nagaland rejected the delimitation of electoral constituencies because, among other things, it was argued that norms valid for plains cannot be blindly applied to hills (*CPO & Ors. vs. UoI & Ors.* 2006). Nagaland, along with six other states, has also opposed the creation of an All-India Judicial Service (*Nagaland Post* 2017b) because it might interfere with constitutional guarantees regarding customary law.

In short, Nagaland's irredentist misdemeanours contest New Delhi's attempts to erase provincial histories and homogenise provincial scales, reduce provinces to mutually exclusive and collectively exhaustive parts of the national scale and create a neatly nested hierarchy of scales contained within the nation-state. Naga counter-mappers not only erase India's international border with Myanmar and interstate borders in the North-East (Map 3.11, note 2 of Chapter 3) but also leave parts of Jammu and Kashmir outside India (GPRN [2007] 2010: 3) and refer to India's North-East as 'Western South East Asia' (*Hindustan Times* 2013).

A final point is in order. To overcome their numerical insignificance, partisans of independence indulge in what is known as 'scale jumping' (Herod 2011: 19) and bond with national and international church, human rights and indigenous rights movements to attract New Delhi's attention, contest the portrayal of their movement as a local law and order problem and signal that they are not isolated. The NSCN-IM's membership of the Hague-based Unrepresented Nations and Peoples Organization (UNPO) in 1993, which was followed by a meeting between Prime Minister Narasimha Rao and the NSCN-IM leadership, is a case in point.[104] Naga organisations such as the Naga Peoples Movement for Human Rights have been active participants of United Nations bodies such as the Permanent Forum on Indigenous Issues. However, to contest the government's claim that the Naga political movement survives only because of foreign props, they simultaneously assert that international support is incidental.[105]

Concluding Remarks

Maps are not sacrosanct and 'can be challenged ... by military action, armed revolt, varying degrees of resistance, political action, actions at law, and even stories, songs, and other expressive behaviour' (Wood 2010: 141). More than any other people in the North-East, Nagas have refused to reconcile with colonial borders. They have deployed a whole range of strategies, including territorial and cartographic irredentism, counter-mapping, scalar competition, scale jumping and competitive developmentalism to challenge colonial-origin borders. Their dissatisfaction with attempts to contain them within a neatly arranged hierarchy of borders affects both government maps and headcounts.

The civil society and the partisans of independence/integration of Naga areas within India use maps as 'rhetorical devices' (Crampton 2001: 238) to 'present arguments' (Barrow 2003: 5) and as tools of resistance. The state government not only condones counter-mapping but also plays the role of counter-mapper blurring the divide between government map-makers and counter-mappers. Counter-mapping can be seen as an example of 'insurgent informational practices' (Wyly 2004: 7) and 'democratization of mapmaking' (Wood 2010: 158), which reminds us that 'maps are not neutral, value-free presentations of the world' (Barrow 2003: 5) and also challenges technocratic hubris that divides the world into expert map-makers and lay users/consumers of maps.

In Nagaland, we are faced with an inherent cartographic indeterminacy (rather than a mere inaccuracy) generated by the encounter between different conceptions of nationhood (Indian and Naga) and understandings of federalism.[106] Interstate ethno-territorial conflicts are both causes and consequences of this indeterminacy. On the Naga side of the border, these conflicts are driven by a combination of political-geographic factors (people are challenging 'artificial' colonial borders) and political-economic factors (competition for resources and political power is driving people to fight for a favourable border). Increasingly, political-geographic arguments are being used to advance political-economic interests, which govern the intensity and direction of Naga irredentist aggression against Assam. Nagaland argues that its dispute with Assam is *positional* in character (that is, concerning the actual location of the border) (NSA, 5:22), but in reality the dispute also involves *territorial* (claims upon neighbouring territory), *functional* (concerning the state's functions along as well as across the border vis-à-vis ethnically similar population) and *transborder resource development* (concerning harnessing of coal and petroleum resources) dimensions.[107]

The resolution of the indeterminacy facing map-making in Nagaland depends on answers to larger questions – *Who is a Naga* and *What is Nagaland?* It cannot be resolved with the help of advanced map-making technologies as it is linked to the as yet inconclusive search for a stable basis for Naga identity and a place for Nagaland within the union. However, governments pretend, or perhaps even believe, that they just need to find the right map or conduct a more accurate survey. The Nagaland government, for instance, complains that the union and Assam governments have 'lost/destroyed' the original maps that favoured its case (Suykens 2013: 184). The obsession with maps betrays a 'cartographic mentality' insofar as proposed solutions revolve 'around the singular cartographic delineation of territory' (Crampton 1996: 353). Nagaland and its neighbours are caught in a 'the territorial trap', an obsession with territorially delineated jurisdictions as fixed, mutually exclusive categories (Agnew 1994). They have failed to devise locally meaningful ways of shared management of agrarian and ecological regions bound by multiple cross-cutting boundaries that have been arbitrarily split by rigid modern borders.

Nagaland's case also highlights the (intra-national) cartographic flexibility of the Indian state in the ethno-geographic periphery. This flexibility is implicated in intra- and inter-scale conflicts within a multi-tiered polity. It is both enabled by and results from the need for strategic ambiguity at different tiers of a government grappling with a nation-building project that is fragile at the edges. Governments use the power to map to maintain ambiguity along intra-national borders that are tainted by colonial arbitrariness and illegitimacy. As a result, map-making becomes a political technology subject to competing considerations across tiers of government. The union government tolerates the cartographic laxity as it helps avoid a strictly legalistic approach that would necessitate the use of force to implement a singular and exclusive solution, particularly when one does not exist. In other words, cartographic flexibility and strategic ambiguity in locating borders in contested territories are mutually constitutive and help governments contain people within fundamentally indeterminate borders.

Until the underlying political problems are resolved, imprecise maps and inaccurate area estimates will continue to affect the whole range of government statistics. First, flawed maps affect the quality of censuses and sample surveys.[108] Specifically in the case of Nagaland, the population of parts of the border area is mapped to both Assam and Nagaland. As a result, the census possibly double counts the population of the disputed area. This would also result in an overlap between the NSSO sampling frames for Assam and Nagaland. Second, the population densities of districts along the Assam border are overestimated as census reports for Nagaland include the disputed territory's population but not its area. Third, villagers over-report their population to attract public services and political patronage that is necessary for survival in the disputed area. Both the governments encourage and even enable settlers to encroach upon forest land but at the same time also express an inability to fulfil civic demands as the border dispute is sub judice. Fourth, given the multiplicity of inconsistent maps of Nagaland, statistics collected by different departments of the state government are, strictly speaking, not comparable because they use different maps and, by implication, collect information from different areas. Fifth, even as it struggles to make ends meet, being entirely dependent upon federal redistribution, the Nagaland government expends considerable efforts to pursue the irredentist project leading to the misallocation of its scarce resources to sparsely populated border with Assam. Last but not the least, the growing 'inaccuracy' in maps after the introduction of advanced map-making technologies suggests that the history of map-making is not a steady progression from less to more accurate maps (Crampton 2001: 238). Not coincidentally, until recently, errors in Nagaland's population projections (Chapters 2 and 4), population (Chapters 4–5) and household consumer expenditure (Chapter 6) also grew despite advances in the respective fields. So, errors in Nagaland's maps have to be understood in relation to errors in other statistics and also political and developmental challenges facing the state.

Notes

1. Three kinds of maps were issued before the 2013 Assembly Elections: (a) legally correct (in respect of the external borders), (b) factually correct (in respect of the disputed territory) and (c) neither. In addition to the constituency maps reproduced in Agrawal and Kumar (2017a), we have printed copies of two identically titled maps ('Nagaland Assembly Constituencies') drawn to the same scale (1 inch = 4 miles and 1.25 inches = 5 miles) that differ in terms of external borders from each other as well as from maps used in this book.

2. Unlike some of the older maps that 'did not demarcate the state's eastern and southern boundaries [with Myanmar and Manipur, respectively]' (Prabhakara 2012: 174), the maps reproduced in this book clearly mark the borders of Nagaland with other states. However, the Assam–Nagaland border is not clearly marked in 'Police Network' and 'Tourist' maps issued in recent years. The latter show the road network in the disputed area, even though some of the road maps do not cover roads in the disputed area (see http://nagalandgis.in/map_catalogue_files/State%20Roads.pdf). Other tourist maps issued by the state government (see http://nagalandgis.in/map_catalogue_files/State%20Tourist%20Map.pdf) cover the area within the borders recognised by the union government and show only a few Naga settlements in the disputed area.

3. There is another category of maps, purportedly, more accurate than the maps discussed in this chapter, namely, maps prepared by the armed forces that are not publicly available (see, for instance, *SoA vs. UoI & Ors.* 1988, order dated 7 March 2005).

4. The Nagaland State Archives (NSA) are strangely devoid of maps. File nos. 163–73 in Index 3 and file nos. 261–315 in Index 5 that contain maps are either with the Directorate of Border Affairs or, at least, not available for researchers. Maps are also missing from several other files in other indexes that ought to have contained maps. The condition of the Assam State Archives (ASA) is a little better in this regard, where researchers can access low resolution maps of the Naga Hills as part of larger maps of Assam.

5. The disputed area along the Assam border is, in fact, an exception within the larger exception that Nagaland has been since the colonial era. Inner lines, Art. 371A and the Armed Forces (Special Powers) Act, 1958, are the most visible markers of this larger exceptionalism that are now integral to the self-perception of Nagas and how they are perceived by others.

6. This chapter is also related to the literature in economics on inter-jurisdictional competition. This literature mostly deals with market regulation, taxation and standards. The possible conflict of interest between national governments and international bodies with regard to statistics has also received some attention (Wade 2012; Michalski and Stoltz 2013).

7. In 1951, GoI (1956: 3, 55, 63) reported two different area estimates for the Naga Hills, provided by the Surveyor General of India and the Assam Survey Department. The estimate of area published in the 1961 Census corresponds to the latter. It is not clear how the discrepancy between the two sources was resolved.

8. *State of Forest Report 2017* notes that Nagaland's *geographical area* was 16,579 square kilometres and the *reporting area for land utilisation* was 16,516 square kilometres, with the difference being accounted for by waterbodies. It is not clear if earlier census publications included only the *reporting area for land utilisation* under *geographical area*.

9. It is not clear if the Indo-Myanmar border has ever been properly surveyed. Presently, the Ministry of Defence seems to be opposed to surveys 'within 50 kms of the international border [with Myanmar]' (*ME* 2014).

10. The NHTA was divided into Kohima, Mokokchung and Tuensang districts, whose borders were 'drawn as to leave, each tribal group, as far as possible, under a single district administrative authority' (GoI 1966: 31). Some Konyak villages to the north and north-east of Mokokchung (that is, parts of Nagnimora and Wakching circles of the present Mon district) and Sangtam villages to the south-east of Mokokchung (that is, parts of Chare and Longkhim circles of the present Tuensang district) were transferred to Tuensang (GoI 1966: 31; see also von Fürer-Haimendorf 1962; Chaube 2012: 150). Parts of Namsang and Tamlu circles of the present Longleng district were earlier under the jurisdiction of Mokokchung (von Fürer-Haimendorf 1962; GoI 1952: 10–15). Likewise, Sumi villages on the western border of Tuensang were transferred to Mokokchung (that is, the present Zunheboto district). Asuto,

Aghunato and Hosephu, which were earlier part of Aghunato circle, and, possibly, parts or whole of Satoi circle of Zunheboto must have originally belonged to Tuensang district (cf. ASA, LIB/R137/S4/13; GoI 1954b; GoI 1966; see also Sema 2015: 106, 119). However, Sitimi and Seyochung circles that have a substantial Sumi population were left behind in Tuensang. We have not been able correct the figures in Table 3.1 for the aforesaid territorial transfers as government publications (see, for instance, GoI 1966: 32) do not provide adequate information about the changes in intra-state borders.

11. The 1961 (Gogoi, Goswami and Borah 2009: 16, 291; Misra 2012: 43; GoN 2013b: 133) and 1971 (GoN 2006: 24; Kashyap 2015) estimates of area continue to be used by researchers and government agencies. In fact, as late as in 2015, a state government website (http://nagaland.nic.in/profile/aglance.htm) mentioned the 1971 area.

12. A similar confusion affects the treatment of borders under the shadow of international disputes. Parts of the same state under the control of different countries are treated differently. The Census clearly notes that it does not have information on Pakistan-occupied Jammu and Kashmir (shaded in grey in maps) and the part of the state transferred by Pakistan to China. The 'General Notes to Provisional Population Totals' (GoI 2011b: x) suggests, 'For working out density of India and the State of Jammu and Kashmir, the entire area and population of those portions of Jammu and Kashmir which are under illegal occupation of Pakistan and China have not been taken into account' (see also GoI n.d.14). However, the territory occupied by China is not shaded in grey, the colour that signifies 'Data Not Available' (GoI 2011f: 13). The Census has also published choropleths with territory under China sharing the colour of Leh district (GoI 2014a).

13. The 10-square kilometre area disputed between Madhya Pradesh and Chhattisgarh (GoI 2011e: 65) and 13-square kilometre disputed between Pondicherry and Andhra Pradesh (GoI 2005a: 169) are not included in either state. Similarly, there is a detailed note on a minor territorial issue involving Maharashtra and Andhra Pradesh: 'One village Ramtapur (code No. 217 and 101 in 1951 and 1961 respectively) of Jukkal circle of Degulur taluka which was transferred under the State Reorganisation Act, 1956 from Maharashtra to Andhra Pradesh, still continues in Nanded district of Maharashtra. The population of this village has, however, been adjusted in Nizamabad district for the year 1901–1951' (GoI 2011b: General Notes). The Survey of India map of Maharashtra does not contain any remark in this regard though (SoI 2004).

14. The border disputes between Assam, Arunachal Pradesh and Meghalaya and between Bihar, Madhya Pradesh and Uttar Pradesh and their respective successor states are noted, but the size of the territory in dispute is not indicated. We are told, 'The interstate boundaries amongst Arunachal Pradesh, Assam and Meghalaya shown on this map are as interpreted from the "North-Eastern Areas (Reorganisation) Act. 1971," but have yet to be verified' (GoI 2011c: ii; 2011f: ii; n.d.4). For the latter group, *Administrative Atlas of India, 2011* notes, 'The State boundaries between Uttarakhand & Uttar Pradesh, Bihar & Jharkhand and

Chhattisgarh & Madhya Pradesh have not been verified by the Governments concerned' (GoI 2011c: ii; 2011f: ii). The SoI map of Bihar carries a similar note (SoI 2002), but there is no such note in Jharkhand's map (SoI 2012a).

15. This difference cannot be explained by the expanding reach of the Census in Tuensang between 1951 and 1961. In 1951, the Census covered only 129.5 square kilometres of Tuensang. A decade later, the coverage increased to 5356.1 square kilometres of Tuensang (GoI 2011b: x, see also note vi in Table 3.1).

16. The SoI map of Nagaland does not indicate the source of information used to draw intra-state borders. In maps of Chhattisgarh and Odisha, the SoI clearly identifies intra-state borders drawn using 'extra-departmental information' that have not been 'departmentally verified' (SoI 2012b; 2014). The maps for Nagaland do not carry a similar note (SoI 2010), even though it is highly unlikely that the SoI has itself verified intra-state borders.

17. The borders of towns are also fluid. Census officials complain that in some cases the reported area of urban settlements has changed erratically over the years (senior census officials, interview, 25 June 2013, Kohima). We do not have sufficient information to comment on town area statistics though. Cadastral surveys can resolve some of these confusions, but these are opposed as they purportedly violate customary laws and land-use practices (*ME* 2018c). Moreover, it is feared that cadastral surveys along Assam border might dilute Nagaland's claim upon the disputed territory under Assam's administrative control (Demo 2014).

18. Other sources suggest that Nagaland controls a larger area: 662.4 square kilometres (Hazarika 2011) or 1,627.70 square kilometres (Gohain 2007: 3281). Gohain claims that 840 square kilometres had been 'encroached' in Golaghat alone, which is unlikely as this almost equals the district's total forest area adjoining Assam–Nagaland border (841.61 square kilometres) that is only partly under Nagaland's administrative control.

19. GoI (1990a) includes two maps 'Administrative Divisions 1981' and 'Tseminyu Circle'. Tseminyu shares a border with Assam in the former but not in the latter. Several earlier sources show the Rengma territory sharing a border with Assam (Luthra 1974: Appendix III; Eaton 1984: 2; GoI 1988a: Map 16). The Rengma-dominated territory has shrunk as Sumis moved into the disputed area adjoining Tseminyu. It seems the Rengma community is not fully aware of the extent of misrepresentation of their territory in government maps. For instance, a recent RSZ complaint to the GIS Cell (18 September 2018) was restricted to the exclusion of Rengmapani village from *Index Map* of 2018.

20. Such discrepancies in Assam's forest statistics are not new or confined to the Assam–Nagaland border though (see Prabhakara [1987] 2012: 213).

21. Senior census officials of Nagaland (interview, 25 June 2013, Kohima) and Assam's border officials (interview, 5 June 2013, Sarupathar) confirmed this. A newspaper reported, 'Allegedly under pressure from Naga militants, villagers insisted on being enumerated by officials from Nagaland' (Karmakar 2010).

22. Census was not conducted in Assam in 1981, while the 1981 Census of Nagaland does not refer to the disputed territory. So, we do not have a direct confirmation

regarding whether Nagaland covered the disputed area. However, B. Bhattacharyya (1994: 55–6) confirms that Nagaland conducted census in Golaghat's reserved forests. Also, several villages located in the disputed area were shown as part of Nihokhu circle of Nagaland in the 1981 *District Census Handbook* for Kohima.

23. *Provisional Population Totals* (*PPT*) Totals do not clearly indicate if both states censused the disputed villages in 2011 and the complete report containing *General Population Tables* (*GPT*) has not yet been published. However, the village lists for the two states contain several common entries (GoI n.d.6).

24. *Nagaland Index Map* of 2013 (Map 3.6) shows about 130 villages in the disputed territory. We confirmed this through field visits as well as discussions with the Western Sumi Hoho (interview, 26 June 2013, Dimapur) and village elders across the disputed area. In fact, according to Assam's border officials, there were 98 Naga-occupied villages in the Golaghat–Dimapur section of the disputed territory (GoA n.d.3). However, the number of inhabited Naga villages reported in the Census of Assam dropped between 2001 and 2011. The 2011 Primary Census Abstract of Assam (GoI 2013d) shows at least 50 uninhabited villages in Sarupathar that were inhabited in 2001 (GoI n.d.2). The reason behind this cannot be ascertained as the *GPT* for 2011 has not yet been published.

25. The Census acknowledges the discrepancy between the estimates provided by the two states: 'population [of the disputed villages] enumerated by Assam is consistently lower than that enumerated by Nagaland' (GoI 2005a: 24). Assam's estimates were not necessarily based on enumeration though as it could not conduct a census in these villages due to 'resistance' (GoI 1996a: 22) or 'strong resistance' (GoI 2008a: 22) by the villagers in both 1991 and 2001. It relied upon figures 'supplied' by the Directorate of Census Operations, Nagaland. We do not have an official statement on how the 2011 Census was conducted in the disputed areas as the corresponding *GPT* has not yet been published. However, after the 2011 Census, one of us interviewed census officials in Assam and Nagaland and found that there was hardly any communication between the two, let alone sharing of information (DCO Assam, interview, 04 June 2013, Guwahati; DCO Nagaland, interview, 24–5 June 2013, Kohima). So, it is possible that Assam's figures are based on indirect estimates, which explains the divergence between the estimates of the two states. Elsewhere, Manipur had to release estimated figures for certain Naga-inhabited subdivisions in 2001 as villagers refused to cooperate when the government tried to verify the headcount (Singh 2006: 1473; Agrawal and Kumar 2019b).

26. The disputed Assam–Nagaland border is divided into six sectors, A through F. The first three sectors cover Homeland/Diphu Reserved Forest, Rengmapani and Haldipari or Haldibari/Nambor South Reserved Forest and Uriamghat/Rengma Reserved Forest, respectively.

27. The village elders of the neighbouring Assamese villages (interview, 6 June 2013, villages in Sector B of the disputed territory) suggested that the drop can be explained by overcount in the 1991 Census. Others confirmed that small Naga villages tried to secure government recognition and attract more development funds by over-reporting headcount (for instance, retired Naga IAS officer, interview,

30 October 2015, Bengaluru; see also Jasokie n.d.2: 37–8; Haralu and Chandola 2012: 76). Yet this is not sufficient to explain the sharp contraction of Golaghat's reported Sumi-speaking population. As argued in Chapter 4, content errors also played a role in this contraction.

28. A Konyak leader (interview, 22 June 2013, Dimapur) claimed that his tribe's traditional boundary with the Ahoms was identified by the grazing pattern of mithuns (*Bos frontalis*).

29. For an exposition of the current Naga understanding of this history, see Yeputhomi (2018b). For an insightful analysis of overlapping realms and cross-cutting ties of kingdoms and communities now known as tribes in western India, see Skaria (1998).

30. In a parallel development, American Baptist missionaries imposed rigid boundaries within the Naga Hills by dividing villages between the converted and unconverted. The converted part was an 'exclusive [but expanding] spatial zone' with 'well defined' boundaries physically segregating the converts (Thomas 2016: 4, 54–6).

31. Not all colonial borders are tainted by unilateralism though. The archives in Kohima and Guwahati abound in correspondence regarding the Manipuri kingdom's attempts to secure its preferred alignment.

32. The British did not merely appropriate tribal territory, but also a very large number of tangible cultural artefacts. For a discussion of the mechanisms, politics and ethics of the cultural appropriation see Kanungo (2014), who suggests that collections in the West house more than 50,000 Naga objects.

33. The British were not the first to map the Ahom–Naga boundary. Mughal chronicles provide information about the extent of the Ahom kingdom including its boundary with the Naga Hills (Habib 1982: 13A–B).

34. The Naga Hills and, more so, the unadministered areas further east were insufficiently surveyed compared to the rest of the British India (GoI 1966: 32). Yet, colonial maps showing variations in, say, population density or sex ratio, covered the unadministered areas, which were not surveyed (see maps reproduced in Singh n.d.). The administered and unadministered parts of the Naga Hills were shaded using the same colour in these maps.

35. 'Backward' Nagas were not the only ones resisting state-sponsored investigations. There was resistance to census elsewhere in the subcontinent (Maheshwari 1996: 35, 137) and even in parts of Europe (Göderle 2016: 69).

36. Christian missionaries were implicitly exempt from the Inner Line Regulations (ILR) (Borgohain and Borgohain 2011: 86). However, post independence even 'Catholic Christian Missionaries who are Indian Citizens' needed an Inner Line Permit (ILP) to enter Baptist dominated Nagaland. In 2006, a Special ILP 'valid for two years' was introduced for Indian Catholic missionaries (GoN n.d.2: Manuals I, XIII).

37. Opinion is divided in contemporary Nagaland as to the motivation behind the introduction of the inner lines. Some argue that the differential administration served colonial interests and reduced Nagas to anthropological curiosities (Sema 1984; S. C. Jamir 1998; 1999). Others, however, believe that these regulations

were established 'to safeguard the Naga identity, and to prevent their exploitation and assimilation by outsiders' (Rio 2012: 93) and 'with a view to protecting and preserving our culture and identity' (Rio 2004: 199; 2006: 66, 213; 2007: 233, 240; 2008: 47–8) and that these archaic regulations can help solve contemporary problems such as 'illegal' immigration (*ME* 2019c).

38. The phrase 'excluded area' was introduced by the British administration in the 1930s only to avoid the anthropologically loaded phrase 'backward tract' (Gundevia 1975: 47–50; Horam 1988: 39–41; Lintner 2012: 54–5; Phanjoubam 2016: 78; Suykens 2013: 172; Hazarika 2018: xxiii, 50). However, this terminological shift has given rise to a popular belief in Nagaland that 'excluded' implies the territories beyond inner lines such as the Naga Hills lay outside British India: 'When the British India Act 1935 came into force, the Naga Hills territory was named as Naga Hills Excluded area in 1937. All these points clearly envisage that Nagaland was never a part of British India' (*ME* 2018q; see also 2018ab). This view has, however, been questioned within Nagaland (NPCC 2000: 7) as colonial sources do not support it. Colonial administrators, for instance, preferred Inner Lines that helped them learn about potential intruders from the hills before it was too late, that is, in case of Nagaland, to the east of the line where the administered territory ended (ASA, Political XXII-10/26; ASA, Lib/R138/S2/06). More generally, district borders depended upon administrative convenience, among other things (NSA, 2:587; ASA, General XVI 64/20).

39. Van Ham and Saul (2008: 16) reproduce a 1932 SoI map, containing white patches, indicating 'unsurveyed' territory in Tuensang and the adjoining parts of Myanmar (see also NPCC 2000: 7).

40. These estimates of the area have been collected from the respective census reports, except for the 1876 estimate that is from Hunter (1879: 198).

41. A Konyak leader (interview, 12 June 2014, Mon) told us that the British used watersheds to divide his community between India and Myanmar, while the community believed that water was meant for drinking and boundaries were decided by men. Nagas though readily embrace colonial borders following watersheds when it is convenient (*Nagaland Post* 2018).

42. Even government officials find it difficult to identify the border on the ground. A retired Naga IAS officer (interview, 9 April 2013, Kohima) recounted an instance when Myanmarese officers found themselves on the wrong side of the border: 'I was posted on the border earlier as ADC. We once caught three Burmese [Myanmarese] enumerators (I don't recall their ethnicity, they looked like us). They seemed to be fairly junior personnel. They said that they were asked to visit such and such villages. I was asked to send them to Dimapur and then to Calcutta, from there to Rangoon. I left them at the border, informing them that they had accidentally crossed over into our territory. I was reprimanded by my senior. I told him that I used my discretion.'

43. An examination of the treatment of Myanmarese Nagas in Nagaland that goes beyond public professions of sympathy and solidarity will require a considerable detour.

44. This is reminiscent of how, unlike their Muslim counterparts, non-Muslim immigrants are invisible in 'mainland' India. It is argued that they are persecuted in their home country and India has a special responsibility towards them being the successor state to British India. The union government amended the Citizenship Act, 1955, to facilitate faster naturalisation of non-Muslim refugees from neighbouring Muslim-majority countries.

45. Several folk tales suggest shared origins of the people of hills and plains as well as Naga and non-Naga tribes (see monographs by colonial officials such as J. H. Hutton and collections of folk tales published by the Central Institute of Indian Languages, Mysore). Stories that bind the hills and plains have inspired some of the best-known contributions to the early modern Assamese literature and cinema (Kumar 2016b). In fact, such stories continue to bind people across the militarised Nagaland–Assam border (Kikon 2019: 14–6).

46. The American Baptist missionaries too played a similar role. They accepted and worked within the colonial state's administrative and political boundaries (Thomas 2016). Equally importantly, they standardised tribal languages without which the tribe-centric reorganisation of the Naga society would not have been feasible.

47. Wouters (2018: 57, 62, 74) accepts the exogenous origin of the tribe-centric organisation of Nagas but adds that they readily embraced the categorisation.

48. An often-ignored, but an important, complaint about dismemberment relates to the disjuncture between the Assam–Nagaland border and the inner line. About 96 per cent of Nagaland's area lies beyond the inner line. There have been recurrent demands to align the two so as to bring the entire area of the state under ILR (for a recent example, see *ME* 2018m) and make Nagaland whole as well as check 'illegal' immigration. This concern about a narrow stretch of land is an instance of the 'anxiety of incompleteness' (Appadurai 2007: 8). For a critique of such demands as historically ill-informed and contrary to Nagaland's claim upon its traditional lands, now under Assam, see Yeputhomi (2018b) and also Demo (2014) for a related discussion. However, most recently, the state government first decided to make ILPs mandatory in the whole of Dimapur (*ME* 2019c) and then shifted focus to a proposed register of indigenous inhabitants of Nagaland (*ME* 2019i). Eventually, the ILR was extended to entire Dimapur (*ME* 2019m).

49. The second strand of the Naga nationalist discourse is centred upon the *uniqueness hypothesis*: Nagas are 'a people who have their own unique history, culture and identity, which mean a unique socio-political community that has existed independently since time immemorial' (*ME* 2015; see also GPRN [2007] 2010: 22).

50. See Wouters (2018: 140) for barricading and Stracey (1968: 133, 136, 162–5, 214), Horam (1988: 83, 98), Dev (1988: 113) and Hazarika (2018: 103) for grouping.

51. For a critique of the competence of the Naga Club to represent all Nagas see Khutso (2018: 149–50).

52. The Federal Government of Nagaland (FGN) constitution has been amended several times, but the text of Art. 1 does not seem to have been revised since 1962 when the provisional constitution was adopted.

53. Jadonang, a millennial Rongmei Naga leader from Manipur and a contemporary of the Naga Club, coined 'Naga Raj' to refer to a kingdom encompassing all Nagas, where they would live free of exploitation, subjugation and humiliation beyond the control of the British and plainsmen (Thomas 2016: 72). Jadonang's movement dwindled as it was squeezed between the colonial state and the emergent Naga middle class, educated in missionary schools (ibid.: 80–9). 'Greater Nagaland' builds upon the Naga Club's *Memorandum to the Simon Commission* and later evangelistic crusades.

54. We are reminded of the tale of Shangmiyang, the Tangkhul giant, whose 'head rested on the Shiroi peak [North Manipur], while his feet reached Thoubal, the furthest point in the Imphal Valley [Manipur] below. His left hand could easily touch the river Chindwin in Burma [Myanmar] and his right hand, the river Brahmaputra [Assam], so many miles away on the other side' (B. K. Bhattacharyya 2005: 168). The origin of this tale is uncertain.

55. As the territory expanded, partisans of integration of hitherto divided Naga areas began producing lists of Naga tribes, but there is enormous variation among sources: 40 (Shimray 2007: 137–8), 49 (NSUD 1996: 69), 'about 50' (Yonuo 1974: 6), 66 (Iralu 2009: 385), 68 (Nuh 2006: 25–6) and 82 (KET 2015: Introduction). Iralu adds, 'Some minor tribes from the Myanmar side may still be missing in this list.' Likewise, Nuh adds the following note to his list: 'Out of the 68 tribes, 50% of the tribes, subject to confirmation for a few, are from Myanmar.' These caveats highlight the indeterminacy at the heart of the 'Greater Nagaland' project.

56. The 'Greater Nagaland' project has been closely associated with religious conversion to Christianity (Thomas 2016: 174–5) as well as ethnic conversions. The latter has not been properly studied in the Naga context, but is reminiscent of ethnic conversions engineered by the expanding Hausa community in Nigeria (Harnischfeger 2006).

57. A discussion of the long-standing debate within the Naga society over internal conflicts is beyond our scope (see Mawon 2017 for a recent example of bitter op-ed clashes between Nagas from Manipur and Nagaland; see also note 70 of this chapter).

58. To delegitimise the demand for Zeliangrong state, the NSCN-IM has, among other things, revoked the tribal status of the Zeliangrong community and has recognised the constituent groups as three separate tribes—Zeme, Liangmai and Rongmei (*ME* 2018ag). Sections of the Zeliangrong community have strongly opposed this divisive move.

59. The campaign against the recognition of 1,313 Rongmeis as an indigenous tribe of Nagaland eligible for affirmative action benefits is a case in point (NTC 2013).

60. Following Göderle (2016: 86), we can add that the way census is conceived, 'The acceptance and acquiescence of the territorial order ... [supported by the state is] the prerequisite for any use of the knowledge provided by the census.'

61. The Naga People's Convention delegation that negotiated the formation of Nagaland had suggested the name 'Nagaland' for 'the new State ... and any other Naga Area which may hereafter come under it'. After the difficulty in listing an

open-ended territory in the First Schedule of the Constitution was 'explained', 'the delegation agreed' to drop the open-ended expression and accepted a precisely demarcated cartographic, administrative and legal correlate of 'Nagaland', namely, 'the territories that were heretofore known as the Naga Hills-Tuensang Area under the Naga Hills-Tuensang Area Act 1957' (NSA, 5:22). The delegation, however, insisted that the new state should be called 'Nagaland'. The then Prime Minister, Jawaharlal Nehru seems to have preferred to call the new state 'Naga Pradesh' (Palat 2015: 156; Thomas 2016: 139). He reportedly approved the use of 'land' in Nagaland in the following words: 'If the Thais can have Thailand, why should the Nagas not have Nagaland?' (Gundevia 1975: 72).

62. Similar parenthetical uses of new and old names can be found in the Kashmir Valley, another site of a long-standing irredentist insurgency.

63. The transition from the NHBCC to NBCC was not problematic for the church as it helped create the new state just as it was complicit in the expansion of the colonial state in the Naga Hills and beyond (Thomas 2016).

64. See, for instance, Vadeo (2018) who claims, 'The Indo-Naga Ceasefire of 1964 covered all the south Naga inhabited areas [in Manipur]. This fact has evidently proved that the Government of India (GOI) has already recognised all south Naga inhabited areas as the land of the Nagas.'

65. Senior government officials in Assam too believe that the Nagaland government colludes with Naga insurgents to 'encroach' land in the disputed territory (Assamese IAS officer 2, interview, 3 June 2013, Guwahati). Such complaints have been made since the mid 1960s (*Hindu* 1967; Stracey 1968: 48–56, 310; Sreedhar Rao 2002: 73–5; B. Bhattacharyya 1994). At least, one observer from within Nagaland – Chalie Kevichusa – has referred to 'illegal villages' established in the foothills by clearing 'reserved forests' that provide refuge to illegal Bangladeshi migrants, who are in turn used as vote banks and cheap labour in Nagaland (Haralu and Chandola 2012: 76). It would, however, be unfair to blame Nagaland alone for the conflict. Assam has also condoned, if not encouraged, settlements in reserved forests and the union government has not responded to Nagaland's repeated pleas for the implementation of the Sixteen Point Agreement with regard to borders and reserved forests (Means 1971; Kinghen 1985; Thakur 2016; Yeputhomi n.d.). For discussions covering concerns of both states, see Borgohain and Borgohain (2011), Prabhakara (2012) and Suykens (2013). The union government has not been entirely neutral in the conflict. While it allowed surrendered Naga insurgents to settle in the disputed territory inside Assam, it also allowed Assam to dominate the joint border management mechanism.

66. At a seminar on the integration of Naga territories, Nagaland's chief minister asserted that 'there is no divergence between my views as an individual and the stand taken by the present Nagaland Government' and assured that organisations working to achieve integration of Naga homeland 'have not only the goodwill, but the active support of my Government' (Rio 2004: 151).

67. Nagaland extended official recognition to a Manipuri Naga tribe settled in Dimapur as an indigenous tribe (*ME* 2013a), but the notification had to be withdrawn as

local Nagas were vehemently opposed to sharing their patrimony with 'outsiders' and to any organisation/entity seen as sympathetic to the government's move.

68. An earlier statement of Nagaland's position indicated that it claimed 1,200 square miles (3,108 square kilometres) of Assam *apart* from the districts of 'North Cachar and Mikir Hills' (Yonuo 1974: 364).

69. The Nagaland government's Directorate of Border Affairs is focused entirely upon the Assam border with hardly any resources committed to monitoring the Manipur and Myanmar borders (GoN 2007: 15–16).

70. A discussion of conflicts between Naga tribes of Nagaland over the disputed territory in Assam is omitted for want of space. These conflicts have claimed many lives and have also led to the renaming of villages of weaker tribes, their eviction from villages, encroachment of their lands and ethnic poaching/conversion (forcing weaker tribes to declare themselves as members of larger tribes). These are a subset of the larger body of intra-Naga conflicts over territory and water resources (see Das 2014: 55 for Chang–Yimchunger boundary; *ME* 2018ae for Zeliang–Sumi boundary in Peren; Sumi Hoho n.d. and Sumi Hoho 2004 for disputes between Sumis and most of the other tribes; Hazarika 2018: xli for a boundary dispute in the Chakhesang area; Kikon 2019: 127 for a dispute between villages in Nagaland's coal belt). In some cases, advanced tribes have also tried to cartographically claim territory of other tribes (Naga state government official, interview, 28 October 2014, Jalukie). For a map that shows most of Dimapur as Angami territory, see Sanyu (1996). The borders of the newly formed Noklak district have not been demarcated to avoid conflict between tribes over the assignment of Chingmei. The dispute between Khezhakeno village of Nagaland and Tunjoy village of Manipur, which predates the formation of Nagaland (NSA, 2:311) and remains unresolved until today (*Nagaland Post* 2017a; 2018), is an example of interstate intra-Naga territorial conflict. An insightful editorial (13 March 1985) of the Ura Mail's Editor late Chalie Kevichusa aptly described territorial conflicts along internal margins: 'There can be no dispute on the claims of the Nagas over Dzukou valley [divided by the Nagaland-Manipur border]. The question on territorial jurisdiction comes only in respect of which Nagas and which villages' (Haralu and Chandola 2012: 81).

71. Nagaland has been working on a foothill road to reduce its dependence upon Assam for intra-state movement (GoN 2007: 8–9). While the discussions on the road began in the early 1980s (Jasokie n.d.1: 20), if not before, the location of the road remains controversial as it is seen as the precursor to the interstate border (Demo 2014). A draft map prepared by the state government that is not included in this chapter as it has not yet been released suggests that long stretches of the road lie in disputed areas under Nagaland's administration.

72. Bharatiya Janata Party (BJP) was a partner in Nagaland's coalition government between 2003 and 2008 and had a token presence in the coalition government in the following decade. In 2018, it emerged as a major coalition partner in the government. Yet its interests are aligned more with Assam, Arunachal Pradesh and Manipur, where it is the main ruling party (see, for instance, *ME* 2018f).

73. The union government has not been actively interested in resolving interstate border and river disputes elsewhere in the country either.

74. The Supreme Court too prefers a resolution through local commissions and mediation (GoI 2014g).

75. Bureaucrats handling such demands in the North-East were 'opposed to conceding even an inch' let alone redrawing borders because they had 'enough headaches already' and feared 'demand and counter demand' as 'there is no knowing when the process will end' (NSA, 2:475). Leaders from within the region too think in similar terms. On the demands for new districts, Neiphiu Rio (interview, 27 May 2015, New Delhi), the then MP of Nagaland in the lower house, said that granting district status to Tseminyu will 'open the floodgates'.

76. Nagaland has built several schools and health centres in the disputed area, see http://nagalandgis.in/Mapcatalogue.aspx. Nagaland State Transport buses that ply through the disputed area serve as a 'proof' for the Naga settlers that 'they form intrinsic part of Nagaland' (Suykens 2013: 177).

77. The Assam government seems to have encouraged settlers in reserved forests through the 1960s and 1970s (Prabhakara 2012: 51–2; Suykens 2013: 175). Thakur (2016: 95) suggests that in the mid 1960s the Assam government decided 'to persuade tough people for settlement' in reserved forests, with preference being given to 'landless peasants' principally 'ex-tea garden' workers and 'Muslim peasants'. Most of our Naga interviewees agreed that the disputed area under Nagaland too witnessed settlement of 'outsiders' (see also Jasokie n.d.2: 37–8; Haralu and Chandola 2012: 76).

78. At least five villages – Wamakenyimsen (unrecognised (UR)) (Tuli circle, Mokokchung), Shuvukhu (UR) (Changpang circle, Wokha), Merapani (Bhandari circle, Wokha), S. Wochan (Ralan circle, Wokha) and Nokyan (Hunta circle, Mon) – are marked beyond the frontier of the disputed territory shown as a part of Nagaland in *Index Map* (Map 3.6). Two of these, Merapani and S. Wochan, are shown within Nagaland's border in the Administrative Circle Map (Map 3.5). The presence of as yet unrecognised villages, that is, recently formed villages, beyond the area under Nagaland's administration suggests that the Assam–Nagaland border is moving into Assam. None of these villages is located around Dimapur, though, where the territory seems to have been saturated.

79. The above observation regarding villages with small populations is also true of Zunheboto, which is the place of origin of Sumis settled in the disputed area in Dimapur's vicinity.

80. The actual growth in the number of villages in Golaghat district should be lesser as the list of villages published by the Census includes Naga villages, which are not under Assam's administration.

81. Competitive developmentalism is not restricted to intra-national contexts in the Indian subcontinent. The phenomenon is also seen along the Indo-Chinese border (Gerwin and Bergmann 2012: 99–102).

82. A recent instance of flooding in Assam due to the alleged unannounced release of water from a dam in Nagaland was followed by a face-off between the police forces

of the two states and jingoistic posturing rather than straightforward coordination between the dam authorities and the irrigation and disaster management departments of the two sides (*ME* 2018n).

83. Some drainage maps do not cover the area beyond the recognised borders of Nagaland though, for instance, http://nagalandgis.in/map_catalogue_files/State%20 Drainage.pdf.

84. The Shukla Commission argued in favour of 'freezing the disputed areas along Assam's borders with Meghalaya, Arunachal Pradesh, Nagaland and Mizoram for, say, 25 years and developing them with Central assistance into infrastructural and industrial hubs for hills-plains interchange. These could provide sites for airfields, railheads, warehousing, cold storages, market yards, regional institutions, medium/ large industry, processing units, and R&R centres for persons displaced by dams and development in the hills. Such innovations could form the basis for creative and cooperative federalism' (GoI 1997b: 4).

85. Just as mapping rendered a territory legible and controllable (Krishna 1994; Painter 2008; Crampton 2010b: 96), enumeration transformed people into 'a natural entity' open to 'human control and management' (Duden 2010: 146).

86. The expression 'Greater Nagaland' came into vogue in the late 1980s (Hazarika 1995: 243), when the NSCN called for the unification of the Naga-inhabited regions of India and Myanmar. Since the late 1990s, 'Greater Nagaland' has also been known as 'Nagalim' (Ao: *limah* = land).

87. 'Nagaland for Christ' (later 'Nagalim for Christ' or 'Nagas for Christ') began as a slogan of the Baptist evangelical crusade before entering the Naga nationalist discourse (Thomas 2016: 89–90, 153, 171) as a political goal with a demographic-geographic correlate (see also notes 30 and 46 of this chapter). For the exclusivist, but expansionist, evangelist-territorial agenda of the Baptist Church in Nagaland, see Thomas (2016: 4, 153–5). 'Nagaland for Christ' is contrasted with the state of Nagaland that is equated with the biblical 'Golden Calf' (Elwin 1961: 63, 67). Competing memorials to martyrs that dot the length and breadth of Nagaland constitue another 'sacred' front/divide in the protracted conflict.

88. For a similar example from Europe, see Urla (1993: 825) on Basque counter-mapping.

89. Senapati district of Manipur is referred to as Tahamzam in Nagaland's government publications (Rio 2006: 212). Manipur counters the nominal irredentism by recognising Naga tribes without suffixing their names with 'Naga', for example, the Mao tribe is recognised as 'Mao' rather than 'Mao Naga'. In Arunachal Pradesh, Assam, Meghalaya and Mizoram, Naga tribes are recognised as 'Naga' that is ideal from the Naga nationalist perspective. Manipur has also bifurcated its Naga-dominated districts to introduce collective action problems (*Indian Express* 2016). Arunachal has recently proposed to recognise Naga tribes using their specific names rather than cover them under 'Any Naga tribes' (*ME* 2018y).

90. Most books on Nagaland referred to in this chapter begin with a discussion on the uncertain origins of 'Naga' and its growing acceptability. For a recent summary of the debates in this regard, see Wouters (2018: 42).

91. Sub-Naga projects mimic the 'Greater Nagaland' rhetoric employed by nationalists against New Delhi (ZPC 1983; KTC 2008; ENPO 2010; Rengma Hoho 2016; *ME* 2018k).

92. Even proposals to rename short stretches of roads in Dimapur can divide Nagas (Merry 2015).

93. The state government's deviant maps carry the following disclaimers (Maps 3.6 and 3.7): 'The boundaries of Nagaland as shown on this map are subject to revision as provided in the 1960 Delhi Agreement,' 'This map is without prejudice to the claims of Nagaland for re-drawing the Assam-Nagaland boundary on the basis of historical and traditional factor' and 'Not Legal'.

94. The Nagaland government's deliberate misinterpretation of interstate borders would not have been covered by the Geospatial Information Regulation Bill, 2016 which proposed to regulate the use of geospatial data and criminalised misrepresentation of borders, as it exempted government bodies (Art. 37).

95. The Supreme Court denied permission for 'additional election booths on the alleged encroached area' and asked Nagaland to maintain status quo (*SoA vs. UoI & Ors.* 1988, order dated 16 December 2002). Unlike Nagaland, Assam maintains *cartographic* status quo, while its field officers maintain a record of polling stations and the number of voters in Assamese villages in the disputed area (Assam government official, interview, 5 June 2013, Sarupathar).

96. Discussing the roots of Nagaland's economic stagnation A. Jamir (2002: 3) pointed out that Nagaland is widely seen as 'a temporary arrangement, pending a final political settlement'.

97. For a discussion of postcolonial cartographic anxiety, see Krishna (1994). He locates cartographic anxiety within a larger postcolonial anxiety, namely, the incomplete transition from 'former colony' to 'not-yet-nation'. This is different from the colonial cartographic anxiety referred to earlier.

98. The British changed the inner lines in Nagaland to suit their economic and political interests, but the arrangement has not been changed after 1947. Also, these lines no longer serve as restrictions on the movement from hills to plains even as the reverse flow continues to be controlled.

99. The union government tries to restrict the possibility of interstate and centre–state statistical-demographic competition/conflict by, say, mandating the use of a historical population estimate for the delimitation of parliamentary seats and federal redistribution. As discussed in Chapter 5, this does not entirely eliminate the scope for statistical conflicts within the union as intra-state competition between districts and communities and interstate territorial conflicts remain unchecked. In fact, even centre–state conflicts involving statistics continue. Goa, for instance, allegedly manipulated financial statistics to bolster its claim to statehood (*Indian Express* 2013). State governments routinely contest unpalatable statistics released by central agencies such as the National Crime Records Bureau (*Outlook* 2013, Kumar 2017d). States also submit 'fictitious reports making tall claims over successful implementation of many developmental works, which actually never take place

122 *Numbers in India's Periphery*

on the ground' (E-pao.net 2013b). Moreover, it can be argued that by postponing delimitation, the centre has actually laid the ground for a more serious interstate conflict as redistribution of seats after several decades will create major losers and gainers.

100. The government that otherwise aims at perfect mobility across the country does not mind the above mentioned impediments that allow it greater autonomy in administering strategically important and politically restive states, while also superficially satisfying public opinion in those states.

101. Taking inspiration from their Indian cousins, Myanmarese Nagas are demanding priority of local customary land use norms over federal laws (*ME* 2019d).

102. The extreme sensitivity to potential alienation of land to outsiders has meant that Naga entrepreneurs cannot collateralise their land to raise loans from banks.

103. The union government had already exempted Nagaland from constitutional amendments aimed at modernising and empowering rural local bodies (Art. 243M).

104. There was a considerable overlap between the maps of Nagalim (http://www.unpo.org/members/7899) and the homeland of the Chin people of Myanmar (https://unpo.org/members/20848), both recognised by the UNPO. Two things are noteworthy. First, the NSCN-IM had joined the UNPO eight years before the Chin National Front. Second, Nagalim's territory is very vaguely marked on the UNPO map even though the NSCN-IM was one of its earliest members. When one of us discussed this with the UNPO (interview, 18 September 2013, The Hague), 'Chin' was still a member of the UNPO. The membership of 'Chin' was discontinued in November 2016. The UNPO's Nagalim map continues to be vague, though.

105. For the incidental role of foreign (missionary) support in the Naga struggle, see Thomas (2016).

106. As journalist Bharat Bhushan (2019) succinctly puts it, the Naga political problem has 'two dimensions – geographical and political. The former relates to a long-standing demand for the unification of all contiguous Naga areas across the Northeast. And the political dimension deals with defining the nature of the relationship that the Nagas wanted with "India".'

107. The above typology of border disputes follows JRV Prescott's fourfold typology that includes territorial, positional, functional and transboundary resource development disputes (Bookman 2013: 149–150), except that we use 'functional' to refer to disputes related to functions of the state both along and across the border.

108. For a discussion on how the absence or poor quality of maps affected intertemporal comparability of censuses in Nepal and resulted in coverage errors, see Kansakar (1977). The use of incorrect maps has contributed to the undercount of tribes in the United States (Lujan 1990: 6, 10). In case of surveys, the use of incorrect maps results in an erroneous sampling frame due to missing population elements, multiplicity problems and incorrect accessing information (cf. Lessler and Kalsbeek 1992: 48).

4

Demographic Somersault

Introduction

A few states/union territories of India reported a decrease in population immediately after decolonisation.[1] The 1941 Census of India overestimated the population of Punjab and Bengal, the two provinces of British India that were directly affected by partition in 1947. In these provinces communities tried to boost their numbers to secure greater political representation and, eventually, a favourable alignment of borders in the event of partition.[2] The overcount was corrected in 1951, resulting in the contraction of the *reported* population (GoI 1954a: 5; Natarajan 1972: vii).[3] While the coverage error (error in the overall headcount) was corrected in 1951, content error (error in the sub-classification of headcount) persisted in Punjab. The 1951 Census data on language were affected by communal competition in Punjab, the Patiala and East Punjab States Union (PEPSU) and Himachal Pradesh.[4] Two union territories, the Andaman and Nicobar Islands (1941–51) and Daman and Diu (1951–61), also reported negative growth rates in the decade of decolonisation. Nagaland's experience is quite different though.

Nagaland registered the highest growth in population across India between 1981 and 2001 (Figures 4.1A and 4.2). However, in 2011, it reported the lowest growth rate as its population contracted in the absence of epidemical disease, famine, natural calamity, war and any major change in its political status and socio-economic conditions. This was the first time that a state in independent India experienced a contraction in population. This chapter examines Nagaland's *demographic somersault*[5] – decades of unusually high growth of the *reported* population followed by its sudden contraction (Figure 4.1B).

Errors in a census can be classified into two broad categories, namely, coverage and content errors. Coverage error 'refers to either an under-count or over-count of units owing to omissions of persons/housing units or duplication/ erroneous inclusion, respectively', whereas content error 'pertains to the error in the characteristics that are reported for the persons or housing units that are enumerated' (UN Secretariate 2010: 10). Content errors affect the distributional accuracy of the headcount, whereas coverage errors affect the accuracy of the overall headcount. Errors in census may not necessarily affect the overall headcount if they are restricted to the composition of population.

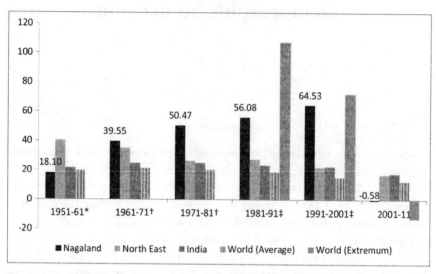

Figure 4.1A   Decadal population growth rates, 1951–2011

Sources: Prepared by authors using (i) 1951–61, Nagaland; 1951–61 and 1991–2011, North-East: authors' computations; (ii) 1961–2011, Nagaland and 1951–2011, India: GoI (2011b; 2013d); (iii) 1961–91, North-East: Sharma and Kar (1997) and (iv) World: United Nations (2011).

Notes: (i) * The growth rates for Nagaland, North-East and India for the period 1951–61 have been computed after excluding Tuensang, where only a small fraction of the population was enumerated in the 1951 Census, and Arunachal Pradesh, which was not covered in 1951. The interpolated populations of Jammu and Kashmir (1951, 1991) and Assam (1981) and estimated population for three subdivisions of Senapati, Manipur (2001) have been used in calculating the decadal growth rates for India (GoI 2011b: x; n.d.21). (ii) † The growth rates have been further adjusted for the periods 1961–71 and 1971–81 to take into account the change in the reference date in 1971. We have not accounted for the ad hoc change in reference dates in 1961 in case of Kohima and Mokokchung (note 12 of this chapter). The growth rate of 'North East' was not adjusted because the 1981 Census did not cover Assam, which accounts for about 70 per cent of the region's population. (iii) ‡ The growth rate of Nagaland was the highest among all the states of India. (iv) World (Extremum) is shown only for 1981–2011, that is, the period during which Nagaland's population grew at abnormal rates compared to the rest of the country. Until 2001, the growth rate of Nagaland was positive. So, 'World (Extremum)' corresponds to the maximum growth rate in the periods 1980–90 and 1990–2000 recorded by any territory listed in the *World Population Prospects 2010*. During 2001–11, the growth rate of Nagaland was negative and 'World (Extremum)' in the period 2000–10 corresponds to the minimum growth rate.

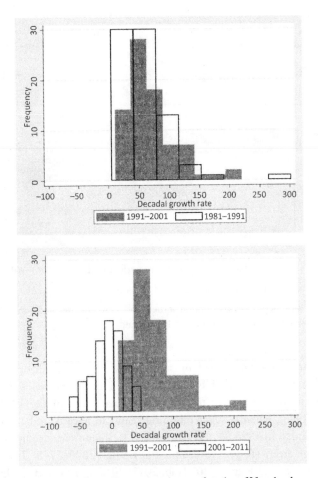

Figure 4.1B   Distribution of population growth rate of circles of Nagaland

Source: Prepared by authors using GoI (1983; 1984c; 2011g; n.d.1; n.d.2).

Note: The borders of circles changed because of inter-circle and inter-district territorial transfers and creation of new circles. The number of circles in the state increased from 69 in 1981 to 114 in 2011. We created a set of 78 circles for which we could generate comparable data for the period 1981–2011. These histograms are plotted for 78 circles.

The literature has examined coverage errors in a wide range of countries. Persistent errors in Nigerian censuses due to ethno-regional conflict over the distribution of federal resources have received sustained scholarly attention (Aluko 1965; Adepoju 1981; Ahonsi 1988; Okolo 1999; Jerven 2013: 56–61; Bookman 2013: 67–8). Lipton (1972) discusses the undercount of Blacks in apartheid-era South Africa. Lujan (1990), McWorter and Alkalimat (1980) and Choldin (1986)

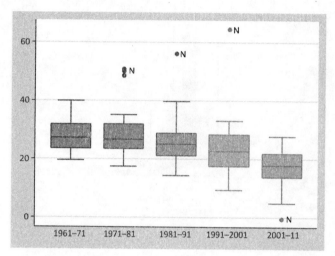

Figure 4.2   Distribution of decadal population growth rate, all states, 1961–2011

Source: Prepared by authors using data from GoI (2011b).

Notes: The box plots depict the distribution of the decadal growth rates across states (excluding UTs). The dots indicate outliers. 'N' indicates Nagaland.

discuss the undercount of American Indian, Black and Hispanic populations in the United States of America (USA), respectively. Housing rationing in erstwhile Yugoslavia offered incentives to over-report headcount in the 1953 Census (Zarkovich 1989), whereas sugar rationing seems to have played a similar role in parts of Sudan in 1993 (A. H. Ahmed n.d.). Bhutan's headcount too suffers from coverage errors (Royal Government of Bhutan 2000: 37–8). In the Indian context, Agrawal and Kumar (2012a–b; 2013; 2018; 2019b) and Guilmoto and Irudaya Rajan (2013) discuss the overcount of population in Nagaland, Manipur and Jammu and Kashmir.

The literature on content errors is much richer than that on coverage errors. Comparisons of censuses conducted before and after wars and political transitions reveal sharp changes in the composition of population of several Central and East European countries (Kertzer and Arel 2002a). Brass (1974) and Gill (2007) discuss unusual changes in Indian census data on languages. Sharad Kulkarni (1991) discusses abnormal increase in the population of Halba/Halbi tribe of Maharashtra due to misreporting by neighbouring non-tribal communities, driven by the perceived benefit from acquiring tribal status (see also Guha 2003). Verma (2013) uncovers the sustained and substantial underreporting of Uttar Pradesh's tribal population due to misclassification. Others examine the treatment of caste (Roy Burman 1998; Sundar 2000; Bhagat 2006; Deshpande and John 2010) and religion (Bhagat 2001; Gill 2007) in postcolonial censuses and the politicisation of these categories.[6]

Another stream of the literature looks at the interrelationship between census/demographic change and politics/elections, ethnic conflict and identity formation (Anderson 2006; Kertzer and Arel 2002a; Horowitz 2000). We shall discuss this aspect of the problem in Chapter 5. Yet another stream of the literature examines the relation between conflicts and fertility (Janus 2013; Morland 2018).

The literature suggests that far from being a passive statistical exercise, census affects and is in turn affected by political processes. This chapter examines Nagaland's demographic somersault using a variety of government and non-governmental sources of data, ranging from decennial censuses to church membership records that cover a long period and adds to the literature on the quality of demographic statistics. It shows that the somersault cannot be explained by conventional demographic factors and clears the ground for the assessment of the political-economic factors in Chapter 5.

This chapter is divided into three parts. We will first discuss how red flags were ignored while Nagaland's population growth was accelerating. We will then show that the census data not only lack internal consistency but are also inconsistent with other sources of demographic information, such as the National Family Health Survey (NFHS), Sample Registration System (SRS), Election Commission of India (ECI), Ministry of Human Resource Development and Baptist and Catholic Churches. We will conclude with a discussion of ad hoc explanations of the demographic somersault and an excursus on content errors.

Red Flags Ignored

In Chapter 2, we pointed out that speeches of chief ministers of Nagaland almost always underestimated the state's population (Table 2.1). We also noted that during the past several decades Nagaland's population repeatedly defied projections as well (Table 4.1 and Figure 2.1).[7] Projection errors in case of Nagaland have, in fact, always been among the highest in the country (GoI 2011b: 168–72). In 1971, the projection error for Nagaland was second only to Goa that joined the union after the 1961 Census. Similarly, in 1981, Sikkim, which joined the union after the 1971 Census, was the only state with a higher projection error than Nagaland. Projection errors were the highest for Nagaland in 1991 and 2001 among all states, and it was second only to Goa in 2011.

The Expert Committee on Population Projections formed in 1974 (GoI 1979a) under-projected the 1991 population of Nagaland by about 21 per cent.[8] This implies that the dynamics of population growth between 1981 and 1991 were inconsistent with the trends in fertility, mortality and migration prevailing in the

Table 4.1   Census and projected populations, Nagaland, 1971–2011

Year	Source	Population (in '000)		Error (%)*
		Projected	Census	
1971	Expert Committee (1968)	439	516.449	–15.00
1981	Expert Committee (1974)	714.5	774.930	–7.80
1991	Expert Committee (1974)	957.9	1,209.546	–20.80
	Expert Committee (1984)	1,137.1	–do–	–5.99
	Standing Committee (1988)	1,097	–do–	–9.30
2001	Expert Committee (1984)	1,571.5	1,990.036	–21.03
	Technical Group (1996)	1,721	–do–	–13.52
2011	Technical Group (1996)	2,185	1,978.502	10.44
	Technical Group (2001)	2,249	–do–	13.67
	DES (2004)‡	3,269.6	–do–	65.25
	PFI-PRB (2007)†	2,426–39	–do–	22.62–23.28

Sources: Prepared by authors using Expert Committee (1968): GoI (2011b: 168), Expert Committee (1974): GoI (1979a: 48–9), Expert Committee (1984): GoI (1988b: 28), Standing Committee (1988): Nath (1991), Technical Group (1996): GoI (1996b: 64), Technical Group (2001): GoI (2006a: 36), DES (2004): GoN (2004b: 28) and PFI-PRB (2007): PFI-PRB (2007: 6, 11).

Notes: (i) 'Error (%)' is the excess of the projected over census population as a share of the census population. Negative (Positive) values indicate under (over)-projection. (ii) ‡GoN (2004b: 28) provides annual projections until 2010. We have extrapolated the population to 2011. (iii) †PFI-PRB (2007) provides two projections, corresponding to low and high fertility scenarios. (iv) The reference date for projections is 1 March of the corresponding year. We could not access the reference date used by Expert Committee (1968). DES and PFI-PRB do not mention a reference date.

preceding decades. The Technical Group on Population Projections constituted in 1996 (GoI 1996b) underestimated the 2001 population by about 14 per cent. The projection errors for Nagaland will increase if adjusted for the gross under-enumeration in the North-East revealed by Post-Enumeration Surveys (PESs).[9] Projections for the next decade were also grossly inaccurate. The Technical Group on Population Projections formed in 2001 (GoI 2006a) overestimated the 2011 population by 14 per cent. The state government overestimated the population by about 65 per cent (GoN 2004b)! The DCO Nagaland told us that the state government was expecting that 'the [2011] population of Nagaland ... would be more than 35 lakhs' (interview, 24 June 2013, Kohima). Interestingly, even after the release of the 2011 Census data, the state government continues to use inflated projections. A state government website reported that the state's population was 2.27 million in 2012 (GoN 2019b), which means the population grew at an incredibly high rate of 15 per cent within a year.

The projection errors stand out for several reasons. First, the underestimation for 2001 despite the use of an inflated baseline (that is, the 1991 Census) means that population growth between 1991 and 2001 was abnormally high. This should have alerted subsequent expert groups to revise their assumptions about demographic change in Nagaland. Second, projections made closer to 2011 were more inaccurate compared to those made earlier. This is also true of projections for 1991. Though projection errors are not directly comparable as expert groups constituted in different decades would have used different models, it is counter-intuitive that projections based on more recent data are more erroneous. Errors should decrease as the forecast horizon becomes narrower (Smith and Sincich 1990: 369). Third, unlike the projections for 1991 and 2001, which were underestimates vis-à-vis the corresponding censuses, the projections for 2011 proved to be overestimates. So, the projections for 2011 not only wrongly estimated the population but also misjudged the direction of change of the *reported* population. Before the publication of the projections for 2011 senior bureaucrats (A. Jamir 2002),[10] the state government (GoN 2003a) and the chief minister (Hazarika 2005) had questioned the reliability of the 2001 Census and civil society organisations had approached the Gauhati High Court to stop the use of the 2001 Census for delimitation (*CPO & Ors. vs. UoI & Ors.* 2006). Moreover, estimates of crude birth rate (CBR) of Nagaland too raised serious doubts about the reliability of past headcounts (cf. Guilmoto and Irudaya Rajan 2001: 723 and 2002: 667). A 2005 household survey conducted for the North East Council raised further doubts. It revealed that in Nagaland the 'size [number of households] of the villages was far smaller than the numbers given by the census. Often the figures were off by as much as four-fifths or in one case by nine-tenths' (Hazarika 2018: 292–3). In short, there were good reasons to critically examine the census data used for projecting population.

The sustained abnormality in Nagaland's growth rates did not receive scholarly attention until after the 2011 Census. Even the administration did not wake up until 2009, when a sample survey conducted in six districts found fewer people compared to the 2001 Census (*Nagaland Post* 2009).[11] There was a growing realisation within the government that flawed statistics made planning difficult. For instance, 'it was found that SSA [Sarva Shiksha Abhiyan] targets could never be met. There was a discrepancy between the numbers of those enrolled and supposed to be enrolled.... Our enrolment rate is very low but we have reached the target. We have very high literacy rate but low enrolment' (DCO Nagaland, interview, 19 September 2012, Kohima). In a consultative meeting convened by the Nagaland government after the 2009 survey, civil society, church, student and tribal organisations, village elders and political parties unanimously agreed that 'previous censuses conducted in Nagaland were defective and inaccurate' and that the next census 'should be conducted properly' (GoN 2009a). The meeting questioned the reliability of both the 2001 Census as well as earlier censuses.

Internal Consistency

The Naga Hills district, formed in 1866, was first censused in 1891 (Census Commissioner India 1893: 209). The 1871–2 and 1881 Censuses and earlier administrative reports presented 'estimates' of the population of the district though. The borders of the district changed over the years as it expanded at the expense of the unadministered areas (Timeline 3.1 and Maps 3.10A–E), but the complete details of the additional area covered in successive censuses are not available. The Naga Tribal Areas were not covered in any census before 1951, when a small part was enumerated for the first time. The population figures for the Naga Hills district before the 1961 Census were in most cases based on estimates rather than direct enumeration. The formation of the Naga Hills-Tuensang Area in 1957, which combined the Naga Hills district and the Tuensang Frontier Division (erstwhile Naga Tribal Areas) and transferred the decision-making power from Shillong to Kohima, was the last major political-administrative change that affected the territory of interest to us. In short, the pre- and post-1957 decennial censuses are not directly comparable because of the sustained increase until 1961 in both the reach of Census Operations (GoI 2011b) as well as changes in the area of the Naga Hills district (GoI 1975a: 4). The pre- and post-1957 censuses are not comparable, even if we restrict the focus to the Naga Hills. There are three reasons for this. First, sufficiently disaggregated data are not available for the period before 1957 as the Naga Hills were a mere district of Assam. Second, the redistribution of territory between districts at the time of the formation of the state also limits comparison. Mokokchung of 1961 includes some areas that were not enumerated in 1951 when they were part of Tuensang (note 10 of Chapter 3). Third, in the late 1950s, villages were grouped in the Naga Hills (that is, the then Kohima and Mokokchung districts) as part of counter-insurgency. However, compared to Mizoram (Nunthara 1981; Hazarika 2018: 98–108), in Nagaland both the scale and duration of grouping were limited and the affected villages were resettled (NSA, 5:22; Stracey 1968: 133, 136, 162–5, 214; Horam 1988: 83, 98; Dev 1988: 113, Hazarika 2018: 103). An interviewee suggested that it seems that even in grouped villages 'people were known to be from their original villages' (Naga IAS officer, interview, 24 June 2013, Kohima). The impact of grouping on the spatial redistribution of population, if any, is not discussed in census reports, which impedes comparisons between 1951 and 1961. We did not find any abnormal change in the population of Angami villages of Kohima subdivision between 1951 and 1961 that can be linked to grouping (GoI 1952; 1966), but we do not have sufficient data for Mokokchung. Comparisons in this chapter are, therefore, restricted to censuses held after 1951.[12]

This section checks if the census data on births, migration, households and age for Nagaland are mutually consistent (*internal consistency*), while the next compares it with other sources (*external consistency*). Before examining the internal and external consistency of census data, we will argue that the problems discussed in this and the following chapters are not artefacts of inappropriate comparisons with other states or errors that have already been identified through PESs.

The Census has been conducting post-enumeration checks/surveys since 1951 to assess the extent of coverage and content errors in enumeration (GoI 2014d). Though we could not access the relevant report for 1951, a 1961 Census publication noted, 'In 1951 Census Post-Enumeration Check was an after thought but in 1961 it was included as a distinct item in the census time schedule' (GoI 1964: 44). The Census usually reports the PES results for regions (group of states), barring 1961 when it reported results for individual states. Separate estimates for the North-East region, including Nagaland, are available only since 2001.

The PES was extended to Nagaland in 2001. In the North-Eastern region, the PES revealed a net omission rate of 7.6 and 12.39 per 1,000 persons in 2001 and 2011, respectively (GoI 2006b: 9; GoI 2014d: Statement 3.2). Assuming the PES results for the North-East to be representative for Nagaland, the PES-adjusted population growth rate of Nagaland was 65.78 and 0.65 per cent in 2001 and 2011, respectively. So, the demographic somersault is not an artefact of the coverage errors identified by the Census itself and, therefore, merits further examination.

The abnormality in Nagaland's population growth is also not an artefact of inappropriate comparisons with other states. The growth rates of Nagaland, where about 90 per cent people follow Christianity and belong to tribal communities, are abnormal even when compared to tribal and Christian populations in other parts of the country (Figure 4.3). The growth of Nagaland's tribal population compared favourably with that of tribes across the country until 1981 and was much higher (in 1991 and 2001) or lower (in 2011) later.[13] Its Christian population always grew much faster than the rest of the country. This is understandable in the period before the 1980s due to the rapid growth of Christianity at the expense of traditional faiths but not in the later period when most Nagas had already converted. In fact, Nagaland's population grew much faster than that of comparable states in the North-East such as Mizoram, where more than 90 per cent of the population is of tribal origin and follows Christianity.

Births and Migration

We will check if births, deaths and documented migration can explain the abnormal changes in Nagaland's population. Population change between two years, say, $t - \tau$ and t, is given by the following fundamental equation (Preston, Heuveline and Guillot 2001: 2):

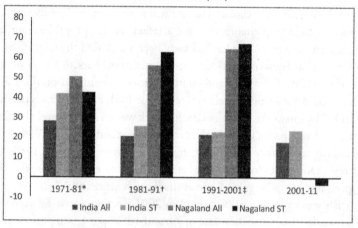

Scheduled Tribes (STs)

■ India All   ■ India ST   ■ Nagaland All   ■ Nagaland ST

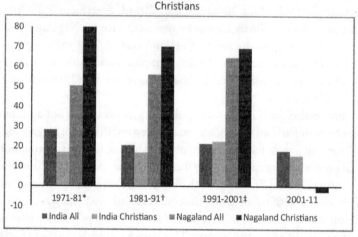

Christians

■ India All   ■ India Christians   ■ Nagaland All   ■ Nagaland Christians

Figure 4.3   Decadal population growth rate, Scheduled Tribes and Christians, 1971–2011

Sources: Prepared by authors using GoI (1973a; 1976c; 1988e; 2018a; n.d.1; n.d.2) for STs and GoI (2004b: xxviii, xxxiii; 2018a) for Christians.

Notes: (i) The growth rate is adjusted to account for the change in the reference date in 1971 (Note ii of Figure 4.1A). (ii) Census could not be conducted in Assam (1981) and Jammu and Kashmir (1991). The growth rates of India (all, ST and Christian populations) have been computed after excluding: (a) * Assam (1971–81), (b) † Assam and Jammu and Kashmir (1981–91) and (c) ‡ Jammu and Kashmir (1991–2001). The exclusions barely affect all-India figures since the share of these states in the country's population and the share of STs and Christians in their population are small. In 2011, Assam and Jammu and Kashmir accounted for 2.58 and 1.04 per cent of India's population, respectively. The population share of STs (Christians) was 12.45 (3.74) per cent in Assam and 11.91 (0.28) per cent in Jammu and Kashmir.

$$\Delta N(t - \tau, t) \equiv B(t - \tau, t) - D(t - \tau, t) + NI(t - \tau, t) \equiv NG(t - \tau, t) + NI(t - \tau, t)$$

(Equation 4.1)

where $\Delta N(t - \tau, t)$, $B(t - \tau, t)$, $D(t - \tau, t)$, $NG(t - \tau, t)$ and $NI(t - \tau, t)$, respectively, denote population change, births, deaths, natural growth and net in-migrants between $t - \tau$ and t. Equation 4.1 simplifies as follows if we decompose natural growth and net in-migration between the 0–9 and 10+ year age groups and note that there are no births in the 10+ year age group:

$$D_{10+}(t - \tau, t) = N_{0-9}(t) + NI_{10+}(t - \tau, t) - \Delta N(t - \tau, t) \geq 0$$

(Equation 4.2)

where $D_{10+}(t - \tau, t)$ is the number of deaths in the 10+ year age group and $N_{0-9}(t)$ is the population of the 0–9 year age group at time 't' that is equal to the sum of natural growth and net in-migration for this age group between $t - \tau$ and t. Tables 4.2A and 4.2B compile information on various components of Equation 4.2. 'Deaths' in Tables 4.2A and 4.2B is the number of deaths in the 10+ year age group if the fundamental equation, which is an identity, is balanced. The number of deaths are positive for 1961–71. However, between 1971 and 2001 the number of deaths in the 10+ year age group have to be *negative* for Nagaland as a whole to balance the fundamental equation. The discrepancy in headcount, defined as the ratio of the unaccounted population to the end of the decade population, increases from 5.25 per cent during 1971–81 to 18.02 per cent during 1991–2001. Thus, internal consistency checks reveal that the Census overestimated Nagaland's population between 1981 and 2001.[14] The estimation of discrepancy for a census decade (Equation 4.2) assumes the base year headcount to be correct, which is not the case in Nagaland. We, therefore, calculated the cumulative discrepancy, which was 26.60 per cent in 2001.

We have been able to estimate only the lower bounds of the discrepancy due to the non-availability of data on death rate for the 10+ year age group and assumptions on the number of migrants noted in Table 4.2A. The actual discrepancy in, say, 1991 will be at least 129,944 plus the total deaths between 1981 and 1991 in the 10+ year age group. Interestingly, the discrepancy-adjusted growth rate of Nagaland (Tables 4.2A and 4.2B) is the highest in the country in 2001 (GoI 2011b).

We also carried out this analysis for rural and urban areas and male and female populations. In rural (urban) areas, the cumulative discrepancy grew from 2.03 (14.44) per cent in 1981 to 25.07 (38.26) per cent in 2001. The discrepancy estimates for the urban sector are very high due to the one-time level effect of the notification of several towns in 1981. The discrepancy of rural (urban) sector

Table 4.2A Decomposition of population changes (rural–urban), Nagaland, 1971–2001

Population/change	Total				Rural				Urban			
	1961–71	1971–81	1981–91	1991–2001	1961–71	1971–81	1981–91	1991–2001	1961–71	1971–81	1981–91	1991–2001
The end of decade population (0)	516,449	774,930	1,209,546	1,990,036	465,055	654,696	1001,323	1,647,249	51,394	120,234	208,223	342,787
Total population change, all ages (1)	147,249	258,481	434,616	780,490	115,012	189,641	346,627	645,926	68,840	87,989	134,564	228,179
Net in-migrants, all ages (2)	22,790	38,064	13,397	-17,657	9,024	23,900	5,436	-22,903	14,421	8,176	7,008	19,983
In-migrants, 0–9 years† (3)	4,199	9,997	3,887	5,718	2,169	5,956	1,745	2,866	4,041	2,142	2,852	5,580
Net in-migrants, 10+ years† (4 = 2 – 3)	18,591	28,067	9,510	-23,375	6,855	17,944	3,691	-25,769	10,380	6,034	4,156	14,403
0–9 years population (5)	134,652	189,739	295,162	445,190	123,025	158,436	243,268	371,715	31,303	51,894	73,475	109,476
Deaths (among 10+ years) (6 = 5 + 4 – 1)	5,994	-40,675	-129,944	-358,675	14,868	-13,261	-99,668	-299,980	-27,157	-30,061	-56,933	-104,300
Cumulative deaths (7)	—	—	-170,619	-529,294	—	—	-112,929	-412,909	—	-57,218	-114,151	-218,451
Discrepancy (%)	—	5.25	10.74	18.02	—	2.03	9.95	18.21	22.59	14.44	16.61	18.27
Cumulative discrepancy (%)	—	—	14.11	26.60	—	—	11.28	25.07	—	27.48	33.30	38.26
Discrepancy adjusted population§ (8 = 0 + 7)			1,038,927	1,460,742			888,394	1234,340		151,005	228,636	352,515
Decadal growth (reported) %	39.88	50.05	56.08	64.53	31.15	40.78	52.94	64.51	133.95	73.18	64.62	66.57
Decadal growth (adjusted§) %	—	—	34.07	40.60	—	—	35.70	38.94	—	25.59	51.41	54.18
Share of urban population (reported) %	9.95	15.52	17.21	17.23								
Share of urban population (adjusted) %			14.53	15.65								

Sources: Authors' computations; GoI (1966; 1976a; 1976b; 1977b; 1985b; 1987; 1988d; 1997f; 1997g; n.d.1; n.d.2; n.d.23).

Notes: (i) 'Net in-migrants' is the difference between in-migrants and out-migrants. 'Discrepancy' is the number of deaths in the 10+ year age group required to balance the fundamental equation. (ii) We do not have data on age profile of (a) out-migrants and assume zero out-migration in the 0–9 year age group and (b) in-migrants to Nagaland from abroad and assume that all of them belong to the 0–9 year age group. Both (a) and (b) lead to the underestimation of 'Net in-migrants, 10+ years' and 'Discrepancy'. Also, in 1971 (1981), all in-migrants in the age group 0–14 (0–12) years have been considered to belong to 0–9 years. This too results in the underestimation of 'Net in-migrants, 10+ years', all ages'. (iii) † There is a difference between the number of in-migrants provided in the sources used in this table (which requires age profile of in-migrants) and Table 4.10. The difference is 0 (1961–71), 163 (1971–81), 138 (1981–91) and 1,146 (1991–2001) and is possibly accounted for by unclassifiable (into rural or urban) in-migrants. These in-migrants have been assumed to belong to 0–9 years resulting in an underestimation of 'Discrepancy'. (iv) Content errors in data on age could bias estimates of discrepancy. However, '0–9 years population' is more likely than not to be underestimated due to age heaping, which would translate into an underestimation of discrepancy. (v) The sum of 'Rural' and 'Urban' may not equal 'Total' because of unclassified migrants. This is particularly the case with out-migrants. (vi) No new towns were notified during 1991–2001, whereas four new towns with a population of 34,956 were notified during 1971–81 followed by the notification of two new towns with a population of 17,162 during 1981–91. We have not accounted for notification of new towns because of unavailability of the corresponding migration data. Accounting for the notification of towns will affect the sectoral decomposition of discrepancy without affecting the total discrepancy. It will increase (decrease) the discrepancy for rural (urban) areas. (vii) § Calculated after adjusting the population of the terminal decades using cumulative deaths.

Table 4.2B   Decomposition of population changes (male–female), Nagaland, 1971–2001

Population/change	Total				Male				Female			
	1961–71	1971–81	1981–91	1991–2001	1961–71	1971–81	1981–91	1991–2001	1961–71	1971–81	1981–91	1991–2001
The end of decade population	516,449	774,930	1,209,546	1,990,036	276,084	415,910	641,282	1,047,141	240,365	359,020	568,264	942,895
Total population change, all ages	147,249	258,481	434,616	780,490	85,057	139,826	225,372	405,859	62,192	118,655	209,244	374,631
Net in-migrants, all ages	22,790	38,064	13,397	–17,657	17,468	25,799	11,050	4,945	5,322	12,265	2,347	–22,602
In-migrants, 0–9 years*†	4,199	9,997	3,887	5,718	2,092	5,084	2,277	3,184	2,107	4,913	1,610	2,534
Net in-migrants, 10+ years*†	18,591	28,067	9,510	–23,375	15,376	20,715	8,773	1,761	3,215	7,352	737	–25,136
0–9 years population	134,652	189,739	295,162	445,190	67,914	96,042	148,763	228,437	66,738	93,697	146,399	216,753
Deaths (among 10+ years)	5,994	–40,675	–129,944	–358,675	–1,767	–23,069	–67,836	–175,661	7,761	–17,606	–62,108	–183,014
Cumulative deaths			–170,619	–529,294			–90,905	–266,566			–79,714	–262,728
Discrepancy (%)	—	5.25	10.74	18.02	—	5.55	10.58	16.78	—	4.90	10.93	19.41
Cumulative discrepancy (%)	—	—	14.11	26.60	—	—	14.18	25.46	—	—	14.03	27.86
Discrepancy adjusted population§			1,038,927	1,460,742			550,377	780,575			488,550	680,167
Decadal growth (reported, %)	39.88	50.05	56.08	64.53	23.04	50.65	54.19	63.29	16.85	49.36	58.28	65.93
Decadal growth (adjusted§, %)	—	—	34.07	40.60	—	—	32.33	41.83	—	—	36.08	39.22
Sex ratio (reported)	871	863	886	900								
Sex ratio (adjusted)			888	871								

Sources and Notes: Sex ratio is the number of females per 1,000 males. See also Table 4.2A.

increases (decreases) after adjusting for the notification of new towns. Likewise, the cumulative discrepancy for male (female) population increased from 5.55 (4.90) to 25.46 (27.86) per cent between 1981 and 2001. The picture that emerges from the analysis in this section is of a pervasive manipulation across sexes as well as urban and rural areas.

Age Profile

Changes in age profile over time can also be used to check the internal consistency of census data. Before the 2011 Census, the chief minister noted that certain age groups had seen an abnormally large increase in population during 1991–2001 (Rio 2010b: 107–8). Other contemporary sources highlighted pervasive over-reporting across age groups (*Nagaland Post* 2009). The intercensal cohort method can be used to examine potential abnormalities in the population of cohorts across censuses (Elo and Preston 1994: 430). Let $N_i(t)$ denote the population of cohort 'i' at the time of the first census 't'. The expected population of this cohort 'τ' years later will be

$$N_i^e(t + \tau) = N_i(t) + B_i(t, t + \tau) - D_i(t, t + \tau) + I_i(t, t + \tau) - O_i(t, t + \tau)$$

(Equation 4.3)

where $B_i(t, t + \tau)$, $D_i(t, t + \tau)$, $I_i(t, t + \tau)$ and $O_i(t, t + \tau)$, respectively, denote the number of births, deaths, in-migrants and out-migrants between t and $t + \tau$. For decennial censuses, $\tau = 10$. Let 'C' denotes the set of age groups 10–19, 20–24, 25–29 … 65–69 and 70+.[15] The number of births will be zero for these groups. If $N_i(t + \tau)$ is the reported population of the ith age group at time $t + \tau$, the ratio of the reported to the expected population can be expressed as[16]

$$R_{i,t+\tau} = \frac{N_i(t + \tau)}{N_i^e(t + \tau)} = \frac{N_i(t + \tau)}{N_i(t) - D_i(t, t + \tau) + I_i(t, t + \tau) - O_i(t, t + \tau)} \forall i \in C$$

(Equation 4.4)

We can use Equation 4.4 to examine the internal consistency of population estimates for the 10+ year age group. $R_{i,t+\tau} > 1$ is indicative of enumeration errors. We assume that death rates are zero for all age groups because of the unavailability of reliable data on age-specific death rates for Nagaland. As a result, Equation 4.4 simplifies to

$$R_{i,t+\tau} = \frac{N_i(t + \tau)}{N_i(t) + I_i(t, t + \tau) - O_i(t, t + \tau)} \forall i \in C \quad \text{(Equation 4.5)}$$

Since $R_{i,t+\tau}$ is likely to be biased downwards in our case,[17] any value of $R_{i,t+\tau}$ even marginally greater than 1 is unlikely and would indicate misreporting/overcount. Figure 4.4 shows decadal changes in $R_{i,t+\tau}$ between 1971 and 2011.[18] The $R_{i,t+\tau}$ curves for both male and female are broadly similar across age groups. Actual populations in most of the age groups under consideration were either

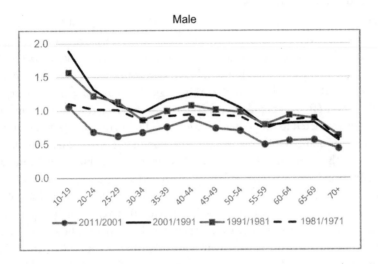

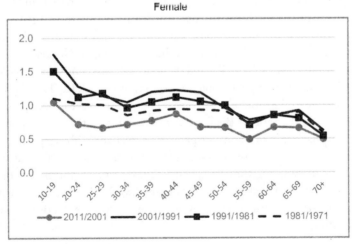

Figure 4.4   Ratio of reported and expected populations, Nagaland, 1971–2011

Sources: Prepared by authors using GoI (1966, 1976a; 1976b; 1977b; 1985b; 1987; 1988d; 1997f; 1997g; 2018a; 2019; n.d.1; n.d.2).

Note: The curves depict the ratio of the actual to expected population (vertical axis) for different age groups (horizontal axis) for four census decades between 1971 and 2011.

lower than or approached the expected population in 1981. However, the same is not true of 1991 and 2001 when $R_{i,t+\tau}$ was quite high for both male and female and all the age groups between 10 and 50 years,[19] except males aged between 30 and 34 years for whom the ratio is close to 1.[20] In 2011, the ratio was markedly below 1, except for those aged 10–19 years, and even approached 0.6 for those aged 25–9 years and 30–4 years.

We have so far not been able to conclude if the headcount of the 60+ year age group was also over-reported, partly, because we do not have data on age-specific death rates.[21] Out-migration of older people to other states is unlikely. So, the share of older age groups in population should increase over time as the life expectancy improves and the out-migration of working-age Nagas increases. The decrease in the share of the 60+ year population in 2001,[22] therefore, suggests that manipulation was largely restricted to the younger age groups. This claim would stand refuted if there was a substantial influx of working-age population from other states leading to a drop in the population share of the 60+ year age group. However, immigrants form a small and *decreasing* part of Nagaland's reported population (Table 4.10) and, in fact, Nagaland witnessed a net out-migration during 1991–2001 (Table 4.2A).

We are unable to analyse the population aged 0–9 years using Equation 4.5 because we do not have reliable estimates of fertility. We can, however, examine the trend in the ratio of the 0–9 year population to the total population. Since the population share of migrants is small, any change in the ratio could be due to changes in the numerator (namely, birth and death rates for those aged 0–9 year) and/or the denominator (total population). The estimates of the CBR based on the Census suggest that the birth rate has been declining in Nagaland – 35.97 in 1991 and 24.1 in 2001 (Table 4.3) – and the above internal consistency checks have revealed that the 10+ year population was over-reported in 2001. This should have caused a decline in the ratio of the 0–9 year population to the overall population. To the contrary, the ratio of the 0–9 year population to the overall population remained unchanged – 24.5 and 24.4 per cent in 1991 and 2001, respectively. This suggests that the 0–9 year population was also over-reported in 2001. Later in this chapter, we will show that the discrepancy in the census data for the school-going age group (6–14 year) peaked in 2001 (Figure 4.5). Thus, we have evidence for pervasive over-reporting across age groups under the very restrictive assumption of zero death rate.

Households

In the run-up to the 2011 Census, the popular media, civil society and government sources singled out villages as the driving force behind the abnormal growth reported in 2001. As discussed at length in the next chapter, villages have an

Table 4.3 Decadal birth, death and natural growth rates, 1971–2021

Decade	Census/survey	Nagaland						India					
		Population growth	Share (0–9)	CBR	CDR	NGR (zero)	NGR (SRS)	Population growth	Share (0–9)	CBR@	CDR	NGR (zero)	NGR (SRS)
1971–81	Census	50.47*	24.5	38.02	n/a	45.23	35.90	24.87*	26.6	34.94	n/a	40.98	23.43
	SRS			21.88	6.87	24.16	16.07			33.67	13.67	39.26	21.90
1981–91	Census	56.08†	24.4	35.97	n/a	42.39	35.64	23.87†	25.5	32.73	n/a	38.00	25.20
	SRS			21.41	5.02	23.60	17.65			28.82	10	32.86	20.50
1991–2001	Census	64.53‡	22.4	24.1	n/a	26.89	21.98	21.54‡	23.2	25.9	n/a	29.14	18.30
	SRS			19.45	4.03	21.24	16.54			24.65	8.95	27.57	16.86
	NFHS**			31.3/30.4	n/a	36.10/34.91	30.88/29.74			28.7/24.8	n/a	32.71/27.76	21.60/17.03
2001–11	Census	-0.58	21.8	21.1	n/a	23.22	18.45	17.70	19.8	21.2	n/a	23.34	14.72
	SRS			16.57	4.05	17.86	13.25			22.96	7.38	25.48	16.72
	NFHS			28.5	n/a	32.45	27.32			23.1	n/a	25.66	16.89
2011–21	SRS	n/a	n/a	14.96	3.40	16.01	12.18	n/a	n/a	21.03	6.71	23.13	15.27
	NFHS			21.4	5.4	23.58	19.57			19	8.4	20.71	12.91

Sources: Prepared by authors using (i) SRS birth and death rates: Srivastava (1987); GoI (1999); SRS Bulletins (2004–19); (ii) Census birth and death rates: GoI (1997c), Guilmoto and Irudaya Rajan (2002; 2013); (iii) NFHS: IIPS and MI (2007 and 2009); IIPS and ICF (2017) and (iv) Other census data: GoI (1976a; 1987; 2018a; n.d.1; n.d.2).

Notes: (i) CBR (CDR) stands for crude birth rate (crude death rate) defined as the number of live births (deaths) per 1000 population. Their estimates are available from 'Census', 'SRS' and 'NFHS'. (ii) 'Share (0–9)' is the population share (in percentage) of those aged 0–9 years and corresponds to the end of the decade. (iii) For *, † and ‡, see notes i and ii of Figure 4.3. (iv) '*'Two waves of NFHS, 1992–3 and 1998–9, were conducted during the census decade 1991–2001. The corresponding CBR estimates are shown respectively separated by a slash '/'. (v) NGR refers to the decadal growth rate of 'closed' or 'no migration' population. Two estimates of NGR have been presented, one, assuming zero death rate (viz., 'NGR (zero)') and the other, using the SRS death rates (viz., 'NGR (SRS)'). NGR is calculated using the following formula: 1 + (NGR/100) = (1 + ((CBR − CDR)/1,000))^10. (vi) CDR from the NFHS is available only for the fourth wave. (vii) Reference period for CBR: (a) 'Census': CBR estimates are 'indirect estimates' based on the reverse survival method for the children aged 0–6 years. Thus, the reference period is six years prior to census (for example, 2004–11 for the 2001–11 decade) (b) 'SRS': The estimates correspond to 1976–81 (average) for 1971–81, 1983–91 (average) for 1981–91, 1991–4 (average) for 1991–2001, 2004–11 (average) for 2001–11 and 2011–17 (average) for 2011–21. Comparable reference periods are used for Nagaland and India. The figures for 1976–81 for Nagaland are based only on the rural sample, but the share of rural population in the state's population was 90 and 85 per cent, respectively, in 1971 and 1981. The SRS birth and death rate estimates are not available for Nagaland for the period prior to 1976 and for 1995–2004. SRS-based estimates exclude Jammu and Kashmir between 1991 and 1997 and Nagaland between 1995 and 2003 due to non-receipt of returns and Mizoram until 1995 as the SRS was not operational in the state. (c) 'NFHS': 1990–2 and 1996–8 (census decade of 1991–2001), 2003–05 (census decade of 2001–11) and 2013–15 (census decade of 2011–21). (viii) @ CBR estimates based on the Census data for India do not include Jammu and Kashmir in 1971–81 and 1981–91 (GoI 1997c). The report is silent on the treatment of Assam in 1981, but the state is unlikely to have been included in the national CBR estimates.

incentive to over-report headcount due to their greater dependence upon public funding and the all-pervading village authorities can facilitate consensual manipulation of records.[23] Moreover, government finds it difficult to cross-check data collected from (remote) villages.

The share of urban Nagaland in the state's overall population stagnated unexpectedly between 1981 and 2001 as the rural population grew at an increasing rate until 2001 (Table 4.2A). During 2001–11, the rural population contracted in most of the districts where new towns were notified. However, Phek's rural population grew despite the notification of a statutory town. So, the notification of new towns alone cannot explain the contraction of rural population. If migration is invoked to explain the reported contraction in rural population, there has to be an unprecedented out-migration of more than 239,713 (87,361, after accounting for the notification of new towns) persons from villages. However, we know of no development that could have triggered an exodus of this scale.[24] In any case, such a massive out-migration should have affected the urban population. The growth in urban population was 134 (66), 73 (59), 65 (65) and 67 (22) per cent, respectively, during 1971–81, 1981–91, 1991–2001 and 2001–11 (figures within parentheses report growth rates after accounting for the notification of new towns). Further, if the contraction in the rural population has to be explained by out-migration to other states and countries, the out-migration has to be at least as large as during the entire period between 1971 and 2001, whereas the actual out-migration during 2001–11 from rural Nagaland to other states was 9,431 and would barely cross 10,000 if we also include out-migrants whose place of origin could not be classified as rural or urban (GoI 2019a). Also, a comparison of all-India and state-level data suggests that in both 2001 and 2011, only about 1 per cent of the speakers of Naga languages of Nagaland lived outside Nagaland.[25]

The overcount of rural population in 2001 most probably explains its contraction in 2011, when stricter enumeration checked ghost entries. The discrepancy in rural population estimated using the fundamental equation (Equation 4.1) increased from 2.03 per cent during 1971–81 to 25.07 per cent during 1991–2001. Over-reporting in rural areas can happen at three levels: ghost villages,[26] ghost households and ghost persons in real households.

Given the influence of villages in the polity and their access to development funding, Nagaland's low population density offers incentives for formation of new villages that in turn have incentive to add ghost entries to secure speedy government recognition.[27] The rate of growth of the number of villages in Nagaland has been much higher than the country as a whole, but it slowed down between 1991 and 2001.[28] So, ghost villages cannot explain the overcount of population in 2001.[29]

Over the past few decades, there has been a steady increase in the rate of growth of the number of households due to the disintegration of joint families, increased mobility and changing social attitudes and family norms. Contrary to this general trend, in Nagaland the growth of the number of households increased from 44 to 51 per cent during 1971–81 and 1991–2001, before dropping to 21 per cent in 2011 (Table 4.4A). Moreover, the average household size in India has been decreasing at an increasing rate since 1981. Nagaland's average household size increased from 5.18 per cent to 6.07 per cent between 1981 and 2001, before contracting by 17.64 per cent between 2001 and 2011 (Table 4.4A). So, ghost households and ghost household members could account for the overcount in 1991 and 2001.[30]

We can estimate the ghost population as follows. Let H and H_s, respectively, denote the number of households and average household size reported in census. The Δ pre-fixed to a variable indicates the number of ghost entries in census. So, ΔH is the number of ghost households and $H - \Delta H$ denotes the true number of households. The ghost population can be estimated using the following equation:

$$\Delta P = HH_s - (H - \Delta H) * (H_s - \Delta H_s) = H_s \Delta H + H \Delta H_s - \Delta H \Delta H_s$$
$$\text{(Equation 4.6)}$$

The ghost population includes people who do not exist as well as out-migrants settled in urban areas within the state or elsewhere who are also counted in villages. We will assume that both the number of households and household size changed between 1971 and 2011 following their respective long-run trends (1971–2011).[31] Under this assumption, in 1991 and 2001, the ghost population in rural areas must have been about 190,000 and 580,000, respectively, that is, 19 and 35 per cent of the state's population (Table 4.4B).[32] These estimates of discrepancy are larger than the estimates based on births and migration (Tables 4.2A–B).[33]

While the ghost population is distributed across the state, one group stands out in this regard. The population of 'Other Nagas', comprising of Nagas not classified elsewhere, grew by 681.67 per cent between 1991 and 2001 (Table 4.13). It accounted for 10.55 per cent of the change in Nagaland's population between 1991 and 2001. 'Other Nagas' contracted by 89.83 per cent during 2001–11 compared to 0.58 and 4.25 per cent contraction in the overall population of the state and Naga population, respectively. The Sumi-dominated Zunheboto is the only district away from the Assam border that reported a substantial increase in the population of 'Other Nagas' between 1991 and 2001. During this period, Sumi strongholds of Dimapur and Zunheboto alone accounted for close to half of the phenomenal growth in the numbers of 'Other Nagas'. The rise and fall in the numbers of 'Other Nagas' can account for some of the discrepancies in Nagaland's population. For instance, the growth rate of Wokha district (95.16 per cent) far exceeds that of Lothas (79.46 per cent), the dominant tribe of the district. The two become comparable if 'Other Nagas' are excluded from the population of Wokha. Likewise, in 2001, Mokokchung's population growth rate drops from

Table 4.4A Households, population and average household size, 1971–2011

Year/characteristic	Nagaland Total		Rural		Urban		India[†] Total		Rural		Urban	
	Number	Growth	Number	Growth	Number	Growth	Number	Growth	Number	Growth	Number	Growth
Households												
1971	104,086		93,987		10,099		99,662,971		78,925,295		20,737,676	
1981	149,480	43.61	124,999	33.27	24,481	143.61	118,832,680	19.23	90,124,596	14.19	28,708,084	38.43
1991	216,982	45.16	174,695	39.76	42,287	72.73	148,165,097	24.68	108,227,175	20.09	39,937,922	39.12
2001	328,057	51.19	263,129	50.62	64,928	53.54	187,096,612	26.28	132,376,300	22.31	54,720,312	37.01
2011	396,002	20.71	277,491	5.46	118,511	82.53	240,975,474	28.80	161,638,587	22.11	79,336,887	44.99
1971–2011[‡]		3.40		2.74		6.35		2.23		1.81		3.41
Population	Number	Growth	Number	Growth	Number	Growth	Number	Growth	Number	Growth	Number	Growth
1971	516,449		465,055		51,394		528,917,868		421,951,334		106,950,831	
1981	774,930	50.05	654,696	41.12	120,234	135.07	659,300,460	24.65	502,880,692	19.18	156,419,768	46.25
1991	1,209,546	56.08	1,001,323	52.94	208,223	73.18	816,169,666	23.79	602,885,849	19.89	213,283,817	36.35
2001	1,990,036	64.53	1,647,249	64.51	342,787	64.62	991,811,100	21.52	711,647,289	18.04	280,163,811	31.36
2011	1,978,502	-0.58	1,407,536	-14.55	570,966	66.57	1,167,108,099	17.67	797,833,758	12.11	369,274,341	31.81
1971–2011[‡]		3.41		2.81		6.20		2.00		1.61		3.15
Household size	Avg. size	Growth	Avg. size	Growth	Avg. size	Growth	Avg. size	Growth	Avg. size	Growth	Avg. size	Growth
1971	4.96		4.95		5.09		5.31		5.35		5.16	
1981	5.18	4.48	5.24	5.90	4.91	-3.52	5.55	4.54	5.58	4.37	5.45	5.65
1991	5.57	7.53	5.73	9.44	4.92	0.26	5.51	-0.71	5.57	-0.17	5.34	-1.99
2001	6.07	8.82	6.26	9.22	5.28	7.22	5.30	-3.77	5.38	-3.49	5.12	-4.13
2011	5.00	-17.64	5.07	-18.97	4.82	-8.74	4.84	-8.64	4.94	-8.19	4.65	-9.09
1971–2011[‡]		0.02		0.06		-0.14		-0.23		-0.20		-0.26

Sources: Prepared by authors using GoI (1973b; 1985a; 1986; 2013d; n.d.1; n.d.2; n.d.9).

Notes: (i) [†] The figures for 'Households' and 'Household size' for India exclude Assam (all years) and Jammu and Kashmir (all years) where census could not be conducted in one of the decades. (ii) 'Growth' indicates decadal growth rates in per cent. [‡] Indicates annual growth rates during 1971–2011.

Table 4.4B   Ghost population in rural Nagaland, 1991 and 2001

Characteristic		1991	2001
CAGR (%, 1971–2011)	Households		2.74
	Households size		0.06
Reported	Households (H)	174,695	263,129
	Households size (H$_s$)	5.73	6.26
Estimated[†]	Households (H–ΔH)	161,495	211,692
	Households size (H$_s$-ΔH$_s$)	5.01	5.04
Ghosts	Households (ΔH)	13,200	51,437
	Households size (ΔH$_s$)	0.72	1.22
	H$_s$*ΔH	75,662	322,010
	H*ΔH$_s$	126,130	320,815
	ΔH*ΔH$_s$	9,531	62,714
Overcount		192,261	580,111
Reported population (rural)		1,001,323	1,647,249
Overcount (%)		19.20	35.22

Source: Authors' calculations, based on Table 4.4A.

Note: (i) [†] Interpolated, using the corresponding 1971 Census estimate (Table 4.4A) and the CAGR (compound annual growth rate) for the period 1971–2011. (ii) The growth rates do not account for rural–urban migration and the reclassification of rural areas as urban, which results in the underestimation of the overcount (see note vi to Table 4.2A).

46.54 to 34.25 per cent after excluding 'Other Nagas'. The adjusted growth rate of Mokokchung is comparable to that of the Ao tribe of Mokokchung (35.76 per cent) that dominates the district. 'Other Nagas' cannot, however, explain the massive overcount in Tuensang and other eastern districts.

Sample Surveys, Administrative Statistics and Church Records

Census estimates can be compared with data from the NFHS and the SRS and data on the gross school enrolment (GSE) (6–14 year population) and electorate (18+ year population).[34] Together, the last two cover almost the entire population. We will cross-check census data using the above sources before examining church membership records.

NFHS and SRS

The NFHS estimates of the CBR are based on the information on the number of children ever born to the women in the reproductive age group (15–49 years) during a reference period of 3 years prior to the day of survey. The SRS is a dual record system that compiles information on births based on continuous enumeration in sample units. While the CBRs from these sources are not directly comparable owing to differences in the methods of data collection and reference periods, they can be used to verify broad trends.[35] We find that the SRS estimates of the CBR are generally lower than those from the NFHS with the estimates based on census lying between the two (Table 4.3).[36]

We estimate the natural growth rate (NGR) for Nagaland and India under two scenarios, assuming zero death rate and the SRS death rates (Table 4.3).[37] The population growth rates of India lie between the NGR estimated under the two scenarios. However, in case of Nagaland the population growth far exceeds NGR until 2001. The CBRs cannot support Nagaland's observed population growth rates even when the crude death rate (CDR) is assumed to be zero. Recall that we found that the fundamental equation is not balanced for Nagaland, even if we assume zero deaths for the 10+ year age group, and that the age data are not inter-temporally consistent, in spite of the assumption of zero death rates for all age groups. Also note that Table 4.3 suggests that Nagaland has not transitioned to a low birth-and-death rate regime that could have explained the decline in population between 2001 and 2011. So, the decline has to be explained by substantial out-migration during 2001–11 and/or the overestimation of population in earlier censuses.

Gross School Enrolment

We can use the GSE data (1963–2011) on children enrolled in primary and middle standards (Classes I–VIII) for information on the population aged 6–14 years to validate the corresponding census population. We will first discuss a few limitations and the internal consistency of the GSE data before comparing it with the census.

The gross enrolment figures underestimate the 6–14 year population as all the children of the school-going age group are not enrolled, and even some of those enrolled drop out due to poor performance, lack of interest, poverty, prevalence of child labour and gender bias. On the other hand, children who spend more than a year in a class, who are enrolled late in schools and whose age has been underreported (allowing them more attempts at examinations and government job interviews) bias the GSE-based estimates of the 6–14 year population upwards. Moreover, state governments have an incentive to over-report enrolment figures to meet targets and attract federal funds linked to student headcounts.[38] We do not have information to estimate the net effect of these factors.

In 1961, the literacy rate of Nagaland was 17.91 per cent, lower than the national average of 24.02 per cent (GoI 1973b). Subsequently, it emerged as one of the more literate states[39] and reported a higher growth in enrolment than the national average (Table 4.5). Both in Nagaland and India, growth in enrolment was lower during 1971–81 than during 1964–71 but increased during 1981–91 before tapering off in the subsequent decade and picking up again after 2001. Thus, the changes in enrolment figures for Nagaland are broadly consistent with that for the rest of the country.

At the national level, the ratio of GSE to the census population (0–14 years)[40] increased steadily from 32 to 53 per cent between 1971 and 2011. However, in Nagaland the ratio *decreased* from 58 per cent in 1971 to 35 per cent in 2001, the year of maximum discrepancy in the Census, before bouncing back to 49 per cent in 2011. A state which was ahead of the rest of the country in terms of the aforesaid ratio as early as in 1971, and has been among the more literate states since the early 1980s, registered a substantial decline in the share of the 0–14 year population in schools. The fall in the school enrolment–population ratio appears to be an artefact of the abnormality in the Census because changes in Nagaland's GSE parallel the trend of the country as a whole. The extent of abnormality in the Census is so much that despite Nagaland's higher rate of growth of enrolment than the national average, the trend of its school enrolment–population ratio diverged from that of the country (Figure 4.5). As the DCO Nagaland (interview, 19 September 2012, Kohima) put it, 'We have very high literacy rate but low enrolment [compared to the corresponding census population].' So, the GSE data suggest that the Census overestimated the population of the 0–14 year age group until 2001.

Electorate

The ECI provides information on the size of the electorate and the number of voters – both disaggregated by gender – for state legislative assembly and parliamentary constituencies. We will examine the data for all 60 assembly constituencies and the only parliamentary constituency of Nagaland.[41] Before that a few observations are in order about the quality of this data. First, the number of voters exceeded the size of the electorate only once, in the 1993 Tenning Assembly Election, when the number of women voters (8,595) exceeded the corresponding electorate (8,534). Second, electorate and voter sex ratios should be comparable if women have not been systematically excluded from the election process and the propensity to vote is gender-invariant. In all assembly constituencies, voter sex ratios mostly lie within 6 per cent of electorate sex ratios.[42] Third, the size of electorates in elections held in the same year or within a year of each other are comparable in most cases. Assembly and parliamentary elections were held in the same year on four occasions (1977, 1989, 1998, 2018),[43] while two assembly elections (1987, 1989), two parliamentary elections (1998, 1999) and two assembly

Table 4.5 GSE and 0–14 years population, 1971–2011

Period	Nagaland					India				
	Literacy§	GSE	GSE growth	Pop. (0–14)	GSE/pop. (0–14)	Literacy†	GSE (in '00s)	GSE growth	Pop. (0–14)	GSE/pop. (0–14)
1971	33.78	112,184	8.48	195,056	57.51	34.45	731,735	3.24	230,334,822	31.77
1981	50.28	136,484	2.96	285,535	47.80	43.57	954,683	2.53	263,107,050	36.28
1991	61.65	209,963	3.79	451,044	46.55	52.21	1,375,010	3.65	312,364,662	44.02
2001	66.59	261,446	2.06	728,409	35.89	64.83	1,614,769	0.38	363,610,812	44.41
2011*	80.11	329,492	3.82	679,032	48.52	74.04	1,971,311	2.03	372,444,116	52.93

Sources: Prepared by authors using (i) Indiastat (n.d.) and http://mhrd.gov.in/statist?field_statistics_category_tid=33 for GSE; (ii) GoI (1976a: 8–9; 1987: 46–7; 2018a; n.d.1; n.d.2) for 'Pop. (0–14)' and (iii) GoI (2011b: 102; 2011g: 34) for literacy rate.

Notes: (i) 'GSE' is the three-year (central) average of enrolment in Classes I–VIII. 'GSE/pop. (0–14)' is the ratio (in %) of GSE and Pop. (0–14). 'We could not access comparable information on GSE for 2012–13. (It seems *Selected Educational Statistics/Statistics of School Education* were last published by the MHRD for 2011–12.) As a result, the GSE values (both for India and Nagaland) for 2010–11 (three-year average) have been used in lieu of 2011–12. (ii) 'GSE growth' is the compound annual growth rate of GSE and has been estimated using a semi-log trend function for the corresponding decade (except for 1971 and 2011, where the reference periods are 1964–71 and 2001–10, respectively). (iii) 'Pop. (0–14)' refers to the census population aged 14 years or below. (iv) † Corresponds to the population aged five years and above for 1971 (1981–2011). The post-1971 censuses provide literacy rate for the population aged seven years or more, whereas in the past it used to be reported for those aged five years or more (GoI 2011b: 102). The population (0–14 years) and literacy figures exclude Assam (1981) and Jammu and Kashmir (1991). (v) § Different census publications use different definitions of literacy and, therefore, provide different headcounts of the literate population. The data reported here are based on GoI (2011g), which reports data for those aged seven years and above. Other sources report the following literacy rates: (a) GoI (1973b: 61): 27.40 (including 0–4 year population) for 1971, (b) GoI (1988c: 68, 71, 73): 42.57 for 1981 and 27.40 for 1971 (both including 0–4 year population), (c) GoI (1997d: 92–5): 61.65 for 1991, 42.57 for 1981 and 27.40 for 1971 (all excluding 0–6 year population as per the report, but it seems that this exclusion was applied only to 1991 and one of the tables for 1981).

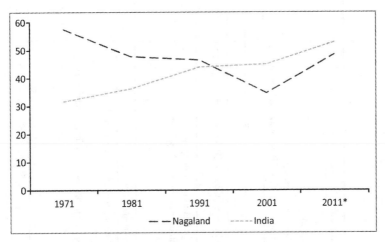

Figure 4.5   Ratio (%) of gross school enrolment to census population (0–14 years), 1971–2011
Sources and *Notes*: See Table 4.5.

(1998, 2013) and parliamentary (1999, 2014) elections were held within two years of each other (Table 4.6). There were substantial differences in three cases. In 1977, the electorate decreased by 70,000 between the parliamentary election (March) and assembly election (November). The March electorate seems to have been inflated due to, say, a delay in summary revision. The 1980 parliamentary electorate was smaller than that of 1977.[44] In 1989, there was a substantial difference (230,595) between the electorates of the assembly and parliamentary elections held on the same day. For some reason, the revised minimum age for voting (18 years) seems to have been applied only in the parliamentary election.[45] Between the 2013 Assembly and 2014 Parliamentary Elections, the electorate reduced by 15,501 in line with the trend of contraction of the electorate between 2011 and 2017 (Table 4.6).

    With the above caveats in place we can compare electoral rolls and censuses. The census estimates are based on compulsory enumeration of *all residents*, while electoral rolls are lists of *citizens eligible to vote* based on voluntary enumeration of individuals possessing documentary evidence of identity and residence (ECI 2006).[46] So, the electorate should be smaller than the census population. If there is no systematic omission of eligible voters from electoral rolls, until 1988 the ratio of the size of the electorate to the census population should provide a lower bound to the proportion of population aged 21 years and above. The voting age was lowered to 18 years in 1988. Henceforth, the ratio should provide a lower bound to the proportion of population aged 18 years and above. The ratio should remain stable or change smoothly unless one or both series are flawed as Nagaland's reported population does not include a large migrant component (Table 4.10).

Table 4.6 Electorate size and voter turnout (%) in Nagaland, 1952–2019

Year	Electorate		Electoral rolls	Voter turnout (%)		Remarks
	Assembly election (AE)	Parliamentary election (PE)		Nagaland	India[*]	
The Naga Hills district (Assam); three seats in Assam State Assembly, one seat in Lok Sabha shared with other autonomous districts (1947–57)						
1952 AE	107,087	—	—	—	—	Election boycotted
1952 PE	—	—	—	—	44.87	Election boycotted
1957 AE	97,548	—	—	—	—	All three candidates won unopposed
1957 PE	—	—	—	—	45.44	Figures for voting in the Naga Hills not available separately
The Naga Hills and Tuensang Area (1957–63)						
1962 PE	—	—	—	—	55.42	
State of Nagaland; 40 seats in Nagaland State Assembly (1963–73) and 6/12 representatives of Tuensang Regional Council (1964–9/1969–74); one seat each in Lok Sabha and Rajya Sabha (1963–)						
1964 AE	124,166	—	—	76.48	—	14 out of 40 candidates won unopposed
1967 PE	—	214,951	—	—	61.04	Candidate won unopposed from Nagaland
1969 AE	176,931	—	—	78.37	—	
1971 PE	—	275,459	—	53.77	55.27	
Elections extended to Tuensang; State Assembly seats increased from 40 to 60 (1974–)						
1974 AE	407,043	—	—	74.35	—	
1977 PE	—	473,257	—	52.83	60.49	2 candidates won unopposed (Akuluto and Tobu)
1977 AE	403,454	—	—	83.26	—	
1980 PE	—	460,083	—	63.90	56.92	One candidate won unopposed (Southern Angami II)
1982 AE	596,453	—	—	74.44	—	
1984 PE	—	594,062	—	66.46	63.56	
59 seats reserved for Scheduled Tribes (1987–)						
1987 AE	581,953	—	—	84.53	—	
1989 AE	582,416	—	—	85.65	—	

	Voting age lowered from 21 to 18 years					
1989 PE	—	813,011	—	74.71	61.95	Turnout highest in the North-East (except Tripura)
1991 PE	—	814,836	—	77.07	56.73	Turnout highest in India (except Lakshadweep)
1993 AE	813,862	—	—	91.53	—	One candidate won unopposed (Northern Angami I)
1996 PE	—	874,518	—	88.32	57.94	Turnout highest in India (except Lakshadweep)
1998 PE	—	926,569	—	45.41	61.97	Turnout lowest in the North-East due to the Naga Hoho's poll boycott
1998 AE	926,569	—	—	78.95	—	43 candidates won unopposed due to the Hoho's poll boycott call
1999 PE	—	955,914	—	76.25	59.99	Turnout highest in India (except Lakshadweep and Sikkim)
2003 AE	1,014,841	—	—	87.85	—	
2004 PE	—	1,041,433	—	91.77	58.07	Turnout highest in India
2007 ER	—	—	1,289,517	—	—	
2008 AE	1,302,266	—	1,303,435	86.19	—	
2009 PE	—	1,321,878	1,321,781	89.99	58.19	Turnout highest in India
2010 ER	—	—	1,331,531	—	—	
2011 ER	—	—	1,342,948	—	—	
2012 ER	—	—	1,229,026	—	—	
2013 AE	1,198,449	—	1,197,313	90.19	—	
2014 PE	—	1,182,972	1,179,881	87.91	66.44	Turnout highest in India
2015 ER	—	—	1,179,635	—	—	
2016 ER	—	—	1,148,317	—	—	
2017 ER	—	—	1,147,338	—	—	
2018 AE	1,195,521	—	1,194,494	83.85	—	One candidate won unopposed (Northern Angami II)
2018 PE	—	1,197,436	1,194,494	85.07	—	Parliamentary bye-election held after the sitting member resigned.
2019 PE	—	1,213,777	1,202,307	83.00	67.40	Turnout highest in India (except Lakshadweep)

Sources: Prepared by authors using election reports and electoral rolls from http://eci.gov.in.

Notes: (i) The electorate before (after) 1993 for assembly elections and 1989 for parliamentary elections corresponds to the population aged 21 (18) years and above. (ii) * The figures reported for India are turnouts in parliamentary elections. (iii) The size of Nagaland's electorate is calculated by aggregating the electorate of all the assembly constituencies. Some ECI reports do not mention the electorate size of constituencies in which there was only one candidate. As a result, the electorate size is not available for Tobu in 1974, the first election held in this constituency, and we have used the 1977 figure. Likewise, the 1993 electorate of 'Northern Angami I' has been substituted by the average of the electorate size in 1989 and 1993. Furthermore, we have used the 2013 figure for Northern Angami II in 2018. (iv) We could access only the post-2007 'Electoral rolls'. The electorate size from 'AE'/'PE' and 'Electoral rolls' differ because of the difference in the reference dates. The maximum difference between these sources is less than 2 per cent though.

The ratio averaged about 62 per cent during 1974–2011 (Figure 4.6). Though the ratio has not behaved smoothly over time, it dropped below the average only twice. It was 57 per cent in the 1987 Assembly Elections and 52 per cent in the 1989 Assembly Elections. As discussed above, this can be attributed to discrepancies in the respective electoral rolls. The ratio also fell below 62 per cent during 1991–2004. As we approach 2001, the census year with maximum discrepancy, the ratio approaches 50 per cent. Since there is a substantial discrepancy in the censuses conducted in 1991 and 2001 and the electoral rolls of this period are mutually consistent insofar as they do not vary abruptly across elections, the abnormality can be attributed to the discrepancy in the corresponding censuses.

The size of the electorate may not provide accurate point estimates of the adult population prior to the 1990s, but the trend estimated with suitable controls can be compared with the growth of the corresponding census population. The ECI (2017) itself carries out such comparisons (see also *ME* 2013e; *Nagaland Post* 2013). We estimate the annual growth of the size of the electorate for three series

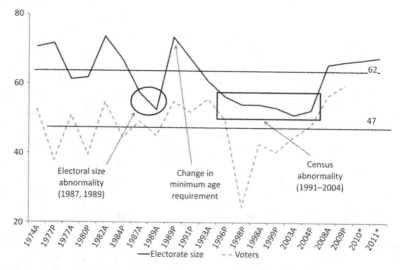

Figure 4.6   Ratios (%) of electorate and voters to census population in Nagaland, 1974–2011

Sources: See Table 4.6.

Notes: (i) The suffixes 'A' and 'P', respectively, indicate assembly and parliamentary elections and * indicates years in which there were no elections. The figures for 2010 and 2011 are based on summary revisions of electoral rolls. (ii) The solid horizontal lines correspond to the averages of the ratios of the size of the electorate (62 per cent) and the number of voters (47 per cent) to the census population. (iii) The census population used in calculating the ratios has been interpolated for elections held in intercensal years. (iv) The ratio for voters dropped sharply in 1998 due to an election boycott.

– assembly, parliamentary and both assembly and parliamentary elections – using an appropriate variant of the following semi-log trend function:

$$\ln\left(Electorate\ size_t\right) = \alpha + \beta t + \delta Type + \gamma_1 D_{1989} * Type + \gamma_2 D_{1993} * (1 - Type) + \varepsilon_t$$

(Equation 4.7)

where 'Type' is a control for the type of election (Type = 0/1 for assembly/parliamentary elections) and D_{1989} and D_{1993} are dummies that assume a value of unity 1989 or 1993 onwards, the year in which the change in voting age became effective in Nagaland. The compound annual growth rate, that is, $(exp^{\beta} - 1)*100$ can be compared with census growth rates. The regressions suggest that during 1974–2009 the electorate grew at the rate of 2.45–2.93 per cent per annum, which would imply a 2.07–2.38 times increase in the population eligible to vote over three decades (Table 4.7). In comparison, the corresponding census population grew at the rate of 4.42 per cent per annum leading to a 3.66 times increase in population between 1971 and 2001.

Together the data on GSE and electorate size corroborate doubts about the reliability of the census population estimates. The ratios of GSE to population[47] and electorate size to population behave abnormally for Nagaland vis-à-vis the corresponding ratios for India and the abnormality peaks around 2001, the year of maximum discrepancy in the census data.

Church Records

The Nagaland Baptist Church Council (NBCC), an umbrella organisation of Baptist churches of Nagaland, is among the oldest supra-tribe organisations of the state. It publishes membership statistics for its constituent tribal church associations that can be added to obtain state-level estimates. We also have data from the Catholic Church. Put together, these two sources provide a lower bound for the Christian population as they account for an overwhelming majority of Nagaland's Christians. The NBCC data suffer from a few shortcomings though: (a) only the baptised members of a family are counted, (b) smaller non-Baptist Protestant churches, such as the Revivalists, Adventists and Pentecostals are not covered, (c) the NBCC does not represent all Naga Baptists of the state,[48] (d) Baptist churches of non-Nagas, except the Kukis, are not included in the NBCC (Gorkha/Nepali Church was added as an associate member in 2011) and (e) the figures for individual congregations that are the basis of aggregate figures may not be accurate (for example, the same figure is repeated in consecutive years, data are missing in a few years and, in some cases, membership figures seem to have been rounded off).[49]

Table 4.7 Growth of electorate and voters in Nagaland

Variable/description	Electorate			Voters	Census (20+ yrs)
	Assembly	*Parliamentary*	*Both*	*Both*	
Panel A: 1974–2009					
Trend	0.0289 (0.001)	0.0242 (0.000)	0.0264 (0.000)	0.0331 (0.000)	
D_{1989}		0.204 (0.026)			
D_{1993}	0.140 (0.249)				
Type			0.0381 (0.482)	-0.231 (0.084)	
D_{1989}*Type			0.186 (0.023)	0.262 (0.145)	
D_{1993}*(1 – Type)			0.165 (0.037)	0.126 (0.478)	
No. of observations	9	10	19	19	
R^2	96.70	97.52	97.04	89.29	
Time period	1974–2008	1977–2009	1974–2009	1974–2009	1971–2001
CAGR	2.93	2.45	2.67	3.36	4.42
Panel B: 1974–2018					
Trend	0.0198 (0.002)	0.0168 (0.000)	0.0181 (0.000)	0.0238 (0.000)	
D_{1989}		0.317 (0.003)			
D_{1993}	0.270 (0.056)				
Type			0.026 (0.701)	-0.244 (0.066)	
D_{1989}*Type			0.289 (0.002)	0.412 (0.013)	
D_{1993}*(1 – Type)			0.311 (0.001)	0.246 (0.116)	
No. of observations	11	12	23	23	
R^2	95.05	95.90	95.41	89.65	
Time period	1974–2018	1977–2018	1974–2018	1974–2018	1971–2011
CAGR	2.00	1.70	1.83	2.41	3.49

Source: Authors' calculations, based on Table 4.6.

Notes: (i) 'Type' = 1 for 'Parliamentary' and 0 for 'Assembly' elections. (ii) The CAGR for 'Census (20+ years)' population is estimated by applying the compound growth rate formula for the census years 1971 and 2001. (iii) p-values are reported within parentheses. See note 67 of Chapter 5 for interpretation of p-values. (iv) Regressions are based on the data from election reports. Data from electoral rolls have not been used in regressions. (v) The dummies for 1989 (D_{1989}) and 1993 (D_{1993}) have been used to capture the impact of change in voting age, in parliamentary and assembly elections, respectively.

Table 4.8   Baptists and Catholics in Nagaland, 1990–2011

Year	Baptists		Catholics		Total§	Census		Total/ census (per cent)
	Number[†]	Decadal growth rate	Number	Decadal growth rate		Number	Decadal growth rate	
1990	223,490	24.16[††]				1056,451		
1991[*]	243,400					1057,940	70.20	
1992	263,310					1115,087		
1993	268,584					1175,321		
1994	280,518					1238,808		
1995	298,348					1305,725		
1996	308,958					1,376,256		
1997	321,269		41,586		577,034	1,450,598		39.78
1998	337,698		42,711		605,541	1,528,955		39.60
1999	337,698		44,459		607,289	1,611,545		37.68
2000	351,081[$]		46,038		631,173	1,698,596		37.16
2001	379,022[$]	55.72	48,196	44.60[‡]	679,899	1,790,349	69.23	37.98
2002	386,368		50,662		694,609	1,785,213		38.91
2003	396,728		50,873		712,086	1,780,093		40.00
2004	406,794		53,031		731,021	1,774,986		41.18
2005	414,256		54,401		744,828	1,769,895		42.08
2006	429,479		55,783		771,581	1,764,818		43.72
2007	454,336[$]		56,727		813,954	1,759,756		46.25
2008	469,491		58,442		840,927	1,754,708		47.92
2009	482,774[$]		57,549[$$]		862,172	1,749,674		49.28
2010	493,259[$]		58,398		880,496	1,744,656		50.47
2011[‡‡]	515,646[$]	36.05	58,252	20.86	917,662	1,739,651	-2.83	52.75

Sources: Prepared by authors using NBCC (2001–11); chancellor, Kohima diocese (interview, 20 September 2012, Kohima); Diocese of Kohima (n.d.); Table 4.11.

Notes: 'Census' corresponds to the Christian population for the state and has been interpolated for intercensal years.

Baptists: (i) [†] Includes police (overwhelmingly Naga) and Kuki churches. [‡‡] Does not include 4,580 members of Association of Gorkha Baptist Churches Nagaland and Nagamese Baptist Churches Association, City Church (Kohima) and Naga Christian Fellowship (Delhi) for which data were published for the first time in 2011. (ii) [††] relates to the period 1980–90 (the membership for 1980 has not been reported in the table). (iii) [*] For want of data, the 1991 church membership is assumed to be the mean of 1990 and 1992. (iv) [$] This figure is the sum of the members of individual Baptist associations and is less than the total published in the corresponding NBCC newsletters for 2001, 2007 and 2009 and more for 2000, 2010 and 2011. Except in 2010 (2.2 per cent), the differences are less than 0.5 per cent. (v) The reference date

Contd

Table 4.8 contd

for church membership data published in a year is generally the preceding December, whereas it is 1 March of the same year for the Census. (vi) We cross-checked the NBCC data with other sources. The difference between Nuh (2006: 191–206) and the NBCC is less than 2 per cent for 1995 and 2005. The NBCC and the CBCC (2000: ix) provide identical figures for 2000.

Catholics: [‡] The average annual growth rate during 1997–2001 is 3.76 per cent implying a decadal (1991–2001) growth rate of 44.60 per cent. [§§] The sum of memberships of parishes and centres is 49,621 in the year 2009 (Diocese of Kohima n.d.), which is less than the membership reported above.

Total: [§] Includes Baptists (divided by 0.6 to adjust for the fact that the NBCC reports only the baptised members) and Catholics but excludes smaller Christian communities.

In Nagaland, non-baptised family members, in most cases children, are treated as part of the 'Christian community' because it is assumed that they 'were being raised in a Christian environment and therefore bore a Christian identity' (Eaton 1984: 15). The NBCC data can be adjusted to account for the non-baptised members in Baptist families assuming (a) the age of baptism is 18 years in all congregations, (b) all adults in Baptist families are baptised and (c) the 18+ year population is 60 per cent of the overall population.[50] The age of baptism and the age structure of population vary over time as well as across tribes and congregations. These estimates of the overall Baptist population are likely to be upper bounds of the baptised population insofar as 'Members' may include those below 18 years as well, while a few adults may not have been baptised. The latter number is unlikely to be sizeable as an overwhelming majority of Nagas had already converted by the late 1980s.

With these caveats in place we can examine the ratio of the adjusted church membership to the Census Christian population.[51] If the assumption regarding the age of baptism is reasonable, the ratio is expected to be slightly less than one for Nagaland as a whole as the numerator does not include all Christians, while it should be almost equal to one for tribes that are almost entirely Baptist. The tribe-level analysis is restricted to Baptists as the Catholic Church's data are organised around parishes rather than tribes. In most cases, this does not affect the ratio as most tribes are largely Baptist. The Catholic Church has a strong presence among Angamis and some of the neighbouring tribes though, and the ratio should be somewhat lower for them.

For both the overall Christian population of Nagaland (Table 4.8) as well as individual Naga tribes (Table 4.9), the ratio was much less than one in the late 1990s. It declined further in the run-up to the 2001 Census much like other such ratios analysed earlier despite the unusually high rate of growth of church membership in the 1990s.[52] The low value of the ratio suggests one/more of the

Table 4.9 Membership of Naga Baptist churches and census population

Tribe	Association	Members			Census population†			Members/census ratio		
		2011†	2001	1992	2011	2001	1991	2011	2001	1991
Ao	ABAM	93,678	68,817	50,762	135,975	139,094	99,536	69	49	51
Angami	ABCC	31,032	21,210	14,989	85,039	74,818	58,445	36	28	26
Chakhesang	CBCC	43,180	31,343	22,000	92,924	80,788	53,500	46	39	41
Chang	CBLT	23,150	15,598	10,600	38,536	36,531	18,222	60	43	58
Pochury	PBCC/CPBC	5,156	3,544	2,928	13,169	9,545	6,023	39	37	49
Rengma	CRBC	12,507	10,905	6,500	37,771	30,580	19,421	33	36	33
Kuki	KBA	3,191	1,926	1,700	11,261	12,117	9,660	28	16	18
Konyak	KBBB	58,102	50,087	39,417	142,541	146,255	81,875	41	34	48
Khiamniungan	KBCA	15,743	10,720	7,951	36,988	22,882	12,999	43	47	61
Lotha	KBES	64,356	42,742	33,136	103,867	88,926	49,552	62	48	67
Phom	PBCA	22,696	14,455	8,154	31,609	69,233	39,203	72	21	21
Sumi	SABAK/SBAK/WSBAK	64,576	48,985	32,974	141,788	145,084	90,468	46	34	36
Sangtam	USBLA	25,619	20,502	12,943	44,996	50,228	31,185	57	41	42
Yimchunger	YBBA	19,037	14,540	7,144	40,183	45,590	21,277	47	32	34
Zeliang	ZBA/ZBCC/LBA	19,823	13,648	7,612	44,926	43,123	21,607	44	32	35
Police	NPBCA	13,800	10,000	4,500						
Total		515,646	379,022	263,310	1,001,573	994,792	612,972	51	38	43

Sources: See Tables 4.8 and 4.12.

Notes: † 'Census population' is 60 per cent of the total population of the tribe as per the respective censuses. This adjustment helps to isolate a comparable sub-set of the census population. Census figures cover all Christians, whereas the NBCC data are restricted to members of its affiliate churches.

following: (a) The census population is inflated, (b) There is a large non-Baptist Naga population, which is highly unlikely and/or (c) Church membership records are incomplete, which is highly unlikely, at least, in the rural areas, where an overwhelming majority of Nagas live. So, we can conclude that the Census overestimated Nagaland's Christian population.

Ad Hoc Explanations

We have so far seen that the census data are both internally inconsistent as well as inconsistent with other sources of demographic information. In this section, we will discuss ad hoc explanations of Nagaland's demographic somersault,[53] but we will not examine ad hoc corrections.[54]

Political Transitions

Nagaland has witnessed four transitions after it was granted statehood. In accordance with the second point of the 1960 Sixteen Point Agreement (NSA, 5:22), Nagaland was placed under the Ministry of External Affairs (MEA) until 1972 (Ramunny 1988: 150, 307–8). It can be argued that census could not be conducted properly leading to under-enumeration in 1961 and 1971 due to a lack of coordination between the Ministry of Home Affairs (MHA), which is responsible for conducting censuses, and the MEA (civil society leader, interview, 26 November 2012, Dimapur).

Another transition is linked to Tuensang district. Art. 371A of the constitution that provides for the autonomy of Nagaland also safeguards the interests of Tuensang district, which was an unadministered area under the British. Between 1964 and 1974, Tuensang was governed by the governor with the assistance of a 35-member Regional Council that vetted legislation before they were applied to the district. The council elected 6 members (later raised to 12) to represent it in the state's legislative assembly and 1 of them served as a minister for Tuensang affairs. This arrangement was abolished in 1974, without the repeal of the relevant constitutional provision, and direct elections were introduced in Tuensang. It could be argued that the transition to the regular administration and the transfer of Nagaland from the MEA to the MHA would have allowed for a more careful enumeration in 1981 in the remote Tuensang and Mon districts. These transitions can at best explain the spike in population growth rate in 1981 due to the reduction in coverage error. The following censuses should have recorded a drop in the growth rate because of a secular decline in fertility and out-migration. To the contrary, the observed growth rates accelerated until 2001.

A third transition relates to the nature of ruling party in the state. The 1991 Census was conducted under the Nagaland People's Council (NPC) government headed by Vamuzo Phesao, a Chokri from Phek. The next census was conducted under the Congress government headed by S. C. Jamir, an Ao from Mokokchung. The 2011 Census was conducted under a Naga People's Front (NPF) government headed by Neiphiu Rio, an Angami from Kohima. The NPC and the NPF are regional parties, whereas the Congress is a left-of-centre national party. Politics in Nagaland is, however, not aligned along the left–right axis, with the two sides having different positions on how to address demographic concerns. In fact, in the 2009 consultative meeting on census, all political parties supported the consensus statement (GoN 2009a; DCO Nagaland, interview, 24 June 2013, Kohima). Moreover, Neiphiu Rio was directly responsible for the 2001 Census as the minister for home affairs in the Jamir-led Congress government, whereas he was the chief minister of the NPF government in 2011. The fourth transition, which happened in the late 1990s when the government and insurgents signed ceasefire agreements, will be discussed in the next section.

Nagaland has also undergone a more general transition that is not directly related to political developments. The period since the 1940s has been marked by intense social and economic change due to the gradual weakening of village-based communities, among other things. Cook (2004) draws attention to the difficulty in counting people when the social structure is changing. However, the structural instability of demographic characteristics of the population due to socio-economic changes should primarily be associated with content errors rather than coverage errors, and the errors should narrow down over time. Instead, Nagaland's headcount was affected by growing coverage errors until 2001.

Insurgency

Census had to be cancelled in Assam (1981) and Jammu and Kashmir (1951 and 1991) during periods of political disturbance.[55] However, census was never cancelled or postponed in Nagaland despite the sustained armed insurgency that subsided only in the late 1990s. This also holds true of the National Sample Survey Office (NSSO) surveys discussed in Chapter 6.

During our fieldwork in Nagaland, we came across several explanations linked to insurgency.[56] The first suggests that changes in the deployment of the armed forces might explain the high growth rate in 2001 as the Census follows the de facto method of enumeration (retired Naga IAS officer, interview, 9 April 2013, Kohima). The government does not release information about the deployment of armed forces, but we can analyse the potential changes in the number of troops.[57]

Insurgency-related fatalities dropped in the aftermath of the cessation of hostilities in the late 1990s (SATP n.d.1), which should have resulted in a reduction of troops deployed in the state. Moreover, the 1999 Kargil War necessitated the relocation of forces from across the North-East to the western border (S. C. Jamir n.d.3: 69; n.d.4: 14; Kumar 2003). The higher concentration of forces along the western border continued at least until 2002 due to Operation Parakram. So, the headcount of armed forces is likely to have dropped in Nagaland in the run-up to the 2001 Census and should have contributed to a drop rather than increase in the population growth rate.

According to the second insurgency-centric explanation, the return of insurgents to the mainstream contributed to the high growth rate recorded in 2001 (retired Naga IAS officer, interview, 9 April 2013, Kohima). A few observations are in order in this regard. First, in all likelihood, the insurgents did not retain too many camp followers in the interest of mobility and security. Second, the process of return of insurgents that began in the 1960s unfolded differently in different parts of the state and is not yet complete. Third, even if we assume that the majority of insurgents resurfaced in the late 1990s, by this time a large number of the fighters were from the Tangkhul tribe of Manipur whose return should not have affected Nagaland's population.[58] Fourth, during our field visits we learnt that the population of Noklak grew at a high rate in the late 1980s due to the return of insurgents (Khiamniungan leaders, interview, 9 June 2014, Noklak) and that the same was expected in Kiphire in 2011 (Naga IAS officer, interview, 24 June 2013, Kohima). However, such claims are not supported by the census data (Table 4.12).

The number of 'underground' people staying permanently with insurgent groups is unlikely to have been in excess of 10,000 in the 1990s.[59] If we assume a ratio of 1:1 between combatants and permanent camp followers and also all those who 'returned' were not counted in the earlier censuses and were recorded as non-immigrant natives in the 2001 Census, the return of insurgents to the mainstream can at best account for about 2.5 per cent of the growth of Nagaland's population between 1991 and 2001.[60] The actual impact is likely to be much smaller though as the aforesaid ratio must have been much larger.

A third insurgency-centric explanation suggests that a drop in death rate after ceasefire agreements between the government and insurgents could account for the abnormal increase in population in 2001. At the time of the 2001 Census, the effect of ceasefire agreements was limited to only four years of the 1991–2001 decade. This effect should have grown in the following decade and contributed to an increase rather than a dramatic decrease in population in 2011. In any case, in the 1990s, in the run-up to ceasefire agreements, the overall insurgency related death rate, including insurgents and civilians, was less than 1 per 1,000 persons per year (authors' calculation based on SATP n.d.1).[61] Therefore, the effect of ceasefire agreements can at best account for less than 0.7 per cent of the population growth between 1991 and 2001.[62]

Together, the return of insurgents to the mainstream and the drop in death rate after the ceasefire cannot explain more than 3.2 per cent of the population growth during 1991–2001, but as mentioned earlier the actual impact is likely to be much smaller and even that would have been partly counterbalanced by the withdrawal of armed forces in the late 1990s.

A fourth explanation relates to expected political changes following the cessation of hostilities between the government and insurgents. People might have feared that a 'Greater Nagaland' comprising of parts of neighbouring states was likely to be formed in the foreseeable future, which would lead to an influx of Naga and related tribes into Nagaland from neighbouring states. This could have pushed Nagas of Nagaland to over-report population to protect their potential shares in an enlarged Nagaland, where they will have to compete with, among others, the well-armed as well as well-educated Tangkhuls of Manipur. We have not been able to find any direct evidence to support this explanation.[63]

Yet another explanation is based on the relationship between conflict and fertility, with higher fertilities serving as an insurance against demographic invasion, among other things.[64] However, as discussed earlier, census-based CBR fell during the period of interest and cannot support the reported population growth rates of Nagaland, even if a zero death rate is assumed (Table 4.3).

Growing Reach of Census

Tuensang was brought under direct administration in 1948 and was not covered by the Census before 1951. The Census covered only 129.5 square kilometres of Tuensang in 1951. In the next census, the coverage increased to 5,356.1 square kilometres and Tuensang's reported population increased from 7,025 in 1951 to 134,275 in 1961 (GoI 2011b: x).[65]

It can be argued that the entire state was nominally covered in 1961, but the coverage expanded gradually on the ground as happened in case of National Sample Surveys (NSSs) (Chapter 6). Given the geographical segregation of tribes (Table 5.1), this could also mean that the coverage might have expanded a few tribes at a time. This can, however, explain only one spike in the growth rates of certain eastern tribes and remote parts of Tuensang. The growth rates should have decreased subsequently with socio-economic progress leading to a drop in fertility. Instead, the growth rates accelerated across Tuensang until 2001. Also, had an incomplete coverage been responsible for the high rate of growth, the abnormality would not have been pervasive across all Naga tribes and districts of Nagaland.

There is another sense in which the growing reach of the Census might explain changes in the reported population. It could be argued that during the peak of the insurgency, enumerators might not have been able to access villages in insurgent strongholds or people did not cooperate.[66] During our fieldwork, census officials and others suggested that in some of the earlier censuses – pre-2011, according to some, and pre-2001, according to others – complete enumeration was not possible in the strongholds of the partisans of independence in districts along the Myanmar border including Mon, Phek and Tuensang (which included Kiphire and Noklak earlier).[67] The partisans might not have wanted to legitimise the state by cooperating with government officials (civil society leader, interview, 21 September 2012, Kohima; Naga IAS officer, interview, 24 June 2013, Kohima). Insurgency was not intense at the time of the 2001[68] and 2011 Censuses, but it affected the 1961 and 1991 Censuses and, to a lesser extent, the 1971 and 1981 Censuses.

Chaube (1999: 524) doubts the veracity of the 1961 Census in Tuensang, where the partisans of independence were influential. However, according to the Census, the enumerators faced problems in Kohima and Mokokchung districts, while 'there were no specific instances of intimidation of the enumerators in Tuensang District' (GoI 1966: 1–2). This is corroborated by the fact that enumeration was completed on time in Tuensang. It took much longer in the other two districts, where despite all efforts enumerators could not reach all the villages and had to occasionally rely upon village headmen because of the opposition of insurgents who threatened villagers and even killed two officials (ibid.).

In any case, if the effect of the politically-motivated boycott of earlier censuses was strong enough to explain the subsequent spike in growth rate reported in the 2001 Census, the population growth rates must have been much lower in the past. However, Nagaland recorded very high and growing population growth rates until 2001. While we have rejected the changing reach of census as an explanation, a related hypothesis linked to the indigenisation of census staff remains to be examined.

It seems whoever is at the losing end finds fault with enumerators.[69] After the 2001 Census, some tribes alleged that in many places the officials did not physically visit sites to enumerate population and in others, they did not inform people in advance (CPO et al. 2003: 2, 5). Likewise, the tribes that suffered a dramatic decline in population in 2011 alleged that this time the enumerators did not conduct house-to-house enumeration and the 2001 Census was the best census ever as enumerators visited every household and counted everyone.

A joint action committee (JAC) comprising of Lotha (Wokha district), Phom (Longleng), Zeliang (Peren) and Sangtam (Kiphire)[70] tribes formed in 2007 claimed that unlike the 2001 Census, the earlier censuses were conducted by enumerators from outside Nagaland, who 'did not have the willingness and the endurance to proceed to the remote village and go from house to house ... and hence ... the population of the Nagaland was underrepresented'.[71] They added that the 2001 Census was conducted by 'local people who have the willingness, means, and endurance to proceed to each and every village and count for every household' (*CPO & Ors. vs. UoI & Ors.* 2006). If this is accepted, it would be difficult to explain the very high population growth in several districts in 1991 and the contraction reported in 2011. In the latter year, enumerators were almost entirely 'local people'.[72] Moreover, it is not clear why Wokha reported a much higher population growth rate in 2001 than Phek. Wokha enjoys a relatively better road connectivity compared to Phek. Also, for various reasons, including shared borders with Myanmar and Naga districts of Manipur, in the past there was a greater presence of insurgents in Phek. So, both on grounds of poor accessibility and disturbed conditions, Phek must have suffered a higher rate of omission in the past and that should have reflected in a relatively higher growth in 2001 when 'local people' served as enumerators.

In the past, officials assigned to census operations might, indeed, not have physically enumerated the population and relied on figures supplied by village authorities, especially, in remote areas (GoI 1966: 1–2; Vamuzo n.d.: 37; 1991: 11–12). However, there is no reason to assume that this tendency was systematically stronger across censuses in only select districts. Moreover, officials, who oversee decennial census operations, are transferred every few years. Therefore, sustained anomalies in specific locations would have to be attributed to local communities.

We can safely conclude that the expanding reach of the Census and consequent reduction in gross omission cannot explain the sustained increase in Nagaland's growth rate until 2001, let alone the subsequent precipitous decline.

Budgetary Constraints

The downsizing of governments after economic liberalisation in the 1990s may have reduced the funding for data collection affecting the quality of training of enumerators and the ability to monitor actual enumeration. Statistical agencies across the world have, indeed, faced budget constraints in the recent decades (Heine and Oltmanns 2016: 201; see also Jerven 2013 for Sub-Saharan Africa, CBC 2007 for Canada). This might hold good for India as a whole and possibly explains why the errors peaked in 2001, the first census conducted after economic liberalisation.[73] However, it cannot explain why Nagaland alone reported abnormal changes in population in that decade (Figure 4.2). Moreover, we have not come across evidence of reduction in the budget for census between 1991 and 2001. The allocation for census operations across the country increased from ₹3 billion in 1991 to ₹12 billion in 2001 and to ₹22 billion in 2011 (Banthia 2001; Chandramouli 2011).

Political-Geographic Explanations

Migration is often cited as the main reason for the abnormal changes in the population of the North-East (Sharma and Kar 1997; Jamwal 2004: 15; Shimray 2007; Amarjeet Singh 2009; Gogoi, Goswami and Borah 2009; Shimray and Devi 2009; Nag 2014). Civil society organisations in the state argued that the abnormal growth can be explained by the influx of at least 312,138 persons between 1991 and 2001 (CPO et al. 2003: 7). If in-migration explains Nagaland's high population growth until 2001, it can as well be argued that out-migration explains the subsequent contraction. Indeed, Chaurasia (2011: 15) implicitly assumes no abnormality in the 2001 Census and uses SRS (2004–9) birth and death rates to project the 2011 population of Nagaland. He overestimates the actual population by 14 per cent and attributes the difference between the projected and actual figures to 'very heavy out-migration (almost 14 per cent) between 2001 and 2011'.

Out-migration is unlikely to explain the contraction in Nagaland's population, as the number of out-migrants during 2001–11 would have to far exceed 81,935, the number of out-migrants during the entire 1971–2001 period (GoI 1977b: 84–5; GoI 1988d: 318–19; GoI n.d.1; n.d.2),[74] whereas the actual figure for the latest census decade was only 23,467 (GoI 2019a). Migration cannot even explain high growth rates during 1971–2001. Migrants constituted about 5 per cent of Nagaland's reported population in both 1991 and 2001 and only 40 per cent of the migrants were from outside the state (Table 4.10).[75] Therefore, the migrants from outside constituted nearly 2 per cent of Nagaland's population in both years. Moreover, the share of in-migrants from other states and countries in Nagaland's population has been *falling* over time, making in-migration an unlikely cause of

Table 4.10   Share of migrants in Nagaland's population, 1971–2011

Characteristic	1971	1981	1991	2001	2011
Share of all in-migrants*	12.64	15.33	5.74	4.36	12.86
share intra-state**	48.29	62.38	61.96	59.24	78.19
share interstate**	42.16	34.00	35.31	38.74	20.94
share international**	9.56	3.62	2.73	2.02	0.88
Share of in-migrants from outside the state	6.54	5.77	2.20	1.78	2.80

Sources: Prepared by authors using GoI (1976b; 1977b; 1985b; 1988d; 1997f; 1997g; 2019a; n.d.1; n.d.2).

Notes: (i) * as proportion of state's total population; ** as proportion of in-migrants. (ii) The migration figures correspond to 'migration by place of last residence'. (iii) We consider only those who changed residence in the intercensal period, that is, the migrants with a reference period of 0–9 years. (iv) The sum of 'interstate' and 'international' may not equal 'in-migrants from outside the state' because of unclassified migrants.

increasing population growth rate during 1981–2001.[76] In fact, as per the 2001 Census, there was net out-migration from the state (GoI n.d.23). We can also argue that in the 1980s and 1990s, the level of conflict and economic development did not vary substantially across Nagaland's neighbourhood to support an influx into Nagaland on a scale that can explain the dramatic increase in its reported population. Even if it is assumed for the sake of argument that an influx can explain the abnormal increase in population, the complementary assumption – there was a reverse flow in the following decade – is highly implausible because in the latest census decade Nagaland did not witness any marked increase in conflict relative to its neighbourhood. In fact, if anything, in-migration should have increased during the 2001–11 period because of the cessation of hostilities and expansion of the economy.

While we have rejected ad hoc invocation of migration as the root cause of changes in Nagaland's population, a political–geographic explanation – people migrate to cope with 'arbitrary' postcolonial borders (Chapter 3) leading to otherwise unexpected shifts in population dynamics – would bear closer scrutiny. We need to check if people could be relocating across colonial and postcolonial borders to recreate whole communities. We will examine the political-geographic hypothesis from the intra-national and inter-national perspectives as Nagas are scattered across Myanmar and north-eastern states of India. Within the North-East, we will focus on the districts of Arunachal Pradesh, Assam and Manipur that share a border with Nagaland (Map 4.1).

Intra-national Migration

The number of potential settlers belonging to Naga and related tribes of Arunachal Pradesh and Assam are too few to account for the changes in Nagaland's population. In Assam, such population is limited to a few villages in Tinsukia district (Sumi Naga) and two larger and older settlements in the districts of Karbi Anglong (Rengma Naga) and Dima Hasao (Zeme Naga). During ethnic conflicts, some Nagas from the last two settlements temporarily relocate to Nagaland, but we have not come across instances of en masse permanent migration. The Sumi, Rengma and Zeme-speaking population of Assam decreased from 30,056 in 1991 to 28,353 in 2001,[77] which is too small to explain the abnormality in the Census of Nagaland even if it is assumed that the entire drop is accounted for by migration to Nagaland. Moreover, this drop is accounted for by content errors in the headcount of Sumis of the disputed area (see the excursus at the end of this chapter), who are in any case included in the population estimates of both Assam and Nagaland.

Map 4.1   Districts of Nagaland and neighbouring states, 2011

Source: Adapted from GoI (2011f).

Note: Map not to scale and may not represent authentic international borders.

In Arunachal Pradesh, the relevant population is limited to a few tribes in districts close to the Nagaland border. Population of these districts grew at rates comparable to the rest of the state in 2001. The decadal population growth rate of tribes in Naga-dominated Tirap, including Changlang that was carved out of Tirap during 1981–91, was 27 (27) per cent in 1991 (2001) compared to 37 (28) per cent for the Scheduled Tribe (ST) population of Arunachal Pradesh (GoI n.d.1; n.d.2).

The migration of north Manipur's large tribal population could possibly account for a part of Nagaland's unaccounted population growth. However, we have not come across any evidence of large-scale movement of people from Manipur to Nagaland in the 1990s.[78] In fact, the districts of Manipur bordering Nagaland – Senapati, Tamenglong and Ukhrul (Map 4.1) – themselves reported high growth rates despite the out-migration of Kukis.[79] The ST population of Ukhrul grew by 32 per cent during 1991–2001 compared to 17 per cent for all STs of Manipur (GoI n.d.1; n.d.2). The ST population of Tamenglong grew at the rate of 28 per cent (GoI n.d.1; n.d.2). The population growth in a few subdivisions of Senapati district was so high that the state government rejected the 2001 Census results and the Census published estimated figures instead (Table 7.3). More importantly, the highest growth rates in Nagaland were reported in districts along the Upper Assam, Arunachal and Myanmar borders, rather than the Manipur border, and there are hardly any Nagas from Manipur in those districts.

To sum up, migration of Nagas from neighbouring states cannot account for the abnormal changes in Nagaland's population.

Unaccounted International Migration

In the early 1980s, the then Chief Minister J. B. Jasokie (n.d.2: 37–8) warned Nagas against encouraging 'unauthorised settlers of foreign nationals [*sic*]' entering Nagaland as 'cheap' labourers (see also GoN 1981: 35). A year or two later, in 1983, *Ura Mail*'s editor, Chalie Kevichusa, noted with alarm that illegal/ undocumented immigrants allegedly from Bangladesh were overflowing from Assam into Nagaland and had emerged as a decisive vote bank in 'four out of five constituencies under Dimapur' (Haralu and Chandola 2012: 76).[80] Hokishe Sema (1986: 151), another chief minister, who was elected from Dimapur, however, suggested that there were barely 5,000 illegal/undocumented immigrants in the state in the early 1980s.

Shimray (2007: 36) refers to an item published in *Nagaland Page* in 1999 (10 August) that alerted Nagas to the danger posed by the 'Bangladeshi' in the following words:

> In Dimapur, all the rickshaw pullers are Bangladeshis and they are a highly aggressive lot in a land where the non-tribals are living a second class living. All these are signs of a growing and highly visible problem – the virtual colonization of Nagaland by Bangladeshi Muslims, locally known as Miyan. But sadly in Nagaland very little attention is being given to this problem, which is much more serious than even the sovereignty issue.[81]

Since then, Nagaland's newspapers have published hundreds of news items, editorials and opinion pieces on this issue. Political and civil society leaders have also held illegal/undocumented immigration responsible for Nagaland's high population growth (S. C. Jamir n.d.4: 12–13; Rio 2010a; see also note 15 of Chapter 2). The alleged Bangladeshi influx could potentially lead to one or more of the following. First, it could result in an explosive growth of the Muslim population, which has indeed been very high (Table 4.11).[82] Given the small base of the reported Muslim population, though, the alleged influx cannot explain the high population growth rates in Nagaland, even if it is assumed that all Muslims are of Bangladeshi origin rather than Indians from other states. The growth of Muslim population cannot explain more than 2 per cent of the change in Nagaland's population between 1991 and 2001.

Table 4.11   Population and decadal growth of religions, Nagaland, 1971–2011

Year	Total	Christians	Hindus	Muslims	Others	Rest
			Population			
1971	516,449	344,798	59,031	2,966	108,159	1,493
1981	774,930	621,590	111,266	11,806	27,852	2,413
1991	1,209,546	1,057,940	122,473	20,642	5,870	7,653
2001	1,990,036	1,790,349	153,162	35,005	6,108	4,601
2011	1,978,502	1,739,651	173,054	48,963	3,214	11,304
			Population shares			
1971	100	66.76	11.43	0.57	20.94	0.29
1981	100	80.21	14.36	1.52	3.59	0.31
1991	100	87.47	10.13	1.71	0.49	0.63
2001	100	89.97	7.70	1.76	0.31	0.23
2011	100	87.93	8.75	2.47	0.16	0.57
			Decadal growth rates			
1971–81	50.05	80.28	88.49	298.04	−74.25	61.62
1981–91	56.08	70.20	10.07	74.84	−78.92	217.16
1991–2001	64.53	69.23	25.06	69.58	4.05	−39.88
2001–11	−0.58	−2.83	12.99	39.87	−47.38	145.69

Sources: Prepared by authors using GoI (1973b; 1988c; 2004b; 2018a; n.d.1; n.d.2).

Notes: (i) 'Rest' includes Buddhists, Jains and Sikhs. (ii) 'Others' includes those who do not belong to any of the religions mentioned in the table.

Second, alleged Bangladeshis could claim to be Bengali or Assamese-speaking Indian Muslims from other states. However, the share of Bengali and Assamese speakers in the state's population declined between 1991 and 2001 (Agrawal and Kumar 2012b: Table 14), which cannot explain the increasing growth rate of the state's population.

Third, the alleged influx could reflect in an abnormal increase in the population of Dimapur, which continues to be the most preferred destination for migrants being the state's economic hub and the only district that was not entirely beyond the inner line. The growth of Dimapur's reported population was not higher than other districts in 2001 though.

Fourth, the alleged influx could reflect in the abnormal increase in the population of the dominant tribes along the Assam border, which can absorb migrants – notably, Sumis of Dimapur and Lothas of Wokha. The growth rate of both the tribes though was lesser than that of all Naga tribes during 1981–91 and comparable to that of other tribes in the state in the subsequent decade (Table 4.12). Indeed, it is difficult to believe that thousands of Bengali-speaking plainsmen allegedly from Bangladesh could get enumerated as Nagas without

Table 4.12 Population, population share and decadal growth of Nagaland's Scheduled Tribes, 1971–2011

Classification	Population					Population share**					Decadal growth			
	1971	1981	1991	2001	2011	1971	1981	1991	2001	2011	1971–81	1981–91	1991–2001	2001–11
All population	516,449	774,930	1,209,546	1,990,036	1,978,502	100	100	100	100	100	50.05	56.08	64.53	-0.58
All Scheduled Tribes	457,602	650,885	1,060,822	1,774,026	1,710,973	88.61	83.99	87.7	89.15	86.48	42.24	62.98	67.23	-3.55
Garo	934	1,473	2,272	1,582	2,346	0.18	0.19	0.19	0.08	0.12	†	54.24	-30.37	48.29
Kachari	4,329	7,212	8,244	7,807	13,034	0.84	0.93	0.68	0.39	0.66	66.6	14.31	-5.3	66.95
Kuki	6,206	9,839	16,100	20,195	18,768	1.20	1.27	1.33	1.01	0.95	58.54	63.63	25.43	-7.07
Mikir	519	440	703	106	218	0.10	0.06	0.06	0.01	0.01	†	†	†	†
Naga, etc.	445,266	630,970	1,029,589	1,741,692	1,667,712	86.22	81.42	85.12	87.52	84.29	41.71	63.18	69.16	-4.25
Angami	43,994	62,557	97,408	124,696	141,732	9.88	9.91	9.46	7.16	8.50	42.19	55.71	28.01	13.66
Ao	74,016	104,578	165,893	231,823	226,625	16.62	16.57	16.11	13.31	13.59	41.29	58.63	39.74	-2.24
Chakhesang and Pochury	43,438	60,771	99,205	150,554	176,822	9.76	9.63	9.64	8.64	10.60	39.9	63.24	51.76	17.45
Chakhesang			89,166	134,646	154,874			8.66	7.73	9.29	†	†	51.01	15.02
Pochury			10,039	15,908	21,948			0.98	0.91	1.32	†	†	58.46	37.97
Chang	16,075	22,375	30,370	60,885	64,226	3.61	3.55	2.95	3.50	3.85	39.19	35.73	100.48	5.49
Khiamniungan	14,338	18,079	21,665	38,137	61,647	3.22	2.87	2.10	2.19	3.70	26.09	19.84	76.03	61.65
Konyak	72,319	83,652	136,458	243,758	237,568	16.24	13.26	13.25	14.00	14.25	15.67	63.13	78.63	-2.54
Lotha	36,638	58,030	82,586	148,210	175,111	8.23	9.20	8.02	8.51	10.38	58.39	42.32	79.46	16.80
Phom	18,019	24,426	65,339	115,389	52,682	4.05	3.87	6.35	6.63	3.16	35.56	167.50	76.60	-54.34

Contd

Table 4.12 contd

Classification	Population					Population share**					Decadal growth			
	1971	1981	1991	2001	2011	1971	1981	1991	2001	2011	1971–81	1981–91	1991–2001	2001–11
Rengma	8,174	15,312	32,368	50,966	62,951	1.84	2.43	3.14	2.93	3.77	87.33	111.39	57.46	23.52
Sangtam	19,315	29,016	51,975	83,714	74,994	4.34	4.60	5.05	4.81	4.50	50.23	79.13	61.07	-10.42
Sumi	64,918	95,312	150,780	241,806	236,313	14.58	15.11	14.64	13.88	14.17	46.82	58.20	60.37	-2.27
Yimchunger	14,146	22,054	35,461	75,983	66,972	3.18	3.50	3.44	4.36	4.02	55.9	60.79	114.27	-11.86
Chirr‡	692	1,560	2,067	19	138	0.16	0.25	0.20	0.00	0.01	†	32.50	†	626.32
Tikhir‡	2,800	3,587	9,177	10,377	7,537	0.63	0.57	0.89	0.60	0.45	28.11	155.84	13.08	-27.37
Makware‡	2,501	612	863	††	10	0.56	0.10	0.08	††	0.00	†	†	†	†
Yimchunger‡	20,139	27,813	47,568	86,379	74,657	4.52	4.41	4.62	4.96	4.48	41.71	63.18	69.16	-4.25
Zeliang	13,883	21,084	36,012	71,871	74,877	3.12	3.34	3.50	4.13	4.49	51.87	70.80	99.58	4.18
Other Nagas§		7,965	11,962	93,504	9,507	0.00	1.26	1.16	5.37	0.57	†	50.18	681.67	-89.83
Unclassified/unspecified*	348	951	3,914	2,644	8,895						†	†	-32.45	236.42
Non-tribal population	58,847	124,045	148,724	216,010	267,529	11.39	16.01	12.30	10.85	13.52	110.79	19.90	45.24	23.85

Sources: Prepared by authors using GoI (1975b; 1988e; n.d.1; n.d.2; 2018a).

Notes: (i) § 'Other Nagas' comprises of the census categories 'Naga' (Those who wrote their tribe name 'Naga') and 'Unclassified Nagas'. These categories are referred together as 'Naga (ST)' in ST-15 table of the 2011 Census. (ii) * 'Unclassified/unspecified' include 'generic tribes, etc.' (whose population – 2,644 – was only reported in 2001 Census) and other miscellaneous non-Naga communities. (iii) ** The population share of Naga tribes is their share in 'Naga, etc.' The population share for 'All Scheduled Tribes', Garo, Kachari, Kuki and Mikir/Karbi and Naga, etc., tribes is their share in 'All population'. (iv) † The growth rate has not been computed if the population in one of the terminal years was less than 1,000 and/or was not reported. (v) †† Population of Makware was not reported in 2001. (vi) ‡ The status of the Makware, Chirr and Tikhir tribes is contested and they are not recognised as separate tribes by the state government. Yimchungers claim that these communities belong to their tribe and the census treats them as speakers of Yimchunger language. Yimchunger‡ includes Chirr, Tikhir and Makware.

being noticed by fiercely territorial hills tribes. So, Bangladeshis could have reported themselves as native non-Nagas, but the population of the latter grew at a relatively modest rate in the 1990s. A 2012 rape case, however, highlighted the possible indigenisation of alleged Bangladeshis as Nagas. The following is a specimen Naga response to this issue.

> Local Nagas were not only employing mians [Bengali-speaking/Bangladeshi Muslims] as cheap labour but even 'accommodating' them as 'citizens' in most 'rural villages of Dimapur district'.... It has become a rule that some local Nagas who have adopted mians as 'sons and daughters' and naming them with Naga names. (*Nagaland Post* 2012a)

The Sumis are blamed for indigenising Muslims in the disputed area to make up for a shortfall in workforce. It is alleged that there is a growing community called 'Sumias':

> The 'Sumias' are the children of intermarriage between the Sumi Naga tribe and immigrants.... In this regard, a student leader asserted: 'These children are also confused about the religion they should adopt. In most cases, they are given Naga names. So, they cannot be detected by the authorities concerned when they apply for advantages like jobs, which are meant only for the indigenous people of Nagaland' (Amarjeet Singh 2009: 23, 40; see also Borgohain and Borgohain 2011: 190; Hazarika 2018: 291–2)[83]

If it is indeed the case that there is a large Sumia community (Sumi mother and Bangladeshi father), the sex ratio of Sumis should have dropped compared to other Naga tribes. However, this is not true (Agrawal and Kumar 2012b: Table 13).

Lastly, the alleged influx could reflect in the massive growth of the 'Unclassified'/'Other Nagas' population, that is, those who identified themselves as Nagas, but did not specify their tribe. Between 1991 and 2001, the population of 'Other Nagas' increased by more than 600 per cent from 11,962 to 93,504 (Table 4.13). 'Other Nagas' are predominantly Christian (about 98 per cent) (GoI n.d.2) and based mostly in districts bordering Assam. If the spike in population growth in 2001 is explained by the erroneous classification of undocumented immigrants as 'Other Nagas', the 2001 Census suffered from content rather than coverage error. In that case, the contraction of 'Other Nagas' by 89 per cent during 2001–11 will have to be explained by massive out-migration or another content error in 2011, but we do not have evidence supporting either.

We have so far used census data to argue that the influx of alleged Bangladeshi immigrants cannot explain abnormal demographic changes in Nagaland. The undocumented migrant population remains to be discussed. In the absence

Table 4.13   'Other Nagas' in Nagaland

District	1991		2001		2011		Decadal growth rate	
	Population	Share	Population	Share	Population	Share	1991–2001	2001–11
Tuensang (1971)	32	0.27	6,466	6.92	3,910	41.13	†	–39.53
Mon	0	0	2,358	2.52	2,970	31.24		
Tuensang	32	0.27	4,108	4.39	940	9.89		
Mokokchung (1971)	1,034	8.64	51,131	54.68	1,662	17.48	5,374.41	–96.75
Mokokchung	601	5.02	20,279	21.69	64	0.67		
Zunheboto	0	0	13,099	14.01	664	6.98		
Wokha	433	3.62	17,753	18.99	934	9.82		
Kohima (1971)	10,896	91.09	35,907	38.4	3,935	41.39	229.54	–89.04
Kohima & Dimapur	10,894	91.07	33,440	35.76	3,371	35.46		
Phek	2	0.02	2,467	2.64	564	5.93		
Total	11,962		93,504		9,507		681.67	–89.83
Share in Naga tribes*		1.16		5.37		0.57		

Sources: Prepared by authors using GoI (n.d.1; n.d.2; 2018a).

Notes: †The growth rate has not been computed if the population in one of the terminal years is very low. * Indicates the share of 'Other Nagas' population in all Naga tribes. See also notes to Table 4.12 and note i to Table 4.14.

of authoritative government figures on the number of illegal/undocumented international immigrants, the public discourse is driven by media reports and statements of politicians and, occasionally, government officials. These sources suggest that the number of alleged Bangladeshi Muslims in the state was between 60,000 and 300,000 during 1999–2004,[84] with some sources even suggesting that the number was close to 500,000 (former minister, interview, 26 October 2014, Dimapur).[85] However, a Naga IPS officer (interview, 21 September 2012, Kohima), rejected these claims as 'simply impossible'. Similarly, a retired Naga IAS officer (interview, 9 April 2013, Kohima) argued, 'Their number cannot be in lakhs.' The above estimates are moot, also because a lot of Bengali-speaking Muslim workers in Nagaland are daily or seasonal migrants from Assam and the 2001 Census reported only 7,984 international immigrants in Nagaland (GoI n.d.2). The high estimates of illegal Bangladeshi immigrants, in fact, appear to be an instance of 'anxiety-laden perceptions of fecundity or illegal immigration of competing groups' that translate into 'overestimates of the population of outgroups' (Horowitz 2000: 194). Perceptions are mistaken for reality even by government agencies.[86] In 2013, the ECI issued the following guidelines for the verification of electoral rolls that assumed the existence of 'illegal immigrants' and issued directives against enrolling them without clarifying how to identify such immigrants.

> If evidence is establish[ed] that the person is illegal immigrant then, the name will be deleted suo moto by the ERO. In order to establish the authenticity of document, the submitted document will be sent back to the issuing authority for verification. No Electoral Photo Identity Card will be issued to any suspected illegal immigrant till claims for citizenship is established. If any Local woman [is] married to any illegal immigrant, the whole family will be treated as illegal immigrant except the woman. (*Nagaland Post* 2013).

While it is commonplace to trace the problem of illegal immigration to Bangladesh, Myanmarese immigrants easily intermingle with kindred tribes. Given the close relationship between Nagas divided by the Indo-Myanmar border, Myanmarese Nagas take shelter in Nagaland in the event of conflict. They have no incentive to register themselves as non-Naga, non-tribal or non-Christian in a state dominated by kindred Christian Naga tribes. Thus, the indigenisation of Myanmarese Nagas who cross the border is not inconceivable and should reflect in population growth rates of districts along Myanmar border in 1991. Between 1981 and 1991, the decadal population growth rate of Konyaks – the largest tribe in the districts along Myanmar border – was a phenomenal 63 per cent compared to 16 per cent in the preceding decade (Table 4.14). However, these high growth rates persisted in 2001. And, this is true of most eastern Naga districts and tribes along the Myanmar border. Thus, the evidence neither clearly supports, nor entirely rules out the possibility of the indigenisation of Myanmarese Nagas, who may have entered the state in the 1980s and the 1990s.

According to one source, until 1991, conflict pushed as many as 100,000 Myanmarese Nagas into Nagaland (Banerjee 1992: 1525).[87] While Myanmar has seen large-scale out-migrations of Shan and Rohingya communities, among others, it still bears emphasis that Banerjee's figure for out-migration is a fourth of his own estimate of Myanmar's Naga population at that time. Most Nagas as well as non-Naga observers strongly disagreed with the possibility of such a large influx from Myanmar. Indeed, unlike Dimapur, the subsistence economy of the eastern districts cannot absorb such a large number of migrants. Moreover, migration from Myanmar is often temporary in nature insofar people cross the border when conflict peaks (Jasokie n.d.1: 19–20; KTC 2008: 3)[88] or they come to access better secular as well as theological education and healthcare facilities (interviews with people in the border districts). A few circles of Noklak, Mon and Kiphire districts are likely to have a sizeable Naga population of Myanamarese origin, but the cumulative figure is unlikely to exceed 30,000.[89] This can account

Table 4.14 Population, population share and decadal growth of Nagaland's districts, 1961–2011

District	Population						Share in state's population						Decadal growth rate				
	1961	1971	1981	1991	2001	2011	1961	1971	1981	1991	2001	2011	1961–71	1971–81	1981–91	1991–2001	2001–11
Tuensang (1971)	134,275	173,003	231,270	382,605	675,470	571,344	36.37	33.50	29.84	31.63	33.94	28.88	28.84	33.68	65.44	76.55	-15.42
Mon			94,156	149,699	260,652	250,260			12.15	12.38	13.10	12.65			58.99	74.12	-3.99
Tuensang			137,114	232,906	414,818	321,084			17.69	19.26	20.84	16.23			69.86	78.11	-22.60
Mokokchung (1971)	130,903	176,126	237,370	337,204	547,263	501,722	35.46	34.10	30.63	27.88	27.50	25.36	34.55	34.77	42.06	62.29	-8.32
Mokokchung			115,177	158,374	232,085	194,622			14.86	13.09	11.66	9.84			37.51	46.54	-16.14
Zunheboto			61,161	96,218	153,955	140,757			7.89	7.95	7.74	7.11			57.32	60.01	-8.57
Wokha			57,854	82,612	161,223	166,343			7.47	6.83	8.10	8.41			42.79	95.16	3.18
Kohima (1971)	104,022	167,320	306,290	489,737	767,303	905,436	28.18	32.40	39.52	40.49	38.56	45.76	60.85	83.06	59.89	56.68	18.00
Kohima & Dimapur			238,850	387,581	619,108	742,018			30.82	32.04	31.11	37.50			62.27	59.74	19.85
Kohima			126,935	209,630	310,084	363,207			16.38	17.33	15.58	18.36			65.15	47.92	17.13
Dimapur*			111,915	177,951	309,024	378,811			14.44	14.71	15.53	19.15			59.01	73.66	22.58
Phek			70,618	102,156	148,195	163,418			9.11	8.45	7.45	8.26			44.66	45.07	10.27
Nagaland	369,200	516,449	774,930	1,209,546	1,990,036	1,978,502	100.00	100.00	100.00	100.00	100.00	100.00	39.88	50.05	56.08	64.53	-0.58

Sources: Prepared by authors using GoI (1973a; 1984b; 2005a; 2018a; n.d.1; n.d.2).

Notes: (i) Tuensang (1971), etc. denote the three districts that existed at the time of the 1971 Census. (ii) The populations of the current and 1971 districts for 1961, 1971 and 1981 have been adjusted for territorial changes (Figure 3.1). (iii) The population of districts under Mokokchung (1971) and Kohima (1971) for 1981 may not add up to that of the corresponding broad divisions because of the transfer of territory. (iv) * Dimapur became a district after the 1991 Census, and its population for 1981 and 1991 is the total population of the corresponding circles under the then Dimapur subdivision.

for less than 4 per cent of the population growth between 1991 and 2001, assuming all the Naga settlers of Myanmarese origin entered and permanently settled in Nagaland during this period.

We cannot cross-check the census data of the countries of origin of unaccounted international migrants in Nagaland. The Census of Myanmar is unreliable for tribal areas and, in any case, provides just two data points for the the period after 1980. Bangladesh's population is almost a hundred times larger than that of Nagaland. So, even if the entire abnormal growth in Nagaland's population is due to Bangladeshis, it is unlikely to leave a noticeable trace in the Census of Bangladesh. Moreover, it may be impractical to trace the abnormal change to Bangladesh because migrants settle among ethnically close communities along the Bangladesh–India border before moving deeper into the Indian territory after acquiring the readily available insignia of Indian citizenship that makes them much more difficult to be detected. To conclude, while we do not have sufficient information to quantify unaccounted international immigration, it is highly implausible that it can explain the abnormal changes in Nagaland's reported population.

Concluding Remarks

We have shown that the population of Nagaland was over-reported during 1981–2001. At the end of this period, the Census had overestimated Nagaland's population by at least 36 per cent. The systematic, sizeable and growing errors in Nagaland's headcount did not attract the attention of the administration and academia though. We examined the internal consistency of the population estimates by analysing changes in (a) births and migration; (b) the population of various age groups and (c) the number of households and mean household size. Births and migration can account for Nagaland's population growth only if we assume a substantial *negative* death rate. There was pervasive overcount of population under the age of 50 years (except the 30–4 year age group), even if we assume zero death and out-migration rates. Also, both the number of households as well as household size were overestimated by the Census. Comparison of the Census with other sources confirms the above conclusions. CBR estimates based on the Census, the NFHS and the SRS cannot explain Nagaland's population growth even under the assumption of zero death rate. We also compared the Census with data on school enrolment (6–14 years) and electorate (18+ years), which cover almost the entire population. The Census diverges from both, and the divergence increases as we approach the year 2001. The church membership data too suggest that the Census overestimated the Christian population.

Having shown that the Census lacks internal consistency for Nagaland and is also inconsistent with other sources of demographic information, we ruled out several ad hoc explanations of the demographic somersault: political transitions in the state, the changing nature of insurgency, the growing reach of the Census and imperfect supervision during enumeration due to budget cuts. We also showed that political-geographic explanations too fail to account for the demographic somersault. The explanations discussed in this chapter suffer from a few common shortcomings. First, they can at best explain a minor fluctuation in Nagaland's population. Second, none of these explanations accounts for the pervasiveness of high population growth rates across tribes, districts, sexes, rural–urban sectors and age groups. Third, none of them explains the demographic somersault – the increasing and very high population growth rates upto 2001 followed by contraction in 2011. The ad hoc explanations can explain a *small* part of either the spike in 2001 or the drop in 2011. An acceptable explanation of the somersault should be parsimonious. It should explain both the abnormally high growth rates as well as the subsequent contraction as manifestations of the same underlying phenomenon.

This chapter has rejected conventional demographic explanations as well as ad hoc and political-geographic explanations of coverage errors in Nagaland's headcount and cleared the ground for the analysis of political-economic explanations. Before we proceed to the next chapter, we will discuss content errors in Nagaland's headcount that have evaded multiple layers of quality checks in successive censuses.[90]

Content Errors: An Excursus

Nagaland's headcount suffers from a variety of content errors, some of which will be briefly mentioned in this excursus, whereas a few major cases will be discussed at some length. Non-indigenous non-Naga immigrants seem to have been reported as members of an indigenous Naga tribe in a few circles on the Assam border. The indigenous non-Naga tribal minorities complain that they are deliberately misclassified, if not undercounted. Likewise, some of the smaller Naga communities such as Tikhirs and Rongmeis fighting for recognition as indigenous tribes are grouped with recognised tribes against their wishes, that is, they are effectively co-opted by larger communities. Even otherwise, members of these communities are often forced to report themselves as belonging to closely related recognised tribes in order to access affirmative action benefits. Another content error relates to the data on Muslims. The Census reports Muslims among Naga tribes including those inhabiting districts along the Myanmar border. In 2011, Konyaks alone account for a fourth of the 20,232 adherents of non-Christian religions among Naga tribes of Nagaland. This seems to be a content error as Konyaks are almost entirely Baptist Christians (note 82 of this chapter).

In addition to the misclassification of smaller communities, the Census reports data for miscellaneous/residual Naga categories referred to as 'Other Nagas' here. The population of 'Other Nagas' grew by 681.67 per cent between 1991 and 2001 and contracted by 89.83 per cent during 2001–11 (Table 4.13). For want of space we cannot go into the details, but it bears mentioning that the growth of this residual category cannot be explained by inter-tribal marriages, disaffiliation of smaller tribes from the officially recognised larger indigenous tribes, detribalisation of Naga society, in-migration of Nagas from other states, indigenisation of non-Naga immigrants and misclassification of individuals belonging to indigenous Naga tribes who report a non-standard appellation in response to the question about their tribal affiliation. The religion tables for 2011 also reported the existence of an unheard of tribe called Viswerna with a population of 3,664.

In the remainder of this excursus we will examine a few major content errors in language data. The ratio of population of a tribe to the population of speakers of its language is equal to one for most Naga communities, except for the cases of content errors discussed below (Table 4.15).

The politically influential Angami community has in the past tried to subsume the languages of Zeliang and Chakhesang communities under Angami/Tenyidie language (Naga IAS officer, interview, 21 September 2012, Kohima; civil society leader, interview, 21 September 2012, Kohima; Naga state government official, interview, 28 October 2011, Jalukie). These attempts were partly successful until the 1980s as Angamis played an important role in spreading Christianity as well as education among Chakhesangs and Zeliangs. In recent decades, these communities have begun to assert their separate (linguistic) identity, even though there is some acceptance of Tenyidie as a (cultural) link language. The changing political fortunes of Tenyidie are reflected in the abnormal changes in the data for Angami language (Table 4.15). A similar problem affects the census data on Chakhesang and Zeliang languages. Chakhesang and Zeliang are portmanteau communities that came into existence in the late 1940s and were recognised as tribes by the state government. Chakhesang consists of the Chakru/Chokri, Khezha and Pochury tribes, while Zeliang consists of the Zeme and Liangmai tribes. These tribes speak eponymous languages. Initially, the members of these communities reported themselves as speakers of the non-existent Chakhesang and Zeliang languages, but the internal cohesion has weakened over time. Pochury, which is itself a portmanteau community, dissociated from Chakhesangs and secured recognition as a separate tribe in the early 1990s. Those who remained within the Chakhesang fold began to assert their separate linguistic identity. This fission and fusion of communities translates into abnormal shifts in the headcount of speakers of the respective languages. Other communities whose language data suffer from content errors include Tikhir who are treated as speakers of Yimchunger.

Table 4.15 Major Naga languages of Nagaland, their decadal growth and tribe–language ratio, 1971–2011

Language	Panel A: population of speakers					Panel B: decadal growth				Panel C: tribe/language ratio**				
	1971	1981	1991	2001	2011	1971–81	1981–91	1991–01	2001–11	1971	1981	1991	2001	2011
Angami, etc.*	79,634	95,176	194,064	281,830	316,476	19.52	103.90	45.23	12.29	1.10	1.31	1.01	0.98	1.01
Angami	68,272	78,643	97,433	131,737	151,883	15.19	23.89	35.21	15.29					
Chakhesang			29,699	9,544	17,919			−67.86	87.75					
Chakru/Chokri			48,083	83,506	91,010			73.67	8.99					
Khezha	11,362	16,533	8,091	40,362	34,218	45.51	−51.06	398.85	−15.22					
Pochury			10,758	16,681	21,446			55.06	28.57					
Ao	73,630	101,598	169,837	257,500	231,084	37.98	67.17	51.62	−10.26	1.01	1.00	0.98	0.90	0.98
Chang	15,813	22,252	32,369	62,347	65,632	40.72	45.47	92.61	5.27	1.02	0.97	0.94	0.98	0.98
Khiamniungan	14,414	17,879	23,543	37,752	61,906	24.04	31.68	60.35	63.98	0.99	1.06	0.92	1.01	1.00
Konyak	72,338	76,071	137,539	248,002	244,135	5.16	80.80	80.31	−1.56	1.00	1.00	0.99	0.98	0.97
Lotha	36,728	57,964	84,384	168,356	177,488	57.82	45.58	99.51	5.42	1.00	1.00	0.98	0.88	0.98
Phom	18,017	24,458	65,336	122,454	53,674	35.75	167.14	87.42	−56.17	1.00	1.01	1.00	0.94	0.98
Rengma	†	15,307	32,811	58,590	61,537		114.35	78.57	5.03	0.97	1.02	0.99	0.87	1.02
Sangtam	20,014	28,471	47,447	84,150	75,841	42.26	66.65	77.36	−9.87	1.01	1.01	1.10	0.99	0.99
Sumi/Sema	64,484	95,528	152,123	92,884	8,268	48.14	59.24	§	§	1.01	1.02	0.99	§	§
Yimchunger	19,609	26,564	45,880	92,092	74,156	35.47	72.71	100.72	−19.48	1.03	1.05	1.04	0.94	1.01
Zeliang	†	‡	33,825	61,492	60,399			81.79	−1.78		0.86	0.88	0.98	1.24
All Nagas§§	414,681	561,268	1,019,158	1,567,449	1,430,596	35.35	81.58	53.80	−8.73	1.07	1.06	0.99	1.04	1.16
Others‡‡			1,511	182,773	241,257									

Sources: Prepared by authors using GoI (1973b; 1990b; n.d.1; n.d.2; 2018c); Table 4.12.

Notes: (i) * Includes Angami, Chakhesang, Chakru/Chokri, Khezha and Pochury. (ii) ** The ratio of population of tribe to speakers of its eponymous language. In the case of Yimchunger language, the corresponding tribal population includes Yimchunger, Chirr, Makware and Tikhir. (iii) 'All Nagas' is the sum of the language speakers shown in the table. (iv) † In 1971, these languages had fewer than 10,000 speakers and were not reported separately. (v) § Not calculated as the census seems to have misclassified Sumi/Sema speakers in 2001 and 2011. (vi) §§ Estimates for 'All Nagas' are affected by the content error in the headcount of Sumi/Sema speakers in 2001 and 2011. (vii) ‡ Zeliang was included under the miscellaneous language category 'Naga', which had 15,571 (15,975) speakers in 1971 (1981). (viii) ‡‡ 'Others' are languages other than scheduled and non-scheduled languages reported in the Census. The figure corresponds to 'Total of Other languages' listed under non-scheduled languages for 1991 and 'Others' for 2001 (Code 123) and 2011 (Code 124).

Another content error in language data relates to the absence of Nagamese, an indigenous link language that is the most widely spoken (second) language of the state. It is not reported in the Census as it is viewed as a non-language, a non-Naga language or a language that endangers the existence of Naga languages. We have so far found only two entries for Nagamese in census reports: 'English is the state/official language and the common speech form used in the state is known as "Nagamese" composed mainly of Assamese, Bengali, Hindi and Nepali. This *peculiar* language is used as a common language next to English' (GoI 1997d: 104, emphasis added; see also GoI 1973b: 72). The only other trace of Nagamese in the census is perhaps found in tables on multilingualism, that is, data on Nagas using Assamese as the second or third language. As per the 2011 Census, 24.58 (11.09) per cent Nagas of Nagaland spoke Assamese as the second (third) language and the corresponding shares for the entire population of Nagaland are 24.92 (11.62) (GoI 2018d). These figures are lower bounds due to the content error in case of Sumi language discussed below and the active hostility among the Naga elite against the recognition/identification of Nagamese as a language of Nagaland. Shahoto (2001: 181) and Tsakise (2001: 166) suggest that those who are reported as speakers of Assamese as a non-mother tongue are, in fact, speakers of Nagamese that is seen as a variant of Assamese. Otherwise, it is difficult to explain the widespread use of Assamese as a second language along the Myanmar border. Nagamese is not the only tribal link language left out of the Census though.[91] Sadri, a major language of eastern India, is also not recorded in the Census (Pattanayak 2001: 49).

Sumi language suffers from the most egregious content error. Unlike the other content errors discussed above, the error in the headcount of Sumi speakers is not driven by communal politics. Sumi is one of the largest tribes of Nagaland. The population of the speakers of the tribe's eponymous language has decreased dramatically as per the 2001 and 2011 Censuses, even though the tribe continues to grow. Since Sumi is spoken by a politically influential community and is among the more developed Naga languages (Kumar 2015i), it is implausible that speakers of the language are abandoning their language and adopting some other language. Moreover, given the tight organic relationship between the tribes of Nagaland and their languages, it is inconceivable that Sumis are abandoning their language when much smaller tribes are asserting their linguistic identity. Indeed, the potential exodus from Sumi language is not reflected in the growth of population of any other language community in the state, and there has not been a corresponding increase in the population of Sumis living outside Nagaland either.

It is possible that the entries for speakers of Sumi language in Zunheboto, where Sumis constitute more than half of the population, were interchanged with that of speakers of 'Other languages'. This ad hoc explanation can at best account for the anomaly in the 2001 data. However, we found a similar error in the 2011 data for Dimapur where the headcount of Sumi speakers was hugely underreported. We will have to assume that the mistake that happened in 2001 with respect to language data for Zunheboto was not only repeated in 2011 but also happened in case of one more district. This is implausible as, unlike Zunheboto, Dimapur is a multi-tribal district and we will have to additionally assume that the mix-up happened only for Sumi speakers.

There is a more plausible explanation of the sharp contraction of the population of Sumi speakers. The Sema tribe changed the spelling of its name to 'Sumi'. The Nagaland government's annual publication *Basic Facts* switched to 'Sumi' in 1995, but the Census continues to use 'Sema'. The 'family-wise grouping ... of languages' followed by the Census includes Sema, but not Sumi (GoI 2018c). The speakers of Sumi must have begun to report their language as Sumi in 2001 and, more so, in 2011, while the Census still uses the old name 'Sema'. As a result, the Census reported a decreasing number of Sema speakers as fewer people identify with the old name of the language. The speakers of Sumi language were reported under 'Others'. Nearly 90 per cent of the Sumi tribe's population was reported in Dimapur and Zunheboto districts. These districts also accounted for about 90 per cent of speakers of 'Others' languages of Nagaland in 2001 as well as 2011. The content error in case of Sumi speakers (see note vi to Table 5.7) can account for 81.5 (94.5) per cent of the speakers of 'Others' languages in 2001 (2011).

Our suspicion that the drop in the population of Sema speakers can be explained by content errors is supported by the fact that older Sema/Sumi settlements in Tinsukia district of Assam (Singh 1998: 2531–2) have not reported a similar anomaly. However, the new Sumi settlements in the disputed area adjoining Dimapur that are populated by recent migrants from Zunheboto district of Nagaland have reported a sharp decrease in the population of Sumi speakers. In other words, while the early twentieth-century settlers continue to identify as Sema, the new migrants identify as Sumi just like their brethren within Nagaland.

We have solved one problem but created several others. First, the Census reports all languages that have more than 10,000 speakers. Why was Sumi with nearly 200,000 speakers not reported separately and, as we speculate, clubbed with 'Others'? Second, it is not clear how Angami, which is increasingly called Tenyidie, seems to have escaped a similar predicament. Third, while the community has started calling itself Sumi (for example, Sumi Hoho and Western Sumi Hoho, the apex bodies of Sumis of Zunheboto and Dimapur), the Census counted them as Sema tribe both in 2001 and 2011. As a result, the reported population of the Sema/Sumi tribe does not show the abnormality seen in the headcount of the speakers of the tribe's eponymous language. Fourth, the Census reports more than one name for several languages, for example, Afghani/Kabuli/Pashto, Arabic/Arbi, Chakru/Chokri, Coorgi/Kodagu, Kurukh/Oraon, Lushai/Mizo, Miri/Mishing and Nissi/Dafla (GoI 2018c). However, the Census has not included the new name in case of Sumi language. A decade later, the ORGI officials (interview, 21 February 2019, New Delhi) were unable to explain how such a serious content error remained undetected despite several layers of checks. The DCO Nagaland (interview, 24 June 2013, Kohima) told us that they 'check things at our end. [And, then] There are manual checks for [coding] mismatch. If the tribe is Angami, but code is SC, then we can easily correct this. Even if tribe is not mentioned, we can find it out from names. ORGI allows for correction in such cases. We do this when we receive data from the Data Centre at Gauhati. Then there is a check at the ORGI's level.' As a result, 'Scope of misclassification is virtually nil after these three layers of cross-checks'.

Notes

1. The Indian experience contrasts with that of Sub-Sahara, where '[u]nderestimation of the population in colonial censuses and overestimation in postcolonial censuses is a general problem' (Jerven 2013: 73, see also 57).
2. The communalisation of census began 'as early as 1911 after separate electorates [for Muslims and Hindus] were introduced in 1909' as communities began to exaggerate 'numbers to secure more seats' (I. Ahmed 1999: 124). By 1941, enumeration 'turned into a complete farce' (ibid.). The then census commissioner of India complained that his department found it difficult to 'defeat an excess of zeal,' while his counterpart in Hyderabad added that the 'whole population was census conscious' and 'trying to increase their numbers' (Husain 1945: iv). Dhulipala (2015: 142) points out that 'redrawing the national boundaries [through the partition of Punjab and Bengal]... along with the exchange of populations was ... already up for public discussion by early 1941'. Assam was another state that was partitioned in 1947. Assam's Muslim League government was 'accused of scheming to have the 1941 Census falsely show a higher Muslim population' through manipulation of categories used to report headcounts (Phanjoubam 2016: 179–80). Cross-cutting religious and linguistic identities shaped the partition of Assam (Dasgupta 2001). For the growing politicisation of census in the run-up to the 1941 Census, government's attempts to shield census operations from communal politics and complaints during and after enumeration, see Maheshwari (1996: 116–36, 139–41).
3. Other reasons for the decrease in the population of Punjab and West Bengal include one of the worst famines of the twentieth century in Bengal and widespread killings and displacement during the partition.
4. The language data of PEPSU and Himachal Pradesh for 1951 were not published to avoid exacerbating linguistic/religious conflict (Gill 2007: 244). It was even 'recommended that the mother tongue question not be canvassed' in these areas in the next census (Mitra 1994: 3209).

5. *Somersault* highlights the deliberate choices of actors both during the decades of abnormal growth as well as the decade of 'contraction'. This is discussed at length in Chapter 5.

6. There are several studies on statistics in colonial India (Barrier 1981; Cohn 1987; Guilmoto 1992; Peabody 2001; Bhagat 2003; Guha 2003; Chaudhury 2012; Walby and Haan 2012; Kalpagam 2014). This literature suggests that the politicisation of census is not a postcolonial development. Political-economic considerations have influenced government data since the earliest phase of colonialism.

7. For an overview of the methodology of population projections used in independent India, see Saluja (2017: 76–85).

8. If multiple projection estimates are available for a census year (Table 4.1), we have referred to only the most recent projection in the text.

9. Unless specified, population estimates have not been adjusted using PES.

10. Some of the most senior government officials (retired Naga IAS officer, interview, 9 April 2013, Kohima), who were directly involved with the 2001 Census in Nagaland, however, told us that they were 'surprised in 2011, when the previous census was shown to be faulty'. Likewise, a senior official in the ORGI (interview, 17 September 2013, New Delhi) told us that he learnt of the problem 'only after the 2011 Census', which is surprising given the numerous letters sent to the ORGI by the Nagaland government as well as civil society (see procedings of *CPO & Ors. vs. UoI & Ors.* 2006; see also Timeline 5.1).

11. In the 1990s, more than one chief minister noted that the population growth rate of the state was very high (Vamuzo 1991: 51; S. C. Jamir n.d.2: 21, 62) and even expressed concern over double-counting (Vamuzo n.d.: 37; 1991: 11–12). It is not clear if these concerns translated into measures to address the problem.

12. The 1961 Census of Nagaland was asynchronous: 'In Kohima district, the enumeration was extended upto 29th May, 1961 while in Mokokchung district, the enumeration was completed only on 28th June, 1961' (GoI 1966: 1). Only Tuensang district seems to have been enumerated as per the schedule. This could affect comparisons between the 1961 Census and later censuses.

13. Certain other parts of the country too reported very high growth in tribal population. As discussed in Chapter 7, political-economic and/or administrative factors explain the abnormalities in most cases.

14. A sharp decrease in Andhra Pradesh's population growth from 24.20 to 14.59 per cent was reported between 1991 and 2001, which seemed incommensurate with changes in the socio-economic correlates of fertility. Kumar and Sharma (2006: 4510) argue that this is indicative of 'a substantial omission of either households or member(s) within households (or both)'. We assessed Andhra Pradesh's census using Equation 4.2 and found D_{10+} (t-τ, t) to be positive during 1971–2001.

15. A few observations on the construction of age groups are in order. First, the class interval used for the terminal age groups, unlike the rest, is not five years. In 1971 and 1981, the Census reported those aged 70 years and above as one category. We have, therefore, considered 70+ as the last age group. Further, $\tau = 10$ and we have

information for the 0–9 year age group but not the 0–4 and 5–9 year age groups. So, the 10–14 and 15–19 year age groups have been clubbed together. Also note that we have omitted the 0–9 year age group from the analysis based on Equation 4.4 as the population $N_i(t)$ cannot be determined for this group.

16. Condran, Himes and Preston (1991) used the ratio to evaluate age and death registration data for Western countries.

17. The denominator of Equations 4.4 and 4.5 are overestimated because for each age group we had to use the aggregate figure for in-migrants from abroad as the data are not available by age groups. Moreover, we assume (a) zero deaths across age groups, (b) the number of out-migrants is zero as we could not find data on the age profile of out-migrants and (c) in 1971 and 1981, in-migrants in the age groups preceding and succeeding age group i were included in i as the age intervals do not coincide with our age groups (the set 'C').

18. We adjusted Equation 4.5 for age heaping or digit preference, that is, over-reporting in ages ending with digits zero and five, which is widespread in developing countries (Begum and Miranda 1979: 99 for Bangladesh; Schwartzberg 1981: 46 and Guilmoto and Irudaya Rajan 2013: 60 for India; Ahonsi 1988: 559 and Jerven 2013: 60 for Nigeria). The age data for Nagaland are also affected by considerations related to elections (GoI 2011c: 2; DCO Nagaland, interview, 19 Sepetmber 2012, Kohima), employment (Vamuzo n.d.: 58; GoN n.d.10: 33) and old-age benefits (S. C. Jamir 2003: 112–13). Age heaping and the manipulation of age vary with age, gender, place (rural/urban), education and social and cultural contexts. The curves adjusted for age heaping are similar to the unadjusted ones presented in Figure 4.4.

19. The 10–49 year age group accounted for 63.98 (67.84) per cent of Nagaland's population in 1991 (2001).

20. The drop around 30–4 years might be a consequence of the assumption of zero death rates for all the age groups or indicative of lesser over-reporting in this age group. We do not have an explanation, but it is not uncommon for a few age groups to behave differently than the rest (see, for instance, Robinson et al. 1993 for the USA).

21. For those aged 50 years and above, $R_{i,t+\tau}$ could be closer to one than shown in Figure 4.4 because the downward bias in $R_{i,t+\tau}$ is unlikely to be uniform across age groups as death rates are usually higher for the older age groups. Thus, the impact of assuming zero death rate will be progressively more pronounced for the older age groups.

22. The share of the 60+ year population in the state was 5.94 per cent in 1981, 5.27 per cent in 1991, 4.54 per cent in 2001 and 5.19 per cent in 2011.

23. For en masse manipulation of electoral rolls and mobilisation of voters in villages, see Wouters (2014; 2018).

24. Rural out-migrants constituted less than 3 per cent of the state's population until 2001. The figure was 0.68 per cent in 2011.

25. The census estimate of the number of speakers of Naga languages of Nagaland who live outside the state, excluding those indigenous to Assam and Manipur, is small, which drops further if we account for the content errors in data on Ao (note 90 of this chapter) and Sumi (excursus of this chapter) languages. Other sources too confirm the low rate of out-migration (Rio 2003: 117; 2007: 120; 2008: 55, 84, 94; 2010b: 59).

26. Elsewhere, ghost (*bhootiya*) villages refer to abandoned villages in the hills of Uttarakhand (Upadhyay 2018). We use 'ghost village' to refer to *new* villages with very small populations.

27. Several of our interviewees (for instance, retired Naga IAS officer, interview, 30 October 2015, Bengaluru) confirmed that very small villages were formed in the disputed area.

28. Note that a large part of increase in the number of villages in Nagaland is accounted for by Dimapur and Wokha (Table 3.3), where the size of villages is smaller than the average size of village in the state (Figure 3.2).

29. At a NBCC meet on Clean Elections Campaign, a senior Naga bureaucrat told the audience that 'Nagaland has the habit of establishing new villages every time. We do not delete names from the old villages' (19 September 2012, Hotel Japfu, Kohima). A census official (interview, 12 December 2018, Kohima) pointed out that even after they settle in a new village, the settlers continue to be counted in their 'parent' village that does not want to lose its votes and development funds, that is, the entire population of the new village is double-counted. Several bureaucrats in neighbouring Manipur too suggested that residents of new villages are often double-counted (interviews, October 2019, Imphal, Senapati and Chandel). We have not corrected the population figures for this type of double-counting because it is not clear for how many years the parent village continues to claim the people of the daughter/new villages as its own. If we assume that new villages are double-counted at least in the first census after their formation and that their mean population size is same as that of older villages, we can account for not more than 20 per cent of the anomaly in the rural population of 2001. Note that the population of new villages is generally smaller than the older ones (note 28 of this chapter). Also, shifting habitat due to *jhum* cultivation that might explain errors in the headcount of other hill states does not seem to be relevant in Nagaland, where the tribes do not move their settlements along with the *jhum* site.

30. During the 2011 Census, enumerators found families with bogus children as well as families that insisted on enumerating children studying elsewhere in their native places (DCO Nagaland, interview, 19 September 2012, Kohima; GoI n.d.10: 17). Manipulation of household size was also reported in the 1991 Census of Nigeria (Yin 2007), 2009 Census of Kenya (Jerven 2013: 73) and 2011 Census of Jammu and Kashmir (Guilmoto and Irudaya Rajan 2013: 63). Van Ham and Saul (2008) travelled through Nagaland in 2002 and reported headcounts of select villages. A comparison of their figures with the 2001 Census suggests that villages over-reported both the number of households as well as inhabitants. We found similar abnormalities in the aftermath of the 2011 Census (note 45 of Chapter 5).

31. We have assumed that the 2011 Census population estimates are reliable. According to the DCO Nagaland (interview, 24 June 2013, Kohima), the ORGI found that the Socio-Economic and Caste Census (SECC) population estimate compared favourably with the 2011 Census and that there was more than 90 per cent 'person-to-person match' between the two sources. However, the 2011 Census too suffers from both content and coverage errors. A few observations are in order in this regard. First, even after adjustments to the 2001 population (Tables 4.2A–B and 4.4A–B) Nagaland's growth rate is the highest among states in 2011. Second, as of 31 December 2018, only 1,260,853 persons had been assigned an Aadhaar number (unique identity number) in Nagaland compared to its population of 1,978,502 as per the 2011 Census. The low enrolment could be an indication of presence of ghost entries in the 2011 Census. Nagaland is among the three states with less than .60 per cent enrolment for Aadhaar (GoI n.d.17). In Assam and Meghalaya, the very low rates of enrolment can be attributed to internal politics. Third, between 1971 and 2011, the share of Nagaland in the country's population grew faster than other states despite the contraction of its population during 2001–11 (Chapter 7). Fourth, Changki (7,718 – population as per the 2001 Census/2,486 – as per the 2011 Census), Chuchuyimlang (7,846/5,674) and Longsa (4,757/3,206) villages in Mokokchung and Kitami village (1,490/430) in Zunheboto have approached the court questioning the reliability of the 2011 Census (DCO, interview, 25 June 2013, Kohima; census official, interview, 11 December 2018, Kohima). Fifth, observers within the state continue to doubt the 2011 figure and suggest that the actual population could be much lower than the census estimate. A former finance minister of Nagaland, for instance, used church statistics to question the census. He argued that 'the Nagaland Baptist Church Council (NBCC) has around three lakh [0.3 million] baptised members and six lakh [0.6 million] associate members; Catholics and people of other communities have over 50,000 baptised members with nearly 1,00,000 associate members each. Hindus, Muslims and others may account for about two lakh [0.2 million], which takes the population to around 14 lakh (1.4 million)' (*Times of India* 2012b, see also Naga 2015). Sixth, the discrepancy in case of the 2011 Census population estimate, as per Equation 4.2, is about 67,000. Last but not the least, the 2011 Census suffers from several content errors some of which are discussed in the excursus at the end of this chapter.

32. Other sources seem to corroborate the estimates of overcount based on the identification of ghost population. Surveys conducted by Nagaland's Health and Family Welfare Department (2004) and Rural Development Department (year not stated, but before 2007) suggest that the census overestimated the overall and rural population (households) at least by 296,070 (48,776) and 295,432 (48,671), respectively (CPO 2007). The latter estimates are based on only tax-paying rural households.

33. The difference between estimates of discrepancy using Equations 4.2 and 4.6 is possibly explained by the fact that the former does not fully eliminate rural overcount as discussed in the notes to Table 4.2A. As a result, despite growing

migration to urban areas, the share of urban population remains stagnant even as per the adjusted population shares in Table 4.2A.

34. It seems paramilitary forces also collect basic demographic data independent of the civilian administration, but the data are not publicly available. The method of data collection is not clear, but it is certainly not based on direct survey/enumeration. A retired census official (interview, 15 September 2012, Delhi) told us that two years before the 2011 Census, a paramilitary official informed him that the population of Longleng district was about 50,000. The population was 50,484 as per the 2011 Census.

35. We use the NFHS and the SRS only for checking if the Census broadly agrees with other sources. Rather than focusing on point estimates, we compare trends revealed by different sources. We do not use SRS or NFHS figures (Table 4.3) to estimate discrepancy in Nagaland's population.

36. The difference in fertility estimates from the NFHS–1 and the SRS has been attributed to, among other things, the possible under-registration of births in the SRS (Narasimhan et al. 1997: 3) and the backward displacement of the most recent births by older respondents in the NFHS (Mari Bhat 1995: 257).

37. NGR and 'Population growth' are not strictly comparable because the latter also includes migration. However, the contribution of migration to Nagaland's population growth is very small (Table 4.10).

38. After the advent of the Sarva Shiksha Abhiyan in 2001, parents have an incentive to enrol children in more than one school to access multiple scholarships and other benefits (former minister, interview, 26 October 2014, Dimapur). Likewise, teachers of government schools have an incentive to over-report enrolment to prevent closure/relocation of their schools because of the exodus of students to private schools. However, both these factors became important after 2001.

39. With a literacy rate of 80.11 per cent in 2011, Nagaland ranked ninth among 28 states (GoI 2011b).

40. The ratio of GSE to the census population (0–14 years) is *not* the same as the *Gross Enrolment Ratio* – the ratio of the 6–14 years enrolled in school to the overall population of this age group.

41. Most comparisons in this section are restricted to 1974–2011 as we do not have reliable population projections for the post-2011 period and almost a third of Nagaland was governed under a non-electoral legislative arrangement before 1974.

42. The two sex ratios diferred by more than 6 per cent only in the 1974 Assembly and the 1977 and 1998 Parliamentary Elections. In 1974, elections were held in the entire state for the first time. The 1977 parliamentary electoral roll seems to have been faulty. The 1998 Election was boycotted by most parties that might explain an incomplete revision of electoral rolls and a less than complete enrolment of new electors.

43. Electoral rolls are prepared for each assembly constituency separately. Except in the erstwhile Jammu and Kashmir, where voter eligibility differed between

parliamentary and assembly elections, the electoral roll of a parliamentary constituency aggregates the rolls of its constituent assembly constituencies (ECI 2006). Hence, assembly and parliamentary electorates can be compared.

44. A civil society leader suggested that the names of illegal immigrants were deleted from electoral rolls in the 1980s (interview, 21 June 2013, Dimapur).

45. The effect of reduction in age may not reflect immediately in electorate size because it is a voter's *duty* to find out whether his/her name has been registered (ECI n.d.). Moreover, in places where population is sparsely distributed over far-flung areas, the spread of information (about the revision of electoral rolls after the lowering of voting age) may take time and electoral officers may not be easily accessible. However, the use of the updated electoral roll in only one of the two elections held on the same day needs an explanation. Three points should be noted in this regard. First, the difference between the electorates of the 1987 and 1989 Assembly Elections was merely 463, which suggests that obsolete rolls might have been used in the 1989 Election. Second, the assembly electorate caught up with the parliamentary electorate in the next election (1993). Third, in 1989, assembly and parliamentary elections were held in eight states, including Nagaland. The size of the electorate was same in both the elections in Sikkim. The size was larger in parliamentary elections in Andhra Pradesh, Goa, Mizoram, Nagaland, Tamil Nadu and Uttar Pradesh, whereas it was smaller in parliamentary elections in Karnataka. The difference was less than 1 per cent in all but three cases (Tamil Nadu – 12 per cent, Mizoram – 20 per cent and Nagaland – 40 per cent). To rule out the possibility that the large discrepancy in case of Nagaland results from typographical errors in election reports, we calculated the total electorate of the state for 1989 by adding up constituency-level electorate data. The latter was found to be equal to the figure for the entire state reported in the highlights section of the relevant election report. We discussed this with several government officials, politicians and civil society leaders in Nagaland, but none of them was even aware of this discrepancy.

46. Electorate also includes service voters, that is, certain classes of government servants posted outside their constituency, who will be counted in their current locations during a census. Service voters are a very small part of the electorate though.

47. Recall that the analysis of age data revealed that anomalies in the population share of the 0–9 year age group peaked in 2001.

48. The Tikhir Baptist Church is not a member of the NBCC, which does not admit congregations of unrecognised tribes as it does not want to get involved in intra-community conflicts (Rev. Anjo Keikung, General Secretary of NBCC, interview, 24 June 2013, Kohima). Tikhir is a very small community though, and its exclusion will not affect our conclusions.

49. For shortcomings a–c, Rev. Anjo Keikung (interviews, 21 November 2012 and 24 June 2013, Kohima). For the rest, NBCC (2001–11).

50. In 2001, the share of the 18+ year age group in India's population was about 59 per cent (GoI n.d.11).

51. Ahead of the 2011 Census, a consultative meeting called by the Nagaland government suggested, 'The church registers may also be used for reference whenever felt necessary by the enumerators' (GoN 2009a). After the 2011 Census, politicians (*Times of India* 2012b) and civil society leaders (Naga 2015) used Church statistics to question census results.

52. According to NBCC (2002: 10) church membership registered a sharp increase during 1990–2000 (56.64 per cent [this should be 57.09 per cent, Table 4.8]) compared to 1980–90 (24.16 per cent). It claims that the former 'indicates some conversion growth'. However, according to the Census, the reported share of Christians in Nagaland's population grew from 80.21 per cent in 1981 to 87.47 in 1991 and 89.97 in 2001 (Table 4.11). So, the Christian share changed sharply during 1981–91 when there were pockets of non-Christian population and not between 1991 and 2001 as suggested in NBCC (2002). The discrepancy between the Census and the NBCC estimates could possibly be explained if there was an increase in the tendency to formally accept baptism among younger cohorts leading to a faster growth of registered members than the growth of those who identify as Christians irrespective of baptism. This is unlikely though. There is a high correlation between marriage and baptism (Rev. Vikuo Rhi, interview, 21 November 2012, Kohima). Since the age of marriage has increased over the years, the age of baptism is also likely to have increased. Further, the growth of Christians among Nagas during 1990–2000 cannot be explained by conversion. The Naga affiliates of the NBCC do not admit non-Nagas into their congregations and the non-Christian Naga community is too small to account for any sizeable change in the Christian Naga population. Moreover, in the 2001 Census, the traditional Naga religions reported a positive growth after many decades of massive contraction (Table 4.11), which again rules out conversion driven growth of the Christian Naga population.

53. Nagaland is one of the most HIV-/AIDS-affected states in India. Agrawal and Kumar (2012a) reject the HIV/AIDS-based explanation of the contraction of Nagaland's population.

54. Radhabinod Koijam, former chief minister of Manipur, suggested that Nagaland's population must have been about 1.6 million in 2001 (Koijam 2001). Nagaland's Chief Minister Neiphiu Rio suggested that the population must have been about 1.4 million in 2001 (Hazarika 2005). If the latter is correct, the growth rate must have been 17 per cent in 2001 and 43 per cent in 2011 and we will have to explain how contrary to changes in socio-economic indicators Nagaland registered a sharp drop in growth rate between 1991 and 2001 and then a substantial increase in the next decade. Rio (interview, 27 May 2015, New Delhi) later noted that his earlier estimate might not be entirely correct. Agrawal and Kumar (2019b) show that the ORGI's ad hoc corrections to the populations of three subdivisions of Senapati district of Manipur create more problems than they solve.

55. Political disturbance does not necessarily result in the cancelation of census. The 1971 Census that was conducted *ahead* of schedule in West Bengal due to 'disturbed

law and order conditions' (GoI 1975a: 1) and the 1961 Census that was extended in Kohima and Mokokchung (GoI 1966: 1) are cases in point.

56. The increase in sex ratio due to underreporting of adult males fearing conscription is a plausible outcome in insurgency-affected areas (see Okolo 1999: 322 for Nigeria). The sex ratio might also increase due to the non-enumeration of men living in insurgent camps and a higher mortality of men in conflict. Nagaland's reported sex ratio has been increasing since 1981, but the discrepancy-adjusted sex ratio does not follow a clear trend. (Table 4.2B).

57. *General Population Tables* (*GPT*) of the 1961 Census specifically note that 'the population figures include a large number of Police and Assam Rifles personnel deployed in Nagaland' (GoI 1966: 2) as this affected both the overall headcount as well as the sex ratio. Here, it bears noting that the security forces were deployed on a large-scale in the Naga Hills including along the Indo-Myanmar border for the first time in the 1950s and after that there have been adjustments in the deployment. In other words, the deployment of armed forces would have had a one-time level effect on the population growth reported in the 1961 Census.

58. As per the 1991 (2001) Census, there were only 1,445 (1,143) Tangkhul speakers in Nagaland.

59. SATP (n.d.24), CDPS (n.d.), Gokhale (1961: 39), Stracey (1968: 82, 130), Alemchiba (1970: 184), Gundevia (1975: 69, 77, 203), Horam (1988: 81), Chaube (2012: 157), Misra (2012: 302) and Hazarika (2018: 77). Several sources suggest that the insurgents' ranks swelled after the 1997 ceasefire (Wouters 2018: 87, 107, see also Stracey 1968: 310 for a similar observation on the 1964 ceasefire).

60. Between 1991 and 2001, Nagaland's reported population grew by 780,490 (Tables 4.2A–B). Assuming 10,000 insurgents and an equal number of camp followers, which is highly unrealistic, not more than 20,000 people would have come overground. This amounts 2.56 per cent of the growth in the reported population.

61. The average population of Nagaland corrected for discrepancies was about 1.25 million in the 1990s (Tables 4.2A–B). The deaths due to insurgency were less than 360 persons per year including armed forces personel (SATP n.d.1). So, it can be safely assumed that the insurgency related death rate was less than 0.29 per 1,000 persons per year or less than 0.29 per cent per decade. The indirect impact of insurgency on death rate – through, say, enhanced morbidity – is difficult to measure. To account for the possible undercounting of deaths and the aforesaid indirect effect, we assume an insurgency-related death rate of 1 per 1,000 persons per year, that is, 1 per cent per decade. The direct as well as indirect effects of the 1997 ceasefire operated only during the very end of the 1991–2001 decade. (In fact, the ceasefires acquired stability nearly half a decade later.) So, the ceasefire would have at most added 0.4 per cent to the decadal growth rate, which accounts for 0.7 per cent of the population growth between 1991 and 2001.

62. This conclusion holds, even if we assume that governments underreport civilian and security personnel casualties and over-report insurgent casualties. The latter

may be a consequence of misclassification of some civilian deaths due to, say, fake encounters or collateral damage. This will not affect the overall headcount of the insurgency-related deaths.

63. The late 1990s and early 2000s were the heydays of cross-border Naga unity. The sentiment soured in the late 2000s though and the Nagaland Tribes Council (NTC), a Nagaland-centric civil society organisation, was launched after the 2013 Assembly Elections ostensibly in response to the extension of affirmative action benefits to Rongmeis, a small Manipuri-origin Naga tribe settled in Dimapur, Peren and, to a lesser extent, Kohima (Kumar 2014a; 2015h).

64. Attane and Courbage (2000: 268, 275) suggest that higher fertility among the non-Sinicised minorities could also be a defence against the demographic invasion by Han settlers. See also Janus (2013) who found a positive correlation between ethnic diversity and fertility, in a setting with weak institutions, for a cross section of countries and Morland (2018: 36–7) who suggests that communities deploy 'hard demographic engineering' strategies such as higher fertility in ethnically diverse countries.

65. During 1951–61, Nagaland's population grew by 73.35 per cent (GoI 2011b: 165), 79.29 per cent (authors' calculations using Eaton 1984: 18) and 14.07 per cent (Gogoi 1990: 91, Sharma and Kar 1997: 77). The adjusted growth rate (after excluding Tuensang in both the terminal years) was only 18.10 per cent.

66. The 1961 *GPT* admitted that 'few if any of the section of the population hostile to the Government and who remained "Underground" (in the jungles) could be enumerated' (GoI 1966: 2; see also Naga IAS officer, interview, 22 November 2012, Kohima for recent decades). It further noted, 'Even otherwise there remained the general difficulty of getting accurate answers ... because of the unpopular system of Poll Tax ... imposed in the early days by the British Administration' (ibid.). However, in the later decades the government began to complain of over-enumeration (Vamuzo n.d.: 37; 1991: 11–12) as the state came to be seen as a resource to be exploited sans moral qualms (Wouters 2018).

67. Until recently, the reach of the NSSs were restricted to 5 kilometres of bus routes in rural Nagaland, while several other surveys completely ignored Nagaland. NSSO suveys could not be conducted in the Kashmir Valley in the 1990s.

68. It can perhaps be argued that the ceasefires between the government and insurgents were not stable during the 2001 Census and, therefore, their impact would be discernible only in the 2011 Census.

69. A former minister (interview, 26 October 2014, Dimapur) from a district that could not inflate as much as other districts alleged that census officials seem to have been bribed in Phek and Longleng. Longleng reported a very high growth rate in 2001, whereas Phek's growth rate was the lowest among the then districts of Nagaland.

70. Yimchungers of Tuensang (included Kiphire in 2001) also seem to have supported the JAC.

71. The presence of 'outsiders' in the census department affected the spellings of place names though. The indigenisation of the staff is reflected in an orthographic shift in Nagaland's census records. (This shift was also aided by the standardisation of Naga languages.) However, several Sumi villages of Dimapur are incorrectly spelled in the 2011 Census. Likewise, the names of a few Naga languages continue to be misspelled in the Census.

72. In its response to the JAC, the CPO pointed out that nearly 89 per cent of all the teachers (who serve as enumerators during census) appointed until 1999 were Nagas (*CPO & Ors. vs. UoI & Ors.* 2006). It is also noteworthy that the consultative meeting called ahead of the 2011 Census, which was attended by representatives of all the communities including those represented by the JAC, admitted that local enumerators condoned manipulation (GoN 2009a). The tribes whose population contracted in 2011 (despite the enumerators being entirely local) complained that this time officials seem to have been committed to deflate the headcount (retired Naga IAS officer, interview, 16 November 2013, Dimapur). In fact, most interviewees told us that their community's population was underreported as the officials were allegedly under strict orders to bring down population. The contraction of population hurt in 2013, when electoral rolls were revised to reflect the decline in population. People complained that officials responsible for updating electoral rolls 'forcibly removed [eligible voters] to suit the census figure' (*ME* 2013e).

73. The Narasimha Rao government that introduced economic reforms was sworn in after the completion of the 1991 Census.

74. This estimate of out-migration corresponds to the reference period of 0–9 years for each census, that is, it counts only those who migrated in the intercensal period. It might double count those who have out-migrated more than once during 1971–2001, say, people who out-migrated in the 1970s and returned in the 1980s before migrating out of the state again in the 1990s. In other words, the magnitude of out-migration during 1971–2001 must have been smaller than the figure reported above (see also note 25 of this chapter).

75. Administrative data on inner line permits (ILPs) throw light on immigration. According to Nagaland's home minister, 'a total of 75,807 ILPs [Inner Line Permits] were issued in 2008–09.... In 2007–08, the number of permits issued was 76,268 ...' (Amarjeet Singh 2009: 37). As per the latest figures, 66,894 inner line permits were issued between January 2015 and September 2018 (*ME* 2018ac). These figures include tourists, businessmen and others who visit for a short duration and also those who enter the state more than once but have to apply for a fresh permit each time. It bears noting that the ILP database is not properly maintained. In 2013, we could access detailed data only for 2007–9 and 2012 and found that the reporting was uneven across districts as well as months.

76. Civil society organisations, however, argued that the population share of in-migrants increased over time and exceeded 25 per cent in 2001 (CPO et al. 2004: 3), that is, they effectively attributed the entire discrepancy to immigration.

77. These figures are based on the data on language as data on tribes are available only for the Naga tribes of Assam as a whole and not for individual Naga tribes. During 1991–2001, the population of all Naga tribes in Assam (based on the data on tribes) increased from 15,354 to 21,706 (GoI n.d.1; n.d.2). We will comment upon the discrepancy between Assam's language and tribe data in Chapter 7.

78. A section of Rongmei Nagas of Manipur's Imphal Valley relocated towards Naga dominated hill districts of Manipur and adjoining Nagaland after the June 2001 uprising in the valley against 'Greater Nagaland'. They returned after the tensions subsided, though, and, in any case, their movement post-dates the 2001 Census.

79. In the mid-1990s, the Naga–Kuki conflict in the hill districts of Manipur sent Kukis away from Naga-dominated areas including Nagaland (civil society leader, interview, 14 November 2013, 25 June 2015, Dimapur; civil society leader, interview, 29 October 2014, Athibung; Oinam 2003; Haokip 2008; KMHR 2009).

80. The electorate of Nagaland grew by about 50 per cent between 1977 and 1982 (Table 4.6) and the two fastest growing constituencies belonged to Dimapur. However, it bears noting that two of the Dimapur's constituencies grew at rates less than the mean (47.83 per cent) as well as median (40.44 per cent) rates of growth of constituencies in the state. Additionally, the electorates of all the constituencies of Zunheboto district, the place of origin of Sumi settlers in Dimapur and the adjoining disputed area, grew at rates much below the mean rate of growth in the state. In fact, Aghunato constituency contracted during this period. So, the abnormal growth in some of the constituencies of Dimapur cannot be attributed solely to alleged illegal immigration as Sumis of Zunheboto have also migrated in large numbers to Dimapur.

81. A similarly apprehensive editorial seems to have been published in *Nagaland Post* in 2002 (Amarjeet Singh 2009: 23–4). The Naga Students' Federation too raised this issue in 2002 (Shimray 2007: 35). For an examination of the role of media in a tragic outburst of the anti-Bangladeshi sentiment, see Kumar (2015c).

82. The Muslim population reported in the Census includes Muslims among Naga tribes. In 2001 (2011), the Census reported 2,034 (5,253) Naga Muslims including 189 (1,346) among Konyaks. One of our Konyak interviewees recalled having come across just one Konyak Muslim a few decades ago and, even, he seems to have relapsed after some time (interview, 22 June 2013, Dimapur). Interestingly, there were only 639 Muslims among Sumis as per the 2011 Census, and their sex ratio was balanced (GoI 2018a), even though they had much greater exposure to Islam than Konyaks. The contribution of Muslims to Nagaland's population growth will decrease if we account for the content errors in the religion data.

83. Many of our interviewees, including a few Sumis, offered similar observations on the issue of indigenisation of Bengali-speaking Muslims. However, after an initial outburst of concern vis-à-vis Sumis, the public debate on the issue assumed a more cautious approach. The naming and shaming of Sumis for letting outsiders marry their girls threatened to disturb the delicate web of inter-tribal relations in the state,

particularly, because Sumis dominate Dimapur. A leading civil society organisation that raised the issue forcefully had to apologise to the Sumi community (*Nagaland Post* 2012b). Most subsequent commentary in Nagaland avoids naming a specific tribe. The focus now is more broadly on non-indigenous people including Nagas from other states trying to settle in Nagaland by marrying 'Naga/indigenous women' (*ME* 2018ad). Other researchers too note the disapproval of mixed marriages in Nagaland (Kikon 2019). Further, fieldwork is needed to locate the alleged Sumias in Nagaland's sociocultural mosaic.

84. See Ghosh (1999); CPO et al. (2004: 3); *Telegraph* (2004); Amarjeet Singh (2009); civil society leader, interview, 24 November 2012; former finance minister, interview, 11 April 2013, Dimapur; civil society leader, interview, 21 June 2013, Dimapur; retired Naga IAS officer, interview, 16 November 2013, Dimapur; Charles Chasie, email communication, 25 November 2013; Member of Parliament Neiphiu Rio, interview, 27 May 2015, New Delhi.

85. Such exaggerated estimates of alleged Bangladeshi Muslim immigrants are not unheard of in the region. For an overview of similar claims in Assam see Hazarika (2018: 197–200).

86. The literature on the politicisation of fertility and population research in India (Jones 1981; Panandiker and Umashankar 1994; Basu 1997; Bhagat 2001; Gill 2007) suggests that 'the use of demographic *arguments* in favour of communalism [exclusive communitarian projects/goals] can lead to exactly the kind of political and social instability that demographic *events* themselves can' (Basu 1997: 10, emphasis in original).

87. Lwin (2003) puts the number of Myanmarese immigrants in India at more than 100,000 but does not specify their distribution across the North-East.

88. In the late 1980s, conflict peaked in Myanmar's Naga areas because of the military's crackdown as well as the internecine fighting among insurgents.

89. Interviews (24 November 2012; 9 June 2014; 13 June 2014 – location and identity of interviewees omitted).

90. We have also noted a possible content error in the estimate of the population of Ao speakers in India. As per the 2011 Census, there were 19,316 speakers of Ao language (including 19,278 speakers of Mongsen dialect of Ao language) in Tripura (including 12,823 in South Tripura) compared to only 4 as per the 2001 Census. However, we will not explore this case further here as it is not directly related to Nagaland's headcount.

91. Non-governmental sources too ignore Nagamese. The language is cursorily covered in the People's Linguistic Survey of India (PLSI 2016: 6–8), while a recent multilingual glossary published locally completely ignores it (KET 2015).

5

Winning Censuses[*]

Introduction

Electoral contests are usually viewed in terms of strategies for winning a plurality or majority of votes. These contests can also be waged at the stages of the choice of electoral system and delimitation of constituencies. The latter involves the choice of rules governing delimitation and the demarcation of constituencies under the rules, both of which are susceptible to political interference. The manipulation of demographic data with the objective of influencing delimitation is another possibility.[1]

A stable constitution and an independent judiciary have meant that the basic structure of India's electoral system is very difficult to change. As a result, political manoeuvring has been restricted to delimitation and electoral contests. Interstate delimitation was frozen in the 1970s and will remain so until the first census taken after 2026.[2] The extended suspension of the interstate delimitation, which was aimed at avoiding interstate conflicts, has shifted the locus of redistributive conflicts to sub-state levels of aggregation and opened up space for intercommunity and inter-district contests. The 2002 delimitation that was supposed to redistribute parliamentary and assembly constituencies *within* states and also redistribute seats between scheduled and non-scheduled communities on the basis of the 2001 Census faced strong opposition in the country's ethno-geographic periphery dominated by the Scheduled Tribes (STs) and religious minorities (Maps 1.2 and 7.4).[3] In Assam, Arunachal Pradesh, Jammu and Kashmir, Jharkhand, Manipur and Nagaland, politically influential communities/regions forced the postponement of the delimitation until after the first census taken after 2026.[4] In Chhattisgarh, Meghalaya, Sikkim and Uttarakhand, the delimitation criteria had to be relaxed in favour of the indigenous communities. In all these cases, concessions were achieved through constitutional amendments,

---

[*] The title of this chapter is adapted from Horowitz (2000: 194).

amendments to delimitation and other relevant legislation or through a departure from the prescribed guidelines at the time of demarcation of constituencies.[5] It is also noteworthy that the government delayed the release of Post-Enumeration Survey (PES) for the 2001 Census 'to avoid needless political controversies' while delimitation was in progress (Bose 2008: 16). In other words, it feared that dissatisfied communities/administrative units could demand adjustments based on the errors identified by the PES.[6] Indeed, some of the aggrieved communities demanded that the Delimitation Commission should adjust census population estimates using the PES data (CPO et al. 2003).

In Nagaland (and parts of Manipur), the impending delimitation triggered the manipulation of census. In Chapter 4, we showed that the Census overestimated Nagaland's population by as much as 36 per cent in 2001 and also that conventional explanations cannot account for the overcount. In this chapter, we will argue that just as 'cartographic carelessness' cannot explain Nagaland's conflicting maps, its erroneous headcounts cannot be attributed to unintended errors, statistical carelessness or, as Guilmoto and Irudaya Rajan (2013: 69) put it, 'statistical incomprehension'. We will not deal with the possibility of unintended/accidental manipulation/misreporting resulting from a lack of familiarity of the enumerator and/or enumerated with the process of enumeration. We will instead discuss deliberate manipulation[7] and, as Guilmoto and Irudaya Rajan (2013: 69) point out in the context of Jammu and Kashmir, argue that 'manipulation is often more a political statement' as government statistics are sites of 'volatile confrontation between state-sponsored categories and etic concepts, between enumerators equipped with tools that are presumed all-terrain and context-free, and myriads of agents actively promoting their local social and political agenda through this encounter'.

We can classify deliberate manipulation of census into four broad types (Figure 5.1): First, *prospective* manipulation to secure a favourable policy change, for example, the creation of a new administrative unit. In this case, if the community does not manipulate headcount, it will not lose anything vis-à-vis the status quo. Second, *pre-emptive* manipulation to check unfavourable policy changes in the future. This applies to manipulation with an eye to prevent the loss of, say, electoral constituencies through delimitation. Third, *defensive* manipulation to ensure that the latest census figures do not contradict manipulated figures reported in the last census or manipulated figures reported to access welfare schemes during the intercensal period. Fourth, *altruistic* manipulation with an eye on the distant future, say, the next generation. We will deal with only the first three as we did not come across intergenerational justifications for the manipulation of census in Nagaland. We will also not discuss the possibility of the state government deliberately condoning overcount, let alone directly inflating numbers, in order to, say, attract more central funds because the current population does not affect federal redistribution.[8]

In this chapter, we will explore the political-economic context of Nagaland's demographic somersault – decades of unusually high population growth followed by a sudden 'contraction' (Figures 4.1A–B). Unlike the bulk of the literature on India's census statistics that is focused on content errors driven by the politicisation of categories of enumeration, administrative fiat or pursuit of political-economic interests (Brass 1974; Schwartzberg 1981: 51; Sharad Kulkarni 1991; Bhagat 2001; 2003; Gill 2007; Verma 2013), this chapter explores political-economic determinants of coverage errors (overcounting of population). Conventional wisdom suggests that under-enumeration is more likely than over-enumeration (GoI 1953b: 1; see also note 54 of Chapter 1). This continues to inform most government and academic discussions of coverage errors in census, but following the discussion in Chapter 4 we will examine over-enumeration in Nagaland.

This chapter contributes to the literature on the political economy and sociology of statistics (Alonso and Starr 1987; Horowitz 2000; Wade 2012; Jerven 2013; Krätke and Byiers 2014; Diaz-Bone and Didier 2016; Heine and Oltmanns 2016; Taylor 2016), quality of demographic statistics (Bose, Gupta and Raychaudhuri 1977; Barrier 1981) and electoral/ethnic politics in tribal-majority states such as Nagaland (Agrawal and Kumar 2012c; 2018; Wouters 2014; 2018). This literature suggests that the deep and multifaceted relationship between statistics and politics is a defining feature of modern states and that government statistics are sites of political contestation.

Ethnic competition is often triggered or enhanced when demographic composition changes, the distribution of political power is under stress and/

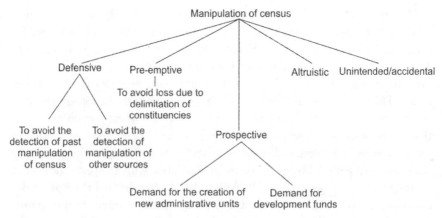

Figure 5.1   Reasons for the manipulation of census
Source: Authors.

or the availability of resources is affected due to newcomers. The fecundity of competing groups and the consequent demographic threat can be a defining feature of ethnic conflict. Janus (2013: 493–4) argues that fertility might be a strategic choice because (a) higher fertility increases voting power and gains from access to political offices, (b) 'if ethnic groups allocate society's resources via conflict or bargaining in the shadow of conflict, then fertility might increase their combat strength' and (c) 'larger groups can more easily impose their language or culture'.[9] In a cross-sectional study of more than 100 countries, he finds that countries with high ethnic diversity and weak institutions reported higher fertility rates.

The alleged threat posed by immigrants looms large over popular imagination in Nagaland, but until 2001 the reported population share of immigrants was very small and declining (Table 4.10). Moreover, immigrants cannot explain exclusively intra/inter-tribal conflicts in the hills of Nagaland. In Chapter 4, we also showed that the reported birth rates cannot support Nagaland's reported population growth rates even under the assumption of zero death rate among those aged 10 years or more. Indeed, the public debate in Nagaland is driven by the politicisation of headcounts and population shares rather than the politicisation of relative fertility rates.[10]

A political economy approach suggests that 'data producers and users have specific personal interests with regard to the scope and design of statistical infrastructure.... As a result, individual rationality and collective rationality may fall apart and create welfare losses for society' (Heine and Oltmanns 2016: 201–2; see also Taylor 2016: 12–14). The focus here is mostly on the supply side, for example, the moral hazard of government officials, the interests of politicians and so on. Government officials often try to maintain consistency between data collected at different times and also between different types of data they collect (GoI n.d.16: 9.2.10; Ahonsi 1988: 557).[11] Otherwise, the manipulation of demographic data by enumerators/officials (Brass 1974: 77–8; Gill 2007; Prabhakara 2012: 32; Verma 2013) mostly leads to content errors rather than coverage errors. While enumerators can, possibly, systematically overcount/ undercount population resulting in coverage errors, this can be only through administrative fiat if the errors are as pervasive and substantial as they were in Nagaland. However, we do not have any evidence that could support such a charge against the administration, even though individual officers may have abetted manipulation. In fact, A. Jamir (2002), Neiphiu Rio (Hazarika 2005) and most of the serving and retired government officials we interviewed suggested that the government and the bureaucracy can be helpless in the face of determined mass violation of law (see also Wouters 2018; Kumar 2019).[12]

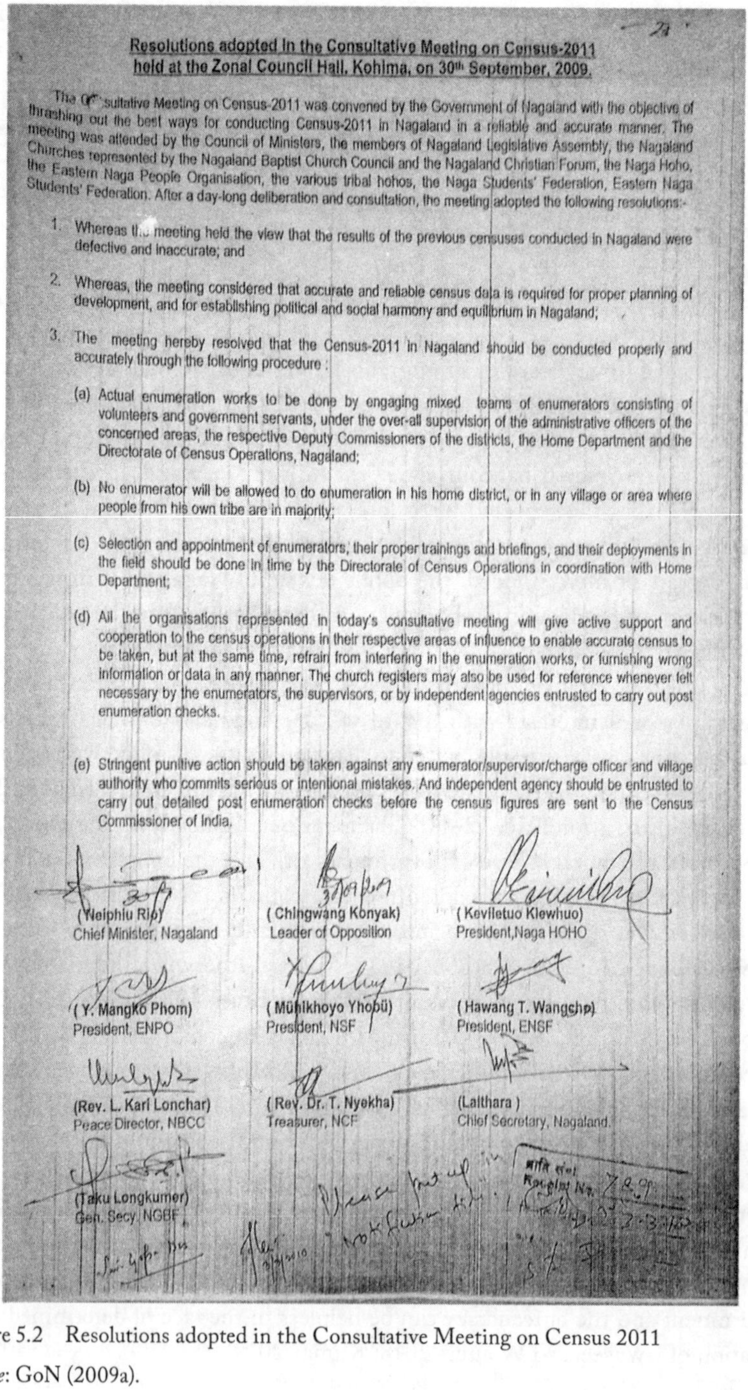

Resolutions adopted in the Consultative Meeting on Census-2011 held at the Zonal Council Hall, Kohima, on 30th September, 2009.

The Consultative Meeting on Census-2011 was convened by the Government of Nagaland with the objective of thrashing out the best ways for conducting Census-2011 in Nagaland in a reliable and accurate manner. The meeting was attended by the Council of Ministers, the members of Nagaland Legislative Assembly, the Nagaland Churches represented by the Nagaland Baptist Church Council and the Nagaland Christian Forum, the Naga Hoho, the Eastern Naga People Organisation, the various tribal hohos, the Naga Students' Federation, Eastern Naga Students' Federation. After a day-long deliberation and consultation, the meeting adopted the following resolutions:-

1. Whereas the meeting held the view that the results of the previous censuses conducted in Nagaland were defective and inaccurate; and

2. Whereas, the meeting considered that accurate and reliable census data is required for proper planning of development, and for establishing political and social harmony and equilibrium in Nagaland;

3. The meeting hereby resolved that the Census-2011 in Nagaland should be conducted properly and accurately through the following procedure :

    (a) Actual enumeration works to be done by engaging mixed teams of enumerators consisting of volunteers and government servants, under the over-all supervision of the administrative officers of the concerned areas, the respective Deputy Commissioners of the districts, the Home Department and the Directorate of Census Operations, Nagaland;

    (b) No enumerator will be allowed to do enumeration in his home district, or in any village or area where people from his own tribe are in majority;

    (c) Selection and appointment of enumerators; their proper trainings and briefings, and their deployments in the field should be done in time by the Directorate of Census Operations in coordination with Home Department;

    (d) All the organisations represented in today's consultative meeting will give active support and cooperation to the census operations in their respective areas of influence to enable accurate census to be taken, but at the same time, refrain from interfering in the enumeration works, or furnishing wrong information or data in any manner. The church registers may also be used for reference whenever felt necessary by the enumerators, the supervisors, or by independent agencies entrusted to carry out post enumeration checks.

    (e) Stringent punitive action should be taken against any enumerator/supervisor/charge officer and village authority who commits serious or intentional mistakes. And independent agency should be entrusted to carry out detailed post enumeration checks before the census figures are sent to the Census Commissioner of India.

(Neiphiu Rio)
Chief Minister, Nagaland

(Chingwang Konyak)
Leader of Opposition

(Keviletuo Kiewhuo)
President, Naga HOHO

(Y. Mangko Phom)
President, ENPO

(Muhlkhoyo Yhobü)
President, NSF

(Hawang T. Wangchp)
President, ENSF

(Rev. L. Karl Lonchar)
Peace Director, NBCC

(Rev. Dr. T. Nyekha)
Treasurer, NCF

(Lalthara)
Chief Secretary, Nagaland

(Taku Longkumer)
Gen. Secy, NGBF

Figure 5.2   Resolutions adopted in the Consultative Meeting on Census 2011

Source: GoN (2009a).

Moreover, the above political-economic approach (for example, Heine and Oltmanns 2016; Taylor 2016) applies to databases in general and has limited explanatory power vis-à-vis phenomena restricted to, say, the demographic-political sphere. We are interested in coverage errors driven by manipulation at the grassroots, that is, bottom-up demand-side manipulation, which is also associated with high voting rates, among other things. We will, therefore, follow Horowitz (2000), who provides a seamless account of the intertwining of political and economic interests, ethnic conflicts and electoral politics.

Non-violent ethnic conflict aggravated in Nagaland after the five-decades-long insurgency subsided in the late 1990s. This was the time when the impending delimitation of electoral constituencies, the demand for new administrative units and the demand for a 'Greater Nagaland' were threatening to disturb the balance of power in the state. This was also the time when Nagas started complaining vociferously against the alleged illegal/undocumented Bangladeshi immigration (Shimray 2007: 35–6; Amarjeet Singh 2009: 23–4).[13] The conjunction of these developments generated uncertainty regarding the distribution of public resources. The manipulation of headcount was one of the forms the contest over resources assumed.[14] Two years before the 2011 Census, a consultative meeting convened by the government suggested that a proper census was an instrument for 'establishing political and social harmony and [inter-community] equilibrium' (Figure 5.2).[15] Horowitz (2000: 194–6) suggests that such intertwining of ethnic conflict and census is not unheard of in the developing world.

> Since numbers count in the quest for political domination, the hope of a group is to enlarge its relative share of the population.... The census is therefore no dreary demographic formality to be left to experts. Disputes over census results in ethnically divided societies are common.... In a severely divided society ... an election can become an ethnic head count. Now it is clear that a census needs to be 'won'.

Likewise, Stephen Olugbemi suggests that

> The close association between the desire for group hegemony and the democratic ethnos of universal suffrage and majority rule are the stimulators of the 'ethnic numbers game' by which groups in competition seek to *adjust* their numerical ratios for sectional hegemonic interests. (Bookman 2013: 20–1, emphasis added)

Horowitz (2000: 326, 332) further argues that in ethnically divided societies, elections are reduced to 'racial censuses' in which a person's vote is predetermined by ethnic identity and are characterised by 'exceptionally high rates of voter turnout' (Horowitz 2000: 326, see also 332).[16] Following Horowitz, we will argue that political-economic factors explain the abnormalities in Nagaland's headcount and very high voting rates in assembly elections. We will first outline the nature of inter-tribal/district and inter-village competition in Nagaland and then discuss the hills–plains divide, the distribution of political and economic power within the state and the patterns and trends of manipulation.

Numbers Games in Nagaland

The politicisation of headcount has been observed in ethnically divided polities. Ethnic conflict, and numbers games, can assume one or more of the following forms: (a) demands for proportional representation in legislature, bureaucracy and other public institutions; (b) manipulation of census; (c) very high voter turnouts; (d) high fertility rate; (e) secessionism; (f) irredentism; (g) internal exit (demand for partition of province/district); (h) movements against 'outsiders' (possibly leading to even physical expulsion and/or genocide of 'others'); (i) assimilation of 'others' and (j) weak institutions, poor public goods provision and corruption (in the sense of nepotism favouring one's own community).[17] Before we discuss the first three at length, we will briefly identify the rest of the manifestations in the context of Nagaland.

While Nagaland has not seen high fertility rates linked to ethnic competition (Chapter 4), it has faced demands for secession from the union (Hazarika 1995; Misra 2012), irredentist demands (Chapter 3), demands for the partition of the state (Kumar 2015d; 2015g), campaigns against alleged illegal Bangladeshi Muslim immigrants leading to occasional expulsions and even killings in rare cases (Kumar 2015c; 2015e; 2015f), violence against Kukis (an indigenous Christian non-Naga tribal minority) and the steady marginalisation of Kukis and Kacharis (an indigenous non-Christian non-Naga tribal minority) (Kumar 2015g). The Against Corruption and Unabated Taxation (ACAUT), a landmark public mobilisation in Nagaland, exposed the poor quality of public infrastructure and services and rampant nepotism in the state. Regarding public institutions of Nagaland, it suffices to say that they invariably find themselves paralysed in face of the slightest hint of conflict between indigenous Naga communities and cannot afford to sympathise with non-Naga minorities. Lastly, despite its head start over other states in the North-East by virtue of being the first state created after decolonisation, Nagaland lags behind the rest of the region in terms of the share of development expenditure in state domestic product (SDP) (GoI 2002; RBI 2004; 2012). A composite infrastructure index covering 80 districts of the North-East ranked 5 of the 11 districts of Nagaland in the bottom quartile, with only the state capital (Kohima) and commercial capital (Dimapur) being in the first quartile (DoNER 2009). The remainder of this section discusses the manipulation of census from inter- and intra-district perspectives and examines elections as ethnic censuses.

Districts and Tribes

S. C. Jamir, who was the chief minister of Nagaland during the 2001 Census, offered a Horowitzian explanation of Wokha district's high growth rates. He (interview, 27 August 2013, Bhubaneshwar) suggested that Wokha over-reported its population to make-up for the loss of an assembly seat in the 1970s.[18] Jamir's argument cannot explain the lower growth rate in Phek, though, which too lost a seat in the 1970s. A year after the 2001 Census (but a year before the 2001 Census was linked to delimitation), Alemtemshi Jamir, a civil servant who later served as the chief secretary, argued that

> the recent population explosion of Nagaland as per the 2001 Census ... is no way related to the ground truth. It is my suspicion that it has more to do with the delimitation of constituencies that was slated for 2001.... The government can be sometimes helpless when it is an act of connivance of *all* the people. (A. Jamir 2002: 8, emphasis added)

Soon after the reference date for the 2002 delimitation was changed from 1991 to 2001, civil society organisations blamed over-reporting, multiple counting and '[f]raudulent enrolment in census of illegal immigrants, foreigners, temporary labourers and non-tribals'[19] (CPO et al. 2003) for the 'considerable and absurd inaccuracies' in the headcount (*CPO & Ors. vs. UoI & Ors.* 2006). Nagaland's member of parliament (MP) in the Lok Sabha too referred to the 'floating' non-indigenous population in parliamentary debates on delimitation in 2003 (Sangtam 2003), but neither the Lok Sabha MP nor the Rajya Sabha MP cast any doubt on the census population estimate (C. A. Jamir 2003; Sangtam 2003). However, after the Delimitation Commission shared its first working paper based on the 2001 Census, Nagaland's Chief Minister Neiphiu Rio admitted that the 2001 Census was vitiated by the impending delimitation.

> All this is because of competition among the tribes, between districts.... The delimitation commission process is also creating problems because some districts are losing seats.... (Hazarika 2005)[20]

He added that a review of results was going to be counterproductive because 'we have had warnings from village and district levels that in the review, the population will increase, not decrease!' (Hazarika 2005).[21] So, census was treated as a determinant of the outcome of state assembly elections.[22] The high population growth reported in 2001 can be explained by ethnic competition for greater political representation, which in turn determines intra-state allocations of development funds (*ME* 2018o), government jobs and government contracts.[23] Nagaland's newspapers and social media abound in allegations of favouritism and press releases and advertisements placed by communities in support of their members in the legislature and bureaucracy. Given the strong sense of belonging to one's village and tribe, leaders and bureaucrats are expected to privilege their 'own' people in the distribution of resources and jobs rather than deliver public goods, or, as Tinyi and Nienu (2018: 174) put it, Naga politicians face a 'trilemma' – 'the responsibility to be true to his office, to help members of his clan, village, and tribe individually, and to bring forth development for his constituency as a whole'.[24] The sorry state of public infrastructure in Dimapur, the commercial capital, is a case in point. Dimapur Town remains neglected as it does not belong to any tribe.

Such communitarian expectations feed a security dilemma that pushes the society towards the collectively worst outcome.[25] The first-past-the-post voting system and the long gaps between delimitations accentuate incentives/compulsions/ desperation to manipulate the determinants of electoral outcomes including population data. The practice of cross-checking electoral rolls with census too nudges people to manipulate the two in tandem (GoI 2011c: viii; *ME* 2013e; *Nagaland Post* 2013; ECI 2017).

Manipulation driven by delimitation and elections was complemented by manipulation linked to the demand for creation of new districts (DCO Nagaland, interview, 25 June 2013, Kohima).[26] District status entails several political and economic benefits.[27] First, each tribe aspires to its own tribal headquarter, that is, an administrative unit where it constitutes a majority or at least dominates the district headquarter.[28] Rio (2007: 217) admitted as much when he noted that creation of new districts helped 'decentralization of Civil Administration, which was necessary in view of the varied customs, traditions, linguistic and geographical factors'. Until 2001, only 7 of the 14 recognised tribes enjoyed this privilege, with Dimapur being a mixed district. Three new districts were formed in 2004 – Kiphire (Sangtam), Longleng (Phom) and Peren (Zeliang). Noklak district (Khiamniungan) was created in 2017, leaving behind just three tribes – Pochury (Meluri in Phek), Rengma (Tseminyu in Kohima) and Yimchunger (Shamator in Tuensang and Pungro in Kiphire) – without their own districts. Other pending demands for districts are fuelled by intra-tribal differences with far-flung circles demanding separation – Aboi (Konyak/Mon) (*ME* 2018t), Tobu (Konyak/Mon) (*ME* 2018u), Bhandari (Lotha/Wokha) (*ME* 2018v) and Pughoboto (Sumi/ Zunheboto) (*ME* 2018w) (also Neiphiu Rio, interview, 27 May 2015, New Delhi; *Telegraph* 2011b).

Second, local people get exclusive access to jobs at the lower rungs of the bureaucracy within a district, which is important given the spread of literacy and the consequent growth in the demand for jobs among the educationally and economically disadvantaged tribes that are hugely under-represented in the public sector. The government is unable to create sufficient public sector jobs to satisfy the employment needs of the growing pool of graduates due to resource crunch and overstaffing. It follows a complex quota system that exasperates new graduates from disadvantaged and smaller tribes, who are excluded from the networks of tribes that dominate the bureaucracy and politics. This reinforces the demand for a separate district where one's community is dominant. Third, local people get compensation for land on which the administrative infrastructure is built and the administration remains in moral debt to the 'original' landowners.[29] Fourth, the government sanctions a hospital and a college for each new district and improves roads and the frequency of bus services.[30] Moreover, district formation obviates the need to travel long distances to reach government offices. Fifth, status as a separate district also guarantees minimal access to central funds.[31] Sixth, local people get priority access to construction-related contracts or they can, at least, claim priority on moral grounds (*Nagaland Post* 2014b; *ME* 2013b; Stracey 1968: 111–12, 134, 232). Contracts encourage 'engineering' activity and entrepreneurship and also create jobs. Lastly, district formation marks the onset of urbanisation. Except Dimapur Town, every other town in Nagaland began as an administrative centre before emerging as an educational and economic hub.

Villages

Villages over-report headcounts to attract more development funds,[32] enhance electoral influence vis-à-vis other villages of the *same* constituency (without necessarily viewing it as linked to delimitation) and strengthen their bargaining power vis-à-vis prospective and elected legislators. People view government data as a unified whole due to the lack of awareness of legal provisions limiting the interlinking of different types of government data. The popular perception is not entirely unreasonable though. First, the same government officials enumerate population, enrol voters and identify poor households. Second, the government cannot overlook any major mismatch between headcounts from different sources, even if they are not formally interconnected. For instance, the Election Commission of India (ECI 2017) checks if the electorate exceeds the 18+ year census population.

The government admits that headcount-linked development funding and political representation fuel numbers games.

Many equated it [Census] with electoral rolls and saw the decadal Census exercise as an opportunity to increase the population in villages and towns to increase the vote bank.... These problems were also compounded by the Developmental model followed in the State in which allocation of funds to Village Development Boards is made on the basis of population and households in a village. This naturally led many to try and increase the fund flow into their villages by showing non-existing population and households in the Census records. (GoI 2011c: viii, 2; see also GoN n.d.3: 1.1; *Nagaland Post* 2009; *Indian Express* 2011)

The widespread practice of en masse voting by clans and villages in favour of consensus candidates, which gurantees conversion of headcount into political power, too provides incentives for investment in the manipulation of headcount.[33]

Manipulation is also closely linked to rural–urban migration. Most of our interviewees and other sources (CPO et al. 2003: 2; *Nagaland Post* 2017c) suggested that it was commonplace for people to get enumerated (in the census) and enrolled (in the electoral rolls) in the town where they were then staying as well as in their native villages. Commenting on the difficulty of arriving at a 'precise population [estimate] of Khonoma [village]', Sanyu (1996: 61) draws attention to the wide gap between the number of actual residents and those who hail from the village:

> According to the Khonoma Baptist Church Census 1985, out of the total population of a little over 6000, only 1945 were living in Khonoma in August 1985.[34] This shows that more than half of the population were living outside the village. Many have jobs in Kohima and others have migrated elsewhere – most to Dimapur area, but most of them keep a close link with the village and are registered in the church membership and electoral rolls.

Likewise in Benreu village of Peren, out of the 3,462 people belonging to the village, only 404 lived there as of November 1996 (Benreu Baptist Church 1997: 60–1).[35] While we do not have comparable published non-governmental statistics for other villages, their experience is unlikely to be different as we have heard similar stories of out-migration in almost all the villages we visited.

Villages (and households) ask migrants to get enrolled/enumerated to protect headcount linked development funds and, more importantly, votes.[36] The latter are an important source of bargaining power within the local political economy comprising of competing villages that in most cases belong to the same tribe and determine illicit payments made by candidates ahead of elections.[37]

Villages also seem to plan for the contingency that they will have to support out-migrants who might return during economic slowdown. It is also plausible that people overstate headcount to secure, say, a minimal food supply through the public distribution system because supplies are erratic, particularly in remote areas, and the quantity is often inadequate. Further, villages overstate their headcount as insurgent factions take away as much as 20 per cent of the development funds. In fact, before development funds reach villages several governmental and non-governmental 'stakeholders' extract their pound of flesh (Wouters 2018), which is another reason why villages overstate their population (and, by implication, developmental needs) and politicians and bureaucrats understandably condone the same.[38]

Villages close to the Myanmar border might have to additionally take into account the occasional influx of kith and kin from across the border. A memorandum of the Khiamniungan community throws light on this.

> In the event of any political turmoil taking place inside Myanmar, Noklak Sub-Division faces a unique problem of influx of refugees from across the border mostly comprising of Khiamniungan tribe. Religious persecution against our own brethrens is a regular feature. They are treated as bonded slaves, tortured and subjected to harsh living and made to survive in the most pitiable condition. With the up-gradation of the present Administratve HQ, we are highly optimistic that it will ameliorate the hardships being faced by them to a considerable extend. (KTC 2008: 3)

The compliance with the diktats of the village community is explained by a combination of factors. First, Naga identity is deeply intertwined with their village: 'Without land it is difficult to claim that you belong to a village. And without belonging to a village, it is difficult to claim that you are a Naga' (Wouters 2018: 60).[39] Second, Naga villages mostly comprise of ethnolinguistically homogenous communities bound by a shared customary law administered by village authorities that combine wide-ranging administrative powers and responsibilities insofar as they control local administration, law and order, land transactions and administer justice. In fact, villages, and even tribal organisations and church leaders,[40] can threaten dissenters with excommunication. In recent times, there have been several instances of threats of excommunication against those who identify ghost voters or oppose the enrolment of ghost voters (*Times of India* 2012b; Wouters 2018: 260–1) or contest against the diktats of village and tribal bodies (Kumar 2017a; *Nagaland Post* 2017d).[41]

Migrants also comply out of self-interest. They try to protect their claim upon agricultural land, which guarantees minimal access to food and also provides employment guarantee during economic slowdown, and maintain access to villages, which serve as safe havens in case of (ethnic) conflict elsewhere (Kumar 2018d).[42] The identification of certain areas as backward makes people eligible for preferential access to public resources, including seats in institutions of higher education and jobs, which provides an additional incentive to keep a foot in the

204 Numbers in India's Periphery

village.[43] Lastly, people try to maintain connection (in the form of documentary evidence of domicile, for example, voter identification card, etc.) with the places where they have property, including their native villages where the local authorities (rather than courts) are the ultimate arbiter of property disputes.[44]

Another aspect of the manipulation of headcount is noteworthy. The remarkable agreement, often perfect matches, between different census tables on, say, language and tribe (Table 4.15), suggest that data were manipulated carefully. Long before the relevant census data were released, in 2002, Yimchungrü (2002) provided a population estimate of Yimchungers that was almost equal to the *combined* census population of Yimchungers and related tribes including Tikhirs. Elsewhere, the village authorities of Yongnyah (Office of the Yongnyah Village Council 2002) and Dzülhami (Dzülhami Village Council 2002) also provided figures that compared favourably with their census population. Either the village authorities themselves falsified the headcount, or others, say, ethno-statistical entrepreneurs, were involved who kept them informed.[45]

To assess the magnitude of multiple counting, we can assume that the number of people counted in more than two locations will be less than those counted in only two locations and so forth and that some migrants (particularly, in-migrants from other states) will be reported only in one location in Nagaland.[46] Thus, multiple counting can be partly accounted for by subtracting intra-state in-migrants and out-migrants to other states from the total population. After this adjustment, the decadal growth rates change to 53, 62 and 63 per cent for 1971–81, 1981–91 and 1991–2001, respectively (Agrawal and Kumar 2012b: Table 9), but are still the highest in the country.

A former finance minister of Nagaland (interview, 11 April 2013, Dimapur; also a former Phom legislator, interview, 19 June 2015, Dimapur) suggested that double-counting can be eliminated by deducting the entire urban population as everyone in the urban areas is also counted in his/her village. However, the non-indigenous people are not counted in Nagaland's villages. Only the urban indigenous tribal population, that is, 226,313 Nagas and 3,691 indigenous non-Naga tribal persons, could have been counted twice in 2001. This correction results in a growth rate of 45.51 per cent in 2001, which is still the highest in the country.

A few more observations regarding manipulation are in order. First, over-reporting numbers to seek greater benefits from government welfare schemes is not unheard of in other states (note 13 of Chapter 1).[47] However, unlike Nagaland, in most cases it did not completely overshadow other determinants of population.

Second, there are crucial differences between manipulation linked to different goals. In case of demand for constituencies and districts, there might be episodic competition over the *means* to development funding (*episodic* manipulation) compared to everyday competition over development funding *per se* (*routine* manipulation). Episodic manipulation of the decennial census can, however, be viewed as an extension of the routine fudging of accounts of development expenditure. Also manipulation inspired by electoral considerations might affect only the voting-age population,[48] unlike the demand for districts that affects the population of all age groups.

Third, the competition over delimitation is part of a broader ethnopolitical competition, which makes it difficult to build and sustain fair institutions that are meta-public goods insofar as they are providers of public goods. Weak institutions are related to poor public goods provision. The quality of census statistics will be affected in ethnically divided societies insofar as these statistics that feed into government planning process are public goods (Heine and Oltmanns 2016: 207; Taylor 2016: 11–12). Nagaland is among the most diverse states of India. Its diversity is ethnically and geographically delineated and these divisions are politically and economically salient.

Fourth, the delimitation-based hypotheses might explain the high growth rate reported in the 1991 Census as well. The 1980s witnessed considerable wrangling over the distribution of constituencies. In 1984 and 1987, the government introduced two constitutional amendments to provide for reservation of seats for tribes in Nagaland's state assembly. Moreover, in 1990, the V. P. Singh government made an abortive attempt to conduct delimitation across the country (Sivaramakrishnan 1997: 3281). In fact, as late as March 2003, when an all-party meeting supported delimitation on the basis of 2001 Census, it was known that the 1991 Census figures would be used for conducting delimitation (Timeline 5.1). Two other developments would have aggravated ethnic and numerical anxieties in the 1980s. First, Dimapur's share in the state's electorate increased sharply (Table 5.3). Second, Sumis displaced Angamis as the dominant community in Dimapur both in terms of population as well as electoral power. At the same time, Dimapur Town displaced Angami-dominated Kohima town as the largest urban settlement of the state (GoI 2018a).

Fifth, even under drastic assumptions, double-counting can at best account for half of the lower bound of the discrepancy calculated in Chapter 4, and Nagaland's adjusted growth rates remain the highest in the country.

Lastly, following information economics, it can be argued that the spike in manipulation in the run-up to delimitation or formation of a new administrative unit is an instance of speculative investment in information by interest groups that tried to push through an irreversible change – a new village, circle/sub-district administrative headquarter or district, once created, is rarely reverted to its earlier status; or a constituency, once delimited, cannot be dissolved before the next delimitation (cf. Heine and Oltmanns 2016: 207–8).[49] Alternatively, it can be argued that interest groups that had been campaigning for a separate district overinvested in raising awareness regarding the instrumental utility of census statistics and mobilising people in the run-up to the 2001 Census 'to protect ... already taken irretrievable, "sunk" investments' (Heine and Mause 2004: 411).

Elections as Ethnic Censuses

In ethnically divided democracies with weak institutions, elections are among the foremost sites of contests for public resources. In Nagaland, the communalisation of elections has happened in two ways. At the micro level, each election held in Nagaland has seen ethnically delineated contests. Candidates cannot win elections outside the stronghold of their tribe (clan/village) within Nagaland (their district). To the best of our knowledge, in the entire history of Nagaland, only one candidate has won an assembly election outside his[50] tribe's stronghold and that too in the 1960s.

At the macro level, tribes oppose any change to their electoral landscape by blocking delimitation even at the intra-district level to preserve the informal ethnolinguistic partition of the state. As a result, elections are often also contests between villages.[51] The intensity of intra-constituency contests can be gauged from, among other things, the high and increasing voting rates. Delimitation would have transferred constituencies to the plains and the consequent reduction in the number of constituencies in the hills would have forced candidates to reach out to communities and villages across the existing constituencies (C. A. Jamir 2003; Sangtam 2003).

With a few exceptions, Nagaland's voting rate in parliamentary elections has always been the highest in the country (Table 4.6). The growth of the number of voters during 1974–2009 (3.36 per cent per annum) has been higher than that of the electorate (2.45–2.93 per cent per annum) (Table 4.7, Panel A). This indicates a growing interest in elections, growing polarisation and/or the deepening/ indigenisation[52] of democracy. Further, controlling for the change in the voting age, the average voter turnout has been higher in the assembly elections compared to the parliamentary elections, which suggests that elections that directly affect redistribution attract greater attention as part of contests over public resources.[53] In this regard, it is also noteworthy that the undivided Tuensang district of 1971 (that includes Kiphire, Longleng, Mon and Noklak), the most disadvantaged region in economic and educational terms, has in *every* election accounted for at least four of the ten constituencies with the highest voting rates and also eight of the ten constituencies with the highest mean voting rates during 1974–2018 (Figure 5.3). Not coincidentally, several of these constituencies overlap with circles that were demanding separate districts and also reported some of the highest population growth rates in 2001 and equally steep reductions in 2011.

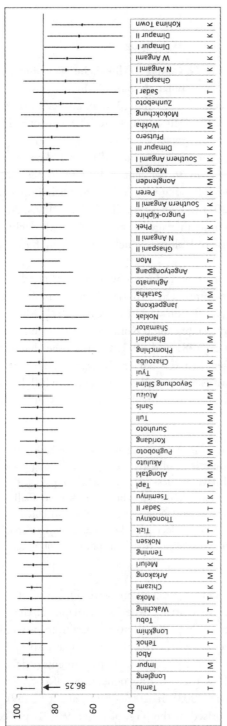

Figure 5.3 Distribution of voting rate by assembly constituencies, Nagaland, 1974–2018

Sources: Prepared by authors using ECI reports.

Notes: (i) T, M and K indicate Tuensang, Mokokchung and Kohima districts of 1971. (ii) The figure shows mean, minimum and maximum voting rates in the assembly elections held over the period 1974–2018 (excluding the year 1998) for all the 60 assembly constituencies. Each vertical line represents one constituency (labelled on the horizontal axis) in such way that the symbol in the middle of the line indicates mean voting rate and the upper and lower ends of the line respectively indicate maximum and minimum voting rates. For instance, the mean, minimum and maximum voting rates observed for 'Tamlu' are approximately 98, 91 and 100 per cent, respectively. The horizontal line at 86.25 indicates the arithmetic mean (across 60 constituencies) of the mean voting rates (1974–2018) of constituencies. The constituencies are arranged in the descending order of the mean voting rates. (iii) Voting rates are not available for uncontested elections in (a) 1974 in 'Akuluto' and 'Tobu', (b) 1977 in 'Southern Angami II', (c) 1993 in 'Northern Angami I' and (d) 2018 in 'Northern Angami II'. The statistics for these constituencies have been computed after excluding the above years.

Dimapur: An Easy Scapegoat

In 1971, there were three districts in Nagaland – Mokokchung, Kohima and Tuensang (Figure 3.1, Map 3.10E). The population share of Mokokchung of 1971 dropped by 10 percentage points between 1961 and 2011, except for 1991–2001 when it managed to temporarily arrest the decline in its share. The share of Kohima of 1971 increased from 28 per cent in 1961 to 46 per cent in 2011, but, in between, its share dropped by about 2 percentage points during 1991–2001. The share of Tuensang district of 1971 declined from 36 per cent in 1961 to 30 per cent in 1981, after which it increased in the following two decades to reach 34 per cent by 2001 before declining again in 2011 to 29 per cent (Table 4.14). Thus, during 1991–2001, Tuensang and Mokokchung managed to arrest the steady decline in their population share at the expense of Kohima, which has all along been a net recipient of migrants.

However, the population did not grow uniformly within the three districts of 1971 (Table 4.14). The Lotha-dominated Wokha district (carved out of Mokokchung) almost doubled its population within a decade (1991–2001) and is the *only* hill district other than the state capital Kohima that reported a large increase in population share between 1981 and 2011. On the other hand, the populations of Kiphire and Longleng, carved out of Tuensang, almost halved between 2001 and 2011. The disparities between the growth rates of hill districts notwithstanding, Dimapur was projected as the real threat. Chief Minister Rio, for instance, argued,

> The delimitation commission process is also creating problems because some districts are losing seats and Dimapur is gaining five seats. Mokokchung seats are dropping by three, Phek will have one less and so on. In the plains, the constituencies are large, Dimapur I has 50,000 voters but the hills have smaller voting numbers, between 12,000 and 20,000. Now these seats are distributed on tribal lines but the ones which the hills are losing are being added to Dimapur which has a three lakh [0.3 million] population. And Dimapur has a lot of non-tribals. (Hazarika 2005)

In 2003, the last election held before 2005, there were 54,533 electors in Ghaspani I constituency of Dimapur district, whereas Dimapur I, the only unreserved assembly constituency, had only 14,221 electors. Apart from overstating Dimapur I's electorate, Rio also overlooked the fact that the Nagas of Nagaland account for a majority of Dimapur district's population. In parliamentary debates, Nagaland's MP too focussed on how the 'floating population' of outsiders in Dimapur affects the tribes (Sangtam 2003). In 2001 (2011), about 61 (59) per cent of Dimapur's population comprised of the STs, of which 91 (91) per cent were Nagas. Indeed, as shown below and contrary to Rio's suggestion, intra-Naga cleavages, rather than the plains/outsider-hills/insider divide, are the primary determinants of ethnic conflict within Nagaland. In the debate on delimitation in the Rajya Sabha, Nagaland's representative C. A. Jamir (2003) said as much when he noted that 'in the past, when this amendment was considered ... [it] created a lot of emotional upheaval among many tribes ... [due to] Assembly segments, which were being carved out by including certain pockets or villages or areas which had no affinity'. His colleague in the Lok Sabha added that 'the people who belong to one community were put [by the proposed delimtation] in another constituency. It did not suit them. In order to elect their own representative, they [candidates] should be from their own community' (Sangtam 2003).

Dimapur is the locus of the intersection of ethnic (tribes versus others, Naga versus non-Naga tribes, tribes/insiders/Nagas versus outsiders and early Naga settlers/'advanced' tribes versus recent Naga settlers/'backward' tribes) and economic (hills versus plains) fault lines. Most of the indigenous non-Naga tribal population of Nagaland is concentrated in Dimapur (55 per cent in 2011) and an adjacent territory in Peren (29 per cent in 2011). Likewise, more than half of the non-tribal population of Nagaland is concentrated in Dimapur district (58 per cent in 2011). Non-indigenous people did not need Inner Line Permits (ILPs) to enter and settle in Dimapur Town, where about 60 per cent of the population is non-tribal (GoI n.d.10: 16).

Dimapur is the only district of Nagaland that is situated almost entirely in the plains. It is also the most urbanised district and dominates the state's economy.[54] With Nagas looking for plains to settle in and seeking a share in the urban economy, clashes with indigenous non-Naga tribes, who claim Dimapur as their traditional territory, Manipuri Naga settlers and non-tribal communities of Dimapur are inevitable. Conflicts between different waves of Naga settlers are also inevitable, but the intra-Naga conflicts are waged tacitly.

Political contests in Dimapur are dominated by a few major Naga tribes including Angami (among the earliest Naga settlers in Dimapur), Ao, Lotha and Sumi (the most populous tribe of Dimapur).[55] Initially, for a brief period, Angamis were the dominant Naga tribe in Dimapur. However, since mid-1970s, Aos and Sumis have dominated the district, with Angamis occasionally managing to win a seat bordering Kohima. There have been violent clashes in Dimapur involving Sumis and Angamis (*Shillong Times* 2012)[56] and Sumis and Tangkhuls from Manipur (*Sangai Express* 2007a; Shishak 2007; *ME* 2013c). Rongmei Naga settlers, a small and politically as well as economically weak community originally from Manipur who live in the heart of Dimapur, are, like alleged illegal Bangladeshi immigrants, easy targets for Nagas from the hill districts of Nagaland trying to find a toehold in the urban economy.

The massive growth in Naga settlements in and around Dimapur notwithstanding; Naga settlers in hot, humid, dusty and mosquito-infested Dimapur continue to view themselves as members of their respective tribes and ancestral villages in the cooler hills. More importantly, when hills' politicians and civil society leaders expressed their resentment against the potential transfer of seats to Dimapur from the hills, they carefully focused their attacks on 'outsiders' deliberately ignoring the fact that Nagas of Dimapur will be the main beneficiaries as 59 out of 60 constituencies were reserved by law for tribes. The unstated fear was the transfer of seats to Sumi- and Ao-dominated Dimapur, which would have destabilised the fragile inter-tribal balance of power in the state. While the origin of this schizophrenic attitude towards Dimapur is beyond the scope of our discussion, it bears emphasising that Nagas have developed a culture of silence on intra-Naga conflicts to preserve inter-tribal unity and, therefore, an external target is needed to contain internal conflicts.[57] Dimapur with its large non-Naga population provides a perfect target.

During the last delimitation of constituencies in 1974, two assembly seats were transferred from Wokha and Phek in the hills to Dimapur. Since then, the disparity in the size of constituencies has grown steadily (Figure 5.4). In 1974, the

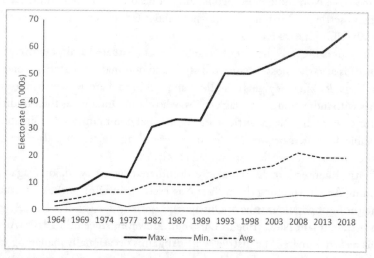

Figure 5.4   Range of electorate size, Nagaland, 1964–2018

Source: Prepared by authors using ECI reports.

Notes: 'Max.' ('Min.') indicates the largest (smallest) assembly constituency in terms of electorate. There were 40 constituencies until 1969 and 60 afterwards. 'Avg.' is the mean electorate size of all constituencies. Mokokchung Town (except Bhandari in 1964 and Moilan Wozhuro in 1969) and Ghaspani I (except Dimapur II in 1974, 1982 and 1987 and Dimapur Town in 1964 and 1969) have been the smallest and largest constituencies, respectively. See also Note iii of Table 4.6.

difference in the electorate size of the largest (Dimapur II in Dimapur district) and smallest (Mokokchung Town in Mokokchung district) constituencies was 10,089. This gap widened to 46,101 in the 1998 Assembly Elections, the last election before the 2001 Census, when Ghaspani I (Dimapur district) and Mokokchung Town were the largest and smallest constituencies, respectively. The size disparity between the largest and smallest constituencies grew in relative terms as well. The sustained disparity indicates the excessive political power wielded by voters in the hills (Figure 5.5).[58] Since historically different Naga tribes have dominated different parts of the state (Table 5.1), the disparity in voting power is a measure of intercommunity/district disparity as well as the potential for conflict between the prospective winners and losers of the process of delimitation.

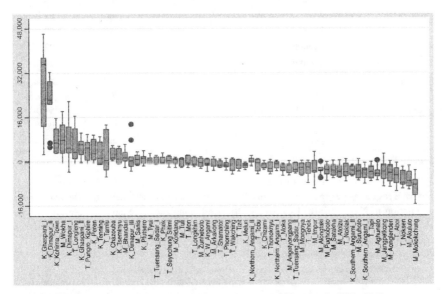

Figure 5.5   Electorate size gap by assembly constituencies, Nagaland, 1974–2018

Sources: Prepared by authors using ECI reports.

Notes: (i) For each constituency, box plots show the distribution of the electorate size gap over 11 Assembly elections during 1974–2018. The electorate size gap is the difference between the electorate size of the constituency and the state's mean electorate size in that year. If the electorate size in a constituency has been around the state's mean, its box plot will be located close to the line passing through zero on the vertical axis. (ii) The constituencies have been sorted in descending order of the mean (1974–2018) electorate size. (iii) The name of each constituency is prefixed with the corresponding 1971 district (K = Kohima, M = Mokokchung, T = Tuensang). K_Chazouba denotes Chazouba constituency in Kohima (1971) district. (iv) The box plot for, say, Ghaspani I indicates that during 1974–2018, the median electorate size gap for this constituency is about 36,000, the first and third quartiles are 14,000 and 38,000, respectively, and the lowest and highest values are about 2,000 and 46,000, respectively. Thus, the electorate of Ghaspani I has exceeded the state average in all years.

212 Numbers in India's Periphery

Table 5.1 Geographical distribution of tribes in Nagaland

Tribe	Primary (secondary) district	Share	
		2001	2011
Ao	Mokokchung	82	74
Lotha	Wokha	89	85
Yimchunger	Tuensang (Kiphire)	95†	56 (34)
Sangtam	Kiphire (Tuensang)	(95†)	45 (43)
Sumi	Zunheboto (Dimapur)	55 (33)	57 (33)
Angami	Kohima	77	81
Rengma	Kohima	95	93
Chakhesang	Phek	91	86
Pochury	Phek	98	93
Konyak	Mon	98	97
Phom	Longleng	98†	89
Chang	Tuensang	94	92
Khiamniungan	Tuensang	97	94
Zeliang	Peren	97‡	92
Kachari	Dimapur	92	72
Kuki	Peren (Dimapur)	51‡ (37)	51 (41)
Garo	Dimapur	90	80
Karbi	Dimapur	44	57

Sources: Prepared by authors using GoI (n.d.1; n.d.2; n.d.9).

Notes: (i) 'Primary (secondary) district' is the district where the largest (second-largest) part of the tribe resides as per the 2011 Census. 'Share' is the share of the district in the tribe's total population in Nagaland. (ii) In 2001, Kiphire and Longleng were part of Tuensang (†) and Peren was part of Kohima (‡). (iii) Kachari, Kuki, Garo and Karbi are indigenous non-Naga tribes, while the rest are indigenous Naga tribes.

The data on electorate provide a measure of the relative demographic weight of Dimapur since the 1960s, especially for intercensal years. Right from 1964, Dimapur has always had fewer seats than suggested by its share in Nagaland's population (Table 5.2) and electorate (Table 5.3).[59] In the 2000s, Dimapur's share in the electorate of Nagaland declined steadily and by 2008 it had fallen to the level of the 1970s, when Dimapur Town's population was about a tenth of what it was in the late 2000s. This steep drop is explained by the fact that Dimapur, which is home to about one-sixth of the state's population and has always been a net recipient of migrants, especially adults including college students and job seekers, accounted for barely 2 per cent of the new electors added to the state's electorate during 1998–2008 (Table 5.3). After 2008, Dimapur's share rebounded to the early-1990s level as the population and electorate of the hills contracted sharply.

Table 5.2 Loss of seats in the state legislative assembly and population growth

Region/district	Existing seats (1974)	Census 1981			Census 1991			Census 2001			Census 2011			Population growth		
		Pop. share	Proj. seats	Loss	Pop. share	Proj. seats	Loss	Pop. share	Proj. seats	Loss	Pop. share	Proj. seats	Loss	1981–91	1991–2001	2001–11
A: 2001 Census districts																
Mon	9	0.1	6	3	0.12	7	2	0.13	8	1	0.13	8	1	89.64	74.12	-3.83
Tuensang	11	0.2	12	-1	0.19	12	-1	0.21	13	-2	0.16	10	1	52.89	78.11	-22.51
Mokokchung	10	0.13	8	2	0.13	8	2	0.12	7	3	0.1	6	4	52	46.54	-16.77
Zunheboto	7	0.08	5	2	0.08	5	2	0.08	5	2	0.07	4	3	32.87	60.01	-8.41
Wokha	4	0.07	4	0	0.07	4	0	0.08	5	-1	0.08	5	-1	43.47	95.16	3.11
Dimapur	5	—	—	—	0.15	9	-4	0.16	9	-4	0.19	11	-6	—	73.66	22.89
Kohima	9	0.32§	19§	-5§	0.17	10	-1	0.16	9	0	0.18	11	-2	62.27§	47.92	17.72
Phek	5	0.09	6	-1	0.08	5	0	0.07	4	1	0.08	5	0	44.66	45.07	10.19
B: 1971 Census districts																
Tuensang	20	0.3	18	2	0.31	19	1	0.34	21	-1	0.29	18	2	65.44	56.68	18.35
Mokokchung	21	0.28	17	4	0.28	17	4	0.28	17	4	0.25	15	6	43.99	62.29	-8.56
Kohima	19	0.41	25	-6	0.4	24	-5	0.39	22	-3	0.46	27	-8	58.25	76.55	-15.3
C: hills vs. plains																
Dimapur	5	—	—	—	0.15	9	-4	0.16	9	-4	0.19	11	-6	—	73.66	22.89
Rest of Nagaland	55	—	—	—	0.85	51	4	0.84	51	4	0.81	49	6	—	62.95	-4.77
Nagaland	60	1	60	0	1	60	0	1	60	0	1	60	0	56.08	64.53	-0.47

Contd

Table 5.2 contd

Region/district	Existing seats (1974)	Census 1981			Census 1991			Census 2001			Census 2011			Population growth		
		Pop. share	Proj. seats	Loss	Pop. share	Proj. seats	Loss	Pop. share	Proj. seats	Loss	Pop. share	Proj. seats	Loss	1981–91	1991–2001	2001–11
D: districts formed in 2004																
Longleng	2	3.32	1.99	0.01	5.60	3.36	-1.36	6.11	3.67	-1.67	2.55	1.53	0.47	163.39	79.58	-58.48
Kiphire	2	3.62	2.17	-0.17	4.16	2.49	-0.49	5.10	3.06	-1.06	3.74	2.24	-0.24	79.29	101.79	-27.04
Peren	2	3.87	2.32	-0.32	4.67	2.80	-0.80	4.56	2.74	-0.74	4.81	2.89	-0.87	88.47	60.62	4.91
E: constituencies (aspiring districts)																
Noklak + Thonoknyu*	2	2.82	1.69	0.31	2.15	1.29	0.71	2.13	1.28	0.72	3.00	1.80	0.20	19.21	62.57	40.11
Pughoboto**	1	1.47	0.88	0.12	1.47	0.88	0.12	1.24	0.74	0.26	0.85	0.51	0.49	56.28	38.79	-31.36
Tseminyu†	1	1.92	1.15	-0.15	2.53	1.52	-0.52	2.66	1.59	-0.59	2.87	1.72	-0.72	105.14	72.85	7.52
Aboi + Moka + Tehok + Tobu‡	4	5.10	3.06	0.94	5.33	3.20	0.80	5.46	3.28	0.72	5.50	3.30	0.70	62.94	68.68	0.09
Bhandari	1	0.68	0.41	0.59	0.63	0.38	0.62	0.68	0.41	0.59	0.87	0.52	0.48	43.94	76.51	27.16

Source: Authors' computations.

Notes: (i) 'Existing seats' are the number of assembly seats as per the 1974 distribution of seats. (ii) 'Pop. share' denotes the population share of the corresponding administrative unit in the state. 'Proj. seats' is the number of seats projected using 'Pop. share'. 'Loss' is the difference between the 'Existing seats' and 'Proj. seats'. (iii) Fractions more than one-half are counted as one, while those less than one-half are ignored (GoI 2008d: 32). (iv) Between 1981 and 1991, Pughoboto and Ghathashi circles were transferred from Kohima to Zunheboto, and Tobu was transferred from Tuensang to Mon. We have assumed the transfers to have occurred before 1981 for the sake of comparison. (v) The figures in Panels B and C are the aggregate of the corresponding figures in Panel A. (vi) '—' indicates unavailability of data for Dimapur for 1981. § Indicates figures for Dimapur and Kohima as a whole. (vii) * Includes Noklak, Nokhu, Panso, Thonoknyu and Chingmei circles (a few villages of Kiusam circle of Kiphire are omitted); ** includes Ghatashi and Pughoboto circles; † includes Tseminyu and Tsogin circles; ‡ includes Aboi, Chen, Angjangyang, Monyakshu, Mopong and Tobu circles due to the difficulty in dividing constituencies between these circles, but the last three seem to be demanding a separate district.

Table 5.3 Electorate and assembly seats, Dimapur and the rest of Nagaland, 1964–2018

Year	Total		Dimapur					Rest of the state				Change in electorate@			
	Electorate size	Assembly seats	Electorate size	Share‡	Assembly seats			Electorate size	Assembly seats			Dimapur		Nagaland	
					Proj.	Existing	Loss		Proj.	Existing	Loss	Absolute	Ratio*	Absolute	Dimapur's share†
1964	124,166	40	13,236	10.66	4	3	-1	110,930	36	37	1				
1969	176,931	40	19,331	10.93	4	3	-1	157,600	36	37	1				
1974§	407,043	60	44,985	11.05	7	5	-2	362,058	53	55	2				
1977	403,454	60	48,944	12.13	7	5	-2	354,510	53	55	2	3,959	0.09	-3,589	—
1982	596,453	60	94,887	15.91	9.5	5	-4.5	501,566	50.5	55	4.5	45,943	0.94	192,999	0.24
1987	581,953	60	124,464	21.39	13	5	-8	457,489	47	55	8	29,577	0.31	-14,500	—
1989	582,416	60	122,637	21.06	13	5	-8	459,779	47	55	8	-1,827	-0.01	463	—
1993§	813,862	60	140,525	17.27	10	5	-5	673,337	50	55	5	17,888	0.15	231,446	0.08
1998	926,569	60	162,439	17.53	10.5	5	-5.5	764,130	49.5	55	5.5	21,914	0.16	112,707	0.19
2003	1,014,841	60	162,517	16.01	10	5	-5	852,324	50	55	5	78	0.0005	88,272	0.001
2008	1,302,266	60	170,785	13.11	8	5	-3	1,131,481	52	55	3	8,268	0.05	287,425	0.03
2013	1,198,449	60	183,253	15.29	9	5	-4	1,015,196	51	55	4	12,468	0.07	-103,817	—
2018§	1,195,521	60	200,924	16.81	10	5	-5	994,597	50	55	5	17,671	0.10	-2,928	—

Source: Prepared by authors using ECI reports.

Notes: (i) 'Proj.' indicates projected seats based on electorate. (ii) 'Loss' is the difference between the existing and projected seats. (iii) 'Change in electorate' is the change over the preceding election year. @ Change is reported for the period after direct elections were introduced in the entire state. (iv) * Ratio of change in electorate (that is, 'Absolute') to Dimapur's electorate of preceding election year. (v) ‡ Share of Dimapur in the electorate of Nagaland. (vi) † Absolute change in Dimapur's electorate divided by the corresponding figure for Nagaland. (vii) § See Note iii of Table 4.6.

As per the 1991 Census, delimitation would have transferred four seats to Dimapur (Table 5.2).[60] In absence of a drastic intervention Dimapur's population share would have grown further, increasing its share of constituencies at the expense of the hills. Threatened by the potential loss of political representation, hill tribes overstated their numbers in the 2001 Census. The Dimapur-based tribes also over-reported their population, but the district's higher rates of literacy, mobility of people and urbanisation, relatively weaker intra-tribe solidarity, less-than-perfect inter-tribal coordination and the lack of clarity about who benefits most from the assignment of additional seats to the district meant that people could not be mobilised as effectively as in the hills to manipulate the headcount.

During 2001–11, the Naga population of Nagaland contracted by 4.25 per cent compared to 0.58 per cent contraction in the overall population of the state (Table 4.12). Each of the 14 recognised Naga tribes reported more than a 14 percentage point drop in their growth rates, while the non-Naga population grew by 25 per cent. Dimapur, the only plains district, reported a positive growth rate, whereas all but two hill districts reported negative growth rates. The share of Naga tribes in Dimapur decreased by 1.5 percentage points during this period despite growing in-migration from the hills. Non-Nagas who account for a sizeable proportion of Dimapur's population had no incentive to overstate their headcount because 59 out of 60 seats in Nagaland are constitutionally reserved for (indigenous) tribes. Moreover, Dimapur-I, the sole unreserved seat, has been dominated by (Sumi) Nagas since the late 1980s. In fact, even earlier, only Angami Nagas and non-Nagas married to Angamis got elected from this constituency. The political economy of Dimapur presents non-Nagas with insurmountable collective action problems. While Nagas were not among the original settlers of Dimapur, they have secured control over this important district by encouraging immigration from the hills, securing reservation of all but one electoral seat for tribes, restricting the number of electoral seats assigned to Dimapur district and ensuring that outsiders who dominate the economy depend on government permits that are mostly issued to Nagas (businessmen, interview, 27 June 2013, Dimapur). Also note that the ability of non-Nagas to influence government statistics is circumscribed by their severe underrepresentation in government jobs that, for instance, means that enumerators are unlikely to belong to their communities.

The Hills: A House Divided

Intra-state delimitation, like the one supposed to be carried out in 2002, does not alter the total number of seats in a state assembly and in Nagaland even the seat share of the STs was exogenously fixed. However, a territorial redistribution of constituencies was bound to create losers in a state like Nagaland where ethnicity is territorially delineated (Table 5.1). While the potential transfer of seats between the hills and Dimapur was restricted to four due to the manipulation of headcount, there was considerable churning within the hills.

Between 1991 and 2001, three hill districts (Mon/Konyak, Wokha/Lotha and Tuensang/Phom, Sangtam and Yimchunger) were able to increase their population share at the expense of other hill districts. These districts stood to gain seats after the reference year for delimitation was changed from 1991 to 2001. The other hill districts (Mon/Konyak, Mokokchung/Ao, Phek/Chakhesang and Zunheboto/Sumi) would have lost seven seats, three to the hill districts of Tuensang and Wokha and four to Dimapur.[61] Even within Tuensang, Longleng and Kiphire stood to gain three seats, while the rest of the areas including Tuensang town were going to lose a seat. This would have meant the dilution of the electoral advantage of the Chang tribe. In fact, towns in other hill districts too feared the loss of exclusive seats.

Moreover, the communities that stood to gain in Dimapur feared the loss of seats in the hills. Sumis and Aos stood to lose two and three seats in their respective hill districts but would have possibly captured two and one out of four seats being transferred to Dimapur. Angamis were not losing any seat in their hill district and would have possibly captured one seat being transferred to Dimapur. Lothas stood to gain a seat in their hill district, and their otherwise dismal prospects in elections in Dimapur could have improved after the addition of more seats to the district. In each of these cases, the part of the tribe based in the hills must have feared that the balance of power within the community could shift to its plains counterpart if seats were added to Dimapur.

Since the tribes were not equally successful at over-enumeration and the four seats to be added to Dimapur in 2001 would have benefitted mostly Sumis and Aos, census proved to be contentious. The Delimitation Commission proposed to maintain status quo of district-wise entitlement of assembly seats in Nagaland and only redistribute the constituencies within each district (Timeline 5.1). However, even this modest proposal was not acceptable as this would have meant transfer of villages to constituencies dominated by other tribal/sub-tribal communities. This would have exposed the newcomers to ethnic conflict as they would have been viewed as divisive, given their potential to ally with *factions* within the majority in that constituency.

The prolonged stalemate over delimitation between 2002 and 2008 exposed the ethnic fault lines within the Naga society. The Chakhesang Public Organization (CPO) filed a petition in the Gauhati High Court against the use of census data vitiated by politically-motivated manipulation for delimitation (*CPO & Ors. vs. UoI & Ors.* 2006). This case, which concluded more than a decade later in 2017 (*ME* 2017e), played a key role in mothballing delimitation in Nagaland.

Chakhesangs (Phek), Aos (Mokokchung) and Sumis (Zunheboto) were opposed to delimitation.

Phek lost a seat in the 1970s. Between 1981 and 2001, 8 out of the 10 circles of Phek grew at rates equal to or less than the state average (Table 5.4). In 2001, Phek's growth rate was the lowest among the then districts of Nagaland. If delimitation was conducted as per the 2001 Census, then Phek would have lost one out of five seats (that is, 20 per cent loss), whereas it would not have lost any seat as per the 1991 (or even 2011[62]) Census (Table 5.2). Chakhesangs of Phek turned against delimitation only after change of reference date from 1991 to 2001 and approached the high court to stop the use of the 2001 Census for delimitation.[63]

The Ao Senden, the apex body of the Ao tribe of Mokokchung, argued that delimitation solely on the basis of population will disturb 'the delicate tribal balance' because vested interests had manipulated the headcount and that loss of seats would affect the 'very existence of the Ao Tribe' (*CPO & Ors. vs. UoI & Ors.* 2006). During 1981–2001, five out of eight circles of Mokokchung (Table 5.4) and both the population of the Ao tribe and Ao language speakers (Tables 4.11 and 4.15) grew at rates much lower than the rest of the state. Moreover, in 1998, 9 of the 10 assembly seats of Mokokchung were much smaller than the average constituency of the state (Table 5.4). As per the 2001 Census, the Ao tribe/Mokokchung district stood to lose 3 seats out of its 10 assembly seats (that is, 30 per cent loss) (Table 5.2). In 2013 (2018), all 10 (10) constituencies of Mokokchung had smaller electorates than the state average and 5 (4) of the 10 smallest constituencies of the state were also located in this district (Figure 5.5). If delimitation is conducted as per the 2011 Census, Mokokchung will lose 4 of its 10 seats (Table 5.2).

The Sumi Hoho, the apex organisation of Sumis, also opposed the delimitation exercise. In its letter to the president, the Sumi Hoho (2002: 1) noted that delimitation (resulting in loss of seats) was 'an act [*sic*] of deprivation of legitimate rights' and that 'hard earned Constituencies through thick and thin by the sweat, tears and blood of the given aspiring populous duly appreciated by the Government of India out of political bargain cannot be whisked away by the cybernetics and inhuman mechanism of the Election Commission'. Between 1981 and 2001, the rate of growth of the Sumi tribe was less than the average for Nagas (Table 4.12). During 1991–2001, 4 of Zunheboto's 11 circles grew faster than the state's average growth rate compared to 2 in the previous decade (Table 5.4).[64] Between 1998 and 2003, all seven constituencies of Zunheboto were smaller than the average constituency (Table 5.4). Zunheboto stood to lose two (three) out of its seven constituencies as per the 2001 (2011) Census (Table 5.2).

The demand for delimitation was, however, strong in parts of south-western Nagaland and eastern districts. A Joint Action Committee (JAC) comprising of

Table 5.4 Voting rate, electorate size and population growth rate

District		Total	Number of constituencies								Total	Number of circles					
			Mean voting rate		1998		2003–8*		2013–18^			Population growth rate					
												1981–91		1991–2001		2001–11	
1971	2011		Above	Below	Above	Below	Above	Below	Above	Below		Above	Below	Above	Below	Above	Below
Tuensang	Longleng	2	2	0	2	0	2	0	1	1	3	3	0	2	1	0	3
	Mon	9	8	1	0	9	0	9	0	9	10	4	6	7	3	5	5
	Tuensang	7	6	1	0	7	1	6	2	5	9	2	7	4	5	5	4
	Kiphire	2	1	1	1	1	1	1	2	0	6	3	3	5	1	1	5
Mokokchung	Mokokchung	10	7	3	1	9	2	8	0	10	8	4	4	3	5	0	8
	Zunheboto	7	5	2	0	7	0	7	1	6	11	2	9	4	7	3	8
	Wokha	4	3	1	4	0	4	0	4	0	8	1	7	4	4	6	2
Kohima	Phek	5	3	2	2	3	3	2	3	2	10	2	8	2	8	8	2
	Peren	2	1	1	2	0	2	0	2	0	5	3	2	2	3	2	3
	Kohima	7	1	6	3	4	2	5	2	5	5	1	4	2	3	5	0
	Dimapur	5	0	5	5	0	4	1	5	0	3	1	2	1	2	2	1
Nagaland		60	37	23	20	40	21	39	22	38	78	26	52	36	42	37	41

Source: Authors' calculations based on various ECI and census reports.

Notes: (i) * The mean electorate of 2003 and 2008. ^ The mean electorate of 2013 and 2018. (ii) 'Above' ('Below') indicate the number of constituencies with mean voting rate or electorate size above (below) or the number of circles with decadal population growth rate above (below) the corresponding state mean. (iii) The respective state-level means are defined as follows: (a) 'Mean voting rate' – the mean of the mean voting rates (1974–2018) for 60 constituencies, (b) 'Electorate size' – the mean across 60 constituencies for the corresponding years and (c) 'Population growth rate' – population growth rate of the state. (iv) The number of circles in the state increased from 69 in 1981 to 114 in 2011 with inter-circle territorial transfers in some cases. We created a set of 78 circles for which we could generate comparable data for the period 1981–2011.

Lotha (Wokha district), Zeliang (Peren), Phom (Longleng), Sangtam (Kiphire/ Tuensang) and Yimchunger (Tuensang/Kiphire) tribes claimed that the 2001 Census 'provides a correct picture' (and 'actual representation') and demanded delimitation (*CPO & Ors. vs. UoI & Ors.* 2006, see also *Telegraph* 2008). Wokha was among the most vociferous supporters of delimitation.[65] Its population nearly doubled between 1991 and 2001, while its population growth rate was lower than the state average in the previous decade. Lothas are among the educationally and economically advanced tribes of Nagaland (Rio 2007: 211). Other educationally and economically advanced tribes such as Ao and Angami registered much lower growth rates (Table 4.12). Wokha would not have lost any seat if the 1991 Census was used for delimitation and would have gained a seat (that is, gain of 25 per cent) as per the 2001 Census (Table 5.2). Between 1991 and 2001, five out of eight circles of Wokha registered growth rates close to or greater than the state's average with three of them reporting growth rates in excess of 100 per cent. Also in 1993, three out of four constituencies of Wokha were smaller than the average constituency of the state, but since 1998, all four have been larger. As per the 2011 Census, Wokha will still gain a seat because unlike other hill districts, its population did not contract (Table 4.14).

Between 1981 and 2001, Konyaks of Mon and Phoms, Yimchungers and Sangtams of Tuensang also reported very high growth rates. During this period, these districts reversed the gradual erosion of their demographic weight and managed to increase their population share from 30 to 34 per cent despite steady out-migration (Table 4.14). Phoms, Sangtams and Yimchungers, the prime beneficiaries, stood to gain three assembly constituencies as per the 2001 Census. Tuensang and Mon share a border with Myanmar and have a relatively difficult terrain, greater forest cover, poorer road coverage and lower literacy. They were exposed to modern education and administration decades after other districts. Even six decades after the formation of the state, Tuensang and its successor districts have a miniscule representation in government jobs and their largely rural economy is hamstrung due to poor infrastructure. Tuensang was also the site of several demands for creation of smaller districts and even a separate state. In short, Tuensang's persistent development deficit offered incentives to manipulate the headcount.

Patterns of Manipulation

Most data on development indicators are available for administrative units rather than tribes. Moreover, the Census provides many more observations for administrative units than for tribes. We have data for 18 tribal communities but as many as 78 administrative units. Communities and administrative units are largely coterminous in Nagaland, though, especially at the level of circles, with the exception of a few urban circles of Kohima, Dimapur and Tuensang. So, inter-tribal competition is largely synonymous with inter-district/circle competition. We will, therefore, use territorial units as the units of analysis to study the correlates of manipulation/over-reporting.

Over-reporting is unobserved and can only be inferred from the reported population. We can construct two measures of over-reporting. Assuming the 1981 and 2011 Censuses to be reasonably reliable (Tables 4.2A–B),[66] we can use the difference between the growth rate of a circle during 1991–2001 and its average decadal growth rate during 1981–2011 as a measure of over-reporting, where $G_{i,j}$ is the growth rate of circle i in period j:

$$Over\text{-}reporting1_i = G_{i,1991-2001} - G_{i,1981-2011,avg} \quad \text{(Equation 5.1)}$$

Another measure can be constructed assuming the natural growth rate does not vary dramatically over a decade, especially in the absence of a demographic transition, major socio-economic changes and high rates of migration. The growth rate during 1991–2001 includes a component of inflation in addition to the natural growth rate, while that for 2001–11 includes a component of correction. Therefore, half of the difference between the two growth rates roughly estimates over-reporting as the natural growth rates cancel out. For the ith circle, the second measure can be expressed as

$$Over\text{-}reporting2_i = \left(G_{i,1991-2001} - G_{i,2001-2011}\right) / 2 \quad \text{(Equation 5.2)}$$

The estimates of the discrepancy in headcount in 2001 calculated using Equations 5.1 and 5.2 by aggregating overcounts over circles are 443,350 and 395,223, respectively, compared to 358,675 (non-cumulative estimate for 2001), calculated using the fundamental equation (Equation 4.1). A few comparative observations about the estimated discrepancies are in order. First, the estimates based on Equations 5.1 and 5.2 use information from at least three censuses. The estimates based on Equation 4.1 are, however, based on pair-wise comparisons of censuses. Second, all the estimates of discrepancy are based on comparisons *within* the Census, that is, do not use data from sources other than the Census. Third, the estimate based on Equation 4.1 is a lower bound on account of the assumptions related to death rates and migration. This partly explains the gap between the estimates based on Equations 4.1, 5.1 and 5.2 and suggests that we have not been able to fully correct the 2001 Census population estimate (see also note 31 of Chapter 4).

We will next discuss the nature of over-reporting (competition among communities), motives behind manipulation (pre-emptive, defensive and prospective) and other correlates of over-reporting (the size of community and the remoteness of administrative units). We will use 1981 as the reference year for our analysis because discrepancies in the Census peaked in 1991 and 2001. In 1981, there were 69 circles that increased to 114 by 2011. We constructed a slightly larger data set consisting of 78 circles for which we could generate comparable figures on population and other characteristics of interest for the period 1981–2011 and then mapped 60 assembly constituencies onto these circles. Table 5.5 summarises the descriptive statistics for the correlates of over-reporting. The results of bivariate and multivariate analyses are presented in Tables 5.6–5.8.[67] The regressions explain about 38 per cent variation in over-reporting.[68]

Competitive Manipulation

A key implication of our discussion is that over-reporting is competitive in nature. Both measures of over-reporting reveal a positive spatial auto-correlation, that is, circles with high (low) over-reporting are surrounded by other circles with high (low) over-reporting (Table 5.5). Also both measures show persistence over distance (Figure 5.6).

The nature of competition can also be understood from the perspective of how over-reporting changes with the number of communities. In a bipolar situation, there is an intense (zero-sum) competition and there are clear winners and losers. As the number of communities increases, the gains and losses are distributed, which induces collective action problems making manipulation less attractive and also difficult. This relationship can be examined by using either the effective number of communities $1/\Sigma_k s_{i,k}^2$ or ethnic fractionalisation index $(1 - \Sigma_k s_{i,k}^2)$, where $s_{i,k}$ is the population share of the kth tribe in the ith circle.[69] Both measures of over-reporting are negatively correlated with the ethnic fractionalisation index and the effective number of communities (Table 5.6: Panels A1–A2). The negative relationship also holds in the multivariate analysis (Table 5.8).

The high spatial dependence of over-reporting and its negative association with ethnic fractionalisation and effective number of communities suggest that (a) over-reporting/competitive manipulation was driven by the demonstration effect of neighbouring circles and (b) manipulation was higher in relatively ethnically homogenous circles.

Role of Public Resources

Popular interest in elections can be treated as a measure of interest in the public pie, which, as argued earlier, is a determinant of manipulation of headcount. Voting rate can be used as a proxy of interest in public resources. We use both the voting rates for the 2003 Assembly Election as well as the long-run average for

Table 5.5 Summary statistics

Variable	Mean	Std. dev.	Minimum	Maximum	Moran's I[§]
Over-reporting1	37.96	40.22	-21.91	204.31	0.118 (0.025)
Over-reporting2	37.88	28.81	-14.61	142.77	0.204 (0.001)
Population growth (1981–91)	57.99	44.51	5.05	302.07	0.192 (0.001)
Population growth (1991–2001)	70.73	41.87	11.67	219.88	0.155 (0.006)
Population growth (2001–11)	-5.04	26.43	-70.27	48.65	0.298 (0.000)
Population (1991, in '000s)	15.51	18.82	1.73	127.73	0.007 (0.370)
Population (1991, in '000s) squared	590.20	2,044.81	2.98	16,313.93	0.010 (0.304)
Share of villages in circle (2001) that lie beyond 10 kilometres of bus route	27.02	28.37	0	100	0.239 (0.000)
Distance of circle headquarter from the nearest town	60.30	44.42	2	202	0.393 (0.000)
Literacy rate (1981)	37.48	14.59	5.52	69.01	0.618 (0.000)
Urban centre (= 1 if circle included an urban area in 2001)	0.12	–	0	1	-0.053 (0.276)
District demand: Group 1 (circles of 3 districts formed in 2004)	0.18	–	0	1	0.407 (0.000)
District demand: Group 2 (other circles demanding district status)	0.19	–	0	1	0.484 (0.000)
Voting rate (2003)[‡]	90.42	7.95	67.95	99.91	0.355 (0.000)
Ratio of electorate size (1993) to population (1991, in %)[‡]	66.42	24.72	26.29	243.38[##]	-0.087 (0.077)
Expected loss of legislative seats (1991, relative value)[†]	0.01	0.30	-0.80	0.31	0.343 (0.000)
Effective number of communities (1991)[††]	1.24	0.59	1	5.52	0.037 (0.163)
Ethnic fractionalisation index (1991)[††]	0.12	0.18	0	0.82	0.118 (0.025)

Source: Authors' computations using GoI (1983; 1984c; 2011g; n.d.1; n.d.2).

Notes: (i) Total number of observations is 78 (see Note (iv) to Table 5.4). (ii) ‡ 60 constituencies were mapped onto 78 circles. (iii) § *Moran's I* measures spatial correlation. *p*-values are reported within parentheses. (iv) ## The ratio is expected to be less than 100, which it is, except for two cases (106 and 243). This could be because of imperfect matching of constituencies and circles. (v) † Calculated using the 1991 data for the 11 districts of 2011 (Tables 5.2 and 5.4). The mean is not zero because of rounding off. (vi) †† Based on the population share of Naga language speakers in each circle. Non-Naga languages have been excluded because of their small sizes.

Table 5.6　Patterns of response to delimitation across circles

Variable/statistic	Over–reporting1	Over–reporting2
Panel A1: correlation with ethnic fractionalisation		
Pearson correlation	–0.17 (0.129)	–0.20 (0.087)
Spearman's rank correlation	–0.37 (0.001)	–0.37 (0.002)
Panel A2: correlation with effective number of communities		
Pearson correlation	–0.12 (0.291)	–0.15 (0.202)
Spearman's rank correlation	–0.37 (0.001)	–0.34 (0.002)
Panel B1: voting rate (2003)		
Voting rate (2003)	1.52 (0.007)	1.30 (0.001)
R^2	0.090	0.129
Panel B2: voting rate (1982–2003)		
Voting rate (1982–2003)	1.04 (0.175)‡	1.09 (0.045)
R^2	0.024	0.052
Panel C: expected loss of seats due to delimitation (pre-emptive manipulation)		
Relative loss (1991)	–10.08 (0.518)	–16.68 (0.133)‡
R^2	0.006	0.03
Panel D: district demand (prospective manipulation)		
District demand: Group 1	31.41 (0.007)	31.32 (0.000)
Intercept	32.31 (0.000)	32.26 (0.000)
R^2	0.09	0.18
Panel E1: ratio of electorate size (1993) to population (1991) (defensive manipulation)		
Electorate 1993/Population 1991	0.39 (0.035)	0.17 (0.206)‡
R^2	0.06	0.02
Panel E2: ratio of electorate size (1998) to population (1991) (defensive manipulation)		
Electorate 1998/population 1991	0.28 (0.067)	0.08 (0.433)
R^2	0.04	0.01
Panel F1: size		
Size (population 1991)	–1.65 (0.009)	–0.66 (0.153)‡
Size squared	0.012 (0.039)	0.004 (0.356)
R^2	0.097	0.042
Panel F2: ln (size)		
ln (population 1991)	–17.56 (0.001)	–9.05 (0.024)
R^2	0.13	0.07
Panel G1: remoteness (share of villages in circle beyond 10 kilometres, 2001)		
Distant villages	0.37 (0.021)	0.27 (0.020)
R^2	0.068	0.070
Panel G2: remoteness (distance of nearest town from circle headquarter, 2001)		
Nearest town	0.39 (0.000)	0.31 (0.000)
R^2	0.19	0.22
N	78	78

Sources: Authors' computations.

Notes: (i) p-values are reported within parentheses. (ii) ‡ Coefficient with t-statistic > 1. See note 67 of this chapter. (iii) Except for Panels A1 and A2, which report correlation coefficients, the rest of the panels report regression coefficients. (iv) Results in Panel D are robust to the inclusion of the other district demand dummy.

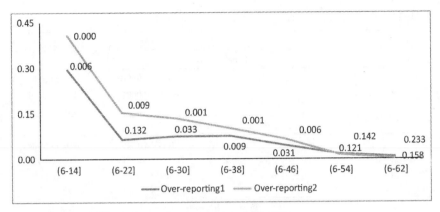

Figure 5.6   Spatial dependence of over-reporting, 1991–2001

Source: Authors' computations.

Notes: (i) The figure shows values of *Moran's I* by distance bands on horizontal axis (in kilometres). (ii) The data labels indicate the corresponding *p*-values.

the period 1981–2003, including all assembly elections between 1982 and 2003 and excluding 1998 that was boycotted by most political parties.

The use of 2003 data can be justified even though we are largely focused on over-reporting in 2001. First, the intensity of voting in the 2003 election, which was the only election conducted in the middle of the delimitation controversy (2002–8),[70] indicates the importance the people attached to elections and by implication their existing constituencies. Second, the 2003 figures are not outliers vis-à-vis the long-run trends. Third, the 1998 Elections held before delimitation were boycotted by the opposition and 43 out of 60 candidates won unopposed, while voting rates were less than the long-run average in the rest of the constituencies.

The 2003 voting rate (Table 5.6: Panel B1) and the long-run average of voting rate (Table 5.6: Panel B2) are positively associated with over-reporting. The multivariate analysis indicates that a 1 percentage point increase in the voting rate is associated with an almost equal increase in over-reporting (Table 5.8). In other words, over-reporting has been higher in circles with higher voting rates. So, circles with a greater interest in accessing government resources over-reported their populations more than others. Manipulation can be driven by different motives discussed as follows (Figure 5.1).

One of the motives behind over-reporting is related to the preservation of benefits of past manipulation. This is *defensive* manipulation. The coefficient of the ratio of electorate size (1993) to population (1991) is positive (Table 5.6: Panels E1–E2), that is, if a circle had more voters relative to its 1991 Census population, then in the subsequent census, it over-reported its population to avoid deletion

Table 5.7   Relationship between population size and growth

Variable	Tribe	Language
Panel A: size		
Size	−0.0002 (0.008)	−0.0004 (0.018)
Intercept	62.97 (0.000)	73.95 (0.000)
R^2	0.125	0.109
Panel B: size and its square		
Size	−0.0002 (0.498)	−0.0008 (0.089)
Size squared	−0.000 (0.867)	0.000 (0.310)
Intercept	61.61 (0.000)	89.61 (0.000)
R^2	0.125	0.129
Panel C: ln (size)		
ln (size)	−12.23 (0.022)	−32.02 (0.002)
Intercept	177.55 (0.002)	395.66 (0.001)
R^2	0.094	0.173
N	56	51

Source: Authors' computations using data from Tables 4.12 and 4.15.

Notes: (i) p-values are reported within parentheses. (ii) The dependent variable is the decadal population growth rate of a tribe or language. The estimates are based on the pooled sample for the period 1971–2011. (iii) The analysis for tribes is restricted to 14 recognised Naga tribes in each decade. Chirr, Makware and Tikhir are excluded as they are treated as Yimchunger speakers by the census and, even otherwise, their population is very small. 'Other Nagas' and unclassifieds, being heterogenous/residual categories, are also excluded. The population of each of the five groups excluded from the analysis fluctuates due to content errors and varies abnormally across censuses (Tables 4.12 and 4.13). (iv) The sample size for language speakers varies from 11 for 1971–81 to 12 for 1981–91 to 14 for the last two decades because of the unavailability of data on Chakru/Chokri (1971 and 1981), Rengma (1971) and Zeliang (1971 and 1981) language speakers. The census report for 1981 mentions that Chakru/Chokri was enumerated under Angami and Zeliang was enumerated under 'Naga'. Zeliang is included in the analysis only for the post-1981 period. The exclusion of Angami in 1971 and 1981 has a minor impact on the magnitude of coefficients but not in their sign and p-values. (v) See also notes to Tables 4.12 and 4.15. (vi) We have corrected the content errors in the data on speakers of Sumi language in 2001 and 2011 (see excursus of Chapter 4) assuming that the populations of the Sumi tribe and Sumi language speakers are equal. This is justified as the two figures are quite close for most tribes (Table 4.15). However, regression results are robust to the exclusion of Sumi language. (vii) The results are also robust to the exclusion of 1971 and/or 2011, the two years that were largely unaffected by inflation of headcount.

of votes. The results are not sensitive to the choice of election year – 1993 and 1998[71] – and also hold good in multivariate regressions. A one percentage point increase in the ratio is associated with a 0.17–0.35 percentage point increase in over-reporting.

Over-reporting linked to the demand for districts is an example of *prospective* manipulation. For want of detailed district-wise allocation of development funds, we test the relationship between development funding and over-reporting by examining the population growth rates of circles that were demanding a separate district.[72] For the purpose of analysis, we created two dummy variables for district demand – one identifying the circles under the three districts formed in 2004 and the other identifying circles still awaiting district status. There is a strong positive correlation between measures of over-reporting and the demand for new districts (Table 5.6: Panel D). In the multivariate analysis, we find a sizable impact of the district demand dummy for districts formed in 2004 on over-reporting (Table 5.8).[73]

A third motivation for manipulation is *pre-emptive* in nature. A community/district had an incentive to over-report population in 2001 if its 1991 Census population share was less than its (a) true 1991 population share because other communities were relatively successful at manipulation in pre-2001 censuses and/or (b) existing seat share in the state legislative assembly. The relative loss to a district i if census population of year k is used for delimitation is given by

$$Relative\ Loss_{i,k} = \frac{Existing\ Seats_i - Expected\ Seats_{i,k}}{Existing\ Seats_i} \quad \text{(Equation 5.3)}$$

$$Expected\ Seats_{i,k} = 60 * \frac{(p+n)_{i,k}}{\sum_j (p+n)_{j,k}} \quad \text{(Equation 5.4)}$$

where p and n denote true population and overcount, if any, and $p + n$ is the population reported in the Census. The correlation between relative loss and both measures of over-reporting is negative, but becomes positive in multivariate regressions (Table 5.6: Panel C). The p-values are high in both bivariate and multivariate regressions. The corresponding t-value of the loss variable exceeds one in some multivariate regressions (Table 5.8), though, which means that its inclusion adds to the model's explanatory power.

The demonstration effect of high growth rates of some of the tribes in the 1980s (Table 4.12) seems to have been very strong leading to pervasive over-reporting in 2001 cutting across circles, districts, age groups, sexes, urban as well as rural areas and tribes (and their languages), which possibly attenuates the impact of the loss variable. Due to competitive manipulation across the state in 2001, the hill districts managed to restrict the potential loss of seats to four, that is equal to the numbers of seats they would have lost to Dimapur if delimitation followed the 1991 Census. The partial correction of accumulated errors of over two decades (1981–2001) in 2011 resulted in a sharp decrease in population across hill districts and tribes. Delimitation as per the 2011 Census would have transferred six seats from the hills to Dimapur.

Size of Community

We also expect a relationship between the size of a community and over-reporting, but the direction of the relationship is ambiguous. On the one hand, the smaller communities have an incentive to over-report more than the larger ones, possibly, because they face an existential crisis. On the other, it might be easier and less costly for the larger communities to over-report. However, larger communities also face greater collective action problems and lesser marginal gains.

The relationship between growth and population size is examined in three different ways. First, we regress the growth rate of each tribe on its population for a pooled sample of four decades, 1971–2011. The coefficients on size as well as log size are negative (Table 5.7). This indicates that compared to the larger tribes, smaller tribes have grown faster. Second, given the close relationship between tribes and their eponymous languages (Table 4.15), we use the number of speakers of a language as a measure of the size of the corresponding tribe. Once again coefficients on speakers and ln (speakers) are negative. In both the cases (tribe and language), the coefficient on the squared term has a very high p-value. Third, we examine the relationship for circles by regressing their growth on the corresponding population (and its square) and ln (population). There is a negative association between population and over-reporting (Table 5.6: Panels F1–F2), that is, there is more over-reporting in smaller circles and over-reporting decreases with population though at a decreasing rate (Table 5.8).[74]

Remoteness

The extent of over-reporting should vary with the difficulty of manipulation. It should be less difficult to manipulate data in remote areas where verification is difficult due to the nature of terrain and, at least until 2001, a greater footprint of insurgency. We use two proxies for remoteness and terrain – the share of villages beyond 10 kilometres of bus route in the circle and distance of the nearest town from the circle headquarter.[75] These variables also account for economic disadvantage because of the weakening in the government's development efforts as the distance from urban areas and roads increases. The lack of connectivity also limits access to markets. So, distant locations also have a greater incentive to manipulate data because of their greater dependence upon the public resources, while the cost of manipulation is lower because communities are relatively homogenous and tightly bound and cross-examination is difficult.

We find that the circles with a greater share of villages more than 10 kilometres away from the nearest bus stop reported above-average population growth rates in the 2001 Census. Moreover, the distance of the nearest town from the headquarter of such circles was more than that of the circles with below-average growth rate. There is a positive correlation between distance variables and over-reporting (Table 5.6: Panels G1–G2). In multivariate regressions, both the proxies of remoteness are positively signed. While the *p*-values of the coefficients of the distance variables increase vis-à-vis the bivariate regression, their inclusion adds to the explanatory power of some of the multivariate models.

We also controlled for urbanisation (whether a circle has an urban settlement) and literacy in the regressions (Table 5.8). The urbanisation variable is a proxy for the potential double-counting of the urban population in their native villages and is positively signed in all specifications. The positive coefficient of the urbanisation variable does not imply greater over-reporting in urban areas; rather, it suggests that there was greater over-reporting in circles that include an urban area due to double-counting.

There is a negative correlation between literacy and voting rate (-0.46, *p*-value < 0.05). Higher levels of literacy are associated with greater representation in the bureaucracy and greater awareness about potential legal and administrative changes including delimitation. However, higher literacy is also correlated with individualism and greater access to opportunities, greater mobility and lesser dependence on community and public resources, which should lead to lesser interest in manipulating government statistics. We found the literacy variable to be positive in all specifications, but the *p*-values of the coefficients are very high. Either the different effects of literacy are cancelling out or the distance variable is capturing the effect of literacy as well. Note that there is a negative correlation between literacy and the distance variables, that is, the share of villages beyond 10 kilometres of bus routes (-0.23, *p*-value < 0.05) and the distance of the nearest town from the circle headquarter (-0.31, *p*-value < 0.05).

Trends of Manipulation

The abnormalities in Nagaland's headcount and electorate size peaked around 2001 and subsided after the government decided to postpone delimitation in 2008 (Timeline 5.1). In 2001, the year with maximum discrepancy in census population (Tables 4.2A–B), the abnormality peaks in the long-run trends of the ratio of children in primary and middle schools to 0–14 year census population (Figure 4.5), ratio of electorate to census population (Figure 4.6), population of those aged less than 50 years except the 30–4 year age group (Figure 4.4), share of 60+ year

Table 5.8 Determinants of over-reporting in Nagaland, 1991–2001

Variable/model	Over-reporting1				Over-reporting2			
	Model 1	Model 2	Model 3	Model 4	Model 5	Model 6	Model 7	Model 8
Population (1991, in '000s)	-2.458	-2.127	-2.681	-2.353	-1.295	-1.030	-1.437	-1.169
	(0.008)	(0.019)	(0.003)	(0.012)	(0.503)	(0.100)	(0.023)	(0.060)
Population (1991, in '000s) squared	0.022	0.017	0.025	0.019	0.012	0.008	0.014	0.009
	(0.002)	(0.005)	(0.000)	(0.002)	(0.022)	(0.053)	(0.006)	(0.022)
Voting rate (2003)	1.058	0.985	1.239	1.178	0.944	0.890	1.062	1.018
	(0.024)	(0.036)	(0.010)	(0.016)	(0.007)	(0.008)	(0.003)	(0.004)
Ratio of electorate size (1993) to population (1991) (in %)	0.372	0.372	0.353	0.353	0.183	0.183	0.171	0.170
	(0.010)	(0.010)	(0.018)	(0.019)	(0.021)	(0.022)	(0.042)	(0.046)
District demand: Group 1 (circles of 3 districts formed in 2004)	29.739	29.106	39.564	40.395	26.688	26.255	33.057	33.598
	(0.195)‡	(0.200)‡	(0.066)	(0.063)	(0.124)‡	(0.127)‡	(0.025)	(0.025)
District demand: Group 2 (other circles demanding district status)	3.959	3.482	3.234	2.844	3.365	2.789	2.851	2.281
	(0.736)	(0.767)	(0.776)	(0.802)	(0.723)	(0.766)	(0.758)	(0.802)
Loss (1991, relative value)	12.302	13.29	14.47	16.049	3.46	3.66	4.885	5.505
	(0.360)‡	(0.330)‡	(0.286)‡	(0.245)‡	(0.725)	(0.710)	(0.623)	(0.581)
Effective number of communities (1991)	-20.274		-23.133		-15.955		-17.883	
	(0.042)		(0.038)		(0.036)		(0.028)	
Ethnic fractionalisation index (1991)		-41.425		-45.281		-39.173		-41.983
		(0.111)‡		(0.116)‡		(0.034)		(0.034)
Urban centre (= 1 if circle was urban area in 2001)	44.815	45.156	43.469	44.350	31.258	31.902	30.212	31.020
	(0.042)	(0.038)	(0.720)	(0.071)	(0.044)	(0.032)	(0.071)	(0.061)
Distance of circle headquarter from the nearest town	0.175	0.192			0.115	0.128		
	(0.237)‡	(0.180)‡			(0.326)‡	(0.260)‡		
Share of villages beyond 10 kilometres of bus route in the circle			0.139	0.135			0.095	0.099
			(0.399)	(0.417)			(0.394)	(0.371)
Literacy rate (1981)	0.209	0.193	0.194	0.171	0.205	0.191	0.196	0.178
	(0.464)	(0.498)	(0.488)	(0.537)	(0.381)	(0.409)	(0.390)	(0.425)

Intercept	-62.099	-77.777	-65.842	-84.202	-50.661	-62.667	-53.152	-67.106
	(0.153)	(0.065)	(0.151)	(0.060)	(0.106)	(0.036)	(0.102)	(0.033)
R^2	0.376	0.373	0.369	0.362	0.38	0.389	0.374	0.381
N	78	78	78	78	78	78	78	78

Source: Authors' computations.

Notes: (i) We have used heteroscedasticity-robust standard errors. (ii) *p*-values are reported within parentheses. (iii) ‡ Coefficient with *t*-statistic > 1. See note 67 of this chapter.

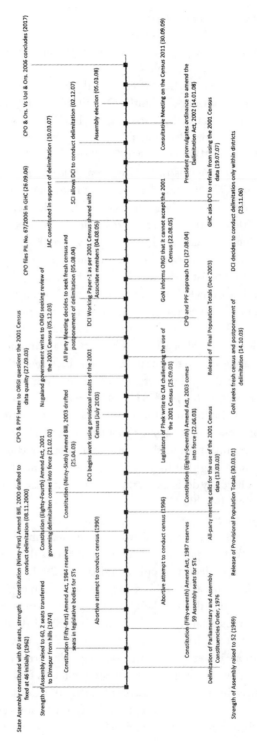

Timeline 5.1 Delimitation and related events in Nagaland

Source: Authors' compilation, using various sources (including *CPO & Ors. vs. UoI & Ors.* 2006; GoI 2008d).

age groups in the population (Chapter 4), household size (Tables 4.4A–B) and rate of urbanisation (Table 4.2A).

As discussed earlier, after steadily increasing until 2011, the electorate contracted continuously until 2017 (Table 4.6).[76] Two characteristics of the decline are noteworthy. First, the decline was so steep that the mean annual growth rate of the electorate falls by about 1 percentage point if we consider the period 1974–2018 instead of 1974–2009 (Table 4.7).[77] Second, the decline was not uniform across districts.[78] Between 2008 and 2013, the electorate of Nagaland shrank by 7.97 per cent, whereas that of Dimapur increased by 7.3 per cent (Table 5.3) even though the Naga population of the district contracted. In 2013, 39 out of the 60 constituencies registered a decline in electorate size relative to 2008. These include Ghaspani I in Dimapur where the decline was marginal. Growth in electorate was marginal in the remaining 21 constituencies, except Dimapur I and III that registered a sizable increase. In 2018, the electorate of 42 out of 59 constituencies including Ghaspani II in Dimapur was smaller than their 2008 electorate.[79] In five constituencies, the size of electorate was smaller in 2018 than in 1998 – Dimapur-I,[80] Impur (Mokokchung), Longleng (Longleng), Tamlu (Longleng) and Tehok (Mon). The last four are among the top five constituencies ranked according to the mean voting rate between 1974 and 2018 (Figure 5.3). In fact, even in 2018, the electorate of Tamlu had not reached the 1993 level.

Moreover, as discussed in Chapter 4, government surveys conducted after 2008 reported a decline in headcounts. A sample survey in 2009 revealed that most parts of Nagaland had a lower population than in 2001 (*Nagaland Post* 2009). The state government 'found that most of the villages recorded exaggerated population figures believing that they would get more financial allocations' (*Indian Express* 2011). Three key decisions of the government eliminated incentives to over-report headcount after 2008.

First, three key sites of manipulation were granted district status in 2004, which eliminated a major driver of manipulation. Our claim is corroborated by the fact that the population share of the circles that continue to demand district status grew or decreased only marginally in 2011.

Second, in early 2008, a presidential ordinance deferred delimitation in Nagaland (and also in Manipur, Assam and Arunachal Pradesh) to until after the first census taken after 2026, that is, in 2031 (GoI 2008b).

Third, 'to encourage the people to come out with correct household and population figures' the government adopted a carrot-and-stick policy. On the one hand, it assured villagers that 'the present level of VDB household grant will not be reduced in any manner as a result of the 2011 Census figures' (Rio 2011: 97–8). On the other, it cautioned that in the future, resources will not be allocated on the basis of census if it is found to have been manipulated (*Indian Express* 2011).

The elimination of incentives to manipulate were complemented by the curtailment of opportunities to manipulate. A vigilant state government alert to the possibility of subversion of data collection, the support of community volunteers and the threat that census data will be compared with church records (GoN 2009a) and followed by biometric surveys (*Assam Tribune* 2011; Neiphu Rio, interview, 27 May 2015, New Delhi) checked the opportunities to manipulate the 2011 Census.[81] In short, both the *incentive* and *opportunity* to overstate headcount had dissipated by 2011. Delimitation as per the 2011 Census will transfer six seats from the hills to Dimapur compared to four as per the 2001 Census.

Concluding Remarks

In this chapter we explored political-economic factors to build a parsimonious explanation of Nagaland's demographic somersault (and high voting rates). We showed that overcounting in 2001 and its (partial) correction in 2011 can account for the somersault. The overcount was driven by political-economic factors including development deficit,[82] demand for new districts, threat of loss of constituencies and need to recover constituencies lost in an earlier delimitation. There was higher over-reporting in circles with (a) a larger share of remote villages, (b) demand for district status and/or preserving old constituencies or creating new ones, (c) larger electorate relative to census population in the 1990s, (d) fewer communities and, thus, clearer demarcation of winners and losers of manipulation, (e) higher voting rates, (f) urban centres and (g) smaller population size. The manipulation of data, which peaked around 2001, subsided after three new districts were created in 2004, delimitation was postponed in 2008 to until after the first census taken after 2026 and the government ostensibly delinked development funding and village size in the run-up to 2011.

The other key findings relate to the hills–plains divide that is coterminous with the insider–outsider divide in popular imagination. While the chief minister and members of parliament highlighted this divide, the Naga fear vis-à-vis non-Nagas of Dimapur seems to be an instance of 'fear of small numbers' (Appadurai 2007). Nagas have been the dominant community in Dimapur both numerically and politically even though both capital and labour are supplied by outsiders. Intra-Naga conflicts shape Dimapur's political landscape. Even Dimapur I (Dimapur Town before 1974), the only unreserved constituency of the state, was dominated until 1988 by Angami Nagas and non-Nagas married to Angamis and afterwards by Sumi Nagas.[83] Sumis also overwhelmingly dominate Naga settlements in the fertile plains in the disputed area that falls in the constituencies of Dimapur. In addition, Sumis are an influential part of every insurgent outfit based in and around Dimapur. The fear of the 'outsider' in Dimapur is, in fact, the fear of Sumi and

Ao dominance over the commercial hub and the only truly multi-ethnic city of the state. The indigenous non-Naga tribes, Rongmei Naga settlers from Manipur, 'illegal' international immigrants (Bangladeshi Muslims) and migrants from plains serve as soft targets that help deflect attention from intra-Naga conflicts.

Recall that Chapter 3 suggested that errors in Nagaland's maps cannot be resolved with the help of better mapmaking technologies as they are rooted in the as-yet inconclusive search for a stable basis for Naga identity and the ongoing dispute over Nagaland's place within the Union of India. This chapter likewise suggests that the errors in Nagaland's census are linked to the fragile balance of power among tribes. Educationally and economically disadvantaged tribes, in particular, and non-Ao/Angami tribes, in general, are competing for a larger share in the public pie – representation in legislature, government jobs, government controlled institutions of professional education and government contracts – whose distribution depends upon *reported* population shares and, in some cases, *measured* educational and economic disadvantage. Moreover, some of the smaller tribes still do not have separate districts for themselves. The 'Greater Nagaland' project that could add large tribes such as Tangkhul, Mao and Rongmei of Manipur to Nagaland is another source of numerical anxiety (and, given the expectations of an imminent conclusion of the Naga peace process, this factor needs attention ahead of the next census). Lastly, the increasingly erratic rainfall, growing pressure on agricultural land in the hills, shrinking *jhum* cycles and the growing gap between villages and towns in terms of health care and education facilities are pushing people from hills to already overcrowded plains, where the economy is not growing fast enough to gainfully absorb in-migrants. Further expansion of the plains economy and the private sector of the economy and the consequent reduction of the dependence of people on the public sector and agriculture is dependent upon the resolution of the dispute over Nagaland's political status and the border dispute between Assam and Nagaland. Conducting census will remain a challenge until communal anxiety is reduced through the resolution of the political dispute over Nagaland's place in the union.

Notes

1. Electoral contest can be viewed as a three-level game, including the choice of electoral system, the choice of specific rules governing elections and elections per se. One of the main differences between the Congress and the Muslim League in the run-up to India's independence involved the choice of electoral system with the latter insisting on a system organised on communal basis. The last colonial census (1941) was affected by widespread competitive manipulation by different groups in Bengal and Punjab, which were partitioned in 1947. The discussion in

this chapter is restricted to the choice of specific rules governing the partition of constituencies and the choice of data used to implement the rules.

2. In the 1960s and 1970s, the growing population and agricultural supply shocks raised the spectre of persistent food shortages and stunted economic growth, which also threatened to undermine India's international strategic autonomy. The government introduced agricultural reforms to tackle the supply-side bottlenecks. It was felt that 'drastic' population control measures involving an element of 'compulsion' were inevitable in 'the larger national interest' (Panandiker and Umashankar 1994: 89–90) to address, among other things, the demand side of the problem of food shortage. The Constitution Amendment (Forty Second) Act, 1976, suspended decennial delimitation as it was feared that states that succeed in meeting family planning targets would lose parliamentary seats. The Eighty-Fourth (2002) and Eighty-Seventh (2003) Amendment Acts retained the interstate distribution of seats based on the 1971 Census.

3. As per the Constitution, the delimitation of constituencies of local bodies is determined by 'the last preceding census of which the relevant figures have been published' (Arts. 243 and 243P). In contrast, the delimitation of parliamentary and state assembly constituencies will continue to be determined by the 1971 and 2001 Censuses, respectively, until the first census taken after 2026. Part IX of the constitution that governs rural local bodies does not apply to Nagaland, while the application of Part IXA that governs urban bodies has been suspended due to opposition from civil society.

4. Delimitation has been a divisive exercise in several other countries. In the United States of America (USA), the reapportionment of seats in the House of Representatives could not be carried out in any state after the 1920 Census and had to wait 'until after the next census' due to objections from the Conservatives who believed that the rural population was underestimated (Prewitt 2003: 16). In Pakistan, where ethno-regional competition forced repeated postponement of censuses, 'no government was prepared to face census results which sharply changed inter-provincial ratios or rural-urban ratios, as these would have resulted in altering the seats allocated to different provinces in the National Assembly as well as the allocation of development funds allocated on the basis of population' (Khan 1998: 481; see also Weiss 1999: 687, 691). See also Adepoju (1981) for Nigeria.

5. In 1987, the government froze the distribution of constituencies between the indigenous tribal people and 'outsiders' in Arunachal Pradesh, Nagaland, Meghalaya and Mizoram. Similar provisions were introduced for Sikkim in 1980 and Tripura in 1992.

6. The results of the 1971 Post-Enumeration Checks were released in 1975 (Agrawal and Kumar 2019a), a year before the publication of the Delimitation of Parliamentary and Assembly Constituencies Order, 1976.

7. We will not discuss the possibility of bottom-up manipulation of census in terms of the defiance of the hegemony of the state, intrusive authority and/or surveillance. In Nagaland, the few instances of defiance, forced or voluntary, involved a withdrawal from the enumeration process rather than its manipulation (Chapter 4).

8. There are several reasons why governments of small states do not have much incentive to manipulate numbers. First, the reference year for federal redistribution was 1971 until the implementation of the recommendations of the Fourteenth Finance Commission (FFC) in 2015 that divided the weight assigned to population between 1971 and 2011 (GoI 2003; 2015a). Second, the actual population and area shares of smaller states at the federal level are less than the corresponding floor value (see, for instance, Table 7.1). In fact, in 2001, even after massive over-reporting Nagaland's share of seats in the parliament was barely more than one. The corrected 2001 share was much less than one, whereas the 2011 share was also less than one. Third, unlike in states such as Punjab (Gill 2007), we have not come across allegations that the government was directly involved in the manipulation of the 2001 Census in Nagaland. It is a different matter that *later* the state government used the inflated headcount to bolster its case for increasing the strength of the state legislative assembly, creating a legislative council for the state and increasing the state's parliamentary representation (see, for instance, GoN 2005b). Months after the state government admitted to errors in the census, Nagaland's MPs complained that despite 'population growth' Nagaland was underrepresented in the parliament (C. A. Jamir 2003; Sangtam 2003). We came across a source which suggested, 'For years, data has been manipulated in Nagaland by village authority, in connivance with state bureaucrats, to boost numbers in order to attract central schemes' (*ME* 2013e), but even this does not suggest the deliberate use of manipulation by the government to secure greater federal transfers at the expense of other states.

9. Attane and Courbage (2000: 268, 275) suggest that in case of China's ethnic minorities, higher fertility seems to be a response to the threat posed by the Han majority and 'a means of affirming identity'. In a different context, Urla (1993: 833–5) points out that the Basque nationalist concern over the loss of language has fuelled campaigns to increase the use of the Basque language in public rather than pronatalism. For a global survey and analysis of the relationship between community size and ethnic conflict, see Bookman (2013).

10. We rarely came across concerns about fertility in Nagaland. On such occasions, the focus was invariably on alleged illegal/undocumented Muslim immigrants. Muslims of Nagaland, a small community (Table 4.11) with a highly skewed sex ratio (Agrawal and Kumar 2012b: Table 13), can barely explain 2 per cent of the population growth between 1991 and 2001. Similarly, the politicisation of population research is irrelevant as there is hardly any demographic research going on in Nagaland, while the public debate is driven entirely by political and bureaucratic statements and opinion pieces in newspapers.

11. In India, the same district administration collects information on population eligible for welfare schemes, conducts enumeration and post-enumeration checks and enrols eligible voters on electoral rolls.

12. See Sharad Kulkarni (1991) for an instance of widespread manipulation of the census in Maharashtra, where officials could/did not intervene, and Zarkovich (1989) for erstwhile Yugoslavia, where people deliberately misled enumerators

and census department had to accept the faulty responses. In most countries, census departments are wary of coercive legalistic approaches to dealing with non-cooperation of people (see Prewitt 2003: 15 for the USA). Kumar (2019) discusses the legal aspect of the government's limited ability to respond to widespread manipulation of headcount at the grassroots.

13. A recent statement of the Lotha Students Union succinctly captures the long-standing Naga concerns over immigration: 'Uncontrolled and unregulated immigration into indigenous societies is a threat to the survival and continuity of sensitive indigenous tribal communities such as ours where trade and commerce is at a nascent stage of adaptation and practice which will take a few years before our own locals are able to compete in trade and commerce with the non-locals in an open market' (*ME* 2018p). These concerns notwithstanding, both Naga insurgent groups and big landlords are deeply dependent upon cheap immigrant labour.

14. Other societies undergoing political or economic transition or turmoil have also witnessed the politicisation of demography (Horowitz 2000; Bookman 2013). In Jammu and Kashmir, census became 'just a pretext for a religious war, led by the competing elites' (Swami 2000). Likewise, in Northern Ireland, where 'the census data has often been used to advance sectarian arguments', 'demography had become even more politicised, a case perhaps of "war by other means"' (Anderson et al. n.d.).

15. In its submission (7 November 2006) to the Gauhati High Court in response to *CPO & Ors. vs. UoI & Ors. 2006*, the Nagaland government argued that the flawed census threatened 'peace equilibrium'.

16. In ethnically divided societies, governments could themselves manipulate data as well as resort to gerrymandering to favour a community. Saudi Arabia's government does not report data on sectarian affiliation to avoid acknowledging the fact that the minority Shia community dominates the oil-rich Eastern Province, while the election system limits the chances of the success of Shia candidates by screening them ahead of elections and distributing Shia majority areas across Sunni majority constituencies (Matthiesen 2015: 4, 191).

17. Bookman's (2013: 32–4) sixfold typology of demographic engineering includes population measurement, pronatalist policies, assimilation, population transfers, boundary changes and economic pressures. Her notion of population measurement, the 'least intrusive method of altering relative numbers', is limited to change in 'how populations are defined and measured … alterations in definitions which de jure result in a change in the ethnic population size, even if they may not de facto change that size'. This can only explain content and coverage errors driven by administrative fiat, but not coverage errors driven by bottom-up manipulation that is of interest to us and is only briefly referred to in Bookman (2013: 20–1). Also, Bookman seems to assume that people necessarily acquiesce to administrative fiat, which is not the case, at least, in Nagaland. However, Morland (2018: 37, 44), who builds on Bookman's typology, acknowledges the autonomous capacity of non-state actors to influence demographic statistics.

18. A Lotha legislator (interview, 23 October 2014, New Delhi) blamed S. C. Jamir's Ao tribe for the reduction of Wokha's seats in 1974. Rengma civil society leaders (interview, 13 December 2018, Tseminyu) believe that Aos were responsible for an alleged loss they suffered in 1964. A retired non-Ao IAS officer (interview, 30 October 2015, Bengaluru) too suggested that Aos manipulated the delimitation process in the early 1970s. While most of our Ao interviewees rejected such allegations, an Ao leader (former minister, interview, 26 October 2014, Dimapur) and a retired Ao IPS officer (interview, 26 October 2014, Dimapur) admitted that the present Mokokchung district, which is overwhelmingly Ao in composition, got an additional seat at the expense of other districts that were carved out of the then Mokokchung.

19. Under the de facto method of enumeration, everyone is counted in the place of her current residence. So, the CPO was effectively demanding the implementation of the de jure method of enumeration under which everyone is counted in the place of her usual residence, even if they are not present there at the time of enumeration. Similar demands have also been raised by tribal leaders in Jharkhand (Venkatesan 2001; *Business Standard* 2016). We have heard similar demands in Manipur (junior government official, interview, 8 October 2019, Senapati).

20. A careful reading of submissions and counter-submissions in *CPO & Ors. vs. UoI & Ors.* (2006) reveals an interesting shift in public discourse in Nagaland. After 2005, the CPO shifted focus from floating population and illegal immigration to manipulation of headcount in rural Nagaland that is almost entirely populated by Naga tribes. Earlier the abnormal increase was explained as illegal immigration including from Bangladesh (CPO et al. 2003), whereas later it was explained as a discrepancy resulting from ghost enumeration (CPO 2007). A similar shift is seen in debates on inflated electoral rolls with post-2011 sources focusing on ghost electors (*Times of India* 2012b; *ME* 2017d).

21. Shürhozelie Liezietsu, who served as the chief minister in 2017, suggested that in some places 'politicians were involved [in manipulation] ... briefing voters and influencing enumerators' (interview, 15 November 2013, Kohima; also civil society leader, interview, 7 June 2014, Tuensang; retired IPS officer, interview, 26 October 2014, Dimapur). K. Therie, a former finance minister, said that 'rural leaders, including ex-pastors and deacons' too encouraged manipulation of numbers and 'summoned and intimidated [officials] for opposing this practice ... forced [them] to give in writing that they [officials] would not lodge any complaints' (*Times of India* 2012b; see also note 45 of this chapter for a related discussion). The government blamed 'vested interests' including 'village councils' for the statistical mess (GoI 2011c: viii; also DCO Nagaland, interview, 25 June 2013, Kohima). Interestingly, later Rio pointed out that the union government 'did not agree for a midterm census' (interview, 27 May 2015, New Delhi), whereas earlier he had said that a recount was not possible due to opposition from the grassroots (Hazarika 2005). The experience of Manipur (Chapter 7) and Nigeria (Adepoju 1981: 29–31; Ahonsi 1988: 557) suggests that recounts do not help in case the first count is manipulated.

22. Delimitation is irrelevant in case of parliamentary elections in Nagaland because ever since its creation the state has had just one Lok Sabha and one Rajya Sabha seat.

23. Tribalism is routinely blamed for the nexus between political representation and share in public pie. The origin of this nexus might be linked to some extent to the union government's expectations of the members of the first legislative assembly in the 1960s. See, for instance, Wouters (2018: 151–2) for how MLAs understood these expectations. Further note that public employment is a source of never-ending debate and dispute, but we have not come across any direct link between the over-reporting of the population and contest over job quotas. The discussion on district formation below will elaborate an indirect relation between the two, though.

24. Nagaland is an example of patronage-democracy, 'a system in which the government monopolises access to basic goods and services valued by a majority of the population, and in which government officials have individualised discretion over how these basic goods and services are distributed … voters decide between politicians, not by assessing their policy positions, but by assessing whether a candidate will favour them in the distribution of patronage' (Chandra 2009).

25. For a simple game-theoretic model of widespread manipulation of headcount, see Kumar (2019).

26. We do not have data to analyse the impact of demands for the creation of new sub-district administrative headquarters on the over-reporting of population. Three points are noteworthy though. First, the sub district demands are distributed across areas that (a) were granted district status in 2004 (Kiphire, Longleng and Peren districts), (b) have not yet been granted district status (select circles of Kohima, Mon, Tuensang, Wokha and Zunheboto districts) and (c) are demanding new sub-districts but not new districts. Most type (a) demands were fulfilled after the grant of district status as the administrative units under the respective circles were upgraded automatically. Second, district demands potentially affect several circles, whereas demands for new sub-district units affect only specific circles. Third, competitive developmentalism along disputed borders is an important driver of the formation of new circles in border areas (Chapter 3).

27. Our discussion is restricted to *ex ante* communal benefits. While district formation could also be linked to *ex ante* individual benefits, the number of individual beneficiaries involved is generally very small and uncertain. The abolition of the Regional Council for Tuensang district and the separation of Mon from Tuensang in 1974 are cases in point. The incumbent chief minister wanted to rework the electoral map ahead of the 1974 Assembly Elections (Dev 1988: 16) and select politicians from the district were seen to be the immediate beneficiaries. There was also a prior demand for separate district, though. Also, note that while we deal with communal benefits, the substance of this discussion remains unchanged as long as individual benefits are distributed within the community. Intra-community equity is sought to be achieved in a roundabout fashion in Nagaland, where a dense

network of civil society organisations involves a large number of people other than bureaucrats and politicians. Several interviewees told us that bureaucrats and politicians are expected to contribute generously to these organisations. See also Wouters (2018) regarding communitarian expectations vis-à-vis politicians and bureaucrats.

28. Tribal headquarter is not an administrative nomenclature, but it is widely used in Nagaland (RSZ and Rengma Hoho leaders, interview, 13 December 2018, Tseminyu; see also ENPO 2010: 2).

29. Rengmas lament that Sumis of the disputed area and Karbis in Karbi Anglong, who enjoy numerical preponderance have failed to honour Rengmas, the original landowners (RSZ and Rengma Hoho leaders, interview, 13 December 2018, Tseminyu). The Kacharis too feel the same about the Naga settlers in Dimapur (identities of interviewees withheld), while Nagas as a whole feel the same about all non-Nagas settled in Nagaland. Nagaland's newspapers abound in news about projects stalled by protests of original landowners, who feel they have not been adequately and appropriately consulted (see also budget speeches of various finance ministers; Rio 2004: 16, 32; 2014: 28, 51). In fact, as Wouters (2018: 119) notes, 'the history of post-statehood governance in Nagaland can be read as a history of tussles between the state government, which requires land to effectuate development, and Naga landowners who hesitate to give up even a square inch of land'.

30. The creation of a separate district also entails the creation of separate district-level customary courts for the major indigenous tribes of the district.

31. The state government constitutes a District Planning and Development Board for each district that ensures access to government funds. Further, special funds disbursed under, for example, the Border Area Development Programme are provided to each district along the international border (*ME* 2018z).

32. It is often alleged that the Mahatma Gandhi National Rural Employment Guarantee Scheme (MGNREGS), which guarantees 100 days of employment per year to rural households, tempts villagers to misreport numbers (Rio 2010b: 107). In 2010–11, Nagaland's approved Labour Budget under the MGNREGS included 336,000 rural households (GoI 2011d) compared to 277,491 rural households reported in the 2011 Census (Table 4.4A). This discrepancy can possibly be accounted for by duplicate and ghost job cards (GoI 2013c). The MGNREGS-based explanation cannot apply to the pre-2005 period. The Village Development Board (VDB) grants, however, pre-date MGNREGS. The VDB grants were revised in 2003 on the basis of the flawed 2001 Census and the number of beneficiary households increased sharply from 139,557 to 205,123 (Rio 2003: 69–70, 90, 98).

33. Wouters (2014) outlines four models of voting in Nagaland that differ in terms of the point of aggregation at which voting/political choices are made – household, clan, village and hereditary chief. These models implicitly assume ethnically homogenous villages and focus on intra-village modes of aggregation of political preferences and communal mobilisation of voters. Even Wouters' exceptional cases are intra-tribal in character. Similarly, the discussion of census as a site of

ethno-political conflict in Das (2017) is restricted to an intra-tribal case. We are interested in choices at the intra-district level that connect with both intra- and inter-tribe/district political-economic competition.

34. Khonoma's population (households/household size) was 2,187 (462/4.73) in 1981, 2,753 (543/5.07) in 1991, 2,917 (589/4.95) in 2001 and 1,943 (424/4.58) in 2011 (GoI 1984a; n.d.1; n.d.2; n.d.9).

35. Benreu's population (households/household size) was 414 (90/4.6) in 1991, 486 (101/4.81) in 2001 and 850 (180/4.72) in 2011 (GoI n.d.1; n.d.2; n.d.9). The 2011 population seems to be highly inflated as the number of households nearly doubled in a decade. We also have information about the population estimate of the neighbouring village of Poilwa, whose population was approximately 2,700 in 2013 as per Baptist Church Poilwa (2013: 26), whereas the corresponding figure was 2,860 and 2,782 (including Poilwa Namci) as per the 2001 and 2011 Censuses, respectively. Another source suggests that there were 600 households in 2002 (Poilwa Village Council 2002), whereas the 2001 Census reported only 398 households.

36. The government itself noted that 'loyalty to one's village and community compelled many to record their names in villages despite actually residing elsewhere' and 'vested interest as well as many Village Councils' too actively tried 'to enroll their natives residing in other parts of the State or Country' (GoI 2011c: viii). During one of our trips from Kolkata to Dimapur, we noticed that several of our co-passengers in their late teens were on their way to their villages to get biometric identification cards.

37. For a first-hand account of the role of bogus votes in Nagaland's elections, see Wouters (2018: 239, 241, 258–62). A Public Interest Litigation filed by the ACAUT claimed that there were as many as 400,000 bogus voters in Nagaland (*ME* 2017d).

38. Extortion by competing insurgent groups is widely held responsible for the over-priced and poor-quality goods and services sold in Nagaland, as traders have to recover their operating expenses (see, for instance, S. C. Jamir 1998: 60, 63). The impact of extortion on public infrastructure, price and quality of goods, private sector economic activity, indigenous entrepreneurship and economic inequality will require a separate discussion.

39. We heard a more or less similar description/explanation of why Nagas remain connected to their villages from a retired Naga IAS officer (interview, 16 November 2013, Dimapur). Villages (Wouters 2018: 56–7) and even clans and khels, spatial subdivisions of villages, have historical personalities (expressed in stereotypes) that presumably shape both individual villagers as well as perceptions about them.

40. Tribal organisations and churches do not have any legal authority either in the customary scheme or under the Art. 371A.

41. Village solidarity is not automatically guaranteed. In addition to threats of excommunication, it is built through an elaborate micro-distribution of power and resources and invocation of local histories (Wouters 2018: 263-7) and regular meetings that everyone including out-migrants (even when their entire family has settled elsewhere) are expected to attend (ibid.: 49). The threat of excommunication

helps check free-riders and dissenters because of dense community networks that extend beyond villages and the near institutionalisation of tribal consociationalism in Nagaland.

42. Even the well-to-do migrants remain engaged with their villages as they play a crucial role as captive support bases in Nagaland's politics, both electoral (retired Naga IAS officer, interview, 16 November 2013, Dimapur; Wouters 2018: 260) and non-electoral (*Nagaland Post* 2019).

43. This is true of most parts of India, including Jammu and Kashmir where one of us has carried out fieldwork. Zhao (2004: 195–9, also 185) notes that 'hundreds of thousands of people who had previously registered as Han' sought 'ethnic minority status' in China because of greater political representation, easier access to universities and relaxed family planning norms (see also Attane and Courbage 2000: 262). Sharad Kulkarni (1991) discusses instances of misreporting to benefit from tribal status. These are examples of competition over preferential access to public resources leading to content errors, that is, people reporting themselves as belonging to another category, and are different from coverage errors, which are of interest to us. Zarkovich's (1989: 607) discussion of the Yugoslavian censuses is closer to our concern. He discusses double-counting, a coverage error, linked to migration. He says, 'An emmigrant is a person who is not closing doors of his house after he left the country.... An emmigrant does not know in advance what his life will look like in the country of his new residence. He likes to keep in his mind the idea of an easy return. This is why his relatives keep him at home in all sorts of lists including those intended to censuses and various surveys.... Should a need arise for a return there will be no formalities as an obstacle. Nor the reputation is useful of a person holding a job abroad. Such a person might be considered rich. That attribute could easily lead to indesirable speculations. Therefore, the best thing is to be just the same as everybody else. The way to achieve this effect is to remain an ordinary resident. This is how the psychology of emmigrants leads to another tendency toward overenumeration.'

44. Intentional manipulation is not the only factor that might explain double-counting. Belated revision of electoral rolls leaving behind the names of government servants transferred to other locations might explain multiple enrolment. However, the number of transferrable positions is too few to explain the magnitude of anomalies and, in any case, cannot explain high growth in remote areas where there is limited government presence. The ignorance of enumerators, who may confound de facto and de jure methods of enumeration, is another possibility (Vipra 1961: 882). This cannot explain the high growth rate in 2001 because it has to be assumed that there was greater ignorance in 2001 than in 1981 and 1991, that is, ignorance increased over time.

45. Van Ham and Saul (2008: 39) visited Yongyah on 31 March 2002 and noted the following: 'We enter the village and face the 2,000 people who live here.' They also report the information supplied by the village council according to which there were 1,286 households and 12,000 people in the village (ibid.: 52). While

the figure 2,000 cannot be taken 'literally', the village council's estimate of more than 12,000 is 'very high' (Peter van Ham, personal communication, 13 October 2013). The population of Yongnyah village in 2002 as per the village council exceeds the 2011 population of the Yongnyah circle that includes 11 villages. A few years after the 2011 Census, one of us visited Kuthur in Tuensang and Nokyan and Noklak in Noklak (8–9 June 2014) and found that village authorities' estimates of population exceeded the 2011 Census estimates by at least 50 per cent. For the role of village leadership in the manipulation of electoral rolls in Chakhesang and Yimchunger villages, see Wouters (2018: 260–2) and Das (2017: 69), respectively. We should add that the inflated figures are not uncritically accepted by everyone. Phom (2001: 150), for instance, questioned the abnormally high growth rate of the Phom tribe since 1981. See also notes 21 and 36 of this chapter.

46. As per PES, which provides results at the level of the North-East region, there was negligible double counting or duplication in 2001 and 2011 (GoI 2006b; 2014d).

47. As discussed earlier (note 8 of this chapter), governments of small states in India do not have an incentive to manipulate headcount. However, in other developing countries, governments seem to have interfered with counting to protect their share in the federal resources, for example, Nigeria (Okolo 1999: 322; Jerven 2013: 57; Fawehinmi 2018) and Pakistan (Khan 1998: 481; Weiss 1999: 687, 691).

48. While delimitation is based on the entire population and not just the voting age population, this nuance might not be widely understood. So, attempts to manipulate headcount might have focussed upon the voting age population. GoI (2011c: 2) supports this reading: 'many misunderstood the exercise to be directly linked with the electoral roll. This lead [*sic*] to the *abnormal* increase in population of villages and towns in order to increase the vote bank. There were also many instances where children's age were manipulated to show them as eligible voters and recorded as such in the Census records' (see Jerven 2013: 60 for possibly a similar manipulation in the 1962 Census in Nigeria).

49. A civil society leader belonging to Longleng, which had seen very high growth rate in 2001 and a steep fall in 2011, said as much. He (interview, 14 June 2014, Longleng) pointed out that the contraction of population did not matter as the district status cannot be revoked. Census officials (interviews, 15 September 2012, New Delhi; 25 June 2013, Kohima) confirmed that this indeed was how Longleng viewed the otherwise unfavourable results of the 2011 Census. There have been three instances of dissolution of constituencies though. Moilan Wozhuro (Wokha district), Yisemyong (Mokokchung district) and Chazouba II (Phek district) were merged with neighbouring constituencies or absorbed in new constituencies in 1974.

50. Nagaland has never elected a woman to the state assembly (Kumar 2017b).

51. Commenting on village politics, a senior government official (Naga IPS officer, interview, 21 September 2012, Kohima) noted: 'Here there is [a] lot of competition between villages. It is matter of prestige to have a candidate from [one's] village. Often Village Councils come together and endorse candidates. Candidates from

big villages are assured victory because people vote en-masse. Even minorities in the village have to follow the diktat of the Village Council' (see also A. N. Jamir 2009; retired Naga IAS officer, interview, 16 November 2013, Dimapur; Wouters 2018). The salience of village politics seems to have changed over time though. The DCO, Nagaland, (interview, 25 June 2013, Kohima) suggested that initially, census used to be an occasion for competition among the tribes, but in the 1980s and 1990s (the period of maximum inflation) districts became the locus of competition before the focus shifted to villages in 2011.

52. Wouters (2018) discusses how the Naga society has adapted democracy to local conditions.

53. Note the negative coefficient of the variable 'Type' in Table 4.7, which suggests voting rates are lower in parliamentary elections.

54. Dimapur Town is the 'Gateway of Nagaland'. At least 80 per cent of outsiders enter Nagaland through Dimapur (*ME* 2018ac). The only functional railhead and civilian airport of Nagaland are located in Dimapur, while Nagaland's most important highway enters the state through this district. The town is also an important transport hub for Manipur and the neighbouring districts of Assam. It is the commercial capital of Nagaland and, perhaps, the second-most important commercial town in the whole of the North-East. It supports most of the non-public sector and non-traditional economy of Nagaland. It accounted for more than two-thirds of Nagaland's registered trade unions (GoN 2008: Table 26.1), as much as 44 per cent of bank loans (Rio 2012: 112) and, until a few years ago, most of the telecommunication network of the state (GoI n.d.10: 12).

55. Tribes with a population share (within the Naga community of Dimapur/overall population of Dimapur) of 5 per cent or more in 2001 [2011] are as follows: Angami (15/8) [13/7], Ao (16/9) [20/11], Lotha (7/4) [9/5] and Sumi (46/26) [40/21] (GoI 2018a; n.d.2).

56. The Sumi–Angami conflict in Dimapur predates the creation of Dimapur district. The Angamis were bitterly opposed to the separation of Dimapur from Kohima (GoN n.d.1). When the Sumi-dominated Dimapur was separated from Kohima, its administrative headquarter had to be placed in the Angami corner of the district (S. C. Jamir, interview, 27 August, 2013, Bhubaneshwar). Lintner (2012: 88–9), in fact, claims that the Sumi–Angami split goes back to the 1960s when the two tribes fought for control over Dimapur. Some of our interviewees suggested that Sardar Gurmukh Singh, a prominent non-local businessman, was murdered in 1984 because, among other things, he was a vocal supporter of district status for Dimapur. Chalie Kevichusa, however, argued that Angamis opposed the formation of Dimapur district to save Nagaland from being flooded by Bangladeshis (Haralu and Chandola 2012: 76–7).

57. The growing fear of being dominated by Tangkhuls of Manipur is, however, unravelling the culture of silence vis-à-vis Manipuri Nagas. Indeed, one of the most sustained mobilisations of the recent years has been directed against Rongmeis, originally from Manipur, effectively telling Maos and Tangkhuls that they are not welcome in Nagaland either. In fact, Tangkhuls were unwelcome even in the

heydays of the National Socialist Council of Nagaland-Isak Muivah (NSCN-IM) because their entry threatened the political-economic equilibrium among Naga tribes of Nagaland (Horam 1988: 26–7).

58. The enormous disparity within as well as between hill districts in terms of voters per constituency is explained by the skewed distribution of political and human capital during the formative years of the state, the 1960s and 1970s (see also note 18 of this chapter).

59. In 2011, Dimapur's population share was 19.15 per cent compared to the electorate share of 13.11 per cent (2008 Assembly Elections) and assembly seat share of 8.33 per cent (Tables 5.2–3).

60. The 2002 Delimitation Commission had awarded nine seats to Dimapur (GoI 2005b). This is equivalent to a gain of four seats. The commission did not, however, get 'into the potentially explosive issue of whether those seats should be general or reserved' (Baruah 2015) because as per the constitution there can be only one unreserved seat in the entire state.

61. Mon appears in the list of districts that improved their shares as well as those that were losing seats. Its population share grew, but that only meant a reduction of potential loss from two seats to one.

62. Certain villages of Phek reported an abnormal increase in population between 2001 and 2011, with the number of households growing by nearly 50 per cent amidst growing out-migration. In some of these villages, family size plummeted sharply resulting in a modest decadal population growth. Wouters (2018: 258–62) reported how threats of violence from powerful villages in Phek circumscribed the administration's ability to delete bogus entries in electoral rolls.

63. Is it possible that some of the tribes manipulated their population in 1991 because the existing legislation mandated the use of the 1991 Census for delimitation? The reference date for delimitation was shifted to 2001 in 2003.

64. The lesser than average growth rates of several circles of Zunheboto can partly be attributed to out-migration to Dimapur, which has accounted for about a third of the Sumi tribe's population in the recent decades (Table 5.1).

65. Lothas strongly believe that the 2001 headcount was 'right' (Lotha legislator, interview, 23 October 2014, New Delhi) and 'if 2001 Census is wrong, then no census in the state is right' (a Lotha speaker at a consultative meeting organised by the Nagaland Tribes Council on 22 June 2013 at Hotel Saramati, Dimapur). A senior insurgent leader belonging to the Lotha tribe too seems to have expressed frustration at the denial of more seats and development funds to his community and argued that this was against the Indian constitution.

66. We are unable to draw firm conclusions regarding the reliability of the 2011 Census until the data from 2021 Census are released. For preliminary observations in this regard, see note 31 of Chapter 4.

67. A lower p-value increases the likelihood of rejecting the null hypothesis of the corresponding coefficient being zero or there being no relation between the corresponding Y and X variables. Conventionally, in economics a p-value of 0.05

or less is considered to be good enough to reject the null hypothesis. In other words, if the p-value exceeds 0.05, one may reject the existence of the relationship between Y and X in a statistical sense. A t-statistic larger than 1 indicates that inclusion of the variable in the model adds to its explanatory power. In other words, from an econometric perspective, the variable is worth retaining in the model. R^2 is the coefficient of determination. It is a measure of goodness of fit and captures the extent of variation in the dependent variable that is explained by the variables included in the model.

68. The analysis is not affected by multi-collinearity as the variance inflation factor is much less than 10, which is considered to be econometrically problematic. We also carried out a spatial regression analysis that yielded results similar to those presented here.

69. We have borrowed 'effective number of communities' from political science, where the effective number of parties is used to count parties weighted by their relative strength (Laakso and Taagepera 1979). The effective number of communities equals the actual number of communities if all of them have identical shares. Otherwise, it will be less than the actual number. Ethnic fractionalisation is measured using the Herfindahl index that increases from zero to one with ethnic diversity. It is closer to zero (one) if the population is divided among few (many) communities. Thus, both the measures assume low values when a few communities dominate and increase as the population shares of communities become equal.

70. The 2008 Assembly Elections was conducted *after* delimitation was indefinitely postponed (Timeline 5.1).

71. The ECI reports data on electorate for 1998. The poll boycott affected the voting rates and, possibly, the revision of electoral rolls.

72. In several cases, district demands were raised long before 2001. The demands for Kiphire and Longleng districts can possibly be traced back to the early 1970s and the late 1980s, respectively (Rio 2004: 14, 30).

73. In multivariate regressions with population growth rate (1991–2001) as the explained variable, the coefficient of the dummy variable for the circles that were granted district status in 2004 was positive and had a very low p-value, while the coefficient of the dummy variable for those circles whose demand was not fulfilled was smaller in magnitude and also had a much higher p-value. A similar regression for 2001–11 showed that coefficient of the dummy variable for the former category of circles was negative and had a high p-value. However, the coefficient continued to be positive (with a lower p-value and t-statistic = 1) for the latter.

74. We have not characterised this relationship as U-shaped because in most cases (Table 5.8: Models 1–8) the population (1991) of only 2 of the 78 circles lies above the estimated point of inflection. Other studies have also found a negative relation between demographic engineering and ethnic dominance. In a sample of 30 countries, Bookman (2013: 39) found that states 'are less likely to implement a multitude of demographic engineering policies' when one ethnic group dominates (that is, fractionalisation is less). Note that Bookman examines manipulation by the state, whereas we are interested in manipulation at the grassroots.

75. We do not have data to control for the quality of roads or the frequency of bus services.

76. A former finance minister of Nagaland claimed that in 2012 there were about 400,000 bogus voters in the electoral rolls since the electorate should be about 60 per cent of the population (*Times of India* 2012b). Half a decade later, the ACAUT too claimed that there were 400,000 bogus voters in the state (*ME* 2017d) even though the electorate had in the meantime shrunk by nearly 200,000 between 2011 and 2017 (Table 4.6).

77. The annual growth in the electorate was 0.16 (−0.95) per cent during 2009–11 (2009–18) compared to 2.64 per cent during 1991–2008.

78. The deletion of bogus entries was not uniform even within districts and depended on the relative political and muscle power of competing villages (Wouters 2018: 258–62).

79. In 2018, Nagaland's electorate began to increase at last. However, the electorate was still about 100,000 less than its 2007 level.

80. Dimapur I's electorate size declined between 1998 and 2008 and increased steadily thereafter.

81. A Naga IAS officer (interview, 25 June 2013, Kohima) recalled that field enumerators under pressure to inflate headcounts eagerly awaited the arrival of biometric machines. Actually, comparison with church registers and biometric enrolment were not part of the official calendar of the 2011 Census. This was not the only instance of potential intersection between church and government statistics. It has been occasionally suggested that 'church pastors should be assigned as registrar, instead of VDB secretary. Since pastors are more influential and regularly available in the station than VDB secretary. Moreover at every birth and death, the pastor's presence is called to offer prayers and in doing so as usual they may not be ignored in recording of events occurred for compulsory registration.' However, the government differs as 'the assignment of works as registrar to the Pastors is not desirable since nature of work differs in regard to religion and government development functionaries are practically quite different' (GoN 2003b).

82. Development deficit refers to poor quality and inadequate public infrastructure (despite massive government spending) and the continued and unsustainable dependence of the economy on public-sector spending.

83. Until 1982 and 1969, respectively, indigenous non-Naga tribes got elected from Dimapur III (known as Dimapur before 1974) and Ghaspani II (Ghaspani before 1974). Otherwise, Nagas have won every single election in Dimapur district, except in Dimapur I where non-Nagas married to Angamis won elections until the late 1980s.

6

Flawed Surveys

Introduction

The poverty headcount ratio for Nagaland estimated using National Sample Survey Office (NSSO) data varies abnormally over the years. Until 2004–5, Nagaland reported one of the lowest rural poverty rates in the country, but by the end of the decade, it was among the states with relatively high poverty rates. A substantial improvement in the *reported* human development and other socio-economic indicators for Nagaland (Agrawal and Kumar 2012b: Table 1), which is largely rural, seem inconsistent with *growing* rural poverty in the recent decade when the state has enjoyed relatively peaceful conditions after a long period of armed conflict. Another puzzling feature of NSSO surveys is the increase in the share of tribal households in its samples for Nagaland from 85 per cent in the 50th round (1993–4) to 96 per cent in the 66th round (2009–10), even though the composition of the corresponding census population has remained stable over the years (Table 4.12).

This chapter analyses the quality of household sample survey data collected by the NSSO. There are several reasons for restricting the focus to NSSO surveys. First, most national level household surveys either do not cover states in India's ethno-geographic periphery or cover them irregularly. The NSSO regularly covers peripheral states including Nagaland. We will argue that even the surveys such as the NSSO that regularly cover these states do not have sufficiently representative samples to generate reliable estimates. The data deficit – the non-availability and/ or the poor quality of data – affects developmental outcomes through its impact on policymaking.[1] Second, the NSSO has been conducting surveys in Nagaland since the 1970s. This provides a reasonably long time series to examine how changes in the sampling design affect survey statistics. Third, other household surveys launched after 1991 do not share sufficient information about the sampling design. In comparison, the NSSO survey reports discuss sampling design in greater detail. Last but not the least, the NSSO data are the most comprehensive and widely used sources of household level statistics for India.

NSSO surveys cover a wide range of household characteristics. We will restrict our attention to monthly per capita consumer expenditure (MPCE), which is of singular importance as it is used to estimate the incidence of poverty. Poverty reduction has been integral to the self-image of the postcolonial Indian state since its inception and several welfare schemes accounting for a substantial proportion of government spending are linked to poverty estimates.[2] NSSO surveys are the primary means through which the government tracks household consumption and poverty.

This chapter contributes to the literature on the quality of survey data, in particular, the problem posed by non-coverage. The literature is largely focused on sampling design and sampling errors (Groves 2004; Groves et al. 2004), while non-sampling errors are relatively under-studied.[3] Non-sampling errors such as survey non-response have received some attention; thanks to the recent rise in non-response rates in developed countries (Meyer, Mok and Sullivan 2015; Hokayem, Bollinger and Ziliak 2015). Non-coverage has received scant attention, that too mostly from a theoretical perspective (Lessler and Kalsbeek 1992).

In the Indian context, few, if any, studies assess the quality of NSSO data in specific sites over a long period and examine how inadequacies in the data generation process affect survey statistics (Agrawal and Kumar 2017b).[4] The *Report of the National Statistical Commission* (GoI n.d. 16), which touched upon several issues related to the quality of NSSO data, did not discuss the deficiencies in NSSO surveys in the context of specific states. The *Report of the Committee on Optimum Sample Sizes for North Eastern States* discussed the problem of small sample size in abstract but did not examine other factors that could affect the representativeness of samples (GoI 2011a). As argued here, the NSSO samples for some of the north-eastern states are affected by frame and sample non-coverage and systematic biases,[5] which are independent of sample size.

Unlike the existing academic literature and official assessments of NSSO surveys, this chapter examines the quality of NSSO data in specific sites over a long period of time. It shows that the reliability of the NSSO data for Nagaland is questionable because of (a) frame non-coverage due to insurgency and restriction of samples to villages within 5 kilometres of bus routes until 2012 and, possibly, the use of outdated bus route maps, (b) the use of imperfect sampling frame and (c) biased samples. As a result, statistics from NSSO surveys in Nagaland are neither representative nor comparable over time. Moreover, consumer expenditure and poverty lines are overestimated because of non-coverage. The degree of non-coverage was so high that in most years between 1993–4 and 2011–12 Nagaland's poverty headcount ratio was one of the lowest in the country despite the possible overestimation of its poverty line.[6] While no other state suffered restrictions on samples in NSSO surveys on such a scale on a sustained basis, states in the country's ethno-geographic periphery such as Jammu and Kashmir, Tripura and Manipur share Nagaland's predicament. We will show that the decline in Nagaland's MPCE and the fluctuation of Jammu and Kashmir's MPCE relative to the rest of the country are partly explained by the changing sampling frame.

This chapter differs from existing evaluations of the NSSO data in another key respect. It explores the context dependence of the quality of survey data by examining the impact of insurgency/political conditions on sample surveys. Politics can impinge upon sample surveys at different stages in the life cycle (Figure 6.1).[7] First, political considerations can intervene at the stage of design of survey. Deaton and Kozel (2005: 196) discuss the possible influence of contesting

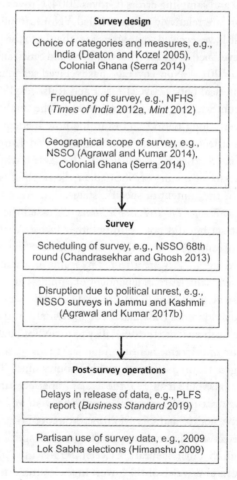

Figure 6.1   Political interventions across the life cycle of sample surveys
Source: Prepared by authors.

political ideologies on NSSO survey design in the late 1990s. Second, the choice of locations and subjects covered can be influenced by political priorities. The sustained exclusion of parts of India's periphery from surveys is indicative of the low priority attached to these regions.[8] This in turns reflects the unequal political and economic power of the periphery.[9] Third, political considerations can interfere with the scheduling of surveys, such as the decision to conduct another quinquennial NSSO survey during 2011–12 soon after the 2009–10 survey (note 27 of Chapter 1).[10] This lends support to the argument that 'as politicians and economic policy advisors work in their own self-interest, one would actually expect over-investment in the production of data' (Heine and Oltmanns 2016: 207). This overinvestment results from the desire 'to protect ... already taken irretrievable, "sunk" investments in certain policy areas' (Heine and Mause 2004: 411).

A fourth possibility explored in this chapter, relates to the disruption of surveys due to political unrest that blocks access to field sites. Agrawal and Kumar (2017b) discuss the disruption of NSSO surveys in peripheral states of India. Sumati Kulkarni (2004: 656) draws attention to the geographical restriction on the National Family Health Survey-II (NFHS-II) due to national security considerations. Lastly, politics could impinge upon surveys when political actors use data that 'appear to lend objective support to political opinions' to mould public opinion (Heine and Oltmanns 2016: 207). The slogan 'Garibi Hatao (Remove poverty)!' played an important role in the landslide victory of Indira Gandhi-led faction of the Congress in the 1971 Parliamentary Elections. After the elections, her government came under enormous pressure due to rising inflation and unemployment and was eventually compelled to impose emergency in 1975 amidst massive protests across the country. In 1973, in the run-up to the Fifth Five Year Plan (1974–9), B. S. Minhas resigned from the Planning Commission due to differences over 'distorted or juggled' data that were used 'to present an unrealistically bright picture of India's prospects' (Weinraub 1973). More recently, in the run-up to the 2014 Parliamentary Elections, the results of the 66th round of the National Sample Survey (NSS) (2009–10), which showed that the employment generation fell significantly short of the target of the Eleventh Five Year Plan, generated a lot of controversy (Chandrasekhar and Ghosh 2011; 2013; *EPW* 2011; *Economic Times* 2012, 2013a–b; *Forbes India* 2013). Academics used NSSO data to support (S. S. Bhalla 2013a–b; 2014a–b; Bhagwati and Panagariya 2014) or question (Chandrasekhar and Ghosh 2014) the economic agenda of political parties.[11] Likewise, NSSO surveys were at the heart of political dogfighting in the run-up to the 2019 Parliamentary Election (CNBC-TV18 2019; *Economic Times* 2019) and even afterwards as the government refused to release the results of the 75th round of NSS that covered consumer expenditure (GoI 2019b; *Times of India* 2019).

The literature examines deliberate/strategic manipulation as the reason behind erroneous statistics, whereas this chapter deals with surveys constrained by the political context. The problem analysed in this chapter is different from cases of active political interference such as China's refusal to participate in the International Comparison Programme (Wade 2012; Coyle 2014: 50–3). It is also different from instances of changes in survey design due to contesting political positions (Deaton and Kozel 2005: 196).

This chapter first introduces the problems of frame and sample non-coverage and then examines non-coverage in NSSO surveys in Nagaland and other states of the North-East and Jammu and Kashmir. This is followed by a discussion on faulty sampling frames and biased samples. After this we examine the impact of non-coverage on MPCE and estimates of poverty rates to illustrate how flawed surveys affect policymaking. The final section discusses the implications of our findings for the quality of government statistics in conflict-prone, underdeveloped regions.

Non-coverage in Sample Surveys

We will first distinguish between different kinds of deficiencies in samples to delineate the problems facing sample surveys in peripheral states of India. Following Groves (2004), errors in sample surveys can be classified into two broad categories: errors of non-observation and observational errors (Figure 6.2).[12] The failure to obtain data on parts of the target population results in 'errors of non-observation' (Kish 1965: 527–8). In contrast, 'observational errors' refer to the deviations of the respondents' responses from their true values (Groves 2004: 11) due to, inter alia, the lack of awareness of respondents, the inability of interviewer to elicit response or the use of improper survey instruments. Observational errors are likely to affect NSSO data in all states, whereas errors of non-observation, specifically non-coverage, are restricted to select states. Depending upon the reason for the non-observation, a threefold classification of resultant errors is possible: sampling errors, errors due to non-coverage and errors due to non-response.

Sampling error arises because the statistic is generated from a subset of the target population and not the entire target population. The 'failure to include some units, or entire sections, of the defined survey population' in the sampling frame is known as non-coverage, whereas non-response is the 'failure to obtain observations on some elements selected and designated for the sample' (Kish 1965: 527–8). Non-coverage occurs when a perfect sampling frame is not available and it is also called frame coverage error (Biemer and Lyberg 2003: 63). Such an error could occur even if a census of the selected sampling frame is attempted (Groves

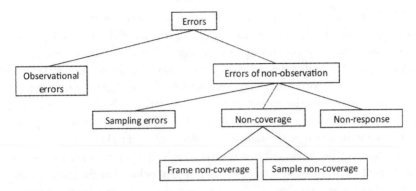

Figure 6.2   Errors in sample surveys
Source: Agrawal and Kumar (2017b: Figure 1).

2004: 11). On the other hand, non-response is a consequence of the inability of respondents to respond to questions, non-cooperation or refusal on the part of respondents to respond to questions, unavailability of respondents and non-return or loss of returned survey schedules. In other words, non-coverage results from the exclusion of certain units from the sampling frame, whereas non-response results from the inability to collect information on a unit included in the frame *and* selected for the sample.

The problem of non-observation in case of NSSO samples in Nagaland can be referred to as *frame non-coverage* because large parts of the state were not included in the sampling frame that was restricted to 5 kilometres of bus routes. In Jammu and Kashmir, too, we observe frame non-coverage due to the exclusion of the Leh and Kargil districts from the sampling frame until recently. There is no specific term in the literature for the areas included in Jammu and Kashmir's sampling frame that could not be surveyed due to unfavourable field conditions. For such omissions, we prefer to use the term 'non-coverage' over 'non-response'.[13] It would be inappropriate to classify the omissions as non-response as the respondent was not approached in the first place. Moreover, Kish (1965: 527–8) treats the failure to include units of the target population in the 'operational sampling frame' as non-coverage and adds that non-coverage 'also refers to "missed units," omissions due to faulty execution of survey procedures' in addition to the problem posed by incomplete frames. The Ladakh region was not part of the sampling frame of Jammu and Kashmir until recently. We can refer to the remaining areas as the *operational* sampling frame. The exclusion of units, which were included in the frame but could not be surveyed due to unfavorable field conditions (for instance, in the Kashmir Valley), will be referred to as *sample non-coverage*. *Frame non-coverage* and *sample non-coverage* together constitute (*overall*) *non-coverage*.

Of the various frame errors that can potentially bias survey estimates, non-coverage is 'perhaps the most serious type of frame error' (Lessler and Kalsbeek, 1992: 48). It biases estimates because of 'zero selection probabilities for some target population units' (Biemer and Lyberg 2003: 66). Groves (2004: 85) points out that 'if a small portion of the target population is missing from the frame, but they have very distinctive values on the survey statistic, then large noncoverage bias may result'. Thus, a bias would result even if the non-coverage rate is small and will not disappear as the sample size increases (ibid.: 11).

In case of a linear descriptive statistic, such as sample mean, the bias is a function of the share of the target population not included in the frame (namely, non-coverage rate) and the difference between the statistics (namely, the means) of those covered in the survey and those left out (Groves 2004: 84–5; Lessler and Kalsbeek 1992: 58–60). In case of a simple random sample, the bias is the product of these two terms. While there is no straightforward way of calculating the bias in case of multi-stage stratified NSSO samples, the population share of the excluded sample First Stage Units (FSUs) can be used to analyse the implications of the bias.

In addition to biasing sample statistics, non-coverage also affects regression analyses. Let y and x respectively denote the explained variable and the set of explanatory variables. We are interested in the impact of non-coverage on the estimates from the following relationship:

$$y = x'\beta + \varepsilon. \tag{Equation 6.1}$$

Here, β is the coefficient vector from a sample without non-coverage. Let β^* be the corresponding coefficient vector from a sample with non-coverage. The relationship between β and β^* is given by (Goldberger 1981)

$$\beta^* = \beta \frac{\theta}{1 - \rho^2(1 - \theta)}. \tag{Equation 6.2}$$

where ρ^2 denotes the coefficient of determination (also known as the R-squared) for the sample without non-coverage and θ is the ratio of variance of y from a sample with non-coverage to one without non-coverage. In Equation 6.1, $\beta^* \neq \beta$ unless ρ^2 equals 1, which is very unlikely in cross-sectional regressions, or θ equals 1. The latter requires variances of y from samples with and without non-coverage to be equal, which too is highly unlikely. Regression analyses that do not account for non-coverage will, therefore, yield biased estimates of coefficients.

NSSO Surveys in Peripheral States

This section examines the changes in the coverage of NSSO surveys in Nagaland, other states of the North-East and Jammu and Kashmir. The NSSO conducts two types of surveys: 'thick' or quinquennial rounds, typically once in five years, and 'thin' or annual rounds. The quinquennial rounds, with a much larger sample, mostly focus on consumer expenditure and employment and unemployment.[14] While we discuss both rounds in this section, the analysis in the remainder of the chapter is restricted to quinquennial rounds.

The share of target population excluded from the frame (namely, frame non-coverage) and sample (namely, sample non-coverage) can be used as a measure of non-coverage. Agrawal and Kumar (2017b: Table 1, Appendix 1) compiled non-coverage rates in NSSO surveys for all quinquennial rounds between 1973–4 and 1987–8 and for all rounds since 1987–8. They also examined an alternative measure of non-coverage, namely, the share of the FSUs in the sampling frame that could not be sampled (ibid.: Table 2). Since the alternative measure assumes that the FSUs are identical in size, which is not realistic, we use it only for sensitivity analysis and for calculating the non-coverage rate in case the information on sampling frame does not help identify the size of the population not covered.

Nagaland

The whole of Nagaland constitutes one NSS region.[15] The NSSO began operations in Nagaland in 1972 (GoN 2013a: 2), that is, about nine years after the formation of the state.[16] Until the 44th round (1988–9), operations were restricted to urban areas. Rural areas were included for the first time in the 44th round, an annual round that focused on the living conditions of tribal population, among other things (GoI 2004a: 55). However, the sampling frame did not fully cover rural Nagaland.

> Due to inaccessible conditions in the Nagaland the (interior) villages located beyond 5 kms. of bus routes (769 [768 as per reports of subsequent rounds that used the same sampling frame] out of a total of 1,119 [1,118] villages in the state) were kept outside the coverage of survey. Samples were drawn *purposively* for the remaining 350 villages of the state, of which 164 were connected by bus-routes and the rest were within 5 kms. of a bus route. The central sample consisted of 120 villages, of which 82 villages were connected by a bus route and 38 villages were within 5 kms. of a bus route. (GoI 1994b: 49, emphasis added)

These numbers do not tally with the 1981 Census, which served as the sampling frame for the 44th round. Our compilation from the *District Census Handbooks* (DCHBs) suggests that there were 1,112 inhabited villages in Nagaland of which only 122 villages were connected by bus routes and 140 villages fell within 5 kilometres of bus routes, while 850 villages were beyond 5 kilometres. The difference between our compilation (262 villages) and the NSSO figures (350 villages) can possibly be explained if the latter used updated village lists[17] and bus route maps to account for changes between 1981 and 1988–9 and included uninhabited villages. However, this seems unlikely. As per the 1991 Census (DCHBs), conducted two years after the 44th round, the total number of inhabited villages was 1,221, of which 338 were connected by bus or fell within 5 kilometres of bus routes and 883 were beyond 5 kilometres of bus routes.

Over the next two-and-a-half decades, NSSO surveys did not include 'interior villages of Nagaland situated beyond five km of any bus route' (GoI 2013a: D1). Nagaland is neither the only insurgency-affected state, nor the only state with difficult terrain. So, it is not clear why the NSSO imposed distance-based restrictions in Nagaland and not in other states of the North-East and Jammu and Kashmir, where sample non-coverage was high in several years (GoI 1989: 2). Andaman and Nicobar is the only other state/union territory where certain villages were regularly excluded on grounds of inaccessibility (NSS Report No. 538: 5).

In the 50th round (1993–4), the NSSO changed the sampling frame after the publication of the 1991 Census.[18] While the sampling frame changed, the number of villages included in the frame continued to be 350 until the 60th round (2004), even though both road coverage and bus routes expanded and the total number of villages in the state increased between 1988–9 and 2004. When the 2001 Census was adopted as the sampling frame in the 61st round (2004–5), the number of villages included in the frame increased from 350 (out of 1,118 villages) to 371 (out of 1,317 villages including uninhabited villages) (GoI 2011a: 34, 45). However, as per the DCHBs for 2001, there were 1,279 inhabited villages in the state, of which 726 were either connected by bus or were located within 5 kilometres of the bus route and 553 were located beyond 5 kilometres.

In the 69th round (2012), the hitherto uncovered villages were included in the sampling frame by forming a special stratum for these villages (NSS Report No. 556: B1). Only four FSUs were allotted to the special stratum compared to 40 FSUs allotted to the non-special stratum. Until the previous round, the non-special strata had 371 villages, while 946 villages were not included in the sampling frame. So, the ratio of the number of villages in the special stratum to those in the non-special stratum is about 2.5, but the corresponding ratio of FSUs allotted to these strata is 0.10.

A few other aspects of non-coverage in Nagaland are noteworthy. First, in contrast to the substantial and persistent frame non-coverage in rural areas between the 47th and 69th rounds (1991–2012), sample non-coverage was restricted to just two rounds (56th and 65th) in which one FSU each could not be surveyed. Second, contrary to its claims, the NSSO did not even include all the villages within 5 kilometres of bus routes in the frame.[19] Third, only five rounds were affected by sample non-coverage in the urban sector and the average sample non-coverage (as per the alternative measure) was less than 2 per cent during this period. The absence of frame non-coverage and a very small sample non-coverage in case of urban areas has limited significance though. Until recently, less than a fifth of the state's reported population lived in urban areas. Moreover, the towns are not evenly distributed across the state. In the period of interest, five out of the seven towns of Nagaland were located closer to the Assam border. Lastly, as the population of states becomes smaller, the sample size requirement decreases at a lesser rate than the population, particularly, in case of highly diverse states. So, the ratio of villages in sample to villages in frame increases as the population of state decreases. However, the ratio is much higher for Nagaland compared to other smaller states (Table 6.1) because the NSSO seemed to meet the sample size requirement by oversampling within the restricted sample.

Other North-Eastern States[20]

NSSO samples are affected by non-coverage in other north-eastern states as well. Frame non-coverage has affected NSSO surveys in Manipur and Tripura. Since the adoption of the 2001 Census as the sampling frame, Manipur's sampling frame has excluded three subdivisions of Senapati district. Yet this was not mentioned in NSS reports. The three subdivisions accounted for about 44.82/59.54 per cent (5.54/9.99 per cent) of the reported population of the district (state) in 2001/2011 (Table 7.3). Similarly, only a few NSS reports mention rural Tripura's exclusion from the sampling frame: 'disturbed villages of Tripura' were outside the sampling frame of the 27th (1972–3) (GoI 1979b: 289), 28th (1973–4) (GoI 2004a: 13–14; 1977a: 49) and 30th (1975–6) (GoI 1984d: 1) rounds. In later rounds the number of surveyed FSUs was often far less than the allotted number (GoI 1989: 2). The problem of frame non-coverage in rural Tripura seems to have been transformed into that of sample non-coverage. Between the 47th and 56th rounds (1991–2001), the average sample non-coverage for rural Tripura was about 19 per cent (25 per cent excluding the 53rd round) (Figure 7.3). On the other hand, urban sample non-coverage was less than 2 per cent.

Frame non-coverage has been minimal in the rest of the North-East, while sample non-coverage has been relatively higher. The average sample non-coverage in urban areas was less than 2.5 per cent except in Arunachal Pradesh, where it was about 8 per cent. The cases of high levels of non-coverage in the rural areas, more than 10 per cent, were restricted to Arunachal Pradesh and Tripura (and Mizoram in the 58th round). Among these states, only Arunachal Pradesh has not seen a steady decline in non-coverage over the years, but its persistently high level of sample non-coverage is not related to political unrest.

Jammu and Kashmir

Jammu and Kashmir is the only state where the scale and persistence of non-coverage is comparable to Nagaland. Not coincidentally, both the states and, to a lesser extent, Manipur and Tripura have been sites of long-standing insurgencies.[21] The coverage of NSSO surveys in Jammu and Kashmir has varied markedly over the years due to geographical remoteness, difficult terrain and, starting in the late 1980s, political unrest. Until the Article 370 was revoked on 5 August 2019, the state was divided into three regions (*four NSS regions*) – Ladakh (*Ladakh*), Kashmir (*Jhelam Valley*) and Jammu (*Outer Hills* and *Mountainous*) – that differ in terms of ethnolinguistic and religious composition. Except for a few rounds, Ladakh was not surveyed until the 63rd round, when it was included in the state sample and, eventually, in the central sample in the 69th round. Kashmir and Jammu were covered regularly by the NSSO starting with the 8th round (1954–5). However, after the onset of insurgency (45th round, 1989–90), all the districts of Kashmir and the contiguous districts of Jammu in the NSS region called Outer Hills were irregularly/incompletely surveyed despite being included in the sampling frame (Agrawal and Kumar 2017b: Table 1).[22] NSSO reports do not provide information about the nature of field conditions, but as shown in Figure 6.3, the degree of non-coverage varies with the intensity of political unrest measured in terms of insurgency-related fatalities.[23] Jammu's Mountainous region is the only NSS region of the state with an uninterrupted NSSO data series. Overall, during 1991–2012 (47th–68th rounds), up to 74 per cent of Jammu and Kashmir's population was not covered by NSSO samples in quinquennial rounds[24] and the state alone accounted for more than 51 (67) per cent of the un-surveyed rural (urban) FSUs of the country although its population share was merely 1 per cent.

A few comparative observations regarding non-coverage are in order. First, sample non-coverage was high in Jammu and Kashmir, whereas frame non-coverage was persistently high in Nagaland. Second, whole districts of Jammu and Kashmir were excluded depending on the intensity of insurgency, whereas in Nagaland all districts were covered, even though the remote villages were left out in most districts. Third, unlike other states, non-coverage affected both rural and urban areas in Jammu and Kashmir. In all other states, urban areas have almost always been part of the sampling frame and, with a very few exceptions, sample non-coverage in urban areas has been very low. Lastly, the ratio of the number of villages in the sample to that in the sampling frame is much higher for Jammu and Kashmir than the national average, but it is lower than the corresponding ratios for most north-eastern states (Table 6.1). The NSSO seems to have allotted more FSUs to Jammu and Kashmir to ensure that a sufficient number of sampling units would be surveyed despite higher non-coverage. However, a

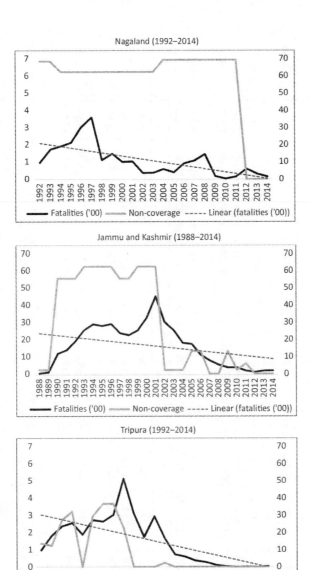

Figure 6.3   Fatalities and non-coverage

Sources: Prepared by authors using Agrawal and Kumar (2017b: Table 1) (non-coverage) and SATP (n.d.1) (fatalities).

Notes: (i) The annual fatalities (in 100s) indicated on the left axis include civilian, security force and terrorist/insurgent fatalities. The degree of non-coverage (in percentage) is indicated on the right axis. (ii) The initial points of graphs vary depending on the onset of insurgency and the availability of data on fatalities. (iii) The estimates of non-coverage rate for Nagaland do not include minor changes in (urban) non-coverage in the 51st (1994–5) and 54th–56th (1998–2001) rounds due to the non-availability of adequate information.

Table 6.1 Some characteristics of NSSO (central) samples, from 2004–5 to 2011–12

Description	Nagaland	Tripura	Assam	Arunachal Pradesh	Meghalaya	Manipur	Mizoram	Sikkim	North-East	Jammu and Kashmir	India
					Panel A						
Total number of villages (as per 2001 Census)#	1,317	870	26,312	4,065	6,034	2,391	817	452	42,258	6,652	638,596
Villages in NSSO sampling frame	371	870	26,312	4,065	6,034	2,228†	817	452	41,149	6,410*	636,127
Average number of villages allotted to the sample in quinquennial (annual) rounds**	89.33 (78.20)	168.00 (158.20)	332.00 (278.00)	145.33 (94.20)	110.67 (92.20)	188.00 (128.00)	80.00 (58.20)	81.33 (60.40)	1,194.67 (947.40)	274.67 (147.20)	7,720 (7,000)
Average number of villages surveyed in quinquennial (annual) rounds**	89.33 (78.00)	168 (158.20)	329.33 (277.60)	141.33 (86.00)	110.33 (91.80)	188.00 (128.00)	79.67 (58.20)	81.33 (59.80)	1,187.33 (937.60)	208.33 (107.20)	7,623.33 (6,267.20)
					Panel B						
Proportion of villages in the frame	28.17	100	100	100	100	93.18	100	100	97.38	96.36	99.61
Ratio of villages allotted to that in the frame in quinquennial (annual) rounds	24.08 (21.08)	19.31 (18.18)	1.26 (1.06)	3.58 (2.32)	1.83 (1.53)	8.44 (5.75)	9.79 (7.12)	17.99 (13.36)	2.9 (2.3)	4.28 (2.30)	1.21 (1.1)
Ratio of villages surveyed to those allotted in quinquennial (annual) rounds	100 (100)	100 (100)	99.2 (100)	97.25 (91.3)	99.7 (100)	100 (100)	99.58 (100)	100 (100)	99.39 (98.97)	75.85 (72.83)	98.75 (89.53)

Sources: Prepared by authors. Panel A (GoI 2011a; http://censusindia.gov.in/Census_Data_2001/Census_data_finder/A_Series/Number_of_Village.htm for Jammu and Kashmir; NSS report nos. 508, 523, 527, 530, 535, 537, 546 and 554). Panel B (authors' calculations).

Notes: (i) # The number of villages include uninhabited villages (GoI 2011a). (ii) * This figure is arrived at by subtracting the 2001 Census villages of Leh (namely, 112 + 1 uninhabited village) and Kargil (namely, 127 + 2 uninhabited villages), which were not included in the sampling frame. (iii) ** These figures are the means of the corresponding rounds during the period 2004–5 to 2011–12. (iv) † Three subdivisions of Senapati district were not included in the sampling frame (*Note on Sample Design and Estimation Procedure*, 63rd round: 27). (v) Figures for annual rounds are reported within parentheses.

higher sample non-coverage has meant that the ratio of the villages surveyed to the villages allotted is the lowest for Jammu and Kashmir in both quinquennial as well as annual rounds.

Flawed Sampling Frames

Sampling frame refers to the list of constituent units of the target population and is a key component of sampling design. The sampling frame must be accurate, complete and updated. In a perfect frame 'every element appears on the list separately, once, only once, and nothing else appears on the list' (Kish 1965: 53).[25] NSSO surveys typically follow a stratified multistage sampling design. The FSUs are villages in the rural sector and blocks in the urban sector. The FSUs are allotted to states and distributed between rural and urban areas within each state in proportion to their populations. Within each district, the NSSO forms rural and urban strata. An intermediate stage is formed in large villages/blocks while households form the ultimate stage units. The number of sample households in a stratum depends on its population share.

The Census provides vital information on the list of villages and the population as well as its distribution at various levels of aggregation (state, district and strata) for NSSO surveys. The NSSO relies upon the Urban Frame Surveys (UFS) to draw samples in the urban areas. The UFS uses the preceding census as the point of departure to partition a territory into mutually exclusive and exhaustive units (GoI n.d. 12). The Census serves as the sampling frame for the urban areas not covered by the UFS.[26] Abnormality in the Census will, therefore, affect NSSO sampling frames for rural areas and, to a lesser extent, urban areas.

In Chapters 4 and 5, we showed that Nagaland's censuses were affected by pervasive manipulation across circles and subgroups of population between 1981 and 2001. The degree of manipulation was higher in remote circles relatively closer to the Myanmar border and circles with a higher tribal population share. So, certain population subgroups are likely to be over-represented in sampling frames based on the 1991 and 2001 Censuses. In other words, the Census of Nagaland was an imperfect sampling frame as it did not contain the population characteristics of interest in proper proportions.

The use of an imperfect sampling frame affected NSSO surveys in Nagaland in two ways. First, the non-coverage rate increased when the 2001 Census was adopted as the sampling frame due to the overestimation of the rural population (Figure 6.3). The overcount was particularly severe in remote areas, which until recently were insufficiently covered by the NSSO. Second, the sampling frames for Nagaland and Assam are likely to overlap with each other. The Census mechanically aggregates the populations of Assam and Nagaland without indicating that both states claim the territory along the border, whose population is accounted for in both the states but without being divided into mutually exclusive parts. So, some of the villages in the disputed territory could, in principle, belong to the sampling frames of both the states. This will have a minor impact on Assam that has more than 25,000 villages, but the disputed area accounts for more than 7.5 per cent of Nagaland's villages (Table 3.3). The population share of these villages is less than 5 per cent of Nagaland's rural population, but they are located in the relatively easily accessible plains and are close to the markets of Dimapur and Golaghat.

The Census is an imperfect sampling frame for Jammu and Kashmir as well. First, census could not be conducted in 1951 (GoI 1953a: 3) and 1991 (GoI 2005a), resulting in the use of outdated sampling frames in the respective decades. Second, the 2011 Census seems to have been affected by manipulation in the Kashmir Valley (Guilmoto and Irudaya Rajan 2013), which has also seen sustained and high levels of sample non-coverage in NSSO surveys in the recent decades. Nagaland and Jammu and Kashmir are not the only states affected by the possible manipulation of the census headcounts though. In recent times, similar problems, albeit on a smaller scale, have been reported in parts of the northern hill districts of Manipur (GoI 2014e), which were excluded from the sampling frame.

Biased Samples

The distance-based restriction on samples skewed NSSO estimates of socio-economic characteristics for Nagaland. A large proportion of Nagaland's villages is located more than 10 kilometres from roads, while NSSO surveys were restricted to villages within 5 kilometres of bus routes. Since bus routes are a subset of roads, the NSSO was not even covering all villages within 5 kilometres of roads.

Geography is a strong determinant of historical patterns of development in Nagaland (and, in fact, in the larger Naga realm extending into Myanmar) because modern administration and education spread to the hills from Assam. Different tribes are concentrated in different parts of the state (Table 5.1), which means they were exposed to modernity in a staggered fashion.

The difficulty of terrain, degree of forest cover and share of rural population increase with distance from Assam or proximity to Myanmar. The density of road network and bus routes and the frequency of bus services too decrease with distance from Assam. So, areas closer to Myanmar have higher rural population as well as more remote villages. Proximity to Myanmar increases the exposure to insurgency as these locations provide easy shelter and escape routes. Lesser urbanisation, difficulty of terrain, greater forest cover and exposure to insurgency negatively affect economic activity.

The geographies of underdevelopment and ethnicity overlap in Nagaland. Both the share of tribal population and the degree of underdevelopment of tribes (measured in terms of, say, literacy) increase with distance from roads and Assam. This spatial divide is powerfully illustrated by the fact that all the tribes residing in districts on the Myanmar border have been designated by the state government as educationally and economically weaker tribes (GoN 2010: 126).

The NSSO's distance-based sampling restriction has meant that remote villages and disadvantaged tribes were less likely to be included in the sample. This resulted in the overestimation of socio-economic indicators such as the average MPCE for the state as households in villages closer to roads and located in more developed districts closer to Assam enjoy a better standard of living.

Data from the 1981 Census, one of the most reliable censuses conducted in the state before 2001 (Tables 4.2A–B), corroborate the geography of underdevelopment outlined above.[27] About 85 per cent of villages in the circles bordering Myanmar were located more than 10 kilometres away from the nearest bus stop compared to 33 per cent along the Assam border. The literacy rate in the circles on the Myanmar border was 16 per cent compared to 44 per cent in the circles on the Assam border. Until recently, there were only two towns in the vast territory adjoining the Myanmar border, compared to four near Assam border. Moreover, the population share of tribes was 97 per cent in the circles on the Myanmar border compared to 82 per cent in the circles on the Assam border (GoI 1984c). As the reach of surveys increased, the share of tribal households in the NSSO samples for Nagaland grew from 85 per cent in the 50th round to 88 in the 55th, 94 in the 61st and 96 in the 66th rounds. The share of tribes in the NSSO samples grew due to the inclusion of more remote villages that are largely populated by tribes as well as the growing migration from villages in the hills to towns in the hills and also to villages and towns in the plains in and around Dimapur.

Compared to the North-East and the country as a whole, a higher proportion of Nagaland's villages included in the sampling frame are sampled even though the state has a much smaller proportion of villages in the sampling frame (Table 6.1). The NSSO seems to 'purposively' (GoI 1994b: 49) oversample the villages within 5 kilometres of bus routes in Nagaland to meet its state-level sample size requirement for the central sample. However, the bias in estimates due to non-coverage will not disappear because there are systematic differences between sampling units included in the sample and those left out.

As in Nagaland, Tripura's tribal communities are concentrated in remote, rural and hilly areas in the eastern part of the state, which were also more susceptible to insurgency. While the NSSO does not clearly indicate the location of villages not covered, most of them are likely to be located in insurgency-prone areas. In other words, the sample must have excluded underdeveloped, hilly, forested and largely rural tribal areas between the 38th (1983) and 56th (2000–1) rounds (Agrawal and Kumar 2017b: Table 2). So, there was a systematic variation between the surveyed and un-surveyed areas in Tripura, which must have biased sample statistics. In Manipur, since the adoption of the 2001 Census as the sampling frame, the NSSO has excluded three subdivisions of the Naga-dominated Senapati district. These subdivisions accounted for 17.15 (5.54) and 24.45 (9.99) per cent of Manipur's reported tribal (overall) population in 2001 and 2011, respectively (Table 7.3).[28]

Jammu and Kashmir is another state where NSSO surveys have been affected by substantial and sustained non-coverage. Several features of non-coverage in the state stand out. In the Jammu region, the areas that were not covered regularly by NSSO surveys are located either along the line of control or share a border with Kashmir and Ladakh. The parts of Jammu covered by the NSSO adjoin the plains of Punjab. The excluded areas have relatively inaccessible terrain (GoI 2013b: Table III.38), greater forest cover and greater exposure to insurgency.[29] Furthermore, the excluded areas have a larger share of Muslim and tribal populations. Kashmir is almost entirely Muslim, while Doda, Punch and Rajouri districts of Jammu, which belong to the NSS region 'Outer Hills' that was not regularly surveyed, have substantial Muslim populations. In 2001, the last three districts accounted for 35 per cent of the tribal population of the state, whereas their share in the state's overall population was 15 per cent. So, the areas of Jammu and Kashmir affected by frame and sample non-coverage were systematically different from the areas included in the sample.

In Jammu and Kashmir, Nagaland and Tripura, non-coverage was higher in areas with greater exposure to insurgency. The degree of non-coverage and the intensity of insurgency measured in terms of overall fatalities are correlated (Figure 6.3). The coefficient of correlation between fatalities and non-coverage is 0.63 for Jammu and Kashmir (1988–2011), 0.60 for Tripura (1992–2011) and –0.48 for Nagaland (1992–2011). A few observations on the negative correlation for Nagaland are in order. First, we see a sustained and a very high degree of frame non-coverage in Nagaland right from the beginning of NSSO surveys and not just a correlation between non-coverage and the intensity of insurgency in specific years. Insurgency predates the introduction of NSSO surveys in Nagaland. This explains the high frame non-coverage since the introduction of NSSO surveys, unlike other states where coverage declined after the onset of insurgency. In Nagaland, non-coverage was 100 per cent until 1972 and between 84 and 90 per cent until 1988, when rural areas were included in the frame for the first time. In the subsequent period (1988–2011), rural frame non-coverage varied between 62 and 69 per cent. So, non-coverage declined in Nagaland in the late 1980s and early 1990s due to a marginal extension of surveys to accessible villages, even though the insurgency peaked during this period. Second, both frame and sample non-coverage respond quickly to an increase in the level of fatalities, but are inertial and resistant to downward revision, due to the risk aversion of the bureaucracy. The downward rigidity is likely to be more pronounced in case of frame non-coverage because the sampling frame is changed once in a decade. Third, there was higher over-reporting of the rural population in the 2001 Census, which served as the sampling frame until the 70th round (2013). This translated into an increase in the frame non-coverage in case of Nagaland even as fatalities steadily declined after mid-1990s due to ceasefires. So, the negative correlation in case of Nagaland is an artefact of defects in the sampling frame and the idiosyncratic factors that governed the expansion of NSSO surveys in the state.

Survey Statistics

We have so far argued that the NSSO samples for Nagaland and Jammu and Kashmir are not representative. The degree of non-coverage varies across districts and survey years due to the expanding reach of roads and bus routes in Nagaland and variations in the intensity and the geographical footprint of insurgency in Jammu and Kashmir. This affects the inter-temporal comparability of survey estimates. In this section, we will discuss the impact of non-coverage on survey statistics. The analysis is restricted to the quinquennial rounds since estimates from these rounds are believed to be representative at the sub-national level.[30]

Non-coverage biases survey statistics. Consider, for instance, MPCE, which is widely used in the estimation of poverty rates and in academic and policy debates on development in India. The MPCE estimates obtained from surveys in Nagaland and Jammu and Kashmir are biased upwards because of the exclusion of relatively inaccessible, economically disadvantaged and insurgency-prone areas (Table 6.2). The average MPCE of Nagaland is close to the maximum average MPCE of states even though its per capita income (PCI) was far below the corresponding maximum. This also holds true for urban Jammu and Kashmir in the year of maximum non-coverage. Before the 66th round, the MPCE of Nagaland and Jammu and Kashmir approached the maximum MPCE in India (Table 6.2), while their PCIs diverged from the corresponding maximum (Figure 6.4).[31] In other words, these states were supporting a much higher level of consumption compared to their PCI.

We can examine the relationship between MPCE and non-coverage rate for Nagaland and Jammu and Kashmir[32] by regressing the ratio of state's MPCE to India's MPCE on the corresponding non-coverage rate.[33] Table 6.3 presents results for three specifications. The first uses a measure of non-coverage based on the share of target population not covered by the survey. The second adds a variable that captures economic growth of the state relative to the median economic

Table 6.2 MPCE and PCI

State	1973–4 (Oct.–Jun.) 28th round		1977–8 32nd round		1983 (Jan.–Dec.) 38th round		1987–8 43rd round		1993–4 50th round		1999–2000 55th round		2004–5 61st round		2009–10 66th round		2011–12 68th round	
	Rural	Urban	Rural	Urban	Rural	Urban	Rural	Urban	Rural	Urban	Rural	Urban	Rural	Urban	Rural	Urban	Rural	Urban
							Panel A: MPCE											
Nagaland	n/a	100.22	n/a	137.30	n/a	196	n/a	367	460	521	941	1,242	1,011	1,498	1,379	1,732	1,757	2,279
Jammu & Kashmir	52.24	55.71	72.86	88.37	128	155	204	271	360	556	677	953	793	1,070	1,244	1,667	1,601	2,320
All India	53.01	70.77	68.89	96.15	112	166	158	250	281	458	486	855	559	1,052	953	1,856	1,287	2,477
India (maximum)	75.51	104.90	114.39	229.58	170	257	244	367	460	556	941	1,243	1,013	1,498	1,763	2,315	2,461	3,346
Nagaland/max (%)		95.54		59.80		76.26		100.00	100.00	93.71	100.00	99.92	99.80	100.00	78.22	74.82	71.39	68.11
J&K/max (%)	69.18	53.11	63.69	38.49	75.29	60.31	83.61	73.84	78.26	100.00	71.94	76.67	78.28	71.43	70.56	72.01	65.05	69.34
							Panel B: PCI per month*											
Nagaland	317.08		354.84		2,159		3,445		9,129		12,594 (16,779)**		30,441		50,263		63,781	
Jammu & Kashmir	291.06		327.35		2,428		2,954		6,543		12,373		21,734		33,650		46,734	
India (maximum)	604.31		709.90		4,181		5,966		16,558		44,349		76,968		149,164		211,570	
Nagaland/max (%)	52.47		49.98		51.64		57.74		55.13		28.40 (37.83)**		39.55		33.70		30.15	
J&K/max (%)	48.16		46.11		58.07		49.51		39.52		27.90		28.24		22.56		22.09	

Sources: Prepared by authors. Panel A: GoI (1977a) for the 28th round; GoI (1986a) for the 32nd round; respective NSS reports for the rest of the rounds. Panel B: Ghosh and De (2005); Reserve Bank of India's *Handbook of Statistics on Indian Economy* for 2012–13 and 2014–15.

Notes: (i) Quinquennial surveys of the NSSO did not cover rural Nagaland before the 50th round (1993–4). (ii) The estimates from the 55th round (1999–2000) are not comparable with the rest of the rounds due to the changes in recall period in questions on consumption (Deaton and Dreze 2002). (iii) The figures for 2009–10 and 2011–12 correspond to the 'Mixed Reference Period.' (iv) Estimates for the 50th round for Nagaland and Jammu and Kashmir have been computed using the distribution of MPCE by fractile groups. (v) 'India (maximum)' is the maximum of the average MPCE or PCI among all states excluding union territories and Delhi. Report no. 502 (50th round) provides information on the average MPCE of only 15 states and 'India (maximum)' values for MPCE for this round are based on 17 states (15 states in the report and Nagaland and Jammu and Kashmir computed by the authors). (vi) * Figures for 1973–4 and 1977–8 correspond to 1960–1 prices, 1983 and 1987–8 to 1980–1 prices, 1993–4 and 1999–2000 to 1993–4 prices and the rest to 2004–5 prices. We have divided PCI by 12 to make it comparable with MPCE. PCI is Net State Domestic Product per capita. (vii) ** The figures in parentheses were obtained by correcting for overcount in 2001 (Chapter 4). (viii) Unless otherwise specified, the survey period is the full agricultural year (that is, from July to June).

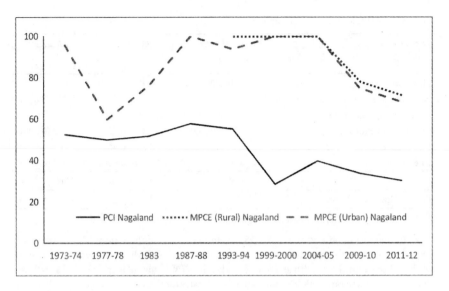

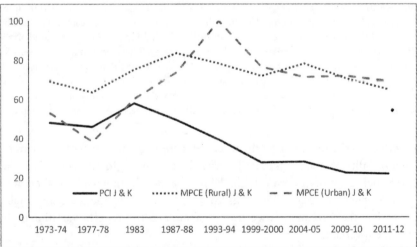

Figure 6.4   PCI and MPCE

Source: Agrawal and Kumar (2017b: Figure 1).

Notes: Each chart shows the ratio (in %) of variable (PCI or MPCE) of the corresponding state to that of the maximum among all the states. In case of Nagaland, MPCE (rural) starts in 1993–4 as the rural areas of the states were not covered in earlier rounds. The pronounced dip in the PCI curve for Nagaland in 1999–2000 is partly an artefact of population overcount.

Table 6.3   MPCE and non-coverage

Dependent variable: MPCE (state)*100/MPCE (India)	Model 1	Model 2	Model 3
Non-coverage rate	0.292 (0.028)	0.293 (0.029)	
Non-coverage rate (alternative measure)			0.236 (0.059)
State dummy (Nagaland = 1)	29.899 (0.000)	30.462 (0.000)	
Sector dummy (urban = 1)	-22.189 (0.004)	-21.745 (0.005)	-26.012 (0.000)
PCI growth[†]		-0.728 (0.461)	
Intercept	116.735 (0.000)	114.626 (0.000)	123.013 (0.000)
R^2	0.65	0.65	0.76
Observations	32	32	14

Source: Authors' calculations based on Agrawal and Kumar (2017b: Tables 1–2).

Notes: (i) Number of observations = 32 (18 for Jammu and Kashmir – 28th, 32nd, 38th, 43rd, 50th, 55th, 61st, 66th and 68th rounds – and 14 for Nagaland where only urban areas were covered in the 28th, 32nd, 38th and 43rd rounds). (ii) [†] 'PCI growth' is constructed as follows. The average growth rate of PCI is calculated for all states for three years preceding each round. We then find the median average growth rate of all states and subtract the median from the averages of Nagaland and Jammu and Kashmir. The variable, thus arrived at, captures the relative position of the state vis-à-vis the median state. (iii) In Model 3, non-coverage, is based on the alternative measure that is restricted to sample non-coverage. This model could be run only for Jammu and Kashmir as sample non-coverage is close to zero for Nagaland across various rounds of NSSO surveys. We could not use the data from 28th and 32nd rounds, both rural as well as urban sectors, even for Jammu and Kashmir because of the unavailability of information on sample non-coverage. (iv) *p*-values are reported within parentheses. See note 67 of Chapter 5.

growth of all the states during the three years preceding the survey to account for the possibility of change in MPCE driven by economic growth, but the *p*-value of the coefficient of growth is high.[34] The last specification uses the alternative measure of non-coverage. The results from the three specifications are comparable and each of the three models accounts for about two-thirds of the variation in the dependent variable.

The results suggest that the ratio is positively correlated with non-coverage. The ratio is higher in years with higher non-coverage, that is, non-coverage is associated with an overestimation of MPCE. It can be argued that the MPCE is higher in these two states because of the higher cost of living on account of inaccessibility, climatic conditions, dietary practices, difficult terrain and, in Nagaland's case, extortion that adds to the price experienced by consumers (see note 38 of Chapter 5). If that is so, expenditure should be high relative to other states in all rounds, rather than in select rounds.

The estimated intercept along with the state and sector dummies indicates that the MPCE of rural Jammu and Kashmir (Nagaland) is about 1.17 (1.47) times higher than that of rural India. The corresponding values for the urban sector are lower, 0.95 for Jammu and Kashmir and 1.24 for Nagaland. In Model 1, 1 percentage point increase in the non-coverage rate increases the ratio of MPCE (state) to MPCE (India) by about 0.30 percentage point. Thus, if non-coverage rate is, for example, 50 per cent, the ratio of MPCE (state) to MPCE (India) will increase by about 15 percentage points. The ratio of MPCE (state) to MPCE (India) in the rural areas would have increased by 20.84 percentage points in Nagaland (for the maximum non-coverage rate, that is, 69.47 per cent in the 61st, 66th and 68th rounds) and 18.76 percentage points in Jammu and Kashmir (for the maximum non-coverage rate, that is, 62.53 per cent during 1993–2002).[35] Assuming non-coverage in Nagaland does not affect India's average MPCE, the estimated average MPCE of Nagaland in 2004–5 would have been ₹894 instead of the reported value of ₹1,011. In other words, Nagaland would have had the fourth-highest average MPCE in the country instead of second.[36]

Policy Variables

The estimation of the incidence of poverty requires information on the poverty line and the distribution of consumer expenditure. Given an expenditure distribution, an overestimated (underestimated) poverty line will lead to overestimation (underestimation) of poverty rate (Figure 6.5). Likewise, poverty rate will be underestimated if the lower end of the distribution is only partially observed or the left tail is thinner than it ought to be because of the unavailability of the consumer expenditure data on poorer groups/remote areas. However, if the poverty line is overestimated and the distribution is only partly observed, as would be the case with Nagaland and Jammu and Kashmir, the overall effect on poverty rate is not unambiguous *a priori*. We will discuss the impact of flawed sample surveys on the poverty estimates of the government-constituted expert groups chaired by Tendulkar (2009) and Rangarajan (2011) (GoI 2014f).[37]

State-specific poverty lines are derived from the national poverty line using state-wise relative (to all-India) prices for the corresponding sector (namely, rural/urban). The Expert Group (Tendulkar) followed a different approach and used the urban poverty ratio for 2004–5, estimated using the Expert Group (Lakdawala) methodology, to recalibrate the urban poverty line for 2004–5.[38] It then derived the state-specific poverty lines for urban areas using state-wise relative (to all-India) urban prices. Once the urban poverty line for a state was arrived at, a within-state rural-relative-to-urban price index was used to estimate the poverty line for the rural areas. The state-level poverty lines for subsequent quinquennial rounds were estimated by applying a state-level price index on the corresponding

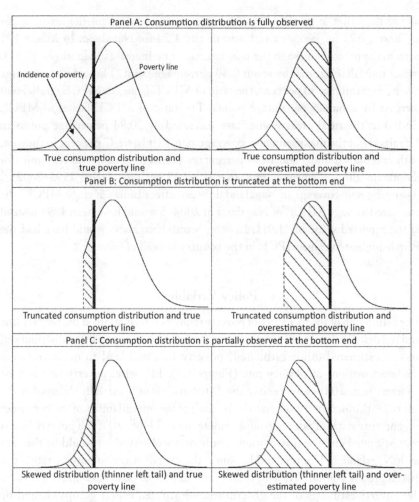

Figure 6.5   Poverty line and consumption distribution

Source: Agrawal and Kumar (2017b).

Notes: The horizontal and vertical axes indicate log MPCE and density, respectively. The lined portion of this hypothetical distribution of MPCE measures the incidence of poverty.

figures for 2004–5. The 2011 Expert Group (Rangarajan) reverted to the practice of estimating separate all-India poverty lines for rural and urban areas. Therefore, state relative to all-India price indices were required for each sector but not the within-state rural-relative-to-urban prices.

The price relatives in both urban and rural sectors are based on NSSO surveys and Consumer Price Index (CPI) (Agricultural Labourers [AL] and Industrial

Workers [IW]). Thus, assuming the all-India consumption distribution of the NSSO is reliable, the state price relatives would be the main source of distortion of the state poverty lines that are based on an adjustment of all-India poverty line using state-specific price relatives.[39] The Expert Group (Tendulkar) used implicit prices from NSSO surveys for most food items, durable goods and education and health services and CPI (AL) and CPI (IW) for entertainment, personal care, other miscellaneous goods and services and durables. The Expert Group (Rangarajan) followed a broadly similar approach (GoI 2014f: 16, 63).

Table 6.4 (Panel A) compiles information on poverty lines for Nagaland and Jammu and Kashmir along with the highest poverty line among all states. In the previous section, we have shown that NSSO surveys overestimated the MPCE for Nagaland and Jammu and Kashmir due to the systematic exclusion of remote and insurgency-affected areas. Non-coverage would have also affected the estimation of the poverty lines via its effect on prices. Insofar as NSSO samples in these states were biased in favour of relatively well-to-do villages and urban areas within the state, it is likely that prices were overestimated.[40]

Indeed this appears to be the case in Nagaland, which had the highest or fairly close to the highest poverty line in the country during 2004–5, 2009–10 and 2011–12 (Table 6.4). During 2009–10, the poverty lines (Tendulkar) for Nagaland were ₹1,017 (rural) and ₹1,148 (urban) compared to the corresponding all-India figures of ₹673 and ₹860, respectively. The next highest poverty lines were ₹850 (Mizoram, one of the most urbanised states of the country and the only north-eastern state to have achieved a negotiated end to insurgency) and ₹830 (Punjab, a leader in agriculture and among highly urbanised states) in the rural sector and ₹1,040 (Delhi, the national capital), ₹1,035 (Sikkim) and ₹1,025 (Goa, among the most urbanised states) in the urban sector.[41] The poverty lines of Jammu and Kashmir are not close to the maximum among states because during 2004–12 the degree of non-coverage was much lower than Nagaland. Also, there is a difference in the nature of non-coverage of the two states. In rural Nagaland, all the remote areas were excluded. However, the non-coverage in Jammu and Kashmir was confined to a few districts and the remaining districts were not affected. Thus, the remote areas of the remaining districts were included in the sample for Jammu and Kashmir. This difference in the nature of non-coverage translates into more biased estimates for rural Nagaland, whose poverty line unlike that of Jammu and Kashmir was almost always one of the highest in the country.

While only Nagaland's poverty lines were severely affected, the poverty ratio was underestimated in both Nagaland and Jammu and Kashmir.[42] Both reported the lowest incidence of rural poverty among all the states at least once in the recent decades (Table 6.4: Panel B). Barring a few instances, Jammu and Kashmir has

Table 6.4 Poverty line and the incidence of poverty

State/India/ratio/rank	2009 Expert Group (Tendulkar)								2011 Expert Group (Rangarajan)			
	Rural				Urban				Rural		Urban	
	1993–4	2004–5	2009–10	2011–12	1993–4	2004–5	2009–10	2011–12	2009–10	2011–12	2009–10	2011–12
	Panel A: poverty line (₹, current prices)											
Nagaland	382	687	1,017	1,270	410	783	1,148	1,302	985	1,230	1,424	1,616
J&K	289	522	723	891	281	603	845	988	848	1,045	1,200	1,403
India (maximum)	382	687	1,017	1,270	410	783	1,148	1,302	1,026	1,231	1,424	1,704
All India	n/a**	447	673	816	n/a**	579	860	1,000	801	972	1,198	1,407
Nagaland/max (%)	100	100	100	100	100	100	100	100	96	100	100	95
J&K/max (%)	76	76	71	70	69	77	74	76	83	85	84	82
	Panel B: poverty incidence (%)											
Nagaland	20.1	10	19.3	19.9	21.8	4.3	25	16.5	11.1	6.1	37.2	32.1
J&K	32.5	14.1	8.1	11.5	6.9	10.4	12.8	7.2	14.4	12.6	32.4	21.6
All India	50.1	41.8	33.8	25.7	31.8	25.7	20.9	13.7	39.6	30.9	35.1	26.4
Nagaland's rank*	2	1	10	14	7	1	21	19	3	2	20	21
J&K's rank*	5	3	1	7	2	4	7	8	5	7	13	12

Sources: Prepared by authors using GoI (2009c; 2014f).

Note: (i) Maximum is among 28 States excluding Union Territories. (ii) * Position of the state when the 28 states are arranged in ascending order of the incidence of poverty. (iii) ** For 1993–4 (All India), GoI (2009c) provides the estimates of the incidence of poverty and not the poverty line. (iv) See also note ii of Table 6.2.

ranked in the lowest quantile, when the states are arranged in the ascending order of the incidence of poverty. Nagaland, on the other hand, has shown substantial volatility.[43] Nagaland was among the two states with the least incidence of rural poverty during 1993–4 and 2004–5, but ranked tenth during 2009–10 in the rural sector. With high poverty lines, one expected a higher incidence of poverty in Nagaland and certainly not the lowest. Nagaland's rank in terms of urban poverty was 7th, 1st and 21st during 1993–4, 2004–5 and 2009–10, respectively.

Were Nagaland and Jammu and Kashmir really better off than most of the Indian states in terms of rural poverty? Or, were a high poverty line and a low poverty rate in Nagaland and a low poverty rate in Jammu and Kashmir artefacts of the inadequacies of NSSO surveys that only partially captured the lower end of the consumption distribution? A high poverty line, a low poverty rate and a low PCI compared to other states, which unlike Nagaland are not economically stagnant, cannot all be simultaneously true. An incomplete MPCE distribution due to the non-coverage of the target population at the bottom end seems to have resulted in an underestimation of the incidence of poverty. The degree of exclusion is so high that despite the overestimation of the poverty line Nagaland reported one of the lowest poverty headcounts (Table 6.4: Panel A). The decline in Nagaland's MPCE relative to the rest of the country over the years is a consequence of the changing sampling frame.[44] Likewise, the non-coverage of remote and disturbed districts explains the underestimation of Jammu and Kashmir's rural poverty.

The estimates from surveys conducted by the respective state governments suggest that expert groups might have underestimated poverty ratio, particularly, in rural areas. Rural Nagaland's incidence of poverty was 62.24 per cent in 2002 (GoN n.d. 4)[45] compared to the Expert Group's (Tendulkar) estimate of 10 per cent for 2004–5. In Jammu and Kashmir, poverty rate was 26.14 per cent in rural and 7.96 in urban during 2007–8 (Government of J&K 2008) compared to the Expert Group's (Tendulkar) estimate of 14 per cent for rural and 10 per cent for urban areas.

Concluding Remarks

Irregular surveys and unrepresentative samples contribute to data deficit in India's ethno-geographic periphery. While small sample sizes are often blamed for unrepresentative samples in the North-East, we highlighted other factors that affect the representativeness of NSSO samples.[46] We argued that NSSO samples are unlikely to be representative for Nagaland because of the arbitrary restriction of its surveys to villages within 5 kilometres of bus routes, whereas the bulk of the rural and tribal population is located farther from these routes. The spatial distribution of population vis-à-vis roads varies across both districts and

NSS rounds that vitiates inter-temporal comparison. Even the recent change in NSSO sampling frame in Nagaland that extends the coverage of NSSO samples to hitherto uncovered villages fails to address this problem as it allocates very few FSUs to them compared to their population share. Sustained non-coverage in Nagaland right from the beginning of NSSO surveys is linked to the long-standing insurgency. Urban Nagaland was first covered by the NSSO in 1972. Rural Nagaland had to wait until 1988–9 and even then only accessible villages were covered, which meant that the areas included in the sample and those excluded differed systematically. We also discussed non-coverage in Jammu and Kashmir and Tripura. Just as in Nagaland, there were systematic differences between the units surveyed and those left out, which affected the representative character of the NSSO samples in these states.

Non-coverage and the incidence of insurgency (as reflected in overall annual fatalities) were shown to be correlated. Non-coverage affects estimates of consumer expenditure and prices, which in turn affect poverty estimates. The changing reach of surveys partly explains the fluctuation of Jammu and Kashmir's MPCE and the decline in Nagaland's MPCE *relative* to the rest of the country.

The unreliability of government statistics in Nagaland and Jammu and Kashmir highlights systemic problems that have wider implications for our understanding of the relationship between state, statistics and policymaking. First, it raises doubts about statistics generated through sample surveys in other conflict-ridden and inaccessible areas such as Naxalism-affected Chhattisgarh. Second, while we have examined only NSSO samples, other demographic and socio-economic surveys conducted in peripheral states are also likely to suffer from similar problems.[47] Third, development schemes will be affected insofar as they are linked to poverty rates estimated from faulty survey data. Fourth, NSSO reports are lacking in information necessary for understanding the sampling frame. Lastly, economically underdeveloped, ethnically divided and politically disturbed states that need better policies are also the states where government statistics are relatively less reliable. Poorly designed policies contribute to underdevelopment, and underdevelopment contributes to political instability, which in turn affects the availability and the quality of statistics by hindering government surveys.

Notes

1. Data deficit results in the exclusion of peripheral states from most academic and policy analyses. Policymakers dealing with the North-East had to use statistics of Assam for the entire region (GoI 2007a). As late as 2004–5, Planning Commission (now, National Institution for Transforming India (NITI) Aayog) used the poverty ratio of Assam for all north-eastern states and Sikkim. Elsewhere, the poverty

ratio of Tamil Nadu is used for Pondicherry and Andaman and Nicobar Islands, while that of Kerala is used for Lakshadweep. The poverty ratio of urban Punjab is used for rural as well as urban Chandigarh. The poverty line of Maharashtra together with the expenditure distribution of Goa/Dadra and Nagar Haveli are used to estimate poverty ratio of Goa/Dadra and Nagar Haveli. The poverty ratio of Goa is in turn used for Daman and Diu. Use of data of neighbouring states is not unheard of in other fields. Nagaland has been classified under Zone V seismic zone (*ME* 2019j). This classification seems to be based on assessments of earthquake-prone neighbouring states, particularly, Assam. For similar examples from the field of demography, see GoI (2006a: 253) and Guilmoto and Irudaya Rajan (2001: 736).

2. The Indira Awas Yojna allots funds to states on the basis of rural housing shortage and poverty ratio (in the ratio of 3:1). Several other schemes such as Antyodaya Anna Yojana (food), Rashtriya Swasthya Bima Yojana (health), Pradhan Mantri Ujjwala Yojana (cooking gas), Deen Dayal Upadhyay Gram Jyoti Yojana (electricity) and National Social Assistance (old age and disability pensions) provide preferential and subsidised access to goods and services to those below the poverty line. Also note that submissions of several states to the Fourteenth Finance Commission (FFC) called for the inclusion of poverty rate in the federal redistribution formula (GoI 2015a).

3. Most texts on survey methodology (Groves et al. 2004; Hansen, Hurwitz and Madow 1953; Kish 1965) have a chapter or two on survey data quality but do not discuss the impact of context-specific factors on data. Moreover, before the 1990s, the discussion on survey data quality in most texts focused largely on sampling errors, thanks to 'elegant mathematical formulas to estimate its magnitude' (Weisberg 2005: 13). Non-sampling errors received greater attention in the 1990s after the advent of the total survey error approach, which stresses that errors can occur at 'every stage of a survey' (ibid.: 16; see also Groves 2004). This approach treats the reduction in non-sampling errors as indispensable for improving survey data quality.

4. The literature on the quality of NSSO data has mostly focused on the reliability of NSSO data in general (Suryanarayana and Iyengar 1986), sampling design and survey schedules (various contributions to Dandekar and Venkataramaiah 1975; Deaton 1997), inconsistencies between the NSSO and other government sources of statistics (Suryanarayana and Iyengar 1986; Minhas 1988; Srinivasan 1994; Deaton and Kozel 2005; Vaidyanathan 2013; Kasturi 2015), impact of respondent characteristics on survey results (Agrawal and Agrawal 2012; Chaudhuri and Saha 2012; see also James and Irudaya Rajan 2004 for NFHS) and the impact of the structure and evolution of the NSSO as an organisation on the quality of data (Vidwans 2002b; Shetty 2012; S. Bhalla 2014).

5. In statistics, the term 'bias' is generally used in the estimation theory, but it also refers to the presence of selective forces in the sampling process (Kruskal and Mosteller 1979: 247).

6. The academic and public debates on poverty in India have focused on the level of poverty line being low (*Economic Times* 2013a), inability of poverty line to capture the multidimensional nature of deprivation (Krishnaji 2012), suitability of concepts and measures adopted by different expert groups on poverty (Suryanarayana 2011), use of price indices to update poverty lines (Deaton 2003; 2008; Minhas et al. 1987), use of inconsistent reference periods across different NSSO surveys and measurement errors (Deaton and Kozel 2005; Deaton 1997; Ravallion 2016) and lack of inter-temporal comparability of poverty headcounts (Suryanarayana 2000). We explore the link between survey data quality and estimates of poverty.

7. Surveys can also be affected by departmental politics within the survey organisation. S. Bhalla (2014), Shetty (2012) and Vidwans (2002b) discuss internal politics at different levels of the NSSO and turf wars among central statistical agencies.

8. In its initial years, the difficulty in accessing remote regions amidst resource constraints and lack of experience might have limited the reach of NSSO surveys. However, the persistence of frame non-coverage in more recent decades is difficult to explain without taking into account *perceptions* about political unrest, the bureaucracy's risk aversion and limited influence of these states in national politics.

9. Serra (2014: 10, 18) and Jerven (2013: 85) point out that in colonial Africa, the geographical locations covered by surveys and items surveyed reflected the political and economic interests of the government.

10. The NFHS-II was delayed due to the lack of funding from the United States Agency for International Development (USAID) because of the sanctions imposed by the United States of America (USA) in the aftermath of India's nuclear tests (Visaria and Irudaya Rajan 1999: 3002). NFHS-IV was delayed due to alleged political interference in the run-up to the 2014 Parliament Election (note 25 of Chapter 1).

11. For a discussion of misuse of data in the run-up to the 2009 Parliament Election, see Himanshu (2009), and on the first anniversary of the demonetisation of high-value currency notes, see Kumar (2017c).

12. Another typology of errors in sample surveys is based on the broad division between sampling and non-sampling errors.

13. The magnitude of the bias in survey statistics is independent of the characterisation of the problem as non-coverage or non-response.

14. The NSSO introduced the Periodic Labour Force Survey (PLFS) in 2017. A thick round covering only consumer expenditure was conducted in 2017–18. It seems the PLFS has replaced the thick rounds on employment and unemployment.

15. The NSS regions are groups of districts having similar agro-ecological characteristics. At present, there are 88 NSS regions (http://mospi.nic.in/Mospi_New/upload/nsso/nss_regions.pdf). See Lahiri (1967) for a discussion on the origin of NSS regions.

16. There are discrepancies between different government sources with regard to the date of commencement of NSSO surveys in Nagaland. GoN (2013a: 2) suggests that the NSSO began operations in Nagaland in 1972, whereas GoI (1976d: 1)

mentions that NSSO began surveys in urban Nagaland in the 23rd round (July 1968–June 1969).

17. The NSSO updates village list 'by excluding the villages urbanised and including the towns de-urbanised after' the last census (Report No. 556: B2).

18. In some earlier NSS rounds (for example, 49th round, 1993), information from the 1991 Census was used only for newly declared towns and for deciding if a district had to be divided into multiple strata (NSS Report No. 429: 20).

19. Even surveys conducted by the state government in recent years do not adequately cover the rural areas. In a recent survey of schools, '192 schools represented the urban areas and only 39 schools represented the rural areas' (*ME* 2018i), even though nearly 70 per cent of the population lives in villages. Most of the rural schools surveyed are likely to be in relatively accessible villages.

20. The discussion of other north-eastern states is based on the alternative measure of non-coverage, namely, the share of the FSUs in the sampling frame that could not be sampled (Agrawal and Kumar 2017b: Table 2).

21. Punjab faced a related problem in a few years during the late 1980s and early 1990s, when in most rounds NSSO surveys were affected by sample non-coverage in the rural sector. In urban areas the non-coverage was restricted to a few rounds, for example, 38th and 49th.

22. Even in some of the earlier rounds, large parts of rural Jammu and Kashmir could not be covered, for example, only 87.5 per cent of the villages could be surveyed in the 38th round (1983). The reason behind this is not clear.

23. After the 45th round (1989–90), the reach of NSSO surveys dropped sharply in Jammu and Kashmir due to 'unfavourable field conditions' (Report No. 407: 2) or 'unavoidable circumstances' (Report No. 407: 18). A few reports allude to (political) disturbances though (Report Nos. 490: 4; 508: 3). Interaction with the NSSO staff revealed that the Srinagar office remained closed at the height of insurgency in the 1990s. Other national surveys such as the NFHS too did not cover Kashmir in the early 1990s (Mari Bhat and Zavier 1999: 3008).

24. According to the alternative measure, the average non-coverage in Jammu and Kashmir's rural and urban sectors, respectively, was 31 and 37 per cent and the corresponding maxima were about 69 and 71 per cent (Agrawal and Kumar 2017b: Table 2).

25. Jessen (1958: 160) underscores the importance of sampling frame by pointing out, 'Some very worthwhile investigations are not undertaken at all because of the lack of an apparent frame; others, because of faulty frames, have ended in a disaster or in cloud of doubt.'

26. After Ladakh was included in the sampling frame (namely, 63rd round), the 2001 Census was used as the sampling frame for Leh and Kargil towns (Report Nos. 535: B1; 549: B3). Until the 66th round the urban areas of Ladakh were treated as non-UFS towns (Report No. 547: B2). Ladakh was covered by the UFS for the first time in the 2007–12 phase (GoI n.d.13).

27. The 2011 Census was first used as the sampling frame very recently in the 71st round (2014), whereas we are interested in the period until the 69th round (2012).

28. All census publications for 2001 and 2011, including those on STs, report figures after excluding the three subdivisions. We assume that these subdivisions are almost entirely populated by tribes, which is indeed the case.

29. Ladakh that was until very recently excluded from the NSSO's sampling frame, is among the most inaccessible parts of the country, but it has not been affected by insurgency. Sumati Kulkarni (2004: 656) pointed out that the selected sampling units of Kargil district of Ladakh region had to be replaced in the NFHS-II survey due to 'national security reasons'. The NFHS fieldwork in the state was scheduled between April and September. This period overlapped with the war triggered by Pakistan's illegal occupation of parts of Kargil.

30. We omit the first quinquennial round (namely, 27th round, 1972–3) and instead use the 28th round (1973–4) because the government relied on MPCE from the latter to estimate the incidence of poverty (GoI 1979c: 10). The report of the Task Force on Projections of Minimum Needs and Effective Consumption Demand (GoI 1979c) does not mention the reason for this. There could be two reasons: (a) 1972–3 was a drought year and (b) substantial changes were made in the NSSO sampling design in the 28th round, including the use of the 1971 Census as the sampling frame (GoI 2004a). GoI (1986b: S-3) notes that the 28th round was conducted to 'meet some ad hoc requirement'. The consumption estimates from the 28th round may not have addressed seasonality adequately since the survey was conducted from October 1973 to June 1974, that is, it was not spread over the full agricultural year (Suryanarayana 2009).

31. The state with maximum PCI could be an outlier. So, we also checked the ranking of states by PCI. Jammu and Kashmir's rank fluctuated between 4 and 6 during 1973–87 and declined gradually from 10 in 1987–8 to 19 in 2011–12, while that of Nagaland fluctuated between 6 and 18 during 1973–2011.

32. Tripura has not been included in the regression analysis as the geography of exclusion is not clear from the NSSO reports.

33. The ratio of a state's MPCE to India's MPCE could deviate from its long run trend because of the changes in the extent of non-coverage and the difference between the MPCE of included and excluded areas. Further note that besides serving as sampling frame, census also provides information for the planning of surveys and auxiliary information for estimation such as sampling weights or multipliers (Kish and Verma 1986). So, the ratio could also deviate because of the use of flawed census as a sampling frame, which affects the distribution of sampling units within the state, and the sampling weights derived from an incorrect census. We have been able to control only the extent of non-coverage in regressions.

34. The growth variable is not available separately for the rural and urban areas.

35. The estimated equation is as follows: $(MP\widehat{CE}_S / MPCE_I) = \hat{\alpha} + \hat{\delta}D_N + \hat{\gamma}Urban + \hat{\beta}NC_S$, where D_N is a dummy variable for Nagaland, the dummy *Urban* = 1 for the urban sector and 0 for the rural sector and subscript s denotes state (Nagaland

or Jammu and Kashmir) and I denotes India. NC_S denotes non-coverage in the sth state. The overestimation of the ratio $MPCE_S/MPCE_I$ due to non-coverage is given by $\hat{\beta}NC_S/(\hat{\alpha} + \hat{\delta})$ for Nagaland (rural), $\hat{\beta}NC_S/(\hat{\alpha} + \hat{\delta} + \hat{\gamma})$ for Nagaland (urban), $\hat{\beta}NC_S/(\hat{\alpha})$ for Jammu and Kashmir (rural) and $\hat{\beta}NC_S/(\hat{\alpha} + \hat{\gamma})$ for Jammu and Kashmir (urban). This translates into an overestimation of the ratio by 14.22 and 4.24 per cent in Nagaland's rural and urban areas, respectively. The corresponding figures for Jammu and Kashmir are 16.07 and 19.85 per cent. The observations on urban Nagaland have been included in the regressions for the sake of completeness as well as to account for occasional sample non-coverage there.

36. We can also quantify the extent of overestimation by calculating the mean of a distribution truncated at the lower end. This distribution would roughly correspond to the distribution of the actual MPCE in Nagaland. As the poorest areas were mostly left out of the surveys, the truncation point could be decided according to the degree of non-coverage. The difference in the means of truncated (observed) and non-truncated (actual) distributions can be used as a measure of the overestimation of MPCE. As per this measure, the MPCE in rural Nagaland is overestimated by more than 100 per cent in all quinquennial rounds since the 50th round. The degree of overestimation for Jammu and Kashmir (both rural and urban each) is above 100 per cent in the 50th and 55th rounds, about 25 in the 61st, about 20 in the 66th and about 4 in the 68th. Observations are not availabed for the areas situated beyond the 5 kilometres of the bus route in Nagaland or in remote areas of insurgency-affected districts of Jammu and Kashmir. While most of them are likely to be located at the bottom of the distribution, we cannot clearly define a truncation point, as the lower end of distribution is under-observed rather than entirely un-observed (Figure 6.5). So, the above estimates should be treated as upper bounds compared to the results of the regressions that provide lower bounds (Table 6.3).

37. The Expert Group (Lakdawala) was the first to provide separate poverty estimates for states, but it used Assam's poverty ratio for all the north-eastern states, including Nagaland. Therefore, analysis in this section is confined to the post-Lakdawala expert groups (namely, Tendulkar and Rangarajan), which provide separate poverty lines and poverty ratios for each state. Note in passing that expert groups have relied on NSSO surveys to estimate poverty rates even though the sampling design permits the generation of unbiased estimates of the mean consumer expenditure rather than its distribution (Suryanarayana 2009: 159).

38. While the poverty ratios for urban India (2004–5) estimated using Lakdawala and Tendulkar methods are identical, the corresponding poverty lines are not because they differ inter alia with respect to the reference period for some items of poverty line basket used in the NSSO surveys. The Expert Group (Lakdawala) used the uniform reference period and the Expert Group (Tendulkar) used the mixed reference period. Estimates of consumer expenditure vary with reference period.

39. GoI (2011a: 9) credits the methodology adopted by the Expert Group (Tendulkar) for estimating state price indicators that in turn enabled the determination of state-specific poverty lines for the smaller states of the North-East.

40. There is a substantial rural–urban difference in prices in India (Bhattacharya and Chatterjee 1971; Majumder, Ray and Sinha 2012).

41. Mari Bhat and Zavier (1999: 3014–15) noted the unusually low fertility and under-five mortality of Nagaland in NFHS-I and suggested that 'there are reasons to believe that NFHS data collection work in these regions had suffered on account of the lack of familiarity of fieldworkers with the terrain'. They did not examine the sampling frame and other contextual factors discussed in this chapter.

42. The degree of underestimation depends on inter alia the density of the MPCE distribution around the poverty line.

43. Poverty in rural Nagaland halved between 1993–4 and 2004–5 but bounced back to the 1993–4 level by 2009–10. In urban Nagaland, the swings are even sharper. Unlike the rural sector, we do not have an explanation for the decline in urban Nagaland's MPCE vis-à-vis India (maximum). Factors such as the increase in rural-to-urban migration and notification of new towns in poorer parts of Nagaland need further exploration. Also note that only Arunachal Pradesh (rural), Jharkhand (urban), Nagaland (rural and urban), Mizoram (rural) recorded an increase in the incidence of poverty between 2004–5 and 2011–12 (GoI 2014f). Further, five states in the North-East including Nagaland also registered an increase in the poverty gap ratio defying the all-India trend (GoI 2015b: Figure 3.10.1). While an increase in measures of poverty is possible, it could also be an artefact of inadequacies in NSSO surveys.

44. The MPCE of Nagaland relative to the maximum MPCE for states declines over time as the number of villages in the sampling frame increases (Figure 6.4). This might appear contradictory to the increase in non-coverage in 2004 (Figure 6.3). The increase in non-coverage was, however, driven by overestimation of headcount in the 2001 Census. The headcounts of rural and remote areas were more erroneous (Tables 4.2A and 5.8).

45. The poverty estimates of the Nagaland government might not be reliable though as the number of households covered by the survey compares favourably with the 2001 Census.

46. In addition to the village level and intra-state factors discussed in this chapter, there are intra-village factors that can bias samples. During our field visits we found that the house of village head was invariably part of the sample in large national surveys such as the NFHS. The inclusion of the village head's household, which is likely to be better off than others, could bias the sample as only a few households are covered in each village. This can have a sizeable impact in largely rural states.

47. The India Human Development Survey (IHDS), another source of socio-economic survey data, is unlikely to be representative for Nagaland. The documentation for IHDS I (2004–5) clearly mentions the that the survey was 'nationally representative' (Desai and Vanneman 2008) but is silent regarding lower levels of aggregation.

The IHDS I sample covered only the economically advanced districts of Nagaland closer to the Assam border. We could not locate the documentation for IHDS II (2011–12), but it seems 'all households surveyed by IHDS-I' were re-interviewed in the second round (IHDS 2011: 3). Likewise, the SRS, a major source of information on vital statistics, is not reliable for states such as Nagaland. As per the SRS bulletin (May 2019), Nagaland has the lowest infant mortality rate (IMR) among all Indian states. Neighbouring Manipur achieved this distinction in 2015. While an investigation into these numbers is beyond our scope, it is hard to believe that Manipur and Nagaland have leapfrogged over states such as Kerala. In fact, the IMR estimates for Nagaland and Manipur from NFHS-4 are two to three times the SRS estimates (IIPS and ICF 2017). This is not the case with other better-performing states such as Kerala and Goa, where the difference between the two sources is small.

Part III
Policy Implications

7

Data, Development and Democracy

[I]n the Reserve Bank [of India] we are handicapped by the reliability of some of
the basic data that we need to use in policy calculations.

—Subbarao (2011)

There should be no fear of being small in number—as a village, town or District,
State or as a people. It is not how many we are that matters, but who we are that
really counts. As Nagas we should be known for our courage, integrity and unity,
irrespective of our numbers.

—Rio (2014: 37–8)

We should judge results, not by statistics or the amount of money spent, but by
the quality of human character that is evolved.

—Jawaharlal Nehru's 'Foreword' to Elwin (1959)

Introduction

In the run-up to the 2011 Census in Nagaland, the government released several
advertisements that framed the exercise in moral terms. One of the posters showed
a Naga idol exhorting people to give correct responses to census questions with
the following words: 'My future must be built on the truth – Correct Census
means strong future!' (Figure 7.1).[1] Politicians (Rio 2010b: 108; 2011: 73–4), civil
society leaders (interviews, 24 November 2012 and 8 April 2013, Dimapur; see
also *CPO & Ors.* vs. *UoI & Ors.* 2006), bureaucrats (Naga IAS officer, interview,
25 June 2013, Kohima) and church leaders (speeches, Clean Election Campaign,
19 September 2012, Hotel Japfu, Kohima) viewed the manipulation of government
statistics as a reflection of individual and collective moral failings and used words
such as 'honesty', 'greed', 'integrity' and 'shame' to describe the problem. The chief
minister argued that the government was helpless in absence of 'a conscious social
decision based on moral values and ethical grounds' (Rio 2010b: 108). He invoked
Naga-Christian values and appealed to all concerned:

to ensure that the Census 2011 [is] conducted properly with truth and honesty. We cannot afford to leave behind for our younger generations a legacy of falsehood and deception. A society cannot be built on the foundation of falsehood and expect to prosper. It goes against our traditional as well as Christian values. We must demonstrate in the right way our traditional qualities of honesty, and uphold the dignity of the Naga people by counting ourselves correctly. (Rio 2011: 73–4)

In his speech on the ocassion of the release of the 2011 Census data, Rio (2014: 37–8) pointed out that his government 'took a political decision' to conduct a clean census but once again linked good quality data to personal integrity. In the run-up to the 2011 Census, the Naga Hoho appealed in similar terms (*Eastern Panorama* 2011) and also implicitly framed the manipulation of census as unbecoming of a modern people.

Since census data is used all over the world by many nations for planning and development, we in Nagaland cannot afford to miss out on this crucial exercise and must assert our rights in demanding that the government utilises the accurate database for planning. (*Meghalaya Times* 2010)

Most of our interviewees, both from within and outside the state, argued or believed that the conflation among census, elections and development policies was unique to Nagaland. This is reflected in statements like 'What has not happened anywhere has happened here' (civil society leader, interview, 23 November 2012, Dimapur) as well as government publications such as *Census 2011: Interesting & Fun Facts* that has an information box with the caption '*It happens only in Nagaland...*' (GoI n.d.10: 20, emphasis in original).

Naga response to the manipulation of government statistics had three layers. First, incorrect responses reflect individual dishonesty. Second, flawed statistics are a matter of collective shame.[2] Third, poor statistics reflect (civilisational)

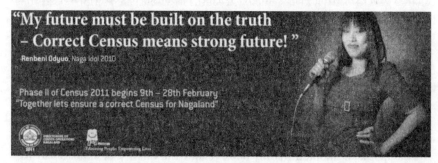

Figure 7.1   Poster exhorting citizens to provide accurate data
Source: GoI (2011c: 6).

backwardness vis-à-vis other societies. So, a manifestation of dysfunctional public institutions in an ethnically divided and economically stagnant setting was transformed into a moral-civilisational problem. While this helped in conducting a relatively clean census in 2011, it diverted attention away from deeper reforms that would have helped prevent the recurrence of similar problems in the future.[3]

Nagas are not alone, though, in viewing the manipulation of statistics in this manner.[4] In the early 1960s, a Nigerian minister suggested that poor statistics were a source of national shame.

> It is our duty as a nation to see to it that we produce population census results which have been thoroughly conducted, verified and appraised, and therefore acceptable, without any shadow of doubt, to all governments of the world and to all international bodies…. The impressions of the manner in which a country conducts its affairs are one of the factors which earn for it the respect or disrespect of the rest of the world. (Aluko 1965: 371)

Such insinuations are misleading. First, manipulation of government statistics in pursuit of mundane objectives is not unheard of in 'advanced' countries. A European administrator related to the Marshall Plan told Morgenstern (1973: 21), 'We shall produce any statistic that we think will help us to get as much money out of the United States as we possibly can. Statistics which we do not have, but which we need to justify our demands, we will simply fabricate.'

Second, comparison of Western countries that until recently had robust institutions and limited ethnic diversity with developing countries having much higher levels of diversity and weaker institutions is unfair. In fact, the United States of America (USA), one of the most ethnically diverse as well as 'advanced' Western countries, has struggled to maintain trust in its censuses (Goldin 2000; Prewitt 2003; 2010). It also bears emphasising that developing countries were exposed to census and other government statistics during the colonial period. The colonial governments actively employed census to accentuate ascriptive divisions based on, say, religion (Bhagat 2001; 2003) even though religion was kept out of the purview of most contemporary Western censuses.

Third, there can be two similar societies, one in which everyone manipulates data and the other in which no one manipulates. Kumar (2019) models the competitive manipulation of census using normal-form games and shows that such interactions are characterised by multiple equilibria, at least one of which does not support manipulation, and societies can move between these equilibria without the threat of punishment.

The approach adopted in this book relates the quality of statistics to the underlying socio-economic and political conditions. It situates data deficit in relation to democracy and development deficits. Poor statistics are, therefore, not a matter of shame rather a problem that needs institutional solutions. The four key chapters examined area, population and household survey statistics and contextualised data deficit.

In Chapter 3 on area, we pointed out that the diversity of mutually inconsistent maps of Nagaland as well as the magnitude of 'errors' in maps grew over the years despite advances in mapmaking technologies.[5] The cartographic diversity is a by-product of the state government's balancing act between an irredentist/ secessionist insurgency and status quoist neighbouring states and the union government. We argued that Nagaland's (external) borders are sites of collision of different conceptions of nationhood and constitutional federalism and that Nagas are constantly reworking their ethnic boundaries and political borders to arrive at a stable basis for their identity. The quality of the maps of Nagaland, therefore, depends upon, among other things, the Indian democracy's ability to address normative conflicts in its ethno-geographic periphery and the emergence of consensus within the Naga society over *Who is a Naga* and *What are his territorial entitlements?*

Chapters 4 and 5 on census showed that the unusual changes in Nagaland's population cannot be explained by demographic and political-geographic factors. As in the case of maps, the anomalies in headcount are driven by a combination of political-economic factors including the dependence of people upon government spending, apportioned according to the reported numbers and measured economic and educational disadvantage of communities/administrative units, and the competition to obtain a larger share in the public pie through a favourable revision of administrative and electoral borders. The quality of data is, therefore, a function of the maturity and perceived fairness of public institutions and the degree of the dependence of people on the state that in turn depends on the development of the economy outside the public sector. Trust in public institutions and development of the economy in turn depend on the resolution of the political dispute over Nagaland's status within the union.

Chapter 6 on sample surveys showed that the National Sample Survey Office (NSSO) surveys lack representativeness and inter-temporal comparability for Nagaland and Jammu and Kashmir due to the use of flawed sampling frames, biased samples and changes in non-coverage across surveys. Between 1993–4 and 2011–12, the extent of non-coverage was so high that Nagaland's rural poverty ratio was among the lowest in the country despite the possible overestimation of its poverty line. The sustained and very high frame non-coverage can be attributed to insurgency and the risk aversion of the (statistical) bureaucracy.

Data deficit deserves urgent attention in light of the systematic, substantial and persistent errors in key government statistics despite conceptual and technological advances in data collection and processing, on the one hand, and the growing clamour for evidence-based policymaking, on the other.[6] In this book, we tried to uncover the context within which government statistics are collected and disseminated and the consequent shortcomings that the general public, policymakers and academics need to be aware of. In this concluding chapter, which tries to generalise the insights from the analysis of different types of statistics from Nagaland, we will situate data deficit in uneven statistical topographies and highlight the mutually constitutive relationship between data, development and democracy deficits reflected among other things in controversies over delimitation. We will argue that there is a need to understand the broader concerns that have to be addressed to improve the quality of data used in policymaking. Following the discussion in the preceding chapters, we will emphasise the need to make statistics more transparent by making adequate metadata available[7] and understand data deficit from the perspectives of the life cycle and interconnectedness of data. We will also emphasise the need to ground proposals for improving the statistical system in the larger context in which data are produced and used rather than allowing technological determinism to drive reforms.

Metadata

The paucity and poor quality of metadata are crucial components of data deficit. There is a growing tendency to treat data as self-contained, requiring minimal, if any, explanation. Descriptive reports seem to be going out of fashion. We will discuss examples related to census, map-making and sample surveys to highlight the lack of attention paid to metadata.

The *Administrative reports* on enumeration and tabulation that provided extensive documentation and insightful commentary on the process of enumeration are hard to find for post-1981 censuses, even though the Census still maintains, 'Along with publishing of the Census data, it would be proper... [to] provide a methodological and administrative report' (GoI n.d.3). *General Population Tables (GPT)*, a key source of valuable qualitative information on, among other things, intercensal territorial realignments, changes in the classification of rural and urban areas and interstate territorial disputes were released only in the form of unannotated Microsoft Excel files after the 2011 Census. In fact, the *GPT* was not published for Nagaland even in 2001. *GPT* were published for other states, but they do not provide adequate information. For instance, Manipur's 2001 *GPT* is silent on the treatment of the population of three subdivisions of Senapati that reported abnormally high growth rates (Agrawal and Kumar 2019b). Likewise, Jammu and Kashmir's 2001 *GPT* did not provide sufficient information on the asynchronous nature of census in the snow-bound areas where enumeration is completed before winter sets in.

In case of maps, we pointed out that the Census and the Survey of India (SoI) do not follow uniform norms for reporting interstate disputes in different parts of the country, for example, Meghalaya's disputes with Assam are treated differently from the latter's disputes with Nagaland. Maps in census reports do not acknowledge the border dispute between Assam and Nagaland. Moreover, the SoI map of Nagaland does not indicate the source of information used to draw internal borders (SoI 2010), though it is highly unlikely that the SoI has itself verified intra-state borders. Maps of Nagaland published by the Registrar General of India (RGI) and the Election Commission of India (ECI) do not identify changes in inter-circle and inter-constituency borders, respectively (Agrawal and Kumar 2017a: Maps 8 and 5).[8] The Census takes shelter behind purported technical difficulties in drawing borders when its maps do not agree with ground reality. Errors in maps affect both the population and population density and result in a potential overlap between the sampling frames of the NSSO for Assam and Nagaland.

In Chapter 6 on sample surveys, we pointed out that NSSO reports do not provide information necessary for understanding the sampling frame for smaller states in the country's troubled ethno-geographic periphery. We highlighted a few instances of lack of attention to essential details regarding the sampling frame. The uncritical acceptance of census is perhaps the foremost among them. The NSSO used the 2001 Census of Nagaland even after the state government had formally questioned the faulty population data. The NSSO did not alert the users to the errors in the Census, let alone discuss its impact, if any, on survey statistics. In fact, the NSSO itself misunderstood the census data. It interpreted the correction in Nagaland's reported population as a contraction and used a negative growth rate to project the rural population after 2013. Another problem relates to the inadequate discussion of variations in non-coverage across rounds. The NSSO reports do not mention the source of information used to identify villages within 5 kilometres of bus routes in Nagaland. As a result, it is not clear why the number of villages in the sampling frame did not change between 1988 and 2004, why the NSSO differs from the Census with regard to the count of villages and why the share of tribal population in its samples has increased over the years in Nagaland. Also, since the publication of the results of the 2001 Census, the NSSO sampling frame for Manipur has excluded three subdivisions of Senapati district, but this was not mentioned in the relevant reports. Non-coverage in case of Tripura was also not appropriately reported. Further, there are unexplained inconsistencies between the NSSO reports and unit-level data. As per the NSSO reports, all urban FSUs (First Stage Units) allocated to Nagaland were surveyed in the 55th round, even though the unit-level data indicate the exclusion of three districts. There is even a disagreement between government reports over the year of commencement of NSSO operations in Nagaland.

Indeed, as data processing capacity grows, data tables are pushing verbal descriptions out of statistical reports. Unannotated data conceal theoretical, ideological and departmental biases and lapses as well as the larger context in which data are located.[9] Government data collection and mapmaking agencies ought to release adequate metadata and administrative reports, without which published statistics cannot be meaningfully interpreted.[10] The Collection of Statistics Rules 2011 (Art. 5.5) stipulates that a minimal set of information regarding data collection should be specified in the notification issued for the collection of data, but it does not mandate the publication of this information along with the final report. Likewise, the National Data Sharing and Accessibility Policy 2012 limits its attention to metadata 'in standardized formats… which enables data discovery and access through departmental portals' and adds that it expects datasets to provide 'information including methods, structure, semantics, and quality control/ assurance' (GoI 2012b: 14–15). The aforesaid rules and policy do not mandate detailed descriptive reports that used to be published earlier and do not apply to the Census, while their applicability to maps generated by the Survey of India and NSSO surveys is not clear.

Life Cycle and Interconnectedness of Data

Discussions of data quality need to take into account the entire life cycle of data from conception to use (Figure 1.1), including what happens after the data are rejected/superseded/corrected. A life cycle approach will facilitate an appreciation of the interlinkages between different kinds of statistics. It will also extend the horizon of the statistical bureaucracy, whose idea of data users is largely limited to government and, to a lesser extent, academic community leaving out lay users/ non-governmental actors, including citizens, politicians and civil society (Figure 7.2). Our discussion shows that the best of the database can be rendered worthless and can even engender conflict if respondents/lay users do not trust them or are compelled by circumstances to resort to manipulation.[11] Nagaland's experience suggests that it helps to educate and engage lay users right from the early stages of the life cycle (GoI 2009a; 2011c). The outreach for the 2011 Census, which is among the better censuses conducted in Nagaland, began as early as 2009 and had the overt support of the political leadership.[12] A key point needs to be clarified through outreach: manipulation does not help. To solve one problem, communities end up creating two more – the deepening of intercommunity conflicts and disruption of development planning.

Another point of interest relates to the systemic impact of errors in basic statistics (Figure 7.3). Errors are transmitted across the statistical system because of the interconnections between data sets and are magnified in the process (cf.

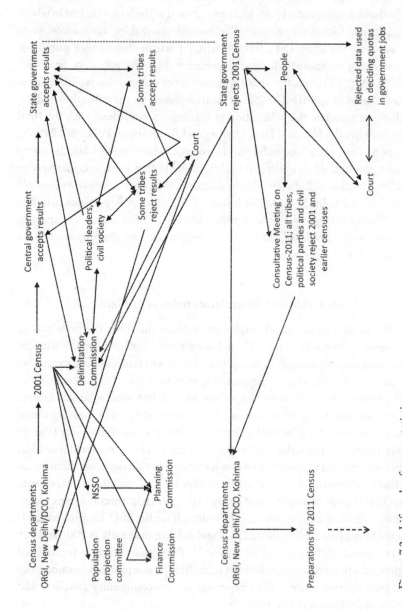

Figure 7.2 Life cycle of census statistics
Source: Authors.

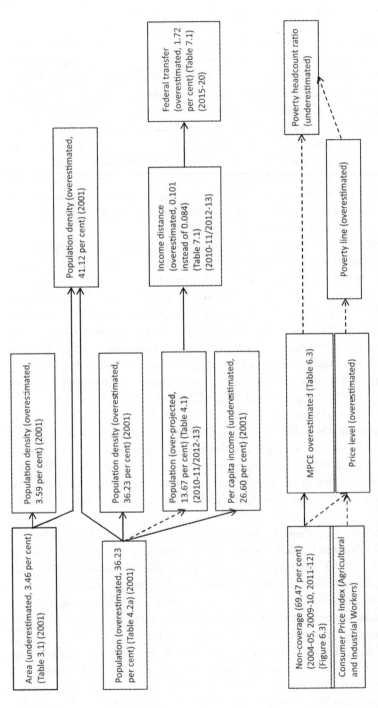

Figure 7.3 Transmission of errors in Nagaland

Source: Authors.

Note: Solid (dashed) arrows identify channels for which we have (have not) been able to quantify the impact of errors.

294 Numbers in India's Periphery

Morgenstern 1973: 50–1). Incorrect maps affected Nagaland's population density estimates. The reported density was overestimated by about 41 per cent in 2001 if we account for errors in both area (Table 3.1) and population (Equation 4.6). Flawed maps also make it difficult to properly account for the population along the Assam–Nagaland border. The population densities of some of the entirely rural border circles is close to 1,000 persons per square kilometre (Table 3.2). The per capita income (PCI) of Nagaland was underestimated by at least 25 per cent due to the overestimation of population. Further, frame non-coverage and the use of flawed censuses as sampling frames and, possibly, outdated bus route maps affected the representativeness of NSSO surveys, leading to an overestimation of rural Nagaland's monthly per capita consumer expenditure (MPCE) relative to rural India's MPCE by at least 14.22 per cent.

At another level, errors in population estimates affected national plans and federal redistribution. Until 2014, most of the transfer of funds from centre to states took place through three channels: (a) the Finance Commission, a constitutional body that determined interstate devolution of federal taxes and also made grants to states (about 60 per cent of all the centre–state transfers), (b) the erstwhile Planning Commission, a non-statutory body[13] that recommended state as well as central plan grants (30–35 per cent) and (c) centrally sponsored schemes and other grants of the union ministries (5 per cent) (Rao and Singh 2001: Table 5; see also Rajaraman 2008: Figure 3). The third channel is highly discretionary in nature (Khemani 2007; Arulampalam et al. 2009). However, the recommendations of the Finance Commission and, to a lesser extent, of the Planning Commission were largely unrestricted by political considerations insofar as these bodies determined transfers mostly on the basis of pre-decided formulae and assessment of the relative condition of states captured through government statistics. While the formulae are uniformly applied to all states, errors in statistics can distort transfers. The distortionary impact of data quality on federal redistribution is mostly overlooked though.[14]

The Planning Commission's transfers were largely ad hoc until 1969, when the Gadgil formula operationalised a systematic mechanism for transfers. The formula was revised in 1980, 1990 and 1991. The Planning Commission first set aside funds for externally aided schemes, Special Area Programmes and so forth. The rest of the amount, known as Normal Central Assistance (NCA), was distributed among Special Category States (SCS) and non-SCS in the ratio of 30 to 70. While the population share of SCS was less than 7 per cent, they received 30 per cent of the NCA. Also, in case of centrally sponsored schemes, the centre financed up to 90 (60) per cent of the budget as grants for SCS (non-SCS) and the remaining 10 (40) per cent was offered as loans. The Gadgil formula provided a basis for the distribution of the 70 per cent of the NCA among the non-SCS (GoI 2009a).

However, there were 'no objective criteria and weight for distribution [of the 30 per cent of the NCA] among the Special Category States. The main considerations were the level of allotment in the previous years, resource position of States and also development needs etc.' (GoI 1997a: 3). For example, in 2007–8 and 2008–9, the NCA was uniformly 10 per cent higher than the preceding years for all SCS (GoI n.d.20). We cannot examine how flawed statistics might have affected the transfer of funds through the Planning Commission to SCS due to the lack of information about the considerations that influenced the quantum of transfers.[15]

Finance commissions decide the inter se (horizontal) distribution of funds using varying combinations of population, area, forest cover, income per capita, fiscal capacity of the states and so forth (GoI 2003; 2009a; 2015a). We will illustrate the impact of flawed statistics on the inter se shares awarded by the Fourteenth Finance Commission (2015–20) that used the 1971 population ($p_{1971,i}$), 2011 population ($p_{2011,i}$), area ($a_{g,i}$) and forest area ($a_{f,i}$) and an income distance index to distribute funds. Income distance is a measure of fiscal capacity, which is a function of the distance between highest SDP per capita among all states and SDP per capita of a state. The inter se share of the ith state (ISS_i) as per the Fourteenth Finance Commission (FFC) is given by the following expression (GoI 2015a: Chapter 8):

$$ISS_i = 0.175 \frac{p_{1971,i}}{\sum_i p_{1971,i}} + 0.10 \frac{p_{2011,i}}{\sum_i p_{2011,i}} + 0.15 \frac{a_{g,i}}{\sum_i a_{g,i}} + 0.075 \frac{a_{f,i}}{\sum_i a_{f,i}}$$

$$+ 0.50 \frac{\left(\left. \frac{Y_i}{p_{\overline{2011,i}}} \right|_{max} - \frac{Y_i}{p_{\overline{2011,i}}} \right) p_{1971,i}}{\sum_i \left(\left. \frac{Y_i}{p_{\overline{2011,i}}} \right|_{max} - \frac{Y_i}{p_{\overline{2011,i}}} \right) p_{1971,i}} \qquad \text{(Equation 7.1)}$$

In Equation 7.1, a floor value of 2 per cent was assigned to the states with lesser share in the country's area. The commission used the 1971 and 2011 Censuses for the corresponding population shares. The FFC was constituted in 2013, but for measuring income distance, it calculated per capita state domestic product (SDP) using intercensal population projections averaged over 2010–11 to 2012–13 ($p_{\overline{2011,i}}$) from the *Report of the Technical Group on Population Projections* (GoI 2006a).[16] As discussed earlier, the Technical Group overestimated Nagaland's population (Table 4.1). The use of inflated estimates resulted in the underestimation of Nagaland's gross state domestic product (GSDP) per capita, which in turn affected the income distance index. If we replace the projected figure for 2011 with the corresponding census population, that is, $p_{\overline{2011}}$ with p_{2011}, we find that Nagaland received an additional ₹3.33 billion (that is, a gain of 1.72 per cent) through devolution (Table 7.1), which is a substantial amount in light of the fact that during 2015–16 the state's own tax revenue was ₹4.27 billion (GoI 2016b: 9). Nagaland's population share for 2011 was also overstated as the Census could not completely eliminate the errors accumulated over decades. As a result, the change in Nagaland's population shares during 1971–2011 was the highest in the country despite the contraction of its population during 2001–11, which further inflated the state's share through the second term of Equation 7.1. This analysis of the impact of errors in population statistics on federal redistribution complements the earlier discussion on the impact of these errors on the delimitation of constituencies. These analyses show that errors in some of the basic statistics transmit across the government statistical system and affect policymaking.

Uneven Statistical Topographies

India has a robust government statistical machinery compared to most developing countries (World Bank n.d.1), but parts of the country suffer from a data deficit

Table 7.1   Federal redistribution, Fourteenth Finance Commission, 2015–20

State	Share of				Income distance	Inter se share (Devolution, in ₹ billion)	Impact on devolution (in ₹ billion)
	Population (1971)	Population (2011)	Area	Forest area			
Weight (%)	17.5	10	15	7.5	50		
Nagaland	0.10	0.17	2.00	1.52	0.10	0.497 (196.44)	
Nagaland[*]					0.08	0.489 (193.11)	-3.33
Assam	2.69	2.62	2.03	3.23	4.07	3.313 (1,308.13)	
Assam[**]			2.00 (1.88)	3.09		3.297 (1,301.84)	-6.29

Sources: GoI (2015a) and authors' calculations.

Notes: (i) 'Inter se share' denotes the share each state receives out of the total amount to be devolved (namely, ₹39,481.87 billion). (ii) [*] Estimated using the 2011 Census population in place of the GoI (2006a) figures that were used by the commission to calculate the per capita SDP. (iii) [**] The area and forest area of Assam have been calculated after accounting for the loss of reserved forests to Nagaland (Table 3.1). Assam's area share has to be further adjusted to 2.00 as the corrected value of area share (namely, 1.88) falls below the floor value (2.00). (iv) Service tax was not levied in Jammu and Kashmir and, therefore, its proceeds were distributed only among the rest of the states. The inter se shares of Assam and Nagaland in service tax proceeds are slightly higher than the figures reported above. Due to the lack of information on the share of service tax proceeds within the divisible pool, the impact on devolution has been calculated using the inter se share reported above. (v) 'Impact' is the additional devolution due to errors in data. See notes ii and iii of this table. The estimate of impact on devolution reported in the table is a lower bound as we have not been able to correct the 2011 Census population (note 31 of Chapter 4).

— either data are unavailable or the available data are of poor quality. Census could not be conducted on a few occasions after 1947: Jammu and Kashmir (1951 and 1991), North Eastern Frontier Agency (NEFA) including Arunachal Pradesh and parts of Nagaland (1951) and Assam (1981) (Map 7.1[a]). The 1951 Census data on language for Punjab, Patiala and East Punjab States Union (PEPSU) and Himachal Pradesh (Gill 2007: 244) and on backward classes (GoI 2009b: 28) were collected but not published. In the 1961 Census, an abridged household schedule was administered for 297,853 out of 336,558 persons in the NEFA (Chaube 2012: Table 6). The Census excluded the Jarawa tribe of Andaman and Nicobar Islands until 1971 (GoI n.d.21), while the Sentinelese have not been enumerated so far.[17] Jammu and Kashmir and the smaller north-eastern states including Nagaland were first covered by the Post-Enumeration Surveys (PESs) in 2001.

Almost all of the areas for which the coverage of the Census has been inadequate in the past lie in the country's ethno-geographic periphery (Map 1.2). Major instances of manipulation of census too occurred in the periphery – Nagaland (1991 and 2001), Manipur (2001 and 2011) and Jammu and Kashmir (2011) (Map 7.1[a]). Most recently, the coverage of Aadhaar registration (12-digit unique identity number) and National Population Register (NPR) has been lower in the North-East and Jammu and Kashmir (Map 7.1[c–d]). This is also true of a recent exercise to identify ration cardholders (*ME* 2019h). Also recall that the Census and Survey of India maps do not precisely mark borders for states in the North-East and in some cases do not even alert users to the inaccuracies therein (Chapter 3). The inter-district borders depicted on the map of Nagaland hosted on Bhuvan, the geospatial platform of the Indian Space Research Organisation, are both outdated and incorrect (ISRO n.d.).

Furthermore, some national-level sample surveys do not cover states in the ethno-geographic periphery (for example, Rural Economic and Demographic Surveys and surveys conducted by the National Nutrition Monitoring Bureau). Other surveys cover these states irregularly (for example, District Level Household and Facility Survey). Even the surveys that cover these states regularly (for example, NSSO surveys) do not adequately cover the entire population or the sample sizes are not large enough to generate reliable estimates.[18] In most years between 1991 and 2012, Jammu and Kashmir and the North-East (particularly, Nagaland, Tripura and a few subdivisions of Manipur) together accounted for more than 40 per cent of the frame and sample non-coverage in NSSO surveys across the country even though their population share was less than 2 per cent (Map 7.1[b]).

Such disparity in coverage across geographies has also been reported in other parts of the world. In Africa, the colonial state was more interested in export-oriented sectors of the economy linked to ports overlooking the inland trade (Jerven 2013: 3). Farmers in colonial Ghana's cocoa-producing areas were, for instance,

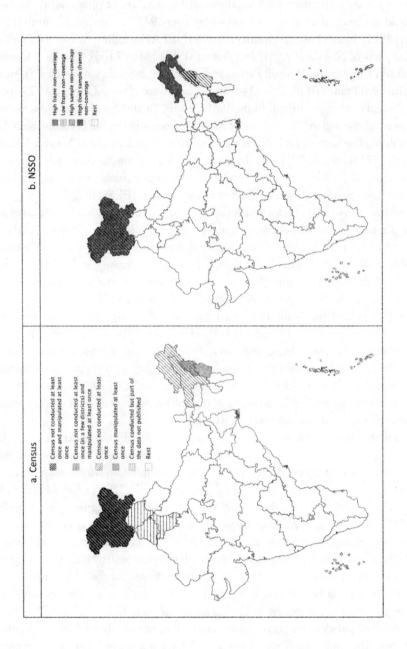

a. Census

Census not conducted at least
once and manipulated at least
once

Census not conducted at least
once (in a few districts) and
manipulated at least once

Census not conducted at least
once

Census manipulated at least
once

Census conducted but part of
the data not published

Rest

b. NSSO

High frame non-coverage

Low frame non-coverage

High sample non-coverage

High (low) sample (frame)
non-coverage

Rest

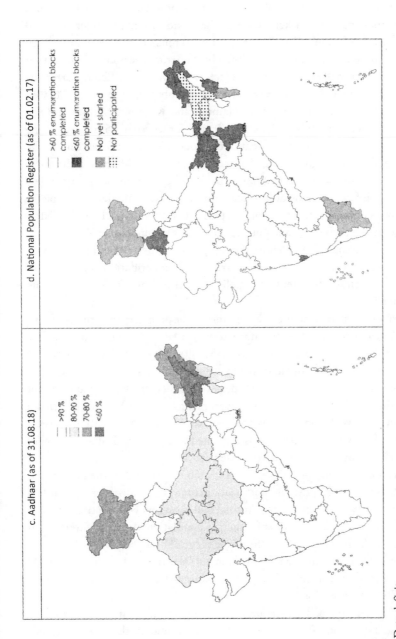

Map 7.1   Data deficit

Source: Prepared by authors using a map template available at https://mapchart.net/india.html and various census reports (a), Chapter 6 (b), data from GoI (n.d.17) (c) and data from GoI (n.d.18) (d).

Note: Maps not to scale and may not represent authentic international borders.

surveyed more rigorously to enable the state to appropriate their wealth (Serra 2014). Informal and non-market sectors of the economy remain under-surveyed around the world (Jerven 2013).[19] Serra (2014: 14) refers to the resultant uneven coverage as 'uneven statistical topography', which mirrors 'the political interests of those in power', 'the will of the state ... to extend its power over different parts of its territory' and is ultimately a manifestation of uneven topography of political power.

The periphery includes nine states (Jammu and Kashmir, Sikkim and the seven north-eastern states; Map 1.2) that account for less than 15 per cent of the country's area but only about 5 per cent of the population and 3.7 per cent of the GDP.[20] Together they control about 5.4 and 7.4 per cent of the seats in the lower and upper houses of the parliament, respectively.[21] Leaving the periphery under-surveyed is, therefore, not politically or economically consequential, which explains the unevenness of India's statistical topography.[22] The attention deficit entailed by small demographic, economic and political footprints is compounded by collective action problems among these states.[23] Lastly, given their size the impact of poor data quality in the peripheral states on, say, federal redistribution is perhaps not large enough to attract the attention of policymakers in New Delhi (see also note 8 of Chapter 5).

Furthermore, sustained political disturbance in the periphery directly constrains surveys. Control over the flow on information is a key objective of insurgencies and counter-insurgencies. Both sides want to control the narrative and access to the site of conflict. This compounds the unevenness of the statistical topography.

The state is weak in low population density areas (Herbst 2000) and cannot deliver quality public goods including government statistics. We can add that a government with weak public goods provision comes in contact with its subjects infrequently and is to that extent less informed about them. India's periphery is characterised by a low population density and a high concentration of ethnolinguistic and religious minorities. This too contributes to the unevenness of the statistical topography. In short, data deficit is not inconceivable in low population density, geographically marginal and insurgency-prone tribal areas.

Even the most elementary statistics such as population are often unreliable in case of tribes, which in turn affects the whole range of headcount-linked statistics and policies. The errors in tribal headcount can be attributed to the ambiguous definition of tribes,[24] the politicisation and manipulation of census due to inter-tribal conflicts/competition, weak state institutions and insurgencies in tribal areas, development and conflict-induced displacement, the relative inaccessibility of tribal habitats, mobility necessitated by tribal economy that often includes shifting cultivation and grazing, contest over the religious identity of tribes and, in tribal-minority states, interference of non-tribal communities.[25] Among these, ambiguous definitions and manipulation of census seem to be the most salient.

'Scheduled Tribes' (STs) is an underspecified constitutional, administrative and enumerative category. According to Art. 366 (25) of the Constitution of India, certain communities are 'deemed under Article 342 to be Scheduled Tribes' and Art. 342 stipulates that such communities are identified through a presidential notification. According to the Ministry of Tribal Affairs, 'The essential characteristics, first laid down by the Lokur Committee, for a community to be identified as Scheduled Tribes are – (a) primitive traits; (b) distinctive culture; (c) shyness of contact with the community at large; (d) geographical isolation; and (e) backwardness – social and economic' (GoI 2007c: 22).[26] These criteria cannot help identify tribes. While the Census of India follows the state-wise list notified by the president, it does not have any clear and stable guidelines for the identification of tribes on the ground (Beteille 1960; Desai 1960; Xaxa 2003; Nongkynrih 2010). The absence of clear guidelines for identifying tribes leaves room for errors and manipulation.

In the absence of a common national list of the STs, the tribal status of communities varies across states, districts of the same state and even seasons. It is not uncommon for a tribe to be recognised under different names in different states, while subgroups of a tribe could be recognised as independent tribes within a state or a few tribes could be collectively recognised as one tribe. Until very recently, the Gond tribe was recognised as an ST in Madhya Pradesh and as a Scheduled Caste (SC) in Uttar Pradesh (Raza and Ahmad 1990: 6). The Bakarwals enjoy ST status only in Jammu and Kashmir and lose that status in winter if they visit grazing grounds in other states. The Barmans of Assam are recognised as an ST in Cachar district but not in Karimganj and Hailakandi districts carved out of Cachar. More generally, Assam's hill (plain) tribes are not treated as tribes in the plains (hills). Similar restrictions were applied in states such as Uttar Pradesh (Verma 2013). Such arbitrary restrictions lead to undercounting as tribal people have in several cases been forced to abandon their home regions because of insurgencies, ecological crises and displacement due to forest/wildlife conservation, mining and development projects. Tribes have also started moving out for better education and employment opportunities.[27] Furthermore, while the identification of a person as a member of a tribe is not conditional upon religious affiliation, the conflation of tribal identity and religion is widespread. In parts of Madhya Pradesh, people of tribal origin were not recorded as STs if they had converted to Christianity (Venkatesan 2001),[28] whereas in parts of the North-East, people were not enumerated as tribes if they had not converted to Christianity (Prabhakara 2012: 108).

The ambiguous criteria used to identify tribes are conducive to manipulation. First, *statistical erasure* of tribal identities has been reported in states such as

Assam (Prabhakara 2012), Uttar Pradesh (Verma 2013) and Jammu and Kashmir. Dominant non-tribal communities suppressed the identity of tribal minorities by not recognising them or by recognising them only in some parts of the state (Figure 7.4[g]).

Second, *statistical marginalisation/submergence* of a tribal community due to the ingress of non-tribal people into the category is another possibility (Figure 7.4[i]). Except the hill states in the North-East and Ladakh, in most places tribes are surrounded by non-tribal people on all sides. This makes the isolation of tribes from non-tribal communities difficult if the latter have an incentive to falsify identity to claim benefits meant for tribes. Parts of Andhra Pradesh, Karnataka and Maharashtra reported abnormal growth of tribal population between 1971 and 1991 Censuses. Sharad Kulkarni (1991: 206) traces the abnormality in population growth to the Removal of Area Restrictions (Amendment) Act of 1976 that delinked Scheduled Areas and STs. He adds that in Maharashtra 'a sub-caste of Koshti caste ... reported to the census enumerators in 1981 that they belonged to the Halba/Halbi tribe ... [Such misreporting] has taken place in the case of many tribes in different states.'[29] Guha (2003: 161–2) adds that Maharashtra reported 'a demographically impossible 200 percent increase' in its tribal population during 1971–81 because of a legislation that 'canceled sales of tribal land to non-tribals made after 1957' but not 'transactions between members of tribal communities'. So, land-scarce non-tribal agricultural communities seem to have tried to expand their access to land by assuming a tribal identity, which they thought would allow them to buy agricultural land from land-surplus tribes. Similar conflicts over land between tribal and non-tribal communities have been reported across the North-East including states such as Assam and Manipur that are discussed in the following section. The anomaly in headcount is also reflected in the mismatch between the data on tribes and languages as the population of the Halba/Halbi tribe increased without a concomitant increase in the speakers of its language (Table 7.2). Furthermore, 'while 96 per cent of the Halba tribe was living in rural areas' in 1971, by 2001 'almost 60 per cent of the tribe had shifted to urban areas' (*Indian Express* 1999; see also Sharad Kulkarni 1991).

Third, manipulation can take the form of *assimilation/co-option* of a tribe under another tribe. In Nagaland, the Tikhir community's population registered an unusually high growth rate in the 1991 Census when it was trying to assert its distinct identity. In the next census, its growth rate dropped by 90 per cent as a larger tribe tried to forcibly assimilate the community (Table 4.12).[30]

Fourth, in many cases the fixed categories used by the Census fail to correctly measure the population, as the underlying entity is fluid. Populations of portmanteau categories such as Chakhesang and Zeliang show sharp variation across censuses because of *fission* and *fusion* of the underlying communities.

Table 7.2   Growth of population of Halba/Halbi tribe, Maharashtra

Year	Population of Halba/ Halbi		Tribe/ language ratio	Decadal growth rate (percentage)			
	Tribe	Language speakers		Halba/Halbi		Maharashtra	
				Tribe	Language	All population	All STs
1971	7,205	2,028	3.55	—	—	—	—
1981	242,819	115,475	2.10	3,270	5,594	25	95
1991	278,378	28,891	9.64	15	–75	26	27
2001	297,923	29,503	10.10	7	2	23	17
2011	261,011	24,950	10.46	–12	–15	16	23

Sources: Prepared by authors using GoI (n.d.1; n.d.2; 2013d; 2018a; 2018c) and Sharad Kulkarni (1991) for the population of Halba/Halbi tribe in 1971 and 1981.

The constituent tribes identify with the census category to various degrees and the degree of identification of each constituent tribe changes along different dimensions of the census category and also over time. For instance, presently, the constituents of Chakhesang identify with Chakhesang qua tribe, whereas the identification with Chakhesang qua language is weak (Figure 7.4[d]). Pochury, which was one of the constituents of Chakhesang, has left the community and achieved recognition as a separate tribe.

Lastly, *ex nihilo genesis* of miscellaneous categories of unclassified/unclassifiable/ ghost tribal population is a possibility (Figure 7.4[e]). In Nagaland, a residual category 'Other Nagas' emerged as the eighth-largest group in 2001 before disappearing into oblivion in 2011 (Tables 4.12 and 4.13). This category largely explains the abnormal population growth reported in at least two districts during 1991–2001.

In short, there is a persistent data deficit along geographical/external margins (states along international border) as well as the social/internal margins (including tribal areas of the 'mainland').[31] As shown in Figure 7.4, the smoothly varying demographic data for India comprise of myriad unexamined local coverage and content errors. Indeed, as discussed in Chapter 2, incorrect statistics have been misinterpreted and used in Nagaland over the decades without the administration, academia and media questioning the quality of data. So, 'What remains an intellectually stimulating problem is how a society adopts to the poor quality of the statistical data it produces; how can research, policymaking and administration thrive on figures of dubious plausibility, never fully accepted nor consistently rejected' (Begum and Miranda 1979: 80).[32]

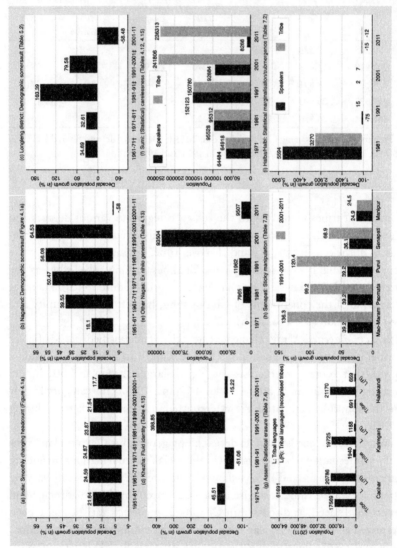

Figure 7.4 Erratic sub-components of the national headcount

Source: Authors.

Delimitation Dilemmas

The founding fathers were alert to potential conflicts over delimitation. The constituent assembly debated the desirability of following a uniform constituency-size criterion across sparsely populated tribal areas and densely populated non-tribal areas. The matter was resolved in favour of tribes to ensure their representation in legislative bodies (Lok Sabha 1999: vol. IV, 659–674). In addition, in most of the tribal areas, the entry of outsiders and land transactions were restricted to protect tribes from demographic marginalisation and dispossession of land (Lok Sabha 1999: vol. IX, 967–1084; Guha 2003: 161–2). However, the initial arrangement merely postponed conflicts that eventually engulfed the country by the 1970s, when the government had to freeze interstate delimitation. The 2002 delimitation, which was restricted to intra-state adjustments, shifted the locus of conflicts to sub-state levels of aggregation. The 2002 delimitation had to be postponed in Nagaland and four other states – Assam, Arunachal Pradesh, Manipur and Jharkhand – and was conducted under constraints in five states – Chhattisgarh, Meghalaya, Sikkim, Tripura and Uttarakhand (Map 7.2). Most of these states belong to the ethno-geographic periphery. This section discusses these states as well as Jammu and Kashmir, where the Delimitation Act did not apply and delimitation was postponed under a state legislation. The fact that delimitation could not be conducted or was conducted under restrictions in 11 out of the then 28 states of the country is revealing. The following discussion is mostly based on secondary sources and serves the purpose of highlighting problems similar to the ones discussed in Nagaland's context. Each of the cases discussed in this section requires fieldwork.

Manipur

In Manipur, three hill districts – Senapati, Ukhrul and Chandel – reported high population growth in the 2001 Census (Table 7.3) despite out-migration of the Naga tribes to the Imphal Valley and other states as well as the out-migration of Kukis from these districts after violent conflicts in the mid-1990s (note 79 of Chapter 4). Moreover, Meiteis, who constitute the majority in the state, are not permitted to buy land in the hills, while the hill people can freely settle in the Meitei-dominated Valley, the educational and economic hub of the state. Therefore, in-migration is unlikely to explain the high growth rates in the Naga-dominated districts such as Senapati. The Manipur government rejected the abnormally high population growth rates reported in the 2001 Census and the ORGI agreed to conduct a recount in Mao-Maram, Paomata and Purul subdivisions of Senapati

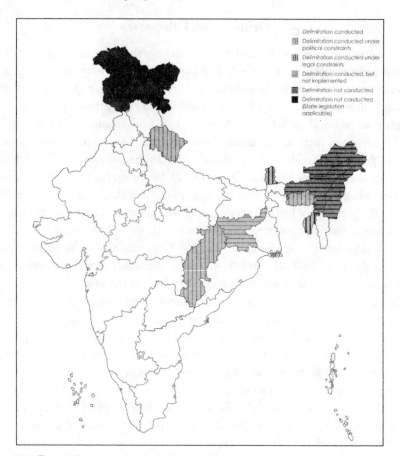

Map 7.2   Regional variations in the 2002 delimitation

Source: Prepared by authors using information available in GoI (2008d) and a map template available at https://mapchart.net/india.html.

Note: Map not to scale and may not represent authentic international borders.

district.[33] Singh suggests that attempts to verify the headcount of these subdivisions met with resistance.

> The government of Manipur started a reenumeration/resurvey from October 7 to October 12, 2003 in the villages which were considered to show abnormal growth. But the people of the concerned districts did not cooperate with the resurvey. (Singh 2006: 1473)

Similarly, reporting on anomalies in the electoral rolls, Laithangbam points out that election officials had gone to these Naga villages after a proper notification for a physical verification of the people said to be residing there. However, in all instances the villages were deserted. (Laithangbam 2004)

According to the Census, 'results for Mao-Maram, Paomata and Purul sub-divisions of Senapati district of Manipur were cancelled due to administrative and technical reasons although a [2001] population census was carried out in these subdivisions also as per schedule' (GoI n.d.22). Delimitation on the basis of the disputed population figures would have transferred five assembly seats to the hill districts of Manipur at the Valley's expense (*Sangai Express* 2007b) (Table 7.3). Political parties opposed to delimitation approached the union government (NENA 2007) and Gauhati High Court (*Manipur Pradesh Congress Committee and Ors vs Union of India and Ors* 2007). The court ordered a recount of the population in nine hill subdivisions. Instead, only three subdivisions were allegedly 'selectively chosen' (ibid.) by the Registrar General, who 'imposed 39 per cent as decadal growth rate … without any field verification' (NENA 2007). The tribes of Senapati continue to complain against the non-implementation of delimitation as per the 2001 Census (E-pao.net 2013a). Unlike Nagaland, there was no constructive public debate on the issue in Manipur. In 2011, the three subdivisions of Senapati once again reported inflated headcounts. The ORGI initially withheld the results for the three subdivisions due to 'administrative reasons' but then belatedly released the 'finalized' figures (GoI 2014e) without any correction. According to the 2011 Census, the population of the three subdivisions has more than doubled within a decade and now Senapati alone accounts for about one-sixth of the state's population. If delimitation is carried out using the 2011 Census, the Valley will lose six assembly seats to the hills (Table 7.3).

The abnormal population changes in Manipur have to be understood in the context of the zero-sum ethno-territorial conflicts between the hills and the Valley as well as between Naga and Kuki tribes in the hills ('Greater Nagaland' has a substantial overlap with Kukiland) and dysfunctional autonomous district councils that have failed to meet the aspirations of the tribes. The over-reporting in 2001 and 2011 was mostly reported from the Naga-dominated hill districts, namely, Senapati (Mao, Maram, Poumai and other Nagas and Kukis) and to a lesser extent Chandel (mixed population of Naga and Kuki tribes) and Ukhrul (Tangkhul Nagas) (Table 7.3). Within Senapati, the three subdivisions along or closer to the border with Nagaland reported more than 175 per cent growth between 1991 and 2011. Churachandpur, which shares a border with Assam, Mizoram and Myanmar and is inhabited by Kuki tribes, did not report high growth rates.

Table 7.3 Distribution of population in Manipur

District/sub-division/region	Population growth				Population share			Assembly seats	Gain†		
	1991–2011	1991–2001(R)	1991–2001(E)	2001–11	1991	2001**	2011		1991	2001**	2011
Manipur	55.45	30.07	24.86	24.50	100	100 (100)	100	60			
Chandel	103.03	66.62	n/a	21.85	3.87	5.16 (4.95)	5.05	2	0.32	1.10 (0.97)	1.03
Ukhrul	68.38	28.83	n/a	30.70	5.95	6.14 (5.89)	6.44	3	0.57	0.68 (0.53)	0.87
Tamenglong	63.02	29.23	n/a	26.15	4.70	4.86 (4.67)	4.93	3	–0.18	–0.08 (–0.20)	–0.04
Churachandpur	55.60	29.36	n/a	20.29	9.59	9.94 (9.54)	9.60	6	–0.25	–0.04 (–0.28)	–0.24
Senapati	129.91	81.96	36.09	68.94	11.34	12.36 (15.87)	16.78	6	0.81	1.42 (3.52)	4.07
Mao-Maram*	228.89	143.12	39.16	136.33	2.70	3.01 (5.05)	5.72				
Pao Mata*	177.15	122.64	39.17	99.15	1.06	1.18 (1.81)	1.89				
Purul*	206.68	168.78	39.16	120.38	1.21	1.35 (2.50)	2.39				
Rest	65.50	33.69	33.69	23.79	6.37	6.82 (6.55)	6.78				
Valley	37.75	19.04	19.04	15.72	64.56	61.54 (59.08)	57.21	40	–1.27	–3.07 (–4.55)	–5.68
Hills	87.68	50.15	35.47	38.54	35.44	38.46 (40.92)	42.79	20	1.27	3.07 (4.55)	5.68

Sources: Prepared by authors using GoI (n.d.1; n.d.2; n.d.9). For the three subdivisions of Senapati district – the Telegraph (2003b) and Pou (2007) for 2001 (R), GoI (n.d.22) for 2001 (E), GoI (2014e) for 2011.

Notes: (i) * Two figures on the population of three subdivisions of Senapati district – reported (R) and estimated (E) – are available for both 2001 and 2011. In 2001, the ORGI did not accept the reported figures citing 'administrative and technical reasons'. Instead, it officially released the figures which were estimated assuming the growth rate to be 39 per cent (see Agrawal and Kumar 2019b for a possible rationale behind this correction). In the 2011 Census, however, the ORGI accepted the reported figures. The magnitude of growth during 2001–11 entailed by these figures is highly unrealistic. (ii) ** Calculations for 2001 are based on officially released figures (namely, E). The figures in parentheses for 2001 are based on reported figures (namely, R). (iii) † 'Gain' is the difference between projected seats as per the relevant census and the 'Assembly seats'. 'Assembly seats' is not reported for subdivisions due to the imperfect match between constituencies and subdivisions. For the same reason 'Gain' has not been calculated for subdivisions within districts. (iv) 'n/a' indicates 'not applicable'.

Assam

In Assam, delimitation threatened to disturb the intercommunity balance of power. The chief minister of Assam informed the Delimitation Commission that 'the ethnic rivalry between the different tribes of Assam … translated into aspirations for separate seats for each tribe' (GoI 2008d: 152). Also, communities recognised as tribes shortly after the 2001 Census objected to delimitation in Assam on grounds that they would be denied their constitutional rights for an extended period until after the first census conducted after 2026.[34] 'Illegal' international immigration was another concern in Assam. The chief minister told the commission that without the completion of the National Register of Citizens (NRC) 'the authenticity of the census figures is questionable' and that a state assembly resolution demanded delimitation 'only on the basis of the NRC to be prepared as per the Assam Accord' (GoI 2008d: 153).

It is noteworthy that Assam's tribal headcount is unreliable with or without NRC because of the arbitrary criteria for the recognition of tribes. First, the plain and hill tribes are not recognised outside their respective regions; for example, Karbis are recognised as tribes only in the autonomous hill districts but not in the plain districts. Second, certain tribes have been denied recognition on specious grounds. According to Prabhakara (2012: 120), the Barmans were 'actually part of the Dimasa Kachari family (hills tribe) that had migrated in historic times to the neighbouring Cachar district, had lost their hills tribe status after moving to the plains, and so were recognized as a plains tribe only in that district. However, when in the 1980s the old Cachar district was restructured into three districts, Cachar, Karimganj, and Hailakandi, the Barmans of Cachar lost their recognition as a plains tribe in Karimganj and Hailakandi.' Third, several indigenous (for example, Koch-Rajbongshi, Moran, Matak and Chutiya) as well as non-indigenous (tea tribes) tribal communities have not yet been recognised as STs anywhere in the state (Prabhakara 2012; Kumar 2016a).

The rationale behind these arbitrary criteria that reduce the tribal headcount seem to be linked to the manner in which power sharing is indexed to census statistics. Delimitation takes into account the population of STs to reserve legislative seats for them. This presents the majority non-tribal communities with an incentive to manipulate the tribal headcount through definitional erasure, undercounting or misclassification. However, other data on identity, for example, language, that are not used for power/resource sharing are less likely to attract interference.[35]

The tribal headcount of Cachar and its successor districts Karimganj and Hailakandi is a case in point. We compiled population estimates for tribes from language tables (Table 7.4). These figures underestimate the tribal headcount

Table 7.4   Population of Scheduled Tribes in the districts of Barak Valley, Assam

Year	Cachar		Karimganj		Hailakandi	
	Tribes	Tribal languages (recognised tribes)	Tribes	Tribal languages (recognised tribes)	Tribes	Tribal languages (recognised tribes)
2011	17,569	61,691 (20,786)	1,940	19,725 (1,188)	691	21,170 (659)
2001	18,631	54,669 (19,187)	2,901	14,719 (960)	821	16,342 (894)
1991	16,563	45,397 (16,351)	1,430	10,357 (298)	715	13,761 (559)

Sources: Prepared by authors using GoI (2018a; n.d.1; n.d.2).

Notes: (i) The figures in 'Tribes' columns indicate ST population in the district and the figures in 'Tribal languages' columns indicate the total number of speakers of the following tribal languages: Adi, Angami, Ao, Bhili, Bhumij, Bodo, Chakhesang, Chakma, Chakru/Chokri, Deori, Dimasa, Gangte, Garo, Gondi, Hajong, Halam, Hmar, Karbi, Kabui, Kharia, Khasi, Koch, Kom, Konda, Korwa, Kui, Kuki, Kurukh, Lalung, Malto, Mishimi, Mishing, Mizo, Mogh, Munda, Mundari, Nissi, Paite, Rabha, Rajbangshi, Rengma, Santali, Savara, Sema, Simte, Tangkhul, Thadou, Tripuri, Vaiphei and Zemi. 'Recognised tribes' includes the speakers of the languages spoken by the officially recognised Scheduled Tribes: Barmans (Only in Cachar), Bodo, Deori, Dimasa, Garo Hojai, Mech, Miri, Rabha, Sonowal and Tiwa/Lalung. (ii) The table begins with the year 1991 because census was not conducted in Assam in 1981. Furthermore, Karimganj and Hailakandi were carved out of Cachar during 1981–91.

as tribal communities are likely to have adopted the language of the non-tribal majority that is used in administrative offices, schools and markets. Still, the reported tribal population of these districts is far less than the population of speakers of all the tribal languages enumerated there. In other words, there are a large number of people who belong to unrecognised tribes and have not been enumerated as STs. Note that the population of *recognised* tribes and the speakers of the corresponding tribal languages are largely comparable.

While the Karimganj district administration admitted that the 2001 figure was 'largely disputed by many, according to whom the ST population was grossly under-enumerated' (GoA n.d.2), the undercounting persisted in 2011. Non-governmental sources suggest that in 2009, there were 105 villages in Karimganj where 'tribes live and their total population will be around 55,000' (*Assam Tribune* 2009). The tribes also suffer economic marginalisation due to the loss of land and access to forests (ibid.).

Jharkhand

Delimitation met with opposition in Jharkhand, where tribes constitute a sizeable minority (about 26 per cent in 2001). Associate members of the Delimitation Commission complained that the intention of Government of India, while creating Jharkhand State, was to give maximum benefit for the tribal people and any decrease in the number of reserved seats for them would be a great injustice. They also expressed their apprehension that the decrease of seven Scheduled Tribe seats [in the state legislative assembly] could be due to the reason that the census figures of 2001 do not reflect the actual Scheduled Tribe population living in villages of Jharkhand. All the Associate Members pleaded with the Commission to take up the matter with the Government of India for rectification of tribal population figures of Jharkhand State before starting the delimitation work. (GoI 2008d: 532)

In fact, even before the 2001 Census was conducted, it was feared that the tribal population could be undercounted due to out-migration. A tribal political party, the Jharkhand Mukti Morcha, 'warned that if the Census is held as scheduled in Jharkhand, a large number of tribal people living away from their homelands would be left out'[36] and was assured by the registrar general 'that a fool-proof system had been evolved to deal with such cases' (Venkatesan 2001). Nothing is known of the foolproof system, however. The Delimitation Commission tried to address the concerns of tribes in a convoluted manner. It suggested that

The grievance of the State of Jharkhand can be mitigated to a small extent if the number of ST seats in the State is increased from 21 to 22 and two (2) seats are reserved for STs in Bihar, thus giving 24 seats to the STs in both the States as per their combined entitlement on the basis of 2001-census. This increase of one seat in the ST quota should in the opinion of the Commission, go in favour of Jharkhand on the ground that the actual entitlement for Jharkhand works out to 21.30 and for Bihar to 2.22, which is a lower fraction vis-à-vis the Jharkhand fraction, and also on the ground that the Bihar Assembly will have 2 ST reserved seats, whereas no seat is reserved for the STs in the existing Bihar Legislative Assembly. (GoI 2008d: 535–6)[37]

Delimitation was eventually postponed as the tribes were demanding a larger share than their population on grounds of their indigeneity. In Uttarakhand, the hills similarly complained of the irony of the marginalisation of the very people who fought for the state's formation. In reality, the hills of Uttarakhand have been rapidly losing population due to out-migration and are dotted with *bhootiya* (ghost/abandoned) villages. The hills (or the leaders from there) feared a loss of nine seats. The Delimitation Commission relaxed the size criterion by 10 per cent for the hill districts and transferred six instead of nine constituencies to the plains (GoI 2008d: 1552). In Jharkhand, the Delimitation Commission did not relax the size criterion in favour of one group as it did in Uttarakhand. In Chhattisgarh, the share of the tribes in the state's population translated into 3.49 parliamentary seats, which would have been rounded off to 3. 'In view of the genuine demand of the public', the commission raised the 'seats reserved for them [STs] in the Lok Sabha ... from three to four' (GoI 2008d: 262).

In all these states, the indigenous communities – tribes in Chhattisgarh and Jharkhand and hill people in Uttarakhand – tried to resist the loss of political power to 'outsiders', whose population share has grown over the years and who have captured land and other resources. Both in Jharkhand and Uttarakhand, the political leadership and the bureaucracy admitted indigeneity as a valid ground for relaxing the principles of delimitation. Prime Minister Manmohan Singh admitted that 'Jharkhand was created to help the tribals and if you reduce their representation in the assembly and parliament, that will be a setback' (*India Today* 2008). Similarly, in case of Uttarakhand, the Delimitation Commission noted that 'in as much as the state was formed for furthering the interest of the hilly region, justice will be served by minimizing the loss of the hill districts' (GoI 2008d: 1552).

Jammu and Kashmir

The Delimitation Act of the union government did not apply to the erstwhile state of Jammu and Kashmir, which used to conduct delimitation under a state legislation. '[I]n April 2002, the J&K Legislative Assembly adopted an amendment to the Jammu and Kashmir Constitution freezing any delimitation exercise till 2026' (Talib 2010). However, at least one Jammu-based political party supported delimitation (ibid.). The controversies over headcount and delimitation are rooted in communal (Hindu–Muslim–Buddhist) and regional (Jammu plains–Jammu hills–Kashmir/Jhelam Valley–Ladakh) conflicts in the state.

The Kashmir Valley fears demographic marginalisation due to potential influx from the densely populated plains of north India. These fears are partly based on the alleged decline in the share of Muslims in the state's census population since 1941. Such claims ignore, among other things, the impact of changing reference dates across censuses that affects the accounting of government servants, who move between the two capitals, Jammu and Srinagar, and nomadic communities that move between Kashmir and Jammu and even other states. The purported demographic threat to the state's Muslim majority remains a fixed component of most political controversies in the state (Panandiker and Umashanker 1994: 96; Guilmoto and Irudaya Rajan 2013: 63; Swami 2014). Indeed, census has become 'just a pretext for a religious war, led by the competing elites of [different parts of the state]' (Swami 2000). The communalisation of census has implications for the quality of the data. Guilmoto and Irudaya Rajan (2013: 63) draw attention to the possible 'deliberate over-reporting of children ... in the Kashmir Valley', where people seem to have inflated 'household population by adding non-existent children'. Explaining the context they note that

> wild rumours started to circulate long before the final operations of the 2011 Census were held in Jammu and Kashmir. It was held that there was a plan to exaggerate the share of the Jammu region.... At a time coinciding with the start of the house listing operations in May 2010, Syed Ali Shah Geelani spoke about 'a planned conspiracy to change the Muslim majority of the state' through the census. This obviously did not happen since the population growth was lowest in Jammu. But this rumour may also have, on the contrary, encouraged people in the rest of the state [Kashmir] to react. (ibid.: 63)

This resulted in a steep drop in child sex ratio 'from 941 to 859 girls per 1,000 boys under seven, by far the largest decline observed among the states between 2001 and 2011' (ibid.: 62).

Interconnected Deficits

The persistent and interlinked errors in Nagaland's maps (Chapter 3), population projections (Chapters 2 and 4), census population estimates (Chapters 4 and 5) and sample surveys (Chapter 6) despite methodological and technological advances challenge the technological determinism of recent proposals for statistical reforms and suggest that data deficit cannot be addressed within the perimeters of the science and technology of data collection. This is corroborated by the fact that the states such as Assam, Jammu and Kashmir, Meghalaya and Nagaland with relatively low rates of enrolment in technology-driven biometric databases including Aadhaar are largely coterminous with areas where conventional databases are deficient (Map 7.1).[38]

While it is true that technology helps cutting delays and, possibly, costs, it does not address the political economic problems at the heart of enumeration and mapping discussed in this book. Consider, for instance, the computer-assisted personal interviewing (CAPI) that is viewed as the solution to many of the problems plaguing government statistics. This method was used in both the Socio-Economic and Caste Census (SECC) (Chandramouli 2015) as well as the 2017–18 Periodic Labour Force Survey (PLFS) with the hope that it will 'speed up data collection and processing to reduce the time lags' (GoI n.d.19). The SECC was marred by severe content errors (Vijayanunni 2015) and the data were not fully released. The PLFS data were not released on schedule allegedly because the results of the survey contested the government's claims regarding creation of jobs (*Business Standard* 2019). Indeed, political interference has emerged as the most critical determinant of the timely release of government data (Agrawal and Kumar 2019a). The insulation of the statistical system from governmental and political interference should, therefore, be an urgent priority. Furthermore, legal solutions to the problem of manipulation of data are often constrained by the very factors that circumscribe data quality.[39] Technological and legalistic solutions that address data deficit in isolation have limited effectiveness as the underlying structural problems will remain unaddressed.[40] A better understanding of the larger context as proposed in this book seems indispensable for the design of statistical reforms.

Soon after its formation Nagaland emerged as one of the biggest recipients of (per capita) funds from the union government (Means 1971: 1014). The government is the biggest employer, consumer and contractor in Nagaland's formal sector. The private sector of the economy remains stunted because the state is inherently capital deficient and constitutional–legal provisions limit the ability of outsiders to invest in the state. Furthermore, rampant extortion by insurgent factions and corruption in the government impede the growth of the private sector, making people dependent upon the public sector. The overall incidence of government employment in Nagaland is very high, 1:15, compared to 1:86 in Assam and 1:140 in Uttar Pradesh (S. C. Jamir 1999: 69–70; the 1991 Census population is used to calculate the ratio). Presently, out of a population of more than 2 million, about 125,000 persons are employed by the state government (ME 2019l). The actual share of public sector in employment in Nagaland would be higher if (a) politicians, contractors and central government employees are included (Chasie 2000: 157) and (b) the overcount of population is accounted for. The high level of dependence upon the government intensifies the competition over public resources financed mostly through federal transfers. Nagaland's experience is not unique though. States in India's ethno-geographic periphery 'were dependent upon central transfers alone (share of divisible pool plus grants) for meeting more than 60% of their expenditure in 2013–14. Government expenditure alone constitutes more than 25% of the gross state domestic product (GSDP) in each of these states (more than 50% in Arunachal Pradesh, Manipur, and Mizoram), and their economies will collapse without the central transfers' (Bhattacharjee 2018: 26). There is a need to rethink the existing capital-intensive, top-down model of development, which has saddled Special Category States with a stagnant economy and burgeoning human capital base. Owing to the gross mismatch between the levels of human and economic development and the dominance of public sector employment and investment in the economy, people perversely believe that economic well-being depends on both economic activity as well as ethno-statistical entrepreneurship. The manipulation of government statistics in Nagaland is, therefore, linked to the struggle over scarce public resources in a stagnant economy, where people

(a) depend on federally supported government spending apportioned according to reported numbers and measured disadvantage and (b) do not trust politicians and bureaucrats from other communities/villages to pursue common good because of weak democratic institutions. So, poor statistics are rooted in a democracy deficit and, in turn, vitiate development planning and contribute to the continued underdevelopment that adds to the ongoing political unrest. In other words, Nagaland's development, democracy and data deficits are interconnected. Nearly half a century of unchecked errors in government maps and statistics in Nagaland and their uncritical use by government agencies raise questions about the Indian state's institutional capacity to design empirically informed policies. A similar predicament faces other Special Category States located in India's landlocked and economically underdeveloped ethno-geographic periphery, where communities compete over a fixed electoral-economic pie.

There are deeper historical–political factors, beyond the immediate bread-and-butter factors discussed earlier, which influence the periphery's data deficit. Most states of the North-East (except the Brahmaputra and Barak Valleys of Assam) and Jammu and Kashmir were poorly integrated with British India due to the colonial scalar politics (Chapter 3) and were cordoned off from the nationalist movement. At the time of the inauguration of the union, these areas were provided with special constitutional and legal guarantees that protected the rights of indigenous inhabitants and restricted the entry of outsiders. However, ethnolinguistic distance, religious differences, border disputes, historical disconnect, economic stagnation and political and administrative mishandling triggered insurgencies.

The Indian state has tried to recover legitimacy through development and democracy and has used counter-insurgency to check armed challenge to the expanding reach of the government. The government has also armed itself with special and emergency laws that severely curtail fundamental human rights and undermine its commitment to democracy. These laws – of which the Armed Forces (Special Powers) Act (AFSPA) is the most egregious – add to the sense of alienation, militarise democracy and contribute to the legitimacy of insurgencies (Map 7.3). In fact, this unpopular law has remained in force despite massive and sustained popular opposition and recommendations of committees appointed by the government such as the Committee to Review the Armed Forces (Special Powers) Act 1958 (2005) and the Committee on Amendments to Criminal Law. Other indicators of democracy deficit include (a) the occasional inability to hold elections (parliamentary and assembly elections in Nagaland in the 1950s; in Assam, Jammu and Kashmir and Punjab in the 1980s and early 1990s and local body elections in Nagaland and Jammu and Kashmir in recent years), (b) appointment of retired army, paramilitary and police officials and bureaucrats with experience in internal security matters as governors in the peripheral states,

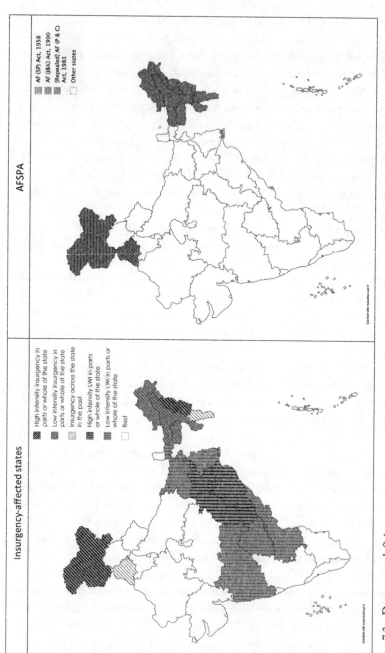

Map 7.3   Democracy deficit

Source: Prepared by authors using information available available at old.satp.org (2011) and a map template available at https://mapchart.net/india.html.

Note: LWI stands for Left Wing Insurgency.

Maps not to scale and may not represent authentic international borders.

(c) involvement of law enforcement agencies in extrajudicial killings (Hazarika 2018) and (d) communalisation of politics and bureaucracy.

Insurgencies, compounded by intra-state ethnic conflicts, have challenged the legitimacy of the state and, as a result, impaired its ability to generate reliable information (cf. Jerven 2013: 112), damaged public institutions and stymied economic development making people dependent upon federally supported state spending (Table 7.5 and Map 7.4). Since the 1960s, the government has not been

Table 7.5 Select macroeconomic indicators of Special Category States

State/group	Ratio of state's own tax revenue to gross central devolution and transfers	Public employment*	Share in state GDP				Employment share in agriculture
			Services		Manufacturing		
	2001–2	2011	1991–2	2001–2	1991–2	2001–2	2004–5
All SCS[†]	0.20	1.62	38.76	47.51	7.89	6.94	
Arunachal Pradesh	0.04	n/a**	37.59	40.91	4.42	2.42	73
Assam	0.33	1.22	34.95	47.96	9.02	7.64	66
Himachal Pradesh	0.32	2.96	37.16	38.55	10.11	11.27	62
Jammu and Kashmir	0.14	1.4	n/a[††]	45.3	n/a[††]	4.12	51
Manipur	0.03	2.53	48.47	49.52	2.74	6.24	59
Meghalaya	0.14	1.25	51.38	52.59	3.8	1.55	71
Mizoram	0.02	0.46	45.47	63.11	6.35	1.37	68
Nagaland	0.03	3.44	59.98	53.34	4.03	1.63	61
Sikkim	0.13	n/a**	43.21	53.52	3.91	3.37	53
Tripura	0.09	3.27	45.31	52.37	4.13	2.65	37
Uttarakhand	0.50	1.27	n/a[‡]	51.85	n/a[‡]	10.03	64
All non-SCS[†]	1.28	0.75	39.67	51.45	17.50	14.39	
All states[†]	1.07	0.80	39.63	51.22	17.11	13.95	58
Data source	RBI (2004)	GoI (2016a)	RBI (2018)				NCEUS (2007)

Notes: (i) * Measured as the ratio (in %) of central and state government employees to the 2011 population. (ii) ** The data on public employees are collected as part of the Employment Market Information Programme. The programme is not operational in certain states due to 'administrative reasons'. (http://www.dget.nic.in/content/students/employment-market-information-program.php). (iii) [†] These figures are weighted means for the corresponding states. (iv) 'All states' excludes union territories except Delhi. (iv) [††] Data not available. (v) [‡] Uttarakhand was formed in 2000.

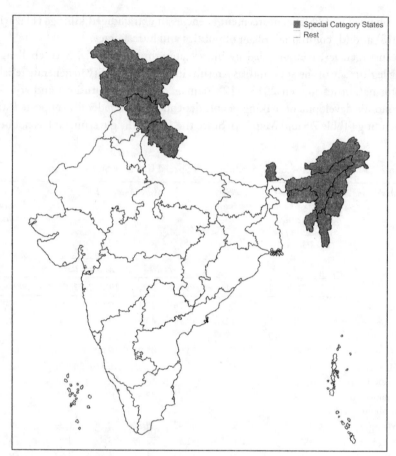

Map 7.4   Special Category States

Source: Authors. Prepared using a map template available at https://mapchart.net/india.html.

Note: The map is based on the categorisation at the time of 2011 Census.

Map not to scale and may not represent authentic international borders.

able to reduce the dependence of these states on federal funding. Agriculture accounts for a greater share of employment and output in SCS than in non-SCS states, while manufacturing accounts for about 7 per cent of the output. Services account for a substantial share of the economy due to massive overstaffing in the government. The government is the biggest actor in the formal sector of these states with a substantial proportion of population employed as public servants (1.62 per cent in SCS compared to 0.75 in non-SCS). The heavy administrative overhead in SCS is made possible by federal transfers. The ratio of state's own tax revenue to gross central devolution and transfers is 0.20 in case of SCS compared to 1.28 for non-SCS. The persistent resource crunch notwithstanding, most SCS in the North-East fail to collect even modest taxes that would help reduce the dependence on the union governement.[41]

To conclude, attempts to mechanically fix data quality through the introduction of better data collection and processing tools will not help as long as the data deficit is embedded in a mutually constitutive relationship with democracy and development deficits.[42] Reforms that fail to appreciate this structural relationship and resort to technological, legal and administrative solutions without strengthening democratic institutions and attending to the development deficit are unlikely to succeed.

Notes

1. The moralistic appeals were backed up by more nuanced arguments. The director of census operations (DCO) (interview, 24 June 2013, Kohima) pointed out that what really counts is the human development of a community, rather than its size, which requires planning supported by good quality statistics. She cited Sikkim as an example of how a smaller state has overcome the limitations of size. A booklet *Census 2011: Interesting & Fun Facts* (GoI n.d.10) fleshed out the DCO's argument. The political leadership of the state seems to have shared this vision (Rio 2014: 37–8).

2. This might be explained by attitudes shaped by (Naga) customary laws that redistribute the guilt of individual wrong-doer across his/her family, clan and village.

3. Public debates are quickly overtaken by moral/Christian self-flagellation in Nagaland, which stifles meaningful debate on institutional reforms (Kumar 2018b). Nagaland's newspapers abound in op-ed contributions such as 'Are Nagas really "honest people"?' (Lohe 2018). For an analysis of the American Baptist origins of this self-flagellation, see Thomas (2016).

4. By the end of nineteenth century, the quality of statistics produced by a country began to be seen as an attribute of its development (Porter 1995: 80) and as a marker of modern civilisation (note 3 of Chapter 1). There were differences within Europe vis-à-vis the relation between state and statistics, but eventually the statistical practices of most of these countries converged irrespective of differences in political systems (Woolf 1989: 590, 601–4) because good quality statistics were seen as means for modernising countries. See Woolf (1989) for Italy and Göderle (2016) for Austria. Postcolonial countries accepted the quality of statistics as a marker of development. A Nepali census official remarked, 'Developing countries are not only economically backward, but also backward in basic data' (Kansakar 1977). In the African context, observers have read poor statistics as 'a sign of the underdevelopment' (Roger Reidel quoted in Jerven 2013: 1). While the above broad-brush correlations might not be tenable, select socio-economic characteristics

have been shown to affect data quality. Chamie (1993: 138) draws attention to a correlation between data quality and the socio-economic development, for example, developing countries with relatively higher death rates have poorer vital registration systems. Irudaya Rajan and James (2008: 33) argue that the quality of demographic data 'has a direct link with the educational status of respondents' and customs/taboos.

5. For a general overview of the changes in the technology of mapmaking in the context of the Indian census, see Singh (n.d.).

6. Agrawal and Kumar (2019a) discuss how delays in the release of Indian census data have grown after the introduction of advanced data processing technologies.

7. India's National Data Sharing and Accessibility Policy defines metadata as the 'information that describes the data source and the time, place, and conditions under which the data were created. Metadata informs the user of who, when, what, where, why, and how data were generated. Metadata allows the data to be traced to a known origin and know quality' (GoI 2012b: 11). In short, metadata is information about how data were collected, processed and tabulated. In case of goverment statistics, information about the legal-administrative framework within which data have been collected should also be part of metadata.

8. Agrawal and Kumar (2019b) draw attention to the lack of metadata on area statistics in census publications of Manipur and its impact on estimates of rural population density.

9. Mitra (1994) gives an insightful account of the scale and scope of qualitative studies undertaken by the Indian Census in the 1960s (see also various contributions to Mohanty and Momin 1996). Such studies are rarely undertaken these days. The departmental differentiation within bureaucracy – for example, there are hardly any anthropologist-cum-administrators in the census department – cannot entirely explain the turn to standalone data tables. On the marginalisation of commentaries in nineteenth-century France, see Porter (1995: 36–7). Hakim (1980: 552) draws attention to a similar trend in Britain where commentaries disappeared after the introduction of computers in 1961. Likewise, Sundar (2000: 116) points out, 'From the 1921 census onwards, in keeping with world-wide trends, economic issues achieved greater importance [in Indian censuses], as did the notion that statistics could speak for themselves, putting a gradual end to the discursive general report in Volume I of the census.'

10. The unavailability of adequate metadata affects both inter-temporal as well as cross-sectional comparisons. Researchers, and even government, calculate measures such as growth rate overlooking changes in non-coverage (see note 65 of Chapter 4 for population growth and Misra and Suresh 2014: Table 4 for employment growth rate).

11. Even 'advanced' countries such as the USA and the United Kingdom (UK) have found it difficult to maintain the sanctity of government statistics in the face of growing public distrust or partisan attacks (Prewitt 2003; 2010). Eurobarometer surveys show a gradually declining trust in government statistics across Europe

(European Commission 2015; Holt 2008). In the USA, rising non-response rates over the past three decades have dented household surveys (Meyer, Mok and Sullivan 2015).

12. For an earlier attempt to engage communities, see Swami (2000) on the 2001 Census of Jammu and Kashmir. See also Okolo (1999: 323) for a similar experiment in Nigeria.

13. In 2015, the Planning Commission was replaced by NITI Aayog, which is supposed to provide strategic and technical advice to the government. Its role in recommending transfer of funds to states is unclear.

14. Government committees implicitly treat official statistics as indisputable. For instance, the Committee for Evolving a Composite Development Index of States argued that 'there is no element of discretion in the allocations' as the index proposed in its report was 'based on publicly available data' (GoI 2013e: iv). The committee did not reflect on the potential distortion in allocations due to the poor quality of data. Moreover, it is not entirely true that the use of government data eliminates discretion. A committee can possibly choose from among different government sources that provide data for a particular socio-economic characteristic.

15. The status of SCS remains unclear after the union government accepted the recommendation of the FFC to raise the tax devolution to states from 32 per cent to 42 per cent. The then union finance minister seemed to suggest that the states in the North-East shall continue to be treated as SCS insofar as funding for 'core of the core' schemes is considered (*Nagaland Post* 2016).

16. The FFC blandly refers to the 'Central Statistics Office' as the source of projections. The projection figures used by the FFC agree with GoI (2006a).

17. GoI (n.d.21) suggests that the Sentinelese have been enumerated after 1971, but as per GoI (n.d.15) the tribe was not covered even in 1981. The figures for 1991 and later censuses seem to be estimates based on observation from a distance.

18. In a few rounds (59th round, Report No. 490: 5; 60th round, Report No. 505: 7) the NSSO sample in Jammu and Kashmir had fewer than the 300 households required to publish state-level estimates (59th round, Report No. 490: 4). Yet results were published to facilitate comparison with earlier rounds.

19. In early nineteenth-century France 'private enterprise of individual manufactures, subsistence agriculture, and cottage industries were seen as backward and mostly ignored' (Woolf 1989: 601).

20. Academic analyses of development problems that mostly omit north-eastern states, Sikkim and Jammu and Kashmir due to lack of data are likely to suffer from sample selection bias because of the omission of states, where data and development deficits are structurally interconnected.

21. The seat share of these states exceeds their population share as each state is entitled to at least one seat in each house of the parliament.

22. Most state-level comparisons in economics are restricted to 'major' states. The coverage of the north-eastern states in national dailies is not only inadequate but also lacks depth (Kumar 2017b; 2018c). Local dailies, on the other hand, avoid

investigations and are often enmeshed with the region's many conflicts (Kumar 2015c; 2017a; 2018a–b). The North-East is also underrepresented in fiction and travelogues published in the 'mainland'. In other words, both government and non-governmental sources of information are deficient vis-à-vis the periphery.

23. Prabhakara (2012: 22, originally published in 1974) argued that 'the weakening and the fragmentation of the NE region has been the consistent policy of the [union] government'. The fragmentation engenders a structural fiscal dependence of the micro-states on New Delhi (Baruah 2005: 43). While this assessment of the consequences of the formation of small states is not entirely incorrect, it is not clear how the centre could have made hostile communities stay together in larger states against their wishes. In fact, in postcolonial India, 'no state was ever created on the initiative of the centre' (Kumar 2000: 3081). Later Prabhakara (2012: 62–3, originally published in 1988) admitted that the smaller hill states were successful and that similar arrangements for plain tribes would have limited conflict in Assam. Naga leaders have all along supported a separate, even though small, state (Sema 1986: 173–4).

24. India's ST population was 19 million in 1951 and rose to 22.5 million after the Scheduled Tribes Order of 1950 was amended in 1956 (Raza and Ahmad 1990: 6; see also Mamoria 1957: 24–5).

25. For a related discussion of under-enumeration of tribes in the USA, see Lujan (1990).

26. For the colonial origins of the category 'tribe', see Skaria (1997) and Roy Burman (2009).

27. Double-counting of tribal migrants cannot be ruled out, though. As discussed in Chapters 4 and 5, at least until 2001, it was not uncommon for tribal people settled in urban Nagaland to get enumerated in their ancestral village as well.

28. SC converts to Christianity might conceal religious identity in government records, including census, to access benefits under affirmative action policies. For an example from Rajasthan, see Sahoo (2018: 34, 45).

29. It seems the government knew of this possibility beforehand but did not adopt any counter-measures (Guha 2003: 162) and, in fact, even accepted the fraudulent claim 'in clear violation of the legal provisions' (Sharad Kulkarni 1991: 206). Unsurprisingly, the population of the Halba/Halbi tribe was not corrected in subsequent censuses.

30. Influential communities also try to manipulate non-governmental sources of information to nominally co-opt others. Ethno-statistical entrepreneurs within the Angami community, for instance, try to boost their community's numbers by recasting its language as Tenyidie and subsuming the languages of neighbouring tribes in Nagaland as well as Manipur. See, for instance, PLSI (2016: 4, 9, 58, 71, 84, 100, 112, 123, 135) which blatantly misinterprets census statistics to suggest that the Tenyimia community is the largest in Nagaland and Angami is one of the largest tribes of Nagaland.

31. The socio-economic/internal margins include slums that too suffer from a data deficit (Srivathsan 2013) that is enmeshed with development and democracy deficits.

32. Over the years, non-governmental and, even, government users of data have found alternatives to government statistics in developing countries. For instance, Chinese Premier Li Keqiang famously admitted to using railway cargo volume, electricity consumption and loans disbursed by banks to gauge the health of his country's economy (Ninan 2018). Others have suggested the use of night light intensity to measure economic activity and urbanisation (Donaldson and Storeygard 2016).

33. In neighbouring Nagaland, the state government rejected the 2001 Census figures for the entire state. However, unlike in Manipur, the ORGI did not endorse the rejection of headcount in Nagaland, possibly, because the state government wanted a fresh census in the entire state.

34. In Uttar Pradesh, a similar objection was initially overruled (ECI 2008: 4–7), but the Supreme Court later ordered readjustment (*Virendra Pratap & Anr. vs. UoI & Ors.*, 2011).

35. This is reminiscent of the 1941 Census in which people inflated headcount anticipating religious partition of their provinces, whereas census was affected by only content errors rather than coverage errors in areas suffering from purely linguistic conflicts: 'in few places where people got excited about the language question, they succeeded only in spoiling the language returns; it did not occur to them to inflate numbers' (GoI 1953b: 1). A mundane but perhaps better-known example is related to contractors, who supplied food to camps set up for partition refugees from Pakistan. They inflated the bills as initially the government did not have an idea of the size of the refugee population. Government statisticians could detect the fraud as the contractors did not inflate the quantity of salt, the most inexpensive food item (Rao 1999: 145–7).

36. After the 2011 Census, the then chairman of the National Commission for the Scheduled Tribes, who belongs to Jharkhand, too argued that the tribal population of the state was underestimated as it did not include tribal people working outside the state (*Business Standard* 2016). Jharkhand's tribes are effectively demanding a de jure census.

37. A plea for a similar adjustment at the inter-district level in Odisha was rejected by the Delimitation Commission (GoI 2008d: 1096).

38. The Naga Students' Federation views Aadhaar card/UID number as a 'big threat to Naga customary law and identity' and is opposed to 'such drastic nationalising policy upon the Nagas pending the final Indo-Naga solution'. It further added that that the 'free enjoyment of social benefits within the fabric of collective social identity is sacred to the Nagas and any denial thereof in the name of identity numerisation is inimical to the social and religious practice of the Nagas' (*ME* 2017c).

39. The Census Act, 1948, stipulates punishment for interfering with the process of enumeration. However, the punitive provisions are rarely used and have not been invoked to deal with cases of widespread manipulation of census at the grassroots (Kumar 2019). DCO Nagaland (interview, 19 September 2012, Kohima) observed that 'no one has ever been punished under the Census Act'.

40. We have not yet seen the end of statistical competition in Nagaland because the current truce is going to breakdown when tribes begin counting their losses due

to deflation. Two interviewees almost suggested that their communities were waiting for the next opportunity to rectify the injustice done to them (Naga state government official, interview, 10 June 2014, Mon; civil society leader, interview, 14 June 2014, Longleng).

41. Baruah (2005: 39) points out 'the routine practices that reproduce the consent of the governed in a modern democracy – for example, the payment of taxes, voting, or provision of key services such as guaranteed public order by the state' are 'either missing or barely present in most parts of Northeast India'. In Nagaland and some of the other peripheral states, the tribal population is exempt from taxation because of underdevelopment and disturbed conditions, which in turn affects the quality of statistics insofar as the ability to collect statistics and taxes are correlated (Jerven 2013: 3, 112). In fact, pre-modern censuses were often motivated by the need to collect information for expanding the tax base.

42. Krätke and Byiers (2014: 7) offer a similar suggestion in the African context when they argue that 'a statistics revolution can only genuinely occur if it can ... overcome some of the existing political economy constraints'.

Appendix

Nagaland in Numbers, 1961–2011

Territory/population	1961	1971	1981	1991	2001	2011	Reference
Area (sq km)	16,487.90	16,527	16,579	16,579	16,579	16,579	Table 3.1
Number of districts	3	3	7	7	8	11	Figure 3.1; Map 3.10E
Number of circles	22*	60	69	88	93	114	Table 3.3; Map 3.10E
Number of towns (including census towns)	3	3	7	9	9	26	Table 4.2A
Number of inhabited villages[†]	814 (14)	960 (6)	1,112 (7)	1,216 (9)	1,278 (39)	1,400 (28)	Table 3.3
Households	80,224	104,086	149,480	216,725	328,057	396,002	Figure 3.2; Table 4.4A
Population	369,200	516,449	774,930	1,209,546	1,990,036	1,978,502	Figures 2.1, 4.1; Tables 4.1, 4.2A–B, 4.14 (Figure 4.6; Tables 4.6, 5.3)
Male	191,027	276,084	415,910	641,282	1,047,141	1,024,649	Table 4.2B
Female	178,173	240,365	359,020	568,264	942,895	953,853	Table 4.2B
Rural	350,043	465,055	654,696	1,001,323	1,647,249	1,407,536	Tables 4.2A, 4.4A
Urban	19,157	51,394	1,20,234	208,223	342,787	570,966	Tables 4.2A, 4.4A
Decadal population growth rate (%)		39.88	50.05	56.08	64.53	-0.58	Figures 2.1, 4.1, 7.4; Tables 4.1, 4.2A–B, 4.14
Population density (persons per sq km)	22.39	31.25	46.74	72.96	120.03	119.34	Table 3.2
Household size	4.60	4.96	5.18	5.58	6.07	5.00	Table 4.4A
Sex ratio	933	871	863	886	900	931	Table 4.2B
Urban share (%)[‡]	5.19	9.95	15.52	17.21	17.23	28.86	Table 4.2A
Literacy rate	21.95	33.78	50.28	61.65	66.59	79.56	Table 4.5

Contd

Contd

Territory/population	1961	1971	1981	1991	2001	2011	Reference
Scheduled Tribes	343,697	457,602	650,885	1,060,822	1,774,026	1,710,973	Figures 4.3, 7.4; Tables 4.12, 4.13, 4.15; Map 1.2
share (%)‡	93.09	88.61	83.99	87.70	89.15	86.48	Tables 4.12
Christians	195,588	344,798	621,590	1,057,940	1,790,349	1,739,651	Figure 4.3; Table 4.11 (Tables 4.8–4.9); Map 1.2
share (%)‡	52.98	66.76	80.21	87.47	89.97	87.93	Table 4.11
Speakers of Non-scheduled languages	354,575	478,630	693,339	1,068,303	1,794,493	1,743,721	Figure 7.4; Table 4.15; Map 1.2
share (%)‡	96.04	92.68	89.47	88.32	90.17	88.13	Table 4.15

Sources: Prepared by author from various census publications.

Notes: (i) * As per GoI (1966), which does not mention the number of circles in Kohima subdivision. † Number of uninhabited villages within parentheses. ‡ Indicates share in the total population of the state. (ii) Statistics reported in this table are not adjusted for content and coverage errors.

Bibliography

Select Interviews

Assam government official. 5 June 2013. Sarupathar, Golaghat, Assam.

Assamese IAS officer 1. 3 June 2013. Guwahati.

Assamese IAS officer 2. 3 June 2013. Guwahati.

Businessmen. 27 June 2013. Dimapur.

Census official. 11 December 2018. Kohima.

Census official. 12 December 2018. Kohima.

Chasie, Charles. E-mail communication. 25 November 2013. Kohima.

————. E-mail communication. 26 November 2014. Kohima.

Civil society leader. 22 June 2013. Dimapur.

Civil society leader (Angami). 24 November 2012. Dimapur.

Civil society leader (Angami). 8 April 2013. Dimapur.

Civil society leader (Chakhesang). 21 September 2012. Kohima.

Civil society leader (Kachari). 21 June 2013. Dimapur.

Civil society leader (Konyak). 22 June 2013. Dimapur.

Civil society leader (Konyak). 12 June 2014. Mon.

Civil society leader (Kuki). 14 November 2013. Dimapur.

Civil society leader (Kuki). 25 June 2015. Dimapur.

Civil society leader (Phom). 14 June 2014. Longleng.

Civil society leader (Rongmei). 19 June 2015. Dimapur.

Civil society leader (Sangtam). 7 June 2014. Tuensang.

Civil society leader (Yimchunger). 23 November 2012. Dimapur.

Civil society leader (Yimchunger). 26 November 2012. Dimapur.

Civil society leader (Yimchunger). 22 June 2013. Dimapur.

Civil society leaders (Khiamniungan). 9 June 2014. Noklak.

Civil society leaders (Kuki). 29 October 2014. Athibung, Peren.

Civil society leaders (Tikhir). 10 April 2013. Dimapur.

Clean Election Campaign, Hotel Japfu (meeting). 19 September 2012. Kohima.

Consultative meeting, the NTC, Hotel Saramati (meeting). 22 June 2013. Dimapur.

DCO Assam. 4 June 2013. Guwahati.

DCO Nagaland. 19 September 2012. Kohima.

DCO Nagaland. 24 June 2013. Kohima.

DCO Nagaland. 25 June 2013. Kohima.

Former minister, Nagaland. 26 October 2014. Dimapur.

Former Phom member of legislative assembly. 19 June 2015. Dimapur.

Gohain, Hiren. 4 June 2013. Guwahati.

Hazarika, Sanjoy. 7 March 2012. New Delhi.

Jamir, S. C., Governor of Odisha and former Chief Minister of Nagaland. 27 August 2013. Bhubaneshwar.

Junior government official. 8 October 2019. Senapati.

Keikung, Rev. Anjo, General Secretary, NBCC. 21 November 2012. Kohima.

————. 24 June 2013. Kohima.

Khing, R, Member of Legislative Assembly, Tseminyu. 13 December 2018. Kohima.

Leaders of the Rengma Hoho and Rengma Selo Zi. 13 December 2018. Tseminyu, Kohima.

Liezietsu, Shürhozelie, President, NPF. 15 November 2013. Kohima.

Lotha member of legislative assembly. 23 October 2014. New Delhi.

Naga IAS officer. 19 September 2012. Kohima.

Naga IAS officer, Clean Election Campaign, Hotel Japfu (meeting). 19 September 2012. Kohima.

Naga IAS officer. 21 September 2012. Kohima.

Naga IAS officer. 22 November 2012. Kohima.

Naga IAS officer. 24 June 2013. Kohima.

Naga IAS officer. 25 June 2013. Kohima.

Naga IPS officer. 21 September 2012. Kohima.

Naga state government official. 28 October 2014. Jalukie, Peren.

Naga state government official. 10 June 2014. Mon.

Office bearers of Western Sumi Hoho. 26 June 2013. Dimapur.

ORGI officials. 21 February 2019. New Delhi.

Program coordinator and treasurer, UNPO. 18 September 2013. The Hague.

Retired census official. 15 September 2012. New Delhi.

Retired Naga IAS officer. 9 April 2013. Kohima.

Retired Naga IAS officer. 16 November 2013. Dimapur.

Retired Naga IAS officer. 30 October 2015. Bengaluru.

Retired Naga IPS officer. 26 October 2014. Dimapur.

Rhi, Rev. Vikuo, Youth Secretary, NBCC. 21 November 2012. Kohima.

Rio, Neiphiu, Member of Parliament and former Chief Minister of Nagaland. 27 May 2015. New Delhi.

Sen, Pronab, former Chief Statistician of India. 11 December 2018. New Delhi.

Senior census officials, Nagaland. 25 June 2013. Kohima.

Senior official incharge of border affairs. 3 June 2013. Guwahati.

Senior official incharge of border affairs. 25 June 2013. Kohima.

Senior official, ORGI. 17 September 2013. New Delhi.

Sreedhar Rao, K., retired IAS officer. 28 April 2013. Bengaluru.
———. 30 May 2013. Bengaluru.
State government official. 7 October 2019. Chandel.
State government official. 8 October 2019. Senapati.
Therie, K., former finance minister. 11 April 2013. Dimapur.
Village elders (Konyak). 13 June 2014. Mon.
Village elders (Yimchunger). 8 June 2014. Kuthur, Tuensang.
Village elders and government officials in Husto, Tohoi and Niuland. 24 June 2015. Dimapur.
Village elders in Dhupguri and Navapur. 6 June 2013. Sarupathar, Golaghat, Assam.
Village elders in Nokyan and Noklak. 9 June 2014. Noklak.
Xavier, Rev. Fr. Sojan, Chancellor, Kohima diocese. 20 September 2012. Kohima.

Archives

Assam State Archives (ASA), Gauhati

Government of Bengal. 24-28/1873: Settlement of the Dispute between Some Banfera Nagas and an Assamese. Papers.
General XVI 64/20: Transfer of the Dimapur Mauza from the Naga Hills to the Sibsagar District.
Home Confidential PLB 70/1971: Assembly (Starred) Question to be Asked by Shri Dullal Ch. Barua, M.L.A. during the Budget Session of the Assembly, 1971 Regarding Setting Up of a Paper Mill by Nagaland Government.
LIB/R130/S1/32: District Naga Hills (1905, 3rd Ed.), Surveyor General of India.
LIB/R136/S1/11: Railways in Assam (1915), Chief Engineer Assam.
LIB/R137/S4/13: Naga Hills District and Tribal Area (1939, Revised 2nd Ed.), Surveyor General of India, No. 83 J/S.E.
Lib/R138/S2/06: Police Stations in the Naga Hills Districts, No. 00.
LIB/R138/S3/17: District Naga Hills (1893, 2nd Ed.). Surveyor General of India.
Political XXII-10/26: Inner line - The Eastern District Boundary of the Naga Hills.
Tribal Area Development TAD/CON-78/54: Unofficial Report Regarding the Constitution of a "Naga Republican Federation" in the Naga Hills Tribal Areas (Naga Constitution).
Tribal Area Development TAD/GA-112/57: Proposal for Exclusion of Borsillah Tea Estate from the Proposed Administrative Unit of Naga Hills District.

Naga Archives and Research Centre, Toulazouma, Dimapur

FGN (Federal Government of Nagaland). 1994. 'The Yehzabo of Nagaland (Constitution) 1994 Revised Edition'. The Ministry of Raliwali.

Kinghen, N. 1985. *Facts about Nagaland–Assam Boundary Affairs*. First edition. Wokha: Lotha Hoho.

NNC. 1951. *Naga Voluntary Plebsicite*. Kohima.

NSCN. 1993. *Free Nagaland Manifesto*. Second edition. Oking.

Office of the Razou Peyu Phek Sub-region Chakhesang. 1992. '1975-1992 Census Report (Letter dated February 22 to Mian Peyhu C/Region, FGN)'. Oking.

Yeputhomi, Hukavi T. (ed.). n.d. 'A Brief Historical Account of Naga Lands in Assam'. The United Naga Tribes Association on Border Areas (UNTABA).

Nagaland State Archives (NSA), Kohima

2:311. Index 2, File 311: Boundary between the Naga Hills District and the Manipur State.

2:475. Index 2, File 475: Memorandums from the Mizo Union Manipur, Cachar and Nagas of Manipur, Setting up of a Separate Constitution for Them and Merger of Mizo Area (Manipur and Cachar) with Mizoram and Naga Hills Districts.

2:587. Index 2, File 587: Correction of the Census Figures in Consequences of the Transfer of the Diger Mauza from the Naga Hills District to the District of Cachar.

5:21. Index 5, File 21: Nine Point Agreement.

5:22. Index 5, File 22: Copy of the Sixteen Point Agreement. (Includes a brief summary of 16 points placed before the prime minister by the delegation).

Society for the Preservation and Promotion of Naga Heritage (SPNH), Frankfurt

Dzülhami Village Council. 2002. 'Gist of the Historical and Cultural Accounts of Dzülha Village'.

Hunter, W. W. 1879. 'Statistical Accoiunt of the District of the Naga Hills'. In *A Statistical Account of Assam*, vol. II, pp. 173–99. London: Trubner & Co.

Office of the Yongnyah Village Council. 2002. *The History of Yongnyah*. 31 March.

Poilwa Village Council. 2002. 'Origin of the Village Folks'.

Yimchungrü, K. Lotan. 2002. *Brief History of Yimchungrü (Naga) Traditional and Culture*.

ZPC (Zeliangrong People's Convention). 1983. 'Memorandum on Zeliangrong Homeland within Indian Union Submitted to Shrimati Indira Gandhi, Prime Minister of India, 28 October, 1983, New Delhi'.

Government

Allen, B. C. 1902. 'Census of India, 1901, Volume IV, Assam, Part I Report'. Shillong: Superintendent of census operations (SCO), Assam.

Census Commissioner, India. 1893 *General Report on the Census of India, 1891*. London: Eyre and Spottiswoode.

Chandramouli, C. 2011. 'Census of India 2011: A Story of Innovations'. Press Information Bureau, New Delhi.

————. 2015. 'Future of the Population Census in India'. UN EGM on Strengthening the Demographic Evidence Base for the Post-2015 Development Agenda, New York. 5–6 October.

DoNER. 2009. 'District Infrastructure Index for North Eastern Region'. Ministry of Development of North Eastern Region, Government of India, New Delhi.

ECI (Election Commission of India). n.d.1. 'A Guide for the Voters'. New Delhi. Available at https://eci.gov.in/files/file/5474-a-guide-for-voters/.

————. n.d.2. 'Delimitation of Assembly and Parliamentary Constituencies'. New Delhi. Available at http://eci.nic.in/delim/Procedure/Delimitation_of_Constituencies.pdf.

————. 2006. 'Compendium of Instructions on Electoral Rolls, EPIC, SLAs & Computerisation 2006 (Upto May 2006)'. New Delhi.

————. 2017. *Electoral Statistics Pocket Book 2017*. New Delhi.

FSI (Forest Survey of India). 1989. *The State of Forest Report 1989*. Dehradun.

————. 1991. *The State of Forest Report 1991*. Dehradun.

————. 2017. *India State of Forest Report 2017*. Dehradun.

GSI (Geological Survey of India). 2011. *Geology and Mineral Resources of Manipur, Mizoram, Nagaland and Tripura*. Miscellaneous publication, no. 30, pt IV, vol. 1 (Part 2). Kolkata.

GoA (Government of Assam). n.d.1. 'Areas of Encroachment by Nagaland' (Courtesy: Anonymous government official).

————. n.d.2. 'Profile of Karimganj District, Assam, India: Population and Demography'. Accessed on 11 May 2013. Available at http://karimganj.gov.in/demo. htm.

————. n.d.3. 'A Brief Note on Assam-Nagaland Border'. (Courtesy: Anonymous government official).

GoI. n.d.1. *Census of India 1991*. Database available as CD.

————. n.d.2. *Census of India 2001*. Database available as CD.

————. n.d.3. 'Census Operations: Dissemination'. Accessed on 12 August 2019. Available at http://censusindia.gov.in/Data_Products/Library/Indian_perceptive_link/ Census_Operation_link/censusoperation.htm#dissemination.

————. n.d.4. 'Indian Railway Map'. Ministry of Railways. Accessed on 18 April 2013. Available at http://www.indianrailways.gov.in/railwayboard/uploads/directorate/ coaching/pdf/IR_Map.pdf.

————. n.d.5. *Census of India 2011, District Census Handbook, Nagaland (all districts)*. Accessed on 20 December 2018. Available at http://www.censusindia.gov. in/2011census/dchb/DCHB.html.

————. n.d.6. 'Area Code Directory: Town and Village Code Directory'. ORGI&CC, New Delhi. Accessed on 29 March 2013. Available at http://censusindia.gov.in/2011- VillageDirectory/index.html.

————. n.d.7. 'History of Census in India'. Drop-in-article on Census No. 5. Accessed on 17 August 2012. Available at http://censusindia.gov.in/Ad_Campaign/drop_in_articles/05-History_of_Census_in_India.pdf.

————. n.d.8. 'The Relevance and Ramifications of Census'. Drop-in-article on Census No. 2. Accessed on 2 August 2012. Available at http://censusindia.gov.in/Ad_Campaign/drop_in_articles/02-Relevance_and_ramifications_of_Census.pdf.

————. n.d.9. 'Census of India 2011, Primary Census Abstract Data Tables (India & States/UTs – Town/Village/Ward Level)'. Accessed on 1 February 2019. Available at http://censusindia.gov.in/pca/pcadata/pca.html.

————. n.d.10. *Census 2011: Interesting & Fun Facts*. Directorate of Census Operations, Kohima.

————. n.d.11. 'Age Structure and Marital Status'. Accessed on 20 July 2019. Available at http://censusindia.gov.in/Census_And_You/age_structure_and_marital_status.aspx.

————. n.d.12. *Urban Frame Survey*. New Delhi: National Sample Survey Office (NSSO). Accessed on 20 July 2019. Accessed on 12 July 2017. Available at http://mospi.nic.in/sites/default/files/publication_reports/UFS/Guidelines_UFS.pdf.

————. n.d.13. *Urban Frame Survey*. New Delhi: NSSO. Available at http://mospi.nic.in/Mospi_New/site/inner.aspx?status=3&menu_id=55.

————. n.d.14. 'India at a Glance'. Accessed on 20 July 2019. Available at http://censusindia.gov.in/Census_Data_2001/India_at_glance/area.aspx.

————. n.d.15. 'Enumeration of Primitive Tribes in A&N Islands: A Challenge', drop-in-article on Census No. 6. Accessed on 5 May 2012. Available at http://censusindia.gov.in/Ad_Campaign/drop_in_articles/06-Enumeration_of_Primitive_Tribes_in_A&N_Islands.pdf.

————. n.d.16. *Report of the National Statistical Commission 2001*. New Delhi: Ministry of Statistics and Programme Implementation (MOSPI). Accessed 11 August 2019. Available at http://www.mospi.gov.in/report-dr-rangarajan-commission.

————. n.d.17. 'State/UT Wise Aadhaar Saturation 31st August, 2018'. Accessed on 6 September 2018. Available at https://www.uidai.gov.in/images/state-wise-aadhaar-saturation.pdf.

————. n.d.18. 'Introduction to NPR'. Accessed on 1 July 2019. Available at http://censusindia.gov.in/2011-Common/IntroductionToNpr.html.

————. n.d.19. 'Periodic Labour Force Survey (PLFS) – Annual Report [July, 2017 – June, 2018] and Quarterly Bulletin [October-December 2018]'. MOSPI, New Delhi. Accessed on 20 August 2019. Available at http://pib.nic.in/newsite/PrintRelease.aspx?relid=190167.

————. n.d.20. 'Index Sheet: Calculation Sheet of Normal Central Assistance on the Basis of Gadgil-Mukherjee Formula'. Planning Commission, New Delhi. Accessed on 12 December 2013. Available at http://planningcommission.nic.in/data/rep_gadgil.pdf.

————. n.d.21. 'Brief Introduction to A-2, Decadal Variation in Population since 1901'. Office of Registrar General of India (ORGI), New Delhi.

————. n.d.22. 'Important Note [Estimated Population Figures, Manipur, 2001]'. Accessed on 28 September 2018. Available at http://censusindia.gov.in/Census_ Data_2001/National_Summary/More_Link/note.aspx.

————. n.d.23. 'Census of India 2001, Data Highlights Migration Tables'. ORGI, New Delhi. Accessed on 10 September 2019. Available at http://censusindia.gov.in/Data_ Products/Data_Highlights/Data_Highlights_link/data_highlights_D1D2D3.pdf.

————. 1932. 'Census of India 1931, Volume III Assam, Part I – Report'. Central Publication Branch, Calcutta.

————. 1952. 'Census 1951, Assam, District Census Handbook, Naga Hills'. SCO, Assam, Tripura and Manipur.

————. 1953a. 'Census of India 1951, Volume I India, Part IA – Report'. Registrar General of India (RGI), New Delhi.

————. 1953b. 'Census of India 1951, Paper No. 1 of 1953, Sample Verification of the 1951 Census Count'. RGI, New Delhi.

————. 1954a. 'Census of India 1951, Paper No. 6, Estimation of Birth and Death Rates in India during 1941-50–1951 Census'. New Delhi.

————. 1954b. 'Census of India. 1951, Assam, Manipur and Tripura, Part I-A, Report'. SCO, Assam, Manipur and Tripura; Shillong.

————. 1956. 'Census of India. 1951, Assam, Manipur and Tripura, Part II-A, General Population Tables'. SCO, Assam, Manipur and Tripura; Shillong.

————. 1964. 'Census of India 1961, Volume 1, India, Part II-A (i) General Population Tables'. Registrar General and Census Commissioner of India (RGCCI), New Delhi.

————. 1966. 'Census of India. 1961, Nagaland, Part II-A, General Population Tables'. SCO, Kohima.

————. 1973a. 'Census of India. 1971, Nagaland, Part II-A, General Population Tables'. Directorate of Census Operations, Kohima.

————. 1973b. 'Census of India 1971, Series 15, A Portrait of Population Nagaland'. Directorate of Census Operations, Nagaland and RGI.

————. 1975a. 'Census of India 1971, Series 1, India, Part II-A (i), General Population Tables'. RGCCI, New Delhi.

————. 1975b. 'Census of India 1971, Series 15, Nagaland, Part II-C (i), Social and Cultural Tables (Tables C-VII and C-VIII Part B with their Appendices) and Special Tables on Scheduled Tribes (Table ST-I to ST-V)'. Directorate of Census Operations, Kohima.

————. 1975c. 'Census of India 1971, Series 1, Paper 1, Scheduled Castes and Scheduled Tribes, Table C-VIII Parts A & B'. RGCCI, New Delhi.

————. 1976a. 'Census of India 1971, Series 1, India, Part II-C (ii), Social and Cultural Tables (Table C-II, C-III Part A & B and C-IV)'.RGCCI, New Delhi.

————. 1976b. 'Census of India 1971, Series 15, Nagaland, Part II D, Migration Tables'. Directorate of Census Operations, Nagaland; Kohima.

————. 1976c. 'Census of India 1971, Series 1, India, Part II-C (i), Social and Cultural Tables'. RGCCI, New Delhi.

————. 1976d. 'The National Sample Survey, Twenty Third Round, July 1968 – June 1969, Number 228, Tables with Notes on Consumer Expenditure'. Ministry of Planning, New Delhi.

————. 1977a. 'Part II: Survey Results, Consumer Expenditure, NSS 28th Round (1973–74)'. *Sarvekshana* 1(1): 49-51 and S1–S131.

————. 1977b. 'Census of India 1971, Series 1 – India, Part II – D (i), Migration Tables, (Tables D–I to D–IV)'. RGCCI, New Delhi.

————. 1979a. 'Census of India 1971, India Series 1, Paper 1 of 1979, Report of the Expert Committee on Population Projections'. Demography Division, ORGI, Ministry of Home Affairs, New Delhi.

————. 1979b. 'Introduction: Consumer Expenditure, NSS 27th Round (October 1972–September 1973)'. *Sarvekshana* 3(1): S289–S290.

————. 1979c. *Report of the Task Force on Projections of Minimum Needs and Effective Consumption Demand*. New Delhi: Perspective Planning Division, Planning Commission.

————. 1983. 'Census of India 1981, Series 15 Nagaland, District Census Handbook' (for Mon, Phek and Wokha districts). Directorate of Census Operations, Nagaland: Kohima and RGI: New Delhi.

————. 1984a. 'Census of India 1981, Nagaland, District Census Handbook, Kohima District'. Kohima: Directorate of Census Operations and New Delhi: RGI.

————. 1984b. 'Census of India 1981, Nagaland, Part II-A, General Population Tables'. Directorate of Census Operations, Kohima.

————. 1984c. 'Census of India 1981, Series 15 Nagaland, District Census Handbook' (for Kohima, Mokokchung, Tuensang and Zunheboto districts). Directorate of Census Operations, Nagaland: Kohima and RGI: New Delhi.

————. 1984d. 'Introduction'. *Sarvekshana* 8(1): 1–2.

————. 1985a. 'Census of India 1981, India, Part II-A (i), General Population Tables'. RGCCI, New Delhi.

————. 1985b. 'Census of India 1981, Nagaland, Part - V A & B, Migration Tables'. Directorate of Census Operations, Nagaland; Kohima.

————. 1986a. 'Some Results on the Second Quinquennial Survey on Consumer Expenditure'. *Sarvekshana* 9(3): S51–S184.

————. 1986b. 'A Report on the Third Quinquennial Survey on Consumer Expenditure'. *Sarvekshana* 9(4): S154–S184.

————. 1987. 'Census of India 1981, Series 1 India, Part IV-A, Social and Cultural Tables (Table C-1 to C-6)'. RGCCI, New Delhi.

————. 1988a. 'Regional Divisions of India – A Cartographic Analysis. Occasional Papers, Series – 1, Volume – XV Nagaland'. RGCCI, New Delhi.

————. 1988b. 'Census of India 1981, Report of the Expert Committee on Population Projections, Occasional Papers–No. 4 of 1988'. ORGI, New Delhi.

————. 1988c. 'Census of India 1971, Nagaland, A Portrait of Population'. Directorate of Census Operations, Nagaland and RGI.

————. 1988d. 'Census of India 1981, Series 1 - India, Part V-A & B (i), Migration Tables (Table D-1 and D-2)'. RGCCI, New Delhi.

————. 1988e. 'Census of India 1981, Series 15 - Nagaland, Part IX, Special Tables for Scheduled Tribes'. RGCCI, New Delhi.

————. 1989. 'Note on Pattern of Consumer Expenditure of Scheduled Caste and Scheduled Tribe Households'. *Sarvekshana* 12(3): 1–23.

————. 1990a. 'Census of India 1981, Survey Report on Village: Tseminyu'. RGCCI, New Delhi.

————. 1990b. 'Census of India 1981, Series 1 - India, Part IV B (i), Population by Language/Mother-Tongue (Table C-7)'. RGCCI, New Delhi.

————. 1991. 'Census of India 1991, Tabulation Plan'. RGCCI, New Delhi.

————. 1994a. 'Census of India 1991, India, Part II-A (I), General Population Tables'. RGCCI, New Delhi.

————. 1994b. 'A Note on an Exploratory Survey of Living Conditions of Tribals of Nagaland, NSS 44th Round (July 88 - June 89)'. *Sarvekshana* 18(1): 49–84.

————. 1996a. 'Census of India 1991, Assam, Part II-A General Population Tables'. Directorate of Census Operations, Guwahati.

————. 1996b. 'Census of India 1991, Population Projections for India and States 1996-2016, Report of the Technical Group on Population Projections Constituted by the Planning Commission'. RGI, New Delhi.

————. 1997a. 'A Background Note on Gadgil Formula for Distribution of Central Assistance for State Plans'. New Delhi: Planning Commission.

————. 1997b. 'Transforming the Northeast: Tackling Backlogs in Basic Minimum Services and Infrastructural Needs (Executive Summary of High Level Commission Report to the Prime Minister Government of India)'. Planning Commission, New Delhi

————. 1997c. 'District Level Estimates of Fertility and Child Mortality for 1991 and Their Inter Relations with other Variables, Occasional Paper No. 1 of 1997'. Registrar General (RG), New Delhi.

————. 1997d. 'Census of India 1991, A Portrait of Population Nagaland'. Directorate of Census Operations, Nagaland; Kohima.

————. 1997e. 'Census of India 1991, Orissa Part II-A General Population Tables'. Directorate of Census Operations, Orissa; Bhubaneshwar.

————. 1997f. 'Census of India 1991 Series-1 India, Part V- D Series, Migration Tables, Volume 2 Part 1'. RGCCI, New Delhi.

————. 1997g. 'Census of India 1991 Series-1 India, Part V-D Series, Migration Tables, Volume 2 Part 2'. RGCCI, New Delhi.

————. 1998. 'Census of India 1991, Series 18 Nagaland, Part II-A, General Population Tables'. Directorate of Census Operations, Nagaland; Kohima.

————. 1999. 'Compendium of India's Fertility and Mortality Indicators 1971-1997 based on the Sample Registration System (SRS)'. RGI, New Delhi.

————. 2002. *National Human Development Report 2001*. Planning Commission, New Delhi.

————. 2003. 'Fifty Years of Fiscal Federalism: Finance Commissions of India'. Twelfth Finance Commission, New Delhi.

————. 2004a. *Evolution of the Sample Design in the Indian National Sample Survey from 1st to 55th Round*. Golden Jubilee Publication. New Delhi: NSSO.

————. 2004b. 'Census of India 2001, The First Report on Religion Data'. RGCCI, New Delhi.

————. 2005a. 'General Population Tables: India, States and Union Territories, Part-I'. RGCCI, New Delhi.

————. 2005b. 'Delimitation of Constituencies – State of Nagaland – Meeting to Discuss Working Paper – 1 Prepared on the Basis of 2001 Census Data (No. 282NL/2005)'. Delimitation Commission of India, New Delhi. 4 August.

————. 2006a. 'Population Projections for India and States 2001-2026, Report of the Technical Group on Population Projections Constituted by the National Commission on Population'. ORGI&CC, New Delhi.

————. 2006b. 'Census of India 2001, Report on Post Enumeration Survey'. ORGI&CC, New Delhi.

———— 2007a. 'Poverty Estimates for 2004-05'. Planning Commission, New Delhi.

————. 2007b. *Report of the National Commission for Religious and Linguistic Minorities, Vol I*. New Delhi: Ministry of Tribal Affairs.

————. 2007c. *Annual Report 2006-07*. New Delhi: Ministry of Tribal Affairs.

————. 2008a. 'Census of India. 2001, General Population Tables Assam'. Directorate of Census Operations, Guwahati.

————. 2008b. 'The Gazette of India Extraordinary, Part II – Section 3 – Sub-section (ii), No. 189, February 8, 2008'. Legislative Department, Ministry of Law and Justice, New Delhi.

————. 2008c. 'Census of India 2001, General Population Tables Orissa'. Directorate of Census Operations, Bhubaneshwar.

————. 2008d. 'Changing Face of Electoral India: Delimitation 2008, Volumes I & II'. Delimitation Commission of India, New Delhi.

————. 2009a. 'Thirteenth Finance Commission 2010–2015, Volume I: Report and Volume II: Annexes'. New Delhi.

————. 2009b. *Manual on Vital Statistics*. New Delhi: Central Statistical Organisation.

————. 2009c. *Report of the Expert Group to Review the Methodology for Estimation of Poverty*. New Delhi: Planning Commission.

————. 2011a. *Report of the Committee on Optimum Sample Sizes for North Eastern States*. New Delhi: NSSO, MOSPI.

————. 2011b. 'Census of India 2011, Provisional Population Totals, Paper 1 of 2011, Series 1 India'. ORGI&CC, New Delhi.

————. 2011c. 'Census of India 2011, Provisional Population Totals, Paper 1 of 2011, Series 14 Nagaland'. Directorate of Census Operations; Kohima.

————. 2011d. *Review Report under MGNREGA in Nagaland*. Release ID: 71648. New Delhi: Press Information Bureau.

————. 2011e. 'Census of India 2011, Provisional Population Totals, Paper 1 of 2011, Series 24 Madhya Pradesh'. Directorate of Census Operations, Bhopal.

————. 2011f. 'Census of India 2011, Administrative Atlas of India'. ORGI&CCI, New Delhi.

————. 2011g. 'Census of India 2011, Provisional Population Totals, Paper 2 Volume 1 of 2011, Series 14 Nagaland'. Directorate of Census Operations, Kohima.

————. 2012a. 'Census of India 2011, Administrative Atlas Nagaland'. ORGI&CCI, New Delhi.

————. 2012b. 'National Data Sharing and Accessibility Policy'. *Gazette of India.* 17 March. New Delhi: Department of Science & Technology.

————. 2013a. *Key Indicators of Household Consumer Expenditure in India, NSS 68th Round, July 2011 – June 2012.* New Delhi: NSSO, MOS&PI.

————. 2013b. *State Development Report, Jammu and Kashmir.* New Delhi: Planning Commission.

————. 2013c. *Report of the Comptroller and Auditor General of India for the Year Ended 31 March 2012,* Report No. 1 of 2013. New Delhi: Comptroller and Auditor General of India.

————. 2013d. 'Census of India. 2011, Primary Census Abstract Data Tables (India & states/UTs – District Level)'. Excel format. Available at http://www.censusindia. gov.in/2011census/population_enumeration.aspx.

————. 2013e. *Report of the Committee for Evolving a Composite Development Index of States.* New Delhi: Ministry of Finance.

————. 2014a. 'Mapping the Adverse Child Sex Ratio in India, Census 2011'. ORGI&CC, New Delhi.

————. 2014b. 'Census of India 2011, Nagaland, District Census Handbook, Dimapur'. Directorate of Census Operations; Kohima.

————. 2014c. *Report of the High Level Committee on Socio-Economic, Health and Educational Status of Tribal Communities of India.* New Delhi: Ministry of Tribal Affairs.

————. 2014d. 'Census of India 2011, Report on Post Enumeration Survey'. ORGI&CC, New Delhi.

————. 2014e. 'Order No. 9/25/2013-CD (Gen) (dated 07.01.14)'. ORGI, New Delhi. Accessed on 2 July 2019. Available at http://www.censusindia.gov.in/2011-Documents/ordermanipur_201401081351.pdf.

————. 2014f. *Report of the Expert Group to Review the Methodology for Measurement of Poverty.* New Delhi: Planning Commission.

————. 2014g. 'Inter-State Border Dispute in North-Eastern States'. Press Information Bureau, New Delhi. 10 December.

————. 2015a. *Report of the Fourteenth Finance Commission.* New Delhi: Fourteenth Finance Commission.

————. 2015b. *Millennium Development Goals, India Country Report 2015.* New Delhi: MOSPI.

————. 2016a. *Statistical Year Book India 2016.* New Delhi: MOSPI.

————. 2016b. 'Finance Accounts (Volume – I) for the Year 2015-2016, Government of Nagaland'. Comptroller and Auditor General of India, New Delhi.

————. 2017. *Report of the Task Force on Improving Employment Data – Draft Report*. New Delhi: Niti Aayog.

————. 2018a. 'Census of India 2011, Population Enumeration Data (Final Population)'. Available at http://www.censusindia.gov.in/2011census/population_enumeration.html.

————. 2018b. 'National Policy on Official Statistics (Draft)'. MOSPI, New Delhi. Available at http://mospi.gov.in/sites/default/files/announcements/draft_policy_17may18.pdf.

————. 2018c. 'Census of India 2011, Paper 1 of 2018, Language, India, States and Union Territories'. RGI, New Delhi.

————. 2018d. 'Census of India 2011, Data on Language and Mother Tongue'. Available at http://www.censusindia.gov.in/2011Census/Language_MTs.html.

————. 2019a. 'Census of India 2011, Population Enumeration Data (Data on Migration)'. Available at http://www.censusindia.gov.in/2011census/population_enumeration.html.

————. 2019b. 'Household Consumer Expenditure Survey'. Press Information Bureau, New Delhi. 15 November.

Government of J&K. 2008. *Below Poverty Line (BPL) Survey-2008: J&K State*. Directorate of Economics and Statistics.

GoN (Government of Nagaland). n.d.1. *Shri Syed M.H. Burney*. Kohima: Rajbhavan. Available at http://www.rajbhavan.nagaland.gov.in/governor_4.html.

————. n.d.2. 'Disclosure as per RTI Act (Section 4(1)(B))'. Office of the Commissioner Nagaland, Kohima.

————. n.d.3. *Evaluation Report on Village Development Board Programme in Wokha District of Nagaland*. Publication No. 20. Kohima: Directorate of Evaluation Government of Nagaland.

————. n.d.4. *[BPL] Census, Dimapur District*. Available at https://www.nagaland.gov.in/portal/portal/StatePortal/UsefulLinks/Census.

————. n.d.5. *Handbook of Rural Development Nagaland*. Kohima: Department of Rural Development.

————. 1970. *Gazetteers of India, Nagaland, Kohima District*. Kohima: Nagaland District Gazetteers Unit.

————. 1979. *Nagaland Basic Facts*. Kohima: Directorate of Information, Publicity and Tourism.

————. 1980. *Nagaland 1980 Basic Facts*. Kohima: Directorate of Information, Publicity and Tourism.

————. 1981. *Nagaland District Gazetteers (Tuensang)*. Kohima: Nagaland District Gazetteers Unit.

————. 2003a. 'Letter to the Registrar General (Sub: Review of Census of 2001 in Respect of Nagaland by Ordering Fresh Census in the State) (No. GAB-20/2/92)'. 5 December. General Administration Branch, Home Department, Kohima..

————. 2003b. *Evaluation Report on Registration of Births and Deaths in Nagaland.* Publication No. 50. Kohima: Directorate of Evaluation, Government of Nagaland.

————. 2004a. *Nagaland State Human Development Report 2004.* Kohima: Department of Planning & Coordination.

————. 2004b. *Population Projection of Nagaland from 2002 to 2010.* Kohima: Directorate of Economics & Statistics.

————. 2005a. *Economic Survey 2002-2003.* Kohima: Directorate of Economics and Statistics.

————. 2005b. 'List of Business, Eighth Session of Tenth Assembly (Thursday, 18th August, 2005)'. Nagaland Legislative Assembly, Kohima.

————. 2006. 'Naga Referencer (Orientation Programme for Legislators of Nagaland, Zonal Council Hall, 18 & 19 April, 2006)'. Department of Parliamentary Affairs, Kohima.

————. 2007. 'Budget Speech of Shri Neiphiu Rio, Chief Minister, Minister In-Charge, Finance for 2007-08'. Finance Department, Kohima. 24 March.

————. 2008. *Statistical Handbook of Nagaland 2008.* Kohima: Directorate of Economics and Statistics.

————. 2009a. 'Resolutions Adopted in the Consultative Meeting on Census-2011 Held at the Zonal Council Hall, Kohima, on 30th September, 2009' (Courtesy: Directorate of Census Operations, Nagaland).

————. 2009b. *Nagaland Basic Facts 2009.* Kohima: Directorate of Information and Public Relations.

————. 2010. 'Compilation of Important Notifications, Orders, Office Memorandums Issued by Various Departments under the Government of Nagaland and Government of India – Volume IV'. Department of Personnel and Administrative Reforms, Kohima.

————. 2013a. *Housing Conditions and Amenities in Nagaland, National Sample Survey 65th Round.* Kohima: Directorate of Economics and Statistics.

————. 2013b. *Nagaland Fifty Years On.* Kohima: The Coffee Table Book Publication Committee, 50 years of Statehood.

————. 2014. *District Human Development Report Longleng 2014.* Kohima: Department of Planning and Coordination.

————. 2017. *Statistical Handbook 2017.* Kohima: Directorate of Economics and Statistics.

————. 2019a. 'Districts – Government of Nagaland: Official Portal'. Accessed on 22 August 2019. Available at https://www.nagaland.gov.in/portal/portal/StatePortal/GovernmentAndPrivateBodies/DistrictProfiles?fontValue=2.

————. 2019b. 'Home – Government of Nagaland: Official Portal'. Accessed on 22 August 2019. Available at https://www.nagaland.gov.in/portal.

Government of Nigeria. n.d. 'History of Population Censuses in Nigeria'. National Population Commission. Accessed on 24 June 2018. Available at http://population.gov.ng/about-us/history-of-population-censuses-in-nigeria/.

Government of Sri Lanka. 2012. 'Census of Population and Housing 2011 – Population of Sri Lanka by District (Preliminary Report (Provisional) – 1)'. Department of Census and Statistics, Colombo.

IIPS and ICF. 2017. *National Family Health Survey (NFHS-4), 2015-16: India*. Mumbai: International Institute for Population Sciences.

IIPS and MI. 2007. *National Family Health Survey (NFHS-3), 2005–06: India: Vols. I and II*. International Institute for Population Sciences, Mumbai; and Macro International.

———. 2009. *National Family Health Survey (NFHS-3), India, 2005–06: Nagaland*. International Institute for Population Sciences, Mumbai; and Macro International.

ISRO. nd. Bhuvan – Indian Geo-Platform of the Indian Space Research Organisation. National Remote Sensing Centre. Available https://bhuvan-app1.nrsc.gov.in/state/NL# (Accessed on 19 July 2019).

Lok Sabha. 1999. *Constituent Assembly Debates, Official Report, Vols. I-IX*. New Delhi: Lok Sabha Secretariat.

Marten, J. T. 1923. 'Census of India 1921, Volume I India, Part II – Tables'. Superintendent of Government Printing, Calcutta.

McSwiney, J. 1912. 'Census of India, 1911, Volume III, Assam, Part II TABLES'. SCO, Assam; Shillong.

Natarajan, D. 1972. *Census of India 1971, Intercensal Growth of Population (Analysis of Extracts from All India Census Reports)*. Census Centenary Monograph No. 3. New Delhi: ORGI.

NCEUS. 2007. *Report on Conditions of Work and Promotion of Livelihoods in the Unorganised Sector*. Report of the National Commission for Enterprises in the Unorganised Sector. New Delhi: Government of India.

Royal Government of Bhutan. 2000. *Bhutan National Human Development Report 2000*. Planning Commission Secretariat.

RBI. 2004. 'State Finances: A Study of Budgets of 2003-04'. Mumbai: Reserve Bank of India.

———. 2012. 'State Finances: A Study of Budgets of 2011-12.' Mumbai: Reserve Bank of India.

———. 2018. 'Handbook of Statistics on Indian States, 2017-18'. Mumbai: Reserve Bank of India.

Singh, A. P. n.d. *Indian Census Cartography - A Journey of 140 Years*. New Delhi: ORGI. Available at http://censusindia.gov.in/2011-common/nsdi/history_census_cartography-drg.pdf.

SoI. 2002. '1:1,000,000 State Map of Bihār'. First edition. Dehradun.

———. 2004. '1:1,000,000 State Map of Mahārāshtra (East)'. First edition. Dehradun.

———. 2010. '1:5,00,000 State Map of Nāgāland'. First edition. Dehradun.

———. 2012a. '1:6,00,000 State Map of Jhārkhand (English)'. Second edition. Dehradun.

———. 2012b. '1:1,000,000 State Map of Odisha (English)'. First edition. Dehradun.

———. 2014. '1:1,000,000 State Map of Chhattīsgarh (English)'. Second edition. Dehradun.

Srivastava, S. C. 1972. *Indian Census in Perspective.* Census Centenary Monograph No. 1. ORGI, New Delhi.

Court Cases

CPO & Ors. vs. UoI & Ors. (Chakhesang Public Organization and Others vs. Union of India and Others). 2006. WP (PIL) No. 67 of 2006. Gauhati High Court.

CPO & Anr. vs. SoN & Ors. (Chakhesang Public Organization and Another vs. The State of Nagaland and Others). 2010. WP (PIL) No. 9 of 2010. Gauhati High Court.

SoA vs. UoI & Ors. (State of Assam vs. Union of India & Others). 1988. Original Suit 2 of 1988. Supreme Court of India.

Virendra Pratap & Anr. vs. UoI & Ors. (Virendra Pratap & Anr. vs. Union of India & Others). 2011. Writ Petition (Civil) No. 540 of 2011.

Civil Society/Political Parties/Insurgent Groups

CPO. 2007. *Public Representation for an Immediate Action to Set Aside the Controversial Census 2001* [Letter Addressed to ORGI]. 8 January.

CPO et al. (Chakhesang Public Organization, Pochury Public Forum, Chakhesang Youth Front, Chakhesang Students Union and Pochury Students Union). 2003. *Total Revision of Provisional Population Total: Census of India 2001 in R/O Nagaland State* [Letter addressed to the Registrar General of India]. 27 September.

———. 2004. *Public Representation against Delimitation of Assembly Constituencies in Nagaland and Phek District in Particular on the Basis of Census 2001* [Letter Addressed to Justice K. Singh (Retd.), Chairman, DCI]. 27 August.

ENPO. 2010. 'Memorandum for Separate State for Eastern Nagaland under Special Provision and Status (of the Erstwhile Tuensang Frontier Division of North East Frontier Agency-NEFA)'. ENPO/Memo-01(Statehood)/PM/GOI/01 dated 25.11.10. Eastern Nagaland People's Organization, Tuensang (Courtesy: Toshi Wungtung).

GPRN. (2007) 2010. *Nagas: Their Pilgrimage for Self-Existence and Quest for Dignity and Peace.* Oking: Ministry of Information & Publicity, Government of the People's Republic of Nagalim (Nagaland).

Haokip, P. S. 2008. *Zale'n-gam: The Kuki Nation.* Revised edition with additional text. Zale'n-gam: Kuki National Organisation.

KMHR. 2009. 'The Plight of the Indigenous Kuki People: Unraveling the story of Deception, Suppression and Marginalization in the Tri Border Area of India, Myanmar & Bangladesh'. Kuki Movement for Human Rights (Courtesy: T. Lunkim).

KSU (Khiamniungan Students' Union). 2013. 'Golden Jubilee Souvenir'. Noklak: Khiamniungan Students' Union (Courtesy: H. Pushing).

KTC. 2008. 'Memorandum Submitted to Shri Neiphiu Rio, Hon'ble Chief Minister of Nagaland, on 8th of October 2008 at Noklak Town during Khiamniungan Tsokum

Festival by the Khiamniungan Tribal Council'. Noklak: Khiamniungan Tribal Council (Courtesy: H. Pushing).

NPCC. 2000. *Bedrock of Naga Society*. Second edition. Kohima: Nagaland Pradesh Congress Committee (I).

NTC. 2013. 'Representation against the Inclusion of Rongmeis as a Recognized Tribe of Nagaland by a Cabinet Decision and Appointment of a Committee by the Government to Study for Inclusion of Mao as a Recognized Tribe in the State of Nagaland'. Letter to the Chief Minister, dated 03.06.13. Nagaland Tribes Council. Unpublished (Courtesy: P. Pius Lotha).

Rengma Hoho. 2016. *Demand for Upgradtion of Tseminyu ADC to District Headquarter* (Letter addressed to the Chief Minister). Ref. No. RH/M-02-2016. 27 July (Courtesy: Kenyuseng Tep).

Sumi Hoho. 2002. 'Letter to the President of India (Delimitation (restructure) of Assembly Constituencies in Nagaland)'. POP/SH/1/2002 (16.11.02). Zunheboto (Courtesy: Hokiye Yepthomi).

———. 2004. 'Sumi Hoho Resolved'. 25 May. Sumi Hoho: Zunheboto (Courtesy: Hokiye Yepthomi).

———. n.d. 'Sumi Hoho under the Presidentiship of Mr. I. Vitokhe Assumi Initiated Unity, Both the Two NSCN Factions and Village/Land Disputes of Sumi Tribe with other Tribes (Neibouring Villages)'. Zunheboto (Courtesy: Hokiye Yepthomi).

TSU (Tikhir Students' Union). 2006. *Magazine cum History*. Anatongre: Tikhir Students' Union (Courtesy: P. Tikhir).

Speeches and Writings of Politicians and Bureaucrats

Dev, S. C. 1988. *Nagaland: The Untold Story*. Calcutta: Gouri Dev.

Jamir, S. C. 1996. 'Speeches of Mr. S.C. Jamir Chief Minister Nagaland 1994-1996'. Directorate of Information and Public Relations, Government of Nagaland; Kohima.

———. 1998. 'Speeches of Mr. S.C. Jamir Chief Minister Nagaland January to December 1997'. Directorate of Information and Public Relations, Government of Nagaland; Kohima.

———. 1999. 'Speeches of Mr. S.C. Jamir Chief Minister Nagaland 1998'. Directorate of Information and Public Relations, Government of Nagaland; Kohima.

Jamir, Alemtemshi. 2002. 'Keynote Address'. In *Dimensions of Development in Nagaland*, ed. C. J. Thomas and G. Das, pp. 1–8. New Delhi: Regency Publications.

Jamir, C. Apok. 2003. 'Uncorrected Rajya Sabha Debate on the Delimitation (Amendment) Bill, 2003'. 16 December. Availabe at http://164.100.47.5/newdebate/deb_ndx/200/16122003/5to6.htm.

Jamir, S. C. 2003. 'Speeches of Mr. S. C. Jamir Chief Minister Nagaland 2002-03'. Department of Information and Public Relations, Government of Nagaland; Kohima.

———. 2016. 'Peace Accord vis-à-vis Future Challenges'. *Morung Express* (*ME*). 1 April.

————. n.d.1. 'Speeches of S.C. Jamir Chief Minister Nagaland (Feb 1984 – Jan 1986)'. Directorate of Information and Public Relations, Government of Nagaland; Kohima.

————. n.d.2. 'Chief Minister S.C. Jamir Speeches Feb '93 to August '94'. Directorate of Information and Public Relations, Government of Nagaland; Kohima.

————. n.d.3. 'Speeches of Mr. S.C. Jamir Chief Minister Nagaland 1999'. Directorate of Information and Public Relations, Government of Nagaland; Kohima.

————. n.d.4. 'Speeches of Mr. S.C. Jamir Chief Minister of Nagaland 2000'. Directorate of Information and Public Relations, Government of Nagaland; Kohima.

————. n.d.5. 'Speeches of Mr. S.C. Jamir Chief Minister Nagaland 2001'. Directorate of Information and Public Relations, Government of Nagaland; Kohima.

Jasokie, J. B. n.d.1. 'Speeches of the Chief Minister Mr. J. B. Jasokie (June 1980 to June 1981)'. Directorate of Information and Publicity, Government of Nagaland; Kohima.

————. n.d.2. 'Speeches of the Chief Minister Nagaland Mr. J. B. Jasokie (July 1981 to August 1982), Vol. II'. Directorate of Information and Publicity, Government of Nagaland; Kohima.

Ramunny, Murkot. 1988. *The World of Nagas*. New Delhi: Northern Book Centre.

Rio, Neiphiu. 2003. 'Speeches of Neiphiu Rio, Chief Minister of Nagaland March 2003 – December 2003'. Directorate of Information and Public Relations, Government of Nagaland; Kohima.

————. 2004. 'Speeches of Neiphiu Rio, Chief Minister of Nagaland January 2004 – December 2004'. Directorate of Information and Public Relations, Government of Nagaland; Kohima.

————. 2006. 'Speeches of Neiphiu Rio, Chief Minister of Nagaland 2006'. Directorate of Information and Public Relations, Government of Nagaland; Kohima.

————. 2007. 'Speeches of Neiphiu Rio, Chief Minster of Nagaland January 2007 - December 2007'. Directorate of Information and Public Relations, Government of Nagaland; Kohima.

————. 2008. 'Speeches of Neiphiu Rio, Chief Minster of Nagaland March 2008 - December 2008'. Directorate of Information and Public Relations, Government of Nagaland; Kohima.

————. 2010a. 'Speech of Shri Neiphiu Rio, Chief Minister at the Conference of the Chief Ministers on Internal Security, New Delhi'. New Delhi. 7 February.

————. 2010b. 'Speeches of Neiphiu Rio, Chief Minister of Nagaland 2009'. Directorate of Information and Public Relations, Government of Nagaland; Kohima.

————. 2011. 'Speeches of Neiphiu Rio, Chief Minster of Nagaland 2010'. Directorate of Information and Public Relations, Government of Nagaland; Kohima.

————. 2012. 'Speeches of Neiphiu Rio, Chief Minister of Nagaland (January– December 2011)'. Directorate of Information and Public Relations, Government of Nagaland; Kohima.

————. 2014. 'Speeches of Neiphiu Rio, Chief Minster of Nagaland January to December 2013'. Directorate of Information and Public Relations, Government of Nagaland; Kohima.

Sangtam, K. A. 2003. 'Consideration and Voting on the Constitution (Ninety-Sixth Amendment) Bill, 2003 (Amendment of Articles 81, 82, 170 and 330)'. Accessed on 12 August 2019. Available at http://eparlib.nic.in/bitstream/123456789/712950/1/5918. pdf.

Sema, Hokishe. 1984. 'A Collection of Speeches and Statements of Shri Hokishe Sema Chief Minister of Nagaland 1969-1974'. Directorate of Information and Publicity, Government of Nagaland; Kohima.

———. 1986. *Emergence of Nagaland: Socio-Economic and Political Transformation and the Future.* New Delhi: Vikas Publishing House Pvt. Ltd.

Sema, Khekiye. 2015. *Encountering Life: Antics of a Govt. Servant.* Dimapur: Heritage Publishing House.

Sreedhar Rao, K. 2002. *Whither Governance: Reflections of an Assam Civilian.* New Delhi: South Asia Foundation.

Stracey, P. D. 1968. *Nagaland Nightmare.* Bombay: Allied Publishers Pvt Ltd.

Vamuzo. n.d. 'Speeches of Vamuzo Chief Minister Nagaland June 1990 – November 1990', vol. II. Directorate of Information and Public Relations, Government of Nagaland; Kohima.

———. 1991. 'Speeches of Vamuzo Chief Minister Nagaland December 1990 - November 1991, Vol. II'. Directorate of Information and Public Relations, Government of Nagaland; Kohima.

Vizol. n.d. 'Vizol's Speeches and Addresses'. Directorate of Information and Public Relations, Kohima.

Churches

Benreu Baptist Church. 1997. 'Centenary Souvenir (Feb. 7-9, 1997)'. Benreu: Benreu Baptist Church Centenary Committee.

CBCC. 2000. 'CBCC Golden Jubilee Souvenir (1950-2000)'. T. Chikri, Pfutsero: Chakhesang Baptist Church Council.

Diocese of Kohima. n.d. 'Directory 2010-2011'. Kohima: Bishop's House (Courtesy: Rev. Fr. Dr. Sojan Xavier).

NBCC. 2001. 'NBCC Newsletter Vol. 1, Issue 2, January-March', p. 5.

———. 2002. 'NBCC Newsletter Vol. 2, Issue 2, January-March', p. 10.

———. 2003. 'NBCC Newsletter Vol. 3, Issue 2, January-March', pp. 9–10 (this issue also contains information for the period 1992–2000).

———. 2004. 'NBCC Newsletter Vol. 4, Issue 2, January-March', p. 10.

———. 2005. 'NBCC Newsletter Vol. 5, Issue 3, January-March', p. 16.

———. 2006. 'NBCC Newsletter Vol. 6, Issue 2, January-March', p. 17.

———. 2007. 'NBCC Newsletter Vol. 7, Issue 2, January-March', p. 5.

———. 2008. 'NBCC Newsletter Vol. 8, Issue 3, April-June', p. 5.

———. 2009. 'NBCC Newsletter Vol. 9 & 10, Issue 3 & 4, April-September', p. 4.

———. 2010. 'NBCC Newsletter Vol. 10, Issue 2, January-March', p. 4.

————. 2011. 'NBCC Newsletter Vol. 12, Issue 1, January-March', p. 4.

Baptist Church Poilwa. 2013. 'Platinium Jubilee Souvenir - Celebrating the 75th Blessed Year of Its Existence'. Platinium Jubilee Committee, Poilwa.

Secondary sources

Abbott, Andrew. 1995. 'Things of Boundaries'. *Social Service Review* 69(4): 545–62.

Abramson, David. 2002. 'Identity counts: the Soviet Legacy and the Census in Uzbekistan'. In *Census and Identity: The Politics of Race, Ethnicity, and Language in National Censuses*, ed. David I. Kertzer and Dominique Arel, pp. 176–201. Cambridge: Cambridge University Press.

Adepoju, Aderanti. 1981., 'Military Rule and Population Issues in Nigeria'. *African Affairs* 80(318): 29–47.

Agnew, John. 1994. 'The Territorial Trap: The Geographical Assumptions of International Relations Theory'. *Review of International Political Economy* 1(1): 53–80.

Agrawal, Ankush and Tushar Agrawal. 2012. 'NSSO's Consumer Expenditure Surveys: An Examination of Respondent Characteristics'. *Sarvekshana* 97: 18–30.

Agrawal, Ankush and Vikas Kumar. 2012a. 'Nagaland's Demographic Somersault'. Working Paper No. 311. Delhi: Institute of Economic Growth.

————. 2012b. 'An Investigation into Changes in Nagaland's Population between 1971 and 2011.' Working Paper No. 316. Delhi: Institute of Economic Growth.

————. 2012c. 'Number Games in Nagaland'. *Hindu*, 12 July [Corrigendum: 14 July 2012].

————. 2013. 'Nagaland's Demographic Somersault'. *Economic and Political Weekly* 48(39): 69–74.

————. 2014. 'Infirmities in NSSO Data for Nagaland'. *Economic and Political Weekly* 49(12): 20–2.

————. 2015. 'Statistical Mirage: Bad Data to Fail Governance'. *Deccan Herald*, 3 June.

————. 2017a. 'Cartographic Conflicts within a Union: Finding Land for Nagaland in India'. *Political Geography* 61: 123–47.

————. 2017b. 'NSSO Surveys along India's Periphery: Data Quality and Implications'. Azim Premji University, Working Paper No. 9.

————. 2018. 'Community, Numbers and Politics in Nagaland'. In *Democracy in Nagaland: Tribes, Traditions, Tensions*, ed. Jelle J. P. Wouters and Zhoto Tunyi. Kohima: The Highlander Books. pp. 57–84.

————. 2019a. 'Delays in the Release of the Indian Census Data'. *Statistical Journal of the IAOS*, forthcoming.

————. 2019b. 'Manipur's Population Conundrum'. Unpublished manuscript.

Ahmed, A. H. n.d. 'The Fifth Population Census in Sudan: A Census with a Full Coverage and a High Accuracy'. UNSD. Available at http://unstats.un.org/unsd/demographic/sources/census/countries/SDN.pdf.

Ahmed, Ishtiaq. 1999. 'The 1947 Partition of Punjab: Arguments Put Forth before the Punjab Boundary Commission by the Parties Involved'. In *Region and Partition: Bengal, Punjab and the Partition of the Subcontinent*, eds. I. Talbot and G. Singh, pp. 116–7. Oxford and New York: Oxford University Press.

Ahonsi, Babatunde A. 1988. 'Deliberate Falsification and Census Data in Nigeria'. *African Affairs* 87(349): 553–62.

Alemchiba, M. 1970. *A Brief Historical Account of Nagaland*. Kohima: Naga Institute of Culture.

Alesina, Alberto, Sule Özler, Nouriel Roubini and Phillip Swagel. 1996. 'Political Instability and Economic Growth'. *Journal of Economic Growth* 1(2): 189–211.

Alesina, Alberto and Eliana La Ferrara. 2005. 'Ethnic Diversity and Economic Performance'. *Journal of Economic Literature* 43(3): 762–800.

Alonso, William and Paul Starr. 1985. 'A Nation of Numbers Watchers'. *The Wilson Quarterly* 9(3): 92–6.

———. 1987. *The Politics of Numbers*. New York: Russell Sage Foundation.

Aluko, S. A. 1965. 'How Many Nigerians? An Analysis of Nigeria's Census Problems, 1901–63'. *Journal of Modern African Studies* 3(3): 371–92.

Aly, Götz and Karl Heinz Roth. 2004. *The Nazi Census Identification and Control in the Third Reich*, trans. Edwin Black and Assenka Oksiloff. Philadelphia: Temple University Press.

Amarjeet Singh, M. 2009. 'A Study on Illegal Immigration into North-East India: The Case of Nagaland.' Occasional Paper No. 8. New Delhi: Institute for Defence Studies and Analyses.

Anderson, Benedict. 2006. *Imagined communities: Reflections on the Origin and Spread of Nationalism*. London and New York: Verso.

Anderson, James, Ian Shuttleworth, Chris Lloyd and Owen McEldowney. n.d. 'Political Demography: The Northern Ireland Census, Discourse and Territoriality'. Available at www.esds.ac.uk/doc/5362%5Cmrdoc%5Cpdf%5Cq5362uguide.pdf.

Anderson, Margo and Stephen E. Fienberg. 2000. '"Partisan Politics at Work: Sampling and the 2000 Census'. *Political Science and Politics* 33(4): 795–9.

Appadurai, Arjun. 2007. *Fear of Small Numbers: An Essay on the Geography of Anger*. Calcutta: Seagull Books.

Arel, D. 2002. 'Demography and Politics in the First Post-Soviet Censuses: Mistrusted State, Contested Identities'. *Population* 57(6): 801–27.

Arulampalam, Wiji, Sugato Dasgupta, Amrita Dhillon and Bhaskar Dutta. 2009. 'Electoral Goals and Center-State Transfers: A Theoretical Model and Empirical Evidence from India'. *Journal of Development Economics* 88(1): 103–19.

Ashraf, Ajaz. 2013. 'An Anglo-Indian Insurance Policy'. *Hindu*, 31 May.

Assam Tribune. 2009. 'Karimganj Tribal Body Demands Reserved Assembly Constituencies'. 14 April.

———. 2011. 'PC Keeps Mum on Population Growth'. 2 April.

Attane, I., and Y. Courbage. 2000. 'Transitional Stages and Identity Boundaries: The Case of Ethnic Minorities in China'. *Population and Environment* 21: 257–80.

Aung, San Yamin. 2018. 'Still No Date for Release of Census Findings on Ethnic Populations'. Irrawaddy. 21 February.

The Avalon Project. n.d. 'Convention on Rights and Duties of States'. Available at http://avalon.law.yale.edu/20th_century/intam03.asp.

Banerjee, Sandeep. 2011. 'Dimaraji Movement: In a Sticky Situation'. *The Northeast Window* 7(7): 6–9.

Banerjee, Sumanta. 1992. 'Dangerous Game in Nagaland'. *Economic and Political Weekly* 27(29): 1525–7.

Banthia, J. K. 2001. 'Mobilising Support for India's Census-Constraints and Challenges'. Paper presented at UNFPA/PARIS21 International Expert Group Meeting: Censuses, Pretoria. 26–9 November.

Baron, James N. and Michael T. Hannan. 1994. 'The Impact of Economics on Contemporary Sociology'. *Journal of Economic Literature* 32(3): 1111–46.

Barrier, N. G. (ed.). 1981. *The Census in British India: New Perspectives*. New Delhi: Manohar Publications.

Barrow, Ian J. 2003. *Making History, Drawing Territory: British Mapping in India, C.1756-1905*. New Delhi: Oxford University Press.

Baruah, Sanjib. 2005. *Durable Disorder: Understanding the Politics of Northeast India*. New Delhi: Oxford University Press.

———. 2015. 'Reimagining Dimapur'. *Indian Express*, 18 March.

Basu, Alaka Malwade. 1997. 'The "Politicization" of Fertility to Achieve Non-Demographic Objectives'. *Population Studies*. 51(1): 5–18.

Beteille, Andre. 1960. 'Question of Defintion'. *Seminar* 14:15–18.

Begum, Sharifa and Armindo Miranda. 1979. 'The Defectiveness of the 1974 Population Census of Bangladesh'. *The Bangladesh Development Studies* 7(3): 79–106.

Behrens, A., C. Uggen and J. Manza. 2003. 'Ballot Manipulation and the "Menace of Negro Domination": Racial Threat and Felon Disenfranchisement in the United States, 1850–2002'. *American Journal of Sociology* 109(3): 559–605.

Bertrand, Marianne and Sendhil Mullainathan. 2001. 'Do People Mean What They Say? Implications for Subjective Survey Data'. *The American Economic Review* 91(2): 67–72.

Bhagat, R.B. 2001. 'Census and the Construction of Communalism in India'. *Economic and Political Weekly* 36(46–7): 4352–6.

———. 2003. 'Role of Census in Racial and Ethnic Construction: US, British and Indian Censuses'. *Economic and Political Weekly*, 38(8): 686–91.

———. 2006. 'Census and Caste Enumeration: British Legacy and Contemporary Practice in India'. *Genus* 62(2): 119–34.

Bhagwati, Jagdish and Arvind Panagariya. 2014. *Why Growth Matters*. New York: Public Affairs.

Bhalla, Sheila. 2014. 'Behind the Post-1991 "Challenge" to the Functional Efficiency of Established Statistical Institutions.' *Economic and Political Weekly* 49(7): 43–50.

Bhalla, Surjit S. 2013a. 'Lessons from the Gujarat model'. *Indian Express*. 26 October.

———. 2013b. 'Gujarat's Muslims: In a Politically Correct Trap?' *Indian Express*. 2 November.

————. 2014a. 'Gujarat's Other Calling Card'. *Financial Express*. 19 April.

————. 2014b. 'The Slur and Troll Campaign'. *Indian Express*. 10 May.

Bhushan, Bharat. 2019. 'Naga Settlement: So Near, and yet so Far'. *Asian Age*. 6 February.

Bhattacharjee G. 2018. 'Is the Special Category Status Really Dead?' *Economic and Political Weekly* 53(20): 25–9.

Bhattacharya, N. and G.S. Chatterjee. 1971. 'On Rural-Urban Differentials in Consumer Prices and per Capita Household Consumption in India by Levels of Living'. *Sankhya* Series B 33(3/4): 355–70.

Bhattacharyya, Bhubaneswar. 1994. *The Troubled Border*. Guwahati: Lawyer's Bookstall.

Bhattacharyya, Birendra Kumar. 2005. *Love in the Time of Insurgency*. New Delhi: Katha.

Biemer, Paul P. 2010. 'Total Survey Error Design, Implementation, and Evaluation'. *Public Opinion Quarterly* 74(5): 817–48.

Biemer, Paul M., Robert M. Groves, Lars E. Lyberg, Nancy A. Mathiowetz and Seymour Sudman (eds.). 2004. *Measurement Errors in Surveys*. Hoboken, NJ: Wiley-Interscience.

Biemer, Paul P. and Lars E. Lyberg. 2003. *Introduction to Survey Quality*. Hoboken, NJ: John Wiley & Sons, Inc.

Bookman, M. Z. 2013. *The Demographic Struggle for Power: The Political Economy of Demographic Engineering in the Modern World*. Oxon: Routledge.

Borgohain, Homen and Pradipta Borgohain. 2011. *Scrolls of Strife: The Endless History of the Nagas*. New Delhi: Rupa.

Boruah, Bhim Kanta. 2014. *Dictionary of Nagamese Language* (Nagamese-English-Assamese). New Delhi: Mittal Publication.

Bose, Ashish. 1991. *Population of India: 1991 Census Results and Methodology*. Delhi: B. R. Publishing Corporation.

————. 1996. 'Foreword'. In *Census as Social Document*, ed. S. P. Mohanty and A. R. Momin, 5–8. Jaipur: Rawat Publications.

————. 2004. 'Census Goldmine: Dissemination of 2001 Data'. *Economic and Political Weekly* 39(32): 3595–7.

————. 2008. 'Accuracy of the 2001 Census: Highlights of Post-Enumeration Survey'. *Economic and Political Weekly* 43(22): 14–16.

Bose, A., D. B. Gupta and G. Raychaudhuri (eds.). 1977. *Population Statistics in India*. Database in Indian Economy Volume III. New Delhi: Vikas.

Bowden, Roger J. 1989. *Statistical Games and Human Affairs: The View from Within*. New York: Cambridge University Press

Bradshaw, Sheldon T. 1996. 'Death, Taxes, and Census Litigation: Do the Equal Protection and Apportionment Clauses Guarantee a Constitutional Right to Census Accuracy?' *The George Washington Law Review* 64(2): 379-413.

Brass, Paul R. 1974. Language, Religion and Politics in North India. New York: Cambridge University Press.

Business Standard. 2016. 'Census 2011 Undercounted Tribal Population in Jharkhand'. 26 February.

————. 2019. 'NSC Members Feel "Sidelined by Govt.", Resign on Row over Jobs, GDP Data'. 30 January.

CBC (Canadian Broadcasting Corporation). 2007. '2006 Census Results Delayed amid Problems'. 13 February. Available at https://www.cbc.ca/news/canada/2006-census-results-delayed-amid-problems-1.676358.

CDPS. n.d. 'Nagaland: Militant Groups' Profile'. Centre For Development and Peace Studies, Guwahati. Available at http://cdpsindia.org/nagaland_mgp.asp.

CNBC-TV18. 2019. 'Congress Accuses Narendra Modi of Destroying Economy, Says Lost 1.1 Crore Jobs Due to PM's DeMo, "Gabbar Singh Tax"'. 8 May.

Cederlöf, Gunnel. 2014. *Founding an Empire on India's North-Eastern Frontiers, 1790-1840: Climate, Commerce, Polity*. New Delhi: Oxford University Press.

Chamie, J. 1994. 'Demography: Population Databases in Development Analysis'. *Journal of Development Economics* 44:131–46.

Chandra, K. 2009. 'Caste in Our Social Imagination'. *Seminar* 601 (September).

Chandrasekhar, S. 1972. *Infant Mortality, Population Growth and Family Planning in India*. Chapel Hill, NC: The University of North Carolina Press.

Chandrasekhar, C. P. and Jayati Ghosh. 2011. 'Latest Employment Trends from the NSSO'. *Hindu BusinessLine*. 12 July.

———. 2013. 'The Employment Bottleneck'. *Hindu BusinessLine*, 8 July.

———. 2014. 'Have Workers in Gujarat Benefited from "Development"?' *Hindu BusinessLine* 31 March.

Chandrasekharan, S. 2013. 'Bhutan: Discrepancy in Population Figures, Need for Caution?' *South Asia Analysis Group* update no. 102.

Chaube, S. K. 1999. 'The Scheduled Tribes and Christianity in India'. *Economic and Political Weekly* 34(9): 524–6.

———. 2012. *Hill Politics in Northeast India*. Third edition. Hyderabad: Orient Blackswan.

Chaudhuri, Siladitya and Amitava Saha. 2012. 'Large-Scale Socio-economic Surveys: Impact of Non-response'. *Economic and Political Weekly* 47(30): 223–31.

Chaudhury, Pradipta. 2012. 'Political Economy of Caste in Northern India, 1901-1931'. Working paper. New Delhi: Centre for Economic Studies and Planning, Jawaharlal Nehru University.

Chaurasia, A. R. 2011. 'Population Growth in India during 2001–2011: An Analysis of Provisional Results of 2011 Population Census'. *Studies in Population and Development* no. 11–02. Bhopal: Shyam Institute.

Choldin, Harvey M. 1986. 'Statistics and Politics: The "Hispanic Issue" in the 1980 Census'. *Demography* 23(3): 403–18.

Chasie, Charles. 2000. *The Naga Imbroglio*. Second edition. Kohima: Standard Printers and Publishers.

Chatterji, Joya. 1999. 'The Fashioning of a Frontier: The Radcliffe Line and Bengal's Border Landscape, 1947-52'. *Modern Asian Studies* 33(1): 185–242.

Chester, Lucy. 2008. 'Boundary Commissions as Tools to Safeguard British Interests at the End of Empire'. *Journal of Historical Geography* 34:494–515.

Cockett, Richard. 2015. *Blood, Dreams and Gold: The Changing Face of Burma*. New Haven, CT: Yale University Press.

Cook, Len. 2004. 'The Quality and Qualities of Population Statistics, and the Place of the Census'. *Census and Society* 36(2): 111–23.

Cohn, Bernard S. 1987. 'The Census, Social Structure and Objectification in South Asia'. In *An Anthropologist among the Historians and Other Essays*, ed. Bernard S. Cohn, 224–54. Delhi: Oxford University Press.

Coleman, David. 2012. 'The Twilight of the Census'. *Population and Development Review* 38(S1): 334–51.

Condran, G. A., C. L. Himes and S. H. Preston. 1991. 'Old-Age Mortality Patterns in Low-Mortality Countries: An Evaluation of Population and Death Data at Advanced Ages, 1950 to the Present'. *Population Bulletin of the United Nations* 30:23–60.

Corbridge, Stuart. 2002. 'The Continuing Struggle for India's Jharkhand: Democracy, Decentralisation and the Politics of Names and Numbers'. *Commonwealth & Comparative Politics* 40(3): 55–71.

Coyle, D. 2014. *GDP: A Brief but Affectionate History*. Princeton, NJ: Princeton University Press.

Crampton, J. W. 1996. 'Bordering on Bosnia.' *GeoJournal* 39(4): 353–61.

———. 2001. 'Maps as Social Constructions: Power, Communication and Visualization'. *Progress in Human Geography* 25(2): 235–52.

———. 2010a. *Mapping A Critical Introduction to Cartography and GIS*. West Sussex: Wiley-Blackwell.

———. 2010b. 'Cartographic Calculations of Territory'. *Progress in Human Geography* 35(1): 92–103.

Crook, Tom and Glen O'Hara (eds.). 2011. *Statistics and the Public Sphere: Numbers and the People in Modern Britain, c. 1800–2000*. New York: Routledge.

Curzon, George. 1908. *The Romanes Lecture, Frontiers*. Second edition. Oxford: Clarendon Press.

Dandekar, V. M. 2004. 'Forty Years after Independence'. In *Indian Economy: Problems and Prospects*, ed. Bimal Jalan, pp. 33–83. New Delhi: Penguin Books.

Dandekar, V. M. and P. Venkataramaiah. 1975. *Database of Indian Economy: Role of Sample Surveys*, vol. II. Calcutta: Statistical Publishing Society and Hyderabad: The Indian Econometric Society.

Das Debjyoti. 2014. 'The Yimchunger Nagas: Local Histories and Changing Identity in Nagaland, Northeast India'. *European Bulletin of Himalayan Research* 45:33–59.

———. 2017. 'The Politics of Census: Fear of Numbers and Competing Claims for Representation in Naga Society'. In *Democratisation in the Himalayas: Interests, Conflicts, and Negotiations*, ed. Vibha Arora and N. Jayaram, 54–78. London and New York: Taylor and Francis.

Dasgupta, Anindita. 2001. 'Denial and Resistance: Sylheti Partition "Refugees" in Assam'. *Contemporary South Asia* 10(3): 343–60.

Deaton, A. 1997. *The Analysis of Household Surveys: A Microeconometric Approach to Development Policy*. Washington, DC: World Bank.

———. 2003. 'Prices and Poverty in India, 1987–2000'. *Economic and Political Weekly* 38(4): 362–8.

————. 2008. 'Price Trends in India and Their Implications for Measuring Poverty'. *Economic and Political Weekly* 43(6): 43–9.

Deaton, A. and J. Dreze. 2002. 'Poverty and Inequality in India: A Re-examination'. *Economic and Political Weekly* 37(36): 3729–48.

Deaton, A. and V. Kozel. 2005. 'Data and Dogma: The Great Indian Poverty Debate'. *The World Bank Research Observer* 20(2): 177–99.

Deininger, K. and L. Squire. 1996. 'Measuring Income Inequality: A New Data Base'. *The World Bank Economic Review* 10:565–91.

Demo, V. 2014. 'Foothill Road Can Become the LOC/LAC between Assam and Nagaland'. *Eastern Mirror.* 28 July.

Desai, A. R. 1960. 'Tribes in transition'. *Seminar* 14:19–24.

Desai, S. and R. Vanneman. 2008. *India Human Development Survey (IHDS), 2005.* Release 1 July. Michigan: ICPSR.

Desiere, S., L. Staelens and M. D'Haese. 2016. 'When the Data Source Writes the Conclusion: Evaluating Agricultural Policies'. *The Journal of Development Studies* 52(9): 1372-87.

Deshpande, S. and M. E. John. 2010. 'The Politics of Not Counting Caste'. *Economic and Political Weekly* 45(25): 39–42.

Desrosières, Alain. 1998. *The Politics of Large Numbers: A History of Statistical Reasoning,* trans. Camille Naish. Boston, MA: Harvard University Press.

————. 2013. 'The History of Statistics as a Genre: Styles of Writing and Social Uses'. *Bulletin de Méthodologie Sociologique* 119:8–23.

Devarajan, Shantayanan. 2013. 'Africa's Statistical Tragedy'. *Review of Income and Wealth* 59:S9–S15.

Dhulipala, Venkat. 2015. *Creating a New Medina: State Power, Islam, and the Quest for Pakistan in Late Colonial North India.* New Delhi: Cambridge University Press.

Diaz-Bone, Rainer and Emmanuel Didier. 2016. 'The Sociology of Quantification – Perspectives on an Emerging Field in the Social Sciences'. *Historical Social Research/ Historische Sozialforschung* 41(2): 7–26.

Diderot, Denis. 2008 [1751]. 'Political arithmetic'. *The Encyclopedia of Diderot & d'Alembert Collaborative Translation Project,* trans. Matthew D'Auria. Ann Arbor, MI: Michigan Publishing, University of Michigan Library. Available at http://hdl.handle.net/2027/spo.did2222.0000.597.

Donaldson, Dave and Adam Storeygard. 2016. 'The View from Above: Applications of Satellite Data in Economics'. *Journal of Economic Perspectives* 30(4): 171–98.

Down to Earth. 2019. 'Language Census: Many Tribal Tongues Now Have Fewer Takers'. 6 July. Available at https://www.downtoearth.org.in/news/environment/language-census-many-tribal-tongues-now-have-fewer-takers-61044.

Duden, Barbara. 2010. 'Population'. In *The Development Dictionary: A Guide to Knowledge as Power,* ed. W. Sachs, 146–57. London: Zed Books.

Eaton, Richard M. 1984. 'Conversion to Christianity among the Nagas, 1876-1971'. *Indian Economic Social History Review* 21(1): 1–44.

Economic Times. 2012. 'Poverty Cutoff Low Due to NSSO Data'. 21 March.

————. 2013a. 'Poverty Line Low, Need to Revisit Methodology, Says Montek Singh Ahluwalia'. 30 July.

————. 2013b. 'NSSO Data Not Necessarily Helps Reach Right Conclusion: Montek Singh Ahluwalia'. 14 February.

————. 2019. 'PM Modi Says Opposition Alliance Will Fail, Clears Air on Jobs Data'. 8 February.

EPW (Economic and Political Weekly). 2011. 'Don't Shoot the Messenger'. 46(28): 7–8.

Economist. 2018. 'How the Big Emerging Economies Climbed the World Bank Business Ranking'. 2 November.

————. 2019. 'What's in a Number: Why Ethiopia Has Postponed Its Census'. 29 March.

Edney, Matthew. 1997. *Mapping an Empire: The Geographical Construction of British India, 1765–1843*. Chicago: The University of Chicago Press.

Elo, Irma T. and Samuel H. Preston. 1994. 'Estimating African-American Mortality from Inaccurate Data'. *Demography* 31(3): 427–58.

Elwin, Verrier. 1959. *A Philosophy for NEFA*. Shillong: North East Frontier Agency.

————. 1961. Nagaland, Shillong: Advisor's Secretariat.

Engineer, Asghar Ali. 2004. 'A Handy Tool for Anti-Minorityism'. *Economic and Political Weekly* 39(39): 4304–5.

Englebert, Pierre, Stacy Tarango and Matthew Carter. 2002. 'Dismemberment and Suffocation: A Contribution to the Debate on African Boundaries'. *Comparative Political Studies* 35:1093–118.

E-pao.net. 2013a. 'Francis Rushes to Delhi, NPO Gears up for Stir'. 25 July. Available at http://e-pao.net/GP.asp?src=28..260713.jul13.

————. 2013b. 'How Manipur Lost Special Category Status?' 8 October. Available at http://e-pao.net/GP.asp?src=16..091013.oct13.

European Commission. 2015. 'Standard Eurobarometer 83: Europeans and Economic Statistic'. Directorate-General for Communication.

Fawehinmi, Feyi. 2018. 'The Story of How Nigeria's Census Figures Became Weaponized'. *Quartz Africa*, 6 March.

Forbes India. 2013. 'India Has More Jobs, but Poorer Jobs'. 13 July.

Gal, Iddo and Irena Ograjenšek. 2017. 'Official Statistics and Statistics Education: Bridging the Gap'. *Journal of Official Statistics* 33(1): 79–100.

Geertz, Clifford. 1973. *The Interpretation of Cultures: Selected Essays*. New York: Basic Books.

Gerwin, Martin and Christoph Bergmann. 2012. 'Geopolitical Relations and Regional Restricturing: The Case of the Kumaon Himalaya, India'. *Erdkunde* 66(2): 91–107.

Ghosh, B. and P. De. 2005. *India Infrastructure Database 2005*. New Delhi: Bookwell.

Ghosh, Subir. 1999. 'Nagalim Has Never Been a Part of India'. *Northeast Daily*. 13 June. Available at http://www.write2kill.in/reports-editorials/northeast/nagalim-has-never-been-a-part-of-india.html.

Gill, Mehar Singh. 2007. 'Politics of Population Census Data in India'. *Economic and Political Weekly* 42(3): 241–9.

Global Times. 2011. 'Backgrounder: China's National Population Censuses'. 28 April.

Goble, Paul. 2015. 'Unpublished Census Provides Rare and Unvarnished Look at Turkmenistan'. *Eurasia Daily Monitor* 12(26).

Göderle, Wolfgang. 2016. 'Administration, Science, and the State: The 1869 Population Census in Austria-Hungary'. *Austrian History Yearbook* 47:61–88.

Gogoi, J. K. 1990. 'Tribal Demography in North-East India: Some Preliminary Observations'. In *Tribal Demography and Development in North East India*, ed. Ashish Bose, Tiplut Nongbri and Nikhlesh Kumar, 85–94. New Delhi: B. R. Publishing Corporationpp.

Gogoi, J. K., H. Goswami and K. C. Borah. 2009. *Project Report on Problems of Border Areas in North East India: Implications for the Thirteenth Finance Commission.* Dibrugarh University, Dibrugarh.

Gohain, Hiren. 2007. 'Violent Borders: Killings in Nagaland-Assam'. *Economic and Political Weekly* 42(32): 3280–3.

Gokhale, B. G. 1961. 'Nagaland: India's Sixteenth State'. *Asian Survey* 1(3): 36–40.

Goldberger, Arthur. 1981. 'Linear Regression after Selection'. *Journal of Econometrics* 15:357–66.

Goldin, David B. 2000. 'Number Wars: A Decade of Census Litigation'. *University of Toledo Law Review* 32:1–17.

Gregg, Paul. 1994. 'Out for the Count: A Social Scientist's Analysis of Unemployment Statistics in the UK'. *Journal of the Royal Statistical Society* 157 (2, series A [Statistics in Society]): 253–70.

Groves, R. M. 2004. *Survey Errors and Survey Costs.* Hoboken, NJ: John Wiley & Sons.

Groves, R. M., Floyd J. F. Jr, M. P. Couper, J. M. Lepkowski, E. Singer and R. Tourangeau. 2004. *Survey Methodology.* Hoboken, NJ: John Wiley & Sons.

Guha, Sumit. 2003. 'The Politics of Identity and Enumeration in India c. 1600–1990'. *Comparative Studies in Society and History* 45(1): 148–67.

Guilmoto, Christophe Z. 1992. 'Chiffrage et déchiffrage: les institutions démographiques dans l'Inde du Sud coloniale' (Counts and accounts demographic institutions in colonial south India). *Annales. Economies, sociétés, civilisations* 47(4–5): 815–40.

Guilmoto, Christophe Z. and S. Irudaya Rajan. 2001. 'Spatial Patterns of Fertility Change in Indian Districts'. *Population and Development Review* 27(4): 713–38.

———. 2002. 'District Level Estimates of Fertility from India's 2001 Census'. *Economic and Political Weekly* 37(7): 665–72.

———. 2013. 'Fertility at the District Level in India: Lessons from the 2011 Census'. *Economic and Political Weekly* 48(23): 59–70.

Gundevia, Y. D. 1975. *War and Peace in Nagaland.* New Delhi: Palit and Palit.

Gyimah-Brempong, K. and T. L. Traynor. 1999. 'Political Instability, Investment, and Economic Growth in Sub Saharan Africa'. *Journal of African Economies* 8(1): 52–86.

Habib, Irfan. 1982. *An Atlas of the Mughal Empire: Political and Economic Maps with Detailed Notes, Bibliography and Index.* New Delhi: Oxford University Press.

Hakim Catherine. 1980. 'Census Reports as Documentary Evidence: The Census Commentaries 1801–1951'. *Sociological Review* 28(3): 551–80.

Hannah, M. G. 2009. 'Calculable Territory and the West German Census Boycott Movements of the 1980s'. *Political Geography* 28:66–75.

Hansen, Morris H., William Hurwitz and William Madow. 1953. *Sample Survey Methods and Theory*, vols. 1 and 2. New York: John Wiley & Sons, Inc.

Haokip, Thongkholal. 2012. 'Is There a Pan-North-East Identity and Solidarity?' *Economic and Political Weekly* 47(36):84–5.

Haralu, L. and M. Chandola (eds.). 2012. *Chalie: A Life Remembered, 1943-1992*. Dimapur: Self-published.

Hazarika, Sanjoy. 1995. *Strangers of the Mist: Tales of War and Peace from India's Northeast*. New Delhi: Penguin Books.

———. 2005. 'Rio Tosses Interim Solution Idea'. *Statesman*. 24 December.

———. 2011. 'Border Battles Turn Deadly across Assam, Northeast'. *Sunday Guardian*, 27 February.

———. 2018. *Strangers No More: New Narratives from India's Northeast*. New Delhi: Aleph Book Company.

He, Kai. 2014. 'Why China Doesn't Want to Be Number One'. *East Asia Forum*. 13 June.

Heine, Klaus and Karsten Mause. 2004. 'Policy Advice as an Investment Problem'. *Kyklos* 57(3): 403–28.

Heine, Klaus and Erich Oltmanns. 2016. 'Towards a Political Economy of Statistics'. *Statistical Journal of the IAOS* 32:201–9.

Herbst, J. 2000. *States and Power in Africa: Comparative Lessons in Authority and Control*. Princeton, NJ: Princeton University Press.

Herod, Andrew. 2011. *Scale*. Oxon: Routledge.

Himanshu. 2009. 'Electoral Politics and the Manipulation of Statistics'. *Economic and Political Weekly* 44(19): 31–5.

Hindu. 1967. 'Nagaland CM Resents Assam's Border Steps'. 20 April.

———. 2012. 'Illegal LPG Connections: Centre Cold to Karnataka Model'. 7 October.

———. 2013. 'We Are Talking More Using Fewer Words'. 3 September.

Hindustan Times. 2013. 'NE Militants Call for I-day Boycott'. 11 August.

———. 2017. 'Rosogolla Originated in West Bengal, Rule GI Authorities, Rejecting Odisha's Claim'. 14 November.

Hokayem, C., C. Bollinger and J. P. Ziliak. 2015. 'The Role of CPS Nonresponse in the Measurement of Poverty'. *Journal of the American Statistical Association* 110(511): 935–45.

Holt, D. Tim. 2008. 'Official Statistics, Public Policy and Public Trust'. *Journal of the Royal Statistical Society A* 171(2): 323–46.

Horam, M. 1988. *Naga Insurgency: The Last Thirty Years*. New Delhi: Cosmo Publications.

Horowitz, Donald L. 2000. *Ethnic Groups in Conflict*. Second edition. Berkeley, CA: University of California Press.

Husain, M. 1945. *Census of India 1941, Vol XXI, Part I-Report*. Hyderabad: Government Central Press.

IHDS (India Human Development Survey). 2011. *India Human Development Survey – II*. February. Available at https://www.ihds.umd.edu/sites/ihds.umd.edu/files/BriefII.pdf.

Indian Express. 1999. 'SC, ST Report Reveals Census Bungling'. 12 January.

———. 2011. 'Census: Nagaland Records Negative Population Growth'. 1 April.

———. 2012. 'Aadhar Helps Weed Out Fake Ration Cards in Andhra'. 18 December.

———. 2013. 'Ex-CM Rane Faked Papers to Push for Goa Statehood: Former Secretary'. 20 December.

———. 2014. 'UPA Panel Set Tough Norms for Tribal Land, NDA Sits On Report'. 9 October.

———. 2016. 'Simply Put: Seven New Districts That Set Manipur Ablaze'. 20 December.

Indiastat. n.d. 'Tables on Gross School Enrolment (Primary and Secondary standards)'. Accessed on 23 February 2012. Available at www.indiastat.com.

Iralu, Kaka D. 2009. *The Naga Saga: A Historical Account of the 62 Years Indo-Naga War and the Story of Those Who Were Never Allowed to Tell It.* Third edition. Kohima: Kaka D. Iralu.

———. 2018. 'Is Naga Integration a Future Naga Dream or a Present Reality?' *ME.* 22 July.

Irudaya Rajan, S. and K. S. James. 2008. 'Third National Family Health Survey in India: Issues, Problems and Prospects'. *Economic and Political Weekly* 43(48): 33–8.

James, K. S. and S. Irudaya Rajan. 2004. 'Respondents and Quality of Survey Data'. *Economic and Political Weekly* 39(7): 659–63.

Jamir, Amongla N. 2009. 'Nagaland: Behind the Curtain'. *Economic and Political Weekly* 44(39): 170–2.

Jamir, M. Sashi. 2019. 'Re-Imagining the Peace Process'. January 17.

Jamwal, N. S. 2004. 'Border Management: Dilemma of Guarding the India-Bangladesh Border'. *Strategic Analysis* 28(1): 5–36.

Janus, Thorsten. 2013 'The Political Economy of Fertility'. *Public Choice* 155(3–4): 493–505.

Jerven, Morten. 2013. *Poor Numbers: How We Are Misled by African Development Statistics and What to Do about It.* Ithaca NY: Cornell University Press.

Jones, Kenneth W. 1981. 'Religious Identity and the Indian Census'. In *The Census in British India: New Perspectives,* ed. N. Gerald Barrier, 73–101. New Delhi: Manohar Publications.

Jones, Reece. 2009a. 'Categories, Borders and Boundaries'. *Progress in Human Geography* 33(2): 174–89.

———. 2009b. 'Sovereignty and Statelessness in the Border Enclaves of India and Bangladesh'. *Political Geography* 28:373–81.

———. 2010. 'The Spatiality of Boundaries'. *Progress in Human Geography* 34(2): 263–7.

Kalpagam, U. 2014. *Rule by Numbers: Governmentality in Colonial India.* New Delhi: Orient BlackSwan.

Kansakar, Vidya Bir Singh. 1977. *Population Censuses of Nepal and the Problems of Data Analysis.* Centre for Economic Development and Administration, Tribhuvan University.

Kanungo, Alok Kumar. 2014. 'Who Owns the Ethno-cultural Past: Cultural Objects of the Nagas in Far Off Museums'. In *50 Years after Daojali-Hading: Emerging Perspectives in the Archaeology of Northeast India Essays in Honour of Tarun Chandra Sharma*, ed. T. Jamir and M. Hazarika, 488–502. New Delhi: Research India Press.

Karmakar, Rahul. 2010. 'Census Weapon for Battle in NE'. *Hindustan Times*. 22 April.

Kashyap, Samudra Gupta. 2015. 'Towards the Govt-Naga Peace Accord: Everything You Need to Know'. *Indian Express*. 4 August.

Kasturi, Kannan. 2015. 'Comparing Census and NSS Data on Employment and Unemployment'. *Economic and Political Weekly* 50(22): 16-19.

Kenett, R. S. and G. Shmueli. 2014. 'On Information Quality'. *Journal of Royal Statistical Society A* 177(1): 3–38.

Kertzer, David I. and Dominique Arel (eds.). 2002a. *Census and Identity: The Politics of Race, Ethnicity, and Language in National Censuses*. Cambridge: Cambridge University Press.

———. 2002b. 'Censuses, Identity Formation, and the Struggle for Political Power'. In *Census and Identity: The Politics of Race, Ethnicity, and Language in National Censuses*, ed. David I. Kertzer and Dominique Arel, 1–42. Cambridge: Cambridge University Press.

KET (Kohima Educational Trust). 2015. *Key Words: A Glossary of Sixteen Nagaland Languages*. Kohima.

Keynes, J. M. 1927. 'The British Balance of Trade, 1925–27'. *Economic Journal* 37(148): 551–65.

Khalidi Omar. 2006. *Muslims in Indian Economy*, Gurgaon: Three Essays Collective.

Khan, Akhtar Hassan. 1998. '1998 Census: The Results and Implications'. *The Pakistan Development Review* 37(4): 481–89.

Khemani, Stuti. 2007. 'Does Delegation of Fiscal Policy to an Independent Agency Make a Difference? Evidence from Intergovernmental Transfers in India'. *Journal of Development Economics* 82(2): 464–84.

Khutso, Riku. 2018. 'Shifting Democratic Experiences of Nagas'. In *Democracy in Nagaland: Tribes, Traditions, Tensions*, ed. Jelle J. P. Wouters and Zhoto Tunyi, 143–56. Kohima: The Highlander Books.

Kiani, Khaleeq. 2019. 'Senate Panel Objects to Distribution of Pool Resources on Population Basis'. *Dawn*, 08 February.

Kikon, Dolly. 2019. *Living with Oil & Coal: Resource Politics and Militarization in Northeast India*. Seattle, WA: University of Washington Press.

Kish, Leslie. 1965. *Survey Sampling*. New York: John Wiley and Sons.

Kish, Leslie and Vijay Verma. 1986. 'Complete Censuses and Surveys'. *Journal of Official Statistics* 2(4): 381–95.

Koijam, Radhabinod. 2001. 'Naga Ceasefire and Manipur'. *Hindu*. 13 July.

Krätke, Florian and Bruce Byiers. 2014. 'The Political Economy of Official Statistics: Implications for the Data Revolution in sub-Saharan Africa'. PARIS21 Partnership in Statistics for Development in the 21st Century, Discussion Paper No. 5.

Krishna, Sankaran. 1994. 'Cartographic Anxiety: Mapping the Body Politic in India'. *Alternatives: Global, Local, Political* 19(4): 507–21.

Krishnaji, N. 2012. 'Abolish the Poverty Line'. *Economic and Political Weekly* 47(15): 10–11.

Kruskal, William and Frederick Mosteller. 1979. 'Representative Sampling, III: The Current Statistical Literature'. *International Statistical Review* 47(3): 245–65.

Kulkarni, Sharad. 1991. 'Distortion of Census Data on Scheduled Tribes'. *Economic and Political Weekly* 26(5): 205–8.

Kulkarni, Sumati. 2004. 'Inputs and Process: An Inside View'. *Economic and Political Weekly* 39(7): 652–8.

Kumar, Hemanshu and Rohini Somanathan. 2009. 'Mapping Indian Districts across Census Years, 1971–2001'. *Economic and Political Weekly* 44(41): 69–88.

Kumar, Pradeep. 2000. 'Demand for New States: Cultural Identity Loses Ground to Urge for Development'. *Economic and Political Weekly* 35(35–6): 3078–82.

Kumar, Sanjay and N. K. Sharma. 2006. 'Riddle of Population Growth Deceleration in Andhra Pradesh during 1991-2001'. *Economic and Political Weekly* 41(42): 4507–12.

Kumar, Vikas. 2003. 'Anatomy of Congress Defeat in Tripura'. *Mainstream* 41(16): 25–6.

Kumar Vikas. 2013. 'India's Missed Opportunity to Review Federal Redistribution'. *East Asia Forum*. 1 November.

———. 2014a. 'Reviving Naga peace process'. *Deccan Herald*. 12 December.

———. 2014b. 'First Nagamese Daily Completes a Year'. The Hoot. 3 December.

———. 2015a. 'The Dumbing Down of Data'. The Hoot. 16 September.

———. 2015b. 'Use of Statistics in Politics not New in India'. *Deccan Herald*. 5 March.

———. 2015c. 'Dimapur Lynching: A Travesty of Reporting'. The Hoot. 6 May.

———. 2015d. 'Frontier Hope for the Doubly Marginalised'. *Deccan Herald*. 8 January.

———. 2015e. 'The Bangladeshi Bugbear'. *Bangalore Mirror*. 17 March.

———. 2015f. 'Lynching Highlights Nagas, Immigrants Acrimony'. *Deccan Herald*. 9 March.

———. 2015g. 'Naga Peace Talks: Need to Guard Interests of Diverse Sections'. *Deccan Herald*. 13 February.

———. 2015h. 'Govt–NSCN Peace Pact: Another Accord of Discord?' *Deccan Herald*. 23 September.

———. 2015i. 'Dual Role of Sumi Newspapers'. The Hoot. 19 January.

———. 2016a. 'Wooing Tribes in Assam: Will It Help BJP?'. *Deccan Herald*. 22 March.

———. 2016b. 'Assam–Nagaland: Artificial Boundaries and Real Problems'. *Deccan Herald*. 26 February.

———. 2017a. 'Naga Papers: Lots of Comment, Little Reporting'. The Hoot. 14 June.

———. 2017b. 'Covering Nagaland's Anti-women's Reservation Agitation'. The Hoot. 14 June.

———. 2017c. 'Demonetisation in Numbers—How Statistics Were Used'. The Hoot. 12 November.

———. 2017d. 'Covering NCRB Data: How Newspapers Fared'. The Hoot. 6 December.

———. 2018a. 'Naga Media, the Elections and "Solutions"'. The Hoot. 18 March.

―――. 2018b. 'Waging Identity Wars in the Nagaland Press'. The Hoot. 8 March.

―――. 2018c. 'Swarajya's Slander in Nagaland'. The Hoot. 9 April.

―――. 2018d. 'India's Deficient Federal Redistribution Debate'. *East Asia Forum*. 11 October.

―――. 2019. 'The Limitations of India's Census Legislation'. Working Paper No. 13. Azim Premji University.

Kundu, A. and D. Kundu. 2011. 'The Census and the "Development" Myth'. *Business Standard*. 8 April.

Laakso, M. and R. Taagepera. 1979. 'Effective Number of Parties: A Measure with Application to West Europe'. *Comparative Political Studies* 12: 3–27.

Lahiri, D. B. 1967. 'Regional Statistics and the Indian National Sample Survey'. *Sankhyā: The Indian Journal of Statistics* 29(3–4, Series B): 213–34.

Laithangbam, I. 2004. 'Naga Tribal Council Plans Blockade'. *Hindu*. 13 November.

Lalasz, Robert. 2006. 'In the News: The Nigerian Census'. Population Reference Bureau.

League of Nations. 1936. 'Convention on Rights and Duties of States Adopted by the Seventh International Conference of American States. Signed at Montevideo, December 26th, 1933'. *Treaty Series, Treaties and International Engagements Registered with the Secretariat of the League of Nations*. 165(3801–24): 19–42.

Legg, S. 2005. 'Foucault's Population Geographies: Classifications, Biopolitics, and Governmental Spaces'. *Population, Space and Place* 11:137–56.

―――. 2009. 'Of Scales, Networks and Assemblages: The League of Nations Apparatus and the Scalar Sovereignty of the Government of India'. *Transactions of the Institute of British Geographers NS* 34:234–53.

―――. 2016. 'Dyarchy: Democracy, Autocracy and the Scalar Sovereignty of Interwar India'. *Comparative Studies in South Asia, Africa and the Middle East* 36(1): 44–65.

Lepenies, P. 2016. *The Power of a Single Number – A Political History of GDP*. New York: Columbia University Press.

Lessler, J. T. and W. D. Kalsbeek. 1992. *Nonsampling Error in Surveys*. John Wiley and Sons

Levitas, Ruth and Will Guy (eds.). 1996. *Interpreting Official Statistics*. London: Routledge.

Lintner, Bertil. 2012. *Great Game East: India, China and the Struggle for Asia's Most Volatile Frontier*. Noida: HarperCollins.

Lipton, M. 1972. 'The South African Census and the Bantustan Policy'. *The World Today* 28(6): 257–71.

Lokniti. 2008. 'A Report on Nagaland Assembly Election 2008'. New Delhi: Centre for the Study of Developing Societies.

Lohe, Z. 2017. 'What a Frenzied Clash of Interest!' *Eastern Mirror*. 15 February.

―――. 2018. 'Are Nagas Really "Honest People"?' *ME*. 13 December.

Longkumer, Arkotong. 2018. 'Along Kingdom's Highway: The Proliferation of Christianity, Education, and Print amongst the Nagas in Northeast India'. *Contemporary South Asia* 27(2): 160–78.

Lujan, Carol. 1990. 'As Simple as One, Two, Three: Census Underenumeration among the American Indians and Alaska Natives'. Undercount Behavioral Research Group Staff Working Paper No. 2.

Luthra, P. N. 1974. 'Nagaland: From a District to a State'. Director of Information and Public Relations, Arunachal Pradesh; Shillong.

Lwin, Saw Min. 2003. 'The General Situation of Migrant Workers from Burma'. *The Human Rights Solidarity* 13:4–5.

Maheshwari, S. R. 1996. *The Census Administration Under the Raj and After*. New Delhi: Concept Publishing Company.

Maier, Mark and Jennifer Imazeki. 2013. *The Data Game: Controversies in Social Science Statistics*. New York: M. E. Sharpe.

Majumder, A., R. Ray and K. Sinha. 2012. 'Calculating Rural–Urban Food Price Differentials from Unit Values in Household Expenditure Surveys: A Comparison with Existing Methods and a New Procedure'. *American Journal of Agricultural Economics* 94(5): 1218–35.

Mari Bhat, P. N. 1995. 'On the Quality of Birth History Data Collected in National Family Health Survey, 1992–93'. *Demography India* 24(1): 245–58.

Mari Bhat, P. N. and Francis Zavier. 1999. 'Findings of National Family Health Survey: Regional Analysis'. *Economic and Political Weekly* 34(42–3): 3008–17, 3019–32.

Matthiesen, Toby. 2015. *The Other Saudis: Shiism, Dissent and Sectarianism*. New York: Cambridge University Press.

Mawon, Somingam. 'Rejoinder to "Can People of outside Decide for the State of Nagaland?" Part 2'. *ME*. 19 April.

McDuie-Ra, Duncan. 2012. *Northeast Migrants in Delhi: Race, Refuge and Retail*. Amsterdam: Amsterdam University Press.

McWorter, Gerald and Abdul Alkalimat. 1980. 'Racism and the Numbers Game: Black People and the 1980 Census'. *The Black Scholar* 11(4): 61–71. (Also, correction in 11(6)).

ME (*Morung Express*). 2011. 'Yimchunger Women Organization Says No to Saramati Region'. 27 February.

———. 2012. 'Dimapur Becoming a Jihadi Hub'. 4 June.

———. 2013a. 'State Govt Says "No Decision on Recognition of Mao Tribe"'. 2 May.

———. 2013b. 'Foothill Road Still in the Pipeline'. 1 December.

———. 2013c. 'Mukalimi Designated Camp Overrun'. 31 December.

———. 2013d. 'AIR Kohima Yearlong Golden Jubilee Celebration'. 24 May.

———. 2013e. 'Nagaland's High Stakes over Census, E-roll'. 30 January.

———. 2014. 'New Parl Secy Assures "Initiative and Direction"'. 31 May.

———. 2015. 'NSCN (IM) on SC Jamir's Article'. 12 January.

———. 2016. 'The Native & the Settler'. 26 September.

———. 2017a. 'Nagaland's Future Not for Sale'. 8 June.

———. 2017b. 'Naga Struggle Is Not a Failure: Rio'. 8 November.

———. 2017c. 'Imposition of Aadhaar a Threat to Naga Customary Law and Identity'. 1 November.

——. 2017d. 'ACAUT Demands Deletion of Four Lakh Bogus Voters'. 11 August.

——. 2017e. 'CPO Hails Delimitation Order by Gauhati HC'. 27 October.

——. 2017f. 'Chümoukedima' Reminds CVC'. 2 November.

——. 2018a. 'NSCN (IM) Refutes Assam Rifles Encounter Claim at Longding District'. 14 July.

——. 2018b. 'Be Cautious with Tangible Solutions'. 30 April.

——. 2018c. 'NTC Advises Govt on Revenue, Land Rights & Citizenship'. 29 June.

——. 2018d. 'Congress Demands Settlement of Border Dispute with Myanmar'. 9 July.

——. 2018e. 'JLF Reiterates Call for Early Naga Solution'. 20 December.

——. 2018f. 'Manipur BJP Submits Memorandum to Union Home Minister Regarding Framework Agreement'. 17 July.

——. 2018g. 'Mizoram Receives Rs 15.18 Crore for Strengthening State Statistical System'. 18 July.

——. 2018h. 'A Wakeup Call'. 6 August.

——. 2018i. 'From Upgradation to Shutdown'. 25 July.

——. 2018j. 'Now Dimasas Want Dimapur in Autonomous State, Report'. 18 July.

——. 2018k. 'Apex Zeliangrong Organizations Respond to NSCN (IM)'. 1 August.

——. 2018l. '120 Unrecognised Villages in Nagaland'. 12 August.

——. 2018m. 'Bring Dimapur under ILP Zone: Naga Hoho'. 9 August.

——. 2018n. 'Doyang Landowners Condemn Attempt by Assam Police to Arrest Head of DHEP, NEEPCO'. 13 August.

——. 2018o. 'Rs 60 Cr LADP Fund Released during 2017–18'. 18 July.

——. 2018p. 'Nagaland: LSU Dismayed by Government Handling of ILP Issue'. 21 June.

——. 2018q. 'Continue to Carry the Torch of Truth and Justice'. 13 August.

——. 2018r. 'Nagas Are Living in a Human Time Bomb'. 25 August.

——. 2018s. 'Clarion Call for Re-unification of Mizo Tribes'. 6 July.

——. 2018t. Demand for Aboi District Stepped Up'. 11 January.

——. 2018u. 'Demand for Tobu District Purely for Development & Admin Convenience'. 15 January.

——. 2018v. 'BDDC Renews Demand for Bhandari District Creation'. 13 June.

——. 2018w. 'Pughoboto Dist Demand Rally Held'. 31 January.

——. 2018x. 'BEFR 1873: Time to Alter ILP's Ambit'. 26 August.

——. 2018y. 'TCLPeF Condemns Attempt to Delete "Any Naga" from ST certificate'. 13 September.

——. 2018z. 'Nagaland: Proceedings from First Day of Second Session of 13th NLA'. 19 September.

——. 2018aa. 'Eight Ongoing EAC Offices Construction in Nagaland'. 20 September.

——. 2018ab. 'Concept for the 100th Year of Naga Club – Celebrating the Legacy'. 19 September.

——. 2018ac. 'Nagaland: 66,894 ILPs Issued in All Districts since 2015'. 18 September.

————. 2018ad. 'Nagaland: JCPI Submits Points of Concern to the State Govt on "Illegal Immigration" Issue'. 5 October.

————. 2018ae. 'WCCZLI Objects to Recognition of Khehoi Village'. 14 October.

————. 2018af. 'Yung Aung Led NSCN (K) Vows to Uphold Principle of Naga Sovereignty'. 20 October.

————. 2018ag. 'NSCN (IM) Derecognizes Apex Zeliangrong Organisations'. 31 July.

————. 2018ah. 'Time for GoI to Prove Its Political Will: UNC'. 14 November.

————. 2018ai. 'It Is "Khiamniungan": Get the Spelling Right, Says KSUK'. 10 December.

————. 2019a. 'Chesezu Village Extend Apology to Sumi Village'. 13 January.

————. 2019b. 'Back to Village: Nagaland Mulls Measures to Curb Rural to Urban Migration'. 2 July.

————. 2019c. 'ILP Will Be Made Applicable to the Entire State including Dimapur: Nagaland Governor'. 21 February.

————. 2019d. 'Recognize Our Customary Tenure and Rights: Nagas to Myanmar Govt'. 28 February.

————. 2019e. 'Border Peace Meeting Held at Saringyim Village'. 30 April.

————. 2019f. 'NSCN (K), Myanmar Army Urged to Exercise Restraint'. 19 May.

————. 2019g. 'ABAM Pledges Rs 36, 56, 282 Lakh to Foothill Road'. 28 June.

————. 2019h. '64% Aadhaar-Ration Cards Linkage in Nagaland'. 30 June.

————. 2019i. 'Nagaland Govt Constitutes Commission to Examine Implementation of RIIN'. 28 July.

————. 2019j. 'Is It Mistaken to Tag Nagaland Earthquake Prone?' 15 September.

————. 2019k. 'Half of State's Population Projected to Live in Urban Areas in Next 20 Years'. 3 October.

————. 2019l. 'The Other Side of Development Expenditure'. 13 March.

————. 2019m. 'Nagaland Govt Expands ILP to Cover Dimapur District'. 11 December.

Means, G. P. 1971. 'Cease-Fire Politics in Nagaland'. *Asian Survey* 11(10): 1005–28.

Meghalaya Times. 2010. 'Nagaland Census Begins, Hoho Urges People to be Honest'. 2 June.

Merry, T. L. 2015. 'Proper Naming of Road in Duncan Bosti'. *Nagaland Post*. 4 July.

Meyer, B. D., W. K. C. Mok and J. X. Sullivan. 2015. 'Household Surveys in Crisis'. *Journal of Economic Perspectives* 29(4): 199–226.

Michalski, T. and G. Stoltz. 2013. 'Do Countries Falsify Economic Data Strategically? Some Evidence That They Do'. *Review of Economics and Statistics* 95(2): 591–616.

Minhas, B S. 1988. 'Validation of Large Scale Sample Survey Data Case of NSS Estimates of Household Consumption Expenditure'. *Sankhya: The Indian Journal of Statistics* 50(3, Series B): 279–326.

Minhas, B. S., L. R. Jain, S. M. Kansal and M. R. Saluja. 1987. 'On the Choice of Appropriate Consumer Price Indices and Data Sets for Estimating the Incidence of Poverty in India'. *Indian Economic Review* 22(1): 19–49.

Mint. 2012. 'Government to Discontinue National Family Health Survey'. 11 April.

Mishra, S. N. 1999. 'The Status of Livestock Statistics in India'. *Journal of Indian Society of Agricultural Statistics* 52(3): 273–89.

Misra, Sangita and A. K. Suresh. 2014. 'Estimating Employment Elasticity of Growth for the Indian Economy', Working Paper Series No. 06. Reserve Bank of India.

Misra, Udayon. 1987. 'Nagaland Elections'. *Economic and Political Weekly* 22(51): 2193–5.

———. 2012. *The Periphery Strikes Back: Challenges to the Nation-State in Assam and Nagaland*. Second edition. Shimla: IIAS.

Mitra, Asok. 1994. 'Census 1961: New Pathways'. *Economic and Political Weekly* 29(51–2): 3207–21.

Mohanty, S. P. 1996. 'Significance of Census Data in the Context of Contemporary Indian Society'. In *Census as Social Document*, ed. S. P. Mohanty and A. R. Momin, 162–7. Jaipur: Rawat Publications.

Mohanty, S. P. and A. R. Momin. 1996 (eds.). *Census as Social Document*. Jaipur: Rawat Publications.

Monmonier, Mark. 1991. *How to Lie with Maps*. Chicago: University of Chicago Press.

Morgenstern, Oskar. 1973. *On the Accuracy of Economic Observations*. Princeton, NJ: Princeton University Press.

Morland, Paul. 2018. *Demographic Engineering: Population Strategies in Ethnic Conflict*. Oxon: Routledge.

Murry, Ezamo. 2014. 'KYONG or LOTHA'. *ME*. 29 November.

Nag, Sajal. 2002. *Contesting Marginality: Ethnicity, Insurgency and Sub-nationalism in North-East India*. New Delhi: Manohar Publishers and Distributors.

———. 2014. 'In Search of the Blue Bird: Auditing Peace Negotiations in Nagaland'. Occasional paper, History and Society New Series No. 60. Nehru Memorial Museum and Library.

Naga, J. N. 2015. 'What Have We Become?' *ME*. 11 February.

Nagaland Page. 2018a. 'Nagaland Assembly Passes Resolution on Naga Integration for 6th Time'. 21 September.

———. 2018b. 'NFHRCC Welcomes ZPO into Its Fold'. 20 September.

———. 2018c. 'Statement by Concerned Tribal Leaderships on Naga Hoho'. 6 December.

Nagaland Post. 2009. 'Nagaland's Inflated Census'. 20 September.

———. 2011. 'Spat over Shamator Census Issue'. 5 March.

———. 2012a. 'Naga Woman Gang Raped; 4 Arrested'. 8 February.

———. 2012b. 'Illegal Migrants Issue a Concern for Nagas: Western Sumi Kukami Hoho (WSKH)'. 5 June.

———. 2013. 'Abnormal Electorate to Population Ratio in Dimapur'. 16 November.

———. 2014a. 'Influx of Illegal Migrants, a Security Problem: Patton'. 23 June.

———. 2014b. 'LLOMBZA Reiterates Stand On Oil-Company'. 1 March.

———. 2014c. '1 Injured in Assam Police Firing'. 23 October.

———. 2016. 'Jaitley Clarifies Changes in Funding Pattern for NE'. 27 November.

———. 2017a. 'Manipur Govt Seeks Centre's Help to Settle Border Dispute with Nagaland'. 3 September.

———. 2017b. 'Nagaland among 7 States Oppose AIJS'. 23 April.

———. 2017c. 'ACAUT Scanner on Bogus Voters'. 7 October.

———. 2017d. 'Civic Body Polls: For Defying Appeal, Senden Excommunicates Individuals for 30 Years'. 21 January.

———. 2018. 'KVC Reacts to TVAC Statement'. 12 December.

———. 2019. 'Transfer of RB Thong "Ambiguous and Bias": RH'. 25 January.

Nagaraj, R. 2009. 'Is Services Sector Output Overestimated? An Inquiry'. *Economic and Political Weekly* 44(5): 40–5.

———. 2015. 'Seeds of Doubt on New GDP Numbers Private Corporate Sector Overestimated?' *Economic and Political Weekly* 50(13): 14–17.

Narasimhan, R. L., Robert D. Retherford, Vinod Mishra, Fred Arnold and T. K. Roy. 1997. *Comparison of Fertility Estimates from India's Sample Registration System and National Family Health Survey.* NFHS Subject Reports Number 4. Mumbai: IIPS and Honolulu: East-West Center Program on Population.

Nath, V. 1991. '1991 Population Census: Some Facts and Policy Issues'. *Economic and Political Weekly* 26(37): 2148–52.

NENA (North East News Agency). 2007. 'Political Parties for Maintenance of Assembly Status Quo'. 3:33. Available at http://www.nenanews.com/ANE%20Aug%2016-31,%2007/mj1.htm.

NDTV. 2018. 'In Rajasthan's Tribal Belt, a Party from Gujarat Challenging BJP, Others'. 6 December.

Ngaihte, S. Thianlalmuan. 2013. 'The Reality of North-East as an Entity'. *Economic and Political Weekly* 48(50): 113–15.

Nibedon, Nirmal. 1978. *Nagaland: The Night of the Guerrillas.* New Delhi: Lancers Publishers.

Ninan, T. N. 2018. 'Political GDP'. *Business Standard.* 1 December.

Nongkynrih, A. K. 2010. 'Scheduled Tribes and the Census: A Sociological Inquiry'. *Economic and Political Weekly* 45(19): 43–7.

Nuh, V. K. 2002. *Nagaland Church and Politics.* Kohima: V. K. Nuh & Bros.

———. 2006. *165 Years History of Naga Baptist Churches.* Kohima: Research Department, Council of Naga Baptist Churches.

Nunthara, C. 1981. 'Grouping of Villages in Mizoram: Its Social and Economic Impact'. *Economic and Political Weekly* 16(1237): 1239–40.

OECD (Organisation for Economic Co-operation and Development). 2017. *Development Co-operation Report 2017: Data for Development.* Paris. Available at http://dx.doi.org/10.1787/dcr-2017-en.

Oinam, Bhagat. 2003. 'Patterns of Ethnic Conflict in the North-East: A Study on Manipur'. *Economic and Political Weekly* 38(21): 2031–7.

Okolo, Abraham. 1999. 'The Nigerian Census: Problems and Prospects'. *The American Statistician* 53(4): 321–5.

Omkarnath, G. 2012. *Economics: A Primer for India.* New Delhi: Orient Blackswan.

Outlook. 2013. 'WB Govt Contests NCRB Report on Crime Against Women'. 12 June.

Painter, Joe. 2008. 'Cartographic Anxiety and the Search for Regionality'. *Environment and Planning A* 40:342–61.

Palat, M. K. 2015. 'Selected Works of Jawaharlal Nehru, Second Series Volume Sixty Two (1st August–31 August 1960)'. Jawaharlal Nehru Memorial Fund, New Delhi.

Panandiker, V. A. Pai and P. K. Umashankar. 1994. 'Fertility Control and Politics in India'. *Population and Development Review* 20:89–104.

PARIS21. 2017. *Partner Report on Support to Statistics: PRESS 2017*. Available at www.paris21.org/sites/default/files/2017-10/PRESS2017_web2.pdf.

Pattanayak, D. P. 2001. 'Tribal Languages in Education'. In *Language Education in Multilingual India*, ed. C. J. Daswani, 48–57. New Delhi: UNESCO.

Peabody, Norbert. 2001. 'Cents, Sense, Census: Human Inventories in Late Pre-colonial and Early Colonial India'. *Comparative Studies in Society and History* 43(4): 819–50.

PFI-PRB. 2007. 'The Future Population of India: A Long-Range Demographic View'. Population Foundation of India, New Delhi; and Population Reference Bureau, Washington, DC.

Phanjoubam, Pradip. 2016. *The Northeast Question: Conflicts and Frontiers*. Oxon: Routledge.

Philipsen, D. 2015. *The Little Big Number: How GDP Came to Rule the World and What to Do about It*. Princeton, NJ: Princeton University Press.

Phom, B. Bauong. 2001. 'Phom'. In *Language Education in Nagaland: Sociolinguistic Dimensions*, ed. Rajesh Sachdeva, 149–55. New Delhi: Regency Publications.

Pioneer. 2016. 'Odisha Hit by Rising Inter-state Border Disputes'. 7 July.

PLSI (People's Linguistic Survey of India). 2016. *The Languages of Nagaland People Linguistic Survey of India: Volume 21, Part 2 (New edition)*. Hyderabad: Orient BlackSwan.

Porter, Theodore M. 1995. *Trust in Numbers: The Pursuit of Objectivity in Science and Public Life*. Princeton, NJ: Princeton University Press.

Pou, John Basho. 2007. '2001 Census and the Black Day'. E-pao.net. 24 January.

Prabhakara, M. S. 2012. *Looking Back into the Future: Identity & Insurgency in Northeast India*. New Delhi: Routledge.

Preston, S. H., P. Heuveline and M. Guillot. 2001. *Demography: Measuring and Modeling Population Processes*. Oxford: Blackwell Publishing.

Prewitt, K. 2003. 'Politics and Science in Census Taking'. Russell Sage Foundation, New York; and Population Reference Bureau, Washington, DC.

———. 2010. 'The U.S. Decennial Census: Politics and Political Science'. *Annual Review of Political Science* 13:237–54.

Rao, C. R. 1973. 'Prasantha Chandra Mahalanobis, 1893-1972'. *Biographical Memoirs of Fellows of the Royal Society* 19:454–92.

———. 1999. *Statistics and Truth: Putting Chance to Work*. Singapore: World Scientific.

Rao, T. J. 2010. 'Official Statistics in India: The Past and the Present'. *Journal of Official Statistics* 26(2): 215–31.

Ravallion, Martin. 2016. *The Economics of Poverty: History, Measurement, and Policy.* New York: Oxford University Press.

Rajaraman, I. 2008. 'The Political Economy of the Indian Fiscal Federation'. *India Policy Forum 2007-08*, 1–51.

Rao, M. Govinda and N. Singh. 2001. 'The Political Economy of Center-State Fiscal Transfers in India', Working Paper No. 107. Stanford Center for International Development.

Raza, Moonis and Aijazuddin Ahmad. 1990. *An Atlas of Tribal India: With Computed Tables of District-Level Data and Its Geographical Interpretation.* New Delhi: Concept Publishing Company.

Robinson, J. Gregory, Bashir Ahmed, Prithwis Das Gupta and Karen A. Woodrow. 1993. 'Estimation of Population Coverage in the 1990 United States Census Based on Demographic Analysis'. *Journal of the American Statistical Association* 88(423): 1061–71.

Rose, Nikolas. 1991. 'Governing by Numbers: Figuring Out Democracy'. *Accounting Organizations and Society* 16(7): 673–92.

Roy Burman, B. K. 1992. *Beyond Mandal and After: Backward Classes in Perspective.* New Delhi: Mittal Publiations.

———. 1998. 'Backward Classes and the Census: Putting the Record Straight'. *Economic and Political Weekly* 33(50): 3178–9.

———. 2009. 'Adivasi: A Contentious Term to Denote Tribes as Indigenous Peoples of India'. *Manistream* 47:32.

Sachdeva, Rajesh (ed.). 2001. *Language Education in Nagaland: Sociolinguistic Dimensions.* Regency Publications: New Delhi.

Sahoo, Sarbeswar. 2018. *Pentecostalism and Politics of Conversion in India.* New Delhi: Cambridge University Press.

Saluja, M. R. 2017. *Measuring India: The Nation's Statistical System.* New Delhi: Oxford University Press.

Sandefur, Justin and Amanda Glassman. 2015. 'The Political Economy of Bad Data: Evidence from African Survey and Administrative Statistics'. *The Journal of Development Studies* 51(2): 116–32.

Sangai Express. 2007a. 'Attack on Tangkhul Community at Nagaland Mob Torch Over 30 Houses at Wungram Colony, Dimapur' 23 April.

———. 2007b. 'SC Snubs Govt on Delimitation Issue'. 15 October.

———. 2018. 'Naga Accord Nearly Final: Will It Be Acceptable to All?' 28 April.

Santschi, Martina. 2008. 'Counting "New Sudan"'. *African Affairs* 107(429): 631–40.

Sanyu, Visier. 1996. *A History of Nagas and Nagaland: Dynamics of Oral Tradition in Village Formation.* New Delhi: Commonwealth Publishers.

SATP (South Asia Terrorism Portal). n.d.1. 'Insurgency Related Killings, 1992-2018'. Available at http://old.satp.org/satporgtp/countries/india/states/nagaland/data_sheets/insurgency_related_killings.htm.

———. n.d.2. 'Terrorist/Insurgent Groups – Nagaland'. Available at http://old.satp.org/satporgtp/countries/india/states/nagaland/terrorist_outfits/index.html.

Saxena, Sadhna. 1997. 'Language and the Nationality Question'. *Economic and Political Weekly* 32(6): 268–72.

Schwartzberg, Joseph E. 1981. 'Sources and Types of Error'. In *The Census in British India: New Perspectives*, edited by N. Gerald Barrier, 41–59. New Delhi: Manohar Publications.

Schweber, Libby. 2001. 'Manipulation and Population Statistics in Nineteenth-Century France and England'. *Social Research* 68(2): 547–82.

Sen, Amartya. 2006. 'What is the Role of Legal and Judicial Reform in the Development Process?' *World Bank Legal Review: Law, Equity, and Development* 2:33–50.

Sentinel. 2012. 'Nagaland Parliamentary Secretary Visits Spot of Murder'. 29 March.

Serajuddin, Umar, Hiroki Uematsu, Christina Wieser, Nobuo Yoshida and Andrew L. Dabalen. 2015. 'Data Deprivation: Another Deprivation to End'. Policy Research Working Paper 7252. Washington, DC: World Bank Group.

Serra, Gerardo. 2014. 'An Uneven Statistical Topography: The Political Economy of Household Budget Surveys in Late Colonial Ghana, 1951–1957'. *Canadian Journal of Development Studies* 35(1): 9–27.

Shahoto, Y. 2001. 'Yimchungrü'. In *Language Education in Nagaland: Sociolinguistic Dimensions,* ed. Rajesh Sachdeva, 175–81. New Delhi: Regency Publications.

Sharma, H. N. and B. K. Kar. 1997. 'Pattern of Population Growth in North-East India'. In *Demographic Transition: The Third World Scenario*, ed. Aijazuddin Ahmad, Daniel Noin and H. N. Sharma, 73–93. Jaipur: Rawat Publications.

Sherani, Sakib. 2016. 'The Data Controversy'. *Dawn.* 24 June.

Shetty, S. L. 2012. 'Dealing with a Deteriorating Statistical Base'. *Economic and Political Weekly* 47(18): 41–4.

Shewly, H. J. 2013 'Abandoned Spaces and Bare Life in the Enclaves of the India-Bangladesh Border'. *Political Geography* 32:23–31.

Shillong Times. 2012. 'Nagaland Returning to Normalcy after Clashes'. 4 September.

Shimray, U. A. 2007. *Naga Population and Integration Movement: Documentation.* New Delhi: Mittal Publications.

Shimray, U. A. and M. D. Usha Devi. 2009. 'Trends and Patterns of Migration: Interface with Education, a Case of the North-Eastern Region'. Social and Economic Change Monographs 15, Institute of Social and Economic Change, Bangalore.

Shishak, Tuisem. 2007. 'Tuisem A. Shishak: A Confession'. *ME.* 24 July.

Siddiqui, Sabrina and Tom McCarthy. 2019. 'Trump Abandons Effort to put Citizenship Question on 2020 Census'. *Gaurdian.* 11 July.

Singh, Khuswant. 1999. *A History of Sikhs*, vol. 2: 1839–1988. New Delhi: Oxford University Press.

Singh, K. S. 1998. *People of India*, vol. 6. India's Communities: N–Z. New Delhi: Anthropological Survey of India; and New Delhi: Oxford University Press.

Singh, W. Kumar. 2006. 'Overestimation of Fertility Rates in Manipur'. *Economic and Political Weekly* 41(15): 1473–80.

Sinlung. 2012. 'Manipur Braces for Kuki Blockade'. 16 November.

Sivaramakrishnan, K. C. 1997. 'Under-Franchise in Urban Areas: Freeze on Delimitation of Constituencies and Resultant Disparities'. *Economic and Political Weekly* 32(51): 3275–81.

Skaria, Ajay. 1997. 'Shades of Wildness Tribe, Caste, and Gender in Western India'. *Journal of Asian Studies* 56(3): 726–45.

———. 1998. 'Being Jangli: The Politics of Wildness'. *Studies in History* 14(2): 193–215.

Smith, Stanley K. and Terry Sincich. 1990. 'The Relationship between the Length of the Base Period and Population Forecast Errors'. *Journal of the American Statistical Association* 85(410): 367–75.

Srinivasan, T. N. 1994. 'Data Base for Development Analysis: An Overview'. *Journal of Development Economics* 44:3–27.

———. 2003. 'India's Statistical System: Critiquing the Report of the National Statistical Commission'. *Economic and Political Weekly* 38(4): 303–6.

Srivastava, S. C. 1987. *Demographic Profile of North East India*. New Delhi: Mittal Publications.

Srivathsan, A. 2013. 'A Count That Just Does Not Add Up'. *Hindu* 25 April.

Starr, Paul. 1987. 'The Sociology of Official Statistics'. In *The Politics of Numbers*, ed. William Alonso and Paul Starr, 7–57. New York: Russell Sage Foundation.

———. 1992. 'Social Categories and Claims in the Liberal State'. *Social Research* 59(2): 263–95.

Steinberg, David I. 2015. *Myanmar: The Dynamics of an Evolving Polity*. Boulder, CO: Lynne Rienner Publishers.

Stepan, Alfred, Juan J. Linz and Yogendra Yadav. 2011. *Crafting State-Nations. India and other Multinational Democracies*. Baltimore, MD: John Hopkins University Press.

Subbarao, D. 2011. 'Statistics in the World of RBI'. Inaugural address at the Statistics Day Conference of Reserve Bank of India, Mumbai. 5 July 5.

Subramanian, S. V., Malavika A. Subramanyam, Sakthivel Selvaraj and Ichiro Kawachi. 2009. 'Are Self-Reports of Health and Morbidities in Developing Countries Misleading? Evidence from India'. *Social Science & Medicine* 68:260–5.

Sundar, N. 2000. 'Caste as Census Category: Implications for Sociology'. *Current Sociology* 48(3): 111–26.

Suryanarayana, M. H. 2000. 'How Real is the Secular Decline in Rural Poverty?' *Economic and Political Weekly* 35(25): 2129–40.

———. 2009. 'Pursuing Inclusion in India: A Story of Specification Errors'. *Indian Growth and Development Review* 2(2): 155–72.

———. 2011. 'Expert Group on Poverty: Confusion Worse Confounded'. *Economic and Political Weekly* 46(46): 36–9.

Suryanarayana, M. H. and Ankush Agrawal. 2013. 'Promoting Human Development in India: Costs of Inequality'. Working Paper Number 109. Brasilia: International Policy Centre for Inclusive Growth.

Suryanarayana, M. H. and N. S. Iyengar. 1986. 'On the Reliability of NSS Data'. *Economic and Political Weekly* 21(6): 261–4.

Suykens, Bert. 2013. 'State-Making and the Suspension of Law in India's Northeast: The Place of Exception in the Assam–Nagaland Border Dispute'. in *Violence on the Margins: States, Conflict, and Borderlands*, ed. Benedikt Korf and Timothy Raeymaekers, pp. 167–89. New York: Palgrave Macmillan.

Swami, P. 2000. 'The Game of Numbers'. *Frontline* 17(21). Accessed on 30 June 2019. Available at https://frontline.thehindu.com/static/html/fl1721/17210360.htm.

———. 2014. 'Demography and Discontent: Crisis of Modernity and Displacement in Undivided Jammu and Kashmir'. In *The Other Kashmir: Society, Culture and Politics in the Karakoram Himalayas*, ed. K. Warikoo, 201–21. New Delhi: IDSA/Pentagon Press.

Talbot, I. and G. Singh (eds.). 1999. *Region and Partition: Bengal, Punjab and the Partition of the Subcontinent*. Karachi: Oxford University Press.

Talib, Arjimand Hussain. 2010. 'Understanding Religious Radicalization: Issues, Threats and Early Warnings in Kashmir Valley'. IPCS Issue Brief No. 149. Institute of Peace and Conflict Studies, New Delhi.

Talukdar, Sushanta. 2014. 'Volatile Boundary'. *Frontline*. 3 October.

Taylor, M. 2016. *The Political Economy of Statistical Capacity: A Theoretical Approach*. Washington, DC: IDB.

Telegraph. 2003a. 'Rio to Warn Delhi on Settlers with Expose'. 25 December.

———. 2003b. 'Villagers Reject Fresh Census in Manipur'. 20 October.

———. 2004. 'Minister Eats His Figures'. 23 July.

———. 2008. 'Bandh as Weapon for Delimitation – 3 Tribes Protest Process Suspension'. 27 January.

———. 2011a. 'NSCN to Mark Areas for "Election"'. 16 March.

———. 2011b. 'Demand Heat on DAN Cries for New Districts and a State Grow Louder in Nagaland'. 17 December.

———. 2014. 'Tracking Maoists to Mapping State Borders'. 22 December.

Times of India. 2010. 'Greater Goa Was a Dream of Ravindra Kelekar'. 16 December.

———. 2012a. 'National Health Survey Not Nixed'. 30 July.

———. 2012b. '4 Lakh Bogus Voters in Nagaland: K Therie'. 17 June.

———. 2012c. 'Naga Groups Want Capital Punishment for Rapists'. 9 February.

———. 2013. 'Nagaland Sets Up Booths in Golaghat, Sivasagar'. 13 February.

———. 2014. 'With Just Two Days to Go for the Telangana Survey, Exodus of Telugus from Chennai Peaks'. 17 August.

———. 2018. 'Nagaland Miscreants Asked Me to Withdraw Candidature'. 25 November.

———. 2019. 'Govt Making History by Driving People into Poverty: Priyanka'. 15 November.

Tinyi, Venusa and C. Nienu. 2018. 'Making Sense of Corruption in Nagaland: A Culturalist Perspective'. In *Democracy in Nagaland: Tribes, Traditions, Tensions*, eds. Jelle J. P. Wouters and Zhoto Tunyi, 159–80. Kohima: The Highlander Books.

Thakur, R. K. 2016. 'Whose Hills? Whose Plains? The Politics of Border'. *Indian Historical Review* 43(1): 83–101.

Thomas, John. 2016. *Evangelising the Nation: Religion and the Formation of Naga Political Identity.* Oxon: Routledge India.

TNI-BCN (Transnational Institute and Burma Centrum Netherlands). 2014. 'Ethnicity without Meaning, Data without Context: The 2014 Census, Identity and Citizenship in Burma/Myanmar'. Burma Policy Briefing Nr 13.

Tooze, Adam J. 2001. *Statistics and the German State, 1900-1945: The Making of Modern Economic Knowledge.* Cambridge: Cambridge University Press.

Tolo News. 2018. 'New Study Estimates Population to Be 34.4 Million'. 30 March.

Tsakise. 2001. 'Sangtam'. In *Language Education in Nagaland: Sociolinguistic Dimensions,* ed. Rajesh Sachdeva, pp. 162–7. New Delhi: Regency Publications.

United Nations. 2011. 'World Population Prospects: The 2010 Revision, CD ROM Edition'. Population Division, Department of Economic and Social Affairs.

UN Secretariate. 2010. 'Post Enumeration Surveys: Operational Guidelines, Technical Report'. World Population and Housing Census Programme, Department of Economics and Social Affairs, New York.

Upadhyay, Kavita. 2018. 'Inside the Ghost Villages of Uttarakhand'. *Indian Express.* 5 August.

Urla, Jacqueline. 1993. 'Cultural Politics in an Age of Statistics: Numbers, Nations, and the Making of Basque Identity'. *American Ethnologist* 20(4): 818–43.

Uvin, Peter. 2002. 'On Counting, Categorizing, and Violence in Burundi and Rwanda'. In *Census and Identity: The Politics of Race, Ethnicity, and Language in National Censuses,* ed. David I. Kertzer and Dominique Arel, 148–75. Cambridge: Cambridge University Press.

Vadeo, Acuyi. 2018. 'Clarification'. *ME.* 3 August.

Vaidyanathan, A. 2013. 'Use and Abuse of the Poverty Line'. *Economic and Political Weekly* 48(44): 37–42.

van Ham, Peter and Jamie Saul. 2008. *Expedition Naga.* New Delhi: Timeless Books.

van Schendel, W. 2002. 'Stateless in South Asia: The Making of the India-Bangladesh Enclaves'. *Journal of Asian Studies* 61(1): 115–47.

Varshney, Ashutosh. 2013. 'How Has Indian Federalism Done?' *Studies in Indian Politics* 1(1): 43–63.

Vashum, R. 1996. 'Some Reflections on Naga Society: An Anthropological Perspective'. In *Nagas at Work,* ed. R. Vashum, A. Iheilung, N. Panmei and L. Longkumer, 61–77. New Delhi: Naga Students' Union Delhi.

Venkatesan, V. 2001. 'Census 2001: The Head-Count and Some Gaps'. *Frontline* 18:5.

Verma, A. K. 2013. 'Tribal "Annihilation" and "Upsurge" in Uttar Pradesh'. *Economic and Political Weekly* 48(51): 52–9.

Vidwans, S. M. 2002a. 'Indian Statistical System at the Crossroads I: Ominous Clouds of Centralisation'. *Economic and Political Weekly* 37(37): 3819–29.

———. 2002b. 'Indian Statistical System at the Crossroads II: Expansion of National Sample Survey'. *Economic and Political Weekly* 37(38): 3943–55.

Vieytez, Eduardo J. Ruiz and Markko Kallonen. 2004. 'Territorial Autonomy and European National Minorities: South Tyrol, Basque Country and Åland Islands'. In *European Yearbook of Minority Issues: 2002–2003* 2(1): 247–81.

Vijayanunni, M. 2015. 'Where is the Caste Data? *Hindu*. 15 July.

Visaria, P. and S. Irudaya Rajan. 1999. 'National Family Health Survey: A Landmark in Indian Surveys'. *Economic and Political Weekly* 34(42–3): 3002–7.

von Fürer-Haimendorf, C. 1962. *The Naked Naga*. Calcutta: Thacker Spink & Co. Private Ltd.

Wade, Robert. 1985. 'On the Sociology of Irrigation: How Do We Know the Truth about Canal Performance?' *Agricultural Administration* 19:63–79.

———. 2012. The Politics behind World Bank Statistics: The Case of China's Income'. *Economic and Political Weekly* 47(25): 17–18.

Walby, Kevin and Michael Haan. 2012. 'Caste Confusion and Census Enumeration in Colonial India, 1871–1921'. *Histoire Sociale* (Social History) 45(90): 301–18.

Weinraub, Bernard. 1973. 'Planning Controversy in India Intensifies as Economist Quits'. *New York Times*. 10 December.

Weisberg, Herbert F. 2005. *The Total Survey Error Approach: A Guide to the New Science of Survey Research*. Chicago and London: University of Chicago Press.

Weiss, Anita M. 1999. 'Much Ado about Counting: The Conflict over Holding a Census in Pakistan'. *Asian Survey* 39(4): 679–93.

Weizman, Eyal. 2007. *Hollow Land: Israel's Architecture of Occupation*. New York: Verso.

Wilkinson, Steven I. 2004. *Votes and Violence: Electoral Competition and Ethnic Riots in India*. New York: Cambridge University Press.

Winichakul, Thongchai. 1994. *Siam Mapped: A History of the Geo-body of a Nation*. Honolulu: University of Hawaii Press.

Wood, Denis. 2010. *Rethinking the Power of Maps*. New York: The Guilford Press.

Woolf, Stuart. 1989. 'Statistics and the Modern State'. *Comparative Studies in Society and History* 31(3): 588–604.

World Bank. n.d.1. 'Statistical Capacity Indicator Dashboard'. Available at http://datatopics.worldbank.org/statisticalcapacity/SCIdashboard.aspx.

———. n.d.2. 'Building Statistical Capacity to Monitor Development Progress'. Available at http://siteresources.worldbank.org/SCBINTRANET/Resources/Building_Statistical_Capacity_to_Monitor_Development_Progress.pdf.

Wouters, Jelle J. P. 2014. 'Performing Democracy in Nagaland: Past Polities and Present Politics'. *Economic and Political Weekly* 49(16): 59–66.

———. 2018. *In the Shadows of Naga Insurgency: Tribes, State, and Violence in Northeast India*. New Delhi: Oxford University Press.

Wyly, Elwin. 2004. 'The New Spatial Politics of Social Data'. Available at http://ibis.geog.ubc.ca/~ewyly/teaching/nov2.pdf.

Xaxa, Virginius. 2003. 'Tribes in India'. In *The Oxford India Companion to Sociology and Social Anthropology*, ed. Veena Das, 373–408. New Delhi: Oxford University Press.

Yeputhomi, Hukavi T. 2018a. 'Integration of Naga Inhabited Areas Is Rightful Claim of the Naga People'. *ME*. 4 July.

———. 2018b. 'The "Inner Line", Its Permit and the Boundary'. *ME*. 30 August.

Yin, Sandra. 2007. 'Objections Surface over Nigerian Census Results'. Population Reference Bureau. Available at http://www.prb.org/Articles/2007/Objections OverNigerianCensus.aspx.

Yonuo, Asoso. 1974. *The Rising Nagas: A Historical and Political Study*. New Delhi: Vivek Publishing House.

Young, Alwyn. 2012. 'The African Growth Miracle'. *Journal of Political Economy* 120(4): 696–739.

Zarkovich, S. S. 1989. 'The Overcount in Censuses of Population'. *Jahrbucher fur Nationalokonomie und Statistik* 206(6): 606–7.

Zhao, Suisheng. 2004. *A Nation-State by Construction: Dynamics of Modern Chinese Nationalism*. Stanford, CA: Stanford University Press.

Zinyü, Mhiesizokho. 2014. *Phizo and the Naga Problem*. Self-published.

Index

insurgency, 158
language, 187n58, 310
population, 307
Sumi–Tangkhul conflict, 209
territory, 116n54
tea tribes, 309
Tenning (circle), 145
Tenyidie. *See* Angami language
Therie, K., 44, 183n31, 204, 238n21, 246n76, 321n15
Thoubal (district), 116n54
Tikhir (tribe)
    assimilation, 174, 302
    church, 185n48
    government statistics and identity, 50
    language, 50, 54n23, 76, 175–6, 226
    insurgency and identity, 102
    population, 168, 204
Tirap (district), 88, 164
Tobu (circle), 68, 200, 214
tribal headquarter, 200, 240n28
tribal languages. *See* languages
tribes. *See* Scheduled Tribes
triple deficit, mutually constitutive, 10–12, 21, 108, 234, 319, 322n31
Tripura, 15, 22–3, 164, 260, 299, 306, 316–18
    content error in census, 191n90
    delimitation, 235n5, 305
    insurgency, 259
    macroeconomic indicators, 317
    NSSO surveys, 35n48, 257–9, 260, 263–4, 290, 297
Tseminyu (circle)
    constituency, 68, 214
    district demand, 41–2, 98, 119n75, 200
    maps, 68, 70, 111n19
Tsogin (circle), 41, 70, 98, 214
Tuensang (district), 66, 172, 212–13, 219
    1971 district, 66, 97, 170, 172, 206–8
    area, 66–8
    census, 111n15, 124, 159–60, 180n12, 220
    delimitation, 188n70, 213–14, 217, 220
    district demand, 200, 239n26
    Eastern Nagaland, 101
    electorate, 220

evolution, 40, 51n1, 69, 109n10, 116n61, 148, 156, 159, 231, 239n27 (*see also* NHTA)
insurgency, 41, 160
maps, 114n39
manipulation of census, 220
'Other Nagas', 143, 170
population, 172, 208
population growth rate, 188n65
tribes, 24, 212, 220
villages, 97, 242n45
voting rates, 206, 220
Tunjoy (village), 118n70

Ukhrul (district), 88, 164, 305, 307–8
undercount/under-enumeration (*see* census, undercount)
unemployment, 45, 48, 181n18, 201, 251, 255, 276n14, 317–8 (*see also* employment)
unemployment statistics/statistics, reliability of, 7, 8, 28n11, 31n23, 31n25, 32n26, 33n32, 251, 255, 276n14 (*see also* employment statistics)
Ghana, 31n23, 297, 300
India,
    census, 130, 159, 296–303
    sample surveys, 47, 139, 249, 255–61, 277n19, 300
    maps, 109n9, 113n34, 114n39
USA, 30n17, 31n23
United Nations, 28n9, 105, 124
United States of America (USA), 4, 13, 26n3, 30n17–18, 31n23, 235n4, 276n10, 287
    statistical controversies in, 30n17–18, 122n108, 125–6, 235n4, 287
United States Agency for International Development (USAID), 276n10
Unrepresented Nations and Peoples Organization (UNPO), 105, 122n104
urban, 134, 142
    area statistics, 111n17
    discrepancy in census, 133–4, 140–1, 302
    double counting (*see* double counting)
    economy, 209